The Collected
Works of
Thomas Müntzer

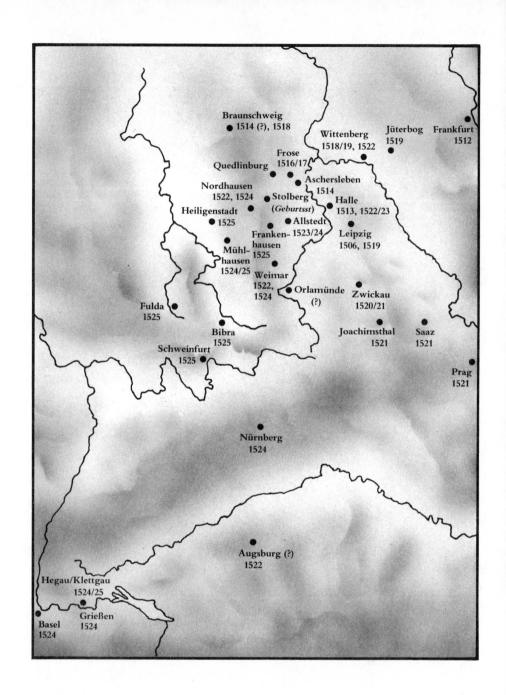

Places and Dates in the Life of Thomas Müntzer

The Collected Works of Thomas Müntzer

Edited and translated by
Peter Matheson

T. & T. CLARK
EDINBURGH

Copyright © T. & T. Clark Ltd, 1988

Typeset by C. R. Barber & Partners, Fort William,
printed and bound by Billing & Sons Ltd, Worcester

for

T. & T. CLARK LTD.
59 George Street, Edinburgh EH2 2LQ

First printed 1988

British Library Cataloguing in Publication Data

Müntzer, Thomas, *1490–1525*
    The collected writings and letters
    of Thomas Müntzer.
    1. Continental Protestant churches.
    Christian doctrine.
    I. Title II. Matheson, Peter
    230′ .4

    ISBN 0–567–09495–2

ACKNOWLEDGEMENTS

This edition is based on the German critical edition by Günther Franz, *Schriften und Briefe*, (Gütersloh, 1968) and grateful acknowledgement is made to the publishers, Gerd Mohn, Gütersloh, for permission to use this; also to the Akademie-Verlag, Berlin, for use of the text of the Mühlausen articles in *Flugschriften der Bauernkriegszeit*, edd. A. Laube, H. Seiffert etc. (Berlin, 1975) pp. 80–2; to Hermann Böhlaus Nachfolger, Weimar, for use of the article by Manfred Bensing and Winfried Trillitzsch, 'Bernhard Dappen, "Articuli ... contra Lutheranos" ...', *Jahrbuch für Regionalgeschichte 2* (1967), 113–47; to the Evangelische Verlagsanstalt, Berlin, for use of *Thomas Müntzer: Theologische Schriften aus dem Jahre 1523*, edd. S. Bräuer, W. Ullmann (Berlin, 1982); to Vandenhoeck und Ruprecht, Göttingen, for citations from Walter Elliger, *Thomas Müntzer: Leben und Werk* (Göttingen, 1975); to VEB Bibliographisches Institut, Leipzig, for use of the map of Müntzer's career in Manfred Bensing, *Thomas Müntzer: mit 74 Abbildungen*, (Leipzig, 1983) p. 34; to the *Wissenschaftliche Zeitschrift der Karl-Marx-Universität* for use of the article by E. Wolfgramm, 'Der Prager Anschlag des Thomas Müntzers' in Vol. 6 (1957), 295–308; to the Zentral-antiquariat der DDR for use of the text of *Thomas Müntzer: Prager Manifest*, intro. by M. Steinmetz, with a contribution on the history of the text by F. de Boor, text and trans. by W. Trillitzsch, facsimile of Latin MS by H-J. Rockar (Leipzig, 1975); and to the Sächsiche Landesbibliothek, Dresden, for permission to use the microfilm in the possession of Dr. Seigfried Bräuer of Müntzer's marginal notes on the *Opera Cypriani*, ed. by Erasmus (Basel, 1520), and the *Opera Tertulliani*, ed. by Beatus Rhenanus (Basel, 1521).

CONTENTS

ABBREVIATIONS

AGBM	*Akten zur Geschichte des Bauernkriegs in Mitteldeutschland.* Vol. 2, edited by W. P. Fuchs, 1942.
ARG	*Archiv für Reformationsgeschichte*
Benzing	*Lutherbibliographie: Verzeichnis der gedruckten Schriften Martin Luthers.* 1966.
Boehmer	*Studien zu Thomas Müntzer.* 1922.
Boehmer-Kirn	*Thomas Müntzers Briefwechsel*, 1931.
Bräuer-Ullmann	*Thomas Müntzer: Theologische Schriften aus dem Jahre 1523*, 1982.
Bubenheimer I, II	'Thomas Müntzer in Braunschweig', *Braunschweigisches Jahrbuch* 65 (1984), 37–78; 66 (1985), 79–113.
CH	*Church History.*
Dismer	Geschichte Glaube Revolution. Zur Schrift-auslegung Thomas Müntzers. 1974.
Elliger	*Thomas Müntzer: Leben und Werk*, 1975.
Emblemata	*Handbuch zur Sinnbildkunst des 16. und 17. Jahrhunderts*, edited by Arthur Henkel, Albrecht Schöne. 1976.
Förstemann	*Neues Urkundenbuch ... der evangelischen Kirchen-reformation.* Vol. I, 1842.
F.	Günther Franz, *Thomas Müntzer: Schriften und Briefe*, 1968.
Friesen and Goertz	*Thomas Müntzer*, edited by A. Friesen and H.-J. Goertz, 1978.
Gess	*Akten und Briefe zur Kirchenpolitik Herzog Georgs von Sachsen*, edited by F. Gess, Vols. 1, 2. 1905, 1917.
Goebke	'Neue Forschungen über Thomas Müntzer ...', *Harz-Zeitschrift*, 1957/1959.
Goertz	*Innere und äussere Ordnung in der Theologie Müntzers.* 1967.
Heidelberg Symposium 1987	Symposium: 'Probleme einer Edition der Schriften und Briefe Thomas Müntzers', Heidelberg, 2-3 April 1967.
Hinrichs	*Thomas Müntzer: Politische Schriften*, 1950.
HZ	*Historische Zeitschrift.*
JEH	*Journal of Ecclesiastical History.*

Kawerau	*Luthers Schriften nach der Reihenfolge der Jahre verzeichnet. Schriften des Vereins fur Reformationsgeschichte* 129, Leipzig, 1917.
Lohmann	*Zur geistigen Entwicklung Thomas Müntzers,* 1931.
LW	*Luther's Works,* 1955ff.
MPL	*Migne, Patrologia Latina.*
MPG	*Migne, Patrologia Graeca.*
MQR	*Mennonite Quarterly Review.*
Schwarz	*Die apokalyptische Theologie Müntzers . . .* 1977.
Scribner	*For the sake of simple folk: popular propaganda for the German Reformation.* 1981.
Th.Lit.Z.	*Theologische Literaturzeitung.*
Vg.	Vulgate.
WA	*Dr Martin Luthers Werke.* Weimar, 1883ff.
WA Br.	*Weimar Ausgabe: Briefe.*
WA TR	*Weimar Ausgabe: Tischreden.*

Bräuer refers to communications received personally or by post from Dr Siegfried Bräuer; Bräuer/Kobuch to the working papers for the forthcoming edition of Müntzer's correspondence in the German Democratic Republic by Drs Bräuer and Kobuch; Scott refers to communications received personally or by post from Dr Tom Scott.

INTRODUCTION

An English edition of Thomas Müntzer's writings requires no justification. It has long been a cause for regret, if not shame, that so few of his writings[1] have been available to the English-speaking world, in view of his prominent role on the Reformation stage. Yet the formidable difficulty of Müntzer's German – his writings have been acknowledged to be 'among the most difficult in the Reformation period'[2] – means that this particular translation can only be put before the reader with the liveliest appreciation of its shortcomings. It is, after all, only when translation is attempted that the limitations to one's understanding of an author are most sharply revealed.

In Müntzer's case the hermeneutical challenge is especially formidable. Contemporary scholarship has yet to resolve the spirited controversies about his theology. Was he primarily a mystic, a Biblical exegete, a social activist or an apocalyptic enthusiast?[3] Virtually every key term can be translated differently according to the interpretive framework chosen.

The avowed aim of this translation is to leave such interpretive questions as open as possible, to abstain from guiding as well as misguiding the reader, while of course indicating where the translation given is debatable.

1. There are excellent translations by James M. Stayer of *Von dem gedichteten Glauben* and the *Protestation oder Erbietung* in MQR 55 (1981), 99–130; and of the *Sermon before the Princes* by George H. Williams in G. H. Williams, A. M. Mergal (edd.), *Spiritual and Anabaptist Writers* (Library of Christian Classics, vol. 25), pp. 47–72; Hans Hillerbrand has translated the *Hochverursachte Schutzrede* in MQR 38 (1964), 22–36; Gordon Rupp has translated many passages from Müntzer, the 'Order and account of the German Rite newly established at Alstet through the servants of God 1523', and the shorter version of the Prague Manifesto, in *Patterns of Reformation* (London, 1969), pp. 157–353, esp. 175–8 and pp. 315–20; cf. also Lowell H. Zuck (ed.) *Christianity and Revolution* (Philadelphia, 1975) who reprints Rupp's translations of the Prague Manifesto and offers brief extracts from a *Sermon before the Princes* (Williams) and *Highly Provoked Defence* (Hillerbrand), from Müntzer's Confession and alleged Recantation (Zuck, Hillerbrand) pp. 31–47; there are also translations by Robert Fowkes: *Sermon to the Princes, Well-warranted speech in my own defense,* Manifesto to the Miners (= Letter 75), in Reinhard Becker (ed.), *German Humanism and the Reformation* (New York, 1982), pp. 257–92; though spirited, Fowkes' translations are unreliable; of considerable interest, on the other hand, is the Italian translation and edition by Emidio Campi, *Thomas Müntzer: Scritti politici (Testi della Riforma, 4)*, Turin, 1972; also the translation of the Stolberg letter by Michael G. Baylor, 'Thomas Müntzer's First Publication', *The Sixteenth Century Journal* 17 (1986), 451–8.

2. Carl Hinrichs, *Thomas Müntzer; Politische Schriften*, p. 7.

3. Cf. Siegried Bräuer, 'Müntzerforschung von 1965 bis 1975', LJ 44 (1977) 127–141; LJ 45 (1978), 102–139.

A second concern has been to convey, however haltingly, something of the vigour and earthiness and freshness of Müntzer's language. Here two principles have been followed. First, the temptation to lapse into an archaic English has been resisted,[4] indeed a conscious effort has been made to capture the vernacular, colloquial flavour of the original. Secondly, while seeking to adhere as closely as possible to the actual wording, Müntzer's own warning to translators, not to 'trace one little figure from another'[5] has provided some guidance. At times the 'spirit' has been granted primacy over the letter.

The linguistic problems are formidable. Müntzer's writings can appear, to the uninitiated, to be written in some strange code. Quite apart from the dense thickets of Biblical references[6] there are many technical terms from mystical, apocalyptic, and protest literature. Spillmann's very useful analysis of Müntzer's vocabulary alerts us to its great variety, to its use of foreign borrowings and of neologisms.[7] Hence the dictionaries frequently fail us, and, as Maron points out, the problems are compounded by the lack of precision and consistency of Müntzer's use of language.[8] It has not always proved possible to give a consistent English rendering to a German term.[9]

Other problems are posed by Müntzer's loose, conversational-style syntax. This reflects, of course, the time-pressure and tensions under which most of his work was written, as well as the personality of Müntzer. Clauses tend to pile up, only loosely hitched together, and

4. The translation of the Sermon on Daniel by G. H. Williams (cf. n. 1. above) tends to adopt an archaic English.

5. In his translation of the Psalms Müntzer sought to do justice to 'German style and form'; he did, however, claim the 'direct leading of the holy spirit' for his very free renderings; cf. the Foreword to his German Church Service Book, p. 000; in practice this led to him on occasion adding his own favourite mystical or apocalyptic terms; the 'God of hosts' becomes the 'God of the poor' (F. p. 36/6), or an 'armed siege-train' appears out of nowhere in Psalm 118[11] (ibid., p. 118/15); difficult phrases can be simply omitted (ibid., p. 97/17) or completely redrafted (ibid., p. 98/1ff.).

6. Müntzer has a profound and remarkably comprehensive knowledge of Scripture; he commutes constantly and consciously between the historical books, the prophets, the writings, the gospels and the epistles and, although he keeps returning to favourite chapters such as Genesis I; or Numbers 19; 2 Kings 23 (Josiah); Jeremiah 23 (false prophets); Daniel 2 (Nebuchadnezzar's dream); Matthew 16; Luke 1 (the Magnificat); John 3; Romans 13; or Revelation 14, to mention only a few, yet it is far harder to state with confidence where the 'centre' of Scripture is for Müntzer than, say, for Savonarola, or Erasmus, or Luther.

7. H. O. Spillmann, Untersuchungen zum Wortschatz in Thomas Müntzers Deutschen Schriften. Berlin, 1971.

8. Gottfried Maron, 'Thomas Müntzer als Theologe des Gerichts,' ZKG 83 (1972) 195.

9. Words such as betrubnis, ergern, unerfarnen, for example. Müntzer himself often uses one word such as 'godless', gottlos, to translate a whole number of Latin terms.

continuity of thought is not always achieved. Sometimes the original thrust of the sentence is partially lost.[10] Prolixity and repetition, a common sixteenth-century failing, are quite frequent, but more characteristic of Müntzer, perhaps, is the compression or telescoping of his thought. It is worth noting that his Latin writings, more circumspectly written for a learned audience, display fewer of these problems.[11]

Perseverance, however, is amply rewarded. Müntzer's language is as fascinating and fresh as his thought: it is direct, startling, sometimes bizarre, hardly every lapsing into bland generality or cliché. The semi-anarchic language, syntax, style reflect his contempt for courtier and schoolman, his quest for a new authenticity.

Müntzer thinks concretely and visually, rather than logically. His writings proceed by a lateral flow of associations – one word, or image, or event, or Biblical theme sparking off another. Exegesis, argument and polemic thus combine in a quite idiosyncratic way; the reader having at times to thread his or her way through a maze of apparent digressions, obscure references, and spectacular abuse. There is, perhaps, some irony and certainly much incongruity about any attempt to apply pedantic, academic analysis to such an iconoclastic figure as Müntzer. His dazzling images and aphorisms, his sharp polarities and polemical broadsides have to be relished, savoured on their own terms. We understand him, if at all, not so much through following his sequences of thought as by imaginatively entering his 'world', in which spiritual and political, mystical and apocalyptic, real and fantastical elements are married in ways quite foreign to us. The strangeness of his language signals the alien universe – sometimes forbidding, sometimes alluring – which he inhabits.

This work makes no claim to be a new critical edition. It is based on the 1968 edition of Franz, but all the Biblical quotations have been re-checked, and the aim is to mediate to the English-speaking world recent advances in scholarship, particularly in Germany. Since the world of Müntzer studies is in ferment, this has proved to be an exacting task. A new critical edition of his correspondence is being prepared by Bräuer and Kobuch in East Germany; and of his writings by Seebass and Wolgast in West Germany;[12] some new material about his early life is still being unearthed;[13] and a translation of his

10. E.g. F. p. 314/3ff.; 322, 1.16ff.; 574/16ff.; or there may be an abrupt shift from the second person to the first, e.g. ibid. p. 408/18ff.; or a second object is inserted, e.g. ibid., p. 313/17ff.

11. The sentences tend to be short, often with quite abrupt transitions.

12. It is anticipated that the edition of the correspondence will appear in 1988/89, that of the writings in 1989/90.

13. Dr Bubenheimer will be publishing, in ZKG 98 (1987), Heft 1, a document

works into modern German is planned;[14] new biographies are being written.[15] For all its undoubted merits at the time, the Franz edition is now very much out of date.

The transitional state of research has posed considerable problems, not least because some areas of Müntzer's work have fared better than others. His printed tracts have, naturally enough, received the lion's share of scholarly attention in the past. The correspondence, by comparison, has been neglected, while the third section of the book – Müntzer's unpublished writings and notes – remains full of as yet unsolved riddles. In Franz's edition, for example, only the most cursory attention was given to his important marginal notes on Tertullian. Such forays as this edition has been constrained to make into such uncharted territory have been made with a due sense of the temerity of such an undertaking. The omission of most of liturgical writings is explained below.[16]

The preparation of this edition has extended over many years, and the debts to a host of friendly advisers are innumerable. They bear, of course, no responsibility for the lacunae and errors which remain. No words can express my gratitude to Dr Siegfried Bräuer for his hospitality, help, advice, encouragement and friendship; I owe a particular debt to Dr Tom Scott's linguistic and historical skills, at the proof-reading stage he not only saved me from errors innumerable but enhanced the whole quality of the translation; I am also deeply indebted to Dr. Kobuch, Dr. Lew Jillings, Dr. Agathe Thornton, Drs. Beverley and Helmut Olssen-Dopfell, to Professor Ulrich Bubenheimer, to Professor Gottfried Seebass, and to my old colleague, Mr. David Wright; to the library staffs of New College, Edinburgh, the British Library, London, and Otago University, Dunedin; to the cheerfully done secretarial work of Miss May Hocking and Mrs. Audrey Way; to a very patient publisher; above all, to my wife, Heinke, to whom it is dedicated.

---

from Muntzer's 'lettersack' which he has identified as a lecture on Jerome, held in Wittenberg 1517/18 by Johannes Aesticampianus; and probably in 1988 a collection of essays, *Thomas Müntzer: Studien und Texte*, which will include a set of questions sent to Müntzer by the Nuremberg patrician, Christopher Fürer, with Müntzer's answers appended, and – from the 'letter-sack' – the so-called list of Plato's writings, and other material.

14. By Professor Siegfried Hoyer.

15. By Dr Tom Scott (to appear in 1989), Professor Günter Vogler (1989), Professor Abraham Friesen; I understand also that Professor Eric Gritsch's biography is being revised.

16. Cf. p. 162 below.

THE CORRESPONDENCE

Müntzer's correspondence, meticulously collected and cared for – no doubt a humanist trait (Nrs. 24, 46) – is even more precious to us than it clearly was to him. There is not, it is true, any marked difference in tone between his treatises and his letters. Both are hewn from the same rugged block. Indeed one could argue that some of his letters, not least those addressed to Luther, Melanchthon, and the Elector, Frederick the Wise of Saxony (Nrs. 13, 31, 40, 45, 64) are among the most disciplined of all his writings. We do not, then, find – as in a Calvin or a Contarini – a 'human' Müntzer in the letters contrasting with a more formal Müntzer elsewhere.

The letters enable us, rather, to reconstruct Müntzer's world, the web of contacts spun by and around him, the extraordinary range of his interests and power of his magnetism; the multiple frontiers on which he so precariously stood. It is, of course, natural that one turns first to the dramatic eloquence of the letters relating to the so-called Peasants' War from the summer of 1524 on (Nrs. 50ff.). Yet the real surprises come much earlier. We are immediately introduced into the heady days of the early Reformation, mirrored by Müntzer's early career: his web of contacts in pre-Reformation Brunswick (Nrs. 1–4) his humanist appetite for books and friendships (Nrs. 7, 8, 9, 15), his ferocious polemical battles with Dominicans, Franciscans and the humanist Egranus (Nrs. 6, 13, 15, 20, 21), his delicate, at times desperate quest for a living to sustain his studies (Nrs. 5, 7, 10), the dire poverty or illness threatening family or friends (Nrs. 14, 16, 17, 18). Against this backdrop excited reports or queries surface about the latest happenings or publications from Wittenberg (Nrs. 8, 16, 26, 28) together with hints of progress in Müntzer's own historical, mystical and theological studies (Nrs. 7, 11, 13).

From the beginning, it appears, Müntzer attracted close friendships, though the bluff, hearty tone (cf. Nr. 10) is less common than that of gratitude for support given (Nrs. 16, 34, 36). Müntzer, it appears, was a 'natural pastor', with a sensitivity and a frankness which bonded a small circle of intimates to him in 'brotherhood' (Nrs. 26, 27, 28, 29, 34, 38). This frankness is also reflected in his rather one-sided correspondence with his mentors in the reforming movement like Agricola (Nrs. 15, 21), Karlstadt (Nrs. 37, 43, 56), Lang (Nr. 51), Luther (Nrs. 13, 40) and Melanchthon (Nr. 31); but while he can regret the ignorance of 'our dear Martin' about the weak in faith, or reprove Melanchthon for his defective understanding of marriage (Nr. 31), his patient and sustained and sadly abortive endeavours to keep in communication with them is impressive. It is paralleled by his equally genuine attempts to engage the sympathy of the Saxon princes for his views (Nrs. 45, 50, 52, 64). We do well to keep this background in mind when dealing with the later confrontational period.

Of the 94 letters 29 are in Latin, the remainder (apart from the odd phrase) in German; after Nr. 51 Müntzer writes only in German. They cover a short period of some seven years. Almost half of them come from his last two years, or rather seventeen months, from 1524–1525. There is almost nothing from 1522, the wretched, restless months after the return from Prague. More surprisingly, almost no letter remains from the five months at the beginning of 1524 in Allstedt. On what principles did Müntzer decide to retain or discard letters? We have clear evidence of him blotting, smudging, cutting, 'purging' some of his extant correspondence. How much was completely 'censored' out of existence? Does so much remain from the later period simply because he had not found time to sift through it?

As this book goes to print a new critical edition of his correspondence is being prepared in the German Democratic Republic by Dr Bräuer and Dr Kobuch. In many respects this is breaking completely new ground: in the redeciphering of all the manuscripts – a formidable and painstaking task – in the tracing of the *Überlieferungsgeschichte*, the transmission and copying of the manuscripts, in the reconstruction of the 'world' of these letters, the social and ecclesiastical and personal networks within which they circulated. The whole contours of Müntzer's correspondence are changing, as dates are revised and a new enumeration developed to take account of letters no longer extant. Some letters are being excised, some new ones added.

For this edition certain decisions, of a somewhat arbitrary nature, have had to be made. In an extraordinary, in my experience unprecedented gesture of openness and generosity the German editors have not only provided extensive information about the progress of their work, but have actually allowed access to their working papers. These are, however, by definition incomplete. Hence, although the debt of this edition to their work is massive, and most gratefully acknowledged, it is their *provisional* conclusions which are cited below as Bräuer/Kobuch. The sole responsibility for errors and lacunae rests with the present editor.

Moreover, since the renumeration is not complete, and some quite new material on the Nuremberg patrician, Christopher Fürer, is to be published by Dr Bubenheimer, this edition, except for the first four letters, and some minor modifications of the rest, will abide by the enumeration of Franz. Since dating has been changed in some

2

instances this produces certain anomalies but the only alternative was to produce an English edition which corresponded neither to Kirn-Franz nor to the forthcoming edition.

Overwhelmingly, the content is religious, frequently being pastoral in tone, with countless references to Müntzer's piety (Nrs. 7, 13, 24, 32, 40), to issues of personal morality (Nrs. 31, 51, 57), to his mystical theology (Nrs. 35, 41, 46, 47, 49, 61) to the need for an adult, disciplined faith (Nrs. 31, 33, 53). To our surprise, perhaps, Müntzer emerges as a 'spiritual director' (Nrs. 48, 57, 61, 69), an interpreter, even, of dreams (Nrs. 62, 63). Nowadays we might call him a therapist or a counsellor; a guru whose advice people sought from far and wide.

This range of gifts – as teacher, pastor, counsellor, liturgist, exegete – tends to be forgotten. His correspondence reminds us of it. It also underlines his literary skills. As a sustained hymn of hate his letter to Ernest of Mansfeld (Nr. 88) has, of course, all the qualities commonly associated with Müntzer, the 'fanatic'. It is however, letters like that of July 1523 to Luther (Nr. 40), or the warning to the 'brothers' in Stolberg (41), or the lyrical epistle to 'George' (Nr. 61) or again the remarkable series of letters to Zeiss (Nrs. 46, 57, 58, 59) which show his real eloquence, his persuasive charm, his originality. He writes with great economy of words, but with an extraordinary profusion of images, positive and negative, which integrate argument and experience in a fascinating, if sometimes misleading manner: the 'key of knowledge', the fish rising to the surface from the murky depths, the 'black crow', the 'sack of gunpowder'. He relates contemporary event to Biblical saga, sets eschatological perspectives to contemporary events, even sees himself in mythical terms: as God's trumpeter or watchman, as a protective bastion or wall, as the courier of God, as Jehu, Gideon, David, John the Baptist. The present becomes a recapitulation of the Biblical past, discipleship a *conformitas* with its sufferings, a concelebration of its triumphs.

Yet when all this has been said we have still barely begun. Müntzer's correspondence certainly throws vivid light on the 'grass-roots' realities of the early Reformation, or, to use his own metaphor, on its less 'ornamental' aspects. Yet it progressively bursts these categories. We note the perplexity of Müntzer and his friends as the alienation from the Wittenbergers gathers pace (Nr. 30, 48), as the latter's theological leadership and then their social and political stances are challenged. The very term 'Christian' comes to acquire a dubious connotation, as Christians have become Turks (Nr. 55) and so-called Christian rulers persecute the faithful (Nr. 57). Christendom is revealed as both sly and foolish (Nr. 67); to obtain justice one has to appeal to the elect beyond the corrupt Christian fold (Nrs. 52, 64).

On the eve of the visit to Prague in 1521 the tone is still anxious, agitated (Nrs. 22, 24) but thereafter an apocalyptic note begins to be sounded (Nr. 25); the summer, the harvest is at hand (Nr. 31), the names of the elect are written in heaven (Nr. 32), the godless are already shaking in their shoes (Nr. 53). The letter to Stolberg (Nr. 41), however, warns us against assuming that a disciplined and individualistic mysticism is being replaced by an enthusiastic, socially-oriented apocalyticism; in fact they complement one another.

The persecution of evangelical fugitives and the Mallerbach incident in 1524 however, harden Müntzer's conviction that it is the elect, schooled in mystical resignation (Nr. 55), fearing God alone, who attract the wrath of the godless tyrants but are alone immune to their threats (Nrs. 47, 49). Political authority is thus relativised; rulers should be loved, not feared, by the elect (Nr. 45); passive resistance is justified (Nr. 50); it becomes imperative to denounce the injustice suffered to the tribunal of the elect throughout the world (Nr. 52); for secular (pagan) political authority has become an idol, an obstacle to the true fear of God; a complete transformation of the world is at hand (Nr. 58).

Müntzer now sees himself increasingly as the advocate of the 'poor people' to whom power should be transferred from the tyrants (Nrs. 57, 84). He seems still, however, relatively unconcerned about their material welfare (Nr. 59) and is far from urging active rebellion. The League of the Elect is an interim, emergency measure of self-defence (Nr. 59), to prevent the elect being decimated by the godless. Yet unless the Saxon princes act decisively and speedily to defend the righteous they will forfeit the confidence of the people (Nrs. 59, 64, 67).

Religious categories are not being replaced at this stage by political ones; they are being broadened to include the latter. Trial, temptation (*anfechtung*), for example, gains a political dimension (Nrs. 67, 72); for the sake of the elect vengeance will have to be loosed on the godless (Nr. 67); the common man, hungry and exploited socially as well as religiously, is everywhere coming to the truth (Nrs. 70, 71).

In fact, Müntzer never develops a political strategy comparable to his liturgical or mystical 'strategies', unless his short-lived hopes for a godly prince (Nr. 45) are accounted such. He moves directly and abruptly from religious reformation to military involvement in the Peasants' War (Nrs. 75ff.), to millenarian propaganda (Nrs. 75, 84), to theocratic, populist justice (Nrs. 78, 83, 84, 85, 86).

In many of his later letters Müntzer writes on behalf of, and in conjunction with, a whole 'community', of Allstedt, or Mühlhausen, or the peasant army. Even in his earlier letters many are not personal, private correspondence, but have a public, proclamatory, didactic, almost 'apostolic' character. They are addressed, in the name of Jesus, to 'dear brothers' and signed not by an individual, nor – after Nr. 43 – in Müntzer's formal capacity as pastor, but as the servant of God, the disturber of the godless, the wielder of the sword of Gideon. Thus his letters, as *Sendbriefe*, open letters, or *Unterrichtung*, as 'instructions' are intimately related to other aspects of his ministry, his liturgies, his sermons, his tracts. The reversion, in his very last letter, to the simple signature, Thomas Müntzer, indicates the collapse of his mission.

Yet this moving, dignified letter (Nr. 94), after defeat and torture and on the eve of his death, reveals again the caring pastor (and husband), the ardent pursuer of divine truth. Largely self-taught, an exile from every kind of security, he emerges in his letters as a very vulnerable person, too open to the sufferings of others for his own good. If he resorted in the end to utopian violence it was because he could not remain passive while others suffered. If he became censorious and dogmatic it was because his genuine questions had remained unanswered. Out of the most unpromising circumstances, and working with very 'ordinary', in his words, 'crude' people he won for himself, for a time, room to create and foster new forms of individual and communal life and thought. If his militancy had been more disciplined and his mysticism less moralistic perhaps the integration he sought might have been achieved. As it is his fragmented vision mirrors the crisis-torn society to which he sought to minister.

1. *Claus, Servant of Hans Pelt, to Müntzer. Halberstadt. 25 July, 1515.*[1]

To the honourable Master Thomas Müntzer,[2] provost in Frose, my good lord and most faithful friend etc.

With all my heart and soul and goods I am at your service. Most learned, worthy, beloved lord, castigator of unrighteousness:[3] I hope your honour and all your friends(?)[4] are well. Your honour should know, too, that I have delivered the five letters of your honour left with Hans Pelt,[5] and have received from the honourable Hans

1. Previously Nr. 3 in Böhmer/Kirn and Franz, due to a falsely transcribed date: 25 July 1517; cf. Ulrich Bubenheimer, 'Thomas Müntzer in Braunschweig' Part 1, *Braunschweigisches Jahrbuch* 65 (1984), 37–77, esp. 44, 67f.; recent research by Bubenheimer and S. Bräuer has thrown quite new light on Müntzer's early career, especially in Brunswick; cf. S. Bräuer 'Thomas Müntzers Beziehungen zur Braunschweiger Frühreformation', *Theologische Literaturzeitung* 109 (1984), 636–8; U. Bubenheimer, 'Thomas Müntzer und der Anfang der Reformation in Braunschweig', *Nederlands Archief voor Kerkgeschiedenis* 65 (1985), 1–30; idem, 'Thomas Müntzer in Braunschweig' Part 2, *Braunschweigisches Jahrbuch* 66 (1985), 79–114; cf. also p. 441 below; at this stage, it is clear that the last word on Müntzer's early life has yet to be spoken; Elliger, p. 9ff., however, has demonstrated that many of Goebke's genealogical conclusions are speculative ('Neue Forschungen über Thomas Müntzer ...' *Harz-Zeitschrift* 9 (1957), 1–30); neither the date of his birth in Stolberg nor the names of his parents have been established with certainty; the dating usually favoured is c. 1488–90; Matthias Montzer, councillor and master of the mint in Stolberg 1484–1501, cannot be his father, for he died in 1501 (Bräuer), and Müntzer's father was still alive in 1521 (cf. Letter 26); Bubenheimer suggests 1482 or earlier as a likely date and that Johann Munther may be his father; 'Thomas Müntzer und der Anfang der Reformation in Braunschweig', NAK 65, 19f.; Bubenheimer I, 73 n. 9; but cf. S. Bräuer 'Zu Müntzers Geburtsjahr', LJ 36, 80–3; a relatively firm date is his immatriculation at the university of Leipzig in 1506 (but cf. Bubenheimer, NAK 65, 21f.); and certainly at Frankfurt university in 1512; his time as an 'assistant' in Aschersleben and Halle no doubt preceded his studies at Frankfurt; cf. p. 437/22ff.; by 1514 he was a priest in Brunswick, which suggests a minimum age of 24; he was also a master of arts; thus by 1515 he was well qualified to be 'provost' to the canonesses of Frose, with ample time to pursue his studies further.

2. *Thoma* [sic] *Monnetarii*; only the form of address is in Latin; Claus has been identified as Claus Winkeler, a resident of Brunswick, employed since 1513 by the merchant Hans Pelt in the collection of debts; cf. Bubenheimer, I, p. 67; on Frose cf. Letter 2, n. 1.

3. *vorfolger der unrechtverdicheyt*; the reference appears to be to personal piety, not social criticism; cf. the reference later on in the letter to the 'fiery love of purity'.

4. The word is illegible; Böhmer/Kirn and Franz suggest *partilats*, which has no obvious meaning; *partilais* (Bräuer/Kobuch) is also incomprehensible.

5. *ick habbe de breffe v, de by Hanss Pelten gesant*; text as amended by Bubenheimer I, 68; clearly when he was away in Frose (cf. p. 441, n. 1 below) Müntzer's post was kept in Pelt's house; Pelt was active as a merchant in Brunswick at least from 1504 on, with extensive trading relations to the Netherlands, Dortmund, Goslar, Halberstadt, Quedlinburg, Magdeburg, Leipzig, Nuremberg, Frankfurt, and other towns; he traded in wool and other goods; he held numerous civic offices, and was an early

Dammann[6] two gulden, at 40 groschen a gulden, and a letter from him to you is enclosed, from which you will readily grasp his intentions. I have also received two gulden, at 31 groschen a gulden, and 40 groschen which his son should have for a book about which he had written to him. In addition he sent him six groschen to help him out. And Henning Binder[7] sends Thomas a parcel, with a letter which should explain everything to you. And I enclose ten groschen to help him out;[8] I really intended to come to see you myself, but had not time to do so, but I will, God willing, be with you soon. Live in health and holiness before God Almighty in the fiery love of purity.[9] And give the good folk my greetings, together with my dear father, grandmother, and mother. God willing, I will be with them soon.[10]

Written with haste on the day of St. James the Apostle, in the year 15. Halberstadt.

Claus, the servant of Hans Pelt.

2.   *Ludolph Wittehovet to Müntzer (Brunswick, 1515–16(?)).*[11]

Written to his honour, Master Thomas Müntzer, provost in Frose,[12] in friendship and respect.

---

supporter of the Reformation in Brunswick, from the later 1520s a pillar of the Lutheran church; Bubenheimer I, 68 n. 1, 71f.; he is not identical with the butcher, Hans Pelt, of Stolberg; cf. also Letters 4, 26, 28 above.

6. *Hanss Tammanz*; held various civic offices in Brunswick between 1510 and 1527; he was again a merchant, a pointer to the circles in which Müntzer moved; he was married to Wynneke, a sister of Ludolph Wittehovet, who may be identical with Müntzer's correspondent in Letter 2; he may have been related to Henning Binder, also mentioned in this letter; the sums of money are clearly to pay Müntzer for instructing his son, among others; he died in 1530; cf. Bubenheimer I, 68 n. 2.

7. *Unde Henick Binder sendet Thomass 1 pack unde eyn breff;* text as amended by Bubenheimer; he was a brewer, serving on the Council for the Hagen district 1516–19; his son, Bartolt, later a goldsmith, may also have been one of Müntzer's pupils; (Bubenheimer I, 68 n. 3); Henning Binder was dead by 11 June 1519; Bräuer, 'T. Müntzers Beziehungen zur Braunschweiger Frühreformation', p. 637.

8. Bubenheimer, II. 84 n. 31, takes this to be a reference to Müntzer himself, but it may be for Binder's son, if he were there; the third person *zw sinem behoeffe* seems odd if Müntzer himself is meant.

9. *Godde dem almechtigen gesunt unde salich leved in der hitzegen leve der reynicheyt.*

10. Elliger, p. 44, characterises the tone of the letter as one of respectful intimacy.

11. This letter is undated; Goebke assumed the letter was written in Aschersleben, shortly after Müntzer became 'provost' in Frose, dating it before 30 August 1516; Böhmer-Kirn dated it 1516–17, from Halberstadt; Franz opted for Aschersleben; Bräuer, however, attributes it, like Letters 1 and 4, to Müntzer's circle of acquaintances in Brunswick, and regards its writer as a one-time pupil of Müntzer; the Wittehovets were a prominent family in Brunswick; op. cit., p.637; Bubenheimer I, 45, 52, 54, 69, identifies the writer with the *Ludolphus Wittehoveth Brunswicensis*, who studied at Wittenberg, held a benefice at St Michael's Church,

First of all, I am yours to command, my dear Master Thomas. You should know that I am sending you this letter by Claus, Pelt's servant,[13] to inform you what I have been thinking about and why I am so very angry. I can only suppose that when your cook requested the heated room,[14] in which I was staying, my dear Master Thomas, that she did not know any fair way[15] to drive me out, but attacked me with wild accusations, and, like a very rogue, betrayed me, creeping behind your coats while telling me the sweetest words she knew. When she went to you, my dear lord, she used words that were three times more shameful: apparently she said[16] that if she wanted the heated room, I should be glad for her to have this. My dear Master Thomas, you should know that I am, God be praised, innocent of what your cook has told you I have committed, or may I perish this very day.[17] But you should know better than to love women; I could never have imagined that you would alienate me from my friends over a matter like this. Still even if I do risk antagonising my friends, I will say nothing but the truth. That is all for the moment; a good night's rest to you all. Please send your good friend[18] a letter by Claus, Pelt's servant, I beg you.

Ludolph Wittehovet

Brunswick from 1503 and, he believes, shared a house owned by Hans Pelt with Müntzer while they carried out their liturgical duties at Our Lady's altar of St Michael's; the letter would then refer to difficulties which arose with Müntzer's cook, when Müntzer was absent in Frose; to some extent the evidence remains circumstantial.

12. The title and office of a *prepositus* in the Gernrode foundation for canonesses in Frose (6 km. from Aschersleben) is as yet undocumented, Bubenheimer I, 55.

13. *bi Clawes Pelten.*

14. *dornsen*; perhaps an indication that the letter was written during the cold season!

15. *myt ghelike.*

16. *Se schol jehe haben ghezaghet*; text as amended by Bubenheimer I, 69; *jehe* has been written in above the line and the reading is uncertain; Böhmer/Kirn and Franz read *scholl me.*

17. Bubenheimer, 1, 54, takes this to mean that Wittehovet has been accused of spreading allegations about Müntzer having affairs with women.

18. *schwager*; can be used to mean 'boon friend' as well as 'brother-in-law'; Bubenheimer I, 54, sees it as referring to Hans Pelt; the translation would then read: 'Please send your brother-in-law, Hans Pelt a letter by means of Claus,' i.e. asking him to settle the controversy; but it seems unlikely that they would want Hans Pelt involved in this squalid quarrel; as yet we have no evidence of kinship between Pelt and Müntzer; it seems best to assume that *dem schwager* refers, rather impersonally, to Wittehovet himself.

3. *Matthew Volmar*[19] *to Müntzer, (Aschersleben?), after 24 August 1516.*

To be delivered to his reverence, Master Thomas, pastor[20] in Frose. Revered sir and most beneficient patron. This present acquaintance of mine is afflicted by a throat ailment, as he himself will explain more fully to your honour. Now he has been reliably informed by some others who suffered from the same ailment and whom your treatment restored to complete health that you, most excellent of men, can cure this same disease. If this is indeed so, I beg you, by the unique bond of love which unites this man and me, to consider my prayers and his well-being and to save and cure him from this venomous ailment. Henceforth you will find me your most obedient servant. Farewell, and may you enjoy the years of Nestor. In haste. Anno Domini 1516 on the Saturday[21] after St. Bartholomew. Your Matthew Volmar.

4. *The Rector of St. Martin's School in Brunswick*[22] *to Müntzer (Brunswick, 1518(?)).*[23]

To his reverence Master Thomas M.,[24] Master of arts and most

19. Born in Aschersleben, 1504 studied in Erfurt; 1509–11 town clerk in Aschersleben, 1512 councillor, 1531 magistrate (Goebke), burgomaster 1542, 1545, 1551, 1557 (Bräuer) d. 1557; in Latin.

20. *domini Thome pastor*; Böhmer-Kirn read *peken*, Franz: *Muther*; Bubenheimer: *parhen* (= *Pfarre*, parish); careful palaeographical investigation suggests it is either *p[ro]vsten* (provost) or *pastor* (Bräuer/Kobuch); the difficulties with the reading led Köhler (HZ 145, 389) to doubt whether the letter was in fact directed to Müntzer, as did G. Vogler, 'T. Müntzer als Student der Viadrina', in G. Haase, J. Winkler (edd.) *Die Oder-Universität Frankfurt* (Weimar, 1983), p. 243; Müntzer's presence in Frose is, however, attested by Letters 1 and 2, and as Elliger remarks, p. 40 n. 36, the apparently unusual request for medical advice may only mean that Müntzer was known to have access to a successful remedy for sore throats!

21. *sabbato post Bartholomei*; (Bräuer/Kobuch), a large ink blot obscures the date; 7ta (F.) is grammatically impossible.

22. It is interesting, as Elliger, p. 46, points out, that neither the writer nor the addressee are named; Bubenheimer has identified the writer as Heinrich Hanner, ordained priest in Hildesheim in 1506, who secured his Master of Arts in Paris and by 1516 was almost certainly Rector, *artium professor*, in the St Martin's school; in June 1518 he matriculated in Wittenberg, in 1523 in Leipzig; 'Thomas Müntzer und der Anfang der Reformation in Braunschweig', NAK 65, 17f; in Latin.

23. Bubenheimer suggests that this undated letter was written in June/July 1517 since its latter paragraphs clearly reflect the controversies raging in Brunswick at that time about the indulgences issued by the Benedictine abbey of Königslutter, some 23 km. from Brunswick; the Dominican John Tetzel had suspended its privileges in favour of the St Peter's indulgence promulgated in Pope Leo X's Bull of 31 March 1515; on the protest of the abbey Duke Henry the Younger of Brunswick-

learned of men, at present a guest of Hans Pelt.[25]

As the person now in charge of the academy of St. Martin's School, Brunswick, but as a disciple[26] to his master, I write to his reverence Master Thomas Müntzer, master of arts, most learned of men, glad to put my mind at his disposal (a rude and very darkened one indeed, but one ready to be instructed and illuminated by sounder information). And I ask Master Thomas to be good enough formally[27] to

---

Wolfenbüttel had intervened and secured the revocation of Tetzel's suspension on 20 June 1517; Elliger, accordingly, dates the letter shortly before 20 June; in view of the likelihood of continuing confusion among the populace Bubenheimer suggests a more flexible dating; he rejects, however, any dependence of Hanner's argumentation on Luther's 95 *Theses* or his *Sermon on Indulgence and Grace* which was printed in Brunswick in a lower Saxon version in 1518; as a Rector, whose pupils would be involved in the ceremonial institution of such indulgence, he had his own professional as well as personal grounds for concern; ibid., 9–15; S. Bräuer argues that the theological and hermeneutical questions raised by the letter do, in fact, show a debt to Luther; accordingly he dates it in 1518 ('Thomas Müntzers Beziehungen zur Braunschweiger Fruhreformation', 637); it does seem improbable that Hanner could have so unerringly hit upon precisely those issues which were central to Luther: remission of guilt by God alone, the role of the sacrament of penance, the authority of the pope, the ordinary person's concern for salvation, the treasure of the gospel; a degree of dependence on Luther and therefore a 1518 date seems the safest conclusion; the indulgences were distributed on 29 June, St Peter and St Paul's day, in Königslutter. The correspondence between Abbot John, his prince, and the relevant officials of the Magdeburg church is found in J. E. Kapp (ed.), *Kleine Nachlese einiger ... zur Erläuterung der Reformationsgeschichte nützlichen Urkunden*, III (Leipzig, 1730) pp. 217–33 (F.)

24. *Thome M.* is repeated twice.

25. Müntzer is back in Brunswick, then, by this time, and staying with Hans Pelt; the letter itself, with its touch of anonymity, is a curious blend of directness and formality; although they live in the same city – indeed just around the corner from one another – (Bräuer), Hanner explicitly requests a written reply; the Rector does not appear to belong to the inner circle of lay friends of Müntzer (cf. Letters 26, 28 below); Bräuer, op. cit., pp. 636–8, has suggested that they cultivated, prior to the Reformation, a form of Bible-orientated, lay mysticism to which Müntzer may have appealed by an early version of his teaching about following the 'bitter Christ' (cf. p. 220/20); Bubenheimer has presented a convincing account of the social milieu in which Müntzer moved: prosperous, mobile merchants and goldsmiths, townspeople closely linked to one another through kinship, commercial interests, communal politics, and early support for the reforming cause; Bubenheimer II, *passim*.

26. The sharp contrast between *qui nunc regit* and *magistri discipulus* does not imply that Müntzer had been the previous Rector with Hanner as his pupil; it simply indicates that the latter was recently appointed; cf. Bubenheimer 1, 43f.; Müntzer could have been Hanner's 'master' in one of the other places where he taught (Halle, Aschersleben?); or there may be a degree of hyperbole in Hanner's language about his debt to Müntzer.

27. *formaliter*, or *finaliter* (Bräuer/Kobuch); *sententialiter* (F.)

communicate and graciously share with him his esteemed judgments about the queries set out in this sheet of paper, as is pleasing to him.

First and foremost, Master Thomas, your aforesaid disciple and pupil does not know what meaning to attach to that clause in the apostolic letters of indulgence from penalty and guilt affirming that guilt is remitted in the sacramental absolution.[28]

Again, what meaning is or can be attached to the firm statement that man cannot absolve a sin which has been perpetrated against God; since the prelates are only men and yet, so we are told, this plenary power has been entrusted to them.[29]

Again, whether or not all that our lord, the pope, intends or desires in this church matter, or is credibly attested in authentic letters as desiring or intending, has in fact been done by him or at his behest in the sight of God.[30]

Again, whether we should put our faith[31] in the letters which are authentic.

Again, whether or not the ordinary layman[32] should put his faith in apostolic letters which are not suspect and are immune from any erroneous falsification, after they have been scrutinised, examined, and received, and publicly examined and promulgated by the prelates; whether, I say, they should take them as gospel,[33] as is said, so that, as such letters argue, he can further his soul's salvation.[34]

---

28. Luther, of course, had preached about the extreme danger that 'the foolish and larger part of the populace will be deceived into believing that by plenary remission all sin has been taken away' (WA I, 65, 20ff.) on 27 July 1516, and on 31 October 1516 in Wittenberg (ibid., pp. 65–9; 94–9); but it seems most unlikely that Hanner would have heard of these sermons, which were not printed; of the 95 *Theses* those with most direct bearing on this point are 36, which speaks of *remissionem plenariam a poena et culpa etiam sine literis veniarum* 'Any truly repentant Christian has a right to full remission of penalty and guilt, even without indulgence letters' (LW 31, 28); cf. also Theses 76, 87 (WA I, 233–8); W. Köhler (ed.), *Dokumente zum Ablassstreit von 1517* (Tübingen, 1902), pp. 127ff.

29. Cf. Thesis 6 'The pope cannot remit any guilt ...' (LW 31, 26).

30. *item utrum dominus (pa)pa in negotio ecclesie faciat et per eum fiat coram deo omne quod intendit et vult et (quod) in literis non suspectis se velle et intendere sufficienter attestatur nec ne*; text as amended by Bubenheimer I, 70f.; much of the 95 *Theses* argues that the pope would be appalled if he knew what was being done in his name; cf. Theses 50, 70, 91.

31. Cf. Thesis 49: *Docendi sunt Christiani, quod veniae papae sunt utiles, si non in eas confidant ...* ('Christians are to be taught that the papal pardons have their value, provided they do not put their trust in them'); Köhler, op. cit., p. 136; and, from the Papal Bull, ibid. 91/31–92/1.

32. The final section of the 95 *Theses* deals with the 'shrewd questions of the laity', esp. 81, 90 and Luther's concern for the misunderstandings and deceit of the common people is evident throughout.

33. *tanquam evangelio*; cf. Theses 53–5.

34. Cf. Thesis 32.

Again, whether or not the treasure of the church[35] (which is the passion of Christ) is in any way augmented by the merit of the saints (as is preached to us).

Again, with nothing but good will in his heart and no trace of evil intent,[36] he asks Master Thomas to explain in as brief compass as possible, what his own view is of the indulgences which of late the friars of the Order of Preachers have been promulgating amongst us, despite the fierce and well-known opposition of the prelates.

Likewise, whether or not the indulgences in Königslutter which were proclaimed many years ago have now been revoked, as some claim.[37]

Thomas, my father,[38] do not be affected by the usual weariness at teaching the unlearned and informing the unlettered, since an aureola of the third kind awaits you.[39] Bear in mind that these are not idle queries but have a bearing on our salvation.

5. *Christian Döring, goldsmith in Wittenberg,[40] to Müntzer. 11 January 1519.*

To his honour, Master Thomas, now resident with the bookseller Christian[41] in the inn at Leipzig.

First of all, my best regards, dear Sir Thomas. This is to let you know that I have talked with Master Bartholomew[42] about you. He

35. Bubenheimer sees a different emphasis from the *95 Theses* (NAK 65, 15 n. 68; but cf. Theses 60, 62).

36. i.e. there is no intention to make Müntzer incriminate himself.

37. Clearly a reference to the suspension of all the indulgences in the dioceses of Magdeburg and Halberstadt by Tetzel; cf. n. 23 above and Bubenheimer I, 71 n. 7; part of the case of Abbot John of Königslutter was that his abbey's indulgence had 420 years of tradition behind it.

38. *pr*, probably *pater*; cf. Bubenheimer, 'Thomas Müntzer . . . in Braunschweig', NAK 65, 19 n. 94; Franz suggests *precor*.

39. Virginity was awarded a white crown, martyrdom a red one, learning a green one; cf. F., p. 348 n. 7; Bensing understands it literally, i.e. that Müntzer was about to be awarded the green wreath of honour for his teaching, and sees it as proof that Müntzer had been Rector of St Martin's before Hanner; *Thomas Müntzer Mit 74 Abbildungen* (Leipzig, 1983) p. 25.

40. One of the most prominent citizens of Wittenberg in the first third of the sixteenth century; cf. N. Müller, *Die Wittenberger Bewegung* (Leipzig, 1911), p. 126, n. 4; Bubenheimer II, 103–11, has pointed to the extraordinarily large numbers of goldsmiths with whom Müntzer had contacts, and suggested that Brunswick goldsmiths may well have put him in touch with Döring.

41. *bey Kristianus Buchfirer*; Christian Breithut (d. 1519) in the Ritterstrasse in Leipzig; cf. *Archiv für Geschichte des Buchwesens* 7 (1966), 1640, Nr. 702.

42. Bartholomew Bernhardi from Feldkirch; b. 1487, from 1518 provost of Kemberg, near Wittenberg; cf. WA, Br. 12, 216f.

says that if you want to become his chaplain, you should come to him at Easter time. If this is your intention you should write to tell him whether you will be coming or not, so that he knows what arrangements to make. A very good night's rest to you, then. Wittenberg, the Tuesday after Epiphany in the year 19.

Christian Döring, goldsmith in Wittenberg.

6.   John of Weida (O.P.) to Müntzer. Naumburg, 12 December 1519.

To the reverend Master[43] Thomas Müntzer, confessor to the nunnery of Beuditz.[44]

I greet you as you well deserve after writings as calumnious as yours. For you add the gall of bitterness and calumny to the sweetness of that love which you commend, although showering it with vituperation and showing not the least evidence of it yourself. This just shows that you are void of all virtue and crammed full of almost every poison of emulation. Finally you profess astonishment at my audacity, at how far I have departed from the truth in pretending to Hermann Färber[45] that I had won over the Mother Superior to oppose the provost.[46] Certainly, if you have looked carefully at the truth, at who the intermediary or rather the nun was who conveyed to me that message from the Mother Superior, you would not have vilified my name so vilely, for it is not the part of a prudent man to form his judgments hastily. For you interpret my words, written with a rustic directness, as menacing, which is quite unbecoming to one of your position, and contrary to the Imperial laws and to the sacred canons. For the interpretation of words pertains to the person who dictates them, not to him who reads or listens to them. May you proceed, then, with your nuns in your accustomed way; I, too, will proceed

43. *magistro*; the letter(s) of Müntzer to which he is replying is lost; in Latin.

44. A Cistercian foundation, near Weissenfels, probably founded in 1232; after Frose, Müntzer's movements are obscure; he seems to have been in Brunswick until about October 1518 when he was expelled; then, probably after brief visits to Leipzig and Wittenberg, he took Franz Günther's place as preacher in Jüterbog around Easter 1519; cf. pp. 447ff.; he probably visited Orlamünde, may have attended the famous Leipzig Disputation in July 1519, and then, by now a convinced Martinian, became confessor to the nuns at Beuditz, presumably for financial reasons; cf. Elliger, p. 69.

45. Cf. Nr. 12, p. 18 below; fields belonging to the Ferber family adjoined those of the monastery (Bräuer/Kobuch).

46. Presumably a reference to Frose, where Müntzer was 'provost'; cf. Letter Nr. 2, n. 11.

without any help[47] from you, as befits a religious man. May you flourish as you wish me to flourish. Naumburg, on 12 December. Brother John of Weida of the order of preachers in the Leipzig house, terminarius in Naumburg.

7.   *Müntzer to Franz Günther. 1 January 1520.*[48]

To the most learned and able Master of arts and of philosophy and Bachelor of sacred Scripture,[49] Franz Günther, my most beloved brother in Christ.

I had no reason to write, dearest of brethren, otherwise I would have written you long ago to say where I was. Do write me about the outcome of your old controversies with the cowled gentlemen. And add something about the attention the people are giving to the divine word, about the state of your own health and that of your sister and tell me, too, what progress you are making in your own private or individual studies, and what books you are reading so I may have cause to congratulate you on your life. I am employed in a nunnery called Beuditz, near Weissenfels. I must needs be content with a shortened rein,[50] but take comfort from the fact that I am not impeded by the nuisance of the Jewish chants and observances,[51] and rejoice that ample time remains for my studies. I read again the first six books of Doctor Augustine,[52] and have gone through other volumes of histories; it has been a bitter cross to me in my Lord Jesus that so far I have been unable to procure many of the authors I need so badly. It is not myself I am concerned about but the Lord Jesus. If it is his wish, he will send me wherever he will, and in the meantime I am content with my lot. Everything is done by God in true judgment on my most wretched self, because I often set myself in the preaching chair without being forced to.[53] I have nothing else to say, not

47. *sine tuo ministerio*; there may be a reference here to conflicting jurisdictions.

48. Written from Beuditz; Franz Günther of Nordhausen studied in Erfurt and Leipzig, clashed with the Franciscans in Jüterbog in early 1519 until his temporary replacement by Müntzer; in August 1520 he became preacher at the Electoral residence of Lochau, when he died in 1528 (F.); cf. pp. 42f.; in Latin.

49. An interesting stress, for Günther had already advanced to be a lecturer on the *Sentences* of Peter Lombard in 1518. (F.)

50. Persius, 4 Satire, V. 52; i.e. his environment is not stimulating.

51. The Choral Office.

52. Amerbach's edition, Basel 1506. (F.)

53. *Non coactus*; presumably the meaning is that he had often preached from a sense of duty, not under the inner compulsion of the Holy Spirit; cf. the reference above to outward compulsion: *Cogor curta suppellectili esse contentus.*

wanting to strain your good-will by my loquacity. May the Lord Jesus be crucified with you. Pray that by faith in the holy Scriptures this may always be my lot, too. Farewell, then, dearest brother; the Kalends of January, the year of our Lord 1520.

Thomas Müntzer, your brother in Christ.

8.   *Müntzer to Achatius Glov, bookseller in Leipzig. Beuditz, 3 January 1520.*

To the honourable and distinguished man, Achatius Glov, bookseller for Master Melchior Lotter; to be found in the Haymarket[54] or below the Town Hall.[55]

The blessing of Christ[56] Jesus be with you, best of friends. You will have forgotten my name. My name is in fact Thomas Müntzer of Stolberg; you called me Thomas of Wittkennaw.[57] This very man is anxious to do business with you. Please see that the name is not changed in the register. I received the chronicle of Eusebius at the time of the disputation;[58] I do not recollect what you charged me. I gladly send 6 groschen for the Hegesippus[59] you sent me, 20 denarii for the two copies of Emser's *Venatio* against Martin.[60] I return intact to your good self the concordance of canon law with Scripture.[61] Tell me how much I owe you for the chronicle of Eusebius,[62] and what the price is of the collected works of Jerome[63] and of the letters and sermons of Saint Augustine.[64] I will buy these within forty days if you write. I would be very indebted if you would send me the acts of the Council of Constance[65] and at the same time the acts of the council of Basel,[66]

54. lit. Hay Street; in Latin.

55. *sub pretorio*, i.e. the vaults beneath the Town Hall. (F.)

56. χρηστι; Jesus is written separately just above the letter.

57. Probably not Wittgenau in Silesia (F.), a small village, but Wittichenau, to the south of Hoyerswerda (Bräuer/Kobuch).

58. Of Leipzig, June–July 1519.

59. The old Latin translation of Josephus, *The Jewish War*; 1510, 1511 published in Paris under name of Hegesippus. (F.)

60. *A venatione Luteriana Aegocerotis assertio*. Leipzig 1519. The words 'and 4 denarii for D. Martin's letter against Eck' have been crossed out. (F.)

61. Perhaps that by Johannes Calderinus; d. 1365? (F.)

62. *The Chronicle of Eusebius*, as translated and expanded by Jerome, had been printed in Paris in 1512, 1518. (F.)

63. The edition by Erasmus, published by Froben in 9 volumes, 1516–1518, Basel. (F.)

64. The *Letters* appeared in Paris in 1517, the *Sermons* in 1516. (F.)

65. Milan, 1511. (F.)

66. Paris, 1512. (F.)

unbound. Farewell, then, in Christ[67] Jesus. The third of the nones of January 1520. Please pass on my kind regards to Master Tulichius.[68]

Thomas Müntzer of Stolberg, confessor to the virgins in Beuditz.

9. *Achatius Glov to Müntzer. Leipzig, 1520 (after 3 January).*

To the honourable Master Thomas of Stolberg, now resident in Beuditz let this letter etc.

First my devoted and hearty good will to you, honourable and gracious Master. I have received in accordance with your communication six groschen for Hegesippus, four groschen for the concordance of the law and the Bible, for which I myself had to pay five groschen, and twenty denarii for the *Aegocerotem* of Emser. So your honour owes me ten groschen for the chronicle of Eusebius, which I do not sell for less than half a florin. I can further inform you that the latest edition of Jerome's works by Erasmus sells for nine or eight and a half florins; likewise the two volumes of the letters and sermons of Augustine cost one and a half florins each, unbound. In this, good Master, I will be most ready to be of service to you. Leipzig at the time of the New Year's Fair, in the year of the Lord 1520.

Achatius Glov, at Melchior Lotter's, servant to your honour.[69]

10. *Henry of Bünau, Archdeacon of Elsterberg,[70] to Müntzer. Leipzig, 21 April 1520.*

To the honourable and worthy gentleman, Master Thomas Müntzer, now in Beuditz, my most gracious and good friend. Greetings! My honourable, worthy, good Sir and Master. I ask you once again not to let anything prevent you from setting off on Wednesday or Thursday and installing yourself in my house, and just act as if you were my vicar.[71] Do your Scripture reading; I will not let you go again.[72] I will

67. χρο.

68. Hermann Tulichius, 1512–20 in Leipzig; worked in M. Lotter's printing press as a proof reader. Luther dedicated the *Babylonian Captivity* (1520) to him. (F.)

69. *Achatius Glov, Melchior Lott dien EW.*

70. Pastor in Elsterberg 1517–1533; the letter, as Bräuer points out, is full of riddles.

71. *conventor.*

72. *Lost bibliam lessen, ich wil euch wider nicht lossn*; the meaning is unclear; either: 'Leave off your Bible reading' (at Beuditz), and come to Elsterberg; or: 'Have the Bible read,' i.e. introducing a reforming order of service will not endanger his staying at Elsterberg.

do all in my power to give your good honour as much help as the Zwickau people will.[73] Do not let yourself be frightened or misled. Talk to my housekeeper, who can give Master Maurice[74] the best advice. If he wants to gain my favour he should stay in the post to which he was first appointed. Give Martin the letter, let nothing hinder you from bringing the letter.[75] Spend the time well in eating, drinking and resting until I arrive. I will not be away long, Jack Pudding,[76] Jack Roast Pudding, my dear sonny boy! Leipzig, the Saturday after Low Sunday, in the year etc., 1520.

Henry of Bünau, archdeacon.

11. *The nun Ursula*[77] *to Müntzer. After mid-May, 1520.*

To the worthy gentleman, Master Thomas, my gracious master etc.

Ave Maria for your salvation. Worthy, kind sir. I send you five of our loaves to remind you that I still have a bone to pick with you,[78] so you can't be left in peace yet. I cannot believe that it was from Tauler or Brother Suso[79] that you learned, or read in their writings, about buying the pretty maidens presents at the fair. Indulge in this to your heart's content; you will certainly find that it does you no harm.[80] I have got the permission of my worthy mistress[81] for this, which her honour kindly and gladly gave me.

S. Ursula Scho.

73. He has clearly heard of the negotiations in train to appoint Müntzer to a temporary post in St. Mary's, Zwickau; cf. Nr. 15, n. 124.

74. Maurice Reynhard; cf. Nr. 17.

75. *Gebt Mart. den briff, lost euch nicht vornehmen, das ir den priff brengk*; Martin could simply be a messenger, but cf. Martin Luther's letter of 30 May 1520 to von Bünau referring to 'Thomas', and promising to try to secure him a chaplain, WABr. 2, 709 (Bräuer); *vornehmen* can mean *zuvorkommen*, Grimm 26, 1357, as translated here; a more common sense is *vernehmen*, 'Do not let it be known that you are bringing the letter,' another possible translation.

76. *Hans Worst*; the cordial tone suggests a friendly relationship; Beuditz is on the route between Elsterberg and Leipzig, so they could easily have met before (Bräuer).

77. Identity unknown; if the signature *Scho.* is an abbreviation for *Scholastica* she was the teacher in her convent, cf. Bräuer, LJ 38 (1971), 130; Franz suggests that the letter was written from Beuditz, between May 1520 and April 1521, when Müntzer had moved on to Zwickau, but there is no firm evidence for place or date.

78. *das ir noch ein dicks mit mir habt*; translation uncertain.

79. Henry Suso's treatise *On Eternal Wisdom*, was much read in monastic houses and could be meant here; Müntzer probably possessed the Augsburg edition of Tauler's sermons, cf. *Protestation*, n. 279 below; he certainly uses Suso's image of the door-mat, cf. below.

80. *vertraigen* = damage; Grimm 12, i, 1928 (Bräuer).

81. The abbess.

12. *Hermann Färber*[82] *to Müntzer. Weissenfels, 6 July 1520.*

To the worthy gentleman, Master Thomas Müntzer, preacher at Zwickau, my good sir.

Many greetings! Worthy, good, dear master. I am always happy to hear that you are well and prosperous. Worthy sir, recently I gave your servant a letter to take to the abbot of Grünhain. Since I have not had an answer, I do not know if the letter was delivered or not. I wanted to get confirmation of this. I am always glad to be of service to you again.

The Friday after St. Ulrich's Day, in (the year) 20. Hermann Färber, citizen of Weissenfels.

Convey to my sister-in-law, the wife of Blasius the pewterer, from me and my wife best wishes for many good nights' rest.

13. *Müntzer to Luther. (Zwickau), 13 July 1520.*

Jesus be with you!

The council has appointed me, most benign father, to seek your advice in my case against those who incriminate me, who rage throughout the day, driven by a spirit of dizziness,[83] dragging me now this way, now that, drenched with the waters of the great sea. They have cited me before the protector of their privileges,[84] in order to make me recant my denunciation not of mendicant monks but of all hypocrites, who for a piece of bread, bring to life the souls of those who are not alive[85] and devour the homes of the widows with their long prayers,[86] not promoting faith in those who are dying, but their own insatiable avarice. I said that such men, whether monks or priests,[87] had seduced the church of God; I said that the laity, too, were likewise guilty who had failed hitherto to pray and sigh for shepherds of souls, hence the Lord had justly set blind watchers over the blind

---

82. Cf. Nr. 6; Hermann Ferber matriculated at Leipzig in 1503, belonging to a rich and influential family in Weissenfels (Bräuer/Kobuch).

83. Isaiah 19[14]; in Latin.

84. The Franciscan Provincial in Breslau, since 1519 Benedict of Löwenberg; cf. Gallus Haselbeck OFM (ed.), *Urkunden, Akten, Briefe und chronikalische Aufzeichnungen zur Geschichte der Thüringischen Ordensprovinz 1521–1600*, I (Fulda, 1925) pp. 2–4; II (Fulda, 1930) pp. 6, 12, 14.

85. Ezek. 13[19], 'You have violated my sanctity before my people ... with scraps of bread. You bring death to those who should not die, and life to those who should not live ...'; Elliger, p. 39 understands it as a reference to almsgiving as assuring salvation.

86. Matthew 23[14] – the hypocritical Scribes and Pharisees.

87. 'or laymen' is crossed out.

sheep.[88] Thus I always bind together monks, priests and laity in a common guilt, excepting no one, sparing no one, admonishing everyone to come to their senses, whether it is opportune or inopportune.[89] I confess that I said openly[90] on Ascension Day[91] that monstrosities wearing the helmets and shields of faith[92] should be shunned, referring to the ceremonies. They kick up an enormous din at this and claim to be defending the church which has already been destroyed elsewhere. They rave on with loud-voiced arguments like that to the ordinary[93] man and denounce me in querulous tones as a blasphemer against holy orders; they say I do not build up the twin forms of love[94] but destroy them etc. I embrace all these insane falsehoods of the adversaries as the sweetest exercise of my faith, being comforted by the gospel: 'If they followed my word, they will follow yours' etc.[95] If they perverted the word of Christ, they pervert mine too. I know that the word of the Lord does not return empty;[96] I know that in every place the eyes of the Lord look down upon both the good and the evil,[97] who cannot design or decide on anything unless it has been planted in their hearts. You are my advocate in the Lord Jesus. I beg you not to lend your ears to those who are defaming me. Do not believe those who have called me inconstant and murderous[98] and have assailed my reputation with six hundred other names. I do not care a snap of the fingers[99] about them; all these things are most pleasing to me through my Christ. Graver struggles are ahead of me; I have a manly trust that God intends notable things through your plans and those of all Christians. My cross is not yet complete; for the whole council supports me and almost the whole town; which from the cradle, as it were, knew how very harmful the avarice of the hypocrites was, and urged me, if you advise it, to appeal to a future council against these harpies and all their ravings. The town council wrote to Duke John to see that they did not molest those preaching the divine word. The town council itself has heard

88. Isaiah 56[10].
89. 2 Timothy 4[2].
90. Or, I confess freely that …' *'Ego fateor plane me dixisse'.*
91. In St. Mary's on 17 May. (F.)
92. Ephesians 6[16f.]
93. *coram plebe.*
94. *geminam charitatem*; Mt. 22[39f.]
95. John 15[20].
96. Isaiah 55[11].
97. Proverbs 15[3]; taken almost word for word from the Vg.
98. Peter Schumann reported Müntzer as declaring in his first sermon that one 'could cut off a pound of flesh from the monks' mouths and there would be mouth enough still.' Clemen, *Egran* 1, 18 n.45, quoted in Elliger, p.78.
99. *strepitus pollicis.*

virtually everything that I have preached. I also expressed my great willingness to meet the representatives of the bishop of Naumburg[100] to give an account of my faith and I expressed my readiness to lay before them all my sermons and amend anything in them which might be found contrary to Christian discretion. The Franciscans are as little satisfied by the one offer as by the other; they burden all men's ears with their stories, they walk around from home to home wailing about their cruel enemy. They say they are being crucified by hunger and are fading away. If you recommend it, I will reply to all these champions; but if I should appeal, write to tell me so. If a disputation should be arranged for them, just propose it. Whatever you suggest I will be prompt to do in the Lord. Sonorous assertions like these will set both your ears ringing:[101]

Christ died once for all, so that he need not die in us; nor should his sacrament be a comfort to us or his example be transformed into imitation. The services of the Mass preserve us from having to suffer in this world.

The new preachers preach nothing but the gospel but this is deplorable: for they contravene the commands of men which need to be observed most. Many things have to be added to the gospel.

One does not need to live according to the gospel all the time.

If poverty were evangelical, kings etc. would not be permitted to own the riches of the world.

If shepherds of souls and the religious ought to give an example of faith by renouncing their riches and thus leading their sheep by word and example, then the same poverty should be observed by princes and kings, so that they should possess nothing and be mendicants.

This is not a precept[102] of the gospel: 'If some one has struck you on the one cheek, offer him the other.' This is a claim of the heretics, to let them persecute the church with impunity, by inhibiting us from invoking the secular arm.

Predestination is an imaginary thing; it should not be included in faith, so that we base our confidence on it rather than on works; the people should not be cautioned against the latter, but the people of Zwickau, dear to me for 24 years, should continue to burn candles and perform the most virtuous works.

Eternal blessedness cannot be predicated of the kingdom of faith

100. Above all Eberhard von Thor and Heinrich Schmiedberg, respectively the deputy and chancellor of Bishop Philip, who was usually non-resident. The Zwickau Council records of 13 June mention a complaint by Schmiedberg about Müntzer's 'crude and extreme' preaching, and it seems Müntzer was interrogated by the episcopal court. (F.)

101. 1 Samuel 3[11].

102. Matthew 5[39]; but a counsel of perfection.

within us,[103] since only in the future will it be our homeland; here we are most uncertain about our blessedness.

All these articles he poured out at once in a sermon to the people.[104]

From the depths of my being I urged this Franciscan father, Tiburtius of Weissenfels, not to broadcast such errors among the people to the peril of their souls, but rather to give me and the council an account of his faith, solidly based on Scriptural passages in their genuine meaning. Crueller than any beast of prey, he said he would do neither the one nor the other but asserted confidently that I would be overthrown by his whole order. Into his chariot he climbed, a furious athlete pouring out curses. I mocked at his fury, dreading nothing, not even a whole cohort of mendicants coming to summon me, tear me to pieces and slay me. It is not my work I am doing, but that of the Lord. I will not suffer, as long as the one spirit inspires me, these mournful chants, these hypocritical antics; I will combat them with unceasing groans and with the trumpet of the word of God, lest the name of the Lord be blasphemed by those who are so anxious to appear as Christians, while their feet are swift to stir up dissension in the people of God[105] and to confuse heaven and earth. If you advise me to write against these assertions with the help of my very trustworthy brothers, Doctor Grosse[106] and his representative and the teacher of Greek,[107] and with the other masters[108] who are assisting me I will do so, so that the adversaries of the cross[109] may learn to revere the name of God and to silence the blasphemous mouth, so that the light which comforts[110] us may shine forth on all who are in the house of the Lord.[111] Please indicate what in all this you regard as Christian. I firmly believe I have been snatched[112] from my original danger for

103. Luke 17[21].

104. Tiburtius of Weissenfels; there was no Franciscan monastery in Weissenfels; Tiburtius was probably born there, and since 1496 at least occasionally preacher in the Zwickau monastery; he was lector at the Zeitz house; cf. Franz Doelle, *Reformationsgeschichtliches aus Sachsen. Vertreibung der Franziskaner aus Altenburg und Zwickau*, (1933), p. 49, n. 32.

105. Romans 3[15].

106. Dr Donat Grosse held the benefice of St. Mary's, but lived in Naumburg; his vicar was Master Wolfgang Zeuner.

107. George Bauer, or Agricola, from Glauchau, 1520–22 Rector of the Greek and Hebrew school which was united in April 1520 with the old Latin school; (F.) (not to be confused with John Agricola of Eisleben).

108. Probably above all Leonhard Nather, Rector of the Latin school and Jerome Nopius. (F.)

109. Philippians 3[18].

110. The term 'consolatio' is the same used in the first thesis attributed to Tiburtius of Weissenfels about the sacrament.

111. Matthew 5[15].

112. *segregatum*.

other struggles with this world. He who plucked me from the loathsome swamp will snatch me from the paw of the beast and the lion and the dragon,[113] so that I will not fear even if I walk in the midst of the shadow of death,[114] for the Lord is with me as a strong warrior.[115] He himself will provide the voice and the wisdom which none of our adversaries will be able to resist.[116] What more can I desire? Fare thee well in Christ, model and beacon to the friends of God!

St. Margaret's Day in the year of the Lord 1520.

Thomas Müntzer, whom you brought to birth by the gospel.[117]

14. *Müntzer to his Father.*[118]

The salvation of Christ be with you, my dear father. I had not expected to find you so lacking in loyalty, indeed so unfair to me, that you would try to deny me my natural rights, as if I were the child of a whore, indeed as if I were a heathen. I am utterly astonished that I have to make good the lack of faith in God that you have long shown, in being unable to support yourself. My mother brought you enough, as many folk in Stolberg and Quedlinburg have told me. She surely earned her bread three times over. You have ... her ...[119]

15. *Agricola to Müntzer. Wittenberg, 2 November 1520.*

To Master Thomas Müntzer, the man and the theologian, preacher at Zwickau, my brother[120] in Christ and cordial friend.

---

113. 2 Timothy 4[17].

114. Psalms 23[4].

115. Jeremiah 20[11].

116. Luke 21[15].

117. *Tomas Munczer quem g[en]uisti per evangelium*; The half-erased words reconstructed by Emmanuel Hirsch; (F.) it seems absolutely clear from the content that the letter was addressed to Luther; cf. Nr. 21, which seems to refer to it, p. 29/12, 25; the attempt to 'erase' physically his debt to Luther should be noted.

118. This draft letter is an extraordinary sight; it is a narrow strip of paper, 6 × 22 cm., smeared with ink and deliberately cut; the inside of it has been used for the book list on p. 000 below; most of the titles come from 1520, only one from 1521, which gives some hint as to the date of this letter; by June 1521 relations with his father had markedly improved (cf. Letter 26), presumably because the quarrel had ended in Müntzer's favour (cf. Letter 22); his father seems to have been living in Brunswick.

119. *Ir habet ir ...*

120. τῷ χριστῷ; in Latin.

[In the name of] God[121]

Greetings, dearest brother, in Christ Jesus.[122] I have to congratulate you on the situation you are in, being found worthy to bear fierce insults for the name of Christ.[123] First and foremost I urge you by the sacred name of Jesus not to do anything publicly that is hateful or harmful to Egranus.[124] We know how importunate and vacillating his disposition is, being void of even the tiniest portion of humanity.

I would have dealt with the portions and pages of the Psalter[125] by now if the printer had not been absent; but when he returns I will apply myself to it with all industry. Finally be a man of valour and be strong in the Lord.[126] For he who has cast himself on the Lord will not be ashamed.[127] I am not a little angry at having being led astray by you; for you did not write down the name of the man whom you have requested me to welcome. So I accosted him with the wrong name. But you have no cause for any worries about me. Everything is falling out excellently as far as my wife is concerned. But those who seemed my best friends have become alienated and gradually I am coming to understand what manner of thing man is, flesh is, trust in men is. Once I believed my towering intellect enabled me to know all this. But now, alas, I recognise that I have been wandering about under the wide heavens to my own great harm. To me the common saw applied: 'In retrospect, even a fool gets the point.'[128]

I will indicate in my next letter[129] the manner of life by which I hope to please God. Farewell, most sweet brother; intercede for me with Christ.

Wittenberg. On the day after All Saints 1520.

John[130] Agricola of Eisleben.

---

121. θεος; the whole letter is written in red ink.

122. χρῶ 'Iησοῦ.

123. τοῦ 'Iησοῦ; Acts 5⁴¹.

124. Johannes Wildenauer from Cheb(Eger), since 1515 the preacher in St. Mary's, the main city church; he had already furthered the evangelical movement in the city, criticising indulgences and the cult of St Anne, and had crossed literary swords with Catholic theologians like Wimpina; having had Müntzer recommended to him by Luther in 1519 he engaged him as substitute preacher when he embarked the following year on a study tour of Switzerland and South Germany; on his return on 1 October 1520 Müntzer transferred to St Catherine's Church and fierce conflicts soon developed between the gradualist, humanist approach of Egranus and that of Müntzer; cf. Nrs. 20, 21; Elliger, pp. 103ff.

125. *Operationes in psalmos*; Suppl. Mel. VI, 1 p. 61f. (F.)

126. Ephesians 6¹⁰.

127. Psalm 55²².

128. ῥέχθεν [sic] δὲτὲ [sic] νήριος ἔγνω Iliad XVII 32 and XX 98 (F.)

129. Not extant.

130. 'Iωαννὴς; Johann Schneider, called Agricola, b. Eisleben c. 1499, student in Leipzig and then 1515–16 Wittenberg; a friend of Luther; attended Leipzig

16. *John Caphan[131] to Müntzer, Wittenberg (c. 20 December 1520).*

To Master Thomas of Zwickau, evangelical sower of the dominical word, my most beloved friend[132] in Christ.[133]

Greetings. I write to tell you that I was eventually successful in my undertaking, although only after the greatest dangers to my life,[134] being far more honourably received by Master Eisleben[135] than I deserved, due above all to the help of your recommendation. For this recommendation I hereby offer you my everlasting thanks and, what is more, will always acknowledge my lasting obligation to you. Further I would not like you to be unaware of this, for[136] Martin has had all the legal codices burnt with the papist bull and many other books of the Romanists. And to explain and justify this action he wrote a pamphlet which I send you with the portions of the Psalms of David,[137] since I imagine you would not want to be without anything new that has appeared. As far as I am concerned I cannot make any conjectures[138] about what fate will bring in the days ahead; I am still dogged by uncertainty and extreme poverty, as has so long been the case; however I have your support; pray with me that God will change things for the better. Hope alone is left to me; otherwise I am done with.[139] Farewell for the moment; and unless the wheel of fortune turns round to produce better days I shall soon be seeing you again. But I beseech you to find some way by which with your intervention and instigation I may secure some lectures (if nothing else) to see me through the summer. As the paper runs out, so do my thoughts. Farewell then.

Wittenberg. Your chaplain John Caphan in the house of Eisleben.

I smiling to you laughing.

Disputation; in later life Court Preacher at Berlin and Superintendent in Brandenburg; d. 1566; he probably met Müntzer in Brunswick; cf. Letters 15, 21.

131. Writer unknown, but seems to be the man referred to in Nr. 15 as recommended to Agricola by Müntzer (F.); Caphan may be a nickname for *Kapaun*, indicating a castrate, cf. Bräuer, LJ 38 (1971), 130; in Latin.

132. 'and brother' has been crossed out.

133. τω χρηστο.

134. *etiam et* crossed out (Bräuer/Kobuch).

135. Agricola.

136. difficult to decipher; *enim* (Bräuer/Kobuch); *nempe* (F.)

137. *Operationes in psalmos* cf. Nr. 15, n. 125; *Why the Pope's Books and those of his Disciples have been burnt.*

138. *tibi* crossed out (Bräuer/Kobuch).

139. *Nisi tu aut Deus aliquo statumene providere in aestate futura* crossed out; 'unless you or God in the coming summer provide some support' (Bräuer/Kobuch).

17. *Maurice Reinhard*[140] *to Müntzer. Elsterberg, 1520.*

To the reverend Master Thomas Müntzer, an astute master of theology,[141] like a parent and a father in his teaching of me, worthy of all my love and respect.

Many greetings. I promised, reverend sir and master, to send bed-sheets, and this I now do, poor and unworthy as they are of your dignity, lest my words be regarded in the same light as the cypress tree.[142] I would send you something more valuable, if the harpies had not dealt with me so. Bear with me patiently. At least you should not lack bed-sheets. I have suffered shipwreck three times now. What I promise to do for you, my reverend sir and master (you will feel I am flattering) I have been unable to carry out immediately because of the loss of other things. I send this, so that you may look after your boys,[143] since I have enough, though no cornucopian superfluity. I am neither able to use nor to enjoy my possessions, nor do I pronounce my own interdiction, like Coriolanus before the city of Rome.[144] Be patient with me and I will return you everything. My feet impede me. I cannot look after my affairs as I would like to because the weakness of my feet overcomes me. Be sure of one thing: you will never look for the true leaves of the cypress in me. Worthy sir, Herr (Wo)lff[145] asks you to be so kind as to send him a piece from the length of cloth you had from me to make into a coat. He will send you the money without delay. I will be a guarantor of that, too, for I intend to collect my belongings and to sell my house. Farewell, in the year[146] 1520 in Elsterberg.

Maurice Reynhart.

140. In Latin; cf. Nrs. 10, 22. He was a cleric, possibly the Maurice Reynhard who gained a bachelor of arts in Leipzig in 1510; he is in debt, ill, and by June 1521 was dead. (F.)

141. On Müntzer's degrees cf. Letter 26 n. 223; above the address there is a faint note in Müntzer's(?) hand: *in Calepino testes t... iam dicitur* (Bräuer/Kobuch).

142. Erasmus in his *Adagia* refers to the fruits of the cypress: of words which sound fine, but are in other respect useless.

143. Müntzer's pupils.

144. Coriolanus is said in 491 BC to have declared that the famine-struck population of Rome should be given corn only on condition that they abandoned the right to have tribunes; the tribunes then condemned him to death.

145. Unknown; last three sentences in German.

146. *ym jar M3; probably a 3 has been mistakenly written for a 5, i.e. M5, 1500;* F. suggests *mindere zal,* i.e. the 'lesser number' which omits the centuries from the date.

18. *Dorothy Albrecht to her cousin, the student George Albrecht in Wittenberg.*

To George Albrecht her dearest cousin, a penniless student of letters in Wittenberg.[147]

My best greetings, dear George. Your resentment[148] really pains me; (but you should not blame) your father and me, dear George. Master Thomas Müntzer himself was with me and put his case to me himself. You need have no worries there; no damage has been done.[149] Dear George, you should know that your father is very weak and his case will not improve unless God is specially gracious to him. My father and I have been wanting to send you a message for ages, but no one was able to call here for[150] it. Dear George, you told your brother Michael that you would come on the fourth Sunday of Lent. Dear George, if you stay away so long, I am really afraid that you will not find him still alive, and your brother will behave wildly, especially as regards your church.[151] He has had a rush of unruly behaviour, and is going wild, as I told you before(?).[152] Dear George, if you cannot come, please let us know; if you cannot come very soon;[153] which may God forfend; lest something happen, and you should blame me and your father. For no one is with your father except old Martin and Laurence, Martin's adviser, if you do not come.[154] That's it then! May God keep you in good health. God grant you a peaceful night. I must lie down now.

I have written as well as I could,
from me Dorothy Albrecht.

---

147. This sentence by Müntzer in Latin; on the top right-hand side he has added, in Latin, the words: 'In the midst of tribulation we fail to recognise God, but after tribulation is over he is made more clear so that tribulation can be understood;' cf. Letter 57 n. 763; a George Albrecht of Rothenburg ob der Tauber immatriculated at Wittenberg on 28 September 1517 (F.); the letter was probably written in 1518/19; cf. Bubenheimer II, 100, n. 155.

148. *onmot* (Bräuer/Kobuch); *armuet* = poverty (F.)

149. Müntzer's relationship to the Albrechts is not clear, but it suggests a visit by him to Rothenburg in Lent 1518 or 1519.

150. *ankoen, ankoem*(?) (Bräuer/Kobuch); *ankern* (F.)

151. *un ess ge wilt zu mit euren broder, zu voran mit eur kilgen*; 'and your brother, and especially your church, will behave wildly' (Jillings).

152. The text is hard to read: *Der hot ein frein genomen und geg wild mit zu wiai hot* (F. *machot) euch vor goschriben ligt* (Bräuer/Kobuch); *frein* not 'friend' (F.) but from MHG *daz vreiden, der vreide* = foolhardiness, rowdyism (Jillings).

153. *das ir nit sse[r] korz werd* (Bräuer/Kobuch).

154. A deliberate(?) smudge: *Den ess ist niment bei dem vater, den der a[lte] Merten un der Leirenzt der Mertin seggeren* (reconstruction by Bräuer/Kobuch); cf. M.H.G. *sacher, secher*, plaintiff, defendant (Jillings); probably not *Schwager*.

19. *Müntzer to the Mayor and Council of Neustadt an der Orla.
Zwickau, 17 January 1521.*

To the honourable, wise and most trustworthy mayor and council of
the town of Neustadt, my gracious and Christian lords.

Salvation and blessedness in Christ Jesus, my wise lords and friends.
According to the word of Christ, on which the holy church is built, I
have set out to comfort the sad in heart, as God commanded his only
son long ago in the words of Isaiah,[155] and as Christ himself says in
Luke, chapter 4: 'The spirit of the Lord is upon me, to comfort the
poor and the deserted and to restore the sick to health.'[156] It is for this
that I am sent, for just as Christ was sent by the father, so we priests are
sent by God (John 20)[157] so that we can comfort the poor consciences;
unless we want to be shepherds who fatten themselves, as Ezechiel
says in chapter 34.[158] My most beloved lords in Christ.[159] I am quite
astonished that our prelates can do nothing but storm away and
burden poor consciences by causing delays in the handling of marital
cases in order to increase their profits, although such matters should
be dealt with as quickly as possible. Your wisdoms will be aware of
the case relating to the married estate which has been before the courts
for so long between Philip Römer and Dorothy of Nuremberg, the
daughter of a citizen[160] of your town. They were engaged to marry, as
Jerome Tuchscherer and Apel Schnetzinger are witnesses and
suitors.[161] Hence I would most urgently request your wisdoms to
summon these witnesses and suitors together with the parents of
Dorothy, so that they can attest whether they have ever promised
anything about the married estate to one another and whether
Dorothy has engaged to marry someone else. In truth, according to
divine law, Philip Römer should have her; even if she[162] had spent
some ten years with someone else in the estate of marriage the first

155. Isaiah 61[2].
156. Luke 4[18f].
157. John 20[21].
158. Ezekiel 34[2ff].
159. Müntzer was already embroiled at this time in fierce controversies with the
episcopal chancellery at Zeitz, and had gained the support of the Zwickau Council
for his refusal to appear before them; his intervention in this Neustadt case which was,
of course, quite outside his pastoral remit, was a further challenge to the Church
courts; cf. Elliger, pp. 115ff.
160. *eynes burgers tochter* (Bräuer/Kobuch – omitted by F.); of C.A.H. Burckhardt,
Neues Archiv für Sächsische Geschichte 3 (1882), 85–6.
161. *freyer*; a respected relative of the bridegroom who would meet the bride's
parents to negotiate the terms of the marriage.
162. *auch so yr eyns zcehen jhar* (F.) should read *auch sso is eyns zcehn jhar*; cf.
Burckhardt, op. cit., p. 85f.

vow must have precedence and be adhered to. Please give me a written statement about this. It is not right to leave these people so long with bad consciences. In the name of God I beg you to be rigorous and thorough in interrogating them about their consciences.[163] (I) will be glad to be of service to your wisdoms in a similar or much greater matter.

Zwickau in the year etc. 21 on Anthony's Day.

Master Thomas Müntzer, preacher in St. Catherine's, Zwickau.

20. *Egranus to Müntzer. (Zwickau, c. 16 February 1521.)*[164]

Egranus to Thomas Müntzer.

That you referred to me so insultingly last Saturday at the castle and in general speak so ill of me when you are in company,[165] and even that you often cry out against me from the pulpit and make me into a devil, is something I have to endure patiently. Perhaps your spirit is instructing you, of which you boast and which (so I hear) you drew up[166] from the water. So just go on and dig both spurs in deep as you intended and have already begun to do. I will be ready for the next escapade, as long as you have me at your disposal; after that another will arrive, for we cannot have you being idle; who knows what good may come of it. You have long since wished a cross on me. And since no one else will give it, then give it to me yourself; I will be glad to accept it and will not pay evil with evil.[167] Just this one thing though, I do ask of you for the sake of Christ: see that what you do is in accord with the truth (for this is what God himself is) lest the simple man be led into error. As far as I am concerned there is no problem. If that does not please you just follow your spirit, and go on in the accustomed way; God willing, from now on I will oppose it neither in words nor deeds. What I have done so far proceeded from

---

163. *wollet sy zu scharff und hart bey yrem gewissen vorhoren*; it destroys the sense to introduce a *nit* (F.), i.e. 'not too rigorously'; Müntzer's rigorist views on marriage (cf. Letters 31, 51) and on the responsibility of ruler or magistrate (cf. p. 248/8ff.; and p. 337/20ff.) coincide here; a false clemency is abhorrent.

164. The date will be c. 16 February 1521, when the Council resolved to summon Egranus and Müntzer and urge them to settle their differences; it is unclear whether the summons of Müntzer to the castle took place before or after that; a covered passage connected St Catherine's, Müntzer's church, with the castle (Bräuer/Kobuch); cf. Letter 15, and the 'Propositions' of Egranus, p. 380ff.

165. *bei der zcech.*

166. *geschöffpt* (sic) in margin, replacing *gesessen*, crossed out.

167. Romans 12[17].

brotherly concern. Ignorant as I am, I wanted to advise my brother. But since he has enough understanding from the spirit itself, which I had not realised, obviously I have erred, so please forgive me and go ahead and arrange matters according to your own sweet will. I will not stand in your way. May God ordain it for the best. Amen.[168]

It was no accident that I have written in German, for I perceive that your spirit despises all scholarship and literature etc.[169]

21. *Agricola to Müntzer, Wittenberg (probably early February 1521).*

To the Christian theologian, Master Thomas Müntzer, preacher at Zwickau, his beloved brother at Zwickau.

[In the name of] God[170]

If ever, good Thomas, you have been accustomed to sound forth on the trumpet,[171] you have surely excelled yourself this time in trumpeting forth on the new moon:[172] I am swept away in admiration for the mighty eloquence[173] by which you have striven to confound heaven and earth, water and fire. For throughout your letter betrays towering anger; every single jot hints at blazing indignation. But I will reply.

First you accuse us of lying in our letters like Ziba, that worst of flatterers;[174] because, led captive by the spirit of giddiness[175] (to use your terms), we wrongly accused you of immodesty. Believe me, Thomas. We know that what we wrote to you about your importunity was not without some substance. I have never mentioned the lack of modesty in your dealings with Egranus. For in that matter we are more or less of one mind, since I recognise plainly that Egranus has no understanding at all of the sacred Scriptures.[176]

---

168. The bottom part of the letter has been torn off; the first 'T' of Thomas is still visible on the back; the following sentence, written at the top of the reverse side by Egranus thus replaces the original conclusion (Bräuer/Kobuch).

169. *dass dein geist ein vorachter ist der kunsth und aller schrift etc.*; *schrift* may well mean the Bible.

170. θεος; letter in Latin.

171. In his letter to Luther of 13 July, Müntzer had talked of combating the mendicants 'with the trumpet of the word of God' (Nr. 13).

172. Psalms 81³.

173. Agricola's sarcasm is reminiscent of that of Egranus in Nr. 20.

174. 2 Samuel 16¹⁻⁴; Ziba was the treacherous servant of Mephibosheth; clearly there were other letters between Müntzer and Agricola which have been lost, cf. Elliger, p. 129f.

175. Isaiah 19¹⁴; cf. p. 18/17 above.

176. Cf. Nr. 15.

Who can fail to see how primitive that man's mind is! Moreover I know from what I had heard at Leipzig and Wittenberg what an infant in true theology the man whom I mention is. But this is the nub of the matter: that you desist from those frenzied attacks on all and sundry in which you forget where you are. Certainly some of those who wish you nothing but good have informed us that you abuse the office of the word, that when you ought to be teaching what is right you impugn others in an unjustified way and even mention them by name. And, to cut this short, they affirmed that YOU BREATHE OUT NOTHING BUT SLAUGHTER AND BLOOD.[177] You wish to know who they were? They were not the sort of people who tell lies. Now when the whole community agrees on something like this, it cannot easily be duped, providing it is actuated by zeal. Those who wanted you to be corrected wrote these things. So there is no reason for you to be so incredibly angry. We have done what we had to do. It is up to you to have due respect for those who justly admonish you. Let the sublimity of your spirit come down to our meagre level. Do not be overweening.[178] For it is written: Do not become conceited.[179] There is no reason at all why you should have to follow the example of Paul in being let down from the wall in a basket.[180] For not even at that time was Paul forced to render an account of his faith, since the plots were secret ones. It is just to avoid these that we ought to appear before the judges. Whether it is Lysias or Porcius or the tribune of Caesar who presides over the tribunal, beware, my good Thomas, of showing a contemptuous spirit. We are of necessity forced to submit; otherwise what need was there for Christ to appear before Pilate? Nor are they a terror to the good but only to the bad.[181] But all this at some other time. For there is not enough time to discuss so many things with you. Farewell in Christ. Set aside this personal hostility, which your letters openly betray. You understand what I am saying. But what you do, do really thoroughly. Look to the interests of the faith and you will receive from the Lord of life greater things than the gift of your life and goods.[182] As to those who are evil and contend against us, censure them, raise up your voice against them, correct them whether it is opportune or inopportune,[183] but in such a way that your modesty is

---

177. Acts 9¹.
178. Μὴ ὑψηλοφρόνει.
179. Μὴ γίνεσθε φρόνιμοι παρ᾽ ἑαυτοῖς.
180. 2 Corinthians 11³³.
181. Romans 13³.
182. Cf. Mark 10²⁸ᶠ.
183. 2 Timothy 4².

evident to all.[184] Farewell and let me hear from you. Greet in my name the master of the school and all the good people.

1521 John Agricola Eisleben.

22. *Müntzer to Stübner (near Zwickau,[185] 8 (?) June 1521).*

To the learned man Master Markus Thoma,[186] his very dear friend, at the bathhouse at Elsterberg.

I heard that you have been here and are firmly resolved to hold to our plan[187] and are therefore ready to make arrangements about the clothes. But it is not convenient to leave the bedding from Master Maurice[188] in your parents' home; your papers can go with mine.[189] I have much household goods[190] left after the mother's death who now rests in the Lord. Since they cannot be taken away at the moment they too can remain in the parental home until a suitable occasion should arise. Dispose of your affairs speedily and be here tomorrow, on Sunday. Our undertaking will brook no delay.[191] I am astonished that

184. Philippians 4[5]; Vg = *modestia*; Elliger, who dates the letter in mid-February, considers that the less aggressive conduct of Müntzer up to Egranus' departure in April may partly be attributable to this letter, op. cit. p. 131.

185. He must have been near Elsterberg, for he requests Stübner to come to him on the following day (F.); on the dating cf. Bräuer/Kobuch; in Latin.

186. Markus Thoma, called Stübner after the bathhouse (*Badestube*) owned by his father in Elsterberg, probably met Müntzer while a student in Wittenberg in 1518, where he may have stayed until June 1521, and then followed Müntzer to Prague (F.); cf. n. 192 below.

187. Franz suggests that Müntzer has jumped a line in transcribing his fair copy and that the Latin text originally read: *Hic te fuisse acceperim et nostri propositi esse tenacem mecum [Bohemiam intrare. Approbo] unde* (instead of *quo*) *destinare digneris vestimenta*; however, as a glance at the original shows, it is far from being a fair copy and the suggested words would not fill a whole line (Bräuer/Kobuch); it is best to leave the text as it stands.

188. Maurice Reinhard (cf. Nr. 17) had been in poor health; there was also an epidemic in Elsterberg in the summer of 1521; (F.)

189. Müntzer was punctilious about keeping his letters; cf. Nr. 24.

190. Those assigned to the priest? (F.); or is Müntzer's mother meant? (Scott).

191. No reason is adduced for the anxiety that, unless they hurry, the journey may be prevented; Elliger, p. 182f., speculates reasonably that he feared the activities of Egranus or his erstwhile Zwickau opponents, and notes the odd fact that Müntzer's letter to Hausmann on the same day (Nr. 25) mentions a previous journey to Bohemia but not his plans to leave again forthwith; the reasons for the conspiratorial haste and secrecy are not far to seek; in the middle of the night of 10 April he had suspected an incendiary attack on his house; he believed traps were being prepared for him day and night (cf. Nr. 25); he had been implicated in the 'wicked mutiny' of the clothmakers on 16 April, and forced to flee Zwickau under cover of darkness (Elliger, p. 174f.); since then he had been to Bohemia and back; he was filled with premonitions of death. (Cf. Nrs. 24, 25.)

Nicholas[192] has neither written nor returned. We cannot let our undertaking drag on any longer. See that you are here tomorrow. I have much to discuss with you, lest Satan should impede our journey. Farewell.[193] Saturday.

Thomas Müntzer, your brother.

23.   *Hans Lebe the Bohemian[194] to Thomas Müntzer (Zwickau, c. 15 June 1521).*

Deliver this letter to Master Thomas Müntzer.[195]

Most beloved father,[196] I crave your favour. I will be glad to do anything for you which the will of God permits.[197] But I cannot accept your invitation to join you, since I have regard for the command of God, although it would be fitting for me to follow you like a son. God's will must be done at all times. For God has given me grace, to separate myself from the Greeks.[198] I, too, am a witness to the cross of Christ, to the discredit and disgrace of the priests,[199] who have to learn from someone who previously had no faith. That must make

192. Nicholas Storch, clothmaker, of an old, but impoverished Zwickau family, reflects the prevalence of 'Bohemian' ideas in and around Zwickau; Peter Schumann, the city chronicler, reports Müntzer as preferring this layman to all the clergy as being someone 'with a profound knowledge of Scripture and expert in the things of the Spirit'; Wappler has pointed to the similarity between the ideas of Storch, Stübner, and Thomas Drechsel (the 'Zwickau Prophets') to those of Nicholas of Wlásenic; this Bohemian peasant, whose ideas had a limited circulation towards the end of the fifteenth century, rejected the clerical estate completely and based faith not only on Scripture but on immediate revelation by the Spirit; Wappler, p. 30, quoted by Elliger, p. 122f.

193. I Thessalonians 2[18].

194. Lebe, of Bohemian origin, as the signature suggests, appears to have come to a lively, personal faith through Müntzer's ministry in Zwickau, the suggestion that he may be identical with the Franciscan, Hans Lew in Hof (F.), can almost certainly be rejected on stylistic grounds (Bräuer), as the latter had a polished, educated style.

195. *Muttzer.*

196. I follow, in the main, the very slightly amended text by Elliger, p. 178.

197. Lit.: Whatever the will of God is, I am glad to grant you.

198. *das ich dy grecen tzu trenne*; F. suggests that *grecen* = Greeks, heathens; Elliger rejects that as meaningless, and takes it to mean 'matter', the 'sleep' in one's eyes, from the word '*Greck*'; the tr. would then read: 'For God has given me grace to rub away the sleep from my eyes;' Elliger's suggestion is possible and an eye-ailment could be meant; the context, however, of the next lines suggests a reference to I Cor. 1.23, to the cross of Christ which is foolishness to the Greeks and shames the wise; cf. Elliger, p. 178, n. 327.

199. *den pfaffen tzu lastern und tzu schanden*; F. reads: *den pfaffen zu lastern und zu schaden.*

them ashamed. It is good, too, that those who have grasped the teaching through you should have it explained to them. Go forth[200] in the name of God and receive the holy spirit of truth. As soon as opportune, God willing, I will join you with Klapst and with Hans, from Freistadt.[261]

Dearest father, if you have any news, be so good as to show it to me; now no more; God be with you!

Hans Lebe the Bohemian.

24. *Müntzer to Michael Gans[202] in Jena (near Zwickau), 15 June 1521.[203]*

To the devoted and faithful Master Michael Gans, living in Jena.

Greetings, most exemplary of friends. I have entrusted my papers to your goodness. Trust no one else with them unless he show you a letter with my seal. I hope to visit you myself next winter until which time I will have been carrying out the office of preaching according to the word. If possible I wish to be all things to all men,[204] until they come to know the crucified by conformity with him in his self-denial. If I should happen to die I shall send a will, written in my own hand, by a sure messenger. Cast away all weariness for the sake of our mutual affection. Greet the civic fathers[205] that they may come to sincerely love me. I will journey throughout the world for the sake of the word, which keeps us all safe. Amen. The year of the Lord 1521 on the day of Vitus and Modestus.

Thomas Müntzer, yours in prayer.

200. *syth yn den namen gott[es]*; Elliger p. 178, suggests *zieht*, which seems sound; cf. the spelling of *geseuge* (witness) p. 32/12; F. reads: *sych yn den namen Gottes*; cf. also the suggestion that *syth = seid* (Bräuer), i.e. 'Be [greeted] in the name of God'.

201. *mit den Klapst and mit den Hans von der Freystat*; the former unknown; the latter, a cloth-worker from Freistadt an der Mühl, in Austria, was a controversial figure, being arrested at the time of Müntzer's dismissal, and again at the end of 1521; he was expelled from Zwickau shortly afterwards; cf. Wappler, p. 40f. (Bräuer/Kobuch).

202. Probably Michael Klausbeck, called Gansau, a wealthy magistrate in Jena; in view of the trust Müntzer puts in him it is puzzling that we know so little about him; he was born in Leipzig, where he matriculated in 1515, BA 1515; held various Council posts in Jena until 1546; cf. Hans Apel, 'Jenas Einwohner aus der Zeit von 1250 bis 1600', *Quellenbuch zur Jenaer Sippengeschichte* (Görlitz, 1937), pp. 143, 101; (Bräuer/Kobuch).

203. In Latin; written from near Zwickau; cf. Letter 22, n. 185.

204. 1 Corinthians 9[22].

205. On Müntzer's connections with Jena nothing is known.

25. *Müntzer to Nicholas Hausmann*[206] *(near Elsterberg), 15 June 1521.*

Thomas Müntzer, a servant of the elect of God, to the reverent and devoted pastor of souls in Zwickau, Master Nicholas Hausmann.

(In the name of) Jesus

You sent a greeting to me through James Lapicida,[207] enquiring how I was. You mentioned that if I had taken the path you had suggested such dangers would not have descended on my head. Dearest friend, I have been taught by the equity of God's commands, directing my hurrying steps by the voice of God; this teaches a spiritual modesty, not a carnal one,[208] disclosed by the lampstand of truth to all the elect of God;[209] nor does it conflict with the action of that most modest servant, Elijah, the prophet when he killed (with the exception of 150 priests) a thousand devotees of Baal.[210] For it was when he seemed most frenzied to the carnally minded that he was at his most modest. In the same way Paul explains himself: If thus far I were pleasing to men I would not be the servant of Christ.[211] But I heard you wanted to please not only the priests but also and above all the nobility, pushing the common throng to the rear. You had heard Egranus publicly blaspheming, but held your peace. In Kirchberg[212] you did not object when he was giving voice to things so ill to the ears that the gentiles abominate them. I ask you, most worthy brother, not to be silent before Zion,[213] not to flatter or put up with such lies, just as you kept your peace in your parish in the presence of many citizens when Egranus, that man accursed to all eternity, said: 'The Church only had the holy spirit in the time of the apostles.' You ought to have purged that blasphemy though it cost you your life and all your goods. You know the fate of dumb dogs.[214] Beware of such! For if you hold your peace and maintain a mendacious pretence of sanctity I will not take your part – not unless it savours of the crucified in his entirety.[215] No disciple who sets himself up above his master will ever

206. Vicar of St. Mary's, Zwickau; in Latin.

207. Not known; = stone-cutter, mason.

208. Cf. Agricola's references to *immodestia* (Nr. 21), and the date at the end of this letter: St Modestus!

209. Cf. Mark 4[22].

210. 1 Kings 18[22] speaks of the death of 450 priests of Baal; cf. Schwarz, p. 62, n. 1 and cf. the Prague Manifesto p. 360/22ff. below.

211. Galatians 1[10].

212. South of Zwickau (F.)

213. Isaiah 62[1]; Vg. *Propter Sion* – for the sake of Zion.

214. Isaiah 56[10]; on Egranus, cf. p. 382/24ff. below.

215. *totum crucifixum* – a favourite theme of Müntzer, the 'bitter' Christ as well as the 'sweet' Christ; cf. 1 Corinthians 2[2].

be able to preach him.[216] Why have you not summoned me to come to you? You would have got a fair judgment if you had genuinely intended converting your people. You know that I could not enter the parish because traps were being set for me there day and night, which finally came out into the open. May you know, may you know, my sweetest brother, that I desire nothing else but my own persecution, so that all may profit and be converted through me. Finally, you should realise that I visited Bohemia not for the sake of my own petty glory, not from a burning desire for money, but in the hope of my coming death. By these words I want to prevent the mystery of the cross, as I have preached it, from being eradicated. If you or my successor Zeidler[217] are intending to root out the tender shoots of the word which I have watered you should be aware that boys and old men[218] will confound you. For it is impossible for the word of God to return void.[219] Nor will that same word allow itself to be directed by the teaching authority of men or to be darkened by the headstrong counsels of the untested and the effeminate. The time of Antichrist is upon us, as Matthew 24 makes so clear: When the Lord introduces the preaching of the Gospel of the kingdom throughout the world then the abomination of desolation is revealed.[220] But no credence is to be given to the reprobate; as in the days of Noah we should care not a straw for them. All of those who say that the late pope[221] was the Antichrist are in error. For he is a true proclaimer of the same, but the fourth beast will have dominion over the whole earth and his kingdom will be greater than all others. I have been delayed in writing these letters. Farewell. In the year of the Lord 1521 on the very day of St. Vitus and St. Modestus.

26. *Hans Pelt*[222] *to Müntzer. (Brunswick), 25 June 1521.*

To his reverence, Master Thomas Müntzer, bachelor of Holy

---

216. Matthew 10[24].

217. *aemulus meus Zeudelerius*, the successor of Egranus of St Mary's where Müntzer had been vicar; *aemulus* can also mean rival, opponent.

218. Joel 2[28].

219. Isaiah 55[11]; the same quotation occurs in his letter to Luther (Nr. 13).

220. Matthew 24[14]f.

221. Julius II.

222. Cf. Letters 1–3 above; text as amended by Bubenheimer I, 71–5; and Bräuer/Kobuch.

Scripture[223] (cordially written to him as preacher at Zwickau)[224] now cordially written to Prague.

Be assured of my poor prayers and willing service at all times, revered and especially good friend in Christ. I am glad to let you know that, God be praised, we are all still well. We hope to hear the same of you. But Hans Ryke[225] has died, may God be gracious to his soul. Pray for him for God's sake. Further, as to your giving me to understand from your letters that you are resigning the poor, small benefice[226] that you hold from the council, so far I have not said anything about it myself,[227] but wanted first to have more information from you. If this is still your intention, and you want to give it up, we, that is, your father,[228] Hans Hornburg[229] and I have someone in mind whom we would like to have it. His name is Marsilius;[230] he is devoted to Christ, following Martin's[231] teachings.

---

223. Elliger, p. 37f., doubts his right to such title; however Vogler points out that he may gave gained his MA before immatriculating at Frankfurt in 1512; the theological records for Frankfurt are not extant, so it is at least possible that he studied theology there; 'Thomas Müntzer als Student der Viadrina', p. 251; other suggested, but unproven, universities he could have studied at are Mainz (Vogler), Paris (Bubenheimer); the latter urges caution about the assumption that the 'Thomas Müntzer of Quedlinburg' who enrolled in Leipzig in 1506 is our Thomas Müntzer; 'Thomas Müntzer ... in Braunschweig', NAK 65, 20–22; normally it took five years to gain a Bachelor of Holy Scripture.

224. The words in brackets crossed out; Letters 26 and 28 belong together; Nr. 26 was originally sent to Zwickau from Brunswick but, as Nr. 28 shows (p. 40/15f.) had only reached Naumburg when the news that Müntzer had left for Prague caused it to be returned to Pelt, who added a postcript (Nr. 28) and sent it on to Prague; it casts a vivid light on the early spread of reforming ideas in the towns.

225. *Ryke*; not Hans Reule of Aschersleben, who had nothing to do with Müntzer, but Hans Rike, the son of Henrik Rike of Brunswick; like Hans Pelt's father the latter was a member of the guild of cloth merchants; Bubenheimer I, 72 n. 8.

226. Cf. pp. 441f. below.

227. *dat sulve noch nicht van my gesecht.*

228. His father appears to be part of the group of reformers; Bubenheimer suggests he may be one of the 'eight Hanses' or 'Johns', mentioned in the letter (p. 38/21), perhaps the Johann Munther engaged in 1509 by Arndt Plaggemeiger of Brunswick to collect debts; but cf. Letter 1 n. 1.

229. *Hornborch*; a merchant and brewer, as the letter shows, a militant and courageous supporter of the reforming cause; expelled from the city in 1521/2, imprisoned by Duke Henry the Younger in 1523; cf. n. 238 below, and Bubenheimer I, 59 n. 51, 73 n. 10; his brother Peter was also an activist.

230. *Marcilius*; a customs clerk in Brunswick, dismissed in 1521 as part of the campaign against the reforming movement and expelled from the city with Hornburg and others; hence the plan to replace Müntzer with him failed; Gregor Harwen was appointed instead; ibid., 58–61.

231. Luther.

If you now want to give it up to him we would ask you to write to the council resigning as from now and requesting the council to bestow it on the said Marsilius since he is in the service of the council here as a collector of tolls. But should you want to retain it, it will be no trouble for me, I will gladly have the benefice renewed for you and will transfer to you such revenues as it produces. I do not know any longer where you are now staying; it has been all too long since you wrote; not till after Easter did we get a letter from you; but there was nothing in it to say where you were. You may have heard, my dear friend, that Martin's books and a painted effigy of him on paper were burnt at Worms, which I am heartily sorry about, and fear that those who have allowed such things to be done must feel uneasy now.[232] Some think that the emperor will publish an edict outlawing anyone who attaches himself to Martin and his teaching. Our hireling priest[233] Arnold is as happy as if he had some 25 cows in calf. He saw fit recently to confront me at a wedding with a statement about your travels[234] and then he got a retort from me, about which he complained that I had so angered him that he was unable either to eat or to drink. I was also involved with Master Gerhard Ryschaw in this new turn of events.[235] He criticised [Martin's] writings strongly without ever having read any of them. So I lent him the one that the doctor had written about the Babylonian Captivity. He kept it for 14 days, and then answered it with a letter on a sheet of paper, written on both sides, in which he singled out eight or ten articles, but adduced no Scriptural proof and advised me under pain of eternal damnation and excommunication not to attach myself to the teaching of Martin. But, God be praised, I know better than that; I notice from his writings that he regards the pope as the head of the Christian churches. I thought of copying his letter and sending it to Master Eisleben,[236] so that he would join the line of Tetzel, Eck, Alveld,

---

232. *und befrochte, idt werde den nicht wol, de sodanss hebben doen lathen.*

233. Arnold von Derlagen, the vicar 'hired' for St Martin's church in Brunswick.

234. *Wuste idt my latest in eyner wertschop iwe reysen vor to leggende; wertschop* can also mean 'inn'; F. reads *ime reyfen,* 'in the ring', or 'group'; the reference to Muntzer's 'travels', which predates Prague, is tantalising; cf. Bubenheimer II, 99f.; also Letter 24 p. 33/18f.

235. *in der wendinge* (Bräuer/Kobuch); *mendynge* (F.); presented to a benefice at St Anne's altar in St Martin's in 1514; apparently remained true to the Old Church; d. 1541; Bubenheimer I, 74.

236. John Agricola: clearly the writer knew that Agricola was the author of the pamphlet: *A brief Address to all who despise Doctor Luther and Christian Freedom – Eine kurze anred zu allen misgunstigen doctor Luthers und der christenlichen freiheit* (ed. Oskar Schade in: *Satiren und Pasquille aus der Reformationszeit.* vol. II (2nd ed. Hanover, 1863) 190–193) (F.).

Emser and Murner;[237] that is what he deserves for his ungrounded views. But I will keep the original here, lest he should now try to deny it. Since all our prelates, spiritual and secular, are opposed to Martin those of us who hold to him will be despised. I have infuriated many with these writings. Please do tell us what you think. I know no one in this town who is a more fervent follower in actual practice of the said Martin than Hans Hornburg who does not want to be a merchant and will not take anything on apart from his brewery, for he only wants enough to live on; he puts his trust in God and has no great concern for temporal goods.[238] I am, I swear by God, still raring to go.[239] In time I, too, hope to let go, but it will be a bitter pill;[240] this does not seem to be possible, so pray God on my behalf that he will give me his grace. But Arndt Pelt[241] has left for Antwerp; there the common folk are a thousand times more attached to the teaching of Christ and to Martin than they are here, I swear to God! I have almost all his writings, except for his very fierce exposition of Daniel 8 on the Antichrist.[242] There is nothing else really that I have to write to you, but my wife and children and servants, my brother Arndt, Hans Hornburg and Hans Kettler[243] all wish you many restful nights. Our Observants are forever warning against us from the pulpit: Do not be led astray by the eight Hanses.[244] But to me they say nothing. Hans Hornburg is under severe attack (from the pulpit) for having eaten flesh during Lent; one has to suffer for the sake of the truth.

Tuesday after the Nativity of John the Baptist in the year 21.

Hans Pelt, wholly yours in Christ.

237. Catholic controversialists, early opponents of Luther. The spelling of *Murnarr* (Narr = a fool) will be a play on words.

238. For Hornburg, discipleship means decisive action; living simply, breaking the Easter fast, demonstratively (cf. l. 22 below), rebuking those he considers unchristian; opponents said that 'The Holy Spirit buzzed around inside him like a fly'; Bubenheimer characterises him as a 'Schwärmer', an 'enthusiast'; 'Thomas Müntzer ... in Braunschweig', NAK 65, 25f.

239. *noch in der lust*; or does it mean: 'still caught in my desires'?

240. *dat wart my suer*; heroic discipleship of the Hornburg variety is not for Pelt; as Bubenheimer points out he represents the moderate wing of the early reformers in Brunswick; ibid., 26f.

241. Bubenheimer I, 75 n. 25, thinks that he is not the brother of the writer, mentioned in l. 18 below.

242. The reference is to Luther's writing: *A Response ... to the book of our fine Master Ambrosius Catharinus ... of May 1521* which interprets Daniel 8[23] as referring to the Pope as Antichrist (WA VII, 722–77).

243. *Ketler*; took the oath of citizenship in the Old Town of Brunswick in 1511, and became in later years a prominent councillor and proponent of the Lutheran cause; Bubenheimer I, 75 n. 31.

244. They would include Hans Pelt; Hans Hornburg; Hans Ketteler; perhaps Hans Munther, and the merchant Jan van Antorp; ibid., n. 32.

27. *Hans Sommerschuh to Müntzer. Zwickau, 31 July 1521.*

To be delivered to the worthy and revered gentleman, Master Thomas Müntzer, now in Prague, my gracious lord.

My most friendly greetings and offer of service to you,[245] my worthy and most gracious dear lord and master. I have always been glad to hear from your Reverence that you are well and prospering according to the will of almighty God; your departure from Zwickau was a terrible blow to me, and something to which as God knows, I was always opposed. Hence I have often had it in mind to write to your Reverence, and your servant who was out here said he would fetch the letter from me. But he failed to do this and that is the reason why I have been so long delayed and have been so slow to write to you. So please do not be angry at me only writing you now. Your Reverence should know that my master and friend Doctor Stuler,[246] God bless him, has died; you were his confessor, and he was particularly well-inclined and favourable to you because of the word of God. If it had been God's will to keep him in life I had hoped to be able to keep you here in Zwickau still, for I often heard him speaking so much about you when he was alive. Since however God has ordained otherwise, as he continues to ordain all things according to his will, and has now destined you to go to Prague, my brotherly love permits no resentment at this. Only begging your Reverence to stand firm through all persecution and to seek life in the word of God, as your Reverence often exhorted us in Zwickau, and thus to stand firm; words which I, too, have taken to heart as all those who love God must do. For it is through such persecution that he is testing you, though to write to you about this and comfort you is far above one such as me.[247] I keep in mind, however, the words which occurred to me once in relation to your Reverence when I was in your little room: If they persecuted and killed the innocent prophets before Christ, and then Christ, the truth himself, and then after him the apostles and the martyrs too for the sake of the truth then they will contrive to be hateful and bloodthirsty to all who speak the truth. For Christ says: The disciple will not be greater than his master.[248] But your Reverence knows and understands all this better than me. But as

---

245. *bev[or]*; = *zuvor*.

246. Erasmus Stuler studied in Leipzig and Bologna, doctor in Zwickau and burgomaster since 1513; notorious for his historical forgeries (F.); an enthusiastic supporter of Müntzer, he urged Court preacher George Spalatin in a letter on 3 September to prevail upon the Elector to give Müntzer his unambiguous support; cf. Elliger, p. 102f.

247. *des ich dan zu geri[ng] bin*.

248. Matthew 10[24f.] Cf. Nr. 25, n. 216.

a hearty listener to your sermons on the words of Christ I have always been heartily inclined and favourably disposed to you and still am. Therefore it is my earnest request to your Reverence to write a letter, if you can, informing me how everything is going; do so, as soon as you can, whenever you have the time. For those who always persecuted your Reverence spread rumours about you, saying that you have been given poison[249] and are very ill; some say that you are dead and much more of that sort. May the almighty God keep you in his grace and his truth; that will be my constant prayer to God; I will always remember you before God. Likewise I beg your Reverence to intercede to God for us all. Zwickau, on the eve of the imprisonment of Peter in 21.

Hans Sommerschuh the Disciple, citizen of Zwickau.

Your Reverence's servant.[250]

28. *Hans Pelt to Müntzer in Prague (Brunswick) 6 September 1521.*[251]

Revered and dear Master Thomas. I had sent this letter to Naumburg, but it was said there that you were in Prague, and we could not believe it, but this Jew[252] said to us that he had seen you being honourably received[253] at Prague and that you have two learned Bohemians with you who translate into Czech the gospel of Christ as they hear you speak and proclaim it to the people. Our priests do not put the best interpretation on your decision however favourable a judgment your views deserved. Please do write to me what you think about the benefice,[254] and to the council, too. Already some people there have petitioned the council for it, and have represented your actions in an unfair light, but the council did not want to take any action, it wanted to have firm grounds first. Please do write, telling me about the benefice and also your judgment about what Christ is working through his word in Bohemia; I believe there are better Christians there than here. Here things are in a bad state at the

---

249. *man hab euch vorgeben.*

250. E W d; apart from this letter we know little about him; he was clearly involved in the covenant of the '12 apostles and 72 disciples' whose armed riot was suppressed on 16 April 1521, precipitating Müntzer's flight from Zwickau; cf. Nr. 22 n. 191; cf. Bräuer/Kobuch.

251. Postcript to Nr. 26; text as amended by Bubenheimer I, 75f, also Bräuer/Kobuch.

252. The letter-carrier.

253. *herliken inhaelen.*

254. Cf. Nr. 26.

moment; the dukes of Brunswick[255] are feuding with the bishop of Hildesheim[256] who also seems to me to pay scant regard to the Gospel, I swear to God. For our consolation we have from Martin at the university of Wittenberg Psalm 36 and Psalm 67 and a fine piece on the Magnificat.[257] Then the emperor had had an edict published against Martin and his followers,[258] to pursue them as outlaws, but I hear that the nobility in Brandenburg, to whom it is addressed, pay no attention to it. I hope that the same will be true now of the other areas too.

I have really nothing else to write about, but I would love to know if you are contented. My wife and children wish you a thousand restful nights. Pray for me and for all of us. This Jew will be here again at Martinmas.[259] Please do send us a message by him. Peter Hummel[260] and Hans Kettler wish you a restful night.

The sixth day after St. Giles in the year 1521.

Hans Pelt.

29. *Veit Goldschmidt and Martin Gentzel,*[261] *monks of St. Peter's in Erfurt, to Müntzer, December 1521.*

Written to[262] Master Thomas Müntzer, revered in Christ Jesus our Lord, Master of the fine arts.

Greetings, best of friends. It was obedience and fear which stopped me answering your letters; I pushed them aside twice, though I understood them well enough when in my right mind. You will be utterly astonished that I have not written to you. Bear in mind the saying: If the cause is absent so is the effect. You know of course that our cells are not secluded. Thus there is the fiercest controversy amongst us. That is as much as I need say to you, best of brothers. For one of the brothers visited my cell. There he read through your letters, not taking them away with him but memorising what was written and said. This he relayed to the lord abbot and so I incurred a

255. *Bruns[wigk]*.
256. *Hildens[hem]*.
257. WA 8, 205–40; 1–35 (Eng. tr. LW 13, 3–37); WA 7, 538–613 (Eng. tr. LW 21, 297–358).
258. Edict of Worms.
259. 11 November.
260. *Hummelen*; took oath of citizenship in the Old Town in 1489; a well-known figure among the early reformers in Brunswick; Bubenheimer I, 76 n. 42.
261. In Latin; on Martin Gentzel of Stolberg, who matriculated in Erfurt 1507, cf. Barbara Frank, *Das Erfurter Peterskloster im 15. Jahrhundert* (Göttingen, 1973), p. 382.
262. *pre[sentes] litterae; per[veniant]*? (F.)

public outburst of indignation from our superior. In the end, wisest of counsellors, my brother Veit and I urged our lord abbot once again to let you inform us about the high points of various doctrines, lest we be called ignorant idiots here. Thereupon the lord abbot promised by the word of truth to send you our scribe. Therefore do not take this ill, but receive our letters with all good will, as you wish to show yourself a speedy and obliging teacher of doctrine. For your expenses and accommodation you will be paid thirty florins and you will stay with us in complete security. Although this is a meagre payment be so kind as to accept it and to correct any error we have made in our Latin. For we have written down whatever was on the tip of our tongue and our friend and your relative, the priest who bears this,[263] will inform you of the other things the lord abbot has entrusted to him, in which you can be of service to us. Be so kind as to receive the present bearer of this letter hospitably. Our very warm greetings; we have prayed for your soul, brother,[264] in our unworthy intercessions. In continuous prayer we shall not be forsaken. Our monastery on the mount of Peter of the order of blessed Benedict in Erfurt in the year of the incarnation 1521.

Veit Goldschmidt, Martin Gentzel, religious brothers.

30.   *Franz Günther*[265] *to Müntzer. Lochau, 25 January 1522.*

To Master Thomas Müntzer, a man devoted to the divine word and the apostolic life, and my brother in Christ. Many greetings.

[In the name of] Jesus

If you fare well in Christ, it is good; I, for my part, am well. They say the Bohemians are not advancing but marking time in some matters pertaining to the gospel, that this completely put you to flight,[266] and you are now said to be staying in Thuringia. If I have any

263. *tibi cognatus presens dominus*; no more is known of this relative.

264. *fr[ater]*, in brackets.

265. Cf. Letter 7; Müntzer had tried to secure Günther to succeed Egranus in Zwickau (F.); Lochau is not a place name but the favourite residence of Elector Frederick the Wise of Saxony, near Torgau; cf. Günter Mühlpfordt, *Deutsche Literaturzeitung* 90 (1969), 635f.; in Latin.

266. *fugavit*; cf. the Prague Manifesto, p. 000 below; Markus Thoma, with Müntzer in Prague, (cf. Letter 22) was with the other 'Zwickau prophets' in Wittenberg at this time, and may have been Günther's informant, though definite evidence that Müntzer had to flee Prague is not available; Günther's letter reflects his uncertainty about Müntzer's whereabouts and views; rumours will have been current about his closeness to the 'Zwickau prophets'; prior to July 1522 his presence in Nordhausen is not attested.

wish at all, I desire that you would desire to be embraced by me and that I should hear your spirit in full flow.[267] On the other hand see that the light which is in you be not darkness.[268] Different men mutter different things about you; The devil is not dead but prowls around like a roaring lion looking for someone to devour.[269] I hope that you have proved the spirit, not fantasizing in the name of Christ but being zealous[270] in his spirit. But may the will of the Lord be done in these times, whatever it may be, and may the breath of his grace afford divine help to us who are perishing. Amen. On the day of Paul's Conversion. Lochau in the year 1522.

Franz Günther, your little brother in Christ, bishop[271] of Lochau.

31. *Müntzer to Melanchthon. (Erfurt), 29 March 1522.*

To the Christian man Phillip Melanchthon, professor of the sacred Scriptures.

Greetings, instrument[272] of Christ. Your theology I embrace with all my heart for it has snatched many souls from the snares of the hunters.[273] That your priests are taking wives I commend, lest the Roman pretence continue to oppress you. What I disapprove[274] of is this: that it is a dumb God whom you adore,[275] for because of your

267. *et ut tuum loquentis spiritum audiam.*
268. Luke 11[35] (Vg).
269. 1 Peter 5[8].
270. *vervens,* for *fervens;* cf. 1 John 4[1].
271. Evangelical pastors often adopted this title; cf. Karlstadt's description of Müntzer as 'bishop of Allstedt', in Letter 56.
272. In Latin; *organum;* Acts 9[15]; R. Schwarz, pp. 35ff., suggests that the occasion for this letter is the controversy following the marriage of the Lutheran pastor of Kemberg, near Wittenberg, Bartholomew Bernhardi, in Spring 1521; an Apologia in Latin and various German translations with a preface by John Lang, mentioned in the postscript of this letter, may well have been attributed to Melanchthon (though in fact written by Karlstadt); the evidence, of course, remains circumstantial; the original is lost, cf. n. 289 below.
273. Cf. Psalms 91[3], 124[7]; *laqueus venantium;* cf. also Psalms 118[61]; there is possibly a reminiscence of Luther's denunciation of the Papacy as Nimrod, the mighty hunter, at the beginning of the Babylonian Captivity; LW 36 p. 12; cf. Nr. 72, p. 137/15; in the medieval period Nimrod was seen as the archetypal tyrant.
274. Müntzer, it will be noted, sets himself up as an independent judge of Wittenberg practice: he embraces this, commends that, disapproves of something else, notes ignorance on several occasions.
275. Isaiah 46[7]; the theme of the 'dumb God' occurs in the controversy with Egranus, p. 382/24ff., in the longer German version of the Prague Manifesto, at the very end, p. 371/8, and in the preface of *A Manifest Exposé of False Faith,* p. 262/17.

ignorance about propagation you cannot distinguish between the elect and the reprobate; as a result you totally reject the coming church in which the knowledge of the Lord will dawn in all its fullness. But this error of your, my most beloved, arises wholly from an ignorance of the living word.[276] Look to the Scriptures, on which we rely to trample down the world; they say quite unambiguously: Man does not live by bread alone but by every word which proceeds from the mouth of God;[277] note that it proceeds from the mouth of God and not from books. It is the testimony to the true word which is found in volumes. For unless it arises from the heart it is the word of man, condemning the turn-coat scribes,[278] who rob the holy oracles, Jeremiah 23.[279] The Lord has never spoken to them, yet they usurp his words. O most beloved, see to it that you prophesy,[280] otherwise your theology will not be worth a cent. Think of your God as at hand and not distant;[281] believe that God is more willing to speak than you are prepared to listen. We are brim full of desires. This hinders the finger of the living God from piercing his tablets.[282] By your arguments you drag men to matrimony although the bond is not yet an immaculate one,[283] but a Satanic brothel, which is as harmful to the church as the most accursed perfumes of the priests.[284] Do not these passionate desires impede your sanctification?[285] How can the spirit be poured out over your flesh[286] and how can you have living colloquy with God when you deny such things? There is no precept (if I may put it like this) which so firmly binds the Christian as that of our

---

276. *vivi verbi*; in his Invocavit sermons (9–16 March 1522) Luther's call for cautious reform included an exhortation on 11 March to clergy contemplating marriage to base their decision on clear texts of Scripture. For Müntzer this is the dead, rather than the living word. LW 51, p. 79f; cf. Elliger, p. 221f; however, as Schwarz, op. cit. p. 40f., points out Müntzer would scarcely have had time to hear of this sermon; Luther's viewpoint was, in any case, very different from Karlstadt's 'biblicist and juridical' argument.

277. Deuteronomy 8³; Matthew 4⁴.

278. Jeremiah 8⁸ *versipelles*, those who shed their skin; a term used later by Bullinger; Heminjard, *Correspondance des Réformateurs IV, 190.*

279. Jeremiah 23³⁰.

280. Exegesis is prophetic, not academic activity; 1 Corinthians 14¹.

281. Jeremiah 23²³.

282. Exodus 31¹⁸, Deuteronomy 9¹⁰; Jeremiah 17¹ (The sin of Judah is recorded with an iron tool, engraved on the tablet of their heart . . .) Joel 2¹³ Vg. *Et scindite corda vestra . . .*

283. Hebrew 13⁴.

284. Amos 6⁶; perhaps a reference to Ecclesiastes 10.1; a favourite verse for Müntzer.

285. 1 Thessalonians 4³ff.

286. Joel 2²⁸.

sanctification. For it first empties the soul, out of desire for God,[287] since it cannot in any way let the pleasures which are inferior to the soul tyrannise over it; for we are to make use of wives as if we did not have them. Give what is due,[288] not as the gentiles do, but as one who knows that God addresses, commands, exhorts you, so that you may know assuredly when [what is due] is required for an elect offspring, so that the fear of God and the spirit of wisdom may hinder the concupiscence of the brute being,[289] lest you be swallowed up.

The phial of the third angel has already been sprinkled on the fountains of the waters (I know this and tremble) and the outpouring of blood has been accomplished; but their mind[290] is oriented towards flesh and blood. Some are chosen, but their minds cannot be opened for the reasons already given. Hence their works are the same as those of the reprobate, with the exception of the fear of God, which separates them from the latter. Two lie in one bed and pursue the same pleasure.[291] For such are the works which I find in you as long as there are contentions among you about the abolition of the Mass.[292] That some hate the abomination of the Papist sacrifice I applaud and commend; for they have acted under the leading of the holy spirit. But they are entangled in errors because they have not imitated the apostolic rite, and used it as a plumb-line. For those who have scattered seed at the command of the Lord ought to tremble; those who preach should examine their auditors when they have finished preaching and those who have displayed the fruits of understanding should be set before the people and the bread and the drink should be

287. *ex voluntate Dei*: Elliger translates 'by the will of God'; the parallelism with *ex ignorantia vivi verbi*, and the Platonic, Augustinian flavour of the sentence, however, suggest the translation given; 'By the will of God' is usually translated by the prepositions *'per'* or *'secundum'*.

288. 1 Corinthians 7³.

289. *bruti concupiscentiam*; Agricola comments on the 'insanity' of limiting marital intercourse to when you hear a 'voice from heaven', and ridicules the idea that a child, elect of God, will spring from this marital embrace; matrimony is only a remedy against fornication; male semen is an effusion of the body like pus, saliva, faeces or urine; (Agricola printed Müntzer's letter with his interpretation of Psalm 19; cf. O. Clemen, *Supplementa Melanchthonia* VI, i. pp. 183ff.)

290. Revelation 16⁴; with its stress on the church of the future, and on the nearness of the 'summer', the whole letter is infused by an urgent sense of imminent judgement; for *lectio* probably read *ratio*, as in l. 12; cf. Schwarz, op. cit., p. 42 n. 32 who interprets the whole letter in terms of Müntzer's expectation of a chiliastic future; the elect cannot make any concessions to the sensual which would cloud their reason and prevent them hearing God's voice.

291. Luke 17³⁴; an extraordinary use of this verse.

292. Luther's *de abroganda missa*, which appeared in January 1522, which deals with the abuses of the Mass, the sparing of the weak, the role of the authorities, may be a key to understanding this letter (Bräuer); WA 8 411–76.

given them, because it is those endowed with the understanding of the testimonies of God, not from books of dead promises but of living promises, who are possessed by the Spirit.[293]

Our most beloved Martin acts ignorantly because he does not want to offend the little ones; but those little ones today are just like the boys who lived to be a hundred years old and were damned.[294] But the tribulation of Christians is already at the door; why you should consider that it is still to come, I do not know. Dear brothers, leave your dallying,[295] the time has come! Do not delay, summer is at the door.[296] Do not make peace with the reprobate, for they impede the mighty working of the word.[297] Do not flatter your princes; otherwise you will live to see your undoing,[298] which may the blessed God forfend. If you deny that purgatory is Christian, you show yourself ignorant of the Scriptures and of the knowledge of the spirit; but I do commend you for rejecting the phantasies of the papists.[299] No one can enter into rest, unless the seven grades of reason are opened to the seven spirits. The denial of purgatory is an abominable error, be warned! Should you wish I will back up all I have said from the Scriptures, from the order of creation,[300] from experience, and from the clear word of God. You delicate biblical scholars, do not hang back. I can do no other.[301]

Farewell, on the fifth day[302] after Annunciation, Thomas Müntzer, messenger of Christ.

Pay no attention to the god of Ekron, your Langius;[303] for he is a reprobate whose undying arrogance has led him to persecute the servant of God.[304]

---

293. Psalms 119²⁵; lit. they have the true 'possessor' i.e. the Holy Spirit; cf. above the reference to the pleasures or lusts as the 'false possessor', or tyrant; and Nr. 49, n. 596.

294. Isaiah 65²⁰; the Invocavit sermon of 9 March is meant; cf. LW 51, p. 72.

295. *last euer merhen*: Saxon dialect word for delay. (F.)

296. Matthew 24³²; cf. Nr. 34, n. 341.

297. 1 Thessalonians 2¹³.

298. 2 Timothy 2¹⁴.

299. By Purgatory Müntzer appears to mean not a purification after death, but before it; cf. Nr. 41A, p. 617f. below; note the influence of Tauler in the following lines.

300. *ordine*.

301. This sentence in German; it ends rather poignantly; *ich kan es nicht anders machen*, i.e. I have no choice, I have to be this blunt.

302. One MS. reads 'sixth'.

303. 2 Kings 1²ᶠ, ¹⁶; cf. Nr. 51; Elliger, p. 215, suggests they had clashed at Erfurt, perhaps preventing Müntzer's stay at St Peter's; cf. Nr. 29.

304. Presumably Müntzer.

32. *Müntzer to an unknown recipient (fragment).*[305] *No date or place given.*

Greetings, brother. It seems to be the general expectation that I will set out to refute what appears perfectly reasonable to everyone else and, indeed this piece of audacity on my part will be sent packing by the clever mouths[306] to Anticyra,[307] since a dose of hellebore seems to be indicated. But in my eyes the views of all wicked men are valueless (even if they make a great noise).[308] For it is the truth – so hateful to these supposed infants[309] – on which my voice will meditate and to which my lips will bear witness against the enemies of the cross until the tongue sticks to my throat.[310] I express nothing but the eternal will of God, with which all the friends of the Lord are to be filled in all wisdom and spiritual understanding, Colossians 1,[311] until the day come when they discern their names mightily and wondrously[312] inscribed in the heavens. Psalm 118.[313] On the other hand, there is no way in which (the names of) those destined for destruction can be written up alongside the righteous. For he who has come to believe that he was chosen before the world was constituted,[314] and has accepted in faith the works of the Lord as altogether credible pointers to this, will not be able to be of this world;[315] rather the world, in its turncoat hatred, will regard him as a lunatic John 17.[316] The name of the Lord has planted our feet firmly on the rock.[317] What is this rock, my brother, if not the solidity of faith in the son of God? To what

305. F. sees this letter as a response to a criticism of Müntzer's harshness to the 'weak' in faith, and as perhaps stemming from the same period as Nr. 31; other themes seem to be present, including that of election, and this, together with the Bible references, e.g. to Psalm 93, suggests that there may be links with Letters 40, 41; Bräuer suggests a dating in Summer 1523 'Die Vorgeschichte von Luthers "Brief an die Fürsten zu Sachsen ..."', LJ 47, 42, n. 10; the recipient will be a fellow-pastor, perhaps a friend like Martin Seligmann (cf. Letter 48); in Latin.

306. *acuto stommate.*

307. City in Phocis, in whose neighbourhood hellebore was found and used in a cure for madness and epilepsy. (F.)

308. Superscribed; the Wittenbergers?

309. *fictis lactentibus*, lit. supposed babes at the breast; i.e. the weak in faith; cf. Nr. 31, p. 46/4ff., and Nr. 33.

310. Proverbs 8[7], Psalms 22[15]; 137[6].

311. Colossians 1[9]; cf. John 15[15].

312. *vehementer, admirabiliter*; seems to add little to the meaning; possibly a reference to 1 Peter 2[9] (Vg.) which refers to the elect, called 'in admirabile lumen suum'.

313. Psalms 118[2] (Vg.) *Beati qui scrutantur testimonia eius*; cf. Luke 10[20].

314. Ephesians 1[4].

315. The words: *summa vigilia* – the loftiest vigils – superscribed.

316. John 17[16, 14].

317. Psalms 40[2].

end? None other than him, who can never be moved! Psalm 92,[318] (God who makes his elect)[319] blessed, immovable to all eternity Psalm 111.[320] This fear of the Lord is the bitter abomination[321] resisted by the imposters, who, without any inkling of the spirit, fix their eyes on the text: Love your enemies;[322] as one angel with outspread wings fixes his eyes on the face of the other above the mercy-seat.[323] The evil-doer is reduced to nothingness at the sight of him, but he glorifies those who fear the Lord. If you have decided like me to adore him with a resolute confession then it will not be I but God in us who will perfect us in one mind in preparation for the day of his coming,[324] he who is to be loved by all who sincerely profess Christ ...

33. Fragment of a letter of Müntzer.[325] No time or place.

Our scribes and pharisees should be given the asses' milk in the skin of Jael, who slew Sisera; compare Judges 4[326] with the text in Isaiah 65:[327] that you may suck and be satisfied from her consoling breasts, not ours. Paul uses milk to train those who are as yet incapable,[328] while our contemporaries see to it that they remain boys for ever, Isaiah 65.[329] God himself laughs at such ceremonies, for he makes our salvation begin and continue to its end in fear.[330] In his last chapter Isaiah makes the same point, though not quite so well as Paul: that you may suck and abound in delights from all the manifestations of her glory. You will be carried to her breasts and be made happy on her knees.[331]

318. Psalms 92[1] (Vg.).

319. These words (*Deus qui electum suum*) superscribed.

320. Psalms 112[6].

321. In Nr. 31 Müntzer described as abominable the denial of purgatory; cf. also Nr. 41.

322. Matthew 5[44].

323. Exodus 25[20]; The reference is to the cherubim above the Ark, perhaps to the holy fear they excite in the beholder.

324. Cf. 1 Corinthians 1[8].

325. In Latin; similar content to the previous fragment, possible part of it (F.); also similarities to Letter 35; since it lacks all the obvious characteristics of a letter, one wonders whether it was the basis of a sermon or meditation on Isaiah 65.

326. Judges 4[19]ff.

327. Isaiah 66[11]; the startling comparison throws light on Müntzer's approach to exegesis.

328. 1 Corinthians 3[1]f.

329. Isaiah 65[20] envisages the end of infant mortality; all boys will live on to a ripe old age; cf. Nr. 31, n. 294 and Nr. 32, n. 309.

330. Isaiah 65[3]ff.

331. Isaiah 66[12].

34. *Johann Esche[332] to Müntzer. No place or date.*

To be delivered to the reverend Master Tho[mas] M[üntzer] with my greeting.

The Lord be with you, my brother Thomas. I received from the brothers, to whom your absence is painful, your greeting[333] and the brief indication of your views. But those with knowledge are not without this consolation, that although we are absent in body yet we are united in the spirit of God,[334] in which we are reborn and forever bound together in one body and in perpetual brotherhood so that we are always present in true love to one other. Hence let us pray for one another, that we may not be found lacking in true faith but be strengthened in the perpetual love with which God loved us.[335] You, best of men, know how the lot of the elect of God, who yearn for the redemption of Israel, can be cast amidst lions, dragons, scorpions,[336] among those who are stiff-necked and hard of heart. But who will be our helper? None other than the Lord who has done wondrous things for those who are his, as we are taught figuratively by the children of Israel.[337] The truth, however, is in the gospel. Who, then, can be greater than his Lord, who is blessed to all eternity, so that we have been found worthy to suffer so many insults, persecutions, and slights for his name.[338] Alas, though, it is yours that torture me more than my own (I swear this as in the presence of God, before whom I do not lie);[339] though I know very well that this all is to your salvation, yet when these dead, insensate and unlearned men with no knowledge of God raise their cavils against the truth they pierce me to the heart. May God repay them according to their deserts, for they are the sort that will not improve after one or two or any number of corrections. What then? Is it not necessary that they should first do such things? But the end is not quite yet, though the Lord knows the end, when he

332. In Latin; the Augustinian monk and later martyr from the Netherlands, Johann van Eschen; like Heinrich Voes, spent some time in the Augustinian house in Eisleben, and was captured in Antwerp on 6 October 1522; the letter refers repeatedly to persecution and suffering and may shortly predate this capture; cf. Hans Pelt's contacts with and references to Antwerp in Letter 26, above; it may be through them that Müntzer's greetings have been conveyed; however, they could have met in Eisleben or in Wittenberg with which the Augustinian house in Antwerp had close links, and the letter could date from an earlier time (Bräuer).

333. *verbum*; abbreviated, reading uncertain.

334. 1 Corinthians 5[3].

335. 1 John 4[19].

336. Ezekiel 2[4, 6].

337. Müntzer, himself, often translates Israel by 'the elect'.

338. Matthew 10[24]; Acts 5[41].

339. Galatians 1[20].

will lead out Israel from captivity. Therefore pray for us, that our flight should not be in winter.[340] The summer is nearly here.[341] But alas, our watchmen act as if they were blind, and our pastors, too, are sruck dumb, unwilling to drive the wolf away.[342] Because they are afraid of losing their temporal welfare they lose their eternal one, too. Perhaps the wheat and the tares have not yet fully ripened.[343] But they are ripening, because the harvest is becoming white.[344] Therefore be mindful of me just as I am always a fellow-sufferer with you, and do not look down on me, because I am your brother. All that I have, then, also belongs to you. So pray to the Lord that he may recall Johann Esch from these perilous snares in which he is entangled;[345] he lives only to do whatever is pleasing to you. If I had known anything to write that would have given you more pleasure[346] than what I did write, I would have done it. Farewell.

35. *Müntzer to an unknown recipient. Nordhausen[347], 14 July 1522.*

Greetings in the name of the virgin's son.

Those who blether away about me denying the doctrine of Christ, as they call it, are fabricating lies.[348] Against them I set the immutable will of God to which I have always adhered. In brief, I confront[349] all impious imposters with the church of Jesus of Nazareth in all its purity[350] as constituted by the fore-ordination of God.[351] What do their complaints about the spirits of men being confused and uncertain[352] matter? The time is imminent which will be really dangerous for all the impious, those who thrust themselves forward – by non-sequiturs[353] all their own – as singled out by divine grace, of which they understand as much as a goose understands the Milky

340. Matthew 24²⁰; Mark 13¹⁸.

341. Matthew 24³²f.; Luke 21³⁰; cf. Müntzer's letter to Melanchthon, Nr. 31, p. 46/9f.

342. Isaiah 56¹⁰.

343. Matthew 13³⁰.

344. The harvest theme is also a favourite one for Müntzer.

345. Psalms 91³.

346. *graciosus* (Bräuer/Kobuch); F. reads *graciorem*, which gives the meaning.

347. In Latin; we know little about Müntzer's movements after his visit to Prague, or when exactly he arrived in Nordhausen; cf. Elliger, pp. 214ff.

348. So far the most abrupt opening to any of Müntzer's letters; the recipient has clearly been attacking his life and doctrine.

349. *exhibeo.*

350. *rectissimam.*

351. *prediffinitione Dei constitutam.*

352. Presumably reference to Müntzer's teaching on predestination.

353. *epicharemate.*

Way in the firmament. For it is the elect who proclaim the marvels of the living word in the law, which have been infallibly written in my heart,[354] and if, by a miraculous dispensation, God should save us we, like Jonah will not be abhorred, as long as we possess our souls in patience.[355] Believe me, I have not lied about a syllable of this, as the divine judgment will show. Put a guard on your mouth, then, lest any guile be detected in the allegation that you and yours are wont to make:[356] Müntzer flees from the scribes and pharisees and hypocrites Mt. 23; for their houses are deserted, lacking a heavenly owner.[357] For they seek their own ends, not those of Jesus Christ.[358] At first, of course, they blabbed on about the need to abandon the sacrifice.[359] But now they would dearly like to deny that, just as the whole populace cries out: Great, great! why did they begin something that they were quite unable to keep up?[360] O you fine witnesses to my Christian life! For producing testimonies that were more than suspect I abominate you. For the glory of the Lord for which these things were undertaken has been exposed to vituperation,[361] that glory which the Lord never allows his own to neglect.

Nordhausen, on the eve of the feast of all the apostles in the year of the Lord 1522 etc.

Thomas Müntzer, a son of shaking[362] to the impious.

36. Johann Buschmann[363] to Müntzer. (Heiligenstadt?), 30 September 1522.

To Thomas Müntzer student of the divine sciences, my most dear brother in Nordhausen.

354. Is this a reference to the allegation that the spirits of men are being confused? note the adverb: *infallibiliter*.

355. Luke 21[19].

356. *asserere* (Bräuer/Kobuch); *assumere* (F.); Psalms 140[3] (Vg.); Ecclesiasticus 22[33].

357. Matthew 23[38]; the spirit, their true 'owner' or possessor has departed; cf. Letter 31, n. 293 and Prague Manifesto, A, p. 357, n. 6 below.

358. Philippians 2[21].

359. The Mass; no doubt a reference to Luther's Invocavit sermons again.

360. Müntzer's critique is both 'radical', and populist (*totus universus populus*).

361. The attacks on Müntzer cast discredit on the cause of God for which he stands.

362. *filius excussionis* cf. Job 38[13] (Vg): *Et tenuisti concutiens extrema terrae, et excussisti impios ex ea*; for Müntzer Sisera, referred to in Letter 33, is a type of 'shaking', cf. his list of Hebrew names, p. 431f. below.

363. In Latin; b. c. 1469 in Heiligenstadt, 1503 studied in Wittenberg, notary for the archbishopric of Mainz in Eichsfeld after 1526. Cf. M. Bensing, 'Thomas Müntzer und Nordhausen ...', *Zeitschrift für Geschichtswissenschaft* 5 (1962), 1109f.; clearly one of a group of friends anxious to help Müntzer, cf. Elliger, p. 236.

Greetings, Thomas, prince of friends. Six days before the present holy day I had the great joy of receiving your letters in the evening and on reading them I passed on your request [364] to Master John Iring[365] in Allendorf by his own letter-carrier and the reply I received you will see from the enclosed letters.[366] Although Alexander,[367] with whom I discussed the matter, and I are both extremely vexed about such prevarication in matters of faith it has, however, come about (in my judgment) at the instigation of our prelates (if it is right to put it like that), who describe and condemn you everywhere as a Martinian[368] and worse. Another person, however, vicar of the church of the blessed Virgin Mary, obtained a parish of his own in the Thuringian region which he put in the care of another priest (although it was difficult to find one). If he had known the situation prior to 23 September[369] there is no doubt that he would have been most happy to commit the care of his sheep to you because, like Alexander, he has always been inclined towards you. But I cannot give you any news about any other position at this wintry time of year. With these few words, farewell; you will always find me eager to be of service to you. Farewell, again. In haste in the year [15]22 on St. Jerome's day.

John Buschmann.

37. *Karlstadt to Müntzer,*[370] *Wittenberg. 21 December 1522.*

To the servant of Christ and dearest of brothers, Thomas Müntzer.

Peace to you from the father of our Lord Jesus Christ. I am bound to wish you this since I see that you have resorted to cursing rather like the cursing of Jeremiah,[371] of which I cannot approve, since in Jeremiah, too, I can see a grain of wheat fallen into the earth but not yet dead.[372] For just like him you seem to me to feel something of the bitterness of mustard, but not yet to feel that you have become the

---

364. Müntzer wished to leave Nordhausen after clashing with the Lutheran Lorenz Süsse and possibly with the Council, and had sought Buschmann's support in finding a new post; cf. Elliger, p. 235f.

365. Pastor in Sooden, d. 1526; cf. Bensing, op. cit. p. 1110.

366. Not extant.

367. Probably Alexander Kindervater, Buschmann's deputy. (F.)

368. Follower of Luther.

369. *ante octavam.*

370. In Latin; answers a (lost) letter of Müntzer; cf. Elliger, pp. 239ff.; the four references to returning to the subject 'some other time' suggest a letter written in haste (F.); the style and syntax is ragged at times to the point of incomprehensibility.

371. Jeremiah 20[14].

372. John 12[24].

least of all men. Surely if you felt yourself the least of all,[373] you, too, would declare yourself unworthy of the glory and honour with which Christ of Nazareth was crowned by that woman.[374] But we can return to this another time. Your letter alerted me to the heavy seas in which you are swimming. Believe me: the Lord chastises his elect with judgement. But though it may for the moment seem to you, too, that you have been struck by a visitation of the enemy, this, too, has been sent by [God's] judgement, namely because of sin. You know how easy it is for us to cast off the will of God since we are separated from it as often and to the extent to which our desires triumph. It is in the land of death that we exist, so the righteousness of Christ does not triumph in us until the life of the flesh is over. But we can return to this another time.[375] I am indeed pleased that in Zwickau some ceremonies are finding no favour. But who would not be pleased, when you strive with such zeal to clamber into the abyss of the divine will, when you strain to be reborn there, where you were the life of God. But we can return to this some other time. I congratulate you on turning only to us for help. Please come alone and ask for me at the house of a citizen called Simon Fleischer where I am staying; because I would like to see you face to face. Not that the idea of seeing you in any way takes my fancy, but so that I can carry out my duty, first to confer with you, and then to see what I can do for you.[376] Then I can say the things which I am unwilling to commit to writing.[377] I will take you to the new lodging I have secured for myself in the country.[378] I think and hope that you will have no cause at all to regret taking the trouble.[379] It is not possible to reply to everything. God is the master of my heart; I have learnt his power and his strong hand by experience. Hence I have said more about visions and dreams than any of the professors. The rest in your presence. Farewell in the joy of[380] Christ Jesus and come as soon as possible . . . my . . . and behold he breathes on my wretched little heart.[381] Farewell. Wittenberg, the day of the apostle Thomas, in the year 1522.   Andrew Karlstadt.

373. Matthew 13[32].
374. A reference to Matthew 26[7]?
375. *palor*(?) crossed out.
376. As in Nr. 36 Müntzer is looking for help to find a new post, and no doubt regarded Karlstadt as more likely to be sympathetic than his colleagues.
377. There is a conspiratorial tone in this part of the letter, curiously married with distrust of Müntzer or at least reservations about him.
378. Probably in Wörlitz, 15 kms. west of Wittenberg; cf. Nr. 43. (F.)
379. *Opinor ac spero, quod neutiquam te laboris paenitebit*; F. interprets this as a reference to working in the fields; the tr. would read then: you will have no cause at all to regret the (experience of) manual labour.
380. *[feli]citer*; (Bräuer/Kobuch).
381. *quam primum [...] en d[...]rum et [e]cce corculum meum anhelat* (Bräuer/Kobuch); cf. *[...]rum meum* (F.).

38.   *Müntzer to unknown Followers in Halle. 19 March 1523.*

Greetings and God's constant mercy be with you, my most beloved brothers. I beg you not to be scandalised by my expulsion,[382] for it is in such trials that the abyss of the soul is emptied so that it is more and more refined and made manifest so that it can draw on the insuperable testimony of the holy spirit. No one can experience God's mercy until he has been forsaken, as Isaiah says clearly in chapters 28 and 54: 'In an instant I forsook you and in great mercy I gathered you up;'[383] this is the same thing of which Christ our saviour speaks: 'When I go away then the comforter comes, the Holy Spirit,'[384] who can only be given to the person who finds no consolation. So let my suffering be a model for yours. Let all the tares shoot up as much as they like; they will all have to come under the flail with the pure wheat;[385] the living God is sharpening his sickle in me so that I will later be able to cut down the red poppies and the little blue flowers. Let this, then, be my greeting to you. God be with you. Let anyone who can afford to do so share with me the wages of the Gospel: 'The labourer is worthy of his wages' (Matthew 10).[386] But if anyone take offence at this, let him give me nothing. Death would be preferable to impugning the honour of God by giving offence in the matter of nourishment. I have two gulden from the lady (abbess) for the whole winter; one I give for the lad, the other I already owe many times over. This lad is loyal to me. In the wretchedness of my expulsion, on the day of St. Joseph in the year of Christ 1523.

Thomas Müntzer, a willing courier of God.[387]

39.   *Engelhard Mohr[388] to Müntzer. Halle, 31 March 1523.*

To Sir Thomas Müntzer, my reverend Master and a friend loved with no common affection.

During the time you were with us, most beloved Thomas, you

382. After Nordhausen Müntzer spent a short and uneasy time in the combined role of preacher in St George's, Halle, and chaplain to the nuns at Marienkammer in Glauchau; cf. Elliger, p. 235f. for a plausible reconstruction of his movements; it is not known whether he was involved in a raid by some 300–400 inhabitants of Halle on the Neuwerk monastery; his reforming views would in any case have sufficed as grounds for his expulsion by the Catholic authorities.

383. Isaiah 28[28(?)]; 54[7].

384. John 16[7].

385. Cf. Matthew 13[24ff.]; note the uneasy tension between humble resignation and anticipated vengeance.

386. Matthew 10[10].

387. This letter is written with great care and precise orthograhy; it can hardly be a draft; yet there is no address or seal-mark; was it ever despatched? (Bräuer/Kobuch).

388. In Latin; Mohr was verger of St. George's, Halle; cf. Elliger, p. 245f.

elucidated several divinely inspired mysteries concerning the inmost being of man and I now regret that I did not take care to listen to what you said about them. But such things appear vain and inadequate, since we have but one master as our sole instructor, who gives us all we want like a loving father and a merciful lord and by whom we all ought to be taught. If we choose not to acknowledge him, he will not acknowledge us. Having long turned this matter[389] over in my mind, on the one hand in faith, but not a faith based on solid rock, but on the other hand weakly hesitating, not knowing the true path, at long last I realised that a man should appear empty of all things, whether belonging to himself or others, just as if he were not there at all. For this realisation I will glorify my God in you, and my saviour Jesus Christ, who alone performs great wonders. But one request I have of you, if a son may bother his father (since you must know that I am burdened with the cares and duties of a verger and am daily tortured by ceremonies).

Could you please draw back the veils around the eucharist for me, so that I can approach it more easily, for I am vexed by all the different customs, ideas and speculations relating to it, though I do doubt whether any little priest can confer the body and the blood, since all they do in his memory is gabble away about a sacrifice of praise, since Christ offered himself up once for all?[390] But they accumulate more and more of these inanely fashioned prayers and will end up, I think, buying themselves a place in the dung-heap. And if it is not too tedious for you please write to me so that he who was once a boy can follow his father's wishes. Farewell and flourish. Halle, on the birth of the virgin 1523, the third day after Psalm Sunday.

Yours always, Engelhard Mohr.

40. Müntzer to Luther.[391] Allstedt, 9 July 1523.

Greetings, father, whose sincerity surpasses that of all the others.[392] Your good opinion was never something I held so cheap that I would

389. lit. *saxum*, 'stone', in anticipation of *petra*, 'rock' in the next line and probably hinting at a Sisyphean task.

390. Obviously Müntzer had taken care not to reveal his own views on these matters while at Halle, although the first half of the letter indicates that he spoke more openly about his mystical views.

391. In Latin; a crucial letter, on the whole reasonable in tone, setting out in brief compass many of Müntzer's central concerns; we may possess some of the preliminary notes for it, cf. p. 404 below; its conciliatory language reflects Müntzer's self-confidence; he had been established in Allstedt since Easter and was finding enthusiastic support for his liturgical reforms; Luther did not reply directly; cf. WAB3, p. 104ff.; the address on the back has been cut off; cf. the end to Letter 13!

392. *Sincerissime inter ceteros pater.*

have lent my ears to any unworthy allegations. After all, from the very beginning I knew for sure that you were not seeking your own interests but those of all men. What really shocked me, however, was that your letters commended to me that most pestilential fellow, Egranus,[393] because with every passing day I realised more clearly what that crow was up to, and that he would soon be casting off the feathers he had stolen and gorge himself on his stinking[394] carcasses, completely turning his back on the ark of righteousness.[395] In short, he emerged in his true colours in that splendid book of his on how to make one's confession,[396] decking himself out vividly for his followers as an unctuous servant of his belly, for in it he commends the church of the ungodly[397] and the evil-doers with such erudition – the most helpful thing he has ever done for the wicked. You wanted this fellow, who was so zealous for his own glory, to be reconciled with me to prevent your enemies attacking you en masse; for my part, I pushed myself forward as an immoveable wall for the glory of God's name.[398] I opposed whole-heartedly this 'proud eye and insatiable spirit with whom I refuse to sup.'[399] As to their blaming me for the disorders at Zwickau[400] all but the blind civic leaders know that during the uprising I was in the baths, with no inkling of what was going on, and that the whole council would have been killed the following night if I had not intervened. Today I am ready to explain everything. On the issue of revelations[401] many lies have been cast in my face by these distinguished brutes. I have never referred to such stupidities, but I will be quite frank with you here about my views. The recognition of the divine will, which should fill us with wisdom through Christ,[402] with a spiritual and infallible understanding, this

393. Cf. Nr. 20; Müntzer's lapse into personalities at this early stage of the letter was hardly calculated to achieve the hoped-for reconciliation with Luther; Bräuer suggests Zeiss may have handed it personally to Luther, 'Die Vorgeschichte . . .', LJ47 (1980) p. 43.

394. Superscribed.

395. Genesis 8[7ff.]; 2 Peter 2[5]; the image of the black crow/vulture haunted Müntzer and was applied to Luther himself in the *Highly Provoked Vindication*.; cf. Phaedrus' fable, The Crow and the Peacock; the topos of the crow stealing other birds' feathers was a common one in the sixteenth century; cf. A. Henkel, A. Schöne (edd.) *Emblemata*, p. 884f.; Jerome also uses the image, cf. MPL XXVI, 601.

396. *A Sermon on Confession* etc.; Panzer Nr. 1518, Weller Nr. 2279.

397. Psalm 26[5].

398. Jeremiah 1[18]; this phrase, added later, is important for Müntzer's self-understanding; cf. the use of the quotation at the beginning of the *Manifest Exposé of False Faith*, p. 260/12; cf. also Nr. 45, p. 68/16 below.

399. Cf. Psalm 101[5]; 1 Corinthians 5[11].

400. The first of the accusations made against him which Müntzer seeks to answer; for the Zwickau incident cf. Elliger, pp. 175ff., Gritsch, p. 40f.

401. The second accusation.

402. 'through Christ' is superscribed.

knowledge of God is to be possessed by all (as the apostle teaches the Colossians),[403] so that we may be seen to be taught by the mouth of the living God and may know with complete certainty that the teaching of Christ was not devised by man but comes to us from the living God without any shadow of deception. For Christ himself wants us to have the judgement over his teaching. May the Lord prevent the opposite happening, for some flies want to contaminate our gentle ointment[404] (which teaches all things). As John 7 says, 'If anyone wishes to do his will, he will know from my teaching whether it derives from God or whether I am just speaking for myself.'[405] No mortal man knows this teaching or knows whether Ch[rist] is mendacious or truthful, unless his will is conformed to the crucified one, unless he, too, has first endured the swells and surges of the waters,[406] which for most of the time are cascading over the heads of the elect from all sides. After a struggle, however, he is rescued again, having cried out hoarsely[407] and learnt to hope against hope[408] and to seek his will alone on the day of visitation that comes after prolonged waiting. Then his feet will be set upon the rock[409] and the Lord who works wonders will appear from afar; at long last authentic testimonies of God will be rendered. But any one who disdains all this, expecting the Lord to be always at hand, is quite at variance with the entire body of Scripture.[410] Nor should those who boast about Christ be believed unless they have his spirit, Romans 8:[411] That he may testify to their spirit that they are sons of God, Isaiah 8.[412] Moreover, no one is a son of God unless he suffers with him[413] and becomes as a sheep for the slaughter all the day long.[414] Let God not spare himself, but forsake him for a while,[415] until at length he is assured that no created thing can detach him from the living God and from the absolutely true testimony of the Scriptures.[416] This assurance

---

403. 1[9ff.]

404. Cf. Ecclesiastes 10[1]; 1 John 2[27]; the 'flies in the ointment' theme is a recurring one.

405. John 7[17].

406. Psalm 93[3].

407. Psalm 69[3].

408. Romans 4[18].

409. Psalm 40[2].

410. Jeremiah 31[3].

411. Romans 8[16].

412. Isaiah 8[16ff.]

413. Romans 8[17].

414. Psalm 44[22].

415. *ne deus sibi parcat*; cf. Romans 11[21] (Vg.), and Isaiah 54[7] (Vg.) possibly there is a reference (to Romans 8[32]: God does not spare his own son).

416. Romans 8[39].

enables him to distinguish by divine revelation between the work of God and that of the malignant spirits; here he draws quite legitimately on really genuine appearances and hidden portents, discerning profound mysteries from the very mouth of God Corinthians, chapter 2;[417] Isaiah 8: 'The people will demand from their God a vision on behalf of the living and the dead for a law and a testimony greater etc.' Anyone who spurned this 'is to be denounced before his king and his God' etc.[418] Dearest of patrons, you know Thomas by name and by character.[419] I am not the sort of person to accept ecstasies and visions unless compelled to by God,[420] and I only give credence to those I do accept if I see they are the work [of God].[421] Nor am I to be seen as leading a perfect life according to the measure of the gift of Christ.[422] Who am I to be worthy of that? The plain text of the Scriptures insists repeatedly that the Holy Spirit does teach us about the things which are to come John 16.[423] For it is his way to bring to pass everything that the fiery shield reveals.[424] I only accept what is testified to by Scripture. You may say that I am ignoring what Moses says in the two texts explained by Jesus Sirach, Ecclesiasticus 34:[425] 'The lot of the senseless man is vanity and mendacity; fools are carried away by dreams.' 'For dreams lead many astray.' Although rather less well than Paul he gives the same explanation for error as the one I gave above. Because they failed to set the wisdom and the testimony of God side by side they deservedly confounded darkness with the vision of God, Micah 3.[426] I am not so arrogant in this matter as to resist being corrected and instructed by your superior testimony so that we may set out together on the way of love. You raise objections about Markus and Nicholas.[427] What manner of men they are is up to them, Galatians 2.[428] I fear and tremble before the divine judgments.

---

417. I Corinthians 2[10ff].

418. Cf. Isaiah 8[19ff]; Müntzer springs back and forward from Isaiah 8 to Romans 8 in this section.

419. From Müntzer's visit to Wittenberg in 1518.

420. *nisi deus me coegerit.*

421. *immo susceptas non credo, nisi videro opus.*

422. Ephesians 4[13].

423. John 16[13].

424. Proverbs 30[5] (Provr. 30 in margin); *cuncta que revelat ignitus clipeus, ea demunire est solitus.*; F. translates *demunire* by 'demolish'; Elliger argues that the 'de' accentuates the meaning of the simple verb to stress completion op. cit., p. 363.

425. Ecclesiasticus 34[1.7.]

426. Micah 3[6].

427. Stübner (cf. Nr. 22) and Storch; cf. Elliger, p. 220; (the third accusation); Müntzer seems to be distancing himself from their 'lack of earnestness' as Lohmann, p. 34, suggests.

428. Galatians 2 refers to the 'testing' of Paul's teaching at Jerusalem.

As to what they said to you, or what they have done, I know nothing about it. You objected that certain terms sickened you.[429] I do not know which they are, but surmise: perseverance, tribulation, gifts of the spirit etc.[430] Best of fathers, I know that the apostle has imposed a rule upon me, that profane novelties and pseudo-knowledge are to be shunned.[431] Believe me! I will say nothing that I cannot back up with the clearest and most apposite of texts. If I fail to do this do not judge me worthy of life. May the Lord preserve you; do renew your old love. Give my regards and greeting in the Lord to Philip, Karlstadt and Jonas, and John . . .[432] and the others in your church. I do not think you really meant what you said,[433] but beseech you to ask whether Christ was not present at the wedding, for the voice of the Lord must always be sought out, especially in so great a mystery, lest the earthern vessels continue to hold water and can never be turned into wine.[434] Perhaps I seem here to resemble Origen. Farewell, again, and lest this letter swell to an immense size, I sound the retreat.

Allstedt in the year of the Lord[435] 1523, the seventh of the Ides of July.

Thomas Müntzer, parish priest of Allstedt.

429. The fourth accusation.

430. *longanimitate, angustia mentis, talento*; in his Table Talk Luther offered a critique of the terms *entgrobung, studirung, verwunderung, langweil, gelassenheit*; WA TR 1, Nr. 1204.

431. 1 Timothy 6[20].

432. pomeranus(?) Bugenhagen; from this and the remaining lines a strip has been torn off; text reconstructed by Trillitzsch (F.) . . . *ceterosque in tua ecclesia saluta et v[ale in] domino. Non arbitror te ex animo dixisse [sed iniur]gio ne Christus adsit nuptiis, vere in-[quiren]dum semper os domini precipuo in tam [magno] mysterio, alioqui vasa illa fictilia aq[uis plena] manerent ne unquam in vinum mutari p[ossent]. Videor hic fortassis Origeni in al[tero] similis. Rursus vale, ne epystola in [immensum] crescat, receptui cano. Ex Alsted anno [1523] 7 Idus Julii*; Braüer (Th. Lit. Z 102 Nr. 3., p. 219) adds *parte* after *Origeno in al[tero]*, with reference to the interpretation of John 2[6] in de principiis, II; *in al[iquo] similis* is another possible reading (Bräuer/Kobuch).

433. Perhaps a reference back to Luther's attitude to Egranus.

434. Obviously a reference to the wedding at Cana (John 2[1ff.]), but what is the significance for Müntzer? Elliger suggests that the reference to Origen in the next sentence is to the latter's sexual rigorism; op. cit., p. 376; the context suggests a broader understanding; the letter to the brothers in Stolberg (Nr. 41) speaks explicitly of 'the man whose loins are crushed waits on the Lord prior to the wedding'; the meaning seems to be that it is only in and through the experience of helplessness, impotence, that the elect can open themselves to the power of God; is Origen's alleged castration thus a symbol of the purification of the elect? cf. *The Sermon to the Princes*, p. 242 below, n. 147.

41A. Draft. An Open Letter to his brothers in Stolberg. 18 July 1523.

To his brothers in Stolberg.[436]

Greetings! What great and remarkable foolishness of the elect friends of God to imagine that God will rush to their aid![437] Though none of them is exactly rushing to embrace suffering. For where there is no poverty of the spirit, the kingdom of Christ cannot commence either. Christ's true reign comes to pass only after the splendour of this world has been completely discarded. It is then that the Lord comes and rules and casts down the tyrants to the ground.[438] After the weakness experienced by the members of the elect in complete self-surrender[439] he supports and endows them with the strength which flows from him. He girds them around with his power; the man whose loins are crushed waits on the Lord prior to the wedding.[440] He who has not discovered anything about such waiting has no God, either, for his feet are not planted on the rock.[442] For all true, godly men must know what to do, so that they cannot be moved; for one's heart becomes a throne for God by realising that it has surely been chosen by God as his possession.[443]

436. This line in Latin.

437. As Elliger, p. 370 remarks, this first draft is pastoral in tone; Müntzer is warning his followers against misunderstanding his message as a glib programme of reform and protest; religious renewal must precede everything else.

438. Psalm 93, just translated by Müntzer for his German Order of Service, cf. p. 000, is the basis for this letter. His translation certainly demonstrates his uninhibited approach to the text! (F., p. 115).

> Clothed in splendour, God shows that it is he who rules.
> He has put on his power and girded himself with it.
> He who is not to be moved makes fast the ends of the earth.
> An unchangeable God, you have made the elect man your throne.
> > (Vg.: *Parata sedes tua ex tunc: a seculo tu es*)
> Above him, O God, the flood waters towered, the flood waters thundered,
> The water courses towered; the great waters thundered.
> An awesome, wondrous man is the Lord in the mighty flood, as the savage ocean swell rages
> In this discovery of his truth, his testimony is not betrayed.
> Man sees he is the house of God when he endures his days with patience.
> > (*in der lanckweil seyner tage* – Vg.: *longitudo*)
> The paean of praise for God's power at the beginning should not be overlooked: the tyrants will be overthrown; the splendour of this world cannot co-exist with that of God.

439. *gelassenheyt*; the mystical terms in this letter are legion: 'friends of God', 'poverty of spirit' etc.

440. Psalm 38[7]; cf. Nr. 40, n. 434.

441. *erharrung*: Luke 12[36].

442. Psalm 40[2].

443. *zu seyner besitzunge* – a favourite expression of Müntzer; cf. Nr. 31, n. 293.

But before one can be sure of salvation torrents of water come again and again with thundering so fearsome[444] that one loses the will to live; for the waves of this wild, surging ocean swallow up[445] many who think they have already[446] won through. So one should not flee these waves but negotiate them skilfully, as wise helmsmen do; for the Lord only gives his holy testimony to someone who has first made his way through perplexity.[447] That is why the hearts of men are so seldom touched with the true spirit of Christ, to whom our souls truly belong;[448] they [want] a foretaste of life eternal before the heart is prepared by the pains of hell for the endless days of eternity. I intended to send you the interpretation of this ninety-second psalm,[449] dear brothers, as soon as I had completed it. Yet you are far too vainglorious; want to achieve great things, but cannot thole it when your preparedness is put to the test.[450] He who cannot endure his hell willingly will endure it all the same – as a laughing-stock, and gnashing his teeth.[451]

41B. An Open Letter to his dear brothers in Stolberg solemnly warning them to shun unjustifiable rebellion.[452]

Salvation in the spirit of Jesus be with you, good brother! What

444. Psalm 93[2,5].

445. *dan dye bulgen dusses wilden meres wag vorslindeth manchen.*

446. *sch(on)*; cf. Bräuer/Ullmann, p. 13, who comment that *schier* (completely) is also possible.

447. *vorwunderunge.*

448. 'spirit of Christ' is written above the line; *warhafftigen besitzer der selen,* following Bräuer/Ullmann, p. 13; cf. n. 443 above.

449. Psalm 93[5].

450. *anfegtung.*

451. Another recurrent theme in Müntzer; cf. the references to purgatory in Letter 31 to Melanchthon, and in Nr. 32; cf. Matthew 13[42,50].

452. Twice as long as the first draft this printed form was rather more judgmental towards the end; it is of course, again based on Müntzer's translation of Psalm 93; it is powerful, eloquent writing, perhaps Müntzer at his very best; it was printed in two virtually identical versions by Nicholas Widemar in Eilenburg in the late summer or early autumn of 1523; its characterisation as a *sendebrieff*, a term Müntzer used for his letters of exhortation to princes or to the elect, but also for the apostolic epistles of the New Testament (Dismer, p. 119) indicates that he expected it to be regarded as authoritative; apart from internal evidence, the occasion for the letter is unknown; Müntzer himself, of course, came from Stolberg, where reforming preaching began early with Johann Spangenberg and Tilemann Platner; the addressees appear to be the members of Müntzer's League or Covenant in Stolberg; note the variation in the form of address from the singular 'good brother' at the beginning, to the plural later on; the former may simply be a misprint; there is a new English translation, with a useful introduction, by Michael Baylor, 'Thomas Müntzer's First Publication', *Sixteenth Century Journal* 17 (1986), 451–8.

Math. 5
Luce 6

Osee 13

Psal. 82

Ro. 4

1 Co. 2

Joan. 6

Joan. 14

eiusdem 16

heights of folly that many of God's elect friends imagine that God will speed to their aid and quickly put Christianity to rights, although no one is really yearning for this or longing to reach poverty in spirit by suffering and endurance. Matthew 5, Luke 6.[453] Until a man has tasted poverty of spirit he does not deserve to be ruled by God; he does not even deserve to be tempted by the devil or the lowliest of the creatures. Hence he must live what he takes to be the good life, following his own will, But if he is to attain to real, unvarnished poverty of spirit, then he must first (by human reckoning) be forsaken by God. The man who is poor in spirit must also leave all creature comforts[454] behind. But as long as the elect cannot bring themselves to show respect for God's work[455] God can do nothing. It accords, then, with his divine and fatherly goodness, that he makes the tyrants rage more and more, Kings 8,[456] so that the countenance of his elect is covered in shame and vice and they are driven to seek the name and glory and honour of God alone Psalm 82.[457] For the lot, or reward of the elect will be identical with that of the damned if they are indolent Luke 12.[458] God's true reign[459] is truly and joyfully inaugurated when the elect come to see what God's work reveals to them in the experience of the spirit. Those people who have not tasted the reverse, bitter side[460] of faith do not know this, for they have not believed against belief, or hoped against hope, or met God's love with hate 1 Corinthians 2.[461] Hence they do not know what harms, or profits, the people of Christ,[462] not having put their faith to the test. They do not want to believe that God himself, in his zealous, unceasing goodness, will instruct man and tell him all he needs to know.[463] That is why the whole world lacks the chief point of salvation, which is faith, not being able to credit that God would deign to be our schoolteacher Matthew 23, James 3.[464] Oh, how great and stiff-necked is that unbelief which contents itself with the dead letter and turns its back on the finger which writes in the heart! 2 Corinthians 3.[465] What

453. Matthew 5[3]; Luke 6[20].

454. *muss alles trostes aller creaturn sich eusseren*; 'creature comforts' is perhaps rather weak; the meaning is something like: 'all material concerns and satisfactions.'

455. God's 'work' is precisely *not* created being but the working of the Law, our 'schoolteacher'; cf. below l. 28f. and Letter 49, pp. 77/4, 79/20ff.

456. 1 Samuel 8[7]; Hosea 13[11].

457. Psalm 83[17f.]

458. Luke 12[45ff.]

459. *warhafftige regiment.*

460. *das bitter widerspyl des glaubens.*

461. Romans 4[18]; 1 Corinthians 2[8ff.]

462. *der christenheit.*

463. John 6[45] 14[26] 16[13]; i.e. immediately, directly, without intermediaries.

464. Matthew 23[8-10]; James 3[15ff.]

465. 2 Corinthians 3[2]; in the margin a large pointing finger.

inkling do such foolish men have of what makes them Christians rather than pagans, or why the Koran should not be as valid as the Gospel. For they cannot refute the opponents from the divine order,[466] which the raka, that is, the wicked,[467] repudiate.[468] So it is all important that we allow God to rule;[469] that we know for sure that our faith does not deceive us, having genuinely suffered the working of the living word and being able to discriminate between the work of God and that of his creatures. As yet the world cannot accept this. We are invested with kingly splendour, with real strength, when we experience the might of God surging through us;[470] but we will be girded around as Peter was. The last chapter of John, Luke 12.[471] Only then will the assembly of the elect lay hold on the whole wide world,[472] which will acquire a Christian government[473] that no sack of gunpowder can ever topple. But because our zeal to grow in the spirit of truth does not increase,[474] our soul is not ready to be a throne for God;[475] but he who sits on the throne of abomination[476] will rule over the man who will not let God rule over him. Hence not even the truth will set him free, but a saucy insolence, which he will have to abandon in shame and sorrow.[477] Therefore every one should watch out for the great waves which pour their torrents of water down on our spirit. He must know his business.[478] A wise helmsman shows his skill by negotiating the great waves; he should not and cannot try to avoid them. Every act of unbelief and sin points the elect to judgment, Psalm 118,[479] for they discover day by day that God does not judge by the standards man employs. But what the world scorns, God raises up, what is folly is wisdom etc.[480] It is for this reason that no one can rule until he has passed through the time of testing, unless he has the

466. *auss der ordenung*.

467. Matthew 5[22]; *rassa* (sic!).

468. 1 Peter 3[15] (giving account of one's faith); cf. *ratio fidei* in margin.

469. Psalm 93[1].

470. *wan wir die krafft Gottes ym durchgang gewar werden*; cf. p. 270/6ff. below; 'we', of course, is the elect.

471. John 21[18]; Luke 12[35]; note the reference to Peter's martyrdom.

472. Cf. Psalm 93[1]; lit. the ends of the earth.

473. *ein christlich regiment*; in view of such phrases it is hard to see how Elliger (p. 373) can claim that any revolutionary ideas were remote from Müntzer's mind at this stage!

474. Romans 10[2].

475. Psalm 93[2].

476. Psalm 1[1]; Psalm 97[7].

477. John 8[32]; Psalm 1[1ff.]

478. Matthew 7[24-7], with Psalm 93.

479. Psalm 119, esp. vs. 123ff.; Dismer, p. 132, suggests v. 176.

480. 1 Corinthians 1[25]; Romans 8[33-6].

living judgement of God Wisdom 6, John 7.[481] For the testimonies of God must be convincing in every respect, since it is they which pass judgement. The matter requires the very highest knowledge in God and from God, so that [the judgement] will endure for ever, lest the house of God, the soul of man, be polluted.[482] It was my intention, good brothers, to have this Psalm 92 or [admonition] printed for you.[483] From what I hear, you combine vainglory with a failure to study; you are negligent; when you are in your cups you talk a great deal about our mission; when sober you are a bunch of milksops. So, my very best brothers, do improve your way of life. Beware of gluttony. Luke 21, 1 Peter 5.[484] Flee from lusts and those who hanker after them 2 Timothy 3.[485] Take a bolder stand than you have done up to now, and write me a letter about how you have invested your talents.[486] God bless you. Give my greetings to all who seek to do God's will, in accordance with the testimony of this teaching.

Allstedt, in the year of the Lord 1523, 18 July.

Thomas Müntzer.

Psal. 92

1 Cor. 3

Psal. 98

Luce 19
Ephe. 4

---

42. *The Magistrate and Community of the Old Town of Frankenhausen to Müntzer. Frankenhausen, 26 July 1523.*

To the honourable pastor of Allstedt, master of arts, our special good[487] friend.

We, Pricius, magistrate[488] Berltz Kulbe, bailiff,[489] and the whole community of the Old Town of Frankenhausen do hereby bear witness that Claus Storbinger sat in prison here in Frankenhausen

---

481. Wisdom 6[5]; John 7[24f.](?)

482. Psalm 93[5]; 1 Corinthians 3[16]; Psalm 99[6]; the printed version reads: in *der lenge der wage.*

483. *Ich war willens lieben brüder, das ich wolte diesen 92 Psalm ader lassen euch haben aussgedrucket*; Dismer, p. 134, reads *aderlassen*, the psalm is a 'blood letting', which is fanciful; *ader* appears regularly for *oder* ('or') and it may be that a word such as *sendebrieff*, or admonitory letter, has been omitted.

484. Luke 21[34]; 1 Peter 5[8].

485. 2 Timothy 3[1-5].

486. Luke 19[11ff.]; Ephesians 4[7(f.)].

487. *guthen* (Bräuer/Kobuch); *g[u]n[sti]gen* (F.); the occasion of this letter is none too clear; presumably Müntzer has enquired about Storbinger in a pastoral capacity; cf. letter 19; F., following Böhmer/Kirn, suggests he may be identical with Nicholas Storch, mentioned in Nr. 40, one of the 'Zwickau prophets', but Elliger, p. 364 n. 16 points to the lack of evidence for this.

488. *schultheysse.*

489. *rotsmeyster.*

some years ago for having brought a suit against his married wife under canon law and having her excommunicated. As a result he had to pledge and promise – and four men had to stand in as surety for him – that he would leave her in peace and bring no more suits against her. He had to do this if he wanted to be freed from prison or be released, for in fact she had no desire to stay with him. We will do whatever we can in this matter. These are the names of the warrantors: Kirsten Ludwig, Johannes Howissen, Clause Wygant, Heinz Müller. At that time they helped him to leave prison, as we have now heard from the elders. We know no more about this matter than what we have heard from the community.

Sunday after James the Apostle's day. 1523.

43. Müntzer to Karlstadt. Allstedt, 29 July 1523.

To his dearest brother Andrew Karlstadt, farmer in Wörlitz.[490]

Greetings, brother in the Lord. What hindered you from writing me I do not know, for you had promised that you would write to me often. I do not know whether you are a layman or a priest, dead or alive, because you have kept silent as far as I am concerned, although you frequently had letter-carriers to hand in Orlamünde. Tell me why you have not even brought about some small renewal of our old love.[491] I will always reply to your letters. As to your complaints about letters being intercepted, that is no problem, for the Lord is looking after our cause. This man Nicholas[492] I send to you as a brother in the Lord. Give him what help you can in the matter of our poor folk. For they have taken away the wealth from our nuns so that it can be distributed to the needy.[493] He himself will give you all the details. You can question him as you would God;[494] he will not fail you, as you know. Have faith in this man. He is sincere in the spirit of God. Farewell. It may be that the Lord wants you as his procurator, so that you may expiate what you have perpetrated under the pompous

490. Cf. Nr. 37, n. 378; in Latin.

491. *veteris charitatis renovationem*; almost an identical formulation to his letter to Luther three weeks earlier; Nr. 40, p. 59/8f.

492. Probably N. Rucker, who may well have accompanied Zeiss on his journey to Wittenberg at this time (Bräuer).

493. *Monialibus enim nostris subtraxerunt census, ut largiantur egenis*; the meaning seems to be that the Allstedt community has refused to pay their tithes to the Cistercian nuns of Naundorf, near Allstedt, and want advice about the administration of a poor fund; cf. Elliger, p. 374.

494. *deum* (God) written in above the line.

regime[495] of Antichrist. I talk to you, most beloved, as I do to myself. Good-bye again. 29 July in the year of the Lord 1523.

Thomas Müntzer parish priest of Allstedt.

Greet your wife in the Lord Jesus. I walk before God in all the original rigour.[496]

44. *Müntzer to Count Ernest von Mansfeld.*[497] *Allstedt 22 September 1523.*

To the noble and high-born count and lord Ernest von Mansfeld and Heldrungen a Christian greeting.[498]

Greetings, noble and well-born count. The intendant[499] and the council at Allstedt have shown me your writing, in which I am accused of using the words 'heretical rascal' and 'scourge of the people'[500] about you. Now this much is true; I know for a fact – because it is notorious – that you have issued a public edict stringently forbidding your subjects to come to my heretical mass and sermons. This led me to say – and I mean to complain to all believers in Christ about it – that you have had the effrontery to ban the holy gospel, and that should you persist (which God forfend) in such senseless banning and raging then I must continue to censure and denounce you and blot you out on paper as long as the blood flows in my veins, and not only to the Christian people, either, but I will have my books accusing you[501] translated into many tongues, and let Turks, pagans and Jews know you for the unbalanced,[502] insane person that you are. And you should realise that in such weighty and righteous matters I would not fear the whole world. Christ sounds the alarm[503] about

495. *in pompatico fastu.*

496. Probably not a reference to celibacy, as it seems probable that he had recently married; possibly, as Elliger suggests, Müntzer's understanding of marriage, as set out in his letter (Nr. 31) to Melanchthon, is meant; Elliger, pp. 375ff.; the reference to Karlstadt's wife suggests that Müntzer did in fact visit Carlstadt in December 1522, for the marriage took place in 1522(F.).

497. Allstedt adjoined the territories of this strongly Catholic prince; Simon Haferitz, pastor of Allstedt's Wigberti church, sent Duke George a similarly defiant letter; he would denounce as a heretic anyone who called the holy gospel heretical! Förstemann 1842, p. 298f.

498. *christlich geschriben.*

499. *schosser.*

500. *schintfessel.*

501. *auch widder euch* (F.: *widder auch*).

502. *verryssen* 'at odds with self and with the world' (Jillings); or perhaps 'scheming'.

503. *schreyhet zeter.*

those who take away the key to the knowledge of God, Luke 11.[504] But the key to the knowledge of God is this: to rule the people so that they learn to fear God alone Romans 13,[505] for the beginning of true Christian wisdom is the fear of the Lord.[506] Now that you, however, want to be feared more than God, as I can prove from your deeds and your edict, you are the one who takes away the key to the knowledge of God and forbids the people to go into the churches, for you can never change for the better.[507] I mean to show that my sermons and new services and the least thing I proclaim is in accord with the holy Bible. But if I am unable to do that then I am ready to forfeit life and limb and all we know on this earth. But if you can only achieve the contrary by armed force please abstain from that, for the sake of God. But if you are intending, as has often been said, to undertake something of this nature you should keep in mind that there will be no end to the trouble it will cause. The prophet says: 'Neither might nor wise counsels can prevail against the Lord.'[508] I am as much a servant of God as you, so tread gently, for the whole world has to be exercised in patience.[509] Don't grab, or the old coat may tear.[510] If you drive me to the printers I will deal with you a thousand times more drastically than Luther with the pope. Be my gracious lord, if you are ready to suffer and show it, but if not, then let God's will be done. Amen.

Allstedt on the day of St. Maurice in the year 1523.

Thomas Müntzer, a disturber of the unbelievers.

45. *Müntzer to Frederick the Wise. Allstedt, 4 October 1523.*

To his Eminence the high-born prince and lord Frederick, Marshal and Elector of the holy Roman Empire, Duke of Saxony, Landgrave of Thuringia and Margrave of Meissen, my most gracious lord.

[In the name of] Jesus the son of God

Most serene, high-born prince and lord, may the upright fear of God and the peace to which the world is hostile be with your electoral Grace. Most gracious lord, ever since the almighty God made me an earnest preacher, it has been my practice to sound the sonorous

504. Luke 11[52].
505. Romans 13[4]; note how Müntzer inverts the usual understanding of this text.
506. Ecclesiasticus 1[16].
507. *und vermoget doch nit eyn bessers*; (Bräuer/Kobuch); *nur. eyn bessers* (F.)
508. Proverbs 21[30].
509. *habt gemach, do dye ganze welt muss gedult mit tragen.*
510. *Gnackt nicht*; cf. Luke 5[36]; cf. p. 270/14ff. below.

marching trumpets[511] so that they resound with zeal for the knowledge of the Lord, sparing no man on this earth who strives against the word of God, as God himself has commanded us through his prophets Isaiah 58.[512] Hence my name (as is proper) is bound to excite alarm, disgust and contempt among the worldly wise. Matthew 5, Luke 6.[513] To the little band of the poor and needy, however, it has the sweet savour of life, while to those who pursue the pleasures of the flesh it is a gruesome abomination presaging their speedy downfall 2 Corinthians 2.[514] And it has come to pass in me, that I have been eaten up by a burning zeal for the poor, wretched, pitiable Christian people, and that is why the godless have frequently loosed their insults at me, Psalm 68,[55] and have driven me without due cause from one city to another Matthew 23[516] and have poured out the most hateful scorn when I defend myself. Jeremiah 20.[517] All this has led me to cast back and forth in my mind Psalm 1[518] how could I throw myself forward as an iron wall to protect the needy Jeremiah 1, Ezechiel 13[519] and I have seen that the Christian people can only be saved from the mouth of the raging lion[520] if one brings out the pure, refined word of God, removing the cover or lid which is concealing it. Matthew 5[521] and if one is quite frank about the truth of the Bible before the whole world Matthew 10,[522] testifying to great and small Acts 26[523] presenting nothing but Christ, the crucified one, to the world 1 Corinthians 1,[524] singing and preaching about him unambiguously and unwearyingly, using a form of church service in which time is not wasted unprofitably, but which builds up the people with psalms and hymns of praise; the basic principles behind the services in German are set out quite clearly in Ephesians 5 and

---

511. *dye lautbaren beweglichen pasaunen*; cf. Nrs. 13, p. 21/16, 21, p. 29/11ff. above; and the Prague Manifesto, p. 362/4f. below.

512. Isaiah 58[1].

513. Matthew 5[11]; Luke 6[22].

514. 2 Corinthians 2[15].

515. Psalms 69[10f.]

516. Matthew 23[34]; Müntzer, of course, could see the parallels to his experience of rejection.

517. Jeremiah 20[7f.]; the ridicule Müntzer encountered is strongly emphasised here.

518. Psalms 1[2]; the righteous man meditating day and night on the law of the Lord, on the one hand, and the way of sinners and the scornful on the other.

519. Jeremiah 1[18]; Ezekiel 13[5]; the pillar of iron, the wall of bronze in Jeremiah is to stand against kings, princes and priests as well as against the people; cf. Nr. 40, p. 56/16 above.

520. Zechariah 11[33ff.]

521. Matthew 5[15]; a favourite verse of Müntzer.

522. Matthew 10[26ff.]

523. Acts 26[22].

524. 1 Corinthians 1[23].

1 Corinthians 14.[525] But no amount of reasonable explanation or protest availed me in this whole matter; throughout the summer the high-born Count Ernest von Mansfeld repeatedly and ever more emphatically forbade his subjects to attend them. Since all this was before the edict of his serene, high-born, and most gracious emperor had been issued,[526] it provoked our and his people to think of rebellion, which in the long run my powers of persuasion would have been unable to restrain. So on the Sunday after the nativity of Mary[527] I publicly appealed to him from the pulpit, urgently inviting him to come to my little flock, saying: I would ask Count Ernest von Mansfeld to appear here with the ordinaries of the diocese and to show in what way my teaching or service is heretical. If, however, he refuse to come (which God forfend) then I will regard him as an evildoer, a rascal and a knave, a Turk and a pagan, and I will prove this with the truth of Scripture. That, and none other, was the form of the words, as I can show. He has dealt with me irregularly, for he now cites the Imperial edict, as if this action of his was embodied in it, although that is clearly not the case. So he should have taken his learned people with him and instructed me in a friendly and modest manner. If I had been vanquished then he should have arraigned me before your electoral grace and thereafter forbidden his people to listen to such services. If it becomes the done thing for human commandments to stand in the way of the gospel Isaiah 29, Matthew 15, Titus I[528] contrary to what the letter of the edict[529] appears to say this will bewilder the people, who should love princes rather than fear them: Romans 13.[530] Princes hold no terrors for the pious. But should that change, then the sword will be taken from them and will be given to the people who burn with zeal so that the godless can be defeated, Daniel 7;[531] and then that noble jewel, peace, will be in abeyance on earth. Revelation 6.[532] He who sits on the white horse

525. Ephesians 5[19]; 1 Corinthians 14, especially v. 19.

526. The Edict of the Imperial government of 6 March 1523; distributed by Frederick the Wise at the end of 1523 (F.); for a fascinating account of the Elector's Fabian tactics in meeting the complaints of Count Ernest von Mansfeld and Duke George of Saxony cf. Förstemann, pp. 228–254.

527. 15 September.

528. Isaiah 29[13f.]; Matthew 15[3]; Titus I[14ff.]

529. Müntzer is probably thinking of the stipulation in the Edict that criticism of preachers 'is not to be understood to mean the prevention or suppression of the evangelical truth.' Yet the main thrust of the Edict, whose mediatorial character is evident enough, offers no support to Müntzer's demands; sermons which could excite disobedience, disunity, and rebellion are forbidden (F.)

530. For Muntzer's interpretation of Romans 13[1ff.] cf. Nr. 44, p. 67/2f.

531. Daniel 7[26]; the saints will receive and retain kingly power for ever.

532. Revelation 6[2]; the rider on the red horse seems to be meant; cf. Schwarz, p. 89, n. 11.

wants to conquer, but it is not for him. O high-born, kindly elector, there is need for diligence here, so that on the day of his wrath our saviour, who sits at God's right hand, (when he himself will pasture the sheep and drive away the wild beasts from the flock) will graciously break the might of the kings Psalm 109, Ezechiel 34.[533] Ah, it would be well pleasing to God if that were not brought about by our negligence. I did not want to conceal any of this from your electoral grace Ezekiel 3.[524] Hence this long exposition. And I would commend all this most urgently to your attention, with the additional request that you would regard my writing favourably and permit me a hearing under divine law, to determine whether my defence is an upright one. It would be intolerable to my conscience and to my duty to the Christian people to yield now, 1 Timothy 3.[535] Your Electoral Grace must also be bold, keeping in mind that God has stood so firmly by Your Electoral Grace from the beginning. May he keep you and your people for evermore. Amen. Allstedt, on Francis' day in the 1523 year of the Lord.

Thomas Müntzer of Stolberg, a servant of God.

46.　*Müntzer to the intendant, John Zeiss.*[536] *Allstedt, 2 December 1523.*

To his dear brother, John Zeiss, intendant in Allstedt.

　　Dear brother, I forgot to mention one thing when answering the assertion that only Christ is required to suffer, while we do not need to suffer anything after his genuine suffering for our sin.[537] The point to note is the delicacy of spirit which gives rise to this wanton proclamation of such unseemly passivity. Compared with Christ, Adam is a model of the damage that has been done; Christ, however, is the very opposite.[538] The disobedience of the creatures is cancelled out by the obedience of the word which became flesh in nature; just as, by the working of faith, our fleshly nature must partly fade away in us who are part of him, as was the case with the whole Christ, our head.[539] Hence Christ has atoned for all the damage done by Adam, so

Roma. 5

Ephe. 2

534. 533. Psalms 110[5]; Ezekiel 34[23ff.]

534. Ezekiel 3[16]; the prophet as watchman.

535. 1 Timothy 3.[4.14f.]

536. The letter is a postscript to Müntzer's writing, *On Counterfeit Faith*; note the similarity between the beginning of the last, fourteenth section, with its address to the 'elect brother' and the beginning of this letter; cf. p. 223/2ff. below.

537. Cf. Nr. 13, p. 20/14 above.

538. *Adam ist ein muster Cristi im schaden, Cristus aber das kegenteil*; Romans 5[12ff.]; in the Gotha MS *ym gegentheyl*.

539. Ephesians 2[5ff.]; in the Gotha MS 'in the Head'.

that the parts may hold together with the whole, as the holy apostle of God clearly says.[540] I fulfil the suffering of Christ which is still outstanding; for the sake of his body, the church.[541] Paul did not want to suffer for the churches except as a member carrying out his allotted task. All of us have to follow in the footsteps of Christ and must be armed with such thoughts. So fancy commentaries will be of no avail to those who imagine that by following their fleshly ways they vanquish those who trust in their works.[542] In fact they, with their fraudulent faith, are poisoning the world much worse than the others with their clownish works. To clarify the distinction, then, they are still neophytes, that is to say, men who have still to be put to the test; they should not be in charge of souls, but for a long time yet should remain catechumens, that is, diligent students of his divine work;[543] they should not teach until they themselves have been taught by God.[544]

This writing of mine is still not in a fit state to release to the mad world.[545] I have still to explain the Scripture in all those chapters in which I have made no reference to Scripture in order to topple the fleshly Biblical scholars, for among them a fraudulent faith has given rise to all manner of wickedness.[546] For this reason it cannot be printed at this time, since it would be going out without any weapons against those who consider themselves well-armed. You should know, too, that this teaching has been attributed to the abbot Joachim, and is being derisively called an eternal gospel.[547] I have every respect for the

540. Colossians 1[21ff.]

541. *vor seinem leib leidet die kirche*; Dismer, p. 34, n. 6, suggests the omission of *leidet*, which is absent in the MS; as Bräuer/Ullmann, p. 9, demonstrate, however, both the Gotha and Nürnberg MSS are later variants on the printed version; 1 Peter 2[21]; 1 Peter 4[13ff.]; Colossians 1[24].

542. Romans 4 sets out Abraham as a model of faith; Matthew 5 is the Sermon on the Mount; 1 Timothy 1 contrasts moral law and Gospel; 11 Timothy 1 talks of the apostle's calling; Isaiah 5 is about the neglect of the vineyard, Israel; John 6 ends with the alienation of many followers of Jesus (the neophytes); Isaiah 54 describes the eventual covenant of peace with Israel; Jeremiah 31 the new covenant.

543. *wergs* = work; Gotha MS *wordt* = word.

544. At this point the Gotha MS ends, except for the following two sentences which Bräuer/Ullmann, p. 10, describe as 'clearly inauthentic': 'This last chapter is especially addressed to someone [to show] which way is the noblest: the sweet or the bitter Christ. I have drawn it to your attention, too, although it very much belongs to these chapters.'

545. 1 Corinthians 2[1]; Matthew 7[15].

546. cf. There is an interesting parallel in Luther's letter to Spalatin of 6 May, 1517; his Penitential Psalms are not ready for the sophisticated Nuremberg readers; *ideo enim sunt tam inermes et sine testimoniis scripture'* WA Br. 1, 96[13-18].

547. Joachim of Fiore, 13th century ascetic, whose theology of history saw the ages of the Father and of the Son soon to be superseded by that of the Spirit, in which the Eternal Gospel will be proclaimed by a new order of the just.

testimony of the abbot Joachim. I have only read his commentary on Jeremiah.[548] But my teaching is from on high; I do not have it from him but from utterances of God which I intend to document at the proper time from all the books of the Bible. Let us leave the matter there and see that we are always careful to keep copies of our correspondence.

Wednesday after St. Andrew's day in the year 1523.

Thomas Müntzer, your brother in the Lord.

47. *Müntzer to Christopher Meinhard in Eisleben. Allstedt, 13 December 1523.*[549]

To my dear brother in the Lord, Christopher Meinhard.

May the grace and peace of the gentle saviour Jesus Christ be with you, my diligent brother in the truth of God. I cannot refrain from setting before your conscience the mighty truth, as God says through David, Psalm 39, 'I will not let my lips be slow' to speak of your truth to all people, so that they may know how to establish their desires on solid rock.[550] Be it known that, following the teaching of Paul, what I say – and will document conclusively with an abundance of Scriptural evidence – is that no one can be saved unless he allows the whole of Scripture to be brought to pass in him by God, Matthew 5.[551] Christ did not come to redeem us in a way that dispensed us from suffering poverty of spirit (by the expulsion of all that is pleasurable to us).[552] His sole task is to see that only the poor are comforted and that those who have not been tested are handed over to the executioner. For anyone who does not conform himself to the son of God is a murderer and a criminal, one who prefers resurrection with Christ to dying with him, who balks both at coming in and going out, like a sheep evading its proper pasture.[553] He must take to heart as earnestly as possible the way in which God is grinding his outward self down to nothing, so that he can grow from day to day in the understanding of God; in this way every one may truly put off the old man, and not be

548. The *Treatise on Jeremiah*, published in Venice in 1516, was incorrectly attributed to Joachim.

549. Cousin and godfather of John Zeiss, intendant of Allstedt. (F.) cf. Letters 49, 71 below; he was a prosperous foundry-master in Eisleben; he died in 1527; cf. Walter Möllenberg (ed.), *Urkundenbuch zur Geschichte des Mansfeldischen Saigerhandels im 16. Jahrhundert* (Halle, 1915), pp. 104, 106f., 112f. etc.; the date as amended by Bräuer/Kobuch, the sixth day after *conceptio Marie*, 8 December.

550. Psalms 39[10] (Vg.); Matthew 7[25]; the marginal reference, š 39, omitted by F.

551. Matthew 5.17–20 (F. suggests v. 18); cf. also the Beatitudes.

552. *durch entsetzung all unser entgetzlykeit.*

553. Cf. Psalms 79[13]; 1 Peter 2[25].

like the untried biblical scholars who stitch a new patch onto the old coat.[554] They purloin one or two little texts but fail to integrate them with the teaching which gushes forth from the genuine source. They are the sort of people who imagine that they can attain to the knowledge of God in a flash, and fail to see how much effort it takes to endure the work of God in the most intense fear of God like the murderers on the cross.[555] This text, and many others like it, shows that they attained their insights while they were asleep, and fail to grasp Scripture as a whole by a close integration of all of it.[556] So I jerk my jaws wide open and bellow to all those untried biblical scholars that the whole of Scripture must come to pass in every man, according to his own measure, before he can be saved. And if anyone wants to deny this, I will prove incontestably that he does not believe a single word of the Bible but is going around with a word that he has purloined. Jeremiah 23.[557] I have comforted you, saying that you should not pray for the dead and that contrary to superstitious ideas, those without knowledge should be commended to the judgement and discipline[558] of God, as Scripture says. The last thing to be concluded from this writing is that I have ceded an inch to the papist wickedness, for I know very well that the entire bliss of those who blaspheme against God rests on their counterfeit purgatory.[559] I have scarcely caught my breath from the masses for the dead.[560] Do my dear friends imagine that I have the least intention of supporting purgatory?[561] That shows you what experienced people they are; as far as righteousness from faith to faith is concerned they cannot compute the number of miles involved.[562] Since the mustard-seed of faith has not even been planted in them how can it begin to multiply?[563] My teaching just cannot permit this condemnation of the

554. Matthew 9[16]; 'untried' = 'not put to the test.'

555. Paper torn off at bottom: *wye vil muhe es eynem kostet, Gottis werk zu erdulden ym hochsten grad der forcht gottis wye dye morder am creutz tragen*; (Bräuer/Kobuch); cf. Luke 23[40]; and p. 72/23ff. above.

556. *gleych wye dye gantze scrift nit vorfast weher yn eyne starke vorgleychung.*

557. Jeremiah 23[30]; the prophets who steal the words of the Lord from one another.

558. *zucht* (F. *recht*) amended Bräuer/Kobuch; presumably refers to infants dying before baptism.

559. *das alle wolfart der gottis lesterer aufm getychten fegfeur stehet.*

560. *Von der studerung der vorstorbnen, hab ich kaum ein weneg atem geholt*; unlike the use of *studerung* in Nr. 49, p. 79/21, and on p. 397/27, Bräuer suggests it means *stundunge* = *Stundengebet*, the Daily Office; in this case prayers for the dead; perhaps one could trans. 'obsession with the dead'.

561. Cf. Nr. 31, n. 299.

562. Romans 1[17]; 'God's way of righting wrong, a way that starts from faith and ends in faith.'

563. Matthew 17[20].

poor and wretched to stand Psalm 68.[564] So burning zeal will devour[565] and swallow up these biblical scholars. You believed[566] that the Scripture does not teach you to pray for the dead; as to what God does with those who have died without experience of faith you must leave it to his judgement. The twenty-fourth chapter of Matthew wisely instructs you to pay careful attention to all created things;[567] as creation is subject to you[568] so you should be subject to God, and when he brings his gospel to pass in you you should not retreat into your house at the time of trial, but avoid doing anything to hinder it[569] and invoke God from the roof-tops.[570] When you are in at the height of the crisis,[571] invoke him freely without being tied to any material thing, and let affliction[572] instruct and discipline you and submerge your unbelief through Jesus Christ, the son of God; may he keep you from harm, Amen! and your wife and children too etc. Allstedt, the sixth day after the feast of the Conception. In spirit and soul. 1 Thessalonians 5.[573]

Thomas Müntzer, a servant of God.

48.   *Martin Seligmann*[574] *to Müntzer. Thalmansfeld, 13 May 1524.*

To his Reverence, Master Thomas Müntzer, a man of singular erudition and my dearest brother in Christ.

564. *Meyne lere kan und mag der elenden erbermlichen orteil nit also slecht lassen hyngehen*; Psalm 69^{32} (Psalm 68^{30} (Vg.)).

565. Psalms 68^{10} (Vg.).

566. *Ir habt gemeynt* (Bräuer/Kobuch); cf. *genunc* (F.).

567. Matthew 24^{32}; the fig-tree, which shows 'summer' is near.

568. Genesis 1^{28}.

569. *das selbyg zu vorhynderung vormeiden.*

570. Matthew 24^{17}; Matthew 10^{27}; this whole passage is compressed and difficult; Müntzer seems to be 'integrating' Psalm 69 (the afflictions of the righteous at the hand of his enemies, and the promise of deliverance) and Matthew 24: as the time of troubles comes, heralding the end of the age, one's attitude to the 'creatures', to created being, becomes critical; one must use them aright, as signs (the fig-tree); yet be ready to cast them off (one's belongings); only if one does this will one be prepared to face conflict, to confess the faith openly, to garner the fruits of affliction, i.e. the revelation and conquest of one's unbelief; in the time of decision between the false and the true prophets, the 'creatures' are pointers, determining where one's true allegiance lies.

571. *do yr den uberswangt thut*; F. translates as 'ecstasy' and refers to Henry Suso (c. 1295–1366); perhaps there is a reference to the exultation of the poor in Psalm 69^{32}; cf. Nr. 49, n. 600.

572. *erbsalikeit*

573. 1 Thessalonians 5^{23}.

574. Of Heilbronn; 1516 curate, later pastor in Thalmansfeld; in Latin.

Many greetings. Even if only a few days have elapsed since I last visited you, dearest brother in Christ, being desirous, above all, to confer with you about the sacred Scriptures, since you are a man of singular erudition and one whose company has given me considerable pleasure for many years; yet love and our mutual friendship compel me to write to you so soon about various rumours which are flying around everywhere. Although I know that they are largely without foundation yet I would like to know what sort of matters were discussed with you at Weimar last week. For a member of the household of our local gentry saw you there and also told me that you had been summoned before the duke.[575] Although I am not unaware that you, who are established on the firmest rock, will survive the dark threats of men, and although I do not believe that any stormy winds can overturn your mind and faith,[576] yet I know that very many people are not at all favourable to you and will leave (as one says) no stone unturned to expel you from where you live, and that some members of that same flock[577] tear at me from behind with their viper-like teeth, claiming that I have deserted the camp of Martin Luther and fled to yours. But I just do not know what these foolish fellows want to achieve with such words, unless perhaps they are out to foster sects of one kind or another. For my part, I was never so bound to the words of any one teacher (as the poet says)[578] that I lost sight of the truth. I will strive to the best of my endeavour to find out what the all-beneficent, and all-powerful God has destined me to do, so that I may be able to obey his will, paying no heed to how these superficial fellows[579] depict me. I beg you, then, most beloved of brothers, to reply when you have the time, telling me what happened and what matters were raised when you met the princes of this world at Weimar and whether the reports about your sharpening your pen against Martin Luther are true, which I will never believe since it would give rise to the most immense conflict. For I want concord and agreement between you; since I could then look forward to both your teachings bringing forth great fruit, not only a hundredfold but a thousandfold. With these words, then, farewell. Pray God that I may

---

575. The chapel at Mallerbach had been destroyed on 24 March 1524; Müntzer had been preaching against it and his 'Confession' in 1525 suggests that he was present when it was sacked; cf. p. 435/14ff. below; Elliger, p. 419, points out that the custodian's account does not support this; AGBM II, 29f.; the magistrate and city council were summoned to Weimar by Duke John but Seligmann's understanding that Müntzer had also been summoned has no documentary support (F.); cf. Elliger, pp. 423ff.

576. Matthew 7[24-7]; lit: the home of...

577. *e quorum grege quidam sunt* added in margin.

578. Horace, *Letters* I, 1, 14: *nullius addictus jurare in verba magistri.*

579. *scioli isti.*

fulfil his will in all things insofar as this is granted me. Please greet Master Balthasar Trochus and Master Simon[580] from me. There is so much about which I could write, but you know that it is not safe to commit everything to letters.[581] Almost all our ceremonies have been abolished with only a few exceptions. The bearer of this present letter will be able to inform you more fully about this.

From Thalmansfeld, on the sixth day after Exaudi, in the year 1524.

Your[582] Martin Seligmann.

49. *Müntzer to Christopher Meinhard[583] in Eisleben. Interpretation of Psalm 18. Allstedt, 30 May 1524.*

Thomas Müntzer to his beloved friend, Christopher Meinhard.[584]

The spirit of wisdom and the understanding of the knowledge of God be with you, my good-hearted brother.

I sense in your letter the really ardent desire for truth, for you show so much determination in your quest for the right way. You will find the clearest exposition of it in the description of the pure fear of God in Psalm 18: 'The heavens tell' etc.[585] There the Holy Spirit instructs you that, first of all, your eyes have to be opened by enduring the work of God, as explained in the Law. You must always set one word alongside another; your heart should concentrate on this, for it is only after the long night that the sun rises from its true starting-point, Psalm 129.[586] A person who has not endured the night will be unable to comprehend the knowledge of God, which proclaims the night to the night, for only after it is over will the true word be revealed in the bright light of day, John 8 and 11.[587] They have to be heavenly men, ready to pursue the glory of God at the cost of their own reputation. One has to walk in the mortification of the flesh every single moment; in particular our reputation has to stink in the nostrils of the godless.[588]

---

580. Simon Haferitz, preacher in Allstedt cf. Letter 44, n. 498; in 1517 Balthasar Trochus, priest in Aschersleben, had published by Melchior Lotter, Leipzig, an extensive *Vocabulorum rerum promptuarium* (Bräuer).

581. Cf. Nr. 37, p. 53/22f.

582. T[uus].

583. Cf. Nr. 47; the MS is not extant; Agricola published it in short sections, interspersed with lengthy critical comments, as *Auslegung des 19. Psalms* (1525).

584. *Suo dilecto Cris Mein*; the rest in German.

585. Psalm 19.

586. Psalm 136[6]; Scripture has to be read as a whole, the Gospel with the Law.

587. John 8[12]; 11[9ff.] (the story of Lazarus); *nox nocti indicat scientiam*, Psalm 18[3] (Vg.).

588. Lazarus!

Then the person who has been tested[589] can preach, and if the listener has previously heard Christ preaching in his heart through the spirit of the fear of God then a real preacher can provide testimony enough. The works of God's hand have to cause the initial consternation;[590] otherwise all preaching and writing will be in vain. A person who has been continuously trained in this can pronounce on everything with flawless judgement. The teaching of such men should echo out to the whole world, and their name to the farthest reaches of the godless, causing the latter, with their senseless violence, to shrink back before the one who will teach them through a new Jehu, 2 Kings 9.[591] God is a friendly bridegroom to his beloved. At first he makes her a despised maid-servant until he can put her to the test. Then he looks upon the things that are lowly and rejects those that are lofty, Psalm 112, 1 Samuel 2, Deuteronomy 32.[592] It may seem as if the godless will stay in power for ever, but the bridegroom comes out of the bedroom like a mighty man that has drunk deeply, for he has slept through all the preparations of his servants Psalm 78.[593] Ah, then is the time for us to urge our case; I think the time has come; get up, why are you slumbering?[594] Just as the LORD went to sleep in the little boat, and it seemed that the tempest raised by the insolence of the godless was going to send the little boat right down to the bottom.[595] Then the bridegroom gets up and leaves his bedroom, as the voice of its true owner is heard in the soul John 3.[596] And then all the elect rejoice with Jesus, and say, Luke 12: 'I must be anointed with a different baptism from that of John, and I will be tormented grievously for undergoing it.'[597] That accords exactly with this psalm: He exulted like a mighty man.[598] He was as splendid as a giant striding along.

When a man becomes aware of his origin in the stormy seas of his agitation,[599] when he is in the very midst of his ecstasy,[600] he must act like a fish which has plunged down from the surface to the murky water at the bottom; it turns around, swims, rises up to the surface of

---

589. *eyn versuchter Gottes*; 'a man under temptation', Gritsch, p. 90.

590. *die ersten verwunderung*.

591. 2 Kings 9[6ff.]

592. Psalm 113[6ff.]; 1 Samuel 2[4-9] (prayer of Hannah); Deuteronomy 32 (Moses excluded from Promised Land).

593. Psalm 78[65].

594. *exurge, quare obdormis*.

595. John 6[16ff.]

596. John 3[27]; cf. Nr. 31, n. 293.

597. Luke 12[50].

598. *Exultavit ut gigas*; Psalm 19[5].

599. *seyner begegnung*; Dismer, p. 213, suggests this may be a misprint for *bewegung* ('movement').

600. *mitten ym schwank*; cf. Nr. 47, n. 571.

the water again and so returns to its original starting-point. The elect cannot stray too far from God, for he sends out his fire, Luke 12, which no one can evade and hinder from stirring his heart, his conscience.[601] Although the elect may commit great and grievous sins the fire of their conscience stirs them to disgust and repulsion at their sins. If they willingly cultivate such feelings of grief and repulsion then they are unable to sin. This is what I call patient endurance,[602] which makes the pleasure-loving swine turn up their noses so derisively. It is they who curse the Old Testament, who are always citing Paul against works, and casting discredit[603] on the Law in the most superficial way; in reality, for all their boasting,[604] they misunderstand Paul.

The law of God is clear;[605] it illumines the eyes of the elect, it covers the eyes of the godless with a cataract; it is unimpeachable when the spirit of the real, pure fear of God is explained by it.[606] This happens, as Christ says, when a man risks his neck for the truth Luke 12.[607] Paul commanded such works of the Law; in brief, they, too, are necessary, although the godless produce their own vain version of a sophistical and fraudulent Paul. Paul never once had a dream; they cite that as proof.[608] To the devil with preachers like that! Paul is speaking about licentious wretches, at a time when the godless were seducing the elect to follow them. Then along come our wild insolent disciples of Bacchus and imagine they have hit the nail on the head by quoting Romans chapter four,[609] (and nothing else) about Abraham receiving God's grace gratuitously; they fail to add the fifteenth chapter of Genesis and Psalm 31, 'Blessed are those',[610] which are quoted in this very chapter by Paul[611] in order to show how God drives man by many a stab to his conscience to an understanding of the grace already dwelling in his heart.

Just as Paul lays great stress on faith without any merit from works,

601. Luke 12[49].

602. *die langweyl*; cf. Nr. 41, A n. 438; there are many parallels between this letter and Nr. 41; cf. also his letter to Luther, p. 59/2ff. above.

603. *verschumpiren*.

604. *solten sie euch zuprasten*.

605. Psalm 19[8].

606. Psalm 19[9].

607. Luke 12[4].

608. *yhr allegat*; Dismer, p. 272, n. 3, argues that the use of *allegat, allegirn* is otherwise unknown in Müntzer, and casts some doubt on the accuracy of Agricola's reproduction of the text; in fact, however, if occurs in his marginal comments on Tertullian's *de resurrectione carnis*, eg. p. 427/12f. below.

609. Romans 4[3]; Spillmann translates *bachanten* by 'wandering scholars' (*vaganti*) or 'bletherers' (F.); *lose* (wild) omitted by F.

610. *Beati quorum*, the initial words of Psalm 31 (Vg.).

611. Romans 4[3, 7].

so do I lay equal stress on the need to endure the work of God, Isaiah 5, John 6.[612] I am in harmony with Paul, not with our biblical scholars who have plundered Paul in a piece-meal way, like the beasts of the belly, Phillippians 3;[613] this is the suffering of the damned and not the working[614] of God.

Hence they produce this fiction of Christ as the fulfiller of the law, so that, by pointing to his cross, they can be exempted from enduring the work of God.[615] Hence this same rotten worm-eaten theology of these old fantasizers is comparable in every respect with the fine fellow in the thorn-bush.[616]

The righteousness of God has to throttle our lack of faith until we come to recognise that all pleasures are sinful and that it is to protect our pleasures that we harden ourselves in sin so implacably. So man must apply himself to understanding these secret pleasures, for they are extremely treacherous. If he does not register disgust, but allows pleasures to rule him and control him,[617] and gives way to them, then nothing can be done to advise or help him. Paul has proclaimed this quite explicitly in 2 Timothy 3.[618] He says: People will be pleasure-loving, devotees of their pleasures, and will say that one cannot endure the work of God, cannot understand it, that is they will deny the value of the study of and meditation on the Law, by which the work of God may be recognised. There you have a brief exposition of Psalm 18. Send me a duplicate or copy of it. In the year 1524, the Monday after the first Sunday of Trinity.

50.   *The Council and commons of Allstedt[619] to Duke John of Saxony. Allstedt, 14 June 1524.*

To his Eminence the highborn prince and lord, to our lord John,

612. Isaiah 5[12, 19]; John 6[28f.]

613. Philippians 3[19]; Müntzer automatically associates the scholars with materialistic attitudes, and this accusation is often associated with that of an atomistic approach to Scripture, which prevents them taking the Law seriously, by relating the Gospel to it.

614. *wirkung*; or 'work of God'.

615. *das werk Gottes.*

616. Proverbs 26[9]: 'Like a thorn that goes up into the hand of a drunkard is a proverb in the mouth of fools;' Peter Lombard, the 'Master of the Sentences', is meant; cf. *On Baptism*, p. 396/10ff. below.

617. *bebegen* for *bewegen*, 'move'.

618. 2 Timothy 3[2-5].

619. Müntzer is not named as a signatory; although much of the language and thought are his we should not assume his sole authorship; dating, as for Nr. 51, follows Bräuer; the occasion for the letter was the arrest of Ziliax Knaut, a member of the Allstedt Council, on 11 June 1524.

Duke of Saxony, landgrave in Thuringia and margrave of Meissen, our most gracious lord and sovereign.

May the true, eternal, upright fear of God be with Your Grace. Gracious Lord, we poor people, the council and people[620] of Allstedt, have been at all times subject and most readily obedience to Your Grace's brother, Duke Frederick, the most noble elector, and intend in the future, too, to render such obedience as is due,[621] to the best of our capabilities; all of which we have proved quite conclusively in the matter of the nuns at Naundorf.[622] Although the latter proved a grievous burden to us yet we let his electoral grace instruct us to give them interest and tithes, although there was no legitimate Christian obligation for us to pay them, so that we might dispose of the matter without any insubordination. But none of this was of any avail, for they have forced their attentions upon us in respect to the Mallerbach chapel, misrepresenting us, together with the others in the neighbourhood, quite unjustifiably and deceitfully. By acting in this vicious, envious way they hope to promote their own godless and unchristian concerns, presenting them in the best light to Your Grace.

However, if their petition to Your Grace is granted, we poor people would be sorely burdened and we could not be answerable to God for helping to maintain and defend this blasphemy against God. For our part we are certainly innocent of this as Holy Scripture testifies. For it is common knowledge that the poor people in their ignorance used to honour and adore the devil at Mallerbach under the name of Mary. And now that this very devil has been destroyed by good-hearted, pious people, are we to lend a hand in arresting and imprisoning them in the name of the devil? For we know by the testimony of the holy apostle Paul that the sword has been given to Your Grace to carry out retribution on the evil-doers and the godless and to honour and protect the pious.[623] Since, however, no real damage has been done by our people, nothing detrimental to the common good, and since all duties and obedience to the most noble elector[624] have been honoured, His Grace would be respecting man more than God,[625] which we can in no wise credit in relation to His Grace and Yours; for we poor people are not requesting protection or any special defence against our enemies – for our last wish is that we poor people should be in any way a burden to Your Grace or to the noble Elector; yet we are in constant danger of death, expecting at any

---

620. *gemeyne.*
621. *das selbige in massen wie geburlich zu volfuren.*
622. Cf. Nr. 48, n. 575.
623. Romans 13⁴.
624. *dem loblichen churf.*
625. i.e. if he were to grant the petition of the nuns.

moment the arrival of our enemies who persecute us relentlessly for the sake of the Gospel with their hate-filled fury. Hence for the sake of God we beseech Your Grace, as a noble Christian prince, to consider and to take to heart what God, our Creator, says himself in the pious words of Moses in Exodus 23: 'You shall not defend the godless.'[626] But because the whole world is now aware that monks and nuns are idolatrous people how can they be legitimately defended by pious Christian princes? We want to put our bodies and goods at the disposal of Your Grace and our noble Elector for whatever you may legitimately demand of us. But that we should continue to allow the devil at Mallerbach to be adored, so that our brothers are surrendered to be sacrifices to him, is as intolerable to us as subjection to the Turks. If this leads to force being used against us then the world, and especially the pious elect of God, will surely know why we are suffering and that we are becoming conformed to Christ Jesus. May Your Grace be preserved by him in the true fear of God.

Allstedt in the Year 1524 of the birth of our saviour.

To Your Princely Grace from the Council and all your obedient commons in Allstedt.[627]

51. *Müntzer to John Lang[628] in Erfurt. Allstedt, (c. June/July) 1524.[629]*

To my brother in Christ, John Lang, servant of God in Erfurt.

Greetings and peace in the Holy Spirit, most beloved friend. As far as your romance is concerned is it only in subdued tones that I may sing the wedding song[630] which the blessed Nathan chanted to his

---

626. Exodus 23[1f.]

627. Note the absence of the magistrate, Nicholas Rucker (Bräuer).

628. In Latin; friend of Luther, previously Prior to the Augustinian Eremites in Erfurt; married widow of the tanner, Heinrich Mattern, around 1524 (F.); in 1523 he had discussions with Müntzer in Allstedt, probably in November; cf. S. Bräuer, 'Vorgeschichte von Luthers "Ein Brief an die Fürsten zu Sachsen ..." 40–70, esp. 47–51.

629. The date of 25 June (F.) is probably too early, for Lang's marriage took place c. 24 June; it could be that Müntzer is responding to an invitation to the wedding ('I would come to you . . .') or to an announcement that it has taken place; in the latter case c. 22 July is possible (cf. Letter 58 p. 100/5f.); the postscript assumes previous correspondence.

630. *Epithalamium*; must refer to Nathan's condemnation of David's liaison with Bathsheba 2 Samuel 12; the Latin is difficult: *Epithalamium, quod sanctus Nathan suo pio cecinit Davidi, tuo ne submissa voce resonem amori, si per id quod gesseris, nomen Dei evangelio iam clarum blasphemantibus dolosis traditum fuerit?* The widow was old and rich (F.); cf. *Exposé*, p. 316/14f. below.

pious [king] David? Has your action in fact exposed the name of God, now so bright because of the Gospel, to crafty blasphemers? But do not be saddened at having been swept away by some passion; the Lord will reveal to you later whether you have wandered away from the just path of his will. Whatever thoughtlessness has led you to neglect, the cross will let you experience. I adjure you, my beloved friend, by the glory of the cross of Christ, not to sweep aside the exhortation of a brother. I would come to you if the duties of a vigilant pastor did not hold me back from going. Farewell in perpetual love, in which[631] may the son of God cause you, with your wife, to be conformed to him in perpetuity.

Allstedt. Thomas Müntzer, servant of the elect of God.

I shall press the labourer George about the 6 groschen which he took from the tanner.

52.   Müntzer to Duke John. Allstedt, 13 July 1524.[632]

To the beloved duke and ruler of Saxony, my dear father and lord, John the elder.

My dear father and lord.[633] My aim is to set before the poor, wretched Christian people the knowledge and faith of God – as Paul did for the Romans in chapter eight[634] – following the unambiguous directions[635] given me by the testimony of God. If, however, I am to be punished for this, then let the whole world witness my proposal: that every nation be informed and alerted about this matter; I will then proclaim with voice and pen the steadfast truth which can be defended before all peoples, despite all those biblical scholars who openly deny the spirit of Christ. If there are any thoughts of delaying or preventing such action on my part the great harm which any further delay could bring about should be carefully considered. For

---

631. *qua* (Bräuer/Kobuch); *quod* (F.).

632. Presumably written just after he had preached his famous sermon on Daniel, cf. pp. 230ff., to Duke John; the main issue is Müntzer's concern to set up a printing-press in Allstedt and the warning delivered to him by the Saxon chancellor, Dr Brück, that anything he wrote would have to be referred first to Weimar for approval; cf. Elliger, p. 463f.

633. Note the contrast with the conventionally fulsome greetings in letter 45; Duke John, co-ruler with his brother, the Elector Frederick, was responsible for the Thüringian territories.

634. Romans 8 deals with the life of the Spirit, present sufferings and the coming glory of the children of God.

635. *wie ich ... unbetriglich geweyset bin.*

the people's hunger for the righteousness of God is an insatiable one; words cannot begin to express it Matthew 5.[636]

In short, it has been revealed that the mouth of those who are depraved will be stopped; for they fear the light John 3.[637] I will not shy away from the light; I demand a hearing; the intolerable affront to the elect requires it.[638] But if you want me to be heard by the Wittenbergers and no one else, that I cannot accept. I want the Romans, the Turks, the heathen there. For I give fair warning, my accusations will confound this uncomprehending Christian world.[639] I know how to give an account of my coming to faith. Thereafter, if you are prepared to let my books circulate, that would please me; but if not, I will commend it to the will of God. I will faithfully give you all my books to read in advance, I will join you in Christ Jesus, our saviour, in whatever the revelation of God declares to you;[640] may he preserve your most beloved self and your people, Amen. Allstedt on Margaret's day, in the year 1524.

Thomas Müntzer, a servant of God.

53. *Müntzer to the God-fearing people of Sangerhausen. Allstedt, c. 15 July 1524.*[641]

I, Thomas Müntzer, wish all the God-fearing people of Sangerhausen the peace which the untried world rejects. Now that God's unshakeable mercy has blessed and instructed you through proper preachers you should not let yourself be led astray by the diverse bletherings of the godless. You should not lose heart, or you will become completely childish, as Paul said in his heart-felt exhortation to the elect in Ephesians 4.[642] See that you are not led around by the nose by empty threats and by the devious tricks of the usurers. For it is certainly true that they are all alarmed that the time is coming when everyone will have to do what is right.[643] This they have never dreamt of doing: not once have they seriously considered it; and they have not the least intention of doing it either. Hence you

636. Matthew 5[6].

637. John 3[19f.]

638. *umb der unerstattlichen ergernus der ausserwelten*, an affront that cannot be made good; the reference seems to be to the Mallerbach affair, cf. Nr. 50.

639. *ich tatele die unvorstendig cristenheit zu podem.*

640. *Was euch die offenbarung Gottis erynnert, das will ich mich mit euch halten in Christo Jesu.*

641. Müntzer's followers in Sangerhausen were being threatened with expulsion, no doubt for forming a league or covenant; cf. Müntzer's Confession, p. 434/22ff.

642. Ephesians 4[14].

643. *das einy der wirt mussen recht thuen.*

should have no fear of such apparitions, Psalm 117.[644] Let God's word be presented to you in the fear of God, as it is written, Psalm 118: Ordain your word to your servant in your fear.[645] Then you will shed all your mistrust and unbelief; then you will find that this is the way to discern God's judgement, in instruction and self-abandonment.[646] But you can only fear God genuinely by running the risks of which we are so foolishly afraid on earth. For our fleshly understanding is by nature incredulous. Let the divine goodness prompt you, whose resources are now so abundant that *more than thirty leagues and covenants of the elect*[647] *have been formed. The same game will be set in motion in every country. To sum up, then, we have to take the consequences; we are in it up to our neck.*[648] Do not let your hearts sink, as has been the case with all tyrants, Numbers 24.[649] It is God's true judgement which has made them so wretchedly stiff-necked, for God will wrench them out by the roots, as Joshua has promised us in chapter 11.[650] Fear only the Lord your God; then your fear will be pure, Psalm 18.[651] Then your faith will be tested like gold in the fire, 1 Peter 1.[652] Then you will find wisdom enough; none of your opponents will be able to counter it. I have often been profoundly surprised, that Christians are more afraid of tyrants than all other peoples are, and yet they can see before their very eyes all the plots[653] of the godless being continually thwarted. The only reason for this is the lack of faith and the timorous preachers. So do not allow yourselves to be deprived of sincere-hearted preachers, for this would mean giving a poor wretched pitiable sack of gunpowder[654] precedence over God and refusing to venture your body, goods and honour for the sake of God; the result will be that you will lose all of them for the sake of the devil.[655] Be sure of this, God will not forsake you. At first it will be a bitter time for you, until you are ready to endure a little affliction for the sake of God;[656] there is

---

644. Psalm 118[6ff.]

645. Psalm 119[38]; this phrase in Latin.

646. *im hynfaren euers herzen.*

647. *anschlege und vorbundnis;* Gritsch translates *anschlege* as 'raids', op. cit. p. 108; cf. n. 653 below; a conspiratorial plan, undertaking is meant; underlined from 'more than thirty ...' to 'Do not let ...', and emphasised by a pointing hand in the margin.

648. *Kurz umb, wir mussen auspaden, wir seint ingesessen.*

649. Numbers 24: Balaam's prophecy of disaster to Balak, king of Moab.

650. Joshua 11[20].

651. Psalm 19[9].

652. 1 Peter 1[7].

653. *anschlege.*

654. Symbol of the coercive power of the ruler, cf. Nr. 41, p. 63/13f. above.

655. A common theme of Müntzer's.

656. Cf. Deuteronomy 4[30f.]

no other way to illumination than through deep affliction John 16.[657]

As a dutiful brother I felt I had to address this message of instruction[658] and comfort to you. Should anything happen to you my pen, my preaching, my singing and speaking will not be far off from you. Just keep your courage up; the godless wretches are already intimidated by the righteousness of God; may the latter strengthen you in Christ Jesus our Lord. Amen.

Allstedt on the Friday after Margaret in the year 1524.

54. *Müntzer to the authorities of Sangerhausen. Allstedt, 15 July 1524.[659]*

May the true, pure fear of God and the peace which the world rejects be with you, my dear lords. Since Jesus Christ, the son of God has said unambiguously: Anyone who is ashamed of my words before men will find that I in turn will be ashamed of him before God my father and his angels Luke 9,[660] I have to bear this in mind, and I am prepared for whatever may befall me and all the ministers of the true word, for all that may happen to an upright servant of God. Since those who are committed to one another cannot leave any member in the lurch when they need protection and help,[661] on my honour I declare this: If you do any harm to Master Tilo Banz[662] I will speak against you, sing against you, write against you, I will do the very worst that I can think up,[663] just as David dealt with his godless persecutors Psalm 17.[664] I have said that I will pursue my enemies,[665] I will track them down, I will not rest until they come down in sin and sorrow. They will fall beneath my feet, big wigs[666] though they be. As if it were not enough that I have had to listen throughout this long year to the way in which you have so slanderously branded my

---

657. John 16[20].

658. *underrichtung*; a formal term, frequently used by Müntzer, for authoritative instruction; e.g. p. 112/33 below.

659. The same date as Nr. 53; the form of address is also similar. As it progresses the letter becomes more and more angry, even threatening in a rather inept way.

660. Luke 9[26].

661. *Nach dem alle glyder schutz und hulf eynem vorfugt in sye nit mugen unterwegen lassen*; Tilo Panse was a pastor in Niederröblingen, in the Allstedt district; cf. Cyriacus Spangenberg, *Mansfeldische Chronik*, IV, 505 (Bräuer).

662. Cf. Müntzer's Confession, p. 434/22ff.

663. *das ich um mher gedenken kan.*

664. Psalm 18[37ff.]; David's enemies are to be consumed, destroyed, beaten fine as dust, cast into the mire.

665. *erwuchsen = erwischen* (F.)

666. *grosse hense.*

teaching as heretical and forbidden the people to come to me and have imprisoned them on this count, now I must sit and watch the slanderous way in which you calumniate your own preachers. You dig out your own stupidity and use it as a fig-leaf[667] to prevent anyone noticing that you are worshippers of man. I know that there are no more idolatrous men in the land than you.[668] Enough of this raging of yours, see yourselves for what you are; otherwise it will not be counted in your favour; keep that in mind.[669] Take my warning to heart in a friendly way; much more of this and I will count nothing in your favour. You want to forbid the word of God and be Christians at the same time? Come, come, what a lot of sense that makes! I tell you, by my solemn word, if you do not improve your conduct in this matter, I will not continue to restrain the people who want to tackle[670] you. You must choose one or the other: you must accept the gospel or you must confess yourselves to be heathens; I am as firm as iron about that.[671] I will complain to the whole world that you are emulating the bluebottle fly which pollutes the ointment of the holy spirit, Ecclesiastes 10.[672] Do not resist the holy spirit;[673] may he illumine you, amen.

Allstedt, in the year of Christ 1524 on the day of the preaching of the holy apostles of God.

55. *Müntzer to the persecuted Christians of Sangerhausen. Allstedt, c. 20 July 1524.*[674]

To all the beloved brothers in Christ in the tyrannical prison at Sangerhausen greetings, not in my own name, but grace and peace in the pure, unfeigned fear of God. Christ Jesus, the tender son of God, has spoken in clear words, in the holy meal of his supper predicting in sad words to his beloved apostles and friends everything that was going to happen: how the pleasure-loving world and the blood-

---

667. *grubet und nemet euren tulpel zum schande decker.*

668. i.e. they do not fear God alone.

669. The threat remains vague.

670. *belestigen.*

671. Lit. 'that is firmer than iron.'

672. Ecclesiastes 10¹, a favourite image; cf. Letter 40, n. 404; *On Following Christ,* p. 396/24 below.

673. Acts 7⁵¹; i.e. in persecuting the prophets.

674. Elliger, p. 474, suggests dating this letter 19–20 July on the grounds that it seems to refer to Duke George of Saxony's instructions of 16 July to his officer in Sangerhausen, Melchior von Kutzleben, to take specific measures against the Protestants; cf. p. 87/12ff. below.

thirsty villains would react when the elect began to recognise the crucified Christ and to grasp hold of true faith. John, too, said in chapter 16, 'You should take no offence at this, for the godless will cast you out of the congregation; indeed the hour is coming when they will believe, as they strangle you, that they are doing God a service.'[675] You should take these words to heart and lock them away in the ground of your heart,[676] because the dangerous time of which St Paul spoke is now upon us: when any one who wants to do the right thing and to revere the holy gospel is bound to be regarded by the godless as a heretic, a rascal, and a wretch, or anything else they can think up.[677] But now I have been informed by some pious folk that you are grievously distressed and under oath to these mad, demented tyrannical people to go to prison again;[678] and that you would be glad of my advice. It is my Christian duty not to refuse this, but you must also see that you abide by it. Since, however, you really want to keep your conscience clear, you must begin by having the pure, upright fear of God and learning to fear God alone, above all created things in heaven and on earth. Through this fear you will come to know and learn what to do and what to leave undone, so as to be pleasing to God. For the beginning of the wisdom of God is the fear of God, as the spirit of God says in Psalm 110 and in the book of Proverbs, chapter 1.[679] So you should sigh for God day and night with your whole heart, crying out and beseeching him to teach you to fear God alone. For if you do not have this pure fear of God you will not be able to withstand any trial. If, however, you do have it then you will gain the victory over every tyrant and they will be so utterly confounded that no words can describe it. The fear of God, however, teaches us that a pious man should be ready to resign himself completely[680] to God's will, ready to venture his body, goods, house and home, children and women-folk, father and mother, and the whole world too for the sake of God.[681] Oh, but that is a terrible abomination to fleshly men, who have devoted all their wits, throughout their lives, to gaining nourishment for themselves, and have not thought at all beyond that.[682] No doubt they thought that God would be sure to save them as long as they believed what everyone believes. This is

---

675. John 16[1f.]

676. Luke 2[19].

677. Cf. 2 Timothy 3[1ff.], [12f.]

678. *und doch angelobet den tollen wansynnigen menschen und tyrannen, euch wider einzustellen ins gefenknis*; the whole town is a prison; cf. p. 86/1f. above and p. 88/35f. below.

679. Psalm 111[10]; Proverbs 1[7].

680. *sol gelassen stehen umb Gottes willen.*

681. Cf. Matthew 10[35ff.]; *sich erwegen* = renounce (F.).

682. Cf. Matthew 6[31f.]

how daft and silly the whole world is nowadays, for no-one is prepared to resign himself to the will of God, although the Lord clearly says in the holy gospel of Matthew, chapter 10: 'He who loves anything more than me, is not worthy of me.'[683] In that text Christ, the son of God, gives the clearest exposition of what true faith is. If, then, you are Christians and believe in Christ Jesus, and that he has redeemed you, then you must start with the pure fear of God, for – as mentioned above – that is where faith begins. To put it in a nutshell,[684] you must fear God alone and nothing else, just as the eternal, living God is to be worshipped and no idol set beside him. There can be no excuses here; the straight path must be followed.[685] If your prince or your superior orders you not to go to one place or another to hear the word of God, or insists that you swear to go there no longer, you should on no account swear this, for in that case the fear of man would be given precedence over the fear of God and set up as your idol. But perhaps you think that you want to please both your prince and God. You will not be able to do that, for if something arrogates to itself a place at God's side, and claims our veneration, then surely, surely it is the devil himself. So be on your watch. But if the murderous rascals[686] allege that you ought to obey your princes and lords, this is how you should answer: A prince and sovereign lord is put there to have authority over temporal goods, and his power extends no further than that, and this is also the view of St Peter and St Paul when they write about man's powers. Hence you should speak up boldly and say this: 'My dear lord, my dear master![687] If our lord the prince has not enough income from the dues and rents which we give him each year then let him take all our goods as well; we will gladly grant him these. But he shall have no authority at all over our souls, for in such matters one has to be more obedient to God than to men;[688] make of that what you want. If you make us suffer on this account, we will denounce this and let the whole world know, and then it will realise why we are suffering, for as far as temporal things are concerned we are willing to do or leave undone whatever is well pleasing in your eyes. What more can we do?'

Therefore, my very dearest brothers, if they demand this you should enter prison or confinement again and stick to these words. If, however, they want to fine you, then pay the devil whatever he wants, but keep your conscience free and clear and do not get it

683. Matthew 10[37].
684. *Summa sumarum* (sic).
685. *sonder die stragke bane naussen gegangen*; cf. Jeremiah 31[9].
686. *die wutrichte* i.e. the magistrates.
687. *lieber her hauptman.*
688. Acts 5[29]; cf. Matthew 22[21].

ensnared in the commands of the tyrants, for it is just that which
Christ our Lord meant when he said in Matthew 10: 'Do not fear
those who can kill your body, for there is nothing more that they can
do after that, but I will show to you whom you should fear: fear him
who, after he has exercised his power to kill the body, has authority
also to cast the soul into the fire of hell; he it is, he it is, he it is whom
you should fear.'[689] Therefore let the tyrants have their pleasure with
you for a little while, for this unbelieving world has not deserved any
better lords and princes. So let them plague you as long as God
permits and until you come to recognise your guilt. For the whole
Christian people is becoming a whore with its adulation of man.[690] It
is adulation of man – one sees that clearly now – when fear of their
lords and princes leads men to deny God's word and his holy name
completely for the sake of their pathetic food and of their stomachs; St
Paul, would call them, as he did the Philippians, beasts ruled by their
stomachs, saying that their God is their stomach.[691] O watch out, my
very dearest brothers, lest you, too, be, or become, part of this same
mob.[692] The devil is a really wily rascal, always luring men with food
and security,[693] for he knows that fleshly men are fond of that. And so
for the sake of it they are forced to deny God. Isn't that a ghastly,
pathetic lack of faith? For if you do not believe that God is mighty
enough, when you risk or abandon your wealth and bodily food and
even your life for the sake of God, to give you different food and
more than before, how will you ever be able to believe that he can
give you eternal life?[694] It is a truly childlike belief that God will give
us our food, but to trust that he will give us eternal life is a
supernatural belief, beyond all human reason. If your faith is found
lacking in small things how is God to entrust you with great ones?[695]

Hence I exhort you, dear brothers, fix your eyes on the model for
all the elect friends of God as they faced the time of trial. If, for
example, you are fond of your possessions, fix your eyes on dear Job,
the holy friend of God; how unperturbed he was! As it is written in
the first chapter of his book, he responded cheerfully when the
messengers came and announced to him that all his children had
perished and all his possessions as well, saying unperturbed: 'It was the
Lord who gave me them and the Lord has taken them away too.'[696]

---

689. Matthew 10[28]; the almost liturgical repetitions omitted by F.
690. *das sie die menschen anbettet.*
691. Philippians 3[19]; cf. Nr. 49 p. 79/3f. above.
692. *haufen.*
693. lit. 'life', *leben.*
694. Matt. 6[25ff.]
695. Cf. Luke 19[17].
696. Job 1[21].

Or if you are afraid for your life, fix your eyes on the example of the holy martyrs, how little value they put on their security, and how they laughed in the very teeth of the tyrants.

Now almighty God loves you as much as he loved dear Job and all the holy martyrs; for he has bought you at as great a cost with the blood of his gentle son Jesus Christ. He will also be as liberal in bestowing his holy spirit on you as he was to them. What, then, can you fear? For I tell you in truth that the time has come when a blood-bath will befall this obstinate world because of its unbelief. Then the possessions which up to then no one was willing to jeopardise for the sake of God will be forfeited for the sake of the devil, and with not a word of thanks; this I know for a fact. So why are you letting yourselves be led around by the nose? For it is common knowledge, and can be proved from the holy bible, that the lords and princes as they behave today are no Christians. Likewise your priests and monks pray to the devil and are still further removed from being Christians. Likewise all your preachers are hypocrites who bow down before men. How much longer will you go on with false expectations? Precious little can be expected of the princes. So anyone who wants to fight the Turks does not need to go far afield; the Turk is in our midst.[697] But deal with him as I have indicated above, act so that the guilt and the blame is theirs and not yours.[698] And speak to them frankly, face to face: 'My dear lord, St Paul teaches us, saying: "The word of God is free and unconstrained."[699] Why, then, do you want to prevent us hearing it? For in the past you did not prevent anyone running to St James and to the devil at Mallerbach,[700] which made widows and orphans and took money and goods out of the country. So will you really prevent us now from making a journey when we need to, will you withhold permission for us to have proper preachers and will you forbid us to listen to others? If that is your will, then I shall regard you as a Turk and not as a Christian prince and lord.' Say that to him frankly and without dissembling[701] and you will stand fast, if you fear God alone and do not dissemble. If you should suffer

697. A theme of Luther, too; Müntzer seems preoccupied with the 'Turk' in his letters at this time.

698. *das yr schuld und ursach zu ynen haben muget und richt sye wyder euch.*

699. 2 Timothy 2⁹.

700. In the text *Heckenbach*, probably a copyist's error; Bräuer suggests the possibility of the Cistercian monastery *Heggbach*, near Biberach, LJ 37 (1971), 130; there is a parallel reference to the 'devil of Mallerbach' in Letter 50, p. 81/11 above, and it seems simplest to assume Mallerbach is meant; conceivably there is some word-play with *dornheck* (Letter 49, p. 79/9f.), the theme of the drunken fool with the thorn in his hand, i.e. heathen ceremonies, cf. *Protestation*, p. 203/10f. below; St James of Compostella in Spain is, presumably, the other centre meant.

701. *frey ungeheuchelt.*

any harm, he will stand by you and carry out his vengeance. But if you dissemble God will so trouble[702] you that you will never come to the truth and will suffer great damage to your salvation from this. For God cannot desert his elect, although at times he may appear to do so, but he will carry out his vengeance at the appointed time.

I felt that it was my Christian duty not to keep this from you, for the honour and praise of God; may he keep your mind[703] in the most steadfast faith. The grace of our Lord Jesus Christ be with you all, Amen.   Allstedt, in haste, 1524.

56.   *Karlstadt to Müntzer. Orlamünde, 19 July 1524.*

To Thomas Müntzer, my dearest brother in Christ, bishop of Allstedt.

Peace be to you from the father of Christ, Amen. My love for you makes it impossible for me to conceal from you what I think, even though I would have preferred not to respond on these issues.[704] So you should not become enraged at me or suspect ill will, or imagine that my attitude to you has become a negative one. For indeed the person who finds fault with you and even wounds you can be the one who is most devoted to you, since the wounds inflicted by someone who loves you are better than the fraudulent kisses of an enemy. This is the spirit in which I am replying to your letters which were very far from pleasant to me.

I am hardly likely to be persuaded that there is any better way of gathering the sheep of Christ than, as Isaiah and Zechariah say, by the word of the truth.[705] Indeed, far be it from me to summon up demons by blasphemies against Christ our God.[706] Moreover, I do not refer to the tricky parts of the Scriptures for guide-lines. But I do urge and beseech you to put an end to the elevation of the host, because it is a blasphemy against Christ crucified. Now I do not think it at all wicked or abhorrent to the divine commands to kindle the people's piety with sacred songs. But when you insert the request for a letter to encourage the people of Schneeberg and the fifteen villages etc.,[707] I

---

702. also *engesten* = ängstigen (F.).

703. *gemuet* – translated by *mens* in the Latin version of the Prague Manifesto, cf. p. 372/14 below.

704. Allstedt had been seeking the support of Orlamünde for its new covenant or league; cf. Elliger, p. 467; cf. the letter from Orlamünde, pp. 93f. below.

705. Isaiah 10.20 (Vg.); Zechariah 8³.

706. 1 Corinthians 10²⁰.

707. The preaching of George Amandus of Schneeberg had been a standing affront to the authorities and led to considerable correspondence between Duke George and Duke John; their condominium made effective action difficult (F.).

find myself quite unable to support your approval of this.[708] For it seems to me that leagues of this kind are altogether contrary to the divine will and cause incalculable harm to souls which have been sprinkled with the spirit of fear; for it is like replacing a walking-stick with a reed[709] – trust in blessing, in the living God, with trust in cursing, in man. You know how wicked that is. And the whole of Scripture testifies how much it alienates fearful[710] minds from God, so that they become feckless, unable to hear the voice of the Lord; and even if Scripture were silent, experience would cry out in the streets that to cast one's trust and heart on man is to have a large, thick foreskin of the heart.[711] Especially since I can hardly think of any sharper sword to despatch us than having to die because our eyes are fixed on the conjectures and rumours[712] of the mob. My hope would be that you and your society[713] would abstain from such letters and conventicles, which have led our countrymen here to fear that we would be tolerating deeds more evil than we would tolerate as robbers or rebels. For my part, I am as astonished by that provocative act as I deplore it, and will say quite plainly that I can have no dealings with you about that sort of undertaking or league.[714] So my counsel is the same as Christ gave, and one which no prophet, either, ever fails to give: that you, together with our most beloved brothers, should rest your hope in the one God who is able to confound your adversaries. On the other hand if your request had been based on the contemplation of the judgements of God you know that I owe you my life as in turn you owe me yours. I will gladly assist you in the work of proclaiming the truth of God, even if death itself be the proof, when I see the Philistine stepping forward and hurling his insults at the camp of God.[715] You add that I should greet my wife from you, which I have done. She greets you and your wife[716] warmly in return and hopes that you may emerge unscathed. I ask you to take this reply well. For I belabour you as one who cares for you. I would like to know why you would prefer my son to be called Abraham rather than Andrew. Farewell in Christ Jesus and may happiness be yours. Greet and comfort our brothers in Christ.

Orlamünde, 19 July 1524.   Your Andrew Karlstadt.

708. *comprobare id, quod tu probas.*
709. 2 Kings 18²¹.
710. Not *crepidas*, (F.) but *trepidas* (Bräuer/Kobuch).
711. Jeremiah 4⁴.
712. *habentibus(?) in vulgi opinionem et auram emissos; auram* = wind, rumour; not *curam* (F.); cf. Ephesians 4¹⁴.
713. *societati.*
714. Cf. p. 84/8ff. above.
715. 1 Samuel 17⁸.
716. Ottilie von Gersen or Görschen; cf. Nr. 43, n. 496, and pp. 459f.

56a. *The statement of the people of Orlamünde to those of Allstedt on the Christian way to fight.*[717]

Divine peace through Christ our Lord. Dear brothers, we have read the statement you sent us and have done our best to understand it, noting your reason for writing to us, that is, the way in which the Christians in your area are being repeatedly thrown into chains and fetters; and then your request that we write back and tell you what we intend to de about it etc. Since we are bound to you like brothers we must be quite frank and say (that is, if we have understood your writings) that we can have no resort to worldly weapons in this matter. This is not what we are commanded to do. For Christ ordered Peter to put his sword away,[718] and did not allow him to use force on his behalf, since the time and hour of his sufferings was close by. So when the time and hour is at hand in which we too have to suffer something for the sake of divine righteousness let us not run for knives and spears and drive out the eternal will of the father by our own violence. After all, we pray every day, 'Your will be done.' But if you want to be armed against your enemy, then put on the strong breast-plate[719] and the invincible armour of faith, of which St Paul writes in Ephesians 6.[720] Then you will genuinely[721] overcome your enemies and put them to shame, for not one hair of yours will be harmed by them.[722] But as to your writing that we should make common cause with you, allying or binding ourselves to you, you adduce the Scriptural passage 2 Kings 23,[723] about Josiah covenanting himself to God, and to the people. We find in this same passage that, when the book of the laws was set before him, Josiah made an engagement with God to walk in the way of the Lord, to give his whole-hearted and entire obedience to his law, commandments, and ceremonies, and to bring back to life[724] the words of the covenant as described in the book, and that the people obeyed this covenant. In other words, the king and the people bound themselves at the same time to God. For if Josiah had bound himself to God and to the people too, his heart would have been divided, inclined both to God's will

---

717. Printed by Hans Luft, Wittenberg c. 19 July 1524; preceded by the letter from Karlstadt to Müntzer of 19 July, (Nr. 56 above) replying to the latter's request that the Orlamünde people join the Allstedt League or Covenant of the Elect.

718. Matthew 26[52].

719. *stecheln.*

720. Ephesians 6[13ff.]

721. *redlich.*

722. Matthew 10[30f.]

723 2 Kings 23[3]; on Müntzer's sermon on this cf. Letter 59.

724. *erwecken.*

and to that of men, although Christ declares, 'No one can serve two masters.'[725] Hence, dear brothers, if we were to ally ourselves to you we would no longer be free Christians, but bound to men, and then the Gospel would really become the object of a grand old hullabaloo.[726] Then the tyrants would dance with joy and declare: These men put their trust in the one God, but they ally with one another; their God is not strong enough to fight for them. Likewise, they want to make sects, disturbances and rebellions of their own. Let them be throttled and slaughtered before they become too powerful for us to handle. Then it would be for this, and not for the sake of the stern righteousness of God, that we would have to die. What would God have to say about this? Would not this bring great dishonour and discredit[727] to the cause of divine truth? This is not the way, dear brothers; rather put all your confidence in God, as King Abijah did, 2 Chron. 13,[728] when he was surrounded by his enemies, and like the children of Israel, when they were pursued by Pharaoh to the Red Sea and yet, confiding in God, were wondrously saved and preserved.[729] Therefore only listen and hearken to what God has really said, each of you according to his talents,[730] and pay no heed if the stiff-necked power of tyranny rises up to resist you. For the apostles and all the saints of God, even Christ himself, were not immune[731] from this. As to giving testimony to your teaching in other respects, insofar as it is of God, we are very glad of the testimony of the holy Spirit and will not be miserly in any way with the gracious gifts distributed by God,[732] and if we are called upon to give an account of our faith we will step forward gaily and answer for it, regardless of whether the full rage of the tyrants arises against us and persecutes us to the point of death. But everything with the help and strength of God. For that reason, dear brothers, learn to do the eternal will of God alone, our heavenly Father, which he has revealed to us through his only son, Christ, in the holy Spirit. Then you will be able to find rest for your hearts in God from all trials and temptations. God grant this to all of us. Amen.

Christ's congregation in Orlamünde.[733]

---

725. Matthew 6[24].
726. *dem evangelio eyn recht cetergeschrey bringen.*
727. *abbruch.*
728. 2 Chronicles 13[esp. v.15].
729. Exodus 14[21ff.]
730. *nach seynem pfund;* cf. Matthew 25[14ff.]
731. *vorhaben.*
732. *und durch die milten gaben Gottis mitgeteilt mit nicht sparen.*
733. For Müntzer's reaction cf. Letter 66, p. 115/21ff.

57. *Müntzer to the intendant, Zeiss. Allstedt, 22 July 1524.*

To my brother John Zeiss, administrator of Allstedt and my very dear friend in Christ.[734]

The pure and undeceived fear of God be with you. I wanted to take measures today to avoid what could be an ugly outcome[735] of the surrounding unrest,[736] and to suggest the steps we could take in the future to prevent anything happening without our planning it, and to communicate this to our sovereign prince with your advice. This will prevent anyone being given the pretext[737] to take action. For almost all the tyrants are busily trying to wipe out the Christian faith. But Hans Reichart's[738] response to the poor people who had been expelled was unjustifiable; it followed the usual practice of the princely administrations and their officials. So those who had been expelled and were on the run asked me then what sort of a gospel ours was. Do we just hand over those who are ready to suffer for the sake of the Christian faith to the butcher's chopping-block in this inhumane way? Then I said that[739] I was completely uninformed about the whole matter; but[740] as soon as I knew about it I would be glad to do what I could, anything in my power. As soon as I had finished with the fugitives Hans Reichart came out of the printer's to meet me. Then I said: What sort of tomfoolery[741] is this? Is this any way to comfort the people who have been expelled for the sake of the gospel? Don't you realise what sort of tomfoolery will result! Then he said that it was you who had instructed him. If the administrator at Sangerhausen[742] or from other districts comes to visit Allstedt then

734. The greeting is in Latin; the rest of the letter in German; this is the first of two letters sent to Zeiss on 22 July; the persecution of adherents of the Reformation, not least by Frederick von Witzleben, had sent a flood of fugitives into Allstedt; this angry and lengthy letter demands a more determined policy of support for the refugees; cf. Gritsch, p. 109f.; Elliger, pp477ff.; no doubt the raids of the League had provoked Witzleben and George of Saxony to retaliate.

735. *dem unflat*; lit. 'foulness', cf. p. 98/7 below.

736. *der umligden emporung.*

737. *unfugliche orsach.*

738. A leader in Müntzer's League of the Elect and in the Council but not, as once thought, Müntzer's printer; cf. S. Bräuer, 'Hans Reichart, der angebliche Allstedter Drucker Müntzers'; he appears to have conveyed to the people what he took to be Zeiss's attitude; born c. 1485/6, he was a tailor, living to be at least 90; in 1542 he presided over the council, and was burgomaster in Allstedt three times between 1566 and 1575; cf. S. Bräuer, '*Thomas Müntzer und der Allstedter Bund*' in J.-G. Rott, S. L. Verheus (edd.), *Anabaptistes et dissidents au XVIe siècle* (Baden, Baden, 1987) p. 100, n. 82.

739. A line from Letter 56 was inserted here by mistake by F., p. 417/1.

740. *aber* omitted by F. (Bräuer/Kobuch).

741. *spyl.*

742. Melchior von Kutzleben.

Allstedt then one must hand the people over to him. Then I replied that this would be all very well if the rulers were not acting contrary to the Christian faith. But now that they had not only acted contrary to the faith but also to their natural law, they ought to be throttled like dogs. And if you administrators[743] in all the districts fail to denounce your neighbour in Schönwerda[744] publicly for being the first to violate the common peace and robbing those subject to him, then you will soon see what will happen to you. Hence I heartily advise you, my dear brother, to think carefully what the consequences are going to be. The fugitives will be arriving every day. Should we win the friendship of the tyrants by leaving the cries of the poor people unheard? That is hardly in accord with the gospel etc. I am telling you that it will set off a terrible collapse of law and order. You cannot go on turning a blind eye to the other territories, as has been customary. For it has become clear as day that they have absolutely no time at all for the Christian faith. As a result their power is at an end and will shortly be handed over to the common people. So act confidently, for wherever the gospel prevails Christians will not be imprisoned[745] at the behest of such wretches. I will be glad to carry out the promise I made to the prince in my own handwriting[746] but I am not going to stand for any nonsense.[747] Seeing that it is the spirit of God which drives me, am I to suffer those who may, perhaps, have ordered you to capture people who have fled for the sake of the gospel, to be judges on my Christian faith? If I knew that for a fact I would write to him again. I advise you to write to the princes yourself (although they may treat it with derision) about that arch-thief Frederick von Witzleben, explaining how he has broken the common peace and become the very epitome of a tyrant and the cause[748] of the whole rebellion. If he is not punished by the other lords for this then the common peace will completely collapse. For from now on no people will trust their own lord; with the result that the people can help their lord as little as the lord the people. As discerning and modest men can see this is the cause of all the slaughter; it is pitiable, and it is enough to make one's heart tremble with fear. The foolish world still derides this and thinks that life goes on as before; it wanders along in a dream until the waters close over its head. May God preserve you from this, dear brother.

743. Again, it is Zeiss who is meant, not Reichart.
744. Owned by the Witzleben family; Frederick von Witzleben supported Ernest von Mansfeld in suppressing the Peasants' Revolt (F.).
745. *eynsetzen.*
746. Nr. 52.
747. *kramanzen.*
748. *orthsprungt.*

Allstedt on the day of Mary Magdalene in the year of our lord 1524.

Thomas Müntzer, your brother.

If anyone wants to be one of the stones in the new churches, let him risk his neck; otherwise he will be rejected by the builders.[749]

Consider this, dear brother; the person who will not risk his neck for the sake of God[750] in these dangerous times, will not be found vindicated in his faith either. He will always find an excuse to avoid having to suffer. As a result he will have to endure all manner of perils for the sake of the devil and be disgraced in the sight of all the elect and finally he will have to die for the sake of the devil; but may God preserve you from all this. Amen.

I had hoped to have issued my little book[751] to go with this message that you have perhaps by now had delivered to Weimar,[752] but I am still thinking about every aspect of it in the light of the will and honour of God, for there is no more dangerous undertaking now than negotiating with those who deride the judgement of God.

Answer to your four questions:

1. The will of God is that of the whole over all his members. To recognise the knowledge and the judgements of God is to explain his will, as Paul writes to the Colossians in chapter one and as is written in Psalm 118,[753] but the work of God flows out from the whole and from each of his members.

2. Doubting is the water, the movement[754] to good and evil. Someone swimming on the water, without anyone to support him[755] lies between death and life etc. But the hope which is attained after doubting has done its work gives man the firmest confirmation. Romans 4, Genesis 13, 22.[756]

3. The judgement on the nature[757] of man seems to be understood by

749. A continuation of the letter in note-form, on the same piece of paper; also in Müntzer's hand.

750. *umb Gottis willen*, omitted by F. (Bräuer/Kobuch); note the contrast with the devil in the next few lines, and Letter 53 n. 655.

751. *On Counterfeit Faith*, dedicated to Zeiss? (F.) It seems more probable that the Testimony to the First Chapter of Luke is meant; cf. Nr. 64, p. 112/31ff. above.

752. *Ich wolte bey disser botschaft, villeychte neulich durch euch zu Weymar gethan, mein buchlein haben gefertigt.*

753. Colossians 1⁹; Psalm 119²ff.; *Gottes kunst und seyne ortheyl zurkennen, ist dye erklerung desselben willens.*

754. *dye bewegung.*

755. *ane behalter.*

756. Romans 4 deals with the faith of Abraham; Genesis 13 the separation from Lot and the promise to Abraham of land and descendants; Genesis 22 the sacrifice of Isaac.

757. *eygenschaft.*

you but all crude externals have to be eliminated[758] before man can begin to smother his nature. Otherwise he always carries an air of pretence about him; he even deceives himself. So one has to watch out when one is inclined to unchastity, and first of all inflict pain on the desires by heightening the awareness[759] of the conflict between the lusts and the thorns of the conscience. If he keeps his conscience alert then the foulness will be eliminated by disgust.[760] For then one can see clearly everything that is leading one to foulness and so becomes hostile to it, first of all confronting the lusts with patient endurance.[761] When this becomes irksome to him he will fall again, so that he has to be driven by his conscience again. The person who can remain steadfast will easily be illumined.

Lord you have taught me from my youth. How great and terrible are the tribulations you have shown me. When I have turned around you have brought me back to life and restored me from the depths of the earth[762]

4. The first real Christian awareness[763] cannot be attained without suffering. For the heart has to be torn away from clinging[764] to this world by wretchedness and pain, until it becomes altogether hostile to this life. The person who has achieved this can choose good days rather than bad with a good conscience, as is clearly indicated by the evangelist John and by Elijah [and] Enoch.[765]
Finally.

There is only one fault in him,[766] a foul worldly matter: one should not menace the fugitives with the authority of their lords, letting them be captured in our town, lest the people become embittered with us. I am telling you that one cannot be too attentive to the new movement of the world in our days.[767] The old loyalties[768] will not fit the bill any more at all, for they are nothing but dregs as the prophet says: the dregs of the cup of indignation are not exhausted, all the impious of the earth will drink of it.[769] Those who have thirsted for blood, will drink blood etc.[770]

---

758. *abber dye groben umbstendigkeyte mussen erst alle vorczert werden.*

759. *myt eynem starken uberschwank des betrachtens.*

760. *in dem entsetzen.*

761. *mit langweyle.*

762. In Latin; cf. Psalm 70[17, 20] (Vg.); cf. Letter 18, n. 147; cf. Prague Manifesto, p. 372/10ff. below.

763. *erinnerung.*

764. *ancleben.*

765. Cf. John 21[22]; 2 Kings 2[11] (Elijah ascends to heaven); Genesis 5[24] (Enoch is 'taken' by God); and the apocryphal books of Enoch (F.); esp. 1 Enoch 5[9], the elect will live 'in eternal gladness and peace, all the days of their life.'

766. The Elector?

767. *dye neue bewegung der itzygen welt.*

768. *anschlege*; cf. Letter 53, p. 84/9; probably in sense of *handschlag*, shaking hands, covenanting together.

769. Psalm 75[8]; quoted in Latin, cf. 74[9] (Vg).

770. Revelation 16[6]; cf. Ezekiel 22[6].

58. *Müntzer to the intendant, Zeiss.*[771] *Allstedt, 22 July 1524.*

To my dearest brother in Christ, John Zeiss, administrator[772] of Allstedt.

Greetings. The affair of the poor people[773] went like this: when Hans Reichart came down from meeting you at the castle he put on an incredibly sad face and reported to them the nature of the warning; they took it to mean that they were to be handed over, and so they came to me and asked if this was our gospel; to sacrifice people on the butcher's block. I was completely taken aback and wondered what had given rise to a question like that. Then they told me. So I said to them: I will write to the intendant; I do not know whether he had the order from the prince. Soon after that I met Hans Reichart coming out of the printers. Then I said to him: 'What sort of tomfoolery will result, if we agree to hand the people over like this?' Then he said that you had given him the orders. Then I said, if the administrator at Sangerhausen[774] or any other tyrants came here they should not think that their old tricks[775] would be tolerated here since they had publicly set out to abolish the Christian faith, but that they would be throttled like mad dogs. There is no other way in which I can speak about the enemies of the Christian faith for I want to convince[776] the whole world that they are demonstrably living devils. But the last thing I wanted was to heap on the pious administrators the fury[777] of the common people. After all I have said in all my sermons that there are still pious ministers of God at the courts of the lords etc. I will not incite the poor people to stay here like a weight around our necks, embittering their enemies, but (advise them) to make their plans more wisely as and when it is beneficial to their cause and to ours; so that they do not get any false encouragement from us. I know full well that everything the tyrants do stems from pure fear and despair. The Witzleben affair is to be judged very differently in times like these. Duke George knows all about it; they are birds of a feather.[778] You should expect only the very best of me.[779] Whenever anything

---

771. A shorter and more sober version of Nr. 57; the short staccato sentences are highly effective.

772. *presidi*; the form of address is in Latin.

773. The fugitives.

774. Melchior von Kutzleben.

775. *kramanzen.*

776. Lit. demonstrate, prove; *nachbrengen.*

777. *ynbrunst.*

778. *es ist eyn kuche*; lit. it's all one cake; 'one deserves the other' (Götze); the people of Schönwerda, persecuted by von Witzleben, had protested to Duke George.

779. *Ir solt euch nicht anderst dan das allerbeste zu myr vorsehen.*

like this happens I will always write to you. Think of the transformation of the world which is now at hand, Daniel 2.[780] God help you, Amen. Allstedt. On the day of Mary Magdalene in the year of the Lord 1524.

The messenger sent by Lang[781] is called Father Lamprecht, previously a Carmelite in Hettstedt,[782] he is coming back here. I will take care of the prince;[783] that is no trouble; the only important thing is to be mindful of the harm that the future can bring.

Thomas Müntzer, your brother in God.

59. *Thomas Müntzer to the intendant, John Zeiss, 25 July 1524.*

To my dearest brother in the Lord, John Zeiss, administrator[784] of Allstedt.

The strength and the power of the holy spirit be with you, my dear brother. Quite recently I have been preaching on the fourth book of Kings, giving my honest advice to the Christian world, as it is set forth in the twenty-second and twenty-third chapter[785] concerning the holy king Josiah. When the priest Hilkiah found the book of the law, he sent for the elders of Judah and Jerusalem and went with all the people into the temple and made a covenant with God, to which the whole congregation assented. Thus each of the elect was to search out and observe[786] the testimony of God with his whole soul and heart. If the Christian people is to risk its life[787] against the murderous oppressors of genuine faith, it really will have to think seriously and diligently about how to prevent the worst of the abominations, which is so adroit at patching itself onto the Christian faith. Luke 5.[788] That is why I wish that our sovereign princes were not so deeply involved with them[789] in this matter. The people are very much aware

780. Daniel 2⁴⁴; the fifth kingdom which will replace and destroy all the preceding ones.

781. John Lang (F.); cf. Nr. 51.

782. Monastery founded in 1451 (F.)

783. *Ich wyl den fursten halten*; the reference is to Duke John of Saxony about whom Zeiss was understandably apprehensive because of the leniency he had shown to Müntzer.

784. *presidi*; the form of address is in Latin.

785. *unterscheyd*; 2 Kings 22, 23; for Karlstadt's exegesis cf. p. 93/21ff. above.

786. *bewaren und erkunden*.

787. Lit. 'blood'.

788. *wirts yhr vil hocher von nöthen sein, das sye zu herzen neme myt vorgewantem vleyss, wye sye vorkomme dem aller ergesten greuel, der sich mit dem christenglauben meysterlich fetzen kan*; Luke 5³⁶.

789. i.e. the oppressors; *also hoch bey yhn eyngethan*; F. follows Böhmer: 'did not carry themselves so proudly'; cf. Letter 64.

that they[790] have risked much in embarking or launching their name and worldly fame into this wild tempest. But (the people) itself may be swept away by such perils and completely lose heart unless (the princes) begin to do more than peer through their fingers, failing to instal genuine priests in their principality, protecting the wicked and making no plans at all which accord with God's most kindly will. For it is as clear as day that the godless rulers themselves have broken the common peace, putting people in chains and fetters for the sake of the Gospel; and our princes maintain an absolute, tight-lipped silence about this. Maintain there is nothing amiss, perhaps because they have been misled by the renegade Biblical scholars. Overlook, too, the fact that the Christian people is as yet ill-prepared[791] to shed its blood for the sake of the faith. Yes, it clings to creaturely things so fiercely that it is about them that all quarrelling and disputes arise. Everyone devotes his entire energies to this, but turns into a block of oak when something is said to him by God. It is incredible impertinence to fall back on traditional ways of administering one's office[792] when the whole world has been so mightily and profoundly altered.

By the love and truth of God I say this to you: the urgency of presenting this to our sovereign princes cannot be over-estimated; do so with all earnestness, without any hesitation, and hold nothing back. Warn them of the danger that their own people may lost heart because of their negligence and urge them to anticipate any trouble in time, while the people still trusts them. In all honesty, then, I have to say this: if they delay things too long they will be much more despised than the other princes. Then people will say: Behold the man who did not make God his helper.[793] Which God forfend! Then there will be toil and trouble, then the land of Germany will be much worse than a death-trap, since men's greed is now approaching its peak. So they must turn their pagan duty and oath to their people into a genuine covenant based on the divine will, so that their people may see with their own eyes that they are doing something. Then the countless hordes of the godless will be pitiably affrighted, not knowing where in the whole wide world they can find refuge, as is written in Numbers 14, Joshua 11.[794] If you administrators want to keep the peace then one sword will have to keep the other in the sheath; no longer will it be in order for you to dissemble with one another, as

---

790. i.e. the Saxon princes.

791. *ungeschickt.*

792. *sich auf den alten gebrauch der ämpter wil vortrosten.*

793. In Latin, from Psalm 51⁹ (Vg.).

794. Numbers 14 (the 'wicked congregation' of Israel, afraid to enter the Promised Land, is defeated by the Amalekites and Canaanites); Joshua 11 (extermination by Joshua of the 'great host' of Jabin and his allies.)

you did when the people had to flee, and you were prepared to hand them over, alleging various reasons all untrue, although in fact it was because of their beliefs. But a sensible covenant[795] must be made, one which will bind together the common man with the pious administrators, solely for the sake of the gospel. Should any rascals or troublemakers join it with the aim of using the covenant for evil ends, they should be handed over to the tyrants or judged by yourselves if this[796] is more convenient. As far as the rendering of feudal duties[796] is concerned particular care must be taken in the covenant that the members of the covenant do not think that they should be dispensed from giving anything to their tyrants; but they should follow the son of God's advice to Peter (Matthew 17)[797] lest some evil men think that we have covenanted ourselves together for the sake of creaturely things.

But the most important thing of all, one that requires the most scrupulous attention, is that no one should put his trust in the covenant, for he who puts his hopes in man is accursed of God Jeremiah 17.[798] It should only be a deterrent to the godless, to make them cease their raging until the elect have been able to search the depths of God's knowledge and wisdom with all the testimony pertaining to them.[799] When the pious make a covenant, even though there be evil-doers in it too, the latter will not succeed in pushing through their evil aims; the bluff honesty[800] of the good folk will prevent them from committing anything like the amount of wickedness that they would otherwise, so that the whole company does not get the blame. The covenant is nothing more than an emergency act of self-defence, something which is admitted by the natural judgement of all rational men. Should those who have not been put to the test say: Why do we need so many covenants? We have covenanted ourselves in baptism; a Christian should, and must suffer. My answer: first learn what baptism is; first learn and see whether you have found God's testimony in you; whether you can stand fast; consider that the whole treasury of the knowledge of God must be known and experienced in its length, width, breadth and depth Ephesians 3.[801] Otherwise all the brazen, fleshly men would

---

795. *beschydner bund*; MHG *bescheiden* = 'informed'; 'a covenant of those who know' (Jillings); cf. Nr. 68, n. 958 below.

796. *Der fronden*; 'Fronen', dues; *fromden* is another possible reading: 'As far as outsiders are concerned ...'; Scott points out that the latter were much more likely to see their princes as tyrants, than the subjects of the Lutheran princes.

797. Matthew 17[26].

798. Jeremiah 17[5]; cf. Karlstadt's arguments in Nr. 56.

799. Cf. l. 33 below.

800. *bydderfreyheit*.

801. Ephesians 3[18].

become martyrs and the arch-seducers would sing them a song or two about their martyrs,[802] and one would swear by the saints that they were martyrs; as a result our cause would be regarded by our descendants as much worse, much fouler[803] than the crudities of the Romans. Your pious rulers must keep that in mind. It is no[804] easy thing to believe and be martyred. But if the elect simply ought to let themselves be martyred on the basis of this counterfeit goodness and faith then the depths of the knavery of the godless would never be exposed and the testimony of God would never be able to develop its true heights either. For all these reasons you should consider taking the advice of God-fearing, reliable people who have the fear of God, who are hostile to avarice, who love the truth from their heart Exodus 18.[805] Then you will find a thousand ways instead of one; you can be confident of that. The Lord is with us like a mighty man;[806] one must have no anxiety about what he plans or he will make your flesh shrink away from the dangers of life, lacking the fear of God; may he keep you in all eternity, Amen.

Allstedt on the day of the apostle James in the year of the Lord 1524.

Thomas Müntzer, your brother.[807]

60. The bookseller Wolfgang Juche to Müntzer. Halle, 26 July 1524.

To the honourable gentleman, Master Thomas Müntzer, now pastor in Allstedt, my gracious lord and f(riend).[808]

I am always at your service Thomas Müntzer, my dear sir. As is well known to your honour, at the moment you have in your possession the book of homilies by Martin,[809] a bound edition costing 1 florin, and I had expected that you would have sent me the money long ago, but a long time[810] has passed and this still has not happened.

---

802. A sarcastic reference to Luther's writing to the martyrs in Ghent; cf. *Vindication*, p. 342/3ff. below.

803. schoder = *schot* (filthy, polluted, like a pig); or MHG schoderen = shiver, shake (Bräuer/Kobuch).

804. *nicht* omitted by F. (Bräuer/Kobuch).

805. Exodus 18[21].

806. *Dominus est nobiscum bellator fortis*, Jeremiah 20[11]; cf. Nr. 49 n. 598.

807. Date in Latin; *Tomas Muntzer, frater tuus* omitted by Franz (Bräuer/Kobuch).

808. *Hern und fr.*; in 1511 a Wolfgang Juche gained citizenship in Halle (Bräuer/Kobuch).

809. Date and price suggest Luther's *Christmas Postil* is meant, Grunenberg, March 1522; Benzing, Nr. 1061; (Bräuer/Kobuch).

810. Müntzer will have bought the book before he came to Allstedt, when he was still preacher at St George's in Halle; cf. Nr. 38. (F.); i.e. from c. December 1521 until at the latest mid-March 1523.

So I now would ask you most earnestly to be so kind as to send the above mentioned florin to me by this messenger and not to leave me in the lurch, because I need the money. After such a long time it really is time to despatch it, for as your honour knows and can well imagine I do not get my books for nothing but have to pay for them. So I would ask you again etc., so that I do not have any further trouble[811] in this matter. That is my friendly request. That will be all for now, except to wish you many thousand 'good nights'. Halle, on St. Anne's Day 1524.

Master Wolfgang Juche, bookseller in Halle.

61. *Müntzer to George.*[812] *No date or place given.*

May the grace and peace of Jesus be with you always, my dear brother, George.

Isaiah 28

Although you came to me for instruction, I failed, as your writing indicates, to give you instruction.[813] It is no wonder, since my pastoral

1 Peter 2

work has kept me busy[814] with many people.[815] Do you know that on that same day I had visitors with me, too, and I had my work cut out

John 10

with them and I was really tired on that day because of the church service as well.[816] Dealing with people these days means the sort of work which a mother has when her children have dirtied

we are a spectacle

themselves.[817] One gets worse; the other is improved after his spirit has been stirred, Psalm 88.[818] Instruction in the faith is not something to be achieved in a day for, as Paul, the holy servant of God, says, 2 Corinthians 4:[819] The outward man diminishes from day to day, but

Luke 5 Matt. 9

the inner man is renewed;[820] thus the more he divests himself of the

811. *erbt.*

812. The internal evidence suggests a clergyman, probably of lower status, who has come to consult Müntzer, having seen or heard about his new German liturgy; cf. Elliger, p. 525; Bräuer/Kobuch plausibly suggest George Amandus, who in December 1523 became pastor in Schneeberg, and urged the introduction of the Mass in German on 25 March 1524; this suggests a date around the turn of the year; the language is reminiscent of *On Counterfeit Faith* and other writings of the summer and autumn of 1523.

813. Cf. Isaiah 28²⁶; the whole chapter refers to the unreceptivity of all but the remnant of Israel to God's teaching.

814. *erbsalig.*

815. cf. 1 Peter 2⁹.

816. John 10¹ᶠᶠ; Jesus as the true shepherd.

817. *spectaculum sumus* in margin; 1 Corinthians 4⁹.

818. Psalm 89³⁰ᶠᶠ (?)

819. 2 Corinthians 4¹⁶.

820. Luke 5³⁶; Matthew 9¹⁶.

old the more he is renewed. He may imagine that he has divested himself of the old; what he has really done is stolen a patch from the new cloth and patched it onto his old coat, becoming as a result worse than if he were a Turk or a pagan masquerading as a Christian man.[821] To stir up faith[822] is something that no man can do for another, as John the Baptist indicates by his baptism;[823] for a preacher will always point straight at the lamb which has been slaughtered, which hurries after the lost sheep in the wilderness.[824] Thus I instructed you concerning the counterfeit faith which has to precede authentic faith,[825] exposing the desires[826] which the Holy Ghost has planted;[827] this brings about a breakthrough through all despair.[828] For the faith of a mustard-seed must cast the great mountain of our self-seeking down into the ocean of all our agitation.[829] Then Christ, the genuine son of God, climbs down to those who by now are completely drowned and have abandoned all hope; he comes to them in the night, when their sadness is at its height,[830] and then the elect think he is a devil, or that he is a phantom, for he says: 'Ah my most beloved, have no fear, it's me; I cannot illumine you in any other way; there is no other way in which I can pour my grace into you.'[831] Then Peter and all the elect with him leap into the sea to meet Jesus and are happy to endure all the agitation of the waters; but the men of Genessaret[832] beg the Lord to depart from their land. These men are the swine that are drowned in the waters[833] and who will never be prepared to teach about how they came to faith.[834] They want to cover up nature with nature,[835] and to use Holy Scripture like a fleshly thing or like the writings of the pagans.[836] Such men cannot abide the swift writer, who does not

821. Matthew 25[31]; the Son of man separates out the sheep and the goats; Galatians 6[7].

822. *Bewegung des glaubens*; cf. Psalm 93[3].

823. Psalm 69[1ff.]

824. Even by Müntzer's standards, a remarkably mixed metaphor! Cf. John 1[26ff.]; Psalm 44[11].

825. Matthew 3[7ff.]; Romans 8[36].

826. *entplossen dye begyr.*

827. 1 Timothy 1[8ff.]

828. *Welche eynen durchbruch thuet*; cf. 2 Timothy 2[11ff., 26]; Matthew 15[22ff.]

829. Matthew 17[20f.]

830. Matthew 14[25f.]; Psalm 69[1ff.]; Matthew 8[23ff.]; cf. Matthew 7[24f.]

831. *In canticis canticorum* in margin; F. refers to Luke 24[23, 37] and sees no reference to the Song of Songs; 5[2] may, however, be meant.

832. *Jo ult* in margin; John 21[7f.]

833. Matthew 8[32]; the various 'lake' stories lead to considerable confusion of metaphors.

834. *dye ankunft yres glaubens.*

835. 2 Peter 2[18].

836. Proverbs 26[24ff.]

write with inks or any other materials but with the stylus of his spirit in the abyss of the souls, where man recognises that he is a son of God and Christ the loftiest of the sons of God. For what all the elect are by grace, he is by his divine nature. And unless man goes this far in his sensitivity to the divine will he will never be able to believe genuinely in the Father or the Son or the Holy Ghost. This is clearly and lucidly expressed in John 7. Christ says: 'He who will do the will of my father will know whether I have spoken for myself or for God my father.'[837] If God's unchangeable will is to be known this can only be by the continual submission of our wills through earnest remorse; it has to be so taken to heart, that one can tell others about it and give an account of the intentions of an earnest, suffering, zealous man. He does not believe in God because the rest of the world believes in this or that; neither in God nor the devil; but because God discloses and reveals himself[838] through the order established in him and in all the creatures;[839] and that man has to perceive and be sure of this, far surer than of all natural things. This business demands a gladsome man, who holds nothing back,[840] but gives his mind to this from day to day. A man like this does not behave like the mad biblical scholars, who display their wares[841] according to the fancies of the world, but he is a repulsive sight to all who have not been put to the test and especially to Christians. How can I know what is of God or the devil, what is mine or the property of others, unless I have got away from myself:[842] 'Reduced to nothing, I know nothing; I was made to resemble a beast of burden in your eyes; yet I am always with you.'[843] Oh, where is our poverty of spirit, if we cannot speak of it because we are too lazy to practise it? How are we to escape, so that God can put it to work? It will take on a quite different profile,[844] than the one it has for the people who take offence so easily.[845] What causes offence is an incomplete or a counterfeit faith, which has to be ruthlessly wiped out, as Christ did for his disciples, since they all had to take offence at his suffering. If, however, one puts all manner of obstacles in the way

837. John 7[17].

838. The words *adder teufel, sondern das sich Got* have been omitted in F. 425, 35 after ... *an Got*; cf. Bräuer, LJ 38 (1971), 130.

839. *auffenbart durch dye ordenung yn sich und yn alle creaturn gesatzt.*

840. *eyn wunsamen und ungesparten menschen; wunsam* = blessed, joyful.

841. *dye ire dinge ... anzeygen.*

842. *das ich myr entworden byn.*

843. Psalm 72[22f.] (Vg.); in Latin.

844. lit. 'nose'.

845. *ergern;* used above, p. 104/20, in the meaning of 'get worse'; the context here – with the reference to the scandal of the Cross – (*ergernuß*) suggests the translation given.

of improvement[846] then one will maintain childish ways alongside it. I beg you, dear George, and the good fellow who was with you, to lend a hand in pressing for the German service to be introduced, and the sooner the better. You will see; God will stand by you. Have no fear, little flock,[847] for it is the pleasure of the strong God of Sabaoth to see his name preached some day before the pompous world. It is high time; arise from the sleep of the heathen ceremonies,[848] for all they will ever do is to harden your hearts more and more from day to day. You must conduct the service daily with the readings from the law and the prophets and the evangelists so that the text will soon be as familiar to the common man as to the preacher. It can be done. As long as you seek no money, or fame, and make no great fuss about it. Oh, oh, it can so easily creep in under the best of motives; a man will swear by the saints,[849] and the same happens when he explains to you his motives. See that Christ is your foundation and that your desire is grounded on that same rock in the tempest.[850] Pay no heed to the edict of the emperor or of Duke George,[851] for they are flesh, and not a God who remains constant, as Isaiah teaches clearly and lucidly in chapter 31 where he is talking of Egypt.[852] All such people are your opponents, too. Be careful that you do not fail to make use of your temporal freedom, because you have it in order to promote the Gospel and it will be taken away from you as it was from Midian.[853]

62. Hans Böttiger[854] to Müntzer. No date or place.

This letter to be delivered to his reverence, Müntzer.

My friendly greetings to you, my dear master[855] in Christ Jesus. My

846. *besserung*; cf. n. 845 above; both meanings of *ergern* are probably present in Müntzer's mind.

847. Luke 12[32].

848. *heydnussen geperde*.

849. i.e. that he is being upright (F.).

850. Matthew 7[25]; lit. 'that your stone is Christ'.

851. Duke George of Saxony.

852. Isaiah 31[3].

853. Numbers 31; the text has '*Madian*'.

854. Like the next letter this is a dream sent to Müntzer for interpretation; cf. p. 108/7f. below; Goebke has identified a monk of this name in Halberstadt, but the name is common enough and the letter may date back to the Zwickau period (1 October 1520 to 15 April 1521) or, more probably, can be assigned to the Allstedt or Mühlhausen period (F.); Bräuer/Kobuch suggest the summer of 1524; the clumsy German does not indicate any great learning! like Nr. 63 it probably comes from a local correspondent; a Hans Böttger has been traced in the 1527 property register of Mittelhausen in the Allstedt district (Bräuer).

855. Müntzer is the revered authority as well as the beloved brother.

dear brother, two (2) ships were sighted on the water, and a large linen sack hung on one of them, and in the ship lay 2 dead people. And he said, 'Dead they be but drowned[856] they are not.' And as for the other ship, it was full of blood;[857] on it someone was washing two fleeces,[858] and great dread encompassed him.[859] Then he spoke, 'Sir, show me[860] your faith,' and the water rose up[861] and from it emerged a nix who wanted to lure me into the water. At that I woke up.[862] I pray you, kindly pray to God so that I may learn from God. That is all now except to say God preserve you.

Hannus Puttyger.

63. Visions of Herold of Liedersdorf (Allstedt, Sommer 1524).[863]

These are the visions which the father saw after Thomas Müntzer was away.

I

I saw a mill near the gate to the Old Town, and the miller was in front of the mill, with Peter Farmut[864] standing beside him. The miller saw me and I saw the master[865] walking along the narrow streets. And the miller said to me: 'Herold, go and call the master over to us.' Then I went and said, 'Master, you are wanted by the miller.' And so off we went together and when we were close to him, I stopped. Then the miller said, 'Herold, you come too.' So I went over to them too,[866] and when we were all together the miller stopped talking and I woke up. And afterwards I went to sleep again. And I

---

856. *nass*, lit. 'wet'.
857. *das ist gbesen al vol pludt.*
858. *und hat sy gbassen ii vel;* last two words in margin.
859. *mit grosser fordt umgeben.*
860. *Er zey mir.*
861. *und das basser hat sich auf dan.*
862. *da mit pyn ich endt munder borden,* i.e. *munter geworden* (Bräuer).
863. As the opening words suggest, this dates from a time when Müntzer was absent from Allstedt, probably either at Weimar (end of July 1524) or after his flight from the city (7/8 August 1524); Liedersdorf is some 8 km. from Allstedt, and the writer appears to be Herold's son; it is possible that 'the father' refers to the old man (and boy) who, according to Agricola, always accompanied Müntzer and told him their dreams; on the back Müntzer has written 'Orlamünde, Karlstadt', presumably indicating an intention to inform the latter about the visions.
864. Cf. Nr. 68 n. 956; Peter Warmuth.
865. *magister.*
866. *Und ich gieng auch hen zuen.*

felt as if I were in Ludersdorf and had climbed up a pear tree,[867] and the tree hung right over a ditch and in the ditch was flowing water, and I shook the tree, and the pears and the leaves[868] fell down, partly into the ditch, partly at the side of the ditch. And when I began to gather them the pears were transformed into chunks of flesh and the longer I went on gathering the more flesh-like they became until the point when I got two pieces of flesh, one piece in each hand, one piece being fatter[869] than the other, and I was there myself and with me was my brother. Then I gave the fattest piece to my brother. And both of us went into the mill and when we entered it a loaf was lying on the table, with part of it cut up. Both of us took some bread and ate it. And the miller came in. Then I said, 'Master of the mill, lend us some bread, please. When we come again, we will bring you some.' Then he said, 'Yes, why not,' And it seemed to me as if I were at home in my own house. Then I looked up and there were three men; they had pulled a man up with a rope and had put the rope over the top of the beams. Then they let him go and quickly pulled him up again. Then I thought, 'Look, are you going to let a man be hanged in your house', and then I thought, 'look, why should you be afraid of him. It's dead he is, and dressed in red-trousers.'

II

I was at a wedding[870] in a barn. I lay on the roof and looked at the people. The bailiff[871] was going the rounds, collecting money. Then I climbed down and wanted to pay 4 groschen. Then I looked for one that was as big as an Annaberger,[872] shaped like this ⊙ , with a face on it. I did not want to give that one, so sat down for a while on a window-seat[873] and looked for another one. This had a little black mark just like this: ⊖ . I did not want to give it away either, so I put it back and looked for two Schneeberger,[874] put them down on the table and looked for pennies worth two groschen to add to them to make up the amount. Then I woke up and afterwards went to sleep again and afterwards came to a house; then I saw someone in the parlour. They were going to cut his head off and I thought: You poor

867. *und steck auff einen bernbaum.*
868. *das lob.*
869. *wetter*; amended from *besser*, better.
870. *wertschaft.*
871. *der richter.*
872. Probably refers to the Schreckenberger or 'Angel's groschen', minted since 1498 in Annaberg and worth a seventh of a Rhenish gold gulden; H. Halke mentions a church 'penny', not a real coin, with the inscription 'Help, St Anne' on it. (F.)
873. *wensten*; perhaps *Wanst* (belly).
874. Minted in Schneeberg from 1496; worth $1/_{21}$ of a golden gulden.

poor man, Now you have to be off and you don't know where to, and then woke up.

III

Then I was at home and put two sacks with corn in them on the horse and wanted to go to the mill and rode up the village towards the mill, and as I came out (of the village) the road was blocked and dug up and, in brief, I wanted to go to the mill and climbed up to a house that was not high, to an attic, and wanted to bring up the sacks. Meanwhile the horse runs away towards the Naumburg forest,[875] and I did not know where the horse got to with its sacks, and woke up.

I was spoken to: 'You are to open the church' and I looked out the keys and went to open up. Then it seemed to me that the door was my sister, and I took the key and turned the broad side[876] of the key upwards and looked for the key-hole but was unable to see the key-hole for blood. So I turned the broad side downwards and then the key went in and I opened and pulled out the lock with one hand and opened the door and got my sister's clothes, which were bloody, and pushed the clothes behind the door and woke up.

64. *Müntzer to Frederick the Wise.*[877] *Allstedt, 3 August 1524.*

To my mighty[878] lord and father Frederick, elector of the dear land of Saxony.

May the pure and upright fear of God and the unconquerable spirit of divine wisdom be with you. This in place of the usual greeting.[879]

The critical situation[880] has made it imperative to prepare for, and take action against, every manifestation of unbelief. Up to now this latter gained its end by pretending to be the Christian church, but

875. Beyernaumburg Forest.

876. *das breyte.*

877. Written just after Müntzer's dramatic summons to Weimar on 1 August to answer accusations of subversive activity in forming the League of the Elect, and of gross attacks on the Elector from the pulpit; he had then, on his return, been informed by Zeiss that his printing-press was to be dismantled; cf. Elliger, pp. 503ff.; Gritsch, pp. 112ff.

878. *Dem thetigen vater und herren*; Hinrichs, p. 165 interprets it to mean 'active for the Gospel'.

879. i.e. Müntzer dispenses here with the usual formal greeting – unlike Nr. 45.

880. *die not . . . foddert*; Müntzer had called the League of the Elect *eyne nothwere* (Nr. 59 p. 102/27); this justification by necessity, emergency had of course been used by Luther in 1520 in his *Appeal to the German Nobility*, LW44, 131.

now it decks itself out in the deceptive form of fleshly and counterfeit benevolence.[881] In view of all this it has been ordained by God that I should be put forward, as Ezekiel says, as a wall in front of our poor, disintegrating Christianity;[882] not just to punish part of it,[883] as some imagine, but to seize it in its entirety by the roots, which God has already done in several places where it was opportune. But Satan is driving the godless scholars to their downfall, like the monks and priests before them, for they let their rascally nature peep out when they treated the holy spirit of Christ as the butt of their scorn and derision,[884] denouncing him as a devil when he appeared in many of the elect. This is what that mendacious man, Luther, does in the scandalous letter about me which he sent to the dukes of Saxony.[885] There is not a hint of a brotherly exhortation in it; he just barges his way in like some pompous tyrant, full of ferocity and hate. I beseech you, therefore, for the sake of God, to consider earnestly what sort of farce may ensue if I pay him back for his loud mouth. I do not want to do this, but the offence which has been given to many pious folk who have heard my teaching in foreign lands and cities makes it difficult to leave it unanswered.

Therefore my frank request, mighty and benevolent lord, is that you should not prevent or forbid my preaching or writing for the edification of the poor Christian people.[886] This would avert any danger arising from actions of the Christian people against the afore-named Luther, which might then prove hard to settle in a harmonious way.

Finally, here is my earnest judgement: The Christian faith which I preach may not be in accord with that of Luther but it is identical with that in the hearts of the elect throughout the earth, Psalm 67.[887] For even if someone were born a Turk he still has the beginning of the same faith, that is, the movement of the holy spirit, as it is written of Cornelius, Acts 10.[888] So if I am to be brought to trial before the Christian people then an invitation, announcement, and communication must be sent to every nation, to those who have, in faith, endured trials quite beyond their strength,[889] have plumbed the

881. In other words the Papal church has been succeeded by a Lutheran one.
882. Ezekiel 4³ (not 13⁵ (F.)); the wall is to besiege Israel.
883. I.e. the Papalist part.
884. *aufs vorachtesten spotvogel machen.*
885. *Letter to the Dukes of Saxony,* LW 40, 45ff.
886. A reference to the suppression of the printing-press.
887. Perhaps Psalm 68³ is meant: *Et justi epulentur, et exsultent in conspectu Dei . . .'* the whole psalm is triumphalist and militant.
888. Acts 10, esp. ⁴⁴⁻⁷.
889. *unuberwintliche;* the same word translated 'unconquerable', above, p. 110/20; cf. Nr. 52 for the idea of an ecumenical tribunal; cf. also pp. 133/10f.

despair of the heart, and are continually meditating on this. People like that I would gladly thole as my judges. That is why I want to avoid the hole and corner trial the Biblical scholars would like to impose on me. Christ declined to incriminate himself before Annas, and said: 'Why ask me? Ask those who have listened to my teaching.'[890] In this way he turned the attention of the godless ruler to the people. So why should I, then, throw pearls to the swine[891] who publicly mock and deride the holy spirit, since Christ has said that they are born of the devil?[892] How can I trust them in some hole and corner? What should induce me to let my patience be exploited to cover up their shame?[893] It would be just the same as their present advice: Christians should suffer and let themselves be martyred and should not defend themselves. That, however, would be of great benefit to the tyrants, a fine cover-up to let them practise their shameful deeds.

I promised our beloved lord, Duke John, your brother, that I would submit my books for examination before having them printed, but I am not willing to thole the exclusive judgement of the poisonous and pompous biblical scholars; there must also be that of the person who can testify with a downcast spirit how he came to his faith. So if it is your will to act as my gracious lord and prince I will broadcast my aforesaid Christian faith to the whole world by word and writing; I will do this in the bright light of day and explain it with all frankness. If, however, this offer should not find acceptance with your benevolence, you should keep in mind that the common folk will lose heart; they will become demoralised about you and the others.[894] For the people have particular confidence in you; moreover, God has given you great powers of insight,[895] compared with other lords and princes. But if you were to misuse them in this matter it would be said of you: Look, that is the man who did not want God for his protector, but who relied upon worldly show. So I sent by our intendant to his lordship, your brother, a written version of my exposition of the Gospel of Luke[896] and an explanation of the godly way to deal with any insurrection that may occur.[897] I do hope that

890. John 18[21].
891. Matthew 7[6]; a favourite text, after the Peasants War, of Nicodemites like Otto Brunfels; cf. Carlo Ginzburg, *Il Nicodemismo* (Turin, 1970).
892. John 8[44].
893. *schantdeckel*; F. sees a reference here to 1 Peter 2[16].
894. *die scheu und vorzagung des gemeynen volks gegen euch und den andern.*
895. *viel vorsichtickeit.*
896. Testimony of the First Chapter of the Gospel of Luke, submitted to Weimar for censorship on 1 August.
897. Cf. Nr. 57 p. 95/3ff.; Hinrichs refers to Nr. 59; Lohmann, p. 56, considers it a lost writing of Müntzer.

you will be guided by it, since the world still holds you in such high esteem; lest Joshua 11[898] be fulfilled in relation to you, about the man who despises the advice of the needy, whose help is God himself. May he preserve you and all your family according to his most loving will.

Allstedt on the day of St. Stephen,[899] in the year of Christ 1524.

Thomas Müntzer, an earnest servant of God.

65. *Müntzer to the Council of Allstedt. No place given. 7 August 1524.*

To his brothers, the magistrates of Allstedt, to be read in the presence of the intendant.[900]

May the peace which the world shuns be yours, my dear brothers. My affairs have constrained me to take my departure. I would beseech you most courteously, therefore, not to be annoyed at me because of this, or to read too much into it. Keep thinking about the action you are required to take to fulfil God's will, according to the guide-lines I gave you from the beginning by the testimony of God: namely, that after a lengthy period of desolation, almighty God will come to you, imparting to you by his most loving will the fullness of illumination, provided you do not deny him. For now, then, may God preserve you in his will. Amen.

The Sunday before Cyriacus in the year of our lord 1524.

Thomas Müntzer, a servant of God.

66. *Two draft letters to Allstedt.[901] 8–15 August(?) 1524.*

A. Instead of the usual greeting I, Thomas Müntzer, wish the perverts among you a perverted God and the innocent among you a

---

898. This chapter, repeatedly cited by Müntzer, pictures the ruthless extirpation of the Canaanite kings and peoples. (F.)

899. *am tage Inventionis Stephani.*

900. After his flight; in view of their failure to support him at Weimar the tone is remarkably measured; cf. Nr. 66, sent on by Zeiss to Elector Frederick, with Letter 67, by 24 August.

901. The relationship of these two writings to one another and to Nr. 67 is disputed; it may be best to regard them as distinct, not as variant drafts for one letter; A is fiercely emotional, expressing anger and hurt as his 'betrayal'; it would seem most natural to place it first; B is a more measured attempt to analyse the situation, to explain the division between 'progressives' and others; Nr. 67, like Nr. 65, is pastoral in tone, patiently explaining his actions, in a remarkably friendly and understanding manner; Scott suggests, very plausibly, that A is addressed to the Council, B to the commons.

gracious[902] and innocent fear of God, Psalm 17.[903] Since your adoration of a mere, wretched man[904] makes you incapable of hearing or seeing anything, the only way of instructing you I know is Isaiah's, who in his first chapter finds oxen and asses far and away preferable to stiff-necked men,[905] and abuses those companions to murderers and thieves whom you obviously adore while at the same time soliciting my opinion on the divinely testified covenant, Isaiah 58,[906] which you are resisting with all your energy. You want to seek out the righteousness of God and the ways of his holy covenant as if you were a people that greatly longed for it, although you know all too well how you would have abandoned me to the cross. I will let the whole Christian people know one day how Nickel Rucker,[907] that supreme Judas Iscariot, and Hans Bosse, and Hans Reichart betrayed me, swearing by the saints to the prince that they would have my neck, and not even blushing to admit this before my very face at the castle. Am I now supposed to disclose the mysteries of the covenant to such renegade Christians, for whom the allegiance and oath they have sworn to a mere man is much more important than the covenant of God? Oh, yes, and I am supposed to betray the people to them as well, now they have got used to betrayal? Stir it up, my dear lords, let the muck give out a good old stink. I hope you will brew a fine beer out of it, since you like drinking filth so much, Psalm 74.[908] I know no way of helping or advising you, having heard you say with my own ears that my teaching was of the devil, who will lead you around for as long as God's fiery will[909] allowed him to play with Job, to bring you to knowledge. Amen.

B. Joy and peace be with you my most beloved, John 16.[910] I beseech you to make an intelligent distinction between real progress and taking offence.[911] Since it is palpably, manifestly clear to you that

---

902. *holtsalige.*

903. Cf. Psalm 28[25f.]; *et cum perverso perverteris* (Vg.); the theme of the *verkarten*, of perversion, recurs in the *Vindication*, p. 327/2 below.

904. Duke John.

905. Isaiah 1[3f.]

906. Isaiah 58[2]; *Esaie 58* in the margin.

907. The magistrate, with the two councillors, had put all the blame on Müntzer at Weimar and again deserted him at Allstedt; on Reichart cf. Nrs. 57, 58; on Rucker and the burgomaster, Hans Bosse, cf. S. Bräuer, 'Die zeitgenössischen Lieder über den Thüringer Aufstand von 1525', *Mühlhäuser Beiträge*, Sonderheft 2 (Mühlhausen, 1979) esp. pp. 37–39; Hans Bosse written in the margin.

908. Psalm 75[8]; cf. the close of Nr. 57.

909. *eynbrunst.*

910. John 16[22].

911. *unterscheyden wollet dye besserung und ergernis kegeneinander;* in Müntzer the

what the enemies of the divine covenant mean by progress is peace and joy, and a life of ease and usury of all kinds, it is no wonder at all that they are worried and terrified at the least agitation,[912] taking offence in the most materialistic way when true progress takes place and the holy people of Christ turns away with all its heart and soul from revering the evil-doers in their fancy gear. Then the world becomes charged with fear of these godless, abandoned men, for as soon as they hear a leaf rustling on a tree they think that an armed man is at hand.[913] So pay no heed if they take offence. For the godless it is just like the time when they wanted to capture Christ, but were worried that it might cause an uprising.[914] The high and mighty, after all, are paid to do what is *not* right. They have not the least intention of ever doing it. So they are opposed to the uprising which all that they have thought and said and done has made inevitable. And then when you resist their antics[915] they accuse you of being seditious. I have made my agreements[916] with many of the friends of God and would have done so with the folk from Orlamünde, too, if they too had wanted to stand by you, as they boasted they would. But they produced a letter,[917] which adduces the ridiculous pretext[918] of the fear of men, which is quite incredible etc. But now that you are so afraid of the godless that you, like the folk from Orlamünde, deny the covenant of God, which you call the old and new testament, there is nothing that I can do. For you know very well that subscribing [to the covenant][919] is not directed against any government but only against shameless tyranny. If your lords should write, let the berry-wine[920] flow; it'll be sure to be drunk. Suffer for the sake of God. I advise you to do this; otherwise you will have too much to suffer for the sake of the devil. With that, then, God preserve you.

---

two terms 'progress', or 'improvement' and 'taking offence' occur almost always together, often in the context of liturgical reform, cf. pp. 167/11, 15ff.; 106/29–107/1; above all p. 117/6ff.; 172/9ff.

912. *in eyner kleynen bewegung.*

913. Leviticus 26³⁶.

914. Cf. Matthew 26⁵.

915. *fratzen.*

916. *anschleg*; the League of the Elect.

917. Cf. Nrs. 56 and 56a.

918. *eynen viserlichen deckel.*

919. *eyn screyben* is amended by Franz, p. 434, n. 11, to *meyn screyben* (my writing) but 'subscription' to the League or Covenant is meant (cf. p. 434/21 below) as Dismer points out, p. 83, n. 3.

920. *bermusth.*

67. *Müntzer to the people of Allstedt.*[921] *Mühlhausen,*[922] *15 August 1524.*

The understanding of the divine will be with you, dear brothers, and with it all the knowledge of God. In my preaching to you I was moved to rebuke very sharply those tyrants over the Christian faith who, under the pretence of governing, put the people in chains and fetters to make them deny the Gospel. It was impossible for me to refrain from doing this, and now I have found it imperative to attack that other group which dared to defend such godless, abandoned men.[923] Truly I had no option but to howl out a warning against these ravenous wolves; it was my duty as a true servant of God, John 10, Isaiah 56, Psalm 76.[924] Yet all I really did was, to put it briefly, to say that a Christian should not offer himself up so pitifully to the butcher's block, and that if the big wigs[925] do not stop this, one should take the reins of government away from them. Now if I have spoken earnestly to the Christian people in this way and they do nothing about it, or are afraid to act on it, what more can I do? Perhaps I am supposed to keep quiet about it, like a dumb dog?[926] What right, then, would I have to live off the altar? I have already told you all about the way in which people tend to react at a time of trial.[927] Perhaps I am just supposed to let it all overwhelm me and suffer death, patiently letting the godless have their way with me[928] and then afterwards they would claim that they had throttled a limb of Satan?[929] No, not on your life! The fear of God within me will not give way to the insolence of anyone else. But after you were reminded of your oath and your allegiance you showed such fear that I could no longer stay with you and be a burden to you – for I would not allow my lips to be constrained in any way from announcing the righteousness of God, Psalm 39, Isaiah 58.[930] And if anything had happened to you as a result, you could not have borne it. So be content, for God's sake. I would have been glad to help you with letters of exhortation, but at no time did you remain unperturbed when fear struck; your confidence was

921. Cf. Nrs. 65, 66 and the letter to the Nordhausen Council of about the same date, Nr 67a.

922. Müntzer had fled to Muhlhausen and remains there until his expulsion on 27 September.

923. Luther and his colleagues.

924. John 10[1ff.] (the hireling shepherd); Isaiah 56[10] (the dumb dogs); Psalm 77[20] (Moses and Aaron the good shepherds).

925. *dye grossen hense.*

926. Isaiah 56[10].

927. *anfechtung*; or: 'should properly act' (Scott).

928. Cf. Nr. 64, p. 110/12 above.

929. *eynen Sathanam.*

930. Psalm 40[9]; Isaiah 58[1] ('lift up your voice like a trumpet').

always defective. You wanted to elude the time of trial, but this is just impossible in an age like ours if we are to do what is right. Be of good courage; preaching like this cannot and will not take place without provoking an enormous scandal; for Christ himself is a stone of scandal. Psalm 117, Matthew 22, Mark 12, Luke 20, Romans 9, Isaiah 28, 1 Peter 2.[931] This sly, but silly Christian people must be scandalised much more than it ever has been since its origins for the sake of the progress which nothing will be able to stop.[932] So do not think of progress in the complacent terms of the world, but as Job does in chapter 28.[933] So on this occasion I will bid you farewell, since the circumstances demand this, in a friendly and gracious spirit, and I am most ready to be of service to you in all sincerity and with unfaltering diligence.

But as far as the threatenings are concerned, to which you reacted in such a fleshly way at the castle, you must have no worries. Your fear of men had to surface, so that I could take in the fact that you could let a man intimidate you so totally, which is an exceptional hindrance to your understanding of the divine will. I then hammered this very point into you in an extraordinary manner, emphasising it for your benefit. I want to be completely friendly to you, if you will let me. But if not (which God for ever forfend) then for his name's sake I must let him loose his vengeance on the evil-doers for the admonition of[934] the godly.

I wanted the mass-books and the vesper-books[935] sent to Mühlhausen. I will pursue this with all diligence, for the people are eager to have them. So make an effort yourselves to get on with one another and let other people have me until the church has been awakened by the fire of scandal. I will continue to write to you and the congregation for your edification, but at the moment I am short of time. God bless you, then, my most beloved in Christ Jesus our Lord.

I would beseech you to give my wife[936] a modicum to sustain her, as long as this does not offend you. Just as you like; I did not preach to you for the sake of money but to seek (the honour of) God's name; may he keep you safe to all eternity. Amen.

Mühlhausen, on the Assumption of Mary in the year of the Lord 1524.   Thomas Müntzer, a servant of God.

931. Psalm 118[9]; Mathew 22[21]; Mark 12[10]; Luke 20[17f.]; Romans 9[32f.]; Isaiah 28[16]; 1 Peter 2[7f.]; a fascinating array of texts.

932. *dan vom anbeynne umb der unuberwintlichen besserung wegen.*

933. Job 28[12f.; 20f., 23ff.], real progress always scandalous cf. Nr. 66, n. 911.

934. *zur innerung.*

935. The type for his German Mass and liturgy.

936. His wife must have stayed behind in Allstedt, together with his famulus; cf. Nr. 68.

67a. Müntzer to the Nordhausen Council; after 28 February 1525.[937]

Grace and peace from God our father and our Lord Jesus Christ.

My dearest brothers in our Lord, since you are our neighbours and, like us, under the authority of the Empire,[938] it is not unfitting that we should open our hearts to you. It has come to our attention – and we are deeply grieved to hear about it – that an inhuman power of Belial has reared itself up in your midst, which, quite arbitrarily, and with scandalous violence, is itching to sacrifice Christian blood to Belial.[939] This arises, as usual, from the hate and blindness of those whose hearts are hardened, and from those who strive to deflect the people of God from the purity of an unfeigned faith[940] and from the recognition of their creator. And from here too springs the tyranny, which (seeks) to destroy the pure fear of God in the hearts of believers, for this is the regular procedure of the devil, devious as he is, to destroy the best for the least, i.e. a living man for a lump of wood or an image. I have it on good authority that this is now the case with you. For Christians this is not only scandalous and ruinous but leads to their deserting the Creator for the sake of creaturely things,[941] which means eternal death. Hence God declares: As far as images are concerned you should not make, adore or love them, nor should you tolerate them if they are made. For if he has forbidden us to praise sun, moon, stars or any elemental power how much more the work of men's hands! Those, however, who do this are to be subject to the death penalty, likewise the prophet who has instructed them.

Most beloved brothers, who ever taught you to set someone in prison because of an image? By doing this you show all too clearly that you defend superstition and images, and subject yourselves to eternal death. For the apostle says[942] that not only those who eat it but

937. Müntzer's authorship is supported by Förstemann, Jordan, Bensing; the MS copies, destroyed in the 2nd World War, were headed 'A writing of the rebel horde to the Nordhausen Council'; the use of Scripture and much of the language is very reminiscent of Müntzer; but it is written in the first person plural which suggests a communal letter with some contribution by Müntzer; cf. Nr. 50, n. 619 above; on 28 February 1525 Müntzer was appointed to St Mary's Church in Mühlhausen; the arrest of Hans Franke's brother c. 3 April in Nordhausen may have occasioned the letter, cf. M. Bensing, *Thomas Müntzer und der Thüringer Aufstand*, p. 84, n. 98; Müntzer would have had contacts in Nordhausen dating from his time there before Allstedt.

938. Written from Mühlhausen, like Nordhausen an Imperial City. (F.)

939. Cf. Letter 50 about the Mallerbach chapel which uses almost identical language 'so that our brothers are surrendered to be sacrifices to him', p.81/12; cf. p. 99/7f. above.

940. Again Müntzer's language.

941. Again, Müntzer's thought, though he seldom uses the word 'creator' for God; it does occur, however in Letter 50, p. 81/4.

942. I Corinthians 11[34](?)

those who approve it, too, deserve to die. Hence your teacher, even if he were an angel,[943] is accursed and liable to death. But this is, of course, also Satan himself at work directing you away from God to the work of human hands, and from pure teaching to lies; therefore in accordance with the punishment laid down by the law he should be stoned. To have anything to do with images is the height of blasphemy against God, whether they be crucifixes or rosaries, for they are dead wooden things, which cannot even help themselves. Are you not ashamed of wanting to defend the saints,[944] since they are holy! But your stupidity probably recognises that they are idols and cannot even help themselves. Therefore have your preachers explain the 13th, 14th, and 15th chapters of the Book of Wisdom; there you will find your blasphemy against God: that the imperishable name of God, which is to be given to the names of his chosen ones,[945] cannot conceivably be given to stone or wood. But if this is done then it is the adultery and whoredom about which Hosea writes,[946] that just as a man breaks his marriage outwardly by penetrating the body of his neighbour with his procreative member, so the same happens in the spirit, as soon as a man amuses himself with images and created things, thereby bringing into derision him who is unlike all images and creaturely things. Therefore listen to us and circumcise the heart with all its desires: 1 Cor. 6; Rom. 2; Deut. 10; Jer. 3.[947] Therefore this is our earnest request to you, to abstain from putting into chains and fetters[948] those members who are redeemed by the blood of our Lord Jesus Christ. Surely, too, the prisoners should be released, if it is unfitting for Christians to desire to kill living creatures for the sake of a piece of wood or an image. Images can be made by men, but not even the whole world can give a man his life. For if the person who smashes an idol which stands there as a blasphemy against God is not committing any wrong but fulfilling the zeal of the Lord, then he earns his favour. But you have done wrong and have slapped God in the face far more brutally than the heathens: John 18; James 2; Luke 22; Matthew 26; Deut. 9.[949] In God's name let the prisoners free; otherwise you bear the guilt for the blood of all righteous men which

---

943. Galatians 1⁸; the reference is to the pastor Laurence Süsse of Nordhausen; cf. *Vindication*, p. 344/6 below.

944. *die h(eiligen)*.

945. Also typically Müntzer; cf. p. 47/12ff. above.

946. Hosea 4[esp. v. 14].

947. 1 Corinthians 6[15ff.]; Romans 2[29]; Deuteronomy 10[16]; Jeremiah 3 [esp. v. 17].

948. A phrase often used by Müntzer; cf. p. 101/9 above.

949. John 18[38] (Pilate); James 2[25] (Rahab); Luke 22[48] and Matthew 26[48ff.] (Judas); Deuteronomy 9[6ff.]; again this idea is very common throughout Müntzer's writings.

has ever been spilt on earth: Matthew 23; Luke 26; Matthew 5;[950] if, as is said, it is your will that they are imprisoned for the sake of wood and image; lest God's wrath be upon you. Do not sacrifice innocent blood; this does not, as you think, do God any service, but your action is taken against him himself, Luke 9; Matthew 21.[951] But if you go ahead and spill blood for this reason, then you are a terrible abomination to God and to all his chosen ones: 2 Cor. 6; Deut. 19.[952] The peace of God be with you, and may he sharpen your wits, to comprehend the truth and the righteousness which the world has not received. Dear brothers, we too were once bemused by the abomination and the loathsome brew,[953] but by his grace his truth now instructs us and impels us to seek the highest good.

68. *Müntzer to his Famulus, Ambrosius Emmen, in Allstedt. Mühlhausen, 3 September 1524.*

To his dearest boy, Ambrosius Emmen, resident[954] in Allstedt.

Greetings, my most beloved son.[955] I thought that I had made the best of provision for you with the carter, who, according to his promise, should have fetched you home eight days ago. I now see, however, that it has come to nothing through the negligence of careless people. I am really longing to see you. If the household goods are a hindrance I would not want this to put you into any jeopardy; just deposit the household goods with Peter Warmuth[956] and come to me. The people in Mühlhausen are slow, for here as elsewhere the folk are rather uncouth;[957] this is God's deliberate design, lest their mother

950. Matthew 23[34f.]; Luke 11[49f.] must be meant; Matthew 5[21ff.](?)

951. Luke 9[54f.]; Matthew 21[38ff.].

952. 2 Corinthians 6[15ff.]; Deuteronomy 19[9ff.] (the cities of refuge).

953. *grundsuppen*; another favourite term of Müntzer; the presumption in favour of Müntzer's authorship must be very strong.

954. *moranti*; tarrying(?)

955. In Latin up to this point; not Müntzer's own son! Dismer, p. 3, suggests he may have been a pupil in Zwickau, but his origins and original contact with Müntzer are still unknown; in the 1530's he was a clerk with Dr. Levin of Emden, a trustee in Magdeburg (Bräuer); the reference to *den vater* in p. 121/8 below, may or may not be to Müntzer's own father; it is the same phrase used in Nr. 63, p. 108/11, to describe Herold of Liedersdorf, and Bensing suspects the 'old man' is meant who accompanied Müntzer and was executed in Mühlhausen at the end of May 1525 (F.); cf. Elliger, p. 15.

956. Cf. Nr. 63; he was a relatively prosperous Allstedt citizen named in Müntzer's Confession (p. 437/4 below) as a founder of the Allstedt League; he died at the battle of Frankenhausen (Bräuer/Kobuch).

957. *ungemustert*.

wit should block the way of the Gospel. It helps my cause in places like this, for where cleverness[958] abounds, deviousness[959] abounds too. Although Duke John has penned a fine letter from Thuringia, it was addressed, due to his fear and diffidence about me, not to the community or even to the council, but to a hypocrite.[960] Such unseemly conduct has met with complete repudiation and rejection and indeed abuse of the aforesaid prince, and it looks to me very much as if things are about to take off.[961] Bring 'father' with you and the little pig and get the advice of this carter about the journey. That's it, then. God preserve you. Amen.

Mühlhausen, Saturday after Aegidius 1524.

Thomas Müntzer.

I have written to the intendant and to the council as well as the community, but I will never again write a word to the Judas Iscariot.[962]

69. *Conrad Grebel and Companions to Müntzer.*[963] *Zürich, 5 September 1524.*

To the truthful and faithful proclaimer of the gospel, Thomas Müntzer of Allstedt in the Harz, our faithful and beloved fellow-brother in Christ etc.

Peace, grace and mercy from God our father and Jesus Christ our lord be with us all, Amen. Dear brother Thomas, for the sake of God do not be taken aback that we address you without using titles,[964] urging you[965] like a brother to contact us by letter; and that we have taken the liberty of initiating a discussion with you without being invited to do so by you and without even being known to you. God's

---

958. *bescheydenheyt.*

959. *seynt auch vil kramantze(n).*

960. *sundern an eynen heuchler*; written in the margin; probably refers to John von Otthera, 'syndic' or city legal adviser and procurator, a counsellor of Philip of Hesse, and a supporter, but a canny one, of the reforming cause in the city (Bräuer/Kobuch); cf. Nr. 70, n. 1016.

961. *dye sache muss aufgehen.*

962. N. Rucker; cf. Nr. 66B.

963. Conrad Grebel and his 'brothers'; named towards the end of this letter, constituted the breakaway group from the Zwinglian reformation in Zürich generally known as the Swiss Brethren. The very fact that they turned to Müntzer for 'correction and instruction' indicates the growing reputation of his books and of his liturgical work in Allstedt, to which this letter was sent. It is not known whether Müntzer actually received it, or whether it was indeed ever sent.

964. Cf. Nr. 64, p. 113/21.

965. *ursachend hinfür.*

son, Jesus Christ, who presents himself as the sole master and head of all those who are to be saved, and calls us to be brothers by the one word that is common to all brothers and believers, has impelled and compelled us to form this friendship and brotherhood and to indicate the following points to you. Your authorship of the two little books[966] about the counterfeit faith was a further reason for us to write. So if you put a favourable interpretation on it, for the sake of Christ, our saviour, it may, God willing, benefit our ministry and activities.

Just as our ancestors fell away from the true God and the knowledge of Jesus Christ and upright faith in him, and from the one true divine word common to us all, from the divine observances, from Christian love and practices, and lived without God, law and gospel, imagining that they would find salvation in useless human and un-Christian observances and ceremonies, but in fact missing the mark completely, as the evangelical preachers have indicated and to some extent still indicate; so now everyone wants to be saved by a hypocritical faith,[967] without the fruits of faith, without the baptism of temptation and trial, without love and hope, without true Christian observances, continuing all the old practices of their own vices and of the ceremonies and observances common to anti-Christ, relating to baptism and the supper of Christ, despising the divine word, and revering the papal word, or the anti-papal preacher's word, which does not conform and accord with the divine word either; as far as this respect for mere men and seductions of every kind is concerned, there is more grave and grievous error now than there has been since the very beginning of the world. We, too, for our sins, were enmeshed in the same error as long as we were content to be listeners and readers of the evangelical preachers, who bear the guilt for all this. But after we resorted to Scripture as well, and studied what it said about a whole variety of points, we became rather better informed and discovered the great and grievous faults of the pastors, of ours too; that we do not earnestly beseech God every day, with constant sighing, to be led away from the destruction of all godly practices and from human abominations and come to true faith and to the observances of God. The cause of all these things is a false laxity,[968] the silencing of the divine word and its adulteration with the human. Yes, we say, that is what causes all the damage and makes all divine things take second place;[969] but there is no need for further analysis and discussion of this.

966. *On Counterfeit Faith; Protestation or Proposition.*
967. *in glichsendem glauben;* 'superficial faith' (C. H. Williams).
968. *dass faltsch schonen.*
969. *macht . . . hinderstellig.*

While we were noting and lamenting all this, your writing against false faith and baptism was brought to us;[970] as a result our knowledge was deepened and confirmed and we were thrilled to have found someone who shared our Christian understanding and who ventured to point out their faults to the evangelical preachers: their false laxity and decisions on all the main points, their erection of their own[971] or even anti-Christ's opinions above God, and against God – which is not the way in which God's ambassadors should act and preach. So by the name, strength, word, spirit and salvation which reaches all Christians through Jesus Christ, our master and our saviour, we would beseech and exhort you as a brother to strive earnestly to preach undaunted the word of God, and it alone, to introduce and defend godly observances, and them alone, and to accept what is found in the pellucid and clear words of Scripture as good and right, and that alone; rejecting, hating, and cursing every proposal,[972] word, observance or opinion deriving from men, even from your own self.

1. We understand that you have put the Mass into German and introduced new German songs and we have seen them. This cannot be right, since we find no teaching about singing in the New Testament, no precedents for it. Paul rebukes rather than praises the Corinthian scholars for murmuring in the congregation, just as if they were singing, like the sing-song way of talking[973] of the Jews and the Italians. 2. Though singing in Latin has developed without any basis in divine doctrine or apostolic precedent and observances, and has not edified anyone or achieved anything worthwhile, it will be still less edifying in German and will make for a formal, pretentious[974] faith. 3. Paul quite unambiguously[975] forbids singing in Ephesians 5 and in Colossians 3;[976] for what he says and teaches is that they should counsel and instruct one another with psalms and spiritual songs and, if one wants to sing, one should sing and give thanks in one's heart. 4. Anything that we are not taught by clear texts and precedents should be as tabu to us if it were written: Don't do that, don't sing. 5. Christ commanded his messengers only to preach the word in the New Testament, and even in the Old. Paul, too, says that the word of Christ, not the song, dwells among us; a bad singer is disheartened;[977]

---

970. The full title of the *Protestation or Proposition* ends with the words: 'and beginning with true Christian faith and baptism'. (F.)

971. *eigens gut dunken.*

972. *anschleg*; 'plan' (Williams).

973. *ire ding pronuncierend in gsangs wiss.*

974. *schinenden.*

975. *heiter.*

976. Ephesians 5[19]; Colossians 3[16].

977. *hat ein verdruss.*

a good singer is arrogant. 6. One should not add to the word what seems good to us or subtract anything from it. 7. If you want to abolish the Mass, it must not be replaced by German songs, which may be your idea or come from Luther. 8. It must be rooted out with the word and the institution of Christ. 9. For it has not been planted by God.

10. The supper of the covenant[978] was instituted and planted by Christ. 11. Only the words of Matthew 26, Mark 14, Luke 22 and 1 Corinthians 11[979] should be used; no more, no less. 12. The minister[980] from the congregation should read them from one of the evangelists or from Paul. 13. They are the words of the covenant meal that was instituted, not words of consecration. 14. It should be ordinary bread, without idols and extras.[981] 15. For the latter produce a hypocritical worship and adoration of the bread and divert attention from inwardness. It should also be an ordinary drinking vessel. 16. That would put an end to the adoration, and bring about true knowledge and understanding of the supper, since the bread is nothing but bread, but in faith is the body of Christ and incorporation with Christ and the brothers; for it is in the spirit and in love that one must eat and drink, as John points out in chapter 6[982] and the others, Paul in Corinthians 10[983] and 11, and as it is clearly taught in Acts 2.[984] So although it is only bread, if faith and brotherly love pave the way, it should be taken with joy; for its congregational use should point out to us that we are truly one bread and body and true brothers and intend to remain so. 18. But if any one should be found there who does not want to live in a brotherly way then he eats to his condemnation, for he eats without discrimination – just as he would at any other time – and dishonours love, the inner bond, and the bread, the external one. 19. For it does not exhort him about the body and blood of Christ, the testament at the cross, that he is to live and suffer for Christ and the brothers, the head and members. 20. Nor should it be administered by you. That is how the Mass became corrupt, when only one person partook; for the supper is a pointer to the covenant,[985] not a Mass or a sacrament; therefore one should not make individual use of it, on the death-bed or anywhere else; nor should the bread be shut away etc., for an individual to use, for no one

---

978. *nachtmal der vereimbarung.*
979. Matthew 26[26ff.]; Mark 14[22ff.]; Luke 22[14ff.]; 1 Corinthians 11[23ff.]
980. *diener;* 'server' (Williams).
981. *on getzen und zusatz.*
982. John 6, esp. v. 63.
983. 1 Corinthians 10[14ff.]; 11[27ff.]
984. Acts 2[46f.]
985. *antzeigung der vereimbarung;* 'expression of friendship' (Williams).

should take the bread of the covenanted for himself alone, unless he is not at one with himself, which is not true of anyone etc. 21. Nor should it be used in temples, as the whole of Scripture and history shows, for this produces a false reverence. 22. It should be used frequently and repeatedly. 23. It should not be used without applying the rule of Christ in Matthew 18;[986] if this happens, then it is not the Lord's Supper, for without it everyone would run to the externals, and the inward thing, the love, would be allowed to vanish, if brothers and false brothers attended or ate together. 24. If you should want to administer it,[987] we would like that to be without priestly clothing and the vestments of the Mass, without singing, without extras. 25. As far as the time is concerned we know that Christ gave it to the apostles during the evening meal and that the Corinthians, too, used the same time. Laying down no particular time etc., for us.

But since your information about the supper of the Lord is much more profound than ours and we are only indicating how we understand the matter; if we are not right then teach us better, and do put an end to the singing and the Mass and act according to the word, and it alone, and bring out the apostolic observances as found in the word and introduce them. If this can't be, it would be better to leave everything in Latin as it is, unchanged, not a half-way house.[988] If the correct practice cannot be introduced then do not administer it either according to the anti-Christ's priestly observances and doctrine or according to your own, but at least teach what it ought to be, as Christ does in John 6, teaching us how to eat and drink his flesh and blood; and pay no heed to corrupt practices[989] or to the anti-Christ's laxity, like these new evangelical preachers who are so very learned but have set up a real idol and planted it throughout the world. It is much better[990] that a few should be informed properly through the word of God, believing the truth and walking in the way of virtue and true observances, than that many should have a false, devious faith based on an adulterated doctrine. Although we exhort and beg you, we also hope that you will do this of your own accord, and exhort you therefore most lovingly to give a really friendly hearing to our brother[991] and admit that you too have been rather indulgent; you – and Karlstadt too – are considered by us to be the purest

---

986. Matthew 18[15-18].
987. *So du ess je zudienen.*
988. *ungeendret und gemitlet.*
989. *sicht nit an den abfal.*
990. *weger.*
991. *unserem bruder also früntlich geloset*; cf. n. 1003 below.

proclaimers[992] and preachers of the purest divine word and both of you, since you quite rightly condemn those who confuse human words and observances with divine, should really tear yourselves away from the priesthood, from benefices and from a whole number of new and old observances, from your own and from traditional opinions, and become completely pure. If your benefices are funded from interest and tithes, which are both usurious, as is the case with us, and the whole congregation does not nourish[993] you, you, too, should divest yourselves of the benefices. You know very well how a pastor should be nourished.

We have great hopes of Jacob Strauss[994] and one or two others who are held in little respect by the negligent Biblical scholars and doctors in Wittenberg. We are similarly rejected by our learned pastors, and in comparison to them; everyone hangs on their words. They achieve this by preaching a sinful, sweet Christ[995] and by their lack of proper discrimination,[996] as you point out in your books, which for those of us who are poor in spirit have been an almost overwhelming source of instruction and strength. And we are of one mind on everything except that we have heard with regret that you have set up tablets,[997] for which we find no authority or precedent in the New Testament. In the Old there certainly had to be external writing, but now in the New it should be written in the fleshly tablets of the heart, as a comparison of both Testaments demonstrates and as we are informed by Paul in 2 Corinthians 3, by Jeremiah 31, in Hebrews 8 and Ezekiel 36.[998] So unless we are wrong – and we do not think or believe we are – you should destroy the tablets again. For they have developed on the authority of personal opinion, which provides no proper nourishment, and would increase and become really idolatrous and take root throughout the world, as was the case with images. It would also create the impression that some external thing was needed and had to be introduced to replace the images in order to instruct the unlearned, although only the external word should be used, as all Biblical precedents and commandments show, and as 1 Corinthians 14 and Colossians 3[999] in particular point out. In time such learning

992. *usskünder.*

993. *ertzücht.*

994. b. in Basel, a preacher 1521/22 in the Tyrol, then in Wertheim, Eisenach; a prominent opponent of usury; cf. H. Bender, *Conrad Grebel, c. 1498–1526;* the founder of the Swiss Brethren. (Scottdale, Penn., 1971), pp. 312–15.

995. Müntzer's language adopted here.

996. *und inen gutz underscheids gebrist.*

997. *taflen;* probably two tablets bearing the Ten Commandments (Williams); painted panels seem unlikely; (F. – *Altarbilder*).

998. 2 Corinthians 3[3]; Jeremiah 31[33]; Hebrews 8[6ff.]; Ezekiel 36[26].

999. 1 Corinthians 14 (on speaking in tongues); Colossians 3[16].

from the one word might come to be rather neglected,[1000] and even if it did no damage I would never devise or introduce anything new; this would be to follow or copy the negligent, false, lax and seductive scholars; I would not devise, teach or introduce a single thing on the authority of personal opinion.

Let the word be your guide and form a Christian congregation with the help of Christ and his rules, as we find them set out in Matthew 18 and applied in the epistles. Gird[1001] yourselves with earnestness and common prayer and fasting, in faith and love, free of the law and of compulsion, and God will help you and your little sheep to be completely purified, and singing and tablets will be discarded. There is more than enough wisdom and advice in Scripture about the way to teach, govern, instruct and edify everyone, of whatever state. Any one who will not improve, and will not believe, but resists the word and the work of God and hardens himself, should not be put to death[1002] but, after Christ and his word and his rules have been preached to him and he has been admonished in the presence of the three witnesses and the congregation, he should – and we speak as those informed by the word of God – be treated as a heathen and a tax-gatherer and allowed to go his way.

One should not protect the gospel and its adherents with the sword, either, nor should they protect themselves, as we have heard from our brother[1003] that you hold and maintain. True believing Christians are sheep in the midst of wolves, sheep for slaughtering, and must be baptised into anxiety and dereliction, tribulation, persecution, suffering and dying, must be tried in the fire and find the fatherland of eternal rest not by throttling their bodily, but their spiritual (foes); then they will attain to it. They make no use of the secular sword or of war, either, for among them killing has been done away with altogether; otherwise we would still be under the old law, though (as far as we can see) even under this law war – once they had conquered the promised land – became a plague. Enough of this.

As far as baptism is concerned your writing pleases us greatly and we would like further information from you. Our information is that without Christ's rules about binding and unbinding not even an adult ought to be baptised. Scripture describes baptism as signifying that

1000. 'This kind of learning from this word only might in time become insidious' (Williams).

1001. *abbruch*; 'decision' (Williams).

1002. Cf. 1 Corinthians 5[5].

1003. The goldsmith Hans Hujuff the Younger, who had come to Zürich from Halle; on Müntzer's contacts with this family cf. Bubenheimer II, 109f.; two sisters of Hans Hujuff, Ottilia and Barbara, were nuns at the Cistercian convent in Glaucha where Müntzer was chaplain from Christmas 1522 to the beginning of March 1523.

sins are washed away by faith and the blood of Christ (converting the heart of the baptised and that of the believer before and after); that it signifies that one is, and should be, dead to sin, walking in newness of life and spirit, and that one will certainly be saved if one lives out the faith as it is signified by the inward baptism; so it is not as if the water strengthens and increases faith, as the Wittenberg scholars say, or is a profound comfort and one's last refuge on the death-bed. Likewise it is not a means of salvation, as Augustine, Tertullian, Theophylactus[1004] and Cyprian have taught, thereby slighting the faith and the suffering of Christ in regard to older adults and slighting the suffering of Christ in regard to the unbaptised little children. We take our stance on the following texts: Genesis 8; Deuteronomy 1, 30, 31; and 1 Corinthians 14; Wisdom 12; likewise 1 Peter 2; Romans 1, 2, 7, 10; Matthew 18, 19; Mark 9, 10; Luke 18 etc.;[1005] that all children who have not yet come to discriminate between the knowledge of good and evil and have not yet eaten from the tree of knowledge will certainly be saved by the suffering of Christ, the new Adam, who has restored to them the life that has been under the curse; for they would only have been subject to death and damnation if Christ had not suffered, not yet having developed the failing of (man's) broken nature; unless one can show us that Christ did not suffer for the children. As to the objection that faith is demanded of all who are to be saved, we exclude children and maintain that they are saved without faith and that they do not have faith, basing ourselves on the aforesaid texts, and we conclude from the description of baptism and from the historical accounts (according to which no child was baptised) and also from the aforesaid texts (which are the only ones to refer to how children should be treated; the rest of Scripture does not refer to children) that the baptism of children is a senseless, idolatrous abomination contrary to all Scripture, and contrary to the Papacy, too; for we find from Cyprian and Augustine that for many years after the time of the apostles believers and unbelievers were baptised side by side, indeed for some six hundred years.[1006] Since you have confessed all this ten times more clearly, and have published your protests against the baptism of children we hope that you are not acting contrary to the divine word, wisdom, and command of God, according to which one should only baptise believers, and are not baptising children. If you and Karlstadt do not write sufficiently

1004. A Byzantine exegete of the eleventh century.

1005. Genesis 8[21]; Deuteronomy 1[39]; 30[6]; 31[13]; 1 Corinthians 14[20]; Wisdom 12[1f., 18f.]; 1 Peter 2[2]; Matthew 18[1-6]; 19[13-15]; Mark 9[33-47]; 10[13-16]; Luke 18[15-17].

1006. G. H. Williams comments: 'Grebel means that adults from believing homes, like Augustine, and converts from among the unbelieving pagans were alike baptised on confession of faith.'

against the baptism of children and all that pertains to it – how and why one should baptise etc. – then I (Conrad Grebel) will pursue my salvation[1007] and complete what I have begun writing to counter all those (you excepted) who hitherto have seductively and deliberately written about baptism, defending in German the senseless, idolatrous form of child baptism, like Luther, Leo, Osiander and the Strassburghers,[1008] and one or two others who have done so in an even more shameful way. Unless God avert it, I like all my companions, am much more certain of being persecuted by the scholars etc. than by other people. We beseech you not to observe or to participate in any of the old observances of anti-Christ such as sacrament, Mass, symbols etc.; but to let the word be your guide and stay, as befits all ambassadors and above all you and Karlstadt, and you will achieve more than all the preachers from all the nations.

Regard us as your brothers and do realise that this writing has arisen out of our great joy and confidence in you for God's sake, and admonish, comfort and strengthen us, as you do so well. Pray to God the Lord on our behalf, that he will come to help us in our belief, for we would gladly believe. And if God enables us to pray, we will also intercede for you and for everyone, so that all of us may walk according to our vocations and estate. May God enable us to do this through Jesus Christ our saviour. Amen. Greet all the brothers, the pastors and the little sheep for us, that they may receive the word of faith and salvation with eagerness and hunger etc.

One more thing. We would appreciate a reply from you; and if you are publishing anything send it by this messenger or by another one. We would also like to be informed whether you and Karlstadt are of one mind. We hope so, and believe it to be the case. We commend this messenger to you, who has also brought a letter to our dear brother Karlstadt. And if you visit Karlstadt it would be a great joy to us if you would reply to us jointly. The messenger is to return to us; the balance of the money he has still to receive from us will be given him on his return.

God be with us.

Wherever we have failed to understand things properly correct and instruct us. Zürich, on the fifth day of the month of autumn in the year 1524 Conrad Grebel, Andreas Kastelberg, Felix Manz, Hans Oggenfuss, Bartholomew Pur, Heinrich Aberli and others who, God willing, are your brothers in Christ; who have written this to you and wish you, all of us, and all the little sheep, until we hear from one

1007. *min heil versuchen*; 'try my hand' (Williams).

1008. Leo Jud was Zwingli's colleague in Zürich; Osiander the Lutheran reformer of Nuremberg; the 'Strassburghers' will be Martin Bucer and Wolfgang Capito.

another again, the true word of God, true faith, love and hope with all peace and grace from God through Christ Jesus. Amen.

To Luther I, C(onrad) Grebel, had intended to write in the name of us all, exhorting him to depart from his false laxity, for which he has no Scriptural authority, and which he and others in his train have planted throughout the world. But tribulation and lack of time have not permitted this. See that you do it, as is your duty etc.

THIS LETTER IS ALSO MEANT FOR THOMAS MÜNTZER. AT ALLSTEDT IN THE HARZ.

Most heartily loved brother Thomas. Although I wrote in the name of all of us and in haste, thinking that this messenger would not wait to give us time to write to Luther, too; in fact, because of the rain, he has had to wait and stay here. So on behalf of my brothers and yours I have written to Luther, too, admonishing him to depart from the false laxity with the weak, which is what they themselves are. Andreas Castelberg has written to Karlstadt. Meanwhile our fellow-citizen and fellow-brother Hans Hujuff of Halle – who was with you for a short while – has received a letter here and a shameful little book of Luther's,[1009] which ill befits anyone who claims, like the apostles, to represent the first fruits (of the Spirit).[1010] Paul's teaching is very different: but the servant of the Lord etc.[1011] I see that he wants to hand you over to the axe and surrender you to the prince, to whom he has shackled his gospel, just as Aaron had to regard Moses as a God. As far as your pamphlet and protestation are concerned I regard you as guiltless, unless you completely reject baptism, and I do not take you to mean this but to condemn the baptism of children and the failure to understand baptism. We intend to study further from your writings and from Scripture what the water means in John 3. Hujuff's brother reports that you preached against the princes, that one should attack them with mailed fist. If it is true that you either defend war, the tablets, singing, or anything else that you did not find in the clear word – just as you did not find these afore-mentioned points – then I exhort you by the salvation which is common to us all, to see that you depart from these and all other human opinions, now and hereafter, and you will become completely pure; for in all other points you please us better than anyone else in these German-speaking, indeed in any countries. If you should fall into the hands of Luther and the dukes let these afore-mentioned points fall and stand by the others like

1009. *Letter to the Princes of Saxony*, LW 40, pp. 40ff.

1010. *der primitie wil sein*, cf. Romans 8[23] (Vg.): 'sed et nos¹ ipsi primitias spiritus habentes'.

1011. *porro servum Domini* etc.; not an exact quotation; cf. Romans 1[1]; 2 Timothy 2[24].

a hero and like a champion of God. Be strong! You have the Bible
(which Luther makes a bible, bauble, babel)[1012] as a defence against the
idolatrous Lutheran laxity which he, and the learned pastors here,
have planted throughout the world; against their devious, negligent
faith; and against their preaching, in which they do not teach Christ as
they should; although they have just opened up the gospel to the
whole word, so that people can read it for themselves, or at least
should do so, but in fact not many do, for everyone hangs on their
lips. There are barely twenty people here who believe the word of
God; others only believe in personalities, in Zwingli, Leo and their
equivalents who are regarded as scholarly in other places. And even if
you have to suffer for it, you know well that this is how it has to be.
Christ still has to suffer in his members. But he will strengthen you
and keep you firm to the end. May God be gracious to you and to us,
for our pastors are equally harsh and rage against us, denouncing us
publicly from the pulpit as scoundrels and Satans disguised as angels
of light.[1013] In time we will also see ourselves engulfed by persecution
at their hands. So intercede with God for us on this account. Once
more we exhort you – for we dare to write to you frankly because of
the love and respect we have for the clarity of your message – not to
do, teach or introduce anything on the basis of human opinions, your
own or those of others but to cast down anything that has been thus
introduced, and introduce, teach etc. only God's clear word and
observances allied with the rule of Christ, an unadulterated baptism
and an unadulterated supper (as we have touched on in the first letter
and as you know far better than a hundred of us). For if you and
Karlstadt, Jacob Strauss and Michael Stiefel[1014] do not bend every
energy to be completely pure (as my brothers and I, however, hope
you will), it would be a wretched gospel which has come into the
world. But you are far purer than our people here and those in
Wittenberg, who slide each day from one distortion of Scripture into
another and from one blindness into a still greater one. It is my belief,
my firm conviction, that they want to become real papists and popes.
Enough for now. May the Lord of hosts with his son Jesus Christ our
saviour and his spirit and his word be with you and with us all.

Conrad Grebel, Andreas Castelberg, Felix Manz, Heinrich Aberli,
Johann Panicellus,[1015] Hans Oggenfuss, Hans Hujuff, your fellow-

1012. *bibel, bubel, babel*; cf. Luther's accusation that to Müntzer the Bible 'means
nothing. It is Bible – Bauble – Babel' etc. LW 40, p. 50; *bubel* may hint, as Williams
suggests, at licentious behaviour.

1013. *Satanas in angelos lucis conversos*; cf. 2 Corinthians 11[14].

1014. A Lutheran pastor (1487–1567) who prophesied the end of the world in
1533 (F.); he was then court preacher to Count Albert von Mansfeld (Bräuer).

1015. Usually known as Hans Brötli.

countryman from Halle; your brothers and, for Luther, seven new little Müntzers.

If you are allowed to continue preaching and nothing happens to you we intend to send you a copy of our writing to Luther and his reply, if he sends us one. We have addressed an exhortation both to him and to our people here, too. In this way, unless God should hinder it, we mean to point out their faults and to have no fears about what may happen to us as a result. The only copy we have kept is of the letter which we have written to Martin, your opponent. Therefore give a friendly reception to our unlearned, unpolished writing and be assured that we have acted with genuine love, for in our message, our trials and our opponents we are identical, though you are more learned and stronger in the spirit. It is because of this very identity that we have addressed or written you at such length. If you should, God willing, greet us as your Christians and reply to us all in a long, joint letter you would make us very happy and kindle still more love for you.

70. *Müntzer to the Church in Mühlhausen. (Mühlhausen), 22 September 1524.*

Thomas Müntzer, a servant of God, to the church in Mühlhausen.[1016]

I am constrained, if I am not to eat my bread in sin,[1017] to advise you and minister to you with all possible diligence. For it is now quite clear to me that the fear of men is what prevents you from coming to any decisions. Now that almighty God has written up for you in clear, bold lettering[1018] the faults, crimes, outrages of your authorities and the whole variety of ways in which they are leading you astray, it is only right that you should make them face up to this, unveiling the

1016. Together with the radical preacher, Henry Pfeiffer, who had already led an abortive coup in Mühlhausen in 1523, Müntzer had submitted to the council in mid-September eleven articles calling for the dissolution of the old council and constitution and the establishment of a revolutionary new order based on the word of God; these demands, which attracted considerable popular support, were rejected by the council on 19 September which used a show of force to disperse the mob; it had just been warned by Luther that Müntzer would spread dangerous and false ideas; WA 15, p. 239; cf. Gritsch; pp. 123ff.; whether Luther's letter actually arrived is not known, cf. WA Br. 3, p. 328; on 27 September both Müntzer and Pfeiffer were expelled from the city; cf. Mühlhausen Articles, p. 455ff. below; a copy of this letter, incorporated in the submission to the Council of the linen-workers' guild (Fuchs, AGBM II, 29f.) was forwarded to the Elector of Saxony and his brother by Dr John von Otthera (Bräuer-Kobuch); cf. Letter 68, n. 960; cf. Tom Scott, 'The "Volksreformation" of Thomas Müntzer ...', JEH 34 (1983), 203.

1017. Cf. Proverbs 4[17].

1018. *mit groben buchstaben.*

full depths of these crimes,[1019] and admonishing them fraternally that to avoid the evil to come they should, for God's sake, accept their dismissal in the interests of you all.

If,[1020] however, they display an arrogant spirit, pursuing their selfish ends and preferring what seems to benefit them and their collective interests; and if they do not renounce office in your favour and make way for the word and for your exercise of justice,[1021] then you should do your duty according to the divine word and have all their crimes, faults, wickedness and all the harm they have done put into print, arraigning such stubborn-headed people before the whole world, and documenting in your accusation the evil they have done, so that you can convict them. There is no doubt that you will be able to confront your authorities with a hundred faults and make them face up to them, so no one will blame you in the slightest[1022] or revile you. For what has alerted you to the full extent of their wickedness is their denunciation of the word of God as heresy; they have no intention of embracing it but rather sacrifice the ministers of the word on the cross.[1023]

So if it does appear in print for the whole world to see, then you can count on the understanding of all Christian people.[1024] They will say: Look, these pious folk have shown far too much patience. They have kept to the divine commandment. So the Christian people will speak of you as an elect people, Deuteronomy 4, 'Look this is a wise people; it is a discerning people; a great people will arise from it. It is a people that will hazard all for God. It will do what is right and will not fear the devil or the world with all its plots, devices and pomposity.'[1025]

Thus by putting it into print – and I will be glad to be of assistance in this – you will be able to argue your case before other governments, and then the turncoat rabble of the godless, when they have retreated,[1026] will be unable to find an honourable refuge in any

1019. *das ir mit weysslich geheymniss solcher mishandelunge zu entdecken.*

1020. *Nemen*; probably a slip of the pen (F.); or Müntzer has forgotten by the end of the sentence that it began: 'If they take it amiss . . .,' and pursued a different line of thought.

1021. *euer rechtfertigunge.*

1022. *do man euch in den geringsten meytheln nicht thadeln wert.*

1023. *aufs crutz opfern.*

1024. Müntzer gave similar advice to the village of Horsmar in the Mühlhausen Articles, cf. p. 457/16ff.; Henry Pfeiffer actually tried to have a denunciation of the Mühlhausen authorities printed in Nuremberg; cf. S. Bräuer's important article, 'Thomas Müntzers Selbstverständnis als Schriftsteller', in *Reform, Reformation und Revolution*, ed. S. Hoyer (Leipzig, 1980), pp. 224–32, esp. p. 228f.

1025. A very loose paraphrase of Deuteronomy 4[6-8] (Vg.).

1026. The two burgomasters who fled Mühlhausen: Johann Wettich and Sebastian Rodemann.

other city. For the common man (God be praised) is acknowledging the truth almost everywhere.[1027] Thus you will render them harmless,[1028] so that they cannot ruffle a hair of your head. Luke 12.[1029]

See that you do not despise the counsel of the wisdom of the divine word, Proverbs 1.[1030] Otherwise, because of your hypocrisy, you will have to suffer for the sake of the devil what, with God on your side, you could have endured easily and without undue distress etc. With that, may God preserve you; he is surely with you. Amen.

The day of Maurice, in the year of Christ 1524.

71. *Müntzer to Christopher Meinhard in Eisleben. (End of November/mid-December 1524).*[1031]

Thomas Müntzer to his dearest brother, Christopher Meinhard,[1032] resident in Eisleben.

Peace in the midst of peacelessness be with you, my dear brother Christopher. Our cause has become like a[1033] beautiful golden ear of wheat, which attracts the love of clever men when they have it in their grasp, but which they cannot imagine ever emerging again, once it has been cast into the earth, John 12.[1034]

You have already heard, a real warning from God,[1035] that Doctor Justus Jonas of Wittenberg excelled himself in entering the lists[1036] against me. Luther's writing,[1037] no less, was triggered off by him, and it is no great surprise to me that I stink so much in the nose of the world, which is shameful for those who fear God but irreparably

1027. This letter reflects the excitement as the Peasants' War gets under way; note Müntzer's tendency to see the cause of the 'common man' and of the 'truth' as identical; cf. Nr. 68, pp. 120/21–121/2.

1028. *untuchtigk.*

1029. *keyn herlin kromen werden;* Luke 12⁷; a millenarian note.

1030. Proverbs 1²⁴ᶠᶠ.

1031. G. Baring, 'Hans Denck und Thomas Müntzer in Nürnberg', ARG 50 (1959), p. 154 dates it at the beginning of December; Müntzer's movements in South Germany and Switzerland are uncertain after a brief stay in Nuremberg to see to the printing of the *Highly Provoked Vindication,* cf. p. 324; the clipped, telescoped, staccato sentences suggest haste; the original is lost.

1032. *Christophoro N*[omen] name (Bräuer/Kobuch); on Meinhard cf. Nrs. 47, 49.

1033. lit. 'the'.

1034. John 12²⁴.

1035. *Ir seid vorhin unterricht durch ermanung Gottes.*

1036. *den plan behalten.*

1037. Presumably the *Letter to the Princes of Saxony,* cf. Nr. 69, n. 1009; another possibility is his letter to Mühlhausen, WA 15, 230–40; Jonas had been cordially greeted by Müntzer in July 1523, cf. Letter 40 on Jonas and Müntzer: cf. Elliger, p. 217f.

miserable and shameful for the soft-living brothers and pussyfoots.[1038] I know how my name tastes as a green shoot before it develops ears. But there are barley pricks on it; the barley bread has to be ground down.[1039] The law will overthrow the godless; all their lamenting will not help them. If once before I scolded them with fire-arms,[1040] now I will thunder against them with God in heaven. They have indulged in their rascally behaviour for long enough; God instructs us clearly that there will be no excuse for them.

I have preached publicly before many hundreds of people, yet they accuse me of crawling into a corner etc.[1041] I have had my teachings published in Nuremberg and they want to curry favour with the Roman Empire by suppressing them.[1042] There is no case for me to answer.

It won't do to say: It's all very well for him to write or to preach; if he had stayed with us his teaching would no doubt have been refuted etc.[1043] I thank God that my grounds for complaint against them are far better than those of Samson against the Philistines etc.[1044] My heart remains undaunted in God my saviour; may he preserve you for ever. Amen. If you can manage it, help me with my sustenance in any way you can.[1045] But if this vexes you then I don't want a cent. Greet John N.; whether he is hostile or favourable to me he will still have to testify for the cause.[1046] He is troubled too much by the wicked and the scandal they cause. Although he may have much to lose before he reaches illumination, not one word proclaimed to him shall fall by the wayside. Ah, how you do carry on when the mask of this devious world has to be lowered! But it has to be; even if they could devour iron,[1047] I still intend to unmask them utterly and awesomely.[1048]

1038. *der sanftlebenden brüder und leisetrettern*; text amended by Bräuer/Kobuch; reminiscent of the title of the *Highly Provoked Vindication and Refutation of the unspiritual, soft-living Flesh in Wittenberg*; cf. also p. 278/30 below.

1039. *gebrochen werden.*

1040. *gescholten mit büchsen*; F. suggests *geschossen*, 'fired'; or should we read *büchern*, with books? The original is missing and the text appears to be corrupt; if we do abide by the reading the 'firing of muskets' should not be taken literally; Müntzer still trusts in his words to cow his opponents; cf. p.136/3f. below; Bräuer/Kobuch adduce an interesting parallel: *mit worten er nit schalt, er schalt in aber mit dem swerte*; Dan. 3502; in M. Lexer, *Mittelhochdeutsches Handwörterbuch*, Bd. 2 (Leipzig, 1874), 696.

1041. Luther wrote Frederick the Wise as early as 21 May: 'That Satan in Allstedt ... makes loud enough threats from his little corner'. (F.)

1042. Cf. n. 1031 above; virtually every copy was confiscated by the Council.

1043. *verlegt sein* in sense of *widerlegt* (refuted).

1044. Judges 14⁴, 15³.

1045. Cf Nr. 67, p. 117/32ff.

1046. *verjehen*; unidentified, probably John Zeiss; cf. Bräuer, LJ 37 (1971), 131.

1047. Cf. Job 41²⁷.

1048. *aufs aller geringste unaussprechlich entbremsen*; apparently the last word only

Note.

I could certainly have started a fine old game with the folk from N(uremberg) if I had wanted to stir up trouble, as this lying world accuses me of doing. But I will certainly make cowards of all my opponents by my words and they will not be able to hide it. Many of the folk in N(uremberg) urged me to preach, but I answered that I had not come to do that, but to testify to my faith in print. When the authorities heard of this, their ears began to jangle; for they love prosperous days. The sweat of the working people[1049] tastes sweet, sweet to them, but it will turn into bitter gall. And then no consultations or mock battles will avail them. The truth will out. No counterfeit enthusiasm for the gospel will avail them. The people are hungry; they must eat; they intend to eat, as Amos says, and Matthew 5, too.[1050]

72. *Müntzer to unknown supporters in Allstedt. Mühlhausen, March 1525(?).*

May the peace of Christ, to which the world is alien,[1051] be with you, most beloved brothers in the Lord. I have heard about the extent of your fall[1052] and can assess this and the terrors of your conscience fairly accurately from the reliable reports I have obtained. I am now constrained to comfort you on these matters – setting before you the holy example of Abraham, a true model and masterly vessel[1053] of divine training in faith. For everything said about him in Holy Scripture is presented[1054] to us not because of his work but as a judgement[1055] on our faith lest we think that God will let us persist in our senseless raging, our hectic, crude life, mocking God and those who are his by the glittering pretence of our counterfeit faith. Paul explains to the Romans in chapter 4 why the Holy Bible so often presents Abraham to us as an example, showing hope contending against hope in him.[1056] For someone who believes in God will often

---

occurs here; cf. *Grimm*, III, 504; *bremse* in this period generally means 'muzzle' and the meaning, 'unmuzzling' = 'unmasking' appears possible in this context.

1049. *handwerksleute*.

1050. Amos 8[11]; Matthew 5[6].

1051. *dem die welt feynd ist*; not *freund* (F.) (Bräuer/Kobuch).

1052. *fahl*; cf. *abfalhen*, p. 137/7 below; Nr.69, n. 989.

1053. *kunstreich werkgefess*.

1054. *vorgewant*.

1055. *umb rechtfertigung unsers glaubens*; cf. Romans 4[22f]; perhaps one should translate: 'for the righteousness of our faith'.

1056. Romans 4[18].

allow himself to conclude – to the extent that the flesh is still alive in him – that our present cause[1057] will not withstand the raging of the tyrants – just like you, my dear brothers, at the service when I was preaching and a thunderstorm passed by overhead. But why should I crave the right to reprove you? You had the pledge of blessedness, the spirit of God (Ephesians[1058] 1), and I warned you against falling away in the time of the visitation by God,[1059] but you imagined this could not be well founded because God let the tyrants vaunt their[1060] power over you. So you fled[1061] the chastisement of the benevolent fatherly rod and preferred, to your burning shame, to seek relief from the messenger of the devil. The result was the protracted agony of your conscience, for you polluted yourselves shamefully in the devil's bath, the lake of fire,[1062] as Revelations 20 puts it. The false prophets will have to go swimming soon enough with their Nimrod,[1063] but you can still be certain of escaping that sort of pleasure bath. If you are willing to recognise your fall, you can certainly still be helped; as you can see from the judgement on Jezebel in Revelation, chapter 2.[1064] You can find comfort, too, in Abraham's fear, Genesis 12[1065] and in the perseverance[1066] of all the saints. Until someone becomes aware of this he cannot be reached because of the evil, just as you tottered around in it for a while.[1067] The distress caused by a fall like this, though, ought to sadden you into penitence. If, as a result of this act of desertion, you let everything slip,[1068] you will just wither away completely; may God in his loving-kindness preserve you from this. Amen. This then is my reason for writing to you again in Christ Jesus. Mühlhausen, in MCCCCC and XXV year.[1069]

Thomas Müntzer, a servant of God to his dear brothers.

1057. *das iczige sach.*

1058. Ephesians 1[13f.]

1059. Jeremiah 46[21]; 50[31].

1060. *mutwilligen.*

1061. lit. 'fell away from'.

1062. *zun warme borne*; Revelation 20[10].

1063. Cf. Nr. 31, n. 273; Müntzer seems to be using a coded language here; presumably the Lutherans are meant, and Nimrod represents the princes.

1064. Revelation 2[20-9].

1065. Genesis 12[4]; there is no explicit reference to the fear of God, but Abraham's obedience will be meant.

1066. *langmutigkeit.*

1067. *ists ym nit vor ubel zu haben, das yr etwan strauchelt.*

1068. *aller ding hinfellig sein.*

1069. Böhmer-Kirn date the letter in August 1524; Bensing, op. cit. p. 83, n. 93, assumes that they contacted him again after his return from South Germany (February 1525). (F.)

1056. Romans 4[18].

73. *George Witzel[1070] to Müntzer. Wenigenlupnitz, 11 March 1525.*

George Witzel to Thomas Müntzer, Greetings.

Although you have been admonished often enough, Müntzer, to return to a saner frame of mind, there is a reason why I, too, sound that call 'Repent' so frequently in your ears. The best of laws stipulates that a factious man should be shunned after one or two admonitions.[1071] On the other hand, as long as there is any hope that you may listen, what objection can there be to a reiteration of the admonition? To begin with, I must ask you what in the name of the immortal God has made you the sort of person you are, what saga has stirred you up? You are not even ashamed of it. What sort of person, you say? One deserving of every ill. Am I lying if I speak of a man of blood, who reveres neither God nor man, who boasts at the top of his voice that Christ has come in the flesh but at the same time prepares to waylay Christ? But why do you grow pale? Why do you gnash your teeth? Is it because a legend is being told about you?[1072] But my licence in reproving you so temptestuously is offensive to you and does the reprover no credit. My real intention is to cure you. Still, if I have spoken a little harshly it is excusable. Yet how can I cure you more effectively than by hoping that your mind (which the copulation of the serpent vitiated) may be healed by holy Israel, by the victor over the serpent, by our king Jesus Christ? Assuredly Leviathan in his ocean has made use of you. You have been a chosen vessel of our adversary, if only you would admit it. If you will not admit it it is idle for me to desire your cure. But this is what I ask with all the energy at my command. Admit it. Admit it, Müntzer, if you can. Submit, so that you may be saved. Behold, the hands of the Lord are full of hyacinths and distil the finest myrrh to restore health.[1073] You have been struck down by the worst of ulcers but if you implore the healer he is at hand and will speedily heal the wound caused by this plague, cicatrising it, and taking away the pus. Only admit the disease and

1070. Witzel was a preacher of Erasmian style, who after initially being attracted by the Reformation returned to the Old Church in the 1530s. He was expelled from his benefice after the suppression of the Peasants' War; cf. Winfried Trusen, *Um die Reform und Einheit der Kirche* (Münster, 1957), p. 11f.; this letter was not published until long after the event in 1534, when he had every interest in demonstrating that he had distanced himself from Müntzer in unmistakable manner prior to the Peasants' War; as an attempt to engage in dialogue it is hardly convincing; the final clauses in particular appear to reflect the knowledge and perspectives of a later period; cf. the forthcoming analysis by Bräuer/Kobuch.

1071. Titus 3[10]; Matthew 18[15-18]; cf. Nr. 69, n. 986.

1072. Cf. Horace, Sermones l, i, 69 (Tantalus, desperately yearns for water; '*quid rides? mutato nomine de te fabula narratur*').

1073. Song of Songs 5[5, 14] (Vg.)

desire to be relieved of it. Do not be ashamed, because of reluctance that something may be uncovered during the healing process; rather be ashamed that it will be impossible to reveal the whole mire[1074] of your tragedy. Secondly I ask you, by the mercy of God, unless your fracture be irremediable, to face seriously what is wrong and put yourself in the hands of the doctor who comes from the bosom of the father. If you have even a glimmering of fear of him then cease to disrupt the straight ways of the Lord and turn back from your very evil designs and plans. If, however, you refuse to admit your guilt again, or even try to wash it away what will be the use of our doctor, Jesus? But what mortal man can deny that you need him? If you yourself dare to deny this, surely this means that no one in the entire world is more insane or shameless than you? I ask you and beseech you again and again, by the salvation of your soul and the common inheritance in the heavens, reserved for all the pious; if it is at all possible, look into yourself. Cast off, tread underfoot, throw away, destroy, reduce to nothing the inclination of your heart, that blackest monster, which depraves everything upright. And may Christ Jesus, that strong and potent David, incite you to this, and help you; whom the unclean spirits flee in every place and abhor, lest they be cast out by him. Müntzer, allow yourself to be cleansed! What does it matter if the demon snatches at you while being cast out and makes you writhe? We will all congratulate you and thank God on your behalf if you acquiesce in our warnings and prayers; What's more you will become the dearest of brothers in our hearts, with whom in future we will be glad to share everything. Only one thing is needed: see to it that you become a different person and blush at your old name. May God grant, according to the riches of his glory, that you may be led by his spirit to desire and attain these things, and to him alone be glory in eternity. Amen.

Lupnitz XI March in the year MDXXV.

Let Müntzer revoke:
The plans of public sedition, in which he is obviously engaged. Likewise the covenant of the gospel as a pretext for opposing everyone who declines to join him.

His writings and teachings about putting to death the ungodly, and let him interpret more fairly the scriptural texts he has usurped to justify this.

His deeds and instructions to others about the violent destruction of temples, statues and altars. And indeed let him take his hands off the other things he has reached for on the pretext of the gospel.

1074. *totam tuae tragoediae lernam*; a reference to the marsh of Lerna, near Argos?

His vile effusions against divinely inspired scripture. His boasts about spirits of some kind. Let him either explain this matter more clearly or cease to make such claims.

His inventions of fantastic visions and dreams etc.

74. *The Christian Community in Langensalza to Pfeiffer. Langensalza, 26 April 1525.*[1075]

To be handed to our dear brother in Mühlhausen.

Dear brother, we have understood your writing[1076] and your offer, thank you cordially for your offer and hope, God willing, to come to a peaceful resolution of our affairs ourselves. God's blessing be with you, then.

26 April in the year 1525.

The Christian Community of Salza.

75. *Müntzer to the people of Allstedt.*[1077] *1525 (c. 26, 27 April).*

May the pure fear of God be with you, dear brothers. How long are you going to slumber, how long are you going to resist God's will[1078] because, in your estimation, he has forsaken you? Ah, how often did I tell you that it had to be like this, that God cannot reveal himself in any other way, that you must remain unperturbed.[1079] If you fail to do so, then your sacrifice is in vain, your heart-sad, heart-felt suffering.[1080] You would then have to start suffering all over again. I tell you this, that if you are unwilling to suffer for the sake of God, then you will have to be martyrs for the devil. So watch out, don't be

1075. On the back: Answer to the (Christian – crossed out) brother in Mühlhausen; almost certainly Pfeiffer, not Müntzer is meant; it is doubtful if it should be included in Müntzer's correspondence.

1076. The letter is lost; Langensalza was not far from Mühlhausen to which Müntzer had once again returned (February–May 1525); hearing that members of his League were in difficulty there Pfeiffer and he had set out with some 400 armed men flying the white flag with the rainbow to help them but found on his arrival, as this letter suggests, that they had resolved the problem themselves; cf. Gritsch, p. 144; Gess, *Akten und Briefe* II, 760; Elliger, pp. 698ff.

1077. One of Müntzer's most famous letters; Luther had it published as *A Shocking History and God's Judgement on Thomas Müntzer*, WA 18, 367; a partial English trs. in E. G. Rupp and B. Drewery (edd.), *Martin Luther* (London, 1970), p. 120f.

1078. *Gott seyn willens nit gestendigk.*

1079. *gelassen.*

1080. *euer herzbetruebtes herzeleyd.*

downcast, or negligent, or flatter any longer the perverted phantasts, the godless evil-doers;[1081] make a start and fight the fight of the Lord! It is high time; keep all your brothers at it, so that they do not scorn the divine testimony and perish as a result. The whole of Germany, France, Italy is awake; the master[1082] wants to set the game in motion, the evil-doers are for it. At Fulda four abbeys were laid waste during Easter week, the peasants in the Klettgau and the Hegau in the Black Forest have risen, three thousand strong, and the size of the peasant host[1083] is growing all the time. My only worry is that the foolish people will agree to a false treaty, because they do not yet realise the gravity of the situation.

Even if there are only three of you whose trust in God is unperturbable and who seek his name and honour alone, you need have no fear of a hundred thousand. So go to it, go to it, go to it! The time has come, the evil-doers are running like scared dogs! Alert the brothers, so that they may be at peace, and testify to their conversion.[1084] It is absolutely crucial – absolutely necessary![1085] Go to it, go to it, go to it! Show no pity, even though Esau suggest kind words to you, Genesis 33.[1086] Pay no attention to the cries of the godless. They will entreat you ever so warmly, they will whimper and wheedle like children. Show no pity, as God has commanded in the words of Moses, Deuteronomy 7;[1087] and he has revealed the same thing to us too. Alert the villages and towns and especially the mine-workers and other good fellows[1088] who will be of use. We cannot slumber any longer.

You see, just as I was writing these words, a message came to me from Salza that the people there want to get hold of the administrator of Duke George from the castle, because he wanted to kill three of them secretly.[1089] The peasants of Eichsfeld have commenced hostile action against their Junkers; in brief, they want no favours from them.[1090] There are many similar happenings to show you the way. You must go to it, go to it, go to it! The time has come. Let Balthasar

1081. Perhaps a reference to Jodocus Kern, sent by Luther to Allstedt; WA Br. 3, 470.

1082. *der meyster will spiel machen*; on *meyster* cf. *Exposé*, p. 262/1f. above.

1083. *der hauf.*

1084. *das sie zur fried kommen und ir bewegung gezeugnus holen.*

1085. *Est ist uber dye mas hoch hoch von noethen.*

1086. Genesis 33⁴.

1087. Deuteronomy 7¹⁻⁵.

1088. *bursse*; groups (F.)

1089. Cf. Nr. 74; the reference is to Sittich von Berlepsch; cf. Elliger, p. 700.

1090. *sie wollen ir keyn gnade haben*; on Friday, 28 April, laden with eight or nine carts full of booty, an Eichsfeld contingent joined the Mühlhausen force at Görmar (F.)

and Bartel Krump, Valentin and Bischof lead the dance![1091] Let this letter go on to the miners. My printer[1092] is coming in the next few days, I've just been told. There is nothing else I can do at the moment, or I would instruct the brothers so thoroughly, that their heart would be much larger than all the castles and weapons of the godless evil-doers throughout the world.

Go to it, go to it, while the fire is hot! Don't let your sword grow cold, don't let it hang down limply! Hammer away ding-dong on the anvils of Nimrod,[1093] cast down their tower to the ground! As long as they live it is impossible for you to rid yourselves of the fear of men. One cannot say anything to you about God as long as they rule over you. Go to it, go to it, while it is day! God goes before you; follow, follow! The whole business can be read up in Matthew 24, Ezekiel 34, Daniel 7, Ezra 16, Revelation 6, and all these texts are explained by Romans 13.[1094]

So do not be deterred. God is with you, as it is written in 2 Chronicles.[1095] This is what God says, 'You should have no fear. You should not shrink from this great host; it is not your fight, but the Lord's. It is not you who fight; stand up like men. Above you, you will see the Lord helping.' When Jehoshaphat heard these words he collapsed. So do the same, with the help of God; and may he strengthen you in the true faith, with no fear of men. Amen.

Mühlhausen in the year 1525.

Thomas Müntzer, a servant of God against the godless.

76. *Statements of captured peasants from Merxleben about a letter of 27 April 1525 written from Volkenroda by Müntzer or the brothers in Mühlhausen to the rebels in Merxleben, 28 July, 1 September 1525.*[1096]

1091. Balthasar Stübener, Bartel Krump, Valentin Krump, and Bischoff from Wolferode; Stübener was regarded as the ring-leader; cf. Müntzer's Confession, p. 000 (F.); even after defeat Bischoff, the pastor in Wolferode, continued to urge resistance to the authorities; on the League members cf. S. Bräuer, '*Thomas Müntzer und der Allstedter Bund*', 85–102.

1092. Unknown; no printed works have survived from this period.

1093. The princes and lords; cf. Genesis 10[8f.] and Nr. 72, n. 1063.

1094. Matthew 24 begins with the prophecy of the destruction of the Temple and is apocalyptic in character throughout; Ezekiel 34 deals with the false and true shepherds and the covenant of peace; Daniel 7 with the kingdom of the saints; Ezra 10 (not 16) with Israel's treason in marrying foreign wives; Revelation 6 with the opening of the seven seals and the great day of wrath; cf. Romans 13[1ff.], as interpreted by Müntzer, Nr. 44, n. 505.

1095. Cf. 2 Chronicles 20[15–18].

1096. The original is lost; this report in the Dresden archives of the interrogation of the Merxleben peasants is the only testimony of its existence and contents.

A.   On the Friday after St. Anne's Day in the year etc. 25 Kunz Rudolph was interrogated in the chamber[1097] at Salza and said the following:

1. . . .

2.   Says, Fritz Schrotter had a letter read out to the six men; it had come to them from Mühlhausen, being brought by Claus Nickel, whom the six men had sent to the Mühlhausen band at Volkenroda. The pastor read this letter to the six men on the meadow; he expects Schrotter's wife will still have the letter.

3.   Says, that the letter's contents were, among other things, that one should keep a close watch for the administrator from Salza,[1098] to prevent him escaping, the tyrant, the bloodhound, for if he got away from Salza, things would not go well.[1099]

B.   In the year etc. 25, on Friday, St. Aegidius' Day. Berthold Bote, also from Merxleben was interrogated about the following points in the chamber at Salza, in the presence of Hartman Goldacker, Sittich von Berlepsch, Gangolph von Kirchheilingen, Christopher von Reckenrode, the official's clerk, and the landknecht:[1100]

1. . . .

2. . . .

3. . . .

4.   Was asked whom the congregation sent to the Mühlhausen host at Volkenroda. Says, it was Claus Nickel that they sent there; he had brought a letter from the Mühlhausen host. The pastor of the congregation read out this letter on the meadow in front of the bakery. What he remembered of it was that Müntzer ordered them to tear down all the castles and homes of the nobility and to leave nothing standing. Secondly the letter included the statement that they should keep a close watch for the administrator, for the tyrant, the bloodhound, so that he did not escape from Salza, for things would not go well, if he got out of Salza; he should be struck dead.

77.   *Müntzer to the people of Frankenhausen. Görmar near Mühlhausen, 29 April 1525.*

To the Frankenhausen community[1101] our very dearest brothers. May the spirit of the true and pure fear of God and of his valiant

----

1097. *hoffstuben*; no torture was used.

1098. Sittich von Berlepsch; cf. Nrs. 74, 75 above.

1099. It was assumed he would use the bridge over the river Unstrut at Merxleben to make good his escape. (F.)

1100. The lowest grade of official.

1101. *gemeine*; cf. Elliger, pp. 709, 733.

strength be with you, my very dearest brothers. We have heard through your letter that we should send two hundred men to help you. We reply that we will not send a small band like that to you but rather that everyone, everyone, as many as we have, wants to come to you, marching through all the country-side, and on the way placing ourselves at your disposal.[1102] You need fear no one. The voice of the Lord says: Look, the strength of my needy people will be increased, who will dare attack them?[1103] So be bold and put your trust in God alone, and he will endow your small band with more strength that you would ever believe. We want to do all we can for you so that our band will enable you to grow in truth and justice to the utmost of our ability[1104] through Jesus Christ. But do see that no fine words persuade you to show a fraudulent[1105] clemency, and your cause will surely prevail.

Görmar, near Mühlhausen, on the eve of Misericordia domini 1525.

The community of Christians[1106] in the field at Mühlhausen.

78. *The Mühlhausen community[1107] to the Langensalza community. In the field near Ebeleben, 30 April 1525.*

To our dear brothers, the whole community of Salza.

May the divine favour, and joy in the holy spirit be with you, our very dearest [brothers]. It has come to our ears that you are not only setting up the kingdom of Saul under your perverse leaders but the pseudo-government of Agag.[1108] None of us brothers can view this with any favour. Since it is by your doing that we have been stirred to action[1109] you must not act so childishly. The evil-doer whom you have recaptured[1110] we would ask you to put to death or at least to

1102. The German is difficult: *wollen zu euch kommen zu eynem durchzog uberall thun und ym itzygem wege unss zu euch vorfugen wyl[le]ns.*

1103. *wehr wyl sich an dye meinen machen?*

1104. *das yhr der warheyt und gerechtigkeyt [z]u[ne]mt von unss[erm haufen] na[c]h [a]llem [u]nss[er]m vormugen* (text reconstructed by Bräuer/Kobuch).

1105. *beschyssnen.*

1106. *Dye gmayne christen.*

1107. Content and style suggest Müntzer as the author.

1108. *das scheinpar regiment Hagag;* in 1 Samuel 15 Saul is condemned by Samuel for disobeying God by sparing Agag; the references seems to be to the dangers of clemency.

1109. *Nachdem ir durch eur verursachunge uns erregt;* hearing of the rising in Langensalza they had set out to help them; Elliger, p. 698.

1110. Sittich von Berlepsch; cf. Nr. 76.

...,[1111] otherwise, contrary to God's warning, you will be warming a serpent in your bosom and turning a wolf into a sheep.[1112] Be on the watch, too, for false preachers; this is our earnest, Christian entreaty. Keep a firm grip on Helbolt.[1113] May our king Jesus Christ bless you, then. Amen.

From the field[1114] at Ebeleben in the year of Christ 1525 on Misericordia domini.

The whole community there.

79. *Müntzer to Count Günther von Schwarzburg.[1115] On the field near Duderstadt, 4 May 1525.*

To Günther the younger, the leader of the Christian congregation in the Schwarzburg territories, to our dear brother in the Lord.

The eternal, unwavering favour of God be with you, my very dearest brother. Your message has been received by our brothers, and your brothers Kurt von Dittichenrode Heinrich Hake, Christopher von Altendorf and Balthasar von Bendeleben[1116] have been received into our covenant, and we have promised them Christian freedom from any molestation or unfair impositions and I have given them a letter of safe-conduct in my own hand, providing it transpires that they do not hinder the righteousness of God or persecute the preachers. But when this has been done it would be right for them voluntarily to offer the congregation provisions for its journeying[1117] and to abstain humbly from hindering Christian unity in the future. I felt I ought to draw this to the attention of your good self in this letter;

1111. *peynigen oder uffs wenigst*; a verb has been omitted.

1112. One of Aesop's fables refers to a hen which hatched out some snake's eggs to the scorn of a swallow which said: 'You fool, why do you rear creatures that ... will make you the first victim of their evil-doing?' Aesop's Fables, Nr. 97; the theme of a man warming or sheltering a snake in his bosom and then being bitten is a common sixteenth-century pictorial or literary image for a benefactor being 'stung'; cf. *Emblemata*, pp. 637ff.

1113. *Den Helbolt*; not known; could Johannes Helmolt be meant, cf. p. 459, n. 1 below?

1114. *aussem felde*.

1115. Cf. Letters 81, 87; Count Günther of Schwarzburg near Sondershausen (1499–1552); joined the League on 30 April 1525 (Bräuer/Kobuch).

1116. Kurt von Dittichenrode, whose seat of Straussberg was near Sondershausen; Heinrich Hake from Tilleda; Christopher von Altendorf from Berga (near Kelbra); Balthasar von Bendeleben from Ichstedt (Bräuer/Kobuch).

1117. *willige nahrung*; perhaps *karung* = compensation. (F.)

may all the blessing of the knowledge of the divine will be yours.

In the field near Duderstadt on the Thursday after Walpurgis in the year of Christ 1525.

Thomas Müntzer, a servant of God.

80. *The Peasants from the district of Sangerhausen[1118] to Müntzer. Frankenhausen, 6 May 1525.*

To Thomas Müntzer, our reverend father in God and trusty master, a friendly greeting.

Reverend sir, our father in God, dear master Thomas Müntzer! We poor country folk from the villages of the whole district[1119] of Sangerhausen want you to know that we country folk, together with the town of Sangerhausen, the council and the bailiff,[1120], have vowed[1121] and sworn a divine covenant, in the love of God and the holy gospel, being ready to offer up our bodies and lives for it. The Naumburg district[1122] has done the same. Further some of us have returned home honourably and with due leave, but some have also deserted us dishonourably and without our knowledge etc. Further they were all forced to go to the castle at Sangerhausen and had to leave all their weapons in the castle. Further they had to take pledges[1123] that they would devote their lives and goods to helping to pursue us. Moreover, the bailiff took away from the men of Riestedt and Blankenheim[1124] all the cattle, sheep, cows, pigs and horses which they had captured at Caldenborn[1125] and intended to add to our booty. We trust that you will give this your best attention and beg you for the sake of God to recognise that we have stuck it out here for a long time under great difficultes, that our poor wives and children have to spend their days and nights in the fields and in the woods because of their great fear of the authorities.

We also got a message today that some folk from the Mansfeld

1118. Cf. Nrs. 54, 57, 59; Elliger, pp. 721ff.

1119. *phleghe.*

1120. Melchior von Kutzleben; cf. Nr. 57, n. 742.

1121. geholtt = *gehuldigt.* (F.)

1122. Beyernaumburg must be meant; the district probably included the villages of Emseloh, Holdenstedt, Liedersdorf, Nienstedt, Sotterhausen. (F.)

1123. *zeychen zcu sych nemhen.*

1124. Both villages are to the north-east of Sangerhausen. (F.)

1125. A monastery of the Augustinian Canons between Sangerhausen and Eisleben.

territories[1126] wanted to flee here because of their fear of the tyrants and were cut to pieces on the way – may God have mercy on them. In haste on the Saturday after Misericordia domini at Frankenhausen.

The whole district of Sangerhausen begs for help as soon as humanly possible to get rid of the [lords] of Sangerhausen because of their ruthlessness. Beg in the name of God for a godly answer, which we will gladly and whole-heartedly accept.

80a. The Frankenhausen Host to the Mühlhausen Community.[1127]
Frankenhausen, 7 May 1525.

To our dear Christian fathers and brothers, gathered at Mühlhausen, etc.

The grace of the most high God, the fear and strength of his holy spirit, be with you all, dear brothers. From our recent letter you heard of our urgent concern,[1128] especially about the extreme threat to us from the power and might of the mounted forces and other warlike preparations of the tyrant at Heldrungen,[1129] Duke George and others. They have presumed so far to assemble these, with the relentless aim of destroying us poor Christians and with us the Christian truth; we are quite unable to resist these opposing forces without your help and support and that of God.[1130]

We have also let you know the situation and resources of our host: that we lack the resources to counter our opponents, and that – now as before – we most earnestly request your help and support. So once again we would reply to your letter and your encouraging promises with the request that you spare no effort to fulfil your promise and your kind written undertaking by speeding on your way to us with

1126. On 5 May Count Albert had set Osterhausen on fire and killed twenty peasants, or miners.

1127. This letter reports a request for help of 29 April, to which Letter 77 is a reply; found among Müntzer's papers, it must have been forewarded to him by the Mühlhausen community; after the battle of Frankenhausen it came into the possession of Philip of Hesse and is now in the Hessisches Staatsarchiv Marburg, Politisches Archiv, Nr. 209, Bl.2r-v; text as amended by Bräuer/Kobuch from Fuchs, AGBM II, 235f., Nr. 1365; cf. Elliger, p. 721f.

1128. habt ir ufs forderlichste vornummen; perhaps: you gave heed in the most helpful way.

1129. Ernest von Mansfield.

1130. dem wir zum gegenteil nicht widderstand vormittels gotlicher und euer beistand und hulfe zu tuen vormogen; perhaps zum gegenteil could be translated 'on the other hand', though it would be unusual; the reference to divine help may well be to the assistance from the League, seen quite concretely as the arm of divine help.

all the artillery, people and resources at your disposal. Unless you do so our Christian blood will be shed in great quantities, which will be a great scandal and detrimental to the holy gospel, since we would never have presumed [to act] without the help of God and yourselves.

So again we beg you to show your Christian and brotherly hearts to us. Come to our help with all the resources at your disposal, within two days at the latest, in order to save innocent Christian blood from the devilish jaws of the wolf. In the oneness of faith and Christian love we will always be in your debt, our dear fathers and brothers. God's will be done, then. Jubilate Sunday in the year 1525.

The whole Christian community and assembly at Frankenhausen.

81. *Müntzer to the Christian brothers of Schmalkalden. 7 May 1525, Mühlhausen.*

To the Christian brothers of Schmalkalden, now encamped at Eisenach.[1131]

May the pure and upright fear of God be with you, my most beloved [brothers]. You should know that we will come to assist and protect you with all the power and resources at our disposal. But our brothers Ernest von Hohnstein and Günther von Schwarzburg[1132] have just asked for the help which we had promised and we are now anxious to put this into effect. If this alarms you, we will come up to your camp, too, with the whole host from this area. We want to do everything in our power to assist you. Just be patient for a short while with our brothers, for it is proving extraordinarly hard work to lick them into shape, for they are much coarser people than anyone could conceive. For in many respects you have become conscious of what it is that oppresses you,[1133] while we are not able to make our folk here aware of this in any whole-hearted way; but because God is driving them forcibly we simply have to work with them. I would dearly like to ask God for the special favour of going back to advise and help you, for I would far prefer to bear all the attendant difficulties[1134] than to start all over again with such clueless people;[1135] yet it is God's will to choose the foolish things and to reject the wise.[1136] Therefore it is

1131. By 11 May Philip of Hesse had already entered Eisenach (F.); cf. Elliger, p. 722.

1132. Allies of the peasants; cf. Nr. 87.

1133. *euers beswerens.*

1134. *mit beswerung.*

1135. *dan mit unwitzigen zu volzyhen vorneuen*; the original is lost; perhaps we should read *vornemen* = i.e. 'to work with'.

1136. 1 Corinthians 1²⁷.

rather weak of you to be so very afraid, when it is plain as a pike-staff[1137] that God is standing by you. Be of good courage, and sing with us: 'A hundred thousand people will not make me afraid, even if they are camped all around me.'[1138] May God give you the spirit of power,[1139] as he will never fail to do through Jesus Christ; may he preserve all of you, who are most beloved of me. Amen. Mühlhausen, Jubilate, in the year 1525.

Thomas Müntzer, with the whole congregation of God at Mühlhausen and from many other districts.

82. *Müntzer to the Mühlhausen Council. Mühlhausen, 8 May 1525.*

To the brothers in Christ at Mühlhausen, to the Council there.[1140] Satan has an extraordinay amount to do; he would like to thwart the common good and does so through his own vessel,[1141] and it is highly desirable that those creating such disruption[1142] should first be summoned before today's circle[1143] and threatened with the direst consequences to prevent them harming your interests as magistrates and those of the city as a whole. But if they will not comply with this, then they should be punished by the authority of the host. Be of good courage. Whenever Judas comes to light, his fate is already sealed. If possible we would ask that this[1144] should be carefully discussed with the whole community[1145] before we leave. God keep you through Jesus Christ. Amen.

Mühlhausen on the Monday after Jubilate in the year 1525.

Thomas Müntzer, a servant of God.

1137. *ir mugets dach wol an der wanth greyfen*; lit. 'as a wall'.

1138. Psalm 3[6]; *vor hundert tausend nit forchten underm volcke* (Bräuer/Kobuch); the Gideon theme is frequently sounded at this time, cf. Nrs. 84, 88, 89.

1139. 2 Timothy 1[7].

1140. Cf. Elliger, p. 722f.

1141. *durch sein eygnen gefhess*; cf. p. 136/20f.; the exact meaning is less than clear; the letter does suggest some caution about A. Drummond's argument that, 'Müntzer's philosophy tended to exclude the God-Devil opposition in favour of a God-Man opposition ...' 'The Divine and Mortal Worlds of Thomas Müntzer', ARG, 71 (1980), 103.

1142. *solche aufrurysche leuthe*.

1143. The circle or ring in which the host made its judicial and other 'theocratic' decisions; cf. Nr. 83, 84, 85, 86 for other examples of the new 'theocratic' justice.

1144. The reference seems to be of the wider question of the administration of justice, not just to the present case.

1145. *gemein*; the same term translated by 'congregation' in Nr. 81. l. 8 above..

83. *Müntzer to the Sondershausen Council. Mühlhausen, 8 May 1525.*

The power and the true, pure fear of God be with you,[1146] my dear brothers.

In chapter 7 of holy Joshua God Almightly pronounced the judgement when Achan[1147] was stoned to death for creating a disturbance[1148] among the people of God. You should pass judgement on[1149] the scoundrel in the same way he would like to punish others although a known adulterer himself. Evil-doers who pursue their own interests like that are not acting on our instructions. So do what is right; do not hesitate. You must be ready when we pass [down] your way;[1150] we must attack the eagle's nest, as Obadiah says.[1151] So be bold! Don't let your heart sink! At the very least you should not spare evil-doers like those from being taken into the strictest custody. Have no pity on them; it is necessary if Germany is not to become a vicious murder-pit. May God bless you. Amen.

Mühlhausen in the year 1525 on the Monday after Jubilate.

Thomas Müntzer, a servant of the congregation of God.

84. *Müntzer to the people of Eisenach. Mühlhausen, 9 May 1525.*

To our dear brothers in the whole Eisenach community.

May the pure, upright fear of God be with you, my dear brothers. Now that God has moved the whole world in a miraculous way towards a recognition of the divine truth, and (the world) is proving this by its great and earnest zeal against the tyrants, as Daniel 7[1152] says clearly: that power should be given to the common folk;[1153] Revelation, chapter 11[1154] also points out that the kingdom of this world is to belong to Christ. This confutes completely the false gloss of those who defend the godless tyrants, who will be confounded by

1146. 2 Timothy 1⁷; as so often the contrast is with a false fear of human authority; cf. Elliger, p. 726.

1147. *Achior* – F. suggests a confusion with the valley of Achor.

1148. *getummel.*

1149. *richten*; Peter Wilde may be meant (Bräuer/Kobuch).

1150. *hyn nidern zyhn.*

1151. Cf. Obadiah, v. 4; Müntzer was planning to attack Count Ernest von Mansfeld.

1152. Daniel 7²⁷.

1153. *dem gemeinen volk*; in Müntzer's German the transition from the people or congregation (*gemeyne*) of the saints to the common folk (*gemeinen volk*) is an easy one; cf. Elliger, p. 727.

1154. Revelation 11¹⁵, ¹⁸.

deeds, not words. For it as clear as day that God is very kindly letting his followers punish the adversaries only in respect to their property, by which they have hindered the kingdom and the righteousness of God from the very beginning, as Christ himself demonstrates by his searching judgement in Matthew 6.[1155] What possible chance does the common man ever have to welcome the pure word for God in sincerity when he is beset by such worries about temporal goods? Matthew 13, Matthew 4, Luke 8.[1156] This is the reason, my dear brothers, why you should not have robbed our fellows so treacherously, going off with their money-chest and their commander.[1157] In its goodness and simplicity the host was taken in by that wonderful disguise[1158] you wore, since you had never ceased to make loud protestations about the righteousness of faith. This action you took against our brothers certainly demonstrates just how devious you are. If you are now prepared to admit this we would ask you amicably to make good the loss. In short, their loss is our common loss, just as their gain benefits us all. You would be well advised not to despise those who are lowly[1159] (as you tend to do) for the Lord raises up those who are weak in order to cast down the mighty from their seats, and those who are foolish to confound the treacherous, traitorous biblical scholars.[1160] If we have to use force to get hold of their property and of our brother, the commander,[1161] you will become painfully aware that the Lord is still alive today; may he stir you up and illumine you so that you recognise the false light, Matthew 6;[1162] for the false servants of the word cause the [true] light to dwindle, to the perpetual ruin of the world, leading the common folk to go viciously astray;[1163] the conflict has become so great that the true light is pronounced darkness and the darkness of those who seek their own interests is supposed to be the light; may the Lord prevent all this happening to you. Amen.

Mühlhausen on the Tuesday after Jubilate in the year of Christ 1525.

Thomas Müntzer, with the sword of Gideon.

1155. Matthew 6[19.24]; cf. Nr. 59, p. 102/9ff., where Müntzer a year previously had taken a very different line.

1156. Matthew 13[3-9. 18-23]; Mark 4[1-20]; Luke 8[4-15]: the parable of the sower.

1157. Hans Sippel (F.)

1158. *larve*; or mask.

1159. Cf. Matthew 18[10].

1160. Luke 1[52]; 1 Corinthians 1[19].

1161. *den houptman*.

1162. Matthew 6[23] ('If then the light in you is darkness ...)'.

1163. *ins gemeine volk lesterlich gerathen*.

85.   *The Assembly at Ehrich*[1164] *to Müntzer. Ehrich, 11 May 1525.*

To be delivered to Thomas Müntzer, who in accordance with the holy, true word of God, is our Christian protector, and our beloved brother in Christ – a Christian message.[1165]

Grace and peace in Christ Jesus, beloved brother in the Lord. We have understood your second letter, too, – the one sent from Ammern on the Wednesday after Jubilate[1166] – and want to inform you also in brotherly love that we have distributed amongst the community as much of the church's property as we have been able to get hold of, giving to the true, living, poor saints even-handedly, according to their needs. We did not want you to be ignorant, either, that we have instituted, to the best of the ability God has granted us, a Christian ordering of the word of God and the supper of Christ amongst us. We poor people also inform you in a Christian spirit that we had before us the honourable Haugs and the Tottlebens[1167] and negotiated with them in a Christian and brotherly way about the sheep; we requested that they should remove them at their convenience within eight days and not trouble our poor community with them thereafter. Haug answered that he would try to dispose of[1168] his sheep within eight days; if he could not he would have to take his chance like anyone else.[1169] But the Tottlebens refuse to concede anything, intending to keep their sheep as they always have, regardless of your, or our whole community. Although we have given them, too, eight days notice they will not accept this in a brotherly or Christian way.

We would like you to know, too, that our Christian brothers, the two villages of Spier and Otterstedt,[1170] and some other villages as well, refuse us (the use of) the wood on the Hainleite. This takes no account of our real shortage, since, particularly in our district, fire has destroyed half our stock; we beg you as our Christian protector[1171]

1164. Lesser or Greater Ehrich, about half-way between Sonderhausen and Langensalza. (F.)

1165. *christlich geschrebn*; note *beschirmer* = protector, which recurs in the next letter.

1166. 10 May; not extant. (F.)

1167. Local members of the nobility; the Tottlebens lived in Greater Ehrich; on 15 February 1525 a judgement in favour of Hans Haug was pronounced in respect of taxes and obligations in Niederspier. (F.)

1168. *anzuwerden.*

1169. *wuhe nit, muss er wagen wye eyn andern.*

1170. Oberspier, Niederspier and Otterstedt, villages between Larger Ehrich and the forested slopes of the Hainleite. (F.)

1171. The special status accorded to Müntzer is interesting; the same word 'protector' occurs in Nr. 86, p. 153/17; cf. Elliger, p. 729.

and brother to be kind enough to remonstrate with them in a Christian way not to refuse us this.

As to the further points which you made as our loving brother; the request to send our cannon and some men to you at Frankenhausen; we would gladly do this, but we sent a number of men last Monday[1172] to join those at Frankenhausen[1173] – those we could spare – and so have no cannon or arms[1174] at all. Most were destroyed on the journey, but if the situation still demands it we will, as Christian brothers, put our lives and goods at the service of the gospel and righteousness as Christian people. Since you are our beloved brother we did not want you to be without a Christian answer and commend you to the grace of God in the Lord Christ. Pray to God for us.

In haste at Ehrich on the Tuesday after Jubilate, in the year etc. 1525.
Your brothers, the Christian assembly and congregation of God at Ehrich.

86. *Hans Burmann to Müntzer. Ehrich, 11 May 1525.*

To be delivered to the Christian protector of the divine word, Thomas Müntzer, my Christian lord and brother.

My Christian lord and brother, grace and peace in Jesus Christ. May I request and plead with you, as a protector and a judge of all evil deeds,[1175] to note that my blessed father held for a long time some parcels of land[1176] which he had inherited, but that one Apel Weinmeister, now living in Thüringenhausen,[1177] used them and confiscated[1178] them from my father three years ago because of some debts, small ones. The latter remain unproven,[1179] yet he has had the use of these lands for three years now, and in the meantime has been instructed by the authorities, to whom I appealed at once in law, to accept the repayment of his alleged debts; I was and still am ready to do this – although from a Christian viewpoint I am not liable to pay them – because I am willing to abide by the aforesaid instruction. The above mentioned person, however, has no intention of following any such instruction, but just pursues his own sweet will in this matter,

---

1172. 8 May. (F.)
1173. Scene of the final battle.
1174. *harnusch*; lit. armour.
1175. Cf. n. 1171 above.
1176. *etzliche lenderige*.
1177. North of Ehrich. (F.)
1178. *ingenohmen*.
1179. *Das selbige ist und* (F. suggests *uns*) *unerwisslich*.

in this matter, knowing that the authorities are powerless. When I wanted to have the lands ploughed, he deprived me of them and refused me access to the lands mentioned above, as the whole community of Ehrich knows. He also promised, three years ago, to hand over some money, and cancel the debt, which had been lent on the security of the lands; this had not been done, either.

In respect of all this I would ask you, as a loving brother and Christian protector to look into this matter for the sake of equity and in the name of God and justice and to find a Christian way to make him hand over the lands to me without any further delay; may the Almighty reward you. Please give your Christian reply to this.

Thursday after Jubilate in the year etc. 1525.

Hans Burmann, living in Ehrich, your Christian brother.

87. *Count Günther von Schwarzburg*[1180] *to Müntzer. Place unknown, 12 May 1525.*

To my dear Christian brother, Master Thomas Müntzer.

Grace and peace in Christ, dear Christian brother. I would be very glad to make my way to Frankenhausen to join you, kind sir.[1181] But there is continual quarrelling[1182] and unrest among the peasants in my territories, which means that every day I have a difficult task keeping the peace among them,[1183] and keeping them happy. Therefore I would ask you, kind sir, to be so good as to explain to the other Christian brothers in an amicable way that I will have to be absent until, once the peasants have quietened down, it is convenient for me to come to you, kind sir. I will be glad to repay this kindness to you, kind sir, in Christian and brotherly love.

Friday after Jubilate in the year etc. 1525.

Günther the younger, head of the Christian congregation, von Schwarzburg by birth.

88. *Müntzer to Count Ernst of Mansfeld. Frankenhausen, 12 May 1525.*

Open letter to brother Ernst of Heldrungen, for his conversion.[1184]

May the outstretched power of God be with you, brother Ernest,

1180. Cf. Nrs. 79, 81.
1181. E.L. = *euer liebden.*
1182. *getzang.*
1183. *sie underlang zu vertragen.*
1184. Comes at the end of the text of the letter, so probably does not belong to the

may you be rooted in his fear and grounded in his righteous will.[1185] I, Thomas Müntzer, one-time pastor of Allstedt, do urge and exhort you, unnecessary though it should be,[1186] to abandon your tyrannical raging for the sake and in the name of the living God and to provoke[1187] the wrath of God no longer. You it was who began the martyring of the Christians; you it was who denounced the holy Christian faith as villainy; you it was who dared to eradicate the Christians. Just tell us,[1188] you miserable, wretched sack of worms, who made you a prince over the people whom God redeemed with his dear blood?[1189] You shall and will have to prove that you are a Christian; you will and shall have to give an account of your faith, as 1 Peter 3 insists.[1190] An absolutely genuine safe-conduct will be given you, so that you can bring your faith into the light of day; this assurance has been given you by the whole community gathered in the ring;[1191] there you will apologise, too, for your manifest tyranny and say who made you so foolish,[1192] as to become a pagan evil-doer like this, to the detriment of all Christians, while professing the Christian name. If you stay away, and do not acquit yourself of the charge laid against you, I will lift up my voice against you for all the world to hear, and all the brethren will be ready to risk their life-blood, as they have been hitherto against the Turk. Then you will be hunted down and wiped out, for everyone will be far keener to gain an indulgence at your expense than those which the pope used to give out.[1193] We don't know any other way of calling you to book.[1194] No feeling of shame penetrates you. God has hardened your heart like that of (King)[1195] Pharaoh; like the kings whom God wanted to destroy, Joshua 5 and 11.[1196] Let the lament rise to God without ceasing that your brazen tyranny, raging like so many wild bulls,[1197] was not detected by the world before now. How were you able to

---

(lost) original copy (F.); Luther printed this letter too in his *Shocking History*; cf. n. 1077 above; cf. Elliger, pp. 755ff.

1185. *Die gestrackt kraft, feste forcht Gottes und der bestendige grund seines gerechten willens sey mit dir.*

1186. *zum ubirflussigen anregen.*

1187. *uber dich erbittern.*

1188. In Luther's edition: *Sihe* (look here).

1189. Note the theocratic understanding of political power.

1190. 1 Peter 3[15].

1191. Cf. n. 1143 above.

1192. *torstlich.*

1193. To the Crusaders.

1194. *Wir wissen nichts anders an dir zu bekomen*; translation by Dr Scott.

1195. Only in Luther's edition.

1196. Judges 5[24ff.] (death of Sisera) and 11[21ff.] (death of Sihon) appear to be meant, (not Joshua); cf. n. 362 above.

1197. *deine grobe, puffel wutende tyranney*; MHG *püffel* = ox (Jillings).

inflict such an astounding amount of irreparable damage? How can anyone but God himself show mercy to you? In brief, you are handed over to destruction[1198] by God's mighty power. If you will not humble yourself before those of little repute[1199] you will be forever disregarded in the sight of the whole Christian people and you will become a martyr for the devil.

So that you know, too, that we are acting under instructions,[1200] I say this: The eternal, living God has commanded that you should be forcibly cast down from your seat;[1201] for you are no use to the Christian people; you are a scourge which chastens the friends of God. God has spoken to you and your like in Ezekiel 34, 39; Daniel 7; Micah 3.[1202] Obadiah the prophet says that your nest has to be torn down and smashed to pieces.[1203]

We want your answer this very evening;[1204] otherwise we will descend on you in the name of God of hosts; so you know what to expect. We shall execute without delay what God has commanded us; so do your best, too. I'm on my way.[1205]

Frankenhausen, Friday after Jubilate in the year of the Lord 1525.
Thomas Müntzer with the sword of Gideon.[1206]

89. *Müntzer to Count Albert von Mansfeld. Frankenhausen, 12 May 1525.*

Written to brother Albert von Mansfeld, for his conversion.[1207]

Fear and trembling upon all who do evil, Romans 2.[1208] Your quite awful misuse of the epistle of Paul distresses me. You want to give the wicked authorities licence to do whatever they like, just as the Pope used Peter and Paul as slave-drivers. Do you think that the Lord God is unable to arouse his uncomprehending people, to depose the tyrants

---

1198. Perhaps an echo of 1 Corinthians 5[5].

1199. *fur den cleynen.*

1200. *das wyrs gestrackten bevell haben.*

1201. Cf. Luke 1[52].

1202. Ezekiel 34 (the false shepherds of Israel); Ezekiel 39 (Gog and Magog); Daniel 7 esp. vs. 12, 27; (the fall of the Beast); Micah 3 (the perverted rulers of Israel).

1203. v. 4; cf. Nr. 83, n. 1151.

1204. *nach heynet.*

1205. *ich fahr daher.*

1206. F. notes on the dissemination of this letter and of Nr. 89 that Leonhard Buchler of Halle admitted on 22 December 1525 to having seen a copy of a letter to von Mansfeld, signed: Thomas Müntzer with the sword of Gideon; cf. Fuchs, AGBM II, Nr. 1962.

1207. Cf. Nr. 88; cf. Elliger, p. 753; original lost; also reproduced in Luther's *Shocking History*; cf. n. 1077 above.

1208. Romans 2[9].

in his wrath? Hosea 13 and 8.[1209] Didn't the mother of Christ speak of you and your like through the holy spirit when she prophesised in Luke 1:[1210] 'The mighty he has cast down from their seats and the lowly (whom you despise) he has raised.' Couldn't you find in your Lutheran pudding[1211] and your Wittenberg soup what Ezekiel has prophesied in his thirty-seventh chapter?[1212] You haven't even been able to detect the flavour, because of that Martinian peasant filth[1213] of yours, of what the same prophet goes on to say in the thirty-ninth chapter,[1214] that God instructs all the birds of the heavens to consume the flesh of the princes; whilst the brute beasts are to drink the blood of the big wigs,[1215] as the secret revelation describes, chapters 18 and 19?[1216] Do you imagine that God is less concerned about his people than he is about you tyrants? Under the name of Christ you want to act the pagan and to use Paul as a cover-up.[1217] But your way will be blocked,[1218] you can be sure of that. If you will admit, Daniel 7,[1219] that God has given power to the common man,[1220] and appear before us to give an account of your faith, we will be glad to permit this and to regard you as our common brother. But if not, then we will not give the least heed to your lame, limp antics but will fight against you as an arch-enemy of the Christian faith; so you know what to expect.

Frankenhausen on Friday after Jubilate in the year 1525.

Thomas Müntzer with the sword of Gideon.

90. *The elected ministers of the Christian congregation of Walkenried to Müntzer. Walkenreid, 13 May 1525.*

A Christian message to our Christian brother, Thomas Müntzer, encamped at Frankenhausen.

Christian love and brotherhood in Christ our saviour. Dear brother, we understood your letter to us very well, and your wish

---

1209. Hosea 13[10f.]; 8[4, 10].

1210. Luke 1[52].

1211. *grutz.*

1212. The vision of the valley of bones; the eternal covenant with Israel, reunited under David; Dismer, p. 91, n. 6, suggests chapter 34 is meant.

1213. *baurendreck*; a curious term of abuse to be applied to Luther by a peasant leader.

1214. *underschied*; Ezekiel 39[4].

1215. *der grossen hansen.*

1216. Revelation 18[2], 19[18].

1217. The reference is to the Lutheran use of Romans 13[1ff.]; Luther of course, accused the peasants of abusing the Christian name to legitimise *their* political and secular ends.

1218. *die pane verlaufen.*

1219. Daniel 7[27].

1220. *der gemeyne*; lit. the community; cf. Nr. 91, n. 1234 below.

that we should make our way to you at Frankenhausen. We have nothing at all against doing that,[1221] our specially dear Christian brother, but we cannot come together so quickly. So we would beg you in a brotherly way to sympathise with our position.[1222] Our host is dissolved and the leaders and ministers of our Christian congregation meet together this coming Sunday,[1223] Cantate, when we can put the letter in their hands and then write to you again in a Christian and brotherly way at our expense and using our letter-carrier. That said, then, dear brother, the peace of Christ be with you.

Walkenried on Saturday after Jubilate 1525.

The elected ministers of the Christian congregation of Walkenried.

91. *Müntzer to the people of Erfurt. Frankenhausen, 13 May 1525.*

To our heartily loved brothers, the whole congregation of Erfurt.[1224]

Strength and comfort in Christ Jesus, most beloved [brothers]. We have heard of your constant love[1225] and that you walk in the truth joyfully and so we are confident that you will not be found lagging behind, unless the Lutheran gruel-sloppers[1226] have softened you up with their grubby soft-heartedness,[1227] as we are credibly informed is the case,[1228] Paul's comment[1229] on those who love pleasure is that nowadays, although they put on the most convincing pose of goodness or godly conduct, they fight the power of God tooth and nail,[1230] as anyone can see if he keeps his eyes open.

So we urgently beg you to give no more credence to platelickers like these, and to let nothing prevent you any longer from helping the ordinary Christian people[1231] to fight with us against the godless, wicked tyrants.

Help us in any way you can, with men and with cannons, so that we can carry out the commands of God himself in Ezekiel, chapter

---

1221. *Das my dan nycht aberedende syn.*

1222. *dass ir met uns wolt haben eyn mytlyding.*

1223. 15 May; in fact they set out towards Frankenhausen on that day, hearing of the defeat of 15 May at Heringen. (F.)

1224. They refused to accept the letter. (F.)

1225. Hans Hut kept Müntzer informed about Erfurt (F.); cf. Elliger, pp. 760ff.

1226. *breyfresser.*

1227. *beschmyrten barmhertzygkeyt.*

1228. *wye wyr des guten gewissen tragen.*

1229. 2 Timothy 3⁴ᶠ·; the reference to those 'holding the form of religion but denying the power of it' was the same accusation made to the Counts of Mansfeld (cf. Nrs. 88, 89).

1230. *myt handt und mund*, lit. 'with hand and mouth'.

1231. *gemeiner christenheyt.*

34,[1232] where he says: 'I will rescue you from those who lord it over you in a tyrannous way. I will drive the wild beasts away from your land.' In chapter 39 of the same prophet God goes on to say: 'Come, you birds of the heaven and devour the flesh of the princes; and you wild beasts drink up the blood of all the big wigs.'[1233] Daniel says the same thing in chapter 7: that power should be given to the common man,[1234] Revelations 18 and 19.[1235] Almost all of the pronouncements[1236] of scripture testify that the creatures must be set free if the pure word of God is to dawn.

If, then, you long for truth then come and join us in the dance, for we want to tread it out evenly,[1237] so that we can really pay back those blasphemers of God for playing about with the poor Christian people as they have. Write to tell us what your view is, for we mean well by you, my very dearest brothers.

Frankenhausen on Saturday after Jubilate in the year of the Lord MCCCCC XXV

Thomas Müntzer on behalf of the ordinary Christian people.

92. *The Peasants at Frankenhausen to the Princes. Frankenhausen, 15 May 1525.*[1238]

We confess Jesus Christ.

We are not here to harm anyone, John 2,[1239] but to see that divine justice is maintained. We are not here to shed blood, either. If your aims are the same, then we have no desire to harm you.[1240] Everyone should be guided by that.

93. *The Princes to the Brothers at Frankenhausen. Frankenhausen, (15 May 1525).*

To be delivered to the brothers at Frankenhausen.[1241]

Since the vicious ways you have adopted and the seductive

1232. Müntzer's words are a loose paraphrase of the whole chapter (already referred to in Nr. 88) with particular reference to vs. 10b, 25.

1233. Ezekiel 39[1ff]; cf. Nr. 88, n. 1202.

1234. *dem gemeinen volk.*

1235. Cf. Nr. 89, n. 1216.

1236. *ortheyl.*

1237. *eben treten;* cf. Revelation 19[15].

1238. The original is lost; reproduced in Hieronymus Emser's *Glaubwürdiger Unterricht,* (true and faithful account) of the battle of Frankenhausen, Dresden, 1525.

1239. Is the reference to Jesus driving the money changers out of the Temple, John 2[14ff]?

1240. On the battle cf. Gritsch, p. 148f.; Elliger, pp. 773ff.

1241. Reproduced by Emser, cf. n. 1238 above; cf. Elliger, pp. 776ff.

teaching of that false gospeller of yours have caused you to commit murder, arson and countless insults to God, blaspheming against our saviour Jesus Christ and in particular the holy and most blessed sacrament and in many other ways, we – as those to whom God has entrusted the sword[1242] – are gathered here to punish you as blasphemers against God. Despite this, however, we are led by Christian love and especially by our conviction that many a poor man has been wickedly seduced to such actions, to decide as follows: If you turn over to us, alive, the false prophet Thomas Müntzer and his immediate following, and throw yourselves completely onto our mercy, our treatment of you and decisions in respect to you will be such that you may yet, if circumstances permit, find favour in our eyes. We expect a speedy reply from you.

94. *Müntzer to the people of Mühlhausen. Heldrungen, 17 May 1525.*

To the Christian community and the Council of Mühlhausen, my dear brothers.[1243]

May salvation and blessedness in the face of fear, death and hell be with you, dear brothers. Since it is God's good pleasure that I should depart hence with an authentic knowledge of the divine name, and in recompense for[1244] certain abuses which the people embraced, not understanding me properly – for they sought only their own interests and the divine truth was defeated as a result – I, too, am heartily content that God has ordained things in this way. For this, like all the deeds God has accomplished, must be judged not by its outward appearance but in the truth, John 7.[1245] Do not allow my death, therefore, to be a stumbling block to you, for it has come to pass for the benefit of the good and the uncomprehending.[1246] Hence I would ask you in a friendly way to see that my wife inherits my property, for example such books and clothes as there are; for God's sake do not let it be taken out on her.[1247] Dear brothers, it is quite crucial that the sort

---

1242. Romans 13[4].

1243. *An dye Christliche gemeyne und Rath zu Molhausen meyne lieben Bruder*; omitted by Franz; (Bräuer); written after the catastrophic battle of Frankenhausen, and his subsequent capture, interrogation, and torture (cf. pp. 433ff. below) and his surrender to his most hated enemy, Ernest von Mansfeld.

1244. *erstattung*; Dr Scott's advice on translation has been invaluable for this letter.

1245. John 7[24].

1246. *unvortstendigen*; F. suggests that the words: 'as a warning to' have been omitted; however, Müntzer's use of *unverstendlich* only four days earlier in a positive way about the common people suggests that the text should stand; cf. Letter 89, p. 156/25.

1247. *und sye nichts umb Gottes willen lassen enthgelden*; cf. p. 440/4 below.

of disaster[1248] which befell the men at Frankenhausen should not be your lot, too; there is no doubt of its root cause: that everyone was more concerned with his own self-interest than in bringing justice to the Christian people.[1249] Therefore make a clear distinction between these;[1250] see to it that you bring no further harm on yourselves. It is for your good that I refer to the Frankenhausen affair, which ended in great bloodshed, that of more than four thousand people in fact. Step forward with the clear, unwavering righteousness of God,[1251] and this will not happen to you. I have often warned you that the only way to escape the punishment of God – which the authorities execute – is to recognise what harm will ensue, and it always can be recognised.[1252] Therefore be on good terms with every man and do not embitter the authorities any more, as many have done by seeking their own interests. That said, then, may the grace of Christ and his spirit preserve you. With this letter in the hand of Christopher Laue[1253] I commend my spirit into the hand of God and wish you the blessing of the father, the son and the holy spirit. Do your best to advise my wife and, finally, flee the shedding of blood, against which I now want to warn you sincerely.[1254] For I know that most of you never had anything to do with this rebellious and self-seeking insurrection, but used every means to oppose and prevent it. To avoid innocent people like yourselves being drawn into grave trouble, as happened to some people at Frankenhausen, you should now shun all gatherings and disturbances and seek the mercy of the princes. I trust that you will find the princes disposed to show you mercy. I wanted to declare this at my departure, to relieve my soul of the weighty burden of conniving at further insurrection, so that innocent blood can cease to be spilt.

From Heldrungen, my prison, and my last farewell.

Wednesday after Cantate in the year etc. 1525.

Thomas Müntzer.

1248. *solche schlappen.*

1249. *dye rechtfertigung der christenheyt.*

1250. *nempt euer sachen eben wahr.*

1251. *gottesgerechtigkeyt* (Bräuer/Kobuch).

1252. *den schaden, welcher altzeyt erkant werden kan* (Bräuer/Kobuch); cf. Elliger, p. 801, n. 63.

1253. Mentioned in the so-called Recantation, pp. 439f.

1254. Eike Wolgasft, *Thomas Müntzer, Ein Verstörer der Ungläubigen* (Göttingen, 1981), p. 113, argues that the farewell and blessing of the previous sentence form a natural conclusion to the letter, and that the concluding lines betray a shift in language and content which reflects the views of the scribe rather than of Müntzer; although Müntzer frequently appears to conclude a writing but then continues it, the final sentences do seem suspiciously conventional and colourless.

1255. *keyner emporung weyter stadt geben*; 'of a weighty burden, that you should support no further insurrection' (Scott).

LITURGY

The creativity and originality of Müntzer's liturgical work is now a commonplace of Reformation scholarship. His relatively short time in Allstedt, from Easter 1523 to August 1524, provided him not only with a respite from the insecurity of a refugee existence but with a leadership role, a position of responsibility, in which his pastoral and liturgical gifts were in constant demand.

His daily services met a need. They probably began at the beginning of April 1523. People flocked to them from adjoining villages and territories. Out of this enthusiastic response to his simplified, reformed German services comes the decision to publish what was to be the first German version of the Mass with music, and a book of common prayer, or order of service. It was an incredibly ambitious, costly undertaking (the musical notation was printed, too), even with the help of the Allstedt Council. Provisional as they were – 'If... a little child can instruct us how to do better, we will be glad to accept this' – the challenge they posed to the Old Church was more momentous than that of any mere theological tractate. As the *Order and Explanation* said, '... the most effective way to silence opposition has always been such reform of worship'. For it was such services which determined the basic rhythm of the religious life of ordinary people, and in fact Müntzer's liturgies were, despite Luther's opposition, to exercise a wide influence from Nuremberg in the South to Pomerania in the North, far beyond the radical camp.

The decision, therefore, to exclude his liturgical writings from this English edition has not been an easy one. In quantitative terms it would have added something like 200 pages to an already large book. More importantly, very special skills are required to evaluate the liturgical (and musical) significance of such texts. Finally, there are quite daunting difficulties involved in translating a translation, in finding a form of English which would do any sort of justice to Müntzer's vernacular rendering of the age-old Latin version.

For the moment, at least, therefore, only the Foreword to the *German Mass* and the Foreword and the *Order and Explanation* of the *German Church Service* have been included, with some very brief samples of Müntzer's prayers. It is hoped that they will suffice to signal in unmistakeable terms the centrality of this aspect of Müntzer's achievement – one which both social historians and theologians have been inclined to overlook. One suspects, for example, that a careful study of his liturgies might have obviated some of the spirited debate about the allegedly Lutheran, or mystical, or apocalyptic basis of Müntzer's theology.

There are still uncertainties about the dating of his three liturgical writings: the *German Church Service*, the *Order and Explanation*, and the *German Mass*. Bräuer suggests plausibly (*Theologische Schriften aus dem Jahr 1523*, p. 52) that the printing of the Service Book began in the Autumn of 1523, ending some four to six months later in early 1524 (the preparation of more than 700 wood-cuts for the music was a lengthy affair), that the *Order and Explanation* appeared around the turn of the year, and that the *Mass* was completed by about August 1524. In the case of the *German Church Service* the Foreword appears to have been published separately a little later. Others, such as Elliger, suggest an earlier dating for the writings.

The Foreword to the *German Church Service* (seen by Smend as a second preface to the *Mass*) is directed mainly against criticism from the Old Church. The Foreword to the Mass, however, refers to 'learned men', driven by envy and fear of the rulers, who have sought to suppress Müntzer's services and will be a reference to the actions of Luther and the Wittenbergers in this regard. The *Order and Explanation*, although it gives evidence of changes which go beyond the printed version in the *German Mass*, is a spirited defence of Müntzer's gradualist approach and indicates that he encountered criticism from radical groups as well. The two cognate terms used for the title, *berechunge* on the title page, and *rechenschafft* at the head of the contents, mean rather more than the English 'Explanation'. Müntzer uses them frequently in the sense of to 'justify', to 'offer grounds for', to 'give an account of'. Thus the writings reflect the raging controversies in Allstedt about the nature and manner of worship. The patient way in which Müntzer adduces historical, Biblical, and even psychological arguments for his liturgies is all the more impressive in this embattled context.

He shows, first of all, appreciation for the diversity of cultural backgrounds. What is appropriate for a liturgy in Italy is not necessarily so for Armenia or Germany. The Latin hegemony which was acceptable in Germany when Christianity there was still in its infancy and the German language 'unformed' is no longer tolerable in present-day circumstances.

The humanist awareness of historical context combines here with Müntzer's apocalyptic views to foster an intriguing concept of development or 'progress'. To absolutise Roman usage is to assert that God is impotent, unable to 'progress further', while in fact the Christian faith is growing as never before (p. 167/16f.). This is a dynamic variation on the normal understanding of reform.

Secondly, he emphasizes Biblical, apostolic grounds for his reforms. The Mass is to be celebrated 'according to the Gospel'. The prophetic, apostolic Pauline practices should be restored.

Thirdly, the reforms should be introduced gently, according to each person's capacity to understand, retaining the traditional well-loved structures and melodies and thus gradually weaning the simple folk away from their superstitious beliefs, while at the same time checking any incipient tendencies to irreverence (p. 172/8). Such outward rites are in any case, unless openly idolatrous, a matter of relative indifference (p. 177/5ff.).

The five different patterns of worship for the Church Year and the five variations on the Mass, are only suggested as possible models, to be shortened, lengthened or omitted altogether at the judgement of the local pastor (p. 177/7ff.).

The general tone, then, despite some spirited polemic, is one of eminent reasonableness and flexibility, a catholic awareness that the church universal cannot, and need not, insist on uniformity of practice. Where, however, the reality of worship is at stake, the symbol pointing to that reality must, as in the administration of the sacrament in both kinds, be the appropriate one. For all its emphasis on inwardness, this is far from a purely spiritualist concept of worship. The sacraments are important. To approach them falsely is to risk damage to one's soul.

His views on baptism are interesting in this respect. The relatively traditional though simplified practice of infant baptism suggested in the *Order and Explanation* has to be read in conjunction with his exposition of baptism in the *Protestation or Proposition*. Infant baptism is, in effect, a provisional baptism, anticipating the time when the baptism of suffering discipleship can be undergone by the adult. (cf. the reference to Matthew 3, and Christ's baptism.) Its meaning lies partly in the congregational participation, signified by the heavy responsibility laid upon the godparents, but Müntzer's characteristic emphasis on the children of the elect (as in Letter 31 to Melanchthon), the *proles electa*, should not be forgotten. The retention of infant baptism, then, despite Müntzer's scorn for 'water-sprinkling', need not be seen as pragmatic concession to conservative pressures.

The main impression, after all, left by the liturgical writings is hardly one of compromise but of a quite startling break with traditional concepts of worship. The role of the priest, for example, is transformed. Although still very much the leader in worship, in teaching, and in spiritual direction he is no longer the mediator. He is defined by his functions, as the diligent pastor, steward, interpreter, watchman, there not to exploit his people materially or to claim any privileged access to God, by 'some private mumbo-jumbo', but to share with all the elect what he, himself, has learnt from Scripture and from his own experience of the spirit of Christ. He will be zealous, devoted to his flock, and fearless, paying 'no heed to the raging of the tyrants', prophet as well as priest (p. 182/25).

Naturally, this has implications for the role of the congregation. They are the elect, promised the key to the knowledge of God, fed not with milk (still less 'dragon's milk') but with the full nourishment of the Gospel which is their 'property', each of them expected to submit, personally and immediately to the 'working of God' in their souls. The elect, priest and laity, function as a unit, as in the consecration of the bread and wine 'which is performed ... by the whole gathered congregation' (p. 174/10f.).

Müntzer does not, however, operate with an exclusivist, perfectionist, understanding of the congregation. The gathering for worship will be a very mixed group, with plenty evidence of ignorance, laziness, hypocrisy and 'crudeness'. Like the catechumens in the Early Church there will be many 'little ones' in desperate need of the teaching of the sermon. We seem closer to the *Volkskirche* than to the gathered church. Yet within every congregation 'there are certainly many pious men ...' (p. 175/1f.), the 'friends of God'. Worship, therefore, is participatory worship. The poor laity, delighting in hymns and Scripture and teaching, not passively listening to papal 'black magic', will thereby be brought to the beginnings of true Christian faith.

Worship, then, as a corporate act, will be open, public, comprehensible, simple. Although the term *geheim* (mystery) is still used for the Mass, in fact the real mystery is now transacted in the abyss of the soul of each individual believer as 'we come to know the immortality of our soul through the new birth of your son' (p. 169/8f.). Here, in the hearts of the elect, the whole witness of Scripture is re-enacted under the sprinkling of the Spirit, as Müntzer explained in December 1523 to Christopher Meinhard (p. 73/11f. above). As the Word complements the Spirit so does corporate worship the spirituality of the individual.

German Church Service Book: some brief selections

A reformed[1] order for Church services in German, which takes away the covering[2] treacherously devised to conceal the Light of the world, which now shines forth again through these hymns and godly psalms; for the edification and growth of the Christian people[3] and in accordance with the unchangeable will of God, but destroying the bombastic ceremonies of the godless. Allstedt.

Foreword to this Service Book[4]

Anticipating all the abuses that would afflict the Christian people, our true saviour Jesus Christ prophesied in the thirteenth chapter of Matthew:[5] 'While men were sleeping (whom he soon afterwards calls angels)[6] the enemy came and sowed tares among the wheat.' It was Christ who began true Christianity. But because of the idleness of the elect the godless were able to pollute it. Hence the dry words of Paul in the twentieth chapter of the Acts of the Apostles:[7] 'Watch out for yourselves and for the whole flock[8] put in your care by the holy spirit. You are to pasture the congregation of God, which he has acquired by his own blood. For I know this, that after my departure ravenous wolves will appear among you, not sparing the flock. Men from your own ranks will rise up and speak perversely, in order to gain the allegiance of the young. So be on your guard!' However, to prevent anyone distorting these words of Christ and Paul to suit himself, following his own fallible reasoning, and so causing further damage to a Church already impeded in its task,[9] one only needs to examine the testimony of all the trustworthy histories. That will show quite clearly that the words of Christ and Paul and of all the holy prophets about the confusion of the Christian people[10] have been fulfilled many times over. Hegesippus, a trustworthy historian and a pupil of the

---

1. *vorordnet*; cf. p. 180/4 below.

2. An image used frequently by Müntzer; cf. also p. 170/6 below.

3. *die zunemenden Christēheyt*, lit. 'the growing Christian people'; growth in faith is meant (cf. *zcunemen in glauben*; p. 169/16f. below), though the context suggests a missionary note, p. 170/6f. below; on the apocalyptic background cf. Schwarz, p. 75.

4. *yns buch disser lobgesenge*; lit. hymn-book.

5. Matthew 13[25, 39]; for 'chapter' Müntzer uses the term *unterschiedt* (division).

6. A characteristically arbitrary piece of exegesis but important for Müntzer's sharp distinction between the elect and the godless.

7. Acts 20[28-31].

8. *herdte*.

9. *die vorhynderte kirche weyther in schaden führe*; probably a reference to the Church's missionary task.

10. *der zurfallen christenheit*; cf. n. 161 below; and cf. n. 3 above.

apostles, states explicitly in the fifth Book of *Memoirs*[11] as does Eusebius in the fourth Book about the Christian Churches,[12] that the holy bride of Christ remained a virgin until after the death of the followers of the apostles, but that from that moment on became an immoral adulteress.[13] From these unambiguous histories, and from others like them, the condition that the Christian people was in six hundred[14] years ago, when our ancestors came to the faith, is not only visible but plain as a pike-staff. In the circumstances of the people at the time the pious, well-meaning fathers (who converted our country) did the best they could. They were Italian and French monks, and as a first step their coming was acceptable.[15] Since the German language at that time was completely unformed,[16] it is quite understandable that they used Latin for the services, and insisted on keeping the people united: for the whole of Asia went its own way all of a sudden.[17] But it would be a bizarre matter[18] indeed if there were never to be any progress beyond that point. From day to day there is a drive for improvement in all man's worldly undertakings;[19] and are we to regard[20] God as so impotent that he cannot progress further in this matter? Certainly not! Christ himself speaks on this point and instructs us to take it with all seriousness:[21] 'A city should stand out quite plainly on a hill. One should not shove[22] a light under a covering. It should shine out for all who are in the house.' 'What then?' as Paul says in I Corinthians 14 and Ephesians 5:[23] 'When the people come together, they should delight one another with songs of praise and psalms, so that anyone joining them may benefit.'

11. F. takes this as a reference to the old Latin translation of Josephus, but clearly Hegesippus himself is meant here; cf. n. 12 below, Letter 8, p. 15/15 above, and Prague Manifesto p. 370/23 below.

12. Eusebius, *Church History*, IV, 22 quotes from the *Memoirs* of Hegesippus: 'Therefore they called the Church a virgin, for it was not yet corrupted by vain discourses.'

13. The theme goes back to the prophets, e.g. Jeremiah 3[6ff.]

14. *wie die christenheit geschigkt gewesen ist.*

15. *Zur besserung war yr ankunft zu dulden*; i.e. until things improved; the reference is probably to the Celtic monks.

16. *ungemustert*; cf. n. 27 below; 'unknown'. (F.)

17. Presumably a reference to the 1054 schism, or possibly to that of Photius in 867.

18. *ein wunderlich spiel*, lit., 'a crazy game'.

19. *vornunftiger wandel*, lit. 'rational behaviour'.

20. *das er sein wergk nicht solte erförer bringen*, i.e. progress beyond the first stage of the conversion of the German people.

21. Matthew 5[14f.]; 10[27].

22. *storzen.*

23. I Corinthians 14[26]; Ephesians 5[19]; 'benefit' translates *gebessert*, i.e. echoing the theme of 'progress'.

This attribution to the Latin words of a power like the incantations of the magicians cannot be tolerated any longer, for the poor people leave the churches more ignorant than they entered them, contrary to what God has declared in Isaiah 54, Jeremiah 31, and John 6,[24] that all the elect should be instructed by God. And Paul says:[25] 'Let the people be edified by songs of praise.' So in order to improve matters[26] I have translated the Psalms in accordance with German style and form[27] but under the intimate and direct leading of the holy spirit,[28] following the sense rather than the letter, for to trace one little figure from another[29] is nauseating nonsense[30] at a time like ours, when we still need much formation in the things of the spirit[31] if we are to be purged of[32] our traditional ways.

There are five services for singing throughout the entire year, the whole Bible being sung instead of the selected readings used previously.[33] The first one is for Advent, starting in the wine month[34] or All Souls Day when the prophetic readings begin. The second on the birth of Christ continues to the Presentation[35] in the Temple, the third – on the suffering of Christ – until Easter. Then the fourth – on the resurrection of Christ – till Pentecost and the fifth – on the holy Spirit[36] – until All Souls Day. In this way Christ will be explained to us through the holy spirit within us, through the testimony about how he was foretold by the prophets, how he was born, died, and rose again, who with his father and the same holy spirit rules eternally and makes us his pupils.

Amen.

Select Collects

O Lord God, keep hard by us, so we can take leave of[37] our dreadful vices, now that we have covenanted[38] ourselves to you for ever through the spirit of Christ, your son, through the holy symbols

---

24. Isaiah 54[13]; Jeremiah 31[34]; John 6[45].
25. Ephesians 5[19]; here Muntzer uses *erbawet*, not *gebessert*; cf. n. 23 above.
26. *zur besserung*.
27. *nach der Deutschen art und musterung*.
28. *in unvorrugklicher geheym das heyligen geists*.
29. *menlein kegen menlein zu mhalen*, i.e. a pedantic imitation.
30. *ein unfletige sache*.
31. *zum geist noch zur zeit vil musterns bedörfen*.
32. *entgröbet*.
33. *an stadt der lection*.
34. October (F.); All Souls Day is on 1 November.
35. *opferung*; 2 February. (F.)
36. Trinity Sunday. (F.)
37. *abzychtung thun*.
38. *vorbunden*.

of his gentle flesh and costly blood, who with you lives and reigns in the unity of the holy spirit etc.

O almighty God, grant that this new birth of your only son, which took place in the flesh, may redeem us from the anti-Christian régime[39] of the godless, which we have merited by our sin, through the same Jesus etc.

O kindly God, open to us the abyss of our souls, that we may come to know the immortality of our soul[40] through the new birth of your son,[41] by the power of his flesh and costly blood who with you lives and ... etc.

O kindly God, you would much rather be gracious to your people than pour out your anger upon anyone. Grant that all the elect may come to hate their sin through the suffering of your son, so that they may receive your comfort through Jesus Christ etc.

O Lord, bring your poor people to recognise your fatherly rod and discipline, so that your congregation may be schooled and grow in faith, as these costly mysteries[42] instruct us, through Jesus Christ etc.

O Lord, pour into us the spirit of love, and make those whom you have fed so abundantly[43] with your Easter lamb, live in harmony in your love through Jesus etc.

O merciful God, you have taught the hearts of your faithful ones[44] by the illumination of the holy spirit; grant that we may reflect and meditate on righteousness in the same spirit so that we may always enjoy his comfort, through Jesus Christ etc.

O Lord, bestow on us the grace of the holy spirit, so that the dew of your goodness may sprinkle the very depths of our heart[45] and make it bring forth good fruit through Jesus etc.

39. *uns erlôse vom entichristischen regiment der gotlosen.*

40. *gemutes*; where it is translated by *mentis* in the Latin version of the Prague Manifesto, F. p. 505/12.

41. i.e. in the soul.

42. i.e. the Mass.

43. *gesetliget.*

44. *deyner getrewen.*

45. *unsern grundt des hertzens*; these eight prayers are all taken from the German Mass; F. pp. 180/1ff.; 183/3ff.; 187/11ff.; 189/6ff.; 192/1ff.; 200/6ff.; 201/10ff; 206/5ff.

Order and Explanation of the German Church Service recently instituted at Allstedt by the servants of God, 1523

Joan. 18
2 Cor. 13
Ephese 2

Luce 12
1 Cho. 4
Math. 5
Luce 24

Luce 11

Joan. 17

Clavis David

Esaic 28

Historia tripartita[56]
Jeremi. 31

Roma. 9

Luce 2

Joan. 17

Ruth 2

Math. 13

Worship conducted by a servant of God should be open and above board, not some private mumbo-jumbo,[46] so that it can edify and set on its feet the whole congregation,[47] which depends for its nourishment on the trustworthy steward distributing the measures of wheat at the due time.[48] He should not treacherously hide the latter away under cover.[49] He should keep nothing hidden or secret from any part of the Christian people or any part of the world either.[50] This tends to be the practice of those who remove the key to the knowledge of God,[51] although the eternal, living God had declared through Isaiah, ch. 22,[52] that all the elect should have it put in their hands.[53] Accordingly we use the psalter to introduce the Mass,[54] since the key of David is on the shoulder of Christ. This begins the whole choral service, and to ensure a proper understanding and not a fragmentary one[55] the whole psalm is sung. This, after all, is what *Introit* happened in the origins of Christianity under the pious followers of the holy apostles.[56] At the very beginning of the service comes the public confession before the altar, and then, when the *introitus* has been sung there follows the *kyrie eleison* so that the friends of God,[57] *Kyrie* realising his eternal mercy, may praise and glorify his name.[58] Then comes the *gloria in excelsis*,[59] in which we give thanks for having been *Gloria* raised by God's son to eternal life[60] and to the enjoyment of God's greatest gifts, and for being returned to our original state.[61] After such

46. *Offenbarlich ampt zu treyben, ist einem knecht Gottis gegeben nit unter dem hutlin tzu spilen*; John 18[20] ('I have spoken openly …'); cf. p. 172/13f. below.

47. 2 Corinthians 13[10]; Ephesians 2[22].

48. 1 Corinthians 4[1f. 17ff.] (Paul and Timothy as trustworthy stewards); sim. Luke 12[42].

49. Matthew 5[15].

50. Luke 24[47f.]

51. Luke 11[52].

52. Isaiah 22[22]; cf. also Revelation 3[7].

53. John 17[8. 26].

54. *geheim Gotis*; cf. Goertz p. 318 n. 3.

55. *one stückwerck*; Isaiah 28[10. 13].

56. Epitome of church histories of Sozomen, Socrates, Theodoret by Cassiodorus in the sixth century.

57. Favourite term of Müntzer's, from German mysticism.

58. Jeremiah 31[7. 31ff.]; Romans 9[15f.. 23ff.]

59. Luke 2[14].

60. John 17[2f.]

61. *in den ersten unsern ursprung.*

thanksgiving the people are comforted with the words of Boaz to his harvesters:[62] 'The Lord be with you', we sing to the sons of God, the ripened wheat.[63] Then the whole church wishes the servant of God a *Salutation* pure spirit (as St. Paul teaches his pupil, Timothy, saying):[64] 'And with your spirit' – lest this needy gathering[65] have a godless man for its preacher.[66] For no one who lacks the spirit of Christ can be a child of God.[67] How can he who has never passively endured[68] the working of God know anything about it?[69] And if he knows nothing of it how can he have anything to say? For so often one blind man is found leading another though he himself has no idea of the way.[70] Hence in the intercessory prayers which follow for the whole assembly of the *Collect* great Christian church[71] we raise up our prayers against the lamentable weaknesses which have penetrated it so deeply[72] and *1st Lesson* which prevent the most glorious name of God from shining out before the entire world.[73] Then prior to God the father letting his most beloved son speak through the gospel the people are reminded by the holy readings[74] and the letters of the dear apostles that every elect person should submit to the working of God.[75] After this the *Gradual* *Gradual* and the *Halleluja* are sung, to encourage everyone[76] to set his *Halleluja* firm trust in the word of God. For by such acts of praise from the psalms he sees how almighty God has dealt with his beloved elect, how he draws them to him, and how they thank him for his fatherly chastisements – for all of his infinite kindness.[77] Before the *Prose* or *Sequence* we sing the psalm *miserere mei deus*[78] etc., to the eighth *Sequence* melody.[79]

Secondly, it should be noted that instead of the [sections from the] epistle and the gospel, we invariably read a whole chapter in order to *2nd Lesson*

62. Ruth 2[4].
63. Matthew 13[23, 38].
64. 2 Timothy 4[22].
65. *durfftige samlung*.
66. Psalm 50[16].
67. Romans 8[9, 14].
68. Lit., 'suffered'.
69. Isaiah 5[12.20]; Psalm 111 [2, 10].
70. Matthew 15[14].
71. The Church universal.
72. Ecclesiasticus 34[18–26] (worship must be sincere); F. amends to Ezekiel 34[2ff.]
73. 1 Corinthians 2[7]; F. amends to 1 Timothy 2[1], but unnecessarily.
74. *gelese*.
75. Wisdom 1[1–15]; F. reads Wisdom 7, incorrectly; Psalm 85[8].
76. *gehertzt werd*.
77. Psalm 44[1ff., 11, 22ff.]; 34; Romans 7[24f.]; 8.
78. Psalm 51 ('Have mercy on me, O God').
79. *im tono peregrino*; the eighth melody, a particular favourite of Müntzer. (F.)

1 Cho. 2

Psal. 117
1 Petri 2

Mar. 16
Collos. v.1

Jere. 31

Actuum 2

1 Chor. 14

depart from the piecemeal approach,[80] and so that the holy scripture of the Bible can become the property of the whole people.[81] This constant hearing of the divine word will also make the superstitious ceremonies or rites in the service redundant. All this, however, is a gradual process, gently easing away from such ceremonies, and guiding the people in their own language, and in the singing to which they are accustomed, just as children are first nourished with milk;[82] this checks any tendencies to irreverence, and yet gives no scope to their evil practices.[83] Although it does, of course, provoke much scandal among our opponents, the most effective way to silence opposition has always been such reform of worship. Hence even in the Mass we sing the epistles and the gospel in our own language, just as the holy apostle Paul had his epistles read out openly before the whole congregation.[84] And Christ our saviour ordered the gospel to be preached to every creature[85] without the addition of subtleties or obscurities; not in Latin or any other extras, for it should be preached with no regard for persons and according to the capacity of each and every man to understand it in his own language.[86]

Roma 10

Matt. 10

Luce 2

Thirdly, after the gospel, on Sundays and feast days, the agreed collection[87] of the main articles of the faith which refutes the crude errors found in the church is sung, lest the pseudo-Christians complain this is being denied, now that the Mass is being presented to the whole world[88] without any mystification.[89] *Creed*

Isaie 1

Psal. 49

Fourthly, comes the sermon, set there so that the singing heard during the service may be explained. For, as David says,[90] 'The explanation of your word gives the little ones understanding.' After the sermon 'Now we beg the holy spirit'[91] is sung, and then comes the *Benedictus* which gives the preacher a moment to catch his breath; in it *Sermon*

Benedictus

80. Isaiah 28[10, 13].
81. 1 Corinthians 2[15].
82. 1 Corinthians 2[5]; 1 Peter 2[2].
83. *yrer bösen weyse kein stat gegeben werd*; Psalm 118[14] ('The Lord is my strength and my song').
84. *offenbar*, cf. n. 46 above; the reference is to Colossians 4[16].
85. Mark 16[15].
86. Jeremiah 31[34]; Acts 2[8]; 1 Corinthians 14 (speaking in tongues).
87. *zu sammen getragen uber ein kommen*; the Nicene creed.
88. Romans 10[18].
89. *unvorholen*; Matthew 10[26f]; Luke 2[30-32].
90. Psalm 119[130]; (*not* Daniel 2[21] (F.)).
91. *Nu bitten wir den heiligen geist.*

we praise God for the preaching of the word of God. There is no offertory[92] during the Mass.

Fifthly the Preface is sung, reminding the Christian people that they have come to know the first born of all creatures in the fullness and knowledge of the will of God and of the knowledge of God which, like all the elect, he has [received] from God himself.

Sixth the *Sanctus* is sung, to explain what a man must be like if he is to handle the sacrament without damage to his soul:[93] namely, that he should, and must know that God is in him, not imagining or conjecturing that God is, as it were, a thousand miles away, but that the heavens and the earth are full, full of God;[94] that the father is continually bringing the son to birth in us, and that the crucified one himself is being brought to our understanding by the holy spirit in the experience of heart-felt sorrow. Moreover [the sanctus explains] that we lack only the will to recognise our blindness and to realise that by putting us to shame God gives us the highest honour, by visiting the body with illness he [assures] the health of the spirit etc.[95] Thus God's name is glorified when ours is dragged in the dust and dishonoured for no cause, and for no fault of our own, etc.[96]

Sanctus

Seventh, to enable us to bear patiently such a high and heavy visitation[97] we follow the pattern which Jesus Christ, the son of God, has commanded his church to follow, to be mindful of him through all our sorrows, so that our soul may yearn and hunger after the bread of life.[98] We need, therefore, to glorify to the utmost these most glorious words of Christ, and to warn everyone against cleaving to this life.[99] For Christ wants his remembrance, his being and his word to dwell in the soul of man, not as in cattle but as in his temple, having been ransomed at such cost by his precious blood.[100]

Words of Institution

92. *kein opffer*; K. Honemeyer suggests that this is a reference, not to the Mass as sacrifice, which would be out of context and banal, but to the practice of the congregation coming forward and laying a gift of money on the altar, 'Thomas Müntzers Allstedter Gottesdienst', in A. Friesen and H.-J. Goertz (edd.), *Thomas Müntzer*, p. 232; Isaiah 1[11]; Psalm 50[9ff.]

93. Colossians 1[22,27f.(?)] ('Christ in you, the hope of glory').

94. 1 Corinthians 15[28]; Jeremiah 23[23]; probably Matthew 21[13] (for Müntzer the temple signifies man's soul); sim. Luke 19[45f.], Mark 11[17]; cf. l. 27 below.

95. 1 Corinthians 1[27f.]; 1 Corinthians 2[3]; Psalm 49[5f.] ('Why should I fear in the evil day?').

96. *on all unser vorwircken und vorwarlosen*; Matthew 5[11].

97. *anfechtung*: trial, tribulation.

98. John 13[16]; 16[20ff., 33]; Lamentations 3 esp.[25f.]; Luke 2[25].

99. Colossians 3[1ff.]

100. 1 Peter 1[18].

Eusebius et alii[101]

1 Chori. 11

Joan 15

Psal. 119

Esaie 40

Nume. 23

Contra officium
Christi[109]
Jo n. 5
Psal. 18
In prima ecclesia
expellebantur
propterea
catecumini[112]
Matt. 18
Matt. 13

Consecration

Eighth, in the primitive church the words of consecration were spoken publicly and this was only departed from because of a fantasy about some shepherds in the fields.[101] But now we sing these same words of consecration publicly in order to avoid the superstition which has arisen in the churches due to the abuse of the Mass. For Christ, the son of God, did not keep these same words secret or speak them to one person only but to everyone, as the text of the gospel shows quite clearly.[102] He speaks in the plural: 'Take and eat etc.', 'take and drink from it, all of you etc.' Moreover, the consecration is a blessing[103] which is performed not just by one person but by the whole gathered congregation. Let that be a retort to our opponents, who persecute us without just cause,[104] saying that we teach even yokels[105] from the fields to celebrate Mass. Any pious, good-hearted man will see from this what sort of respect they have for the son of God, as if he were some painted puppet,[106] or the Mass some act of magic like the incantations used to conjure up the devil.[107] They dare to imagine that one can conjure up Christ, the son of God, with incantations, too, as and when man's arrogance finds this desirable. No, not so! Christ only meets the needs of the hungry in spirit; the godless he leaves unsatisfied.[108] What can Christ do for those whom he finds coming to the sacrament without a hungry, unsatisfied soul?[110] He must needs be perverse with the perverse and good with the good.[111] What use is the symbol to a person who scorns the

---

101. Eusebius and others; cf. Eusebius' *Church History* VII, 9; Tertullian, *De spectaculis*, 25; Ambrose, *De mysteriis* IX, 54; all imply that the words of consecration were said out loud, the congregation responding, 'Amen'.
This must be a reference to the story told by John Moschus (c. 550–619) in his *Pratum Spirituale* (MPG LXXXVII, 2, col. 3079–3083); some Syrian shepherd boys, whiling away the time by celebrating a mock Mass, pronounced the words of consecration with which they were very familiar, since the priests pronounced them in a loud clear voice. No sooner had they done this when a bolt of lightning destroyed the mock altar. When the awful truth was eventually extracted from the terrified boys by the local bishop they were promptly incarcerated in a monastery. This, allegedly, led to the practice of saying the word of consecration silently to prevent such profanation.

102. 1 Corinthians 11[23ff.]

103. *termung*; i.e. *Wandlung*; 'transformation' (Bräuer/Ullmann).

104. John 15[25]; Psalm 120[2].

105. *die rossbuben auff dem felde*; cf. n. 101 above; precise reference unclear.

106. *ein gemaltes menlin oder ein gaukelspiel do man den teuffel mit worten beschweret, betzaubert.*

107. Isaiah 40[18ff.]; Numbers 23[23].

108. Cf. Luke 1[53].

109. Against the office of Christ.

110. John 5[38ff.(?)].

111. Psalm 18[26].

reality?[112] Within every gathering, however, there are certainly many pious men, and for the sake of their faith he truly comes to it to satisfy their souls etc.[113]

Ninth. The formula for the consecration, or the Lord's Supper is sung, using the same melody as for the *Preface*, and with the following words:[114] 'The day before Jesus chose to suffer he took the bread in his holy, worthy hands and raised his eyes to heaven to you, God, his almighty father; he thanked you, blessed it, and broke it, and gave it to his disciples, saying: 'Take, and eat from this, all of you.' Raising his hand the priest says: 'This is my body, which is given up for you.' Then the minister will turn, take the cup facing the people and say: 'Likewise in the same way, when they had eaten, he took the cup in his holy, worthy hands, and thanked you and blessed it, and gave it to his disciples, saying:[117] 'This is the cup of my blood, of the new and eternal testament, a sacrament[118] of faith, which was spilt for you and for many for the forgiveness of sin.' Again turning towards the altar he says; 'You should remember me every single time you do this.'

Tenth. Immediately after the elevation, to the same melody, the *Our Father* following words are sung: 'Therefore let us all make our prayers as Jesus Christ, the true son of God, has taught us, saying: 'Our Father in heaven' etc., to which all the people respond by singing: 'Amen'.[119] Then so that we can catch breath for a moment, there will be silence, during which the priest will divide up the sacrament for the communicants and will sing: 'From eternity to eternity'. Then the common people will answer: 'Amen'. The priest will respond: 'The peace of the Lord be with you for ever.'[120] Then the people will *The Peace* answer 'And with your spirit.' Soon after this, that their minds may be focussed during the Mass on the death and resurrection of Christ and helped to understand it better, all the people will sing three times: 'O lamb of God, you who take away the sin of the world etc.', which *Agnus Dei* is the confession of John,[122] who baptised Jesus, adding from the gospel of Luke XVII: 'Have mercy on us',[123] and the last time: 'Give us

Margin notes (left):
minister oculos
at sacrificium[115]
er sich umb.[116]

. 14
ult.
nibus
lis[121] Pauli
s 1
4. 3
. 3
8
cas calcanei mei
ndat me[127]
1. 2
2

---

112. In the primitive church the catechumens were sent out because of this.
113. Matthew 18[20]; Matthew 13[8ff].
114. Cf. 1 Corinthians 11[23f].
115. The minister raises his eyes and makes ready the sacrifice.
116. He turns round.
117. 1 Corinthians 11[25].
118. *ein geheim.*
119. 1 Corinthians 14[16].
120. Luke 24[36].
121. In all the letters of Paul.
122. John 1[29].
123. Luke 17[13].

your peace'. For Christ died and rose again because of our sin, desiring to justify us,[124] which he alone does, and which we must passively accept. On such [evidence of] faith[125] the most revered sacrament is given to the people during the *agnus Dei*,[126] omitting the hypocritical confession of the papists. For in every sermon they are collectively exhorted that everyone should keep in mind his old life and past lusts and see how richly merited his cross is etc.[127] Man commits sin. God exacts penance for it, and it is for man to come to terms with this.[128] No man can have a good, pure, and peaceable conscience before God unless he recognises this whole-heartedly.[129] That is why the third *agnus Dei* is concluded with: 'Give us your peace', and 'Let your servant, O Lord, go in peace according to your word.'[130] For only the long-suffering are worthy of the saviour of life, etc.

Eleventh. The most revered sacrament is then distributed in both kinds, notwithstanding the gossip of the hucksters[131] in this market-place or that, in this group or that. For if we do not receive the sacrament, the holy symbol, how are we to understand the reality which is signified by the symbol? Hence after the communion one says to the people: 'Thank God', and 'Bless the Lord etc.' *Benediction*

Communio

Finally, no one should be surprised that we hold the Mass in German in Allstedt. The full reasons for this can be expounded at a more opportune time. There is nothing new, either, about adopting a different pattern from that of Rome. The church in Milan has a very different way of conducting the Mass than in Rome: every diocese has its own peculiar ceremonies or rites. Why should we not do the same when circumstances permit it?[132] For we are German people in Allstedt, not Italians, and want to burrow our way through the great confusion[133] and find out what it is that we should believe. The sole way we can do this properly is by acting according to the very word of God. The Croatians, who are of the Roman allegiance, hold the Mass and their other services in their own tongue. The Armenians, a great people, use the vernacular, too, and show the people the sacrament on the paten. Likewise the Bohemians have many differing

Luce. 12

---

124. 1 Peter 3[18]; v. 15, frequently cited on the need to confess one's faith, may be meant; cf. Dismer, p. 126.

125. *Auff solchen glauben.*

126. Lamb of God.

127. Lamentations 3[39ff]; Psalm 48[5] ('the iniquity of my heels shall compass me about').

128. *es gehort dem menschen, sich dorin zu richten.*

129. Romans 2[1ff.]

130. Luke 2[29].

131. *grempeler.*

132. Luke 12[57].

133. *das getumle.*

practices in their vernacular Mass. Likewise the Mozarabs[134] and the Russians have many other rites but that does not make them into devils. Likewise in the country[135] where the Christian faith first began there are some fourteen sects, all of which have different practices from us. O! what blind, ignorant men we are to vaunt ourselves as the only Christians in outward ostentation, quarrelling madly among ourselves more like beasts than men! Surely every servant of the word of God has the authority to teach the people of his parish a pattern of worship using psalms and songs of praise from the Bible readings to edify them. As Paul says so clearly in Ephesians 5:[136] 'You should', he says, 'be filled with the holy spirit, and greet one another with psalms and songs of praise and spiritual hymns and tunes,[137] singing and playing before the Lord and giving thanks at all times for one another.' 1 Corinthians 14[138] says the same. If we are going to call it un-Christian to sing and read in German in the churches, how will we fare when we have to bear witness about how we have been moved to faith.[139]

How Baptism is Conducted

If one of our children is being baptised the god-parents are exhorted – as they value the salvation of their souls – to pay good heed to what happens in baptism,[140] so that later on, when the child is growing up, they can report it to him, so that in time the baptism can be understood. Hence Psalm 68[141] is read in German, explaining how man is born to toil in fear and want,[142] and how the great waves rise over his neck etc. Then we read the third chapter of Matthew[143] on the baptism of Christ, which shows how Christ came to us as we were drowning[144] and saved us from the raging waves. Christ, however, soon climbed out of the water again; the waves did not overpower him as they did us, though for the sake of all righteousness he had to go through with it. We poor, wretched, pitiable men have for so long reduced baptism to mere fantasy and water-sprinkling. Salt is presented to the child, saying: 'N., receive the salt of wisdom, so you may learn to distinguish good and evil in the spirit of wisdom, and

134. Descendants of the Christian Visigothic kingdom in Spain.
135. Palestine.
136. Ephesians 5[18ff.]
137. *leissen*.
138. 1 Corinthians 14[25].
139. *unser bewegung zum glauben sollen vortragen*.
140. *was man bey der touffe handelt*.
141. Psalm 69.
142. *wie ein erbtsaliger mensch zu angst und noth geborn ist*.
143. Matthew 3[13ff.]
144. Lit. 'drowned'.

never be trodden down by the devil.' Then the child is addressed: 'Come in to the people of Christ, so God may find you like the pure wheat.' The creed is then spoken in the baptismal service and the works and pomp and deceit of the devil are renounced. While oil is being put on the breast and the back of the child the priest declares: 'Rejoice, N., that you are now encompassed by the eternal loving kindness of God.' If the priest is ready to baptise he asks: 'Do you want to be baptised?' If the god-parents say, 'Yes,' then the priest declares: 'I baptise you in the name of the father and the son and the holy spirit.[145] Amen. May God, who has conceived you of his eternal love, grant that you may avoid the oil of the sinner.'[146] And putting the bonnet[147] [on the child] he says: 'Put on the new garment; put away the old one; do not patch the old garment with a new patch, lest when you come before the awesome judge you may not be able to endure.'[148] Then, as the candle [is given]: 'N., let Christ be your light; see that you light is not darkness,[149] but let the life of Christ be your mirror, that you may live to all eternity. Amen.'

Binding People together in Marriage
We allow no fooling around here,[150] but read out to them in German Psalm 127, *beati omnes*,[151] then we read from Chapter Two of the gospel of John about the marriage[152] and give them some advice etc.

Bringing the Sacrament to the Sick
This is the way the sacrament is given to the sick: They make a general confession. Then from the gospel, Luke 12 is read:[153] 'In whatever house you go etc.' After that, 'I believe in God the father.' After that, The Lord's Prayer. Then the Lord's Supper is read aloud: 'The day before Jesus chose to suffer etc.' After distributing the sacrament one says, 'O Lamb of God etc.' and thanks God, and exhorts the sick man to prepare himself for the cross etc.

Burial of the Dead
Luce. 1 Omitting the wake we sing the *Benedictus*[154] as we fetch the dead. All the people follow the body and join in the singing of the *Benedictus*.

145. Cf. Matthew 28[19].
146. Cf. Psalm 141[5], and the Prague Manifesto, p. 373/13 below.
147. *imponendo mitram.*
148. Matthew 9[16]; cf. 2 Corinthians 5[10].
149. Cf. Matthew 6[23].
150. *Do halten wir keinen schertz mit.*
151. Psalm 128, 'Blessed is everyone ...'
152. *wirtschafft;* John 2[1ff.]
153. Presumably Luke 10[5] is meant.
154. Luke 1[68-79].

Then after the burial the people sing: 'In the midst of life etc.'[155] We then go into the church, where the priest sings the epistle: 'We do not want you to be ignorant' etc.;[156] the gospel is John 5 on the raising of the dead[157] and we conclude with the hymn: 'in the midst of life etc.'

If, however, a little child can instruct us how to do better, we will be glad to accept this.

155. *Media vita in morte*, translated into German in the 15th century. (F.)
156. 1 Thessalonians 4[13ff.]
157. John 5[24-9].

German Evangelical Mass

The Mass in German according to the Gospel. Hitherto the Mass has been in Latin and treated by the papalist priests as a sacrifice, to the great detriment of the Christian faith. Now, in these critical times, it has been reformed, thus exposing the abominable idolatry so long perpetrated by such abuses of the Mass. Thomas Müntzer. Allstedt 1524.

Foreword

To all the elect friends of God I, Thomas Müntzer, a servant of God, wish grace, peace, and the pure and upright fear of God. Some church services and hymns in the German tongue have been issued recently at my initiative,[158] since for a long time services have been conducted by the papal priests and monks in Latin, to the detriment of the Christian faith. Hateful envy, however, has moved some learned men to take this exceeding ill of me. They have done their best to prevent them being used, for they have come to the conclusion that I am trying in this way to bring back and justify the old papal ceremonies, masses, matins and vespers. Their accusation in fact runs clean contrary to my aim and intention, which is to rescue people's poor, pitiable, blind consciences by producing a shortened form[159] of what the devious, false priests, monks and nuns had previously chanted and read in the churches and monasteries in Latin, thus withholding it from the masses of the poor laity, to the destruction of the faith, the gospel, the word of God, and contrary to the clear, lucid teaching of the holy apostle Paul in 1 Cor. 14.[160] Hence my genuine intention remains to this day that of helping our poor, confused[161] Christian people by [providing] services in German, whether they be masses, matins or vespers, which will enable every good-hearted person to see and hear and understand how these abandoned papal villains have robbed our poor Christian people of Scripture, to their great detriment; and how they have kept from them their true interpretation, while at the same time having the nerve to gobble up the possessions of the poor folk. Their deceitful conduct is described by Christ in Matthew 23, by St. Paul in 2 Timothy 3,[162] and indeed by the holy apostle Peter too in 2 Peter 2,[163] as well as by all the dear

---

158. *The German Church Service*, cf. p. 166ff. above; a new facsimile edition of the *German Mass*, edited by Siegfried Bräuer, will be published by the Evangelische Verlagsanstalt, Berlin, in 1988.

159. *auff ein kleyne zeyt vortragen*; F. understands *vorgetragen*.

160. i.e. the gifts of the Spirit are for the edification of all.

161. *zurfallenden*, lit. 'disintegrating'; cf. p. 166/25 above.

162. Matthew 23[2ff.]; 2 Timothy 3[2-7.]

163. 2 Peter 2[1.]

prophets. But since the poor common man has been so accustomed to putting his faith in mere pretences, in truly idolatrous ceremonies in the churches, with all their chants and readings and papal black magic,[164] it is only right and proper that – as the preachers of the gospel[165] admit themselves – considerations should be shown for the weak. 1 Corinthians 3.[166] Surely there could be no better or fairer way of showing such consideration than by using German versions of these same services,[167] so that their poor, weak consciences are not torn away abruptly from their bearings, or fobbed off with whatever new-fangled songs[168] happen to turn up, but can be led by the psalms and songs, now they are translated from Latin to German, to the word of God and the right understanding of the Bible readings. I will also enable them to appreciate the intentions of the good fathers who originally established these liturgies to build up faith at its first beginnings.[169] Another reason is that consciences, torn away from the pretences of the churches will be drawn by the chants and psalms of God expounded by the readings, so that they do not remain as coarse and uncomprehending as a chopping-block.[170]

No one, then, should take it amiss that I have only issued five services, for my intention is that everyone should feel free to shorten or lengthen them himself as circumstances dictate. Likewise with such hymns as *et in terra* or *patrem*,[171] which sometimes drone on and become tedious, it is up to the individual to include them or omit them, whichever is more convenient. I have no intention of perpetuating or restoring the papal abomination by them. Whatever has been instituted and commanded by men, like these songs and their music, and not instituted and commanded by God, can be added to or subtracted from by anyone at their discretion. He may continue using the service for one of the great feasts as long as he likes, singing for example, from the Pentecost liturgy until Advent, or right through Advent to Christmas; the Christmas service can be used till the Purification of Mary;[172] the service for the Passion of Christ can be sung from the Purification of Mary until Easter, or right on until Pentecost, as seems best to whoever is in charge. The main thing is

---

164. *gramentzen*.
165. i.e. supporters of reformation.
166. 1 Corinthians 3[1ff.]
167. *lobgesenge*, 'songs of praise', as in p. 180/9 above.
168. *mit losen unbewerten liedlen*.
169. *zu erbawung des glaubens als zur ankunfft*.
170. *hackebloch*; a favourite smile of Müntzer.
171. The Gloria and the Lord's Prayer.
172. 2 February.

that the psalms are sung and read properly for the poor layman, for it is in them that the working of the holy spirit can be clearly discerned: how one should walk before God and come to the beginnings of the true Christian faith. How faith should be maintained in the face of great temptation[173] is also very clearly expounded by the holy spirit in the psalms. That is why St. Paul teaches that one should find discipline and delight in spiritual hymns and psalms. Ephesians 5.[174] This means, then, that these delicate priests must start racking their brains for the sake of the poor folk, or else abandon their priestly trade. Have they any right to laze around, only delivering one sermon on Sunday, and playing the lordling[175] for the rest of the week? No, by no means! I know very well that they will turn up[176] their noses at this, and make a fool of it all. It is nonetheless true. There can be no excuse for them. For until the crudeness of the ordinary man, his ignorance and hypocrisy, are refined somewhat by hymns in German, there can be little progress in setting our poor, crude Christian people on its feet again, whatever anyone says.[177] Hence the ordinary man should pay no attention at all to these lazy wretches, the priests, who want to spare their delicate constitutions and claim that they want, and indeed have to offer milk first.[178] Milk! It is dragons' milk that they are offering! They are scared for their skins, and imagine they can be at the same time preachers of the faith and of the gospel. When will their faith be tested like gold in the fire? 1 Peter 1.[179] As St Paul teaches us, the priest must be ready to follow Christ as he did. 1 Corinthians 11[180] He should pay no heed to the raging of the tyrants, but administer the testament of Christ[181] publicly, and sing and preach in German, so that men can become Christ-formed.[182] Romans 8.[183] Then all the greed, the usury and the devious tricks of the priests, monks, and nuns, who, for all their fine appearances, at present stand in the way of faith, will topple over immediately, torn out at the roots. God help us all thereto. Amen.

173. *anfechtung.*
174. Ephesians 5[19].
175. *juncker.*
176. *dovor rümpffen.*
177. Radicals like the Swiss Brethren who reject all music in worship?
178. The argument has shifted from the genuine need to take account of the weak in faith by providing transitional liturgies to the false use of Paul's argument about the weak to justify pastoral timidity in the face of princely opposition to reformation; cf. 1 Corinthians 3[1ff.]
179. 1 Peter 1[7].
180. 1 Corinthians 11[1ff.]
181. *das testament Christi*; i.e. the Lord's Supper – 'this is the new covenant (Vg. testamentum) in my blood', ibid. v. 25.
182. *christformig.*
183. Romans 8[29].

PROTESTATION OR PROPOSITION

The autumn of 1523 saw Müntzer increasingly in conflict with the strongly Catholic Ernest von Mansfeld, many of whose Catholic subjects had come flocking to Müntzer's services. In forbidding this the Count had justified himself by reference to the Imperial Mandate of 6 March 1523 which had proscribed new religious polemics in the expectation of a General Council settling the controversies.

Müntzer had denounced the Count's actions and when the latter complained to the Allstedt Council wrote a defiant letter to him (Nr. 44) on 22 September and another a few days later to his Elector, Frederick the Wise (Nr. 45). This letter calls for the setting up of an independent tribunal of the elect to which Müntzer could present his case. It twice uses the root-form *protestir, protesteren*, which appears in the title of this writing as *Protestation*, 'declaration'; and contains many verbal and thematic parallels to the *Protestation*. The use of the 'trumpet' theme from the Prague Manifesto and the quotation from Acts 26[26] (Paul's hearing before Festus is no 'hole-and-corner' affair) make it clear that by *protesteren* the proclamation or public testimony to the Gospel is meant. It is, after all, the suppression of this public ministry and worship that is at issue. The actual term *erbieten* ('proposition' or 'proposal') does not occur in the letter but Müntzer does indicate his readiness to have his views tested by 'divine law' (p. 70/10 above) and to retract them if proved wrong – precisely his 'proposition' here and in letter 52.

This suggestion of an impartial hearing may seem totally impractical (Elliger, p. 402); he had, however, already challenged Count Ernest to send his representatives to Allstedt to debate the issue. One should bear in mind also Luther's own appeals from the Pope to a free and Christian General Council and the rash of 'impartial' civic disputations at this time. Müntzer's critique of Biblicism and of the universities, and his implicit rejection of the Christendom concept only accentuate this dramatic crisis of authority. Apolitical, then, as this writing may at first sight appear, it is directed against arbitrary secular intervention by Count Ernest and should be read in conjunction with his blunt warning to the Saxon Elector that the sword has to be taken from the tyrant and given to the elect.

It is, in fact, part of a whole cluster of writings of which the most important is *On Counterfeit Faith*. Until recently it was believed to have followed closely on the heels of the latter. The consensus of scholarly opinion, however, (Bräuer, Dismer, Elliger, Stayer) now tends to support the view that the *Protestation* was published first, in December 1523. As its initial words put it, it was to 'hail the new year'. When Münzter wrote to Zeiss on 2 December 1523, he had still to add the Biblical quotations to the writing which became known as *On Counterfeit Faith*. On the Gotha manuscript of the latter there is a marginal note: 'In the same year 1524 Müntzer had published a pamphlet entitled *Protestation or Proposition of Thomas Müntzer*, (F., p. 569). The priority of the *Protestation*, accordingly, seems probable, although to all intents and purposes they can be taken as complementary and contemporaneous.

Not unlike Calvin's *Institutes*, Müntzer's *Protestation* is both an apologia for a persecuted minority and a conscious exposition of the Christian faith. Although it is a plea for a hearing, in its later sections one senses Müntzer's apprehension that, like his crucified Lord, only rejection and suffering lie ahead for him. For if, as he believes, the Christian Church lies in ruins, how is one to persuade those who are responsible for, and indeed benefit from, this state of affairs to change their ways? How convince those proud of their insights that they are blind? How shock the 'conventional' Roman or Lutheran Christians out of their complacency, without totally alienating them?

It is a carefully organised piece of writing. With brevity, liveliness and homely imagery it engages the reader from the start, luring the 'brethren', the 'elect friends of God', to whom it is primarily addressed into ever deeper waters. It is poetry masquerading as prose. Pole-vaulting over Christian conventions and territories it uses the new medium of the printing press as an eschatological tool to summon a court of the elect from all nations and tribes. Before this bar, and none other, Müntzer is willing to appear. In fact, throughout this book that is what he is already doing: presenting his case to the elect, documenting it so abundantly from Scripture that both margins of the page are frequently needed, appealing beyond Rome and Wittenberg to the higher court of what we would, today, call world opinion. Müntzer remains humanist enough for the myth of beginnings to compel him. Truth lies in the beginning of things: for the Church in its apostolic purity, for the individual in his or her initiation into faith. This cannot possibly be infant (or rather 'infantile') baptism. As long as this, with its ludicrous accessories, is maintained there can be no growth in faith.

In one sense – the cultic sense – Müntzer is not particularly concerned about baptism, as his contemporaneous liturgies illustrate. It is, however, absolutely crucial for him to demonstrate that it is only by way of despair, madness, error, crime, sin, unbelief – all adult prerogatives – that true initiation into faith can take place, as fear of the Lord becomes sudden and desperate reality.

The fear of the Lord is the beginning of all beginnings: the groaning, yearning of the elect friends of God, conscious of their virtual submergence in, and over-shadowing by, the towering arrogance of the godless. To reach the living waters of apostolic Christianity the elect have to turn their backs both on the hypocritical moralism of the Roman Church and on the counterfeit faith of the Lutherans, and to foster the disciplined nurture of their children in a Christ-formed life.

The aim of this discipline is freedom: to free the elect from the grotesque insensitivity, or hardening, which blinds people to the superficiality and two-facedness of contemporary Christianity. In her apostolic days the daughter of Sion, the Church, did not confuse inner reality with outward symbols but separated herself sharply from the godless world by the catechumenate. There is no evidence in Scripture of children being baptised, or indeed of the water baptism of Mary and the disciples.

True baptism, then, is no longer understood. The very foundations of the Church, as a result, are unsound, built on sand, on dregs. In reality this water baptism of children means that Christianity has become infantile, drunk on the wine of licentious living. That is its new foundation, its *grundsuppe*.

The theoretical basis is supplied by the piecemeal interpretation of Scripture by the academics, the biblical scholars. A true exegesis of John 1–7, on the other hand, reading it as a whole and integrating it with the prophets of the Old Testament, makes it clear that the waters of true baptism flow from the side of Christ on the Cross; they are the waters of tribulation in which one's spirit moves in God, so that the bride (the Church) can hear the voice of the bridegroom (Christ).

Historically, the result of shunning the true baptism of the spirit has been tyrannical dogmatism, a burgeoning of pagan superstitions and an inversion of all genuine priorities. The Germans inherited all this when they were converted.

The resultant degeneration of the Church into a number of feuding sects should prompt self-criticism, for heresies are only permitted by God where the Church has neglected its genuine task. They make manifest the unbelief with which the Church refuses to come to terms.

Müntzer moves to an interesting assessment of Biblical authority in the light of the claims of other religions. The Bible is not a quarry for texts to defend oneself and condemn others. Islam and Judaism have their own sacred writings; they are not likely to be impressed by the authoritarianism of a corrupt Church, with its 'honey-sweet', indulgent Christ.

Until, then, we are purged of our creaturely attachments the Bible remains a closed book. If one is not to confound true faith with mere plagiarism, one needs to experience the power of God in the abyss of the soul.

Thus the controversy between Rome and Wittenberg about justification by faith is irrelevant. Without God's work in our hearts, as confirmed by Scripture, we remain in bondage to our natural reasoning and inclinations.

The serried array of Biblical texts indicates the centrality of sections 17 and 18. There can be no two-level Christianity, one for the learned cleric, who indolently and patronisingly palms off anxious enquiries, and another for the humble laity. All the elect have the same terrible anxieties and require sensitive pastoral care, which only those who have experienced such tribulations can give. Such pastors can expect to be rejected by the world; and they should welcome correction by others.

Müntzer, too, is ready to admit his errors before an impartial tribunal; indeed this is precisely his proposal or 'proposition': that he and his adversaries be summoned to such a tribunal. The need to reform the clergy of both confessions is urgent. He will take no steps to protect himself, any more than Christ did. He begs his opponents – without much hope – not to condemn him in advance without a fair hearing.

Few of the themes developed here are new. The need for 'separation' of the elect and for personal experience; the broad ecumenical perspective, the pastoral concern, the critique of blind preachers who 'steal Scripture' are all to be found in the Prague Manifesto. The pointed polemic against the Biblical scholars, however, is new, as are many of the questions about the authority of the Church, of Scripture, and of infant baptism. Almost as important is what is missing: the egocentricity of the Prague Manifesto, the obscure semi-Gnostic vocabulary, and most of the apocalyptic material.

A relatively clear analysis of the situation of the church is the result. Above all, the use of Scripture is quite remarkable, not only in its range but in its coherence and originality, binding together the Psalms and the Prophets with Paul and John, and both Testaments with the testament of human experience. We are, in one sense, not far from the mystical exegesis of a Juan Valdes. Yet, of course, Müntzer's grasp of historical reality is much firmer, his concern to change structures of church life more urgent, his conception of the church of the elect quite different from the individualistic piety of the *spirituali*. This is quite a new brand of popular mysticism, though as yet its social dimensions are only fleetingly apparent, as in section 11 where Jezebel becomes archetypal for the persecutor of the faithful, strutting around as a 'painted' cosmetic believer; and probably also in section 2 with its cannibalistic motif: 'all [God's] creatures are being gobbled up'.

Finally, a word on the language of this tract. It is conversational or exhortatory in tone rather than soberly didactic, not unlike, one suspects, his sermons. The dialogue in section 17 is earthy and entertaining, yet typically complemented by a barrage of Biblical texts, which deserve the most careful attention. The imagery is often drawn from the fields or from domestic life: the plough, the tree-stump, the thorn-hedges, the mustard seed, the fatted pigs, the dog with its teeth clamped on to a sausage, the sorrowing mother, the white-washed house; then there is the more exotic bestiary of lions and wolves (often interchangeable with dogs and pigs), of Cerberus and the 'horned apes' who war against the saints (Daniel 7^{21}) and an inexhaustible mine of Biblical imagery, often subtly transmuted: the daughter of Sion, the house built on sand, the 'waters' imagery in John and the prophets, the unforgettable Jezebel depiction. Some of the strangest images, as in the Prague Manifesto, refer to eating: the 'honey-sweet Christ', the *grundsuppe*, the dregs, the *suplin*, for which the 'dumb dogs' scrabble, (cf. notes 76, 124, 256), with which their mouths stink, and which has become the treacherous, intoxicating foundation on which the church is built.

Yet, the images, as in sections 9, 11, 12, conclude or supplement arguments and do not replace them. Despite the cascades of questions and expostulations, the biting shafts of sarcasm, even the occasional aphorism, the flow of thought remains clear, or – should one say – the flow of images remains thoughtful.

Protestation or Proposition[1]

A protestation or proposition by Thomas Müntzer from Stolberg in the Harz mountains, now pastor of Allstedt, about his teachings, beginning with true Christian faith and baptism[2]. 1524. Are you listening, world? I preach to you – as the new year begins[3] – Jesus Christ, he who was crucified, and you and me with him. If it appeals to you accept it, if not, cast it aside.

First

I, Thomas Müntzer, from Stolberg in the Harz, a servant[4] of the living God, by the unchanging will and unwavering mercy of God the father, do commend to you all, elect friends[5] of God, the pure and upright fear of the Lord. This I do in the holy spirit, wishing you also the peace against which the world has set its face. After the head of the household,[6] all-wise and watchful, destined you to be pure wheat and placed you in fruitful and profitable soil,[7] your development has been such that (one could weep to God in vexation) it is hard to see any great difference between you and the tares.[8] For you are hopelessly outshone by the godless sons of wickedness,[9] with their skulking, underhand ways; they tower so high above you, to the front and to the rear, that your piteous and wretched groaning[10] at the lofty pretensions of the cornflowers and the red blooming roses and the prickly thistles[11] has been totally blotted out, surrendered to scorn and

Ro. 1
Malach. 3
Psal. 18
Joan. 14

Math. 13
Marci. 4
Luce. 8
Esaye. 5
Joan. 15
Ecclast. 8
Roma. 8
Can. 2
Treno. 4

1. *Protestation oder empietung*; Stayer: 'Protestation or Demonstration'; Elliger, p. 395 n. 137 translates *empietung* as 'explanatory proof'; cf. p. 208/16 below; the term 'Protestation', perhaps most famously used in the submission of the Lutheran Estates of the Diet of Speyers in 1529, should not be understood in the modern sense of 'protest'; it implies both a testimony, and an assertion of one's rights by submitting a declaration; Müntzer uses *protestatio* elsewhere in the sense of testimony, not least in the title to the Prague Manifesto, cf. p. 362 below; cf. also p. 69/1f. below and p. 68/21 above; on *empietung* cf. p. 202/8 below, 209/2 below, and especially Letters 52 82/21 below and 64 111/32 below; 'proposition' or 'proposal' appear to be the best rendering.

2. *seine lere betreffende und zum anfang von dem rechten christenglawben und der tawffe*; Stayer: 'on the beginning of a genuine Christian faith'; cf. the beginning of section 20; on Müntzer's view of baptism cf. G. Seebass, 'Zum Zeichen der Erwählten ...', in *Umstrittenes Täufertum* ... (Göttingen, 1977), esp. pp. 147–53.

3. 1524.

4. Romans 1[1]; Malachi 3[1]; Psalm 19[11ff.]

5. John 14 esp. vs. 23, 27; cf. *Counterfeit Faith* n. 9.

6. *haussvatter*.

7. Matthew 13[1ff.]; Mark 4[1ff.]; Luke 8[5ff.] (parable of the sower).

8. Isaiah 5 (Israel as God's vineyard); John 15[esp. v. 14] (Christ the true vine).

9. Ecclesiastes 8[10ff.]

10. Romans 8[22f.]

11. Song of Songs 2[2]; in this period the image of the cornflowers and thistles

derision,[12] an ugly sight indeed. Yet no one can doubt that this heart-felt groaning and yearning to follow God's will[13] is the one infallible mark of true apostolic Christianity, gushing out of the hard rock from which the living waters flow,[14] the origin and starting-point for the elect. There is absolutely no other way to help our poor, wretched, pitiable, needy, crude[15] and corrupt Christian people[16] than to direct the elect towards this[17] with all possible urgency, sparing neither work nor effort.[18]

Esaye. 40

Joan. 1

Joan. 4

Psal. 15

Psal. 17

Psal. 76

Joan. 14
Roma 3
De opposito[18]

Second

Ezech. 23

Unless this is done the Christian church will remain even more demented and crazy than all the nations on the face of the earth.[19] Since the beginnings of time, such stiff-necked folly has never raged so clearly, so blatantly, so foully as it does today.[20] All the devious wiles of all sorts of honey-sweet lewdness have reached their height, tricked out[21] at great expense, sometimes with counterfeit faith, sometimes with hypocritical works. So all God's creatures are being gobbled up, as abruptly as one would toss a lewd fellow into hell. This is what awaits the godless.[22]

Third

The first step is to face up to what is wrong with the foolish world[23] and why it has come about,[24] for otherwise it will be impossible for

Timothe. 1

im. 3

atores
tum depicti
n[20]

per totam

---

among the wheat is a common one, sometimes indicating the eventual victory of goodness; *Emblemata*, p. 320.

12. Lamentations 4[15].

13. Isaiah 40[3ff.]; John 1[6ff.]; cf. Prague Manifesto, p. 372/3 below.

14. John 4[13f.]; Psalm 16[5, 11]; 18[2].

15. *groben*; mystical term indicating bondage to material concerns.

16. *christenheyt*.

17. Psalm 77[1ff.]; John 14[16f.]

18. Romans 3[1ff., 31] ('Is the law overthrown? On the contrary!').

19. Ezechiel 23 (the adultery of Oholah, i.e. Samaria, and Oholibah, i.e. Jerusalem); 1 Timothy 1[19f.], 2 Timothy 1[15] (apostasy of Hymenaeus, Alexander, Phygelus, Hermogenes).

20. 2 Timothy 3[1ff.]; in the margin: 'the arrogant lovers of pleasure are cosmetic Christians'.

21. Lit. 'made use of, and concealed themselves with'; cf. 1 Timothy 2[9].

22. Sentence structure as in Bräuer/Ullmann: *das auch jeelich alle creaturn vorschlungen seint, wie man einen buben in die hellen wirfft, also viel wirt den gotlossen vortragen*; jerlich (F.) cf. n. 18 above for Müntzer's understanding of Romans; *jeelich*, abuptly, as suggested by Heidelberg Müntzer Symposium, 1987; cf. Numbers 16[30], the story of Korah.

23. Luke 12[2f.]; Mark 8[15ff.] and Luke 9[41ff.]?

24. *mit alle seinem ursprunge*; 'from its origin on' (Stayer following Bräuer/Ullmann); origin and causation are closely linked in Müntzer; cf. p. 193/10 below.

Luce 9
Per totam Esaiam et
omnes prophetas[25]
Prove. 12
Roma. 13
Joan. 8
Osec. 4
Mat. 24
Prove. 13
Roma. 8
Ephe. 1

the father to set aside his gracious rod. For those whom God has chosen,[25] and who have brought such intolerble abuses upon the Christian people as a whole, must be liberated by the heart-felt truth. Thus it is a disgusting abomination, sitting in the holy place of God,[26] that a child is supposed to live without discipline and as free as the beast in the field.[27] For the sole comfort for the wretched churches is the expectation that the elect will be Christ-formed and pursue God's work in suffering and discipline of all kinds.[28]

Fourth

Josue. 7

1 Timo. 4

Ad Titum 1

Jacobi 1

quem si negaveris

probo cum[31]

Joan. 8

Gala. 5

Likewise the most careful scrutiny must be made of how we Christians have come to have such totally hardened minds,[29] turning our precious Christian faith into such a tawdry bauble, and gaining no real faith at all.[30] We talk big about the truth, we excel in writing great tomes littered with blots and saying: 'I believe, I believe,' although in fact we spend our days in empty quarrels and in worrying about material things.[32] Day by day we become more usurious[33] and yet dare to say: 'I believe the whole Christian faith, accept its truth, and have a firm strong confidence in God etc.' My fine fellow, you have no idea what it is that you say 'Yes' to, or 'No' to. You have not allowed God to root out your thorns and thistles the least little bit.[34] You don't believe it? Your faith in higher things is sure to be fraudulent, for you are unreliable and hesitant about small things. Who would trust you with matters of ultimate importance?[35]

1 Eimo. 1

Esaic. 5

Math. 6

Mat. 25
Vom kegentey

Fifth

Zacha. 9

Daughter of Zion,[37] remember what you were like many years

25. Müntzer thinks here of Israel, God's chosen people, yet repeatedly chastised by 'Isaiah and all the prophets' (margin) for its sins; cf. Proverbs 12[1]; Romans 13[1ff.]

26. John 8 (Jesus' controversy with the Pharisees); Hosea 4[6ff.]; Matthew 24[15ff.]; Ephesians 1[1].

27. wie ein vihe.

28. Proverbs 13[1]; Romans 8[12ff., 29]; Ephesians 1[1, 17ff.]

29. Joshua 7 (sin of Achan); 1 Timothy 4[1f.]

30. zum solchen leichtfertigen dinge . . . one alle ukerkommung; i.e. no real blessing or salvation; cf. the use of the words in the Exposé of False Faith; F. pp. 272/7; 275/23; Titus 1[10ff.]; James 1[22ff., 26].

31 'if you deny this, I affirm it'; F. refers to James 1[12]; probably the reference is to the Pharisees in John 8.

32. Galatians 5[13-26]; 1 Timothy 1[3-11].

33. in broad sense of 'covetous'.

34. Isaiah 5 (vineyard of Israel); Matthew 6 (criticism of hypocrites, materialism).

35. Matthew 25[21].

36. 'On the contrary'.

37. Zechariah 9[9]; Matthew 21[4]; the reference is eschatological as well as historical; the apostolic church will be renewed as Christ enters Jerusalem again (the church).

ago, in the time of the apostles and their pupils, who kept a close and earnest watch[38] lest the enemy, the antagonist of all the pious, should scatter weeds among the wheat.[39] To prevent this only adults were admitted, and after a lengthy period of instruction as church-pupils, being called catechumens because of this teaching. There was no such superstition then of trusting more in the holy symbols than in inward reality.[42] Words fail me! He[44] has never once produced a single thought from any of the works of the Church Fathers, from their beginning to their end, to prove what true baptism is. I would be obliged if any of our learned men of letters could show me a single instance from the holy letters[45] where an immature[46] little child was baptised by CHRIST or his apostles,[47] or if they could prove that we are commanded to have our children baptised in the way it is done today. What's more – since you brag so much about it – you will find nowhere that Mary, the mother of God, or the disciples of CHRIST, were baptised with water.[48] If it were necessary for our salvation, we would much rather embrace a honey-sweet CHRIST and have good Greek or German wine[50] poured over us than submit in such ignorance to this sprinkling with water.

Matt. 21
Ezech. 3
Math. 13
Kegenteyl[40]
Deine handt soltu
niemant bald
aufflegen[41]
1 Timo. 5
Jere. 7
Mat. 12
Ein guter man etc.[43]

1 Chor. 15
Esaie 22
Im kegenteil[49]
Esaic.43
von vorstandt[50]

Sixth

True baptism is not understood. That is why initiation into the Christian Church has become crude monkey-play.[51] The biblical

38. Ezekiel 3[16f.] (called to be a watchman over Israel).

39. Matthew 13[25].

40. Cf. n. 36 above.

41. 1 Timothy 5[22a]; cf. ibid. 3[6], n. 261 below.

42. *auffs ynnerliche wesen*; Jeremiah 7[4-11. 21-8]; Matthew 12[1-14].

43. Matthew 12[35] (A good man ...).

44. *er*; Luther must be meant, though it is interesting that at this stage his name is not explicitly given.

45. Scripture; a play on words: the literalistic (*buchstabische*) scholars fail to prove their case from their chosen authority, the holy *buchstaben*, letters, of the Bible.

46. *unmündiges*, 'immature'; not yet able to distinguish between good and evil; cf. Deuteronomy 1[39].

47. *bothen*, 'messengers'.

48. 1 Corinthians 15[29ff.]; (Paul boasts of those whose baptism is death to the old life and resurrection to new); cf. Isaiah 22[12f.]

49. 'On the contrary'; i.e., far from being understood true baptism has been betrayed.

50. *mit guther malvhasier und wein*; Greek wine from Napoli di Malvasia (F.); cf. Isaiah 43[23ff.] (false worship); as the marginal comment ('about understanding') shows, Müntzer is stressing the meaningless of the rite.

51. Amos 5 esp. v. 21 (lament for the virgin Israel, perversion of justice and worship); Matthew 7[13f.. 15. 21. 24ff.]

scholars have totally betrayed their sorrowing, wretched mother,[52] the dear Christian church, by building it on sandy ground.[53] Quoting texts out of context, they have cited John 3;[55] 'Whoever is not baptised in water and the holy spirit will not come into the kingdom of God.' These words are the very truth but, together with the entire, consistent message of the evangelist John, their meaning is being withheld from the poor Christian church. For the knowledge of God to which the books of the Bible testify requires a careful comparison[57] of all the clear statements to be found in both Testaments, 1 Corinthians 2.[58] Our Biblical scholars have not opened their eyes to the real truth.[60] They have imagined that the third chapter is not yoked with the seventh, where the voice of wisdom declares: 'If someone is thirsty, let him come to me and drink. For, as Scripture says, whoever believes in me, streams of water will flow from his body, living waters.'[61] He speaks here of the holy spirit which believers will in the future be receiving.[62] So you see, my dear fellow, that the evangelist expounds himself, speaking of the waters as the prophets do, for – as John explains in the first chapter by reference to Isaiah[63] – the waters are the movement of our spirit in God's.[64] Now in the second chapter[65] these waters of ours become wine. Our 'movement' begins to long to suffer.[66] John baptises in the third chapter,[67] since until there are many waters,[68] and much movement, the voice of the bridegroom cannot be heard and understood. In the fourth chapter[69] the waters gush out of the ground of the fountain of life. In the fifth John[70] shows straight away his agreement with all the

Marginal references (left): Jere. 5. 6 / Kegenteyl[54] / 1 Cho. 2 / Dz ist untergestzt[56] / Math. 5 / Luce von Maria[59] / Joan. 9 / Isaie 55 / Josue 7 / Nume. 19 / Psal. 68 / Psal. 92 / Esaie 40 / Jere. 2 / Proverb. 5 / Psal. 143 / Esaie 8 / Jere. 17 / Esaie 11 / 33 eiusdem

Marginal references (right): Psal. 17 / Psal. 22 / Psal. 28 / Psal. 79 / Can. 4 / Ecci. 39

---

52. Jeremiah 5, 8 esp. 8[25] (God's wrath against false worship); F. cites Jeremiah 6 by mistake.

53. Matthew 7[24ff.]

54. Cf. n. 36 above.

55. John 3[5].

56. 'That is suppressed', i.e. the true meaning of John.

57. *vorgleichung*, i.e. synthesis; esp. of Law and Gospel, cf. Matthew 5[17ff.]

58. 1 Corinthians 2[6–12] (God's hidden wisdom revealed through the Spirit).

59. Luke about Mary; cf. *Exposé of False Faith*, p. 266/19ff. below.

60. John 9[39ff.]

61. John 7[37f.]; Isaiah 55[1ff.]

62. Joshua 7[5b]; Numbers 19[12. 19].

63. John 1[23]; Isaiah 40[3]; Jeremiah 2[13]; Proverbs 5[15]; Psalm 144[7].

64. Psalm 69[1ff.. 14f.]; Psalm 18[5(?). 16(?)]; Psalm 23[2f.]; Psalm 29[3. 10]. Psalm 80[5f.]; Song of Solomon 4[15]; Ecclesiasticus 39[13f.. 17. 22] (F. suggests Ezekiel 39); Psalm 93[3f.]

65. John 2[9].

66. Lit. 'our movements', 'stirrings' (Stayer).

67. John 3[23].

68. Isaiah 8[5–8].

69. John 4[14]; cf. Jeremiah 17[13].

70. John 5[1–5] (the Pool of Bethseda).

prophets on the movement of the waters.[71] In the sixth[72] the true son of God is seen wandering over the waters after the storm. In broadening the understanding of this the seventh chapter is in harmony with the third, and the third with all the others. Nicodemus was moved to come to CHRIST by signs; hence Christ directs him to water as he did to other Biblical scholars, too.[73] Much as it may vex them, there is to be no other sign than that of Jonah.[74]

Luce 11
Matt. 12

Seventh

See, then, if you can get firm ground under your feet,[75] for in the church the muddy, sandy ground shakes and boils like some awful brew.[76] Here is the origin of the evil that confronts all the elect,[77] together with all the other heathenish ceremonies and rites which have burgeoned so seductively, the whole abomination in the holy place.[78] Ever since immature children have been made Christians and the catechumens abolished, Christians themselves have become children, despite Paul's prohibition of this,[79] for then all understanding vanished from the church.[80] Then true baptism was obscured by this wearisome and hypocritical god-parent business, which attracts great enthusiasm and pomposity,[81] people clinging to it like a dog to its sausage. Good grief, not even Cerberus[82] could devour a brew like this. Then along came that loose woman in her scarlet apparel,[84] the shedder of blood, the Roman church;[85] she had a difference of views with all the other churches, believing her ceremonies and rites — although they were raked together[86] from

Margin notes: Psal. 7, 27, 36 / Prove. 28 / Deutr. 28 / Esaie 8 / coniuratio[80] / Apoca. 18 / Psal. 2 / Judic. 20 / Diversa et una sententia impiorum / Gene. 26 / Exodi. 18

Left margin notes: 4 et 19 / 14 / s. 2 / tice[81] / is formis niarum dei[83] / 44

71. Isaiah 11[9]; cf. 12[3]; 33[21].

72. John 6[19].

73. John 3[1-5]; 7[37-9].

74. *Auffs zeychen Jone ist auch kein ander*; cf. Luke 11[29]; Matthew 12[39] there appears no need to read *das* for *auffs*, as F. suggests.

75. *zum grunde kommen*; 'come upon the basis' (Stayer).

76. *grundsuppen* 'dregs' (a play on words with *grund*, foundation, basis).

77. Psalm 7[6ff]; 28[1ff]; 37[12ff]; (God as the Rock of the righteous against the ungodly); Proverbs 28[10, 14, 18].

78. Matthew 24[15]; Daniel 9[16-18]; cf. 2 Thessalonians 2[4].

79. 1 Corinthians 14[20].

80. Deuteronomy 28 (blessings and curses, esp. v. 28); Isaiah 8[21ff]; 2 Thessalonians 2[10ff]; *coniuratio* = conspiracy, cf. Isaiah 8[10], (and 30[1ff]) and Psalm 2[1ff].

81. Amos 6[1ff]; *pompatice* = pompously.

82. The monstrous dog, with snake-like body, that guards the entrance to Hades; cf. Revelation 18[3].

83. 'On the true forms of ceremonies of the Spirit of God'.

84. Revelation 17[3f].

85. The mother becomes the whore, the church of martyrs the shedder of blood; cf. *Exposé of False Faith* p. 312/28 below; the terrible passage in Judges 20 illustrates immorality; similarly Genesis 26[7].

86. *zusammen gestuppelt*; cf. Ezekiel 44[6f]; Leviticus 10[1ff]; Deuteronomy 4[2, 15ff., 25ff].

paganism – to be the best ones, and all others to be odious abominations.[87] Honestly, even to talk about it pains me. The whole of Asia was excommunicated,[88] surrendered to the devil – as is the wont of those who think in such a worldly way – on account of a bagatelle[89] like this, because the fathers there celebrated Easter on 14 April. The same happened with all the others. Thus the Romans left the whole world in the most lamentable desolation, driving the others to break off fellowship with us – and all because of their wretched brew[90] and their petty nonsense.[91] What a lamentable business! The lands which were so dearly bought with the precious blood of the apostles are surrendered to the devil for the sake of a few measly rites![92] That is why God has made us blinder than all other nations and given us up to such mighty errors.[93] It is because we have no understanding of baptism that our sole preoccupation[94] is with ceremonies and church rituals.

Marginal notes left: Exo. 12 / Ephe. 4 / Roma. 1 / Psal. 94 / Deutr. 28 / Mat. 24 / 2 Thess. 2 / 2 Timo. 2 / 1 Timo. 4

Marginal notes right: Levi. 9 et 10 / Deutro. 4 / In der clagung und Math. 24 vom grewel der vorwustunge[95]

Eighth

We[96] were almost the last to come to the Christian faith, through the missions of the Romans and other sects. From the beginning we were taught from Scripture to hate all the sects,[97] with the result that deep suspicion of them has become second nature to us whether justified or not. Because of this our attention to the central issues of the

Marginal notes left: Numeri 12 et 14 / Rom. 1 / Deutr. 32 / oblitus es[100] / Psal. 13

---

87. Is Exodus 18 adduced as an example of true worship? Cf. v. 12.

88. The so-called Quartodeciman controversy about the date of Easter between Rome and Asia Minor, beginning with Victor I and Polycrates of Ephesus in the second century; the Eastern Church celebrated Easter on the date for the Jewish Passover, irrespective of the day of the week, the Western Church on Sunday; cf. Eusebius, *Church History* (V, 24, 9) which Müntzer avidly read; cf. Prague Manifesto, p. 377/12 below; he may also have in mind the schism between the Eastern and Western churches from 1054; cf. Exodus 12 (institution of the Passover).

89. *kinderspiel*, 'child's game'.

90. Cf. n. 76 above.

91. *geschnorres*; 'mooching' (Stayer); *geschnurr, geschnörr* = petty things, which refer back to *kinderspiel* (n. 89) and forward to *geringe geperde*; cf. Grimm V, 3953; *geschnurr* can also mean 'muttering'; cf. p. 190/11 above, and p. 181/22 above; a further possibility is suggested by the Modern German *schnorren*, to exploit someone's goodwill, to wheedle, scrounge.

92. Cf. Ephesians 4 (exhortation to charity and unity).

93. Romans 1[18ff., 24f., 26]; Psalm 95[8ff.]; Deuteronomy 28[37]; Matthew 24[15]; 2 Thessalonians 2[11]; 2 Timothy 2[23]; 1 Timothy 4[1ff.]

94. *Das wir keinen andern gewissen, dann.*

95. 'In the Lamentations of Jeremiah and Matthew 24 on the abomination of desolation'.

96. The Germans.

97. Numbers 13[31ff.], 14 (the Israelites complain about Moses and Aaron); Romans 1[18ff.] (stifling of the truth).

faith was so dissipated[98] by ferocious quarrels that we didn't once pause to think of the origin of faith in the heart. Not one of the doctors of the church gave us even a glimpse of this.[99] I declare this quite openly – to arouse pity for us, not scorn.[100] Hence the head of the household, kind as he is, has let his precious field be ruined with so many tares, or rather by great tree-stumps.[101] If our forefathers had read Isaiah 5[102] they would at least have caught a whiff of it. This much is certain: whenever the mighty God of hosts allows errors and heresy to sprout up, he proves that people are not growing in faith, or have a faith which is devious and full of wiles.[103] What right have they to condemn heretics when their own faith has not been forged in the fire![104] The son of God says[105] that when he sends the holy spirit he will surely punish the world for its unbelief. Since they do not want to recognise it in themselves,[106] they must see it in those who are quite clearly unbelievers, whether they want to or not.[107] For just as the latter have gone astray in our self-opinionated eyes,[108] so have we in the eyes of God. It is because we consider that we have a healthy faith that we spurn a doctor and God keeps hurling one affliction after another upon us.[109] So we wander around in this blindness and obscurity, refusing to believe anyone who tells us that we are blind, quite blind.[110]

Isaie 19
Zacha. 12
Esaie 42, 56
Treno. 4
Sopho. 1

Ninth

If our eyes are to be opened, my most beloved brothers, we have first to recognise our blindness,[111] of which the most obvious marks are the counterfeit faith and the hypocritical works which follow from it. But we must not follow the example of the biblical scholars in

Math. 9
Joan. 9
Esaie 6
Luce 8
Ephe. 4
Matth. 13

---

98. *Daruber ist unser sache unter uns auch also weitleufftig worden.*

99. *lassen erfurgutzen*, 'let it peep out'; Psalm 14[1].

100. Deuteronomy 32 (judgement on the apostasy of Israel; cf. v. 18 *oblitus es*, 'You forsook the creator'); v. 36.

101. Romans 3[10ff.]; Matthew 13[24-30]; 21[33] (*de impiis agri [colis]*), about the wicked farm-labourers).

102. Isaiah 5[1ff.]

103. Jeremiah 2 (apostasy of Israel); Deuteronomy 28; 1 Timothy 1, (both quoted for third time) Titus 1[10ff.]

104. Romans 2[1ff.]

105. John 16[8].

106. *Das sie yhn nicht wollen in yhn selbern erkennen*; Isaiah 1[esp. 1ff.]

107. Isaiah 19[21ff.]; 33[1].

108. *gutdunckenden*, following our own judgement, not the Spirit of God; cf. 2 Peter 1[20f.]

109. 2 Kings 6 (famine in Samaria); Matthew 9[12].

110. Zechariah 12[1ff.]; Isaiah 42[19ff.]; 56[10ff., 6ff.]; Lamentations 4[13f.]; Zephaniah 1[17].

111. Matthew 9[27ff., 12]; cf. Isaiah 35[5]; Isaiah 6[10]; Luke 8[9f.]

John, chapter 9,[112] whose stubborn and ignorant minds[113] are attested by the miracle of the blind man. For they said: 'We know that God speaks through Moses'; just as today, my dear brothers, your biblical scholars say: 'We know that Scripture is right'. The truth is that its rightness is there to kill you, not to make you alive, for it is not set on earth for that.[114] Rather it is written for us ignorant people, so that the holy faith, the mustard seed,[115] should taste as bitter[116] as if there were no Scripture at all, bringing about a tremendous, irresistible[117] feeling of consternation. Am I really going to accept Scripture just because the church gives it its outward approval, with no further knowledge of how one arrives at faith? What would I be doing? If I were to cast my eyes around the whole circumference of the earth and look at all its peoples, then I would notice that the heathen believe, too, that their gods are pious saints, subject to the highest God.[118] The Turks, too, boast of their Mohammed as highly as we of our Christ. Moreover the Jews, outwardly at least, seem to have firmer ground under their feet than other impetuous, ignorant people, for when they quarrel with others it is about Scripture (which is a quarrel with some point to it) while we quarrel only about status and material goods. The Jews' traditions go back some four thousand years,[119] while we devise a new regulation every day, which we only abide by for the sake of money or status, until we get our own way.[120] For all our laws sing the same feeble song: Expiravit.[121] They help their brothers; we rob ours; we love no one so much as ourselves. See, then, my most precious brothers, this is the truth and kindly meant (though to our unaccustomed palate[122] a bitter tasting herb):[123] we Christians throughout the world have gorged ourselves so excessively with foul

Marginal notes (right): Marci 4 / Ro. 15 / Joan. 9 / 2 Timo. 3 / 2 Chor. 3 / Math. 17 / Luce 17 / Psal. 118 / Psal. 96 / Ezech. 20, 33

Marginal notes (left): Jere. 2 / Osee. 4 / Jere. 6, 8, 22 / Esaie. 10 / Jere. 2 / We denen, die bose gesetz machen[120] / Joan. 8 / Psal. 48 / Psal. 88

---

112. John 9[29].

113. Ephesians 4[14]; Matthew 13[13ff]; Mark 4[11f]; Romans 15[31(?)].

114. 2 Timothy 3[4, 8]; 2 Corinthians 3[6f] ('the letter killeth').

115. Matthew 17[19f]; Luke 17[5f].

116. Psalm 119, a sustained paean of praise for the Law, despite the persecutions suffered, e.g. vs. 81–87; Psalm 97 (God as a devouring fire).

117. *unaussschlalichen*, inescapable.

118. Jeremiah 2[10] ('has a nation ever changed its gods, though they were no gods?').

119. *Die Juden haben yre gewonheit nach anlegender sach von viertausent jarn.*

120. *bis das wir das unser uberkommen*; in margin: 'Woe to those who make unjust laws.'

121. Jeremiah 6[13ff]; 8[10ff]; 22[1ff. 13ff. 17]; Isaiah 10[1ff]; Ezekiel 20 (God refuses to be inquired of by Israel, because of its rebellion); 33[30ff]; Wiechert suspects a reference to Ovid, *Metamorphoses* V, 106: *Medios animam exspiravit in ignis* (F.).

122. *gemuth*, lit. 'disposition'.

123. John 8[45]; Psalm 49[13ff]; 89[48ff] (all earthly things pass away, but God delivers his people).

dregs[124] that our mouth reeks hideously and unrecognisably from the stink of them.

Tenth

Let us scrutinise first the faith of the intelligent heathen. We find that they confess there is a God who is himself immoveable, and that all the pious who have been of any special benefit to the world, become associates of God – much the same way as we tend to speak of the saints.[125] Since, being such delicate plants,[127] we cannot bear to suffer at all, we call upon the saints in our distress, though we would claim that in doing this we are not pagans at all but Christians. As is obvious, this means that many a decent fellow[128] will lose his neck yet before we come to recognise our wickedness properly.

Eleventh

If I then go on to look at the Turks I find that in the Koran, which Mohammed has written, JESUS of Nazareth was the son of a pure virgin but (he goes on to say) it cannot be true that he was nailed to a cross. The reason: God, one and mighty,[129] is far too gentle to allow evil men to perpetrate this.[131] Hence (he says) God kept faith with his son by putting an evil-doer in his place to be crucified, thus deceiving the stupid men,[132] who did not even perceive the almighty power of God. Judge for yourself, you miserable, false brother:[133] isn't our whole world today party to a similar fantastic, sensual, deceptively attractive way of looking at things,[134] although it still likes to dress up neatly in Holy Scripture. It makes a great song and dance about the faith of the apostles and the prophets, but apparently the only price we need to pay for the faith so bitterly gained by them[135] is to stagger

[margin: Esaic. 3 et 49; Psal. 70; Psal. 139; Psal. 140; 1 Chor. 15; Esaic. 22; 1. Reg. 21; Apoca. 2]

124. *unflatige hefen*; cf. Prague Manifesto p. 372/30 below; and Joel 2[20b].

125. Deuteronomy 32[8]; Psalm 18[26] ('with the perverse you show yourself perverse').

126. 'Does not promote truth, their help'; (the help the saints give in material troubles does not help us to discern the truth).

127. *kreuter*; takes up again the image of the mustard-seed, the bitter herb of truth; which Zedekiah cannot face, for example: Jeremiah 32[1ff.]

128. *manchen byddern*; cf. p. 205/23 below; Luke 19[27].

129. Isaiah 28[2].

130. The fantasy of the godless; the piety of the godless; cf. n. 151 below.

131. Amos 9 (God will bring doom on Israel; only a remnant will be spared); Luke 12[49ff.]

132. Cf. n. 130 above.

133. Cf. n. 44 above.

134. *geist*; Proverbs 7 (the adulteress seduces from wisdom); Ecclesiasticus 22[9-22] (wisdom and folly); Isaiah 3[16ff.]

135. Isaiah 49[4. 7. 9. 14]; Psalm 71[4. 10. 12f.. 20]; 140; 141[8]; (sufferings of the righteous).

[left margin notes: 2; rverso ris[125]; t zur warheit, das sy; 6; ginatione m; npiorum[130]]

round mad-drunk.[136] Come on, my dear lords, give up! Toss the Matt. 23
cosmetic jars to the devil, don't paint yourselves like Jezebel, who Apoca. 17
likes to do Naboth to death.[137] As yet, however, the dogs have not
completely devoured her; she still lives on, a real tough specimen,[138]
torturing the servants of God.

Twelfth

First, dear Christians, let us give ourselves a jolt,[139] and see if we, Prove. 18
too, are like the heathen.[140] The heathen worship Lady Venus, Juno Justus prior acc
etc., so as to assure themselves of fine children and avoid the pains of fui [sic]
childbirth, and they have other gods as well.[141] In the very same way Jere. 2
we call upon the mother of God, honouring her conception,[142] and Contra canticum
then go on to call upon St. Margaret, contrary to the explicit text of Marie magnific
the Bible: 'You shall give birth to your children in pain'.[143] We never
recall that we conceived our children in the fear of God.[144] Does it Prove. 19
strike you how our whole life rages in open idolatry against the totus liber nihil
sonat[144]
equitable will of God?[145] We still cannot see this. We refuse to do so.[146] widder dz vatte
The reason is that faith in God, as taught nowadays by the unreliable unser[145]
biblical scholars, is (one could weep to God) reaching ever greater
heights of folly,[147] heights never previously seen. As a result we too Osee 4
have become arrogant[148] — just like our opponents[149] — and are inclined Joan. 9
promptly to throw to the dogs anyone who does not hold our views 2 Timo. 3
in every respect. It is a great lack of humility that brings this about. 1. ciusdem 4
The real reason is that many people have no eyes for the work of Amos 6

---

136. I Corinthians 15[32f.]; Isaiah 22[12f.].

137. I Kings 21; lit. 'strangle'.

138. *lebt ach, hat ein hartes leben*; cf. 2 Kings 9[30ff.]; Revelation 2[21ff.]; Matthew 23[34f.]; Revelation 17[6]; the repetition of *lebt, leben*, with the idea of Jezebel only being as yet half-devoured by the dogs, has a certain parallel in Müntzer's almost equally gruesome depiction of Luther's tough flesh in the cooking-pot! *Highly Provoked Vindication*, p. 348/19ff. below.

139. *uns selbern ... bey der nasen rucken*, 'pull ourselves by the nose'.

140. Proverbs 18[17] (Vg.) *Justus, prior est accusator sui*; 'the first to accuse the just man is himself'; i.e. let us be self-critical!

141. Jeremiah 2[20ff., 28].

142. 'Contrary to the song of Mary, the Magnificat'; Mary seeks to understand the meaning of her child's birth, not to evade the pain of it; cf. n. 126 above.

143. Genesis 3[16]; St Margaret is one of the fourteen Auxiliary Saints.

144. Proverbs 19[23] (The fear of God leads to life); 'this is the nub of the whole book'; cf. letter 31, p. 44/17ff. above.

145. Contrary to the Lord's Prayer ('Your will be done ...'); Hosea 4[1ff.]

146. John 9[27].

147. I Timothy 4[1ff., 7]; Amos 6[8].

148. 2 Timothy 3[2].

149. The Roman Church.

et eiusdem
totum

textum Esaie
naginatione
m¹⁵¹

3
ım¹⁵²

11

.

.

2

.

2
.
.

5
8
3 in fine¹⁶²

Mat. 13
Luc. 8
Mar.
Joani. 15
Psal. 129

Job 5
Jere. 8
Ephe. 3

Matt. 22

Psal. 131

Sapie. 5

Contra textum:
Coll. 1¹⁶²
1 Pe. 2
Ephe. 1

God;¹⁵⁰ they imagine that all one needs to do to come to the Christian faith is to think about what CHRIST has said. No, my dear man, what you must do is endure patiently,¹⁵¹ and learn how God himself will root out your weeds, thistles and thorns from the rich soil which is your heart.¹⁵² Otherwise nothing good will grow there, only the raging devil in the guise of light,¹⁵³ and showy corn-cockles etc. There is nothing for it! Even if you have already devoured all the books of the Bible you still must suffer the sharp edge of the plough-share. For you will never have faith unless God himself gives it you,¹⁵⁴ and instructs you in it. If that is to happen, then at first, my dear biblical scholar, the book will be closed to you, too.¹⁵⁵ For even if you burst¹⁵⁶ in the effort, neither reason nor any created being can open it for you. God has to gird your loins;¹⁵⁷ yes, you must let God, working in you, strip of all the clothing of creaturely origin¹⁵⁸ which you have been wearing, and you must not do what the clever ones do, producing one saying here, another there, without a scrupulous comparison with the whole spirit of Scripture.¹⁵⁹ Otherwise we will have confused the window with the door.¹⁶⁰ Even if we come across one apposite text,¹⁶¹ it will be quite inadequate unless we relate it to another. To take an example: if one says: 'CHRIST has achieved everything on his own', that is really quite inadequate. If you do not see the head in relation to its members, how can you hope to follow in

150. Isaiah 30¹ff.·⁹ff.; 5 (vineyard of Israel); 'and the whole book', Matthew 13²³ff. (not Matthew 19; cf. Schwarz p. 69 n. 25); Luke 8¹⁵; John 15¹ff. (the true vine); Psalm 130⁶ (cf. Dismer, p. 102 n. 5).

151. Psalm 30⁵; Isaiah 28⁷ff.; 'contrary to the text in Isaiah 28 about the fantasy of the godless'; Job 5¹⁷; Jeremiah 8¹⁸ff..

152. Ephesians 3¹⁶ff.; 1 Corinthians 3⁶ff.; (God the gardener); Psalm 36⁸ (the psalm contrasts the wicked and the upright).

153. geschwunden yns liecht; 2 Corinthians 11¹⁴.

154. Luke 9¹²⁻¹⁷; John 6⁵⁻¹⁵; (feeding of the five thousand); Isaiah 54¹⁻³; Jeremiah 31; (end to barrenness and mourning); cf. Isaiah 28²⁴⁻⁶.

155. Isaiah 29¹¹ᶠ.

156. zupresten.

157. Cf. Genesis 32²⁴ᶠ. (Jacob's struggle with the angel); Psalm 38⁷; cf. also Luke 12³⁵.

158. von allen creaturn angezogen; Matthew 22¹¹ff. (the man without a wedding garment); cf. Revelation 3⁵; Psalm 132⁹; (clothed in righteousness); Luke 12²⁷ᶠ. (God clothes the faithful); Wisdom 5¹⁶⁻²⁰; Isaiah 28⁵ᶠ. (the crowning and arming of the righteous creation to punish the wicked); Ephesians 4²²ff..

159. 1 Corinthians 2¹¹ff..

160. John 10¹.

161. ein urteil; Müntzer's word for a Scriptural text which speaks to a specific situation; 'a single statement' (Stayer); Maron sees his whole theology as one of 'Judgement', the entire Bible being for him a book of oracles (Urteile), ZKG 83 (1972), 195–225.

his footsteps?[162] I suppose on a good, warm[163] fur, or on a silk-cushion.[164]

Thirteenth

1 Joan. 2
Luce 19
Zacharias
Math. 7
contra Eph. 2 et 3[166]
Prove. 5

The Romans distributed indulgences, and remitted penalty and guilt, and are we, straight away, to build on a similar foundation?[165] That would be equivalent to having an old house white-washed and saying it was new. We would be doing the same if we preached a honey-sweet CHRIST, well-pleasing to our murderous nature.[166] Yes, what would we achieve if it didn't have to suffer anything and Christ gave everything gratuitously? Wouldn't we just be blowing the same fanfare as the Turk?[167] He denies the history of CHRIST, our saviour;[168] and we wanted to deny it secretly, or rather thievingly; so that we do not need to suffer and can let the wheat and the thorns vaunt themselves side by side.[169] O no, my brothers, that is not the right way to life; it is contrary to the clear texts of Matthew 7, 1 Peter 2, 1 John 2 and John 14,[170] though, as mentioned above, it is very acceptable to our nature. In brief it has to be the narrow way, so that a text[171] is not studied according to outward appearances, but according to the most loving will of God in his living word and tested in crises of faith[172] of all kinds, as CHRIST says himself in the seventh chapter mentioned above.[173] Only then does a person realise that his house – he himself, that is – is built on the immoveable rock.[174] St Peter (like us) did not understand the need for such a solidly based building and so, although he was founded on the rock,[175] he still had to fall,[176] for he

Joan. 10
1 Petri. 2

Contra tempus
messis[169]
Joan. 4
Matt. 13
Luce 8
Marci 4
Math. 7
Joannis 7
Hebre. 4

1 Chor. 6
2 Chor. 6
Psal. 92
Mat. 16

Luce 22
1 Petri. 1

162. Matthew 7[21]; Luke 6[46]; against the text 1 Colossians[18, 24]; Ephesians 1[23]; 1 Peter 2[21]; Song of Songs 5 (the love song of the bride and bridegroom, the Church and Christ); 1 Corinthians 3[23] ('at the end').

163. *einen gutten warmen kalten peltzs*; the German adds 'cold' after 'warm'.

164. Probably a reference to the licentious priests and prophets of Isaiah 28[7ff.]

165. 1 John 2[1–6]; Luke 19[1–10] (Zacchaeus gives away half his riches) cf. Zechariah 1[6]; 3[3–5]; 5[8ff.]; Matthew 7[13f.(?)].

166. *der morderischen unser natur*; 'against Ephesians 2 and 3'; cf. esp. 2[3ff.], 3[13]; Proverbs 5[3] (cf. 25[27]).

167. *in ein loch blassen*; instead of the new song of the holy spirit; cf. the Prague Manifesto; p. 362/5 below.

168. John 10[11, 17].

169. 'Against the time of the harvest': John 4[35]; Matthew 13[7, 22]; Luke 8[7, 14]; Mark 4[7, 18f.]

170. Matthew 7[13f.] (cf. n. 165 above); 1 Peter 2[21]; 1 John 2[3ff.]; John 14[6].

171. *alle urteil*; cf. n. 161 above.

172. *anfechtung*.

173. Matthew 7[13–23].

174. 1 Corinthians 6[19f.]; 2 Corinthians 6[16–18]; Psalm 93[1f., 5].

175. Matthew 16[18] (not Luther's exegesis of this text(!)).

176. Luke 22[54–62].

was not all of a piece.[177] His faith did not diminish as a result of his fall but increased markedly.[178] After the fall he recognised his temerity and it was then, and only then, that he became quite resolute. But we have to realise that the apostles and all the prophets could not face the words of God[179] until all the weeds and the temerity of a counterfeit faith had been hoed away.[180] And we biblical scholars like to think that it is enough to have the Scripture and that we do not have to be conscious of the power of God, although it says clearly in the first chapter of Romans that the gospel is a power of God,[181] that is, to those from whom it is not concealed.[182] For I have to know whether it is God who said this and not the devil; I have to distinguish the work of both of them in the ground of the soul.[183] Otherwise I will let myself be hoodwinked in a way which only catches the wind,[184] such as the biblical scholars, who have not been put to the test, practise on themselves and on others, Matthew 7.[185] Their speech has not the might of God, for they say quite unabashedly that they have no other belief or spirit than the one they have stolen from Scripture.[186] Only they don't say that it is stolen, but believed. The light of nature has such a high conceit of itself[187] that it fancies that [faith] is so easily come by.

Roma. 8
Certior sum, quod nequio [sic][178]
Joan. 5
2 Timo. 3

kondt die nicht, noch t Gottis[182]

Actorum per universum librum[183]

manens redentes, non

Joan. 10
Jere. 13

Fourteenth

The mark is missed completely if one preaches that faith and not works have to justify us.[188] This is to talk immodestly.[189] For it does not confront one's nature with the fact that man comes to faith by the work of God and that this is the first and the main thing for which one must wait.[190] Otherwise faith is not worth a cent[191] and is a lie from

---

177. *er war nicht allenthalben vorfasset*; he had not, as today's slang puts it, 'got his act together'.

178. 1 Peter 1[6f.]; Romans 8[35–9], esp. v. 38 (Vg.): *Certus sum enim quia neque mors . . .*

179. *mit Gottis wortten nicht bestehn kundten.*

180. John 6[39ff.]; 2 Timothy 3.

181. Romans 1[16].

182. 'You err, knowing neither the Scripture nor the power of God'; Matthew 22[29].

183. 'The whole book of Acts'.

184. Proverbs 11[29]; Isaiah 64[6].

185. Matthew 7[29]; Jeremiah 2[8].

186. Cf. John 5[37–40]; v. 38 (Vg.): *Et verbum eius non habetis in vobis manens: quia quem misit ille, huic vos non creditis* John 10[22–39] (in controversy with 'the Jews' Jesus refers to his works as evidence for his words).

187. Jeremiah 13[15, 17].

188. Philippians 3[9].

189. 1 Corinthians 9[16].

190. Colossians 4[2ff.]; Psalm 19[1ff.]; Jeremiah 17[15f.]; Isaiah 5[21]; cf. p. 387/5 below.

191. *nicht eines pfifferlings wert.*

Mat. 5
Psal. 33
Psal. 9 et 67, 71, 73,
87, 108

1 Cho. 2

Luce 2
Psal. 1

Joan. 3
Math. 5 et 10

1 Tim. 1
2 Ti. 4
Ro. 4

Esa. 25

Ro. 25 (sic!)

Jere. 13
Joan. 10

beginning to end, being based on our efforts.[192] One has to explain how it feels to be poor in spirit[193] and confirm this by the tribulations of the fathers from, and in, the Bible.[194] For with all his written[195] promises God reveals how his almighty power has been active in all his elect.[196] Thus the whole context of every word [of Scripture] is related to a coming event[197] and the devious theft of the letter disappears.[198]

Fifteenth

Esaie 43
Esaie 15
Roma 4 et 10
Luce 18
Mat. 26
Mar. 14
Luce 22
Joan. 13

Titum 1
Esa. 29

Mat. 15

Act. 10

Prove. 11

I have put my proposition or set of conditions before you in different ways and at considerable length, my most beloved brothers, because I know very well (for God's sake, forgive me) that at the moment you have no intention either of embarking on faith or on upright works,[199] for those who champion the gospel at the moment praise faith above all things. That is what the self-opinionated light of nature likes to believe.[200] O, if all that were required was faith how easy it would be for you to come to it! [The light of nature] goes on: 'Yes, there is no doubt about it, you are born of Christian parents,[201] you have never once doubted, and you will continue to stand firm.'[202]

Lu. 18 gloriatur[202]

Yes, yes, I am a good Christian. O, can I come to salvation so easily? Shame, shame on the priests! O, these cursed men, how bitter they have made things for me etc. For people then think they can come to salvation in this wind-catching way; they neither read nor attend to a single thing one writes about faith and works;[203] they just want to be

Luce 10

---

192. 1 Timothy 1[3ff.]; 2 Timothy 4[3ff.]; Romans 4[14].

193. Matthew 5[3]; Psalm 34[esp. v.6].

194. Romans 4[18f.]; Psalm 10, 68, 72[12ff.]; 74; 88; 109; (the Psalms relate the sufferings of the righteous at the hands of the wicked).

195. *buchstabischen*.

196. Isaiah 25[4f.]; 1 Corinthian. 2[4f.]; Romans 15[8f.] (not Romans 25); Luke 2[29ff.]; Psalm 1[3].

197. *Also wirt der gantze context aller wort in einer nahen gelegenheit vorfasset*; 'is brought together into a tight inter-relationship' (Stayer, following Bräuer and Ullmann); F. understands *nahen gelegenheit* as the 'near future'; Jeremiah 13[12ff.] refers to coming judgement on Israel; Isaiah 43[9ff., 18f.] to God is imminent salvation of Israel, as the true interpretation of his will.

198. John 10[1]; John 3[19]; Matthew 5[21-43] ('You have heard . . . But I say'); Matthew 10 (persecution awaiting the disciples).

199. Isaiah 43[8, 10]; Isaiah 15[5(?)]; Luke 18[8]; Romans 4, 10; Matthew 26; Mark 14; Luke 22, John 13 (the betrayal of Jesus by Peter).

200. Titus 1[16]; Isaiah 29[13]; Matthew 15[8].

201. Acts 10 (the conversion of the centurion – not of Jewish birth).

202. Luke 18[11]; Proverbs 11[2] (references to pride); in margin: 'he boasts'.

203. Luke 10[16].

good evangelical folk by using many vainglorious words.[204] That is a momentous, crude, and clumsy error. Would that it were recognised as such! There are still many who favour it as a pretext to pursue a loose life.

Roma.

Sixteenth

But, on the other hand, there are a number of honest people[205] who do not let their consciences be stilled by such frivolous chat, who realise and recognise that in truth the way to heaven must be a very narrow one[206] — which cannot be discovered through any fleshly enjoyment; the trouble is that this leads them to fall into a hedge of thorns,[207] that is into heathen ceremonies and rites, into excesses of fasting and praying, and to think that now they have discovered the way. Aha! those who let themselves be stilled by that and do not continue to be shaken about and to long to reach beyond themselves[208] are beyond all help. They become arrogant devils and are damned beyond all hope.[209] But those who gnaw their way through counterfeit faith and outward works — which even the very crudest sinners do through their crimes[210] — see that the word, on which true faith depends, is not a hundred thousand miles from them[211] but they see how it springs out of the abyss of the heart; they notice how it is derived from the living God. They are well aware that one has to be sober, to bid all the lusts farewell and exert oneself to the utmost in the expectation of a word or promise of this kind from God.[212] For a man does not believe because he has heard it from other people. Whether the whole world accepts or rejects it, that, too, is a matter of indifference to him, just as the fourth chapter of John witnesses.[213] But his inward eyes have waited for a long, long time on the Lord and on his hands, that is to say, on his divine work,[214] so that

Mat. 5

Mat. 7
Luce 6
Psal. 57
Paulus ad Romanis [sic]

Mar. 6

Esaie.

Roma. 10
Jere. 23
Deutr. 30
Joan. 4
Mat. 16
1 Petri. 5
Math. 13

---

204. Presumably Müntzer means Luther's stress on justification by faith, based on Romans.

205. Matthew 5[1ff.] and Luke 6[20ff.]; (the Beatitudes).

206. Matthew 7[13f.]

207. *in eine dornhecken*; cf. Psalm 58[9] (Vg.: *Priusquam intelligerent spinae vestrae rhamnum*); cf. On Baptism p. 396/11 below.

208. *sich sehnen uber sich*; cf. section one above, p. 189/2.

209. Mark 6[1-6].

210. Isaiah; cf. Isaiah 9[18] (wickedness devours the thorns, i.e. the ceremonies).

211. Romans 10[8]; Jeremiah 23[23]; Deuteronomy 30[11ff.]

212. Matthew 16[1-4]; 1 Peter 5[8ff.]; Matthew 13[20-22]; Luke 8[13-14]; Mark 4[16-19].

213. John 4[44].

214. Romans 14, 15 (the strong and the weak in faith; cf. 14[20], 15[18f.]; Psalm 128[2] (Vg.: *Labores manuum tuarum quia manducabis*).

until the whole process of edification is complete[215] he profits from all the dividends which the spirit bestows.[216] This is the way in which one has to become receptive to the unwavering mercy of God.[217]

Seventeenth

It is the zealous expectation of the word that is the first step to being a Christian.[218] This expectation must begin by enduring the word patiently, and there must be no confidence at all that we will be forgiven eternally because of our works.[220] Then a person thinks he has no trace of faith. As far as he can see there is no faith to be found in him. He feels or finds a feeble[222] desire for true faith, which is so faint that he is scarcely and only after great difficulty aware of it.[223] But finally it has to burst out and he cries 'O, what a wretched man I am, what is going on in my heart? My conscience devours the very marrow of my being, my strength, everything that makes me what I am.[225] What on earth am I to do now? I am at my wits' end,[226] and receive no comfort from God or man.[227] For God is plaguing me with my conscience, my lack of belief, my despair and with blaspheming against him. Outwardly I am visited by sickness, poverty, wretchedness and every manner of distress, by the deeds of evil men etc.[228] And the inward stresses are far greater than the outward ones.[229] What wouldn't I give to be able to believe truly, since everything

Marginal references (left): Psal. 16 et 17, 58, 105; Psal. 102; Daniel 9; Prove. 10; Psal. 20; Apo. 4 et 5 oppositum[224]; Mat. 23; Luce 11; Psal. 101; Treno. 1; Eccs. 7 et per universum librum; Job. 4, 39; Mar. 9 adiuva incredulitatem meam[230]; Psal. 18; Lu. 2, 17; Roma. 1; Psal. 62; Psal. 16; Zacha 2

Marginal references (right): Psa. 35, 129 Sustinuit anima mea[219]; Esaie. 54 ad punctum dereliqui te[221] Ro. 8; 1 Pc. 4 Pro. 12 Mat. 12; Job. 6 et per to Sophonie 2

---

215. 2 Timothy 3[17]; edification in the literal sense of the building of temple of the spirit; cf. 1 Corinthians 3[9ff.]; 14[3f., 12, 26]; Corinthians 5[1-5]; 10[8]; 12[19].

216. Luke 19[11-27]; Matthew 25[14-30].

217. Proverbs 18[2, 10].

218. Psalm 17[1ff.]; 18[1ff., 6]; 59[1ff.]; 106[1ff., 47]; 35[1ff., 17ff.]

219. Cf. Psalm 130[5f.]: 'my soul waits'.

220. *do muss gar kein trost in ewiger vortzeihung zu unserm werck sein*; 'we must eternally derive no consolation whatever from our own work' (Stayer, following Bräuer and Ullmann); F. takes *vortzeihung* to mean *Verziehung* or 'postponement'; yet the beginning of section 13 appears to deal with the same theme of forgiveness based on human remedies, using the cognate form, *vortzeigt*, which recurs in section 15 also, *vortzeigt mir*; cf. Psalm 103[10]; Daniel 9[esp. v. 18]; Proverbs 10[17].

221. Isaiah 54[7] ('For a brief moment I forsook you').

222. *durfftiges*, lit. 'meagre'.

223. Romans 8[esp. vs. 22f., 26]; Psalm 21[2].

224. Revelation 4; 5 (holiness of God and the Lamb on the throne); in margin: 'on the contrary': Matthew 23[6]; Luke 11[43] (the scribes and Pharisees in the best seats in the synagogue).

225. Proverbs 12[1]; 1 Peter 4[1f.]; Matthew 12[33ff.(?)]; Psalm 102[3ff.]; Lamentations 1[esp. v. 13]; cf. also Romans 7[24].

226. *Ich bin yrre worden*: 'I have gone astray' (Stayer); cf. p. 206/1 below.

227. *der creatur*.

228. Job 6 and passim; Ecclesiastes 7 and passim; Zephaniah 2.

229. Job 4[12-16]; Job 39 (man's ignorance).

seems to depend on this.[230] If only I knew what the right way was![231] Then I'd be ready to run to the ends of the earth to obtain it.'[232] Then the pious biblical scholars[233] when such disheartened people come to them (who are the very best there are) saying,[234] 'Dear, estimable, honourable, most learned sir' and a lot of similar rubbish: 'I am a poor devil at my wits' end. I really have no faith in God or man. I feel so bad that I really don't know if I would rather be dead or alive.[235] For God's sake give me some good advice,[236] for I suspect that the devil has got hold of me.' Then the learned gentlemen, who are always enormously irritated at having to open their mouths, for one word from them costs many a pretty penny,[237] reply: 'Now, now, my good chap; if you won't believe, then go to the devil!'[238] Then the poor creature will answer: 'I'm sorry, most learned doctor, I would really like to believe, but unbelief smothers all my good intentions. How in the world should I deal with it?' Then the learned man says:[239] 'Well, my dear fellow, you should not be concerning yourself with such lofty matters. Just have simple faith and chase these ideas away. It is pure fantasy. Go back to your own folk and cheer up, then you'll forget your worries.'[240] You see, my dear brother, this is the sort of consolation which holds sway in the churches – the only sort![241] Such consolation has made all serious Christian discipleship abominable in men's eyes.[242]

Matt. 23
Lu. 18
Isaie 53
Psal. 118
Job. 3
Jere. 20
Psal. 72
Psal. 118
Job. 7
Michee 3
Matt. 23
Marci 9
Prove. 24

Oho, hoch ist die
weyssheit der
narren[239]
1. Cho. 15
Esaie 22
Treno. 1
Matt. 24

in fine
et Esaie 24

Eighteenth

When a sincere Christian[243] becomes worried that such sharp and bitter thoughts and terrible anxiety will drive him silly, right out of his mind,[244] his rational nature becomes exceedingly suspicious. Surely this is the first [step] of unbelief, that you do not trust your

Psal. 118

et 26

Matt. 16 et 6
Marci 8
Luce 19 et 17

230. Mark 9[24] ('help my unbelief'); Luke 17[5f.]

231. Romans 1[19]; Psalm 19[7ff.]; 63[1ff.]; 17[1ff.]

232. Luke 2[15]; Zechariah 2[6f.]

233. Matthew 23; Luke 18[1, 9ff.] (F. reads Luke 11 incorrectly).

234. Isaiah 53[4ff.]; Psalm 119[1ff.]

235. Job 3; Jeremiah 20[14ff.]; Job 7[16, 21.]

236. Psalm 73[24]; Psalm 119[esp. vs. 34, 71(?)].

237. vil rother pfennig, lit. 'many golden pennies'; Micah 3[11]; Matthew 23[16-25.]

238. Mark 9[42].

239. 'Aha what lofty wisdom the fools have,' cf. Proverbs 24[7] (Vg.: Excelsa stulto sapientia); Luke 11[35f., 52.]

240. I Corinthians 15[32]; Isaiah 22[13]; Matthew 24[37ff., 48ff.]

241. Lamentations 1[2]; Matthew 23[37.]

242. John 7[49]; Hosea 4[1ff.]; Isaiah 24[4ff.]

243. Psalm 119[1ff.]

244. Wisdom 5[4].

creator, who is so gracious and kind, to keep your sanity[245] for you? It is here one sees quite clearly our lack of faith.[246] If we scholars are to devote ourselves to such matters we must stretch our brains[247] much more.[248] Hence the idle scholars say: 'Of course, if we were to confront the ordinary man with such lofty teachings he would become mad and lose his wits'. They go on to say: 'CHRIST says that one should not throw pearls to pigs.[250] What can the poor, crude man make of such high and spiritual teachings?[251] They should be reserved only for the scholars.' No, no, my dear sir,[252] St Peter tells you who the pigs for fattening are.[253] They are all the unfaithful false scholars,[254] from whatever sect you care to mention, who approve of gluttony and boozing and devote themselves to their lusts, living in luxury and snarling[255] like dogs with sharp teeth if one contradicts one word they say.[256]

Margin notes:
Deutro. 1. 32
1. Cho. 4
Eiusdem 2 et 4
Prove. 24
Math. 7
contra totum
Esaiam[251]

Contra Esaiam 11[251]
Luce 11

2 Pe. 2
Prove. 26
Luce 11
Mat. 7

Furantur clavem
Stumme hunde, um
der gelben suplin
willen[256]

Isaie 28
Phil. 3
Esa. 56
Psa. 21

Nineteenth

These fattened pigs are called false prophets by CHRIST: they neither remove the rafters from their own eyes nor from those of others.[257] The narrow way they make broad;[258] the sweet they call bitter; the light darkness, Isaiah 5.[259] In their own eyes they are the clever ones. I would ask them for the sake of God to abstain from such insolence. And what they should preach in awe and trembling[260] is something they have yet to experience themselves;[261] and they should believe that there are many, many infants at the breast whom God

Margin notes:
Mat. 7

Phil. 3

Mat. 7

In variis psalmis
testimonium[259]

Phil. 2

Esaie. 66

Non fit Neophitus[261]

Zacha. 5

---

245. Lit. 'your head'.

246. Isaiah 8[12f.]; 26[3]; Ezekiel 7[25ff.]; Matthew 16[6ff., 25f.]; 6[25ff.]; Mark 8[34ff.]; Luke 19[41ff.]; 17[33]; Deuteronomy 1[26ff.]; 32[5ff., 15ff.]

247. *unser köpffe höcher nutzen.*

248. 1 Corinthians 4[6-8, 18ff.]; 2[esp. 10ff.]

249. Proverbs 24[30ff.]

250. Matthew 7[6].

251. 'Contrary to the whole of Isaiah'; 'contrary to Isaiah 11'; cf. Isaiah 11[1-5]; cf. Luke 11[52] (they steal the key . . .).

252. *domine.*

253. 2 Peter 2[22]; F. reads 2 Peter 1, though corrects this on p. 238 n. 192; Proverbs 26[11].

254. Luke 11[52]; Matthew 7[15(?), 6(?)].

255. *greynen*, in sense of 'baring their teeth'; cf. Psalm 22[13] (snarling lions).

256. 'Dumb dogs, for the sake of their golden broth'; lit. yellow; or perhaps from *gel* = rich; Isaiah 56[10ff.]; 28[7]; Philippians 3[2, 19].

257. Matthew 7[15, 3ff.]

258. Philippians 3[2, 18f.]; cf. Matthew 7[14].

259. 'As various psalms testify'.

260. Philippians 2[12].

261. Müntzer's view is that this is impossible; cf. the marginal reference to 1 Timothy 3[6] (he should not be a recent convert); and *On Counterfeit Faith*, p. 215/4f. below.

will use to spread his name abroad.[262] For all who do this will, in the eyes of the world, be trodden underfoot like worms as Christ was.[263] They will not behave as the messengers from Gadarene did towards the Lord,[264] asking him to leave their land, although he had only come to it to offer[265] his word there to the needy; but they wanted to receive it without any sacrifice[266] of their lusts. Which is impossible.[267] Hence, dear brothers, if people mean well by us and treat us well we should not, like the horned apes or the big bluebottle flies, regard this as a great humiliation,[269] but should think of the saying of Solomon: 'The wounds inflicted by the lover are better than the kisses of a deceiver.'[270] And the prophet says, too: 'My beloved people, those who call you holy and good deceive you.'[271] When a wise man is punished he improves his life. A fool or idiot pays no heed to the word of wisdom. One has to say to him what he wants to hear. May God in his mercy preserve you from this, dear brothers, to all eternity. Amen.

Twentieth

In this proposition and set of conditions[272] I have dealt in summary form with the damge which has been done to the church[273] through the defective understanding of baptism and through counterfeit faith. If I am in error here, I will let myself be amicably corrected before an impartial congregation,[274] but in the full light of day and not without

Esaie 5
Jere. 2
Psal. 78
In domo unanimos[274]

I. Petri 3
Joan. 18
Luce 9

262. Zechariah 5 refers to a flying scroll with a curse on all who steal or swear falsely, presumably the 'false prophets'; thus denunciation, exhortation to change, renewed denunciation follow one another so fast that Müntzer's meaning is hard to follow; the reference to infants cannot be polemic against infant baptism, however, as the following sentences show; and Isaiah 66[10f., 18] requires a positive interpretation.

263. *wie die hinfelligen regenwurmer mit Christo*; 'perishable earthworms' (Stayer, following Bräuer/Ullmann) is incorrect; cf. Psalm 22[6f.] and n. 279 below; cf. also *Sermon to the Princes*, n. 36, p. 233 below; Psalm 23[4].

264. Matthew 8[34]; Mark 5[17].

265. *entpiethen*; cognate of the word Müntzer uses in the title of this work.

266. *schaden*, 'harm'.

267. Proverbs 1[7, 10ff.]; 3[11f.]; 5[1–5]; 8[10ff.]; 10[esp. vs. 2, 11]; 12[1]; 13[1]; 19[1, 27]; 22[1, 22f.]; 23[1–5, 19–21, 27ff.].

268. *wenn es gut mit uns gemeint und gehandelt ist*; i.e. if they reprove us for our good.

269. i.e. the priests and the scholars; 'horned apes' could be a word play on oxen, (cf. p. 114/4 above) a symbol of stupidity, and apes, cf. *affenspiel* (pp. 191/21 above, 272/29 below); perhaps one should read *hornissen* (hornets) as suggested by the Heidelberg Müntzer Symposium (1987); cf. Revelation 12[3], 13[1] and Ecclesiastes 10[1]; on 'humiliation' *schmach*, cf. Psalm 22[6], n. 263 above, and n. 279 below.

270. Cf. Proverbs 27[6].

271. Isaiah 3[12b]; cf. Jeremiah 23[16ff.] (F.).

272. As at the beginning of section 15 a slight variation on the title of the work.

273. Isaiah 5 (Israel as God's vineyard); Jeremiah 2 (the apostasy of Israel); Psalm 79 (Jerusalem in ruins).

274. *ungefherlichen*, not dangerous, non-hostile; A reads *unanimes*; cf. the marginal

sufficient witnesses, or in some obscure corner.[275] I hope by this initiative to bring about an improvement in the teaching of the evangelical preachers; nor have I any desire to despise our backward and slow Roman brothers.[276] All I ask is that judgement should be delivered on me before the whole world and not in some obscure corner. For this I pledge myself, life and limb,[277] scorning any devious defence by human hand,[278] through Jesus CHRIST, the true son of God; may he have you in his keeping for ever. Amen.

Nolite prohibe non est adversu vos, pro vobis

I. Chori. 9

Twenty-first

I have had weighty reasons for publishing my submission, for the door cloth[279] must be raised to the shaft of the cross, lest the teaching of CHRIST suffer at all on my account.[280] If anyone should find weaknesses in it,[281] let him write amicably[282] and I will give him full measure in return, lest he judge anyone else without due cause.[283] May JESUS CHRIST, the gentle son of God, aid us in this, who makes us his brothers.[284] Amen.

Joan 18
Joan. 10
Michee 2 et 3
1. Chor. 4
2 Tim. 2
Luce 6
Ephe. 4

Twenty-second

I am willing to present evidence for my case,[285] and I would appreciate if those of you who have not been put to the test did not turn up your noses in derision, but I would like to be interrogated

Joan. 10

Jere 1 et 15

note, 'one in the Lord' and 1 Peter 3[8] (have unity in spirit; Vg.: *omnes unanimes*); cf. also v. 15; i.e. Müntzer rejects, as elsewhere, the idea of a trial in Wittenberg; cf. introduction, p. 183 above.

275. John 18 (the trial of Jesus before the high priest and then Pilate).

276. Luke 9[50] ('Do not forbid him; for he that is not against you is for you').

277. Cf. The Prague Manifesto p. 351/5f. below.

278. A reference to Luther's spiriting away to the security of the Wartburg after the Diet of Worms in 1521; cf. p. 348/4ff. below; 1 Corinthians 9[1-3(?)].

279. *fusshadder*, foot-cloth; cf. Müntzer's translation of Psalm 22[6ff.] in his German Order of Service; '*Aber ich bin ein worm und kein mensch, ein schmach der leuthe und ein fusshader der buben*'; F., p. 74/2f.; *fusshader* translates *abjectio plebis* (Vg.), i.e. a doormat is Müntzer's term for something treated with utter contempt, trodden underfoot like a worm; cf. the *Sermon to the Princes* p. 234/11 below, in addition, of course, there is a reference to Luke 23[36 par]; Stayer, following Bräuer, refers to Heinrich Suso, Autobiography, ch. 20 in Georg Hofmann, (ed.) *Heinrich Seuse, Deutsche mystische Schriften* (Darmstadt 1966), 67–8; for Suso an old foot-cloth torn this way and that by dogs, symbolises the humiliation a Christian must undergo.

280. John 18 (betrayal of Jesus by Peter); John 10[1ff.] (the good shepherd); Micah 2[6]; 3[5-7].

281. *Wer do gebrechen ane hat*; 1 Corinthians 4[3-5].

282. 2 Timothy 2[25].

283. Luke 6[37f.].

284. Ephesians 4[25].

285. *meinen grund beweysen*.

with my opponents before men of all nations and all faiths. If you will   Ezechi. 13
pay the piper[286] my poor body is completely at your disposal.[287] Don't
be too quick with a hasty judgement[288] for the sake of the mercy of
God. AMEN.

Finis

---

286. *Wolt yr es euch lassen kosten*; 'If you want a price for that' (Stayer).

287. John 10[11]; Jeremiah 1[18f.] (cf. *Exposé of False Faith*, p. 260/12 below), 15[15ff., 20];
Ezekiel 13 (Ezekiel and the false prophets).

288. *mit schwindem urteyl*; cf. p. 276/10 below; Bräuer points to a parallel in
Tauler's *Predigten* (ed. F. Vetter, *Deutsche Texte des Mittelalters*, XI, Berlin, 1910)
p. 73/12f.

ON COUNTERFEIT FAITH

There are four important clues to this influential little writing. Firstly, it is intimately linked in its language and its ideas to the *Protestation*. Secondly, it was printed together with Müntzer's letter to Hans Zeiss on 2 December 1523 (Nr. 46.); thirdly there is the rather mysterious relationship to the list of questions posed by Spalatin, the court-preacher of Weimar, probably in mid-November. Finally, Müntzer himself advises the reader in section 14 that it should be read as an exposition of Matthew 16.

The letter to Zeiss is informative about the genesis of the book, showing that the biblical references were added later as an 'armoury' against the Wittenbergers. It also underlines the Christ-centredness of Müntzer's thought. The new humanity in Christ is reached through suffering obedience, as the members conform themselves with their head, the parts with the whole. This concept of unitive discipleship had already emerged in his controversy with Egranus and the Prague Manifesto, and many of the same themes are to be found in 'On the Incarnation of Christ' and 'On Following Christ', pp. 388ff., 396ff.

As a piece of literature it is not wholly successful. The Biblical references are sometimes, as in section 3, hard to follow. The beginning is rather abrupt and the continuity of thought is poor. Sometimes, too, the themes are presented in such a telescoped style as to be virtually unintelligible without consulting the *Protestation*, which had appeared shortly before.

Müntzer's rhetoric does, however, begin to take wing as he moves into the Biblical material – where Abraham, Moses, Peter figure as archetypes of authentic faith; and by the central sections has attained lyrical heights he will seldom surpass. In comparison with the more historical and practical emphasis of the *Protestation* it is much more of a treatise on spirituality.

The very first sentence has, at first sight, a strongly Lutheran ring: faith rests on the promise of Christ. Yet this certainty of faith, so important for Müntzer at Zwickau and Prague, is understood in a distinctive way. It is based, as the first biblical reference, to Isaiah 53, shows, on one who is depised and rejected by believing Israel.

Before we can attain it we have to be purged, 'ploughed', our deafened faculties awakened (cf. the reference in the *Protestation*, sections 8, 9 to our 'blindness'). As in the *Protestation*, section 3, and 'On Following Christ', faith means, in effect, being Christ-formed. Müntzer is wrestling with the problem of a merely nominal Christianity, of a pretended, superficial, unreal faith. To describe the latter, he uses the term *geticht*, *gedichtet* (also used by Luther); it has the meaning of 'dreamed-up', 'invented', or, as Stayer translates, 'imaginary'; yet it is pervasive enough, and 'counterfeit' may be the best English rendering, expressing its fraudulent plausibility.

The Bible unmasks this false religiosity. John the Baptist, for example, points to the incredulity with which Christ himself was met. Thus Scripture is a powerful 'negative' witness, putting us to the test, killing our old self. Its history of the chequered path to salvation challenges us to take the narrow path which leads, via unbelief, to authentic faith. But it cannot, as the delicate biblical scholars suggest, provide a substitute for personal faith. Even the enlightened pagans, as the *Protestation* had already indicated, are closer to true faith than this.

From section 3 on, Müntzer illustrates how for Abraham, Moses, Peter God's promise becomes (astonishing collocation!) a plague; it conflicts with all that the light of nature tells us. Only painfully and gradually do the elect learn to discriminate between the things of God and of the devil, to understand the order of creation. For Heaven cannot be gate-crashed with mere words and promises. If Abraham despaired, if Moses disbelieved, if the apostles misunderstood everything – with the bearer of revelation before their very eyes and ears – surely it is evident that without the living word there is no hope for us.

For our soul is a desert, a raging ocean, a battle-ground of apocalyptic dimensions. Until we allow the whole, dialectical message of Scripture to expose our inner fraudulence we cannot even begin to believe.

Heart has to cry out to heart, the earnest preacher (section 9) has to stir the waters of the soul, so that it can be receptive to the work of God, to the gentle son of God, until it is ready to suffer with the Lord. The vocabulary here is very close to that of 'On Following Christ,' pp. 396ff.

In sections 10 and 11 image is piled on image. The sheep who need the salt of wisdom are being poisoned by sweetness. The false shepherd, the stranger, is a salamander or a leopard, changing his appearance every moment. He leaves the thorns and thistles standing. He is a sneak-thief. In effect he wants the honey of religion, not the bitterness of Christ.

The positive images follow: God is the master-mason, Christ (the whole Christ) is the door, the corner-stone, the true measure, the bridegroom for whom one takes off the garment of the old life (Luke 6[29] being pressed into service to document the latter). In another strange conflation the 'jot or tittle' of Matthew 5[18] becomes the farthing from the parable of the talents.

It is all rather breathless, but also very striking and moving; it culminates in the 'song of the elect' in section 12, who joyously face the suffering that lies ahead, confident of its ultimate transfiguration into glory. There is a reference to the 'new song' of Psalm 40.

To the academics, however, Christ is not the foundation-stone but a stumbling-block; they combine the defects of the sign-seeking Jews and the rationalist Greeks; and they build on the shifting sand, the *grundsuppe*, or dregs of which the *Protestation* had spoken.

The final section is a rather magnificent coda, based on Matthew 16, with its denunciation of the leaven of the Pharisees, its Petrine texts (heavenly revelation, the rock, the keys) the all-too human (or Satanic!) reaction of the disciples to the prediction of suffering, the call to leave self and take up the cross.

Hell has to be endured before it can be overcome. That is the crux of the whole writing. An outward respect for Scripture can co-exist happily with the chaos of our desires, for Scripture is itself a creature. If, however, the book is to be opened and its inward reality reached, then the bitter mustard seed or yeast of faith will have to consume us until true poverty of spirit is reached. Then we will be taught by God alone, by his work in our soul, and will repudiate utterly all that is creaturely.

How did contemporaries read this book? For some, as Letter 69 documents for the Swiss Brethren, it represented an extraordinary break-through, an undergirding and deepening of their own stance. On the other hand, how would a Spalatin assess it? Where would his interest or comprehension tail off? At the polemical language against the (unspecified) biblical scholars? At the mystical terminology? How convincing would he find the antithesis between authentic and counterfeit faith?

The polemic against the affluent, self-confident, 'positivist' scholars is certainly swingeing; it is, however, only part of the call to separate those ready to suffer the ploughing of the spirit from those possessed by the devil – mentioned in section 2, 4, 8. Likewise the mystical language of conformity, of *gelassenheit*, of endurance, simplicity, transfiguration is subordinate to the advocacy of true discipleship.

This writing, best known for its striking aphorisms, is, from beginning to end, a mosaic of images, often paradoxical, almost exclusively male, predominantly biblical: the two-edged sword, the stone of stumbling and stability, the wine press which crushes us, so that we can mature in faith. Sometimes the images become confused; in section 5 the 'gate-crashing' pigs shrink back; sometimes, as in the canine image of section 4, the sense is obscure.

Yet these images, the language of the soul, are part of the strength of this writing, bridging the chasm to Scripture, delving below the surface of words, the 'false light of nature'. Müntzer's hermeneutic links John and the prophets, Psalm 40 and Matthew 16, Isaiah 53 and the Synoptic gospels. It is, apparently, in the abyss of the image that God and man meet. The sole public activity needed is earnest preaching, exposition of the soul as well as of Scripture, which will cut through the superficiality of our inherited faith, reveal its effective atheism, and point the way forward towards growth in Christ.

On Counterfeit Faith;[1] following the recent *Protestation* issued by Thomas Müntzer, pastor at Allstedt 1524.
Against the Counterfeit Faith among the Christian People.

First

Isaie. 53
Roma. 10
Math. 13
Luce. 8
Marci. 4

Christian faith is an assurance[3] that one can rely on the word and promise of CHRIST.[4] Now if anyone is to grasp hold of this word with an upright, unfeigned[5] heart his ears must first be swept free of the droning of all sorrows and lusts.[6] For a man can no more claim

Luce. 9
1 Timo. 1
Psal. 129
Luce. 12
Jacobi. 1
Mathei. 23
Luce. 6
Joan. 13
Ephe. 4
Roma. 8

that he is a Christian before his cross has made him receptive[7] to God's work and word than a field can produce a heavy crop of wheat until it has been ploughed.[8] The elect friend of God[9] who yearns for and endures the word[10] is no counterfeit hearer, but a diligent pupil of his master,[11] constantly and ardently watching all that he does, seeking to be found conformable to him in every respect, to the best of his ability.[12]

Second

Joan. 1
Psal. 18
Roma. 5

Whenever a person hears or sees something pointing him to CHRIST he takes it as a miraculous indication[13] of how to chase

---

1. *getichten glawben*; *getict* is translated 'imaginary' by Stayer; cf. *eingebildet* (Bräuer/Ullmann); it is often used by Luther, and is quite basic for Müntzer, being the opposite to 'authentic', 'real'; cf. 1 Timothy 1[5] (Vg. *fide non ficta*).

2. *auf nechst protestation aussgangen*; another possible translation would be: 'issued in advance of ...'; cf. pp. 183f. above.

3. *sicherung*, not a normal expression of Müntzer's; Spalatin's sixth question asks: How can we be sure (*certi*) of our faith?; cf. introduction, p. 210; cf. also pp. 224f.; this section contains a brief definition of faith, cf. Spalatin's first question: What is true faith? and his second question: How is faith born?

4. Isaiah 53 [esp. v. 1]; Romans 10[esp. v. 17] (faith comes from what is heard); this sounds very Lutheran.

5. *ungeticht*.

6. *vom gethön der sorgen und luste*; 'from the wax of ...' (Stayer), which seems misleading; cf. *gedön*, F. p. 162/12; Matthew 13[14ff.. 22]; Luke 8[14]; Mark 4[19] (parable of sower); cf. Dismer, pp. 241–3, for a different elucidation of some of the citations.

7. *entpfinlich*.

8. The 'ploughing' of the soul is a recurrent theme in Müntzer; cf. the *Protestation* p. 199/8 above; cf. Isaiah 28[24-6]; Luke 9[23]; 1 Timothy 1[5].

9. *freundt Gottis*; term much used by Müntzer, drawing on German mysticism, rather than citing Biblical passages like John 15[14f.]; Romans 8, however, referred to in the margin, speaks of sons, children of God.

10. *In sulcher erharrung erleydet*; Psalm 130[5f.] ('I wait for the Lord'); Luke 12[35ff.] ('Let your loins be girded ...').

11. James 1[22ff.] (a key passage); Matthew 23[10]; Luke 6[40. 46-9]; John 13[16].

12. Ephesians 4[7. 13]; Romans 8[29] (cf. n. 9 above).

13. *gezeugnis*; Scripture is testimony to faith, not its sole ground or authority; cf. Spalatin's third question: Where do we seek faith? John 1[7-13]; Psalm 19[7] (a favourite psalm).

away, do to death, reduce to pulp his unbelief.[14] He sees the whole of holy scripture in this way, as a two-edged sword,[15] everything it contains being there, in the first instance, to choke us to death, not to vivify us.[16] A person who has never been put to the test, who makes a great show of the words of God, will catch nothing but the wind.[17] Just think how sorely God has tried all his elect from the very beginning,[18] not even sparing his only son,[19] since he destined him to be the true goal of blessedness, showing us that the narrow way is the only way[20] – and one which the self-indulgent biblical scholars are never going to find.[21] This is why an elect friend of God cannot come to faith lightly.[22] The more boastful people are about their faith, the more fraudulent and counterfeit it will be,[23] unless – like all the men of the Bible – they can give an account of how they came to their faith.[24] Such deluded and self-opinionated men[25] will never deserve to be regarded as intelligent pagans,[27] far less Christians. It is people such as they who take on the appearance of angels of light;[28] we should be on our guard against them as much as against the devil himself.

Third

God caused Abraham to be miserable and forsaken so that he would put his trust in God alone, not in any created being.[29]

14. *unglauben*; cf. 1 Timothy 1[13]; Romans 5[3ff.] ('we rejoice in our sufferings').

15. Hebrews 4[12]; cf. *Protestation*, p. 196/5 above.

16. 2 Corinthians 3[6] (Vg: *littera enim occidit*); Deuteronomy 32[39–41] (Vg: *ego occidam* ...); *würgen*, 'choke', is an emphatic variant of 'kill', and recalls the parable of the sower (cf. n. 6. above).

17. Cf. *Protestation*, p. 202/21 above.

18. 1 Samuel 2[6. 31ff.]; Ecclesiasticus 34[12ff.]; Psalm 1 (separation of wicked from righteous); Proverbs 25[4] and 1 Peter 1[6f.] refer to the refining of silver or gold; Wisdom 3[esp. v. 5.] (God has put them to the test).

19. Romans 8[32].

20. 1 Peter 2[21]; Matthew 7[13f.]; this is also a main theme of the *Protestation*, esp. sections 13, 14; cf. also Philippians 3[14].

21. Matthew 23 (Müntzer never tires of citing this chapter with its denunciation of the scribes and Pharisees).

22. Cf. *Protestation*, p. 202/18 above; cf. Spalatin's question 4: How is faith acquired?; 1 Peter 1[6f.]

23. Matthew 8[25f.]; 9[11ff. 8]; Wisdom 5[1ff. 8]; Ecclesiastics 19[23] (Vg.: *Et est qui emittit verbum certum enarrans veritatem. Est qui nequiter humiliat se, et interiora ejus plena sunt dolo*).

24. *yrs glaubens ankunfft und rechenschafft*; 1 Peter 3[15].

25. 'lovers of pleasure are corrupted in their judgement', cf. 2 Timothy 3[4]; 1 Timothy 3[6].

26. 'Whatever ...' Cf. Romans 15[4].

27. Cf. *Protestation*, p. 197/3 above.

28. For comparison: 2 Corinthians 11[14]; Jeremiah 31[31ff.] (i.e. false and true faith); lit. 'the angel of light'.

29. 'throughout Scripture'; Romans 4[18ff.]; Genesis 12; 13; 14; 22 (sacrifice of Isaac).

per totam
scripturam[29]

Psal. 118

Psal. 35

Actuum 7
Sapien. 2
Philippen 3
Ephe. 3
Judas predigte
Cristum und hatte
den Beutel am halse.
Jo. 12[37]

1 Corin. 2
Luce. 2
Psal. 1
Mathei. 5
Joan. 8
Luce 22

Roma. 7
Roma. 7

Joan. ultimo
Zacharias
Elisabet, Maria
omnes difficiles ad
credendum[42]

Therefore he was plagued[30] by the promise of God. In order that [the experience of being forsaken] should always come just before the promise,[31] he was plagued by a remote hope of consolation, one which seemed very far-fetched indeed to the light of nature,[32] St Stephen points this out in his reproof to the delicate, finger-pointing[33] biblical scholars in the Acts of the Apostles.[34] The damned always want to grasp hold on CHRIST at the height of his dereliction,[35] while at the same time keeping a tight hold on themselves.[36] We have to read the tenth and eleventh chapters (and the thirteenth) of the book of creation in the light of the twelfth, where everything is resolved,[38] and Abraham pronounced worthy to see the coming day of CHRIST after all his distress and toil.[39] From the very start this has always been God's way. If the light of nature had to be obliterated so radically in Abraham, how much more will this be true of us?[40]

Fourth

Moses, who illustrates how the law leads to a recognition of the false light of nature, had no faith in God's living promise.[41] Before he could come to an unfeigned trust in God his unbelief had to be made quite clear to him. Otherwise he could not have been sure that the devil would not plant himself in his path in the guise of a dog.[43] For

---

30. *gepeiniget*; for Müntzer the biblical plagues were parables; cf. his marginal notes on Tertullian, p. 423/7f. below.

31. *So sie nuhe schire solte angehn fur der zusage*; *sie* must refer to Abraham's *gelassenheit*, his 'being forsaken', prior to the fulfilment of the promise.

32. *mit weit herstregktem trost, welchen er nach der liecht der natur weithleufftig befand*; Psalm 119[19]; 36[7].

33. *spitzfingerischen*; Müntzer refers elsewhere to the scholars pointing their finger at people; cf. On Following Christ, p. 397/26f. below.

34. Acts 7[2ff., 51f.]

35. *den hochgelassenen Christum fassen*; forsaken like Abraham (*elende und gelassen*, p. 215/18 above); Philippians 3[10]; Ephesians 3[11-13].

36. *sich in selbst furhalten*; instead of 'longing to reach beyond themselves', Declaration, p. 203/13 above; 'want to be extremely self-centred' (Stayer); Wisdom 2[esp vs 21f.]; cf. also Romans 14[7].

37. 'Judas preached Christ with the money-bag around his neck'; John 12[5ff.]

38. *verfassen*; the words *und das dreizehnte*, 'and the thirteenth', in the MS have been omitted from the printed version; cf. Dismer, p. 204.

39. *erbselickeit*; Luke 2 (birth of Jesus); cf. Philippians 1[6].

40. 1 Corinthians 2[4f., 13]; Psalm 1[1f.]; Matthew 5[14(?)]; John 8[12]; Luke 22 (Peter betrays Jesus).

41. Cf. Exodus 3[11]; 4[1, 10ff.]; 6[30]; Romans 7[7ff.] (law reveals sin).

42. John 21[4]; Zechariah, Elisabeth, Mary all had difficulties in coming to faith; cf. Expose of False Faith, p. 286/5f. and p. 322/12ff. below.

43. *das der tewffel yme keinen hund vorn lerben schlug*; 'Larve, Schnauze' (F.); cf. Exodus 11[7] 'against ... the people of Israel ... not a dog shall growl'; perhaps it is meant metaphorically: 'that the Devil was not pulling the wool over his eyes'

Moses might well have taken God for a devil if he had not recognised the distinction between the directness[44] of God and the deviousness of the creature laid down in the order between God and the creatures.[45] Even should the entire world accept that something is God-given the man who is poor in spirit will only be satisfied if it accords with what he has found after tribulation.[46]

Fifth

In short let any honest, pious member of the elect go through the books of the Bible without any particular bias or axe to grind.[47] There he will discover that none of the fathers – the patriarchs, prophets, the apostles least of all – came to faith without great difficulty.[48] None wanted to gatecrash like these mad, lecherous swine we know, who shrink back from the ferocity of the winds, the raging of the waves, and from all the great waters of wisdom.[49] For in their hearts they are very well aware[50] that a great storm like that would be their undoing. For all their fine promises[51] they are like the foolish man who builds on sand, although such buildings must collapse etc.[52]

Sixth

God's messengers[53] had listened to the bearer of the gospel himself; CHRIST told Peter that neither flesh nor blood had revealed the truth to him but God himself.[54] Yet even so they were unable to respond to a single one of the promises with anything but scandalous apostasy, to their red-faced shame. For the depths of their unbelief had to be tested. Not one of them would believe that Christ was risen when it happened.[55] They thought him a ghost or an apparition.[56]

(Stayer): *larventier* = *teufel*, the devil; here, as elsewhere, I am indebted to Dr Tom Scott for advice on the translation.

44. *einfeltigkayt*; cf.

45. *nach der ordenung die in got und creaturn gesatzt ist* Genesis 1[26ff.]; Luke 4[1ff.] (Jesus tempted by the devil); on God and the creatures cf. Prague Manifesto, p. 357, n. 6 below.

46. Isaiah 61[1-3].

47. *ane groll sunderlichs gesuchs*; 1 Corinthians 10[9-11].

48. Ephesians 2[1ff.]; Matthew 8[26]; 11[25f.]

49. Matthew 7[6, 21]; is there a reference to 8[30ff.]?

50. *Dann yre gewissen mergken wol*; Proverbs 10[24] (What the wicked dread will happen to them).

51. *vorheischungen*.

52. Matthew 7[24-7]; Ecclesiasticus 8[15] ('Do not travel with a reckless fellow, lest he imposes on you ... you will both be ruined by his folly').

53. *boten*, 'apostles'; cf. Spalatin's question 7: how should faith be tested?

54. Matthew 16[17].

55. Luke 24[11, 16, 25, 31, 48f.]; John 15[26f.]; Ecclesiasticus 10[12] ('The beginning of human pride is to desert the Lord').

56. Luke 24[37].

Isayc. 61

And what a fine opinion we have of ourselves, who have not yet been put to the test, having recourse to counterfeit faith and a fictitious picture of God's mercy; we imagine we can storm the heavens with the help of a natural promise or assurance.[57] O no, most beloved Christians, let us use the holy Scriptures as they were meant to be used; to do us to death (as we have argued above)! For the living word which brings us to life is heard only by the soul which has been purged.[58] So let us be led by the teaching of the spirit and not of the flesh[59] and recognise the consistent message of every part of Scripture, which both consoles and affrights us;[60] not seizing on one passage here, another there.[61] Until fraudulent faith is completely exposed, the outward word is invariably believed, but they fail to find the door when the storm comes.[62] Hence if people are ever to get rid of their feigned faith and be rightly instructed in upright faith they must first be reduced to confusion and [come to recognise their] total ignorance.[63]

2 Cor. 3

Psal. 118

Isa. 28

1 Cor. 2
Luce. 2
1 Regum 2

Luce. 8

Math. 13

Marci. 4

Psal. 118

Seventh

Jerc. 1

Joan. 2

Psal. 66

Jerc. 23

When the preacher who has been under God's judgement[64] has the words of God put in his mouth they are not accompanied by honey-sweet words and hypocrisy[65] but with a consuming and truly earnest zeal[66] to root out, tear down and scatter the counterfeit Christians and destroy every scrap of the wicked faith which, like artful thieves, they have stolen from others by eavesdropping on them or reading their books.[67]

Eighth

Joan. 9

Isaic. 6

Our poor, wretched, pitiable, lamentable Christian people cannot be helped because they do not recognise what is wrong with them;[68]

---

57. *ein natürlich promission ader zusage*; i.e. one which appeals to our human nature; cf. Isaiah 61[2] ('the day of vengeance of our Lord').

58. 2 Corinthians 3[3.6]; Psalm 119[71.120(?)] (Vg.: *Confige timore tuo carnes meas: a judiciis enim tuis timui.*)

59. 1 Corinthians 2[13].

60. Like Simeon who, led by the Spirit, interprets Jesus' birth in the light of Isaiah, Luke 2[25ff.]; and Eli, told that his wicked sons will die, 1 Samuel 2[27–36].

61. Isaiah 28[9f.]

62. Luke 8[24f.]; John 10[1ff.]; cf. p. 199/15f. above.

63. Matthew 13[54.14ff.]; Mark 4[37–41]; Psalm 119[71].

64. *rechtfertigen*; question 8 asks: Who are the truly faithful?

65. Jeremiah 1[6.9f.]

66. John 2[17]; Psalm 67[2].

67. Jeremiah 23[30].

68. This seems to take up question 2: How is faith born?; John 10[39ff.]; Isaiah 6[9f.]; Luke 8[9f.]; Matthew 13[14f.]; Mark 4[33f.]

because they use the mere form of true faith as a fig-leaf[69] and declined to abandon their counterfeit faith they are impervious to advice and assistance. The same fault is common to all; none will recognise that when they first came to faith[70] they are on the same level as Turks, pagans, Jews, and all unbelievers.[71] On the contrary, each dons his cap and preens himself[72] about his faith and his good deeds, although he really knows nothing about the source or foundation of either.[73] For this reason our crude and clumsy forefathers handed over the whole world (themselves only excepted) to the devil,[75] and declined to be accountable to anyone themselves, thereby bringing about all the sects and schisms, most of which have been due to disputes about ceremonies or rites[76] (whether it was counterfeit or true faith being blissfully ignored).[77]

Ninth

If our wretched, crude Christian people is to be saved from such grievous abominations,[78] the first, and all-important, step is to listen to an earnest preacher who, like John the baptiser, will cry out piteously and dolefully in the waste places of the mad, raging hearts of men,[79] so that through God's work they may find the way to become receptive to God's word; after they have been stirred up in different ways[80] they will be shown the fountain of blessedness,[81] the son of God, like a gentle little lamb which gave no cry when it was slaughtered.[82] In this way he bore the sin of the world, enabling us, sheep like him,[83] to be conscious all the day long that we, too, are to be butchered; not to growl or complain about our suffering like whining

---

69. *schandtdeckel*; pretext.

70. *in der ankunfft seines glawbens*.

71. Matthew 9[10ff.(?)] (Jesus eats with tax-gatherers and sinners); Luke 19[1-10] (Zacchaeus); Matthew 18[1ff.] ('unless you turn and become like children ...')

72. *mutzet und putzet* in the original not *nutzet* (F.); 'crowns himself and dresses himself up' (Stayer); cf. *Exposé*, p. 292/18 below.

73. 1 Peter 3[15]; 1 Timothy 1[6f.]

74. The whole of Romans.

75. Luke 18[10-14]; cf. section 7 of the *Protestation*.

76. Acts 10[9-16] (forbidden foods); Romans 11[8ff.]

77. *unangesehen wider getichten nach rechten glawben*; i.e. trivialities displace the central issue; cf. the *Protestation*, section 7.

78. Question 5 asks: How are we to be taught faith for our profit and well-being?

79. Psalm 119[136(?)]; John 3[23ff.]; Isaiah 40[3]; Psalm 63[1].

80. *nach manchfeltiger bewegung*; Psalm 30[1ff.]; 69[1ff.]; cf. John 5[7] and the *Protestation*, section 6.

81. Psalm 36[9]; John 4[13f.]

82. Isaiah 53[7]; John 1[29]; copy in British Library reads *Joannis*; not *Joannis I* as in F.

83. Romans 8[36]; Psalm 44[11. 22]; cf. Letter 40 to Luther, p. 57/25f. above (Stayer).

Isaic. 5

Mathei. 20
Psal. 94

dogs,[84] but to be like the sheep of his pasture,[85] which he only makes over to us[86] in suffering, with the salt of his wisdom.

Tenth

Ezech. 34

Isaic 5

dicunt amarum
dulce[88]

Oppositum

2 Cor. 1[89]

Pardus[92]

Jere. 13 c.ct

Joan. 10

Prover. 10

Sapien. 5

Prover. 9

Sheep are poisoned by bad pastures, but nourished by salt.[87] To preach a sweet Christ to the fleshly world[88] is the most potent poison that has been given to the dear sheep of Christ from the very beginning. For a man who accepts this wants to be God-formed, but has not the least desire, indeed is totally disinclined, to become Christ-formed. Further – and at the most basic level[90] – he is not even true to himself,[91] but changes his appearance in all he sets his hand to like a salamander or a leopard.[92] Hence the insistence of Christ:[93] 'My sheep hear my voice and pay no heed to the voice of the stranger.' The stranger is anyone who neglects[94] the way to eternal life, leaves the thorns and thistles standing, and proclaims: 'Believe! believe! Be firm, be firm with a strong, strong faith, one which will drive piles into the ground.'[95]

Eleventh

Joan. 10

1 Cor. 1 ct 2

Prover. 5

Psal. 117

Mathei. 21

There is no other basis of faith than the whole Christ; half will not do;[96] for one does not sneak into a house by the window.[97] Any one who rejects the bitter CHRIST will gorge himself to death on honey.[98] CHRIST is a corner-stone.[99] Just as he had to be shaped,[100] so we have to be knocked into shape by the master-mason[101] if we are to

---

84. Matthew 20[11f.]

85. Isaiah 5[17]; Psalm 95[7].

86. *vortregt*; 'admits' (Stayer); the German is awkward; Bräuer/Ullmann reconstruct: *[wir], die er mit dem Salz seiner Weisheit in Leiden und nicht anders erträgt*; but cf. the use of *vortragung* in the letter to Zeiss, p. 70/24 above.

87. Ezekiel 34[18f., 31].

88. Isaiah 5[20] (Vg.: *dicunt amarum dulce*).

89. The opposite; 2 Corinthians 1[5ff.]

90. *zum allerundtersten*.

91. *yhm selbern nicht enlich*; cf. the reference to Peter in the *Protestation*, section 13.

92. *wie ein molchelein ader panthertier*; cf. Jeremiah 13[23, 25] (though the Biblical text insists the leopard cannot change!); cf. *pardus* (panther) in margin.

93. John 10[27, 4f.]

94. *vorwildert*, allows to go wild; Proverbs 10[9] (Vg.: *depravat vias suas*); Wisdom 5[6]; cf. 2 Peter 2[2].

95. Proverbs 9[1] (seven pillars of wisdom).

96. 1 Corinthians 1[12ff.]; 2[2f.]

97. John 10[1ff.]

98. Proverbs 5[3].

99. Psalm 118[22] ('The stone which the builders rejected ...'); Matthew 21[42]; Ephesians 2[20f.]

100. *Wie mit dem ym polliren ist umbgehalten*.

101. *werckmeister*.

grow into a true living building.[102] Not a cent[103] must go missing at any time of our lives; every Christian must stand up to scrutiny from top to toe, and must strain his utmost, according to his talent or gift, to measure up to [Christ].[104] Only he who dies with CHRIST can rise with him.[105] How can anyone be living the true life if he has not once taken off his old garment?[106] Therefore those who console before they sadden are thieves and murderers; they want to spring into action before CHRIST comes;[107] they have no idea what it is to which they say 'Yes' or 'No'.[108]

Twelfth

CHRIST, unchanging like his father,[109] has shown no more winsome love to his elect than this:[110] that he has laboured to make them as sheep for the slaughter;[111] the damned, on the other hand, will only be able to think about being expelled and killed and their name vanishing from the earth.[112] Remembering this, anyone who looks at the little lamb, and sees how it takes away the sin of the world, will say:[113] 'I have heard with my ears how the old fathers in the Bible dealt

---

102. Ephesians 2[21f.]

103. *meytlin*; *Meit* is the smallest copper coin (F.); Matthew 5[18] (not a jot or tittle).

104. *und demselbigen nach seinem pfund ader masse auffs höchste gleich zu werden*; Romans 8[29]; 5[1-5]; cf. also 12[3].

105. Cf. Romans 8[17].

106. Luke 6[29(t)] ('When a man takes your coat …').

107. John 10[1. 10ff.] (the false shepherds).

108. 1 Timothy 1[7].

109. *unwandelbar mit seinem vatter*; 'unchangeably [one] with his Father' (Stayer, following Bräuer/Ullmann); the reference is certainly to John 10, cited in the previous section, with its reference in v. 30 to oneship with the Father; the main emphasis however seems to be the constancy of Father and Son, unlike the salamander-like false shepherds; cf. v. 28f. 'no one can snatch them from my care … and no one can snatch them out of the Father's care.'

110. Cf. Spalatin's question 10; How can faith maintain itself under trials? 1 John 3[1ff.] ('How great is the love that the Father has shown to us!'); cf. also 1 John 1[3].

111. *die do dienen in die kuchen*; Romans 8[36].

112. Wisdom 2[4]; The German is difficult: *das sie nohr sinnen, wie sie werden vortrieben umbrengen und yr gedechtnus von der erden werde auffgehaben*; 'who can only brood about how they be driven away, killed …' (Stayer, following Franz); the argument in Wisdom 2, however, is that because life is short and oblivion inescapable, one should enjoy life, oppress the poor and the widow (v. 10), kill the righteous (v. 20); thus there is more of a case for the active meaning of the verbs than usually admitted; the context, however, is not a contrast between persecutors and persecuted, but of allegedly worldly Christians relying, like Luther, on secular support (after the Diet of Worms) and of the true followers of the Cross; the passive meaning seems, therefore, the correct one; cf. the *Protestation* n. 278.

113. Psalm 44[1ff.]; song of the elect; end of the song (this should be at the end of the twelfth section).

Genc. 32
Finis cantici[113]
Psal. 53

Joan. 10
Psal. 118
Luce. 10
Psal. 39
Psal. 39
Isai. 26

with God and he with them, none of them becoming one with him until he had overcome through his suffering (assigned to him before all time).[114] Thus we are transfigured by the glory of God from splendour to splendour'.[115] This is what the Lord says:[116] 'No one can tear out of my grasp the sheep given me by my father.' This means the pasture of the sheep which is assigned to them in heaven.[117] For after all the butchery it says:[118] O Lord, shake off your sleep. Why do you turn your face away from me? Help me for the sake of your name to plant my feet firmly on the rock. Then I shall say: You alone have done it. Then I will not allow my lips to be sealed, but will proclaim in your great church the righteousness which you alone have set in train.[119]

Thirteenth

Ephc. 2
Roma. 9
Math. 16 ct 23 ct 7
2 Cor 2
Psal. 48

On such a foundation true Christianity,[120] destined for eternal life, is built. One only attains it after learning to watch our for, and get rid of the yeast of those wicked scholars[121] who dare to convert the pure word of God into their yeast with their worm-eaten, hobbling clap-trap.[122] For the result of all their teaching is that men strut around with their untried faith, vainly confident,[123] and imagining they will be man enough to cope with any crisis, armed with their bland assurances. In reality, they have not learnt at all how a man can achieve this.

114. Genesis 32[24-32] (Jacob wrestles with the angel); Psalm 54[3f.]

115. *Das machet die erglastung Gottis im liechte zum liechte gelangen; erglasten, überglasten* are used by Müntzer for the glory of God transfiguring us; this passage seems close to 2 Corinthians 3[18]; cf. also 1 Corinthians 2[7] (God's secret wisdom, purpose bringing us to our glory).

116. John 10[28].

117. Psalm 119[89]; Luke 10[20]; Psalm 40[7] (name written in heaven).

118. Psalm 44[23f.]; 40[13, 17].

119. Isaiah 26[4]; Psalm 40[2f., 9f.]

120. Ephesians 2[20f.]; Romans 9[32f.] (Christ both the foundation-stone and the stone of stumbling).

121. Mathew 16[6]; 23; 7[15].

122. *wurmfressigen lamen tzotten*; cf. the parallels in Luther WA 10[287, 8f.]; Müntzer usually talks of *lahme Fratzen*; there may be a continuation of the sheep symbolism of the previous section, and a reference to Ezekiel 34[18ff.] ('My flock has to eat what you have trampled and ... churned up'); cf. Psalm 49[13ff.] (wicked are sheep whose bodies will rot in Sheol) cf. also Mark 9[48] (the devouring worm is the fate of those whose self-seeking causes others to stumble).

123. *das sich die menschen falschs in einer getichten weise mit unversuchtem glawben auffbrüsten*; lit., that men brag of something false in a feigned manner with untried faith; 2 Corinthians 2 (Paul's tears and distress at the failings of the Corinthians).

Fourteenth

Read through the whole of the sixteenth chapter of Matthew, you elect brother, every word of it! There you will find that no one can believe in CHRIST until he has first conformed himself to him.[124] Through experiencing unbelief the elect leaves behind him all the counterfeit faith he has learnt, heard or read from Scripture;[125] for he sees that an outward testimony cannot create inward reality,[126] but can only do what it was created to do.[127] Hence he is not deflected by anything said by those lacking in experience,[128] but, eagerly pursues revelation, like Peter, who is a pioneer for all who follow, saying:[129] 'I know full well that CHRIST is the son of the living God.' For the unbelief, concealed in my flesh and blood,[130] is half-smothered[131] by the desires, which the mustard seed and the good yeast penetrate and devour,[132] and thus break through in the whole [reality of] unbelief.[133] One has to have gone through despair and the most extreme reverses. Hell has to be endured, before one can take due precautions against its engulfing gates, with all their wiles.[134] The faith of the damned and of the elect is arrived at very differently.[135] The godless man is only too happy to accept Scripture.[136] He builds up a strong faith on the fact that someone has suffered before him. But when it comes to facing the little lamb who opens up the book,[137] he has no intention at all of losing his life,[138] or of conforming himself to the lamb, but hopes in

124. John 12[26]; Matthew 7[21].

125. Jeremiah 8[8].

126. *kan in ime kein wesen machen*; Romans 8[16] ('the Spirit bears witness with our spirit . . .'); 2 Corinthians 3[3, 6].

127. Scripture is itself part of the created world!

128. Matthew 7[21]; 2 Peter 2[esp. v.3].

129. Matthew 16[16]; 14[28, 33].

130. Matthew 7[15] (wolves disguised as sheep).

131. *ist uberwunden fast zum teil*; or: 'utterly smothered in part by the desires' (Scott).

132. *die das senffkorn und guter sawerteig durchfressen und dringen*; 'which eat their way through . . . the mustard seed and good leaven' (Stayer); this is grammatically difficult and makes no sense; as the next paragraph shows the mustard seed is the tiny beginning of true faith; likewise yeast penetrates, is not penetrated itself.

133. *machen den durchbruch in allem unglauben*, 'break through unbelief everywhere' (Stayer, following Bräuer); for Müntzer the desires are the thorns in the parable of the sower; they obscure not only true faith but the depths of unbelief; by eating their way through them authentic faith comes face to face with the reality of unbelief; cf. 1 Samuel 2[22ff.] (the immorality of Eli's sons); cf. p. 203/15ff. above.

134. The opposite; note this particularly; Psalm 24[7-9]; cf. Matthew 16[18]; Psalm 49[13f.]

135. *Es ist nicht ein annemen des vordampten und ausserwelten* 'The damned and the elect do not accept the same thing' (Stayer).

136. Isaiah 29[13f.]

137. Revelation 5[7ff.]

138. *sele.*

Psal. 39
Isaie 22
Luce 4
Isaie 61
Luce 17
2 Cor. 4
Isaie 54
Joan. 6

his worldly way to save his skin with proof-texts.[139] That is all wrong.

The scholar cannot grasp the meaning of Scripture, although the whole of it has been expounded to him in a human way, and although he may be about to burst apart [with all his knowledge]; he has to wait[140] until the key of David[141] has revealed it to him, until he has been trodden underfoot with all his habitual ways in the wine-press.[142] There he will attain such poverty of spirit[143] as to acknowledge that there is no faith in him at all; only the desire to learn true faith. This, then, is the faith which becomes as small as a mustard seed.[144] Then man must see how he is to endure the work of God, in order that he may grow from day to day in the knowledge of God. Then man will be taught by God alone, person to person, and not by any created being.[145] Everything known to created being will become bitter gall to him, since its ways are perverse. God preserve all his elect from them, and save them when they have fallen into them. CHRIST bring this to pass. Amen.

Appendix to *On Counterfeit Faith*. Questions of George Spalatin.
(Allstedt(?), mid-November(?) 1523)

Questions transmitted to Master Thomas Müntzer 1523[146]

1. Which, and what,[147] is truly Christian faith?
2. How is faith born?
3. Where does one seek faith and enquire about it?
4. How can faith be secured?

139. lit. 'clear texts'.
140. Psalm 40[1].
141. Isaiah 22[22].
142. *do er zuknyrschet wirt in alle seiner angenomen weisse*; 'where all his assured manner is crushed' (Stayer).
143. Isaiah 61[1-3].
144. Luke 17[6].
145. Isaiah 54[1, 5ff., 11]; John 6[45].
146. *Interrogationes magistro Thomas Muntzero transmissae MDXXIII*; F., p. 569; it is not clear how, if at all, these questions, found among Spalatin's papers, relate to *On Counterfeit Faith*; following the discovery of the Gotha manuscript of *On Counterfeit Faith* (which is reproduced in Bräuer/Ullmann, pp. 22–9) Franz, p. 569, came to the conclusion that 'from this manuscript it is evident that the writing, *On Counterfeit Faith*, is the answer to the questions which Spalatin posed to Müntzer'; more cautiously Elliger, p. 405, concluded that 'it is conceivable that the recently discovered, contemporary manuscript copy of the treatise is a somewhat inexact copy made, perhaps in Allstedt, of a revision of the first draft which was specially made by Müntzer for Spalatin'; the basis of these judgements is the note at the end of

5. How are we to be taught faith to our profit and well-being?[148]
6. How can we be sure of our faith?
7. How can, and ought, each individual test his faith?
8. Who are the true followers of Christ?
9. What are the trials under which faith is born, bears seed, and grows?
10. How can faith maintain itself under trials and emerge as conqueror?
11. Which faith saves and how?

To which Thomas Müntzer wrote back to me, G. Spalatin, as follows, in his own hand:[149]

Spalatin's quotations, and the following comments, in Spalatin's hand, on the Gotha manuscript: 'Against Counterfeit faith (*Contra fidem fictitiam*). 1524. Thomas Müntzer. All these have been scrutinised and sent on with a brief evaluation.' (Bräuer/Ullmann, p. 22); Bräuer/Ullmann, p. 9ff., 19f., point out that the Gotha manuscript is not in Müntzer's hand (as Franz and Elliger acknowledge); that it is very similar to a manuscript discovered by Gottfried Seebass in the Nuremberg archives – and attributed to Christian Hitz of Salzburg(!); that a careful analysis of the Gotha and Nuremberg manuscripts shows that they are both *secondary* variants on the printed text, and presumably were circulated in this Nicodemite form after Müntzer's death (the Gotha manuscript, for example, carefully removes all personal references to Müntzer as author and to Zeiss as recipient of the appended Letter 46); moreover they argue that Müntzer would never have agreed to tackle the question of faith in the terms set by Spalatin's questions, which presuppose that faith can be taught systematically; most of these conclusions appear incontestable; and thus the Gotha manuscript cannot be regarded as an early form of *On Counterfeit Faith* and certainly not as the handwritten response to his questions to which Spalatin refers; we need not doubt, however, that Spalatin received such a response (and he seems to take care to distinguish it from the printed version of *On Counterfeit Faith*) to the questions he despatched to Müntzer in 1523, perhaps, in November when he was in Allstedt, as Elliger, p. 403, suggests; the theme, and many of the specific questions he raises are indeed dealt with by *On Counterfeit Faith*; a tentative conclusion, therefore, might be that there is some relationship between Spalatin's questions and the genesis of *On Counterfeit Faith*; (cf. notes 3, 13, 22, 53, 67, 78, 110); as yet, however, its precise nature cannot be determined, and Elliger's certainty, p. 404, shared by Stayer, 'Thomas Müntzer's Protestation and Imaginary Faith', MQR 55, (1981) 102, that Müntzer's response is 'identical in content' with *On Counterfeit Faith* goes well beyond the evidence; however, as this edition goes to print (May, 1988) Professor Seebass informs me that he has grounds for believing that the Gotha manuscript is, after all, a first draft of *On Counterfeit Faith*; and that Letter 46 relates not to the latter but to the *Protestation*.

147. *Quid et que*.
148. *utiliter et salubriter*.
149. Cf. n. 146 above.

SERMON TO THE PRINCES

This sermon, 'one of the most remarkable sermons of the Reformation Era' (Williams), was preached by Müntzer on his own home ground in Allstedt on 13 July 1524. Among the select audience were Duke John of Saxony, brother of the Elector, and his stoutly Lutheran son, John Frederick. The latter was fast gaining a somewhat inquisitorial reputation. Duke John, on the other hand, had an open ear to radicals such as the court preacher, Wolfgang Stein, and Jacob Strauss, who were urging the implementation of Mosaic Law, and hence was likely to give Müntzer a charitable hearing.[1]

Some of the circumstances are less than clear. The sermon took place in the aftermath of the Mallerbach affair (cf. Letter 50) and amidst Luther's growing alarm at Müntzer's conduct. On 18 June he had already dubbed him 'that Satan in Allstedt'[2] in a letter to Prince John Frederick. Through Zeiss, the Elector's representative in Allstedt, Müntzer had repeatedly been requesting an impartial hearing for his views (cf. Letter Nr. 52).

On 1 July Duke John passed through Allstedt with his son and a large following on his way to Halberstadt, and again stayed a night with Zeiss in the castle at Allstedt on 12 July. It seems clear that the sermon was preached in the morning of 13 July by Müntzer before the princes although the possibility of 2 July cannot be excluded. It cannot have been a 'trial sermon' (Hinrichs, Franz) as the princes did not regard themselves as judges in such theological matters. Elliger believes, however, that it was commissioned by the princes on 1 July for their return visit.[3] The sermon's careful structure and preparation might seem to lend some weight to that view. Bräuer however points out that there is no reference at all to the sermon in the documents relating to the princes' stay in Allstedt and suggests that, through Zeiss, Müntzer himself may have sought the chance to preach to them, perhaps as late as the evening of 12 June.[4] It may well have been an impromptu, informal affair, held in the *hofstube* rather than in the church, for we know that the princes left directly after their morning meal (Bräuer). There would have been little time available and certainly none for the sermon in its present, printed form. This may not wholly convince, but it is certainly curious that the

---

1. Cf. S. Bräuer, 'Die Vorgeschichte von Luthers Brief an die Fürsten,' *Luther Jahrbuch* 47 (1980), 47ff.
2. WA Br 3, 307, 169.
3. Elliger, p. 442.
4. Bräuer, 'Vorgeschichte', p. 66.

correspondence between Duke John and his brother, the Elector, does not even mention such a sensational event.[5]

By 20 July Zeiss was able to send a copy of it to Spalatin. It is likely that this was the revised, much extended version on which the printed copy was based, but we do not know if the latter was available by then. With its compromising title, 'preached ... before the great and revered dukes of Saxony', and its advocacy of princely enforcement of a radical reformation, it may well have been the last straw which provoked Luther to pen his *Letter to the Princes of Saxony*.[6] It should be read in conjunction with Letters 50–55.

The sermon weaves in and out of Daniel 2. The dream of Nebuchadnezzar, the apocalyptic predictions of the chapter, and the conflict between Daniel and the 'wise' courtiers, are used most effectively to highlight Müntzer's clash with Luther and his challenge to his 'brothers', the Saxon rulers, to initiate a drastic, all-embracing reformation.

In language reminiscent of the Prague Manifesto the sermon begins by recalling the need for devoted servants, watchmen, or shepherds, to reform the corruption and idolatry which the devil and his false prophets have sown among the people of God. The early polemic is mainly against the priests, the Masses and the monkish superstitions of the Old Church (despite some digs at 'counterfeit faith'); with its emphasis on an apostolic, Scripture-oriented Church it would be quite acceptable to the Lutheran princes.

As, however, the emphasis shifts from the Church to Christ the apocalyptic note becomes predominant. Christ, the corner-stone, the stone hewn miraculously from the mountain, will smash the 'divided kingdom', and go on to fill the whole earth. This stone is also identified as the mountain which crashes into the sea, and it is the rock from which living water flows.[7]

Müntzer's Christ is the Christ of the spirit, of the soul, not the idolatrous, 'painted puppet' of outward religiosity; he is the Christ of the humble, not of those who pride themselves on status and title. The 'wooden' stupidity of priest and people contrasts with the rock-like strength of Christ.

Müntzer then maps out the true path to salvation. Although interrupted by polemic against Luther and by the first digression about dreams or visions, it is developed systematically as (i) giving absolute primacy to the fear of God, (ii) looking frankly at the

---

5. Ibid., p. 68; note the give-away reference to 'this little book' p. 251/7 below, which reminds us that there will have been little similarity between the delivered sermon and the lengthy printed version.

6. LW 40, 49–59; cf. Bräuer, 'Vorgeschichte', p. 69.

7. Cf. footnotes 31, 32, to the text of the Sermon.

abomination of contemporary wickedness (iii) showing full confidence in God's love for his elect, and (iv) abandoning all material comforts. This apparent legalism allows God's 'work' to take place in the soul, and is a precondition to any discernment of the truth, to recognising oneself as a temple of the Spirit. Brother Softlife (Luther) will never achieve this.

Dreams or visions are acknowledged to be difficult to interpret.[8] The rationalist, hypocritical biblical scholars reject them entirely because they presuppose an immediate, personal, transfiguring communion with God which they lack, relying on their 'stolen' Scripture. True visions come to us in tribulation, unprompted and unsought; they can be confirmed by Scripture and they lead on to the purer knowledge of God in our heart. They are, as for St Peter, only a step towards our final illumination.

The previous vague references to the end of the divided kingdom are now clarified. The fourth Empire, the Roman, had coincided in its cruelty with the birth of Christ. Now the end of the fifth is 'in full swing' as the 'full and final reformation' of the world – secular as well as ecclesiastical – is imminent. Its unstable mixture of iron and clay will be smashed by the stone of Christ. The poor laity are more alert to this than the princes or priests, and are now ready to challenge tyranny. Hence the Saxon dukes have to take a firm stance, and to trust the new Daniel (Müntzer) to reconcile the people with them and to explain their dreams.

A new concept of the Christian prince is required, who will, like the Old Testament kings, wield his sword to destroy the evil-doer and protect the good. Romans 13 is reinterpreted to validate an active, 'angelic' ministry of justice and vengeance by the prince.[9] Müntzer also rejects the use of Daniel 2[33], the stone hewn 'not by human hands', to support Luther's view that political or military means must not be used to spread the Gospel.[10]

There is no room for a hypocritical clemency. The princes, for the sake of order, are entrusted with power on behalf of the elect. If they fail to use the sword, it will be taken from them. Godless rulers, as Christ, Paul, and the law agree, should be killed, and that includes the false clergy, for God is taking power into his own hands. The transformation of the world is imminent.

8. Cf. Letter 40, p. 56/23ff. above.

9. On Müntzer's interpretation of Romans 13 of Letters 44, p. 67/2 above; 45, p. 69/25ff. above; 75, p. 142/13ff. above.

10. Cf. the Elector's letter of 27 June to the Allstedt Council arguing that force was unnecessary; that the oppression of the Gospel would collapse without human intervention – *on menschlich gewalt, handt und unterdrucken*; Förstemann, *Bauernkrieg*, p. 168, quoted by Elliger, p. 441.

We have no indication how effective the sermon was, though even in this revised form it does throw some light on Müntzer's homiletical skills. It moves, on the whole coherently, towards a stirring conclusion and draws constantly on the content and imagery of Daniel. It is enhanced by lively dialogue and the usual succession of vivid images. It is hard to conceive of the audience being bored! Müntzer, however, had no illusions about the offence it would give.[11] The sharp polarities of elect and godless, prophet and soothsayer, Christ and Antichrist prepare the listener for the ruthless campaign against the wicked which is announced at the end of the sermon. Müntzer's view that ultimate good and evil manifest themselves simultaneously[12] heightens the sense of crisis, especially when the identification between Israel's exile and Christ's humiliation and the present situation of the Church is so clearly drawn. Again, the personalisation of the issues in the figure of Daniel is a masterly stroke.

There is much of interest in the exegesis, which frequently draws together the Law, the Prophets, the Gospels and Paul, illustrating Müntzer's concern for an integrated use of Scripture. Frequently, however, this leads to strange conflations of texts which have little in common except a shared image.

Some of the metaphors used by Muntzer are also strangely mixed, yet the vivid visual images certainly enhance the writing: the flies in the ointment, the field covered with scrub, the eels and snakes copulating in a heap, the deceptive beauty of the cornflower among the wheat, the scholars devouring thousands of Bibles, the tottering structure of a Church without a corner-stone.

With historical examples, Biblical quotations, striking contrasts, polemical thrusts, rhetorical questions, sarcasm, exhortation and veiled threats, Müntzer drives home his chilling vision: that the prophecy of Daniel remained as true in his day as ever.

11. Cf. p. 251/7 below.
12. Cf. pp. 233/1f., 236/18ff.; a similar thought is developed in the *Exposé*, p. 280/17ff. below, and in Letter 60, p. 103/6ff. above.

INTERPRETATION OF THE SECOND CHAPTER OF DANIEL

Interpretation of the second chapter[1] of the prophet Daniel, preached by Thomas Müntzer, servant of the word of God, in the castle at Allstedt before the great[2] and revered dukes and rulers of Saxony. Allstedt 1524.

First of all the text of the above chapter from the prophet Daniel's predictions was read out and translated in its straightforward meaning,[3] and then the whole sermon was delivered in accordance with the text as follows:[4]

In view of the wretched, ruinous condition of the poor Christian Church[5] it should be realised that no advice or help can be given until we have industrious, unflagging servants of God who are ready, day in, day out, to promote the knowledge of the Biblical books through singing, reading, and preaching. This will mean, however, that either the heads of our delicate priests get used to taking some hard knocks, or else they will have to abandon their trade.[6] What alternative is there, while ravaging wolves are so grievously devastating the Christian people, like God's vineyard described in Isaiah 5, Psalm 79?[7] St Paul, after all, teaches us to school ourselves in songs of divine praise, Ephesians 5.[8] For our situation today is the same as that of the good prophets Isaiah, Jeremiah, Ezekiel, and the others, when the whole congregation of God's elect had become completely caught up in idolatrous ways. As a result, not even God could help them, but had to let them be captured and transported and tormented under the heathen until they learned to recognise his holy name again, as Isaiah 29, Jeremiah 15, Ezekiel 36 and Psalm 88 testify.[9] Nonetheless, in our own time and that of our fathers, our poor Christian people has shown even greater obstinacy while going to incredible lengths to claim the divine name for itself, Luke 21, 2 Timothy 3.[10] The devil, of

1. *unterschied.*
2. *tetigen*: used regularly by Müntzer to translate Vg. *magnus* (great, mighty) e.g. Psalm 110[2]: *Magna opera Domini* is translated *Die wergk des Herren seint tetigk*; F., p. 94/12; on *vorstehern*, cf. *Exposé*, p. 316/1f. below.
3. 'Read out verse by verse from the Vulgate and translated' (Hinrichs).
4. *mit verfassen des text gesatzt.*
5. *christenheyt.*
6. *oder seins hantwercks abgehen.*
7. Isaiah 5[ff.]; Psalm 80[9-14].
8. v. 19.
9. Isaiah 29[17-24]; Jeremiah 15[11-16]; Ezekiel 36[20f., 23]; Psalm 89[31-8] (Dismer, p. 22 n. 4, suggests 89[17, 25]).
10. Luke 21[5]; Timothy 3[5] (pride in the Temple, the outward show of religion);

230

course, and his servants, love to deck themselves out like this, 2 Cor. 1,[11] and do it so alluringly that the true friends[12] of God are seduced, and – despite the most determined efforts – are almost incapable of seeing their mistake, as Mt. 24[13] points out so clearly. The cause of all this is the counterfeit sanctity and the hypocritical absolution of the godless enemies of God, who say that the Christian Church cannot err, although – if error is to be avoided – she should be being built up continually by the word of God and kept free from error.[14] She should also admit the sin which keeps her in ignorance, Lev. 4, Hosea 4, Malachi 2, Isaiah 1.[15] There can, however, be no doubt that Christ, the son of God, and his apostles and his holy prophets before him, founded a pure and true Christianity, and cast the pure wheat into the field, that is, planted the precious word of God in the hearts of the elect, as we read in Mt. 12, Mark 4, Luke 8 and Ezek. 36.[16] But the lazy, negligent servants of these churches were not willing to perfect and protect this work by watching over it zealously. They pursued their own interests, not those of Jesus Christ, Philip 2.[17] Hence they stood by while the tares, that is, the damage done by the godless, gained a firm hold, Psalm 79.[18] They could do this because the cornerstone mentioned in the text was still small;[19] Isaiah 28 refers to it.[20] It is true that it has not yet filled the whole world, but very soon this will come to pass; the world will be full, completely full. So the foundation stone that was laid at the infant beginnings of Christianity was speedily discarded by the masons, that is, by those in power, Psalm 117, Luke 20.[21] What I am saying, then, is that after its beginnings the Church throughout the world became a tottering

---

'divine name' is collective designation for divine family, people (Hinrichs); = 'divine origin' (Streller).

11. 2 Corinthians 11[3ff]; like women who fail to cover their hair at worship.

12. Biblical and mystical term frequently used by Müntzer for the elect; Tauler sees the friendship as union, the friend being 'another I, between the two there is the most intimate communion, the blending of the divine spirit with the human', *The Book of Spiritual Poverty XX*; cf. John 15[15], quoted by Tauler, Isaiah 41[8] (Abraham is God's friend); cf. also James 2[23].

13. Matthew 24[24] (the elect deceived by false messiahs and prophets).

14. Here the polemic is against the Roman Church.

15. Leviticus 4[3f]; Hosea 4[6]; Malachi 2[1-7]; Isaiah 1[10-17]; a strange group of texts!

16. Matthew 13[4ff] (the London copy reads Matth. 13; cf. Dismer, p. 95 n. 1); Mark 4[26-9]; Luke 8[5-15]; Ezekiel 36[29], the Ezekiel reference is in the context of an identification of the wheat and of the 'new spirit'.

17. Philippians 2[21].

18. Psalm 80[12-16]; cf. n. 7 above.

19. Daniel 2[34f]; in Nebuchadnezzar's dream the stone shatters the image of the other kingdoms, then takes their place.

20. Isaiah 28[16].

21. Psalm 118[22f]; Luke 20[18].

structure, until the time of the divided kingdom; Luke 21, Ezra 4, and this second chapter of Daniel.[22] For Hegesippus and Eusebius (in the fourth book, chapter 22, of his history of the Christian churches) say that the Christian congregation ceased to be a virgin after the pupils of the apostles had died.[23] Soon after that she became an adulteress, as predicted by the good apostles, 2 Peter 2.[24] And in the histories of the apostles St Paul addressed the shepherds of the sheep of God in these clear, unequivocal words, Acts 20;[25] 'Keep a close eye on yourselves and on the whole flock over which the holy spirit has made you watchmen, to nourish the congregation of God, which he has redeemed by his blood. For I know that after my departure ravaging wolves will come, which will not spare the flock. Men will also rise up in your midst, who will teach perverse ideas in order to get the disciples to follow them. So be on your guard!' We find the same in the letter of the holy apostle Jude; Revelation 16 refers to it, too.[26] That is why our lord, Christ, warns us to be on the look-out for false prophets in Matthew 7.[27] Now it is all too clear (one could weep aloud to God) that nothing is so scorned and despised as the spirit of Christ. And yet no one can be saved until the holy spirit has assured him of his salvation, as it is written in Romans 8, Luke 12, John 6 and 17.[28] But how are poor, little worms like us to arrive at this as long as we regard with such awe the status which the godless have?[29] Alas! Christ, the gentle son of God, is a mere scarecrow or a painted puppet[30] in our eyes compared with the great titles and names of this world, although he is the true stone, hurled from the great mountain into the sea, into the pomp and affluence of this world, Psalm 45.[31] He is the stone torn from the great mountain without human hands, who is called Jesus

22. Luke 21[10]; Ezra 4; Daniel 2[25]; (dissension, war, the rise and fall of kingdoms); Müntzer's own age is seen as the last of these kingdoms, a mixture of iron and clay, which may represent the secular and clerical powers (Williams).

23. Hegesippus, fragments of whose second-century *Memoirs* were preserved by Eusebius, talks of the 'false Christs, false prophets, false apostles who divided the unity of the Church ...' *Church History*, IV, 22; already quoted in the Prague Manifesto, p. 377/12ff. below.

24. 2 Peter 2; Hinrichs points to v. 14, but the whole chapter is relevant, with its references to false prophets (v. 1) and to the betrayal of Christ (v. 20ff.).

25. Acts 20[28-31].

26. Jude[4-19]; Revelation 16[6, 13f.]

27. Matthew 7[15].

28. Romans 8[9]; Luke 12[12]; John 6[63]; the last reference seems to be to John 16[7ff.], not to John 17; Dismer, p. 232 n. 7, suggests John 17[22f.]

29. *weil wir die wirdickeit der gotlosen in solcher achtbarkeit halten.*

30. *wie ein hanffpotze oder gemalts menlin.*

31. Daniel 2[45]; Psalm 46[2]; an extraordinary conflation of texts; the meaning seems to be that Christ's coming agitates the powers of this world; cf. Wisdom 5[23].

Christ, 1 Cor. 10.[32] He was born at the very time that wickedness was moving towards its climax,[33] Luke 1, 2,[34] in the time of Octavian, when the whole world was on the move to be taxed. Then a wretched sack of filth, a man quite devoid of spiritual power,[35] sought to possess the whole world, although all he could derive from it was pomp and pride. Indeed he managed to convince himself that he alone was great. How diminutive in comparison Jesus Christ, the corner-stone, appeared in men's eyes! He was despatched to the cattle stall like so much refuse,[36] Psalm 21.[37] Afterwards the biblical scholars rejected him, Psalm 117, Mt. 21, Mark 12, Luke 20[38] as they still do today. Indeed in the end they made a game out of the Passion,[39] after the pupils of the dear apostles had died. The spirit of Christ became the butt of their derision, as it still is, as Psalm 68 testifies.[40] They have run off with him quite blatantly, like thieves and murderers, John 10.[41] They have robbed the sheep of Christ of the true voice and transformed the true, crucified Christ into a mere idol of their imaginations.[42] How did that come about? I would answer: They rejected the true knowledge of God[43] and set up in its place a pretty, fine, golden god of their own making, before which the poor peasants smack their lips, as Hosea clearly said in chapter 4 and Jeremiah, Lamentations chapter 4: 'Those who once ate good spiced dishes now have filth and dung set before them.'[44] The shame of it! Of this

32. 1 Corinthians 10[4]; Schwarz, p. 9 points to a very similar use of Daniel 2[34f.] by the Bohemian Brethren.

33. *gleich do die haubtschalkeit im schwang ging*; 'when that greatest of all bondage (slavery) prevailed' (Williams); a possible translation since in Middle High German *schalk* had this meaning of servitude; Müntzer's use of the term elsewhere speaks against it; cf. pp. 235/5, and 247/4 below; F., p. 97/10.

34. Luke 1[51]; 2[1].

35. *amechtiger im geist*; Augustus, prototype of the godless tyrant.

36. *ein hinwerffen der menschen*; 'like an outcast of men' (Williams); cf. in the next line *verworffen* (rejected).

37. Psalm 22[6]; the inversion of truth: Christ is regarded as a worm, scorned by men.

38. Psalm 118[22]; Matthew 21[15ff.]; Mark 12[10]; Luke 20[17] (the stone rejected by the builders).

39. *die passion mit ym gespilet*; 'they have been re-enacting the Passion with him' (Williams).

40. Psalm 69[11ff.]   41. John 10[1].

42. *zum lauttern fantastischen götzen*.

43. *die reyne kunst Gottis*: 'pure handwork' (Williams); (Müntzer would use *handtwerk* for 'handwork', as on p. 237/24 below); Hinrichs points correctly to the mystical background of the term *kunst* and its connotations of unmediated illumination.

44. As often, a grotesquely mixed metaphor; Hosea 4[8ff.] (the priests and prophets, in a land without knowledge, feed on the sin of the people); Lamentations 4[5] (*qui nutriebantur in croceis, amplexati sunt stercora*).

lamentable abomination (of which Christ himself speaks in Matthew 24)[45] that he should be ridiculed so pitiably by these devilish Masses, by such superstitious sermons, rituals and behaviour; for they worship after all, nothing but an idol carved of wood. Truly a superstitious, wooden priest and a coarse, clumsy and gnarled[46] people, unable to comprehend the simplest pronouncement of God! Isn't that a sin, a shame, a cause for grief? I have come to the conclusion that the beasts of the belly, Phil. 3,[47] and the pigs, described in Matt. 7 and 2 Peter 2,[48] have trodden the precious stone, Jesus Christ, completely underfoot, to the best of their ability. He has become a doormat[49] for the whole world. Hence all the unbelieving Turks, pagans, and Jews have had an easy time ridiculing us and regarding us as fools; one is, after all, bound to regard as mad those who refuse to hear any mention of the spirit of their faith.[50]

Hence the suffering of Christ is nothing but a fairground spectacle[51] in the eyes of these abandoned scoundrels, of whom Psalm 68 speaks.[52] No mercenary[53] would be so depraved. And so, my dear brothers,[54] if we are to rise up out of this mire and become true pupils of God, taught by God himself, John 6, Mt. 23,[55] we will need the vast resources of his strength, sent down to us from above, in order to punish such unspeakable wickedness and nullify[56] it. We will need, that is, the very clearest wisdom of God, Wisdom 9, which can only spring from the pure unfeigned fear of God.[57] This alone can equip us with its mighty arm to exercise vengeance on the enemies of God with burning zeal to God, as is written in Wisdom 5, John 2, Psalm 68.[58] No rational or human considerations should serve to excuse them, for, like the pretty cornflower[59] among the golden ears of wheat, the shape taken by the godless can be incredibly attractive and

45. Matthew 24[15].
46. *knuttelisch*.
47. Philippians 3[19].
48. Matthew 7[6] (a favourite text for later Nicodemites like Otto Brunfels); 2 Peter 2[22].
49. *fusshadder*.
50. *yres glaubens geist*.
51. *jarmerckt*; fairground present (Hinrichs).
52. Psalm 69[11].
53. *spitzknecht* (mercenary); the reference is to Luke 23[36par.]; cf. *Protestation* n. 279.
54. The dukes!
55. John 6[33]; Matthew 23[9].
56. *schwechen*.
57. Wisdom 9[10]; cf. Psalm 111[10].
58. Wisdom 5[18]; John 2[17]; Psalm 69[9]; the text from Wisdom draws together the concepts of judgement and wisdom, so important for Müntzer in this sermon.
59. *kornblume*; 'poppy' (Williams).

deceptive, Ecclesiastes 8.[60] It takes the wisdom of God to recognise it.

Secondly, we must have another, careful look at this abomination, which despises the stone. However, if we are to see him[61] as he really is then we have to become conscious every day of the revelation of God. How rare and scarce that has become in this scoundrelly world! For the sly proposals[62] of our crafty scholars will rain down on us the whole time, and hinder us still more from progressing in the pure knowledge of God, Wisdom 4, Psalm 36.[63] This sort of thing has to be averted[64] by the fear of God. If we preserved this, and this alone, in our hearts – in its purity and entirety – then the holy people of Christ would easily come to the spirit of wisdom and the revelation of the divine will. All this is found in Scripture, Psalm 144, Psalm 110, Proverbs 1.[65] But the fear of God must be pure, unsullied by any fear of men or creaturely things, Psalm 18, Isaiah 66, Luke 12.[66] How desperately we need a fear like this! For just as it is impossible to serve two masters and be saved, so it is impossible to fear both God and created things and be saved, Mt. 6.[67] And God is unable to have mercy upon us (as the mother of Christ, our Lord, says)[68] unless we fear him, and him alone, from the bottom of our hearts. Hence God says: 'If I am your father, where is the honour due to me? If I am your master, where is the fear due to me?,' Malachi 1.[69] So, my beloved princes, it is necessary, in these very dangerous days, 1 Tim. 4,[70] for us to show the utmost diligence in tackling such underhand acts of wickedness. As the books of the Bible record, this has been done by all our dear fathers from the beginning of the world. For this is a dangerous time and these are evil days, 2 Tim. 3, Eph. 5.[71] Why? The sole reason is that the sterling power of God has been so lamentably defiled and dishonoured. For the profligate biblical scholars seduce the poor, coarse people with their endless chatter, (just as the prophet Micah says in chapter 3).[72] This seems to be the way of all but a few of the biblical scholars today. With very few exceptions they teach that God

60. Ecclesiastes 8[14] (just and unjust hard to distinguish); cf. Vg.: while living the wicked *in loco sancto erant, et laudabantur in civitate quasi iustorum operum.*

61. Christ.

62. *anschlege.*

63. Wisdom 4[12]; Psalm 37[12, 32].

64. *solchem muss man vorkummen;* 'Such a person one must stave off' (Williams).

65. Psalm 145[18f.]; Psalm 111[5,10]; Proverbs 1[7].

66. Psalm 19[9]; Isaiah 66[2]; Luke 12[4f.]

67. Matthew 6[24].

68. Luke 1[50].

69. Malachi 1[6].

70. 1 Timothy 4[1ff.]

71. 2 Timothy 3[1]; Ephesians 5[16].

72. Micah 3[11]; *grob* (coarse) in the sense of 'ignorant'.

no longer reveals his divine mysteries to his dear friends through genuine visions or direct words etc. So they adhere to their bookish[73] ways, Ecclesiasticus 34[74] and make a laughing-stock[75] of those who have experience of the revelation of God, as the godless once did with Jeremiah, Jer. 20:[76] 'Say, friend, have you had a message from God recently? Or have you been questioning or consulting him recently? Is the spirit of Christ in you?' They go on like this, pouring out contempt and scorn. What happened in Jeremiah's time was no small matter, was it? Jeremiah warned the poor blind people how painful their imprisonment in Babylon would be, just as the pious Lot warned his sons-in-law, Gen. 19.[77] But it all seemed absurd to them. They said to the good prophets: 'Yes, yes, how nice of God to issue these fatherly warnings.' But what happened then to this crowd of smart alecs during their imprisonment in Babylon? Just this: they were put to shame by the pagan king Nebuchadnezzar! Take a look at our text![78] He[79] accepted what God said to him, although he was a terrible devastator and scourge of the chosen people, who had sinned against God. But it is because of the blindness and stubbornness of the people of God[80] that the pinnacle of all goodness had to be revealed to the world, as St Paul and Ezekiel say in Romans 11 and Ezekiel 23.[81] So for your instruction let me say this: almighty God informed this heathen king not only about matters which would come about many years in the future – to the incredible mortification of the stiff-necked members of the people of God, who would not believe any of the prophets. Those of our own generation who have not been put to the test come under the same judgement. They have no awareness of God's punishment, even though it is there before their eyes. What more can almighty God do for us? He can only withhold his goodness from us.

Now comes the text:[82] 'King Nebuchadnezzar had a dream, but it eluded him etc.'

What should we say about this? Talking about men's dreams is no easy matter; it is not something we are used to, and is invidious, because from the very beginning up to now the whole world has been

---

73. *unerfarnen*; without experience (of trials).
74. Ecclesiasticus 34[10].
75. *ein sprichwort*; cf. Deuteronomy 28[37]; Psalm 69[11].
76. Jeremiah 20[7f.]
77. Genesis 19[14].
78. Daniel 2[47].
79. Nebuchadnezzar.
80. Israel.
81. Romans 11 esp. vs. 11, 15, 22, 25f.; Ezekiel 23[4, 9] (the harlotry of Oholibah or Jerusalem).
82. Daniel 2[1-13]; cf. Vg. *et somnium eius fugit ab eo.*

led astray by the interpreters of dreams, as is written in Deuteronomy 13, Ecclesiasticus 34.[83] That is why this chapter states that the king was unwilling to believe the clever soothsayers and interpreters of dreams. For he said: 'First tell me what my dream was, and then give me the interpretation. Otherwise all I will get from you is deception and lies.' What was the result? They could not even begin to recount the dream and said: 'Dear king, no man on the face of the earth can tell you what the dream is; only the gods can, and they have no communion with men on earth.' To their mind they really talked sense, but they had no faith in God, for they were godless flatterers and hypocrites who said what their masters wanted to hear, as is the case today with the biblical scholars who like the choicest morsels at court. But it is against them that the words of Jeremiah 5 and 8[84] are directed. And so much more! The text[85] says that one would need men who had communion with heaven.[86] Now! What a bitter pill that is for such smart alecs,[87] although St Paul stressed the same point to the Philippians in chapter 3.[88] Despite this such scholars still arrogate to themselves the interpretation of the mysteries of God. What a vast number of scoundrels like them there are in the world, with the affrontery to make such claims! Isaiah 58[89] describes this sort of men: 'They seek to know my ways as if they were a people who lived by my righteousness.' Such biblical scholars are like the soothsayers, who publicly deny that there is any revelation from God, but in fact obstruct the holy spirit's work. They set themselves up as instructors to the whole world, and anything which does not suit their academic approach is branded at once as devilish, although they themselves are not assured of their own salvation, essential as that is, Rom. 8.[90] They can chatter away beautifully about faith and brew up a drunken faith for poor, confused consciences. The reason for all this is their uninformed judgement, based on their abhorrence of the poisonous, accursed dreams of the monks, through whose odious deceptions the devil realised all his plans. Indeed, he was able to deceive many pious but uninformed members of the elect, who gave immediate and total credence to these visions and dreams, with all their mad beliefs. Add to this their monastic rules and the wild, hypocritical idolatry[91]

83. Deuteronomy 13[2ff.]; Ecclesiasticus 34[5ff.]
84. Jeremiah 5[13,31]; 8[8f.]
85. Daniel 2[28].
86. *die do gemeynschafft im hymmel hetten.*
87. *den klüglingen ein bitter kraut.*
88. Philippians 3[20].
89. Isaiah 58[2].
90. Romans 8[14ff.]
91. *losse pockfintzerey*; a neologism; possibly a combination of *vinserie* (Middle Low German, 'hypocrisy') and *Bock*: to give hypocritical adoration to a

prescribed to them by the devil, against which the Colossians were strongly warned by St Paul in the second chapter![92] But the accursed monkish dreamers did not know how to become aware of the power of God, and adhered stubbornly to their perverse views. Nowadays they are being exposed to the whole world for the idle good-for-nothings that they are, their sin and shame emerging more clearly every day. They are still too crazed to recognise their blindness. It is nothing but this superstition which seduced them, and up to this present day is still seducing them, into ever worse paths. For since they have no experience of the coming of the holy spirit,[93] who is our instructor[94] in the fear of God, they spurn divine wisdom and are unable to differentiate the good from the bad (when it masquerades as goodness). It is against such people that God cries out in Isaiah 5:[95] 'Woe to you, who call good bad and bad good.' That is why the pious take care not to throw away the good with the bad, as St Paul says in 1 Thessalonians 5:[96] 'You should not despise prophecy, but put it all to the test, and keep what is good in it etc.'

Third, take to heart this teaching,[97] that there is no limit to God's loving-kindness to his elect. For if he can warn them in the least important matters, Deut. 1, 32, Mt. 23,[98] he will do so in the greatest, provided that, with their great unbelief, they can receive his warning. For here this text of Daniel agrees exactly with St. Paul's words in 1 Corinthians 2, and goes back to the blessed Isaiah, chapter 64,[99] who says: 'What no eye has seen, no ear heard, and no human heart contained, has been prepared by God for those who love him. But God has revealed it to us through his spirit, for the spirit searches all things, even the depths of the godhead etc.' Hence our earnest teaching is, in brief, that we need knowledge – not just some windy faith – so we can discern what has come to us from God, from the devil, or from nature. For if our natural reason is to be taken captive and made subject to faith, 2 Cor. 10,[100] then it must be brought to the very limits of its own judgement,[101] as indicated in Romans 1 and

---

goat = superstition (Hinrichs); 'black magic' (Williams).

92. Colossians 2[8].

93. *on alle erfarne ankunfft des heyligen geystes.*

94. *des meysters*; 'the overcomer' (Williams), similarly F. but, in my view, incorrectly; cf. F., p. 293/3 and Prague Manifesto p. 371/8, 16 below; also p. 248/8 below.

95. Isaiah 5[20].   96. 1 Thessalonians 5[19ff.]

97. *solt yr die meynung wissen*; perhaps the reference is to the disposition (*meynung*) of God to the elect (F.); but cf. l. 27f. below.

98. Deuteronomy 1[42]; 32[6]; Matthew 23[37].

99. 1 Corinthians 2[9f.]; Isaiah 64[4].

100. 2 Corinthians 10[5, 13].

101. *so muss er kummen auff den letzten grad aller seyner urteyl.*

Baruch 3.[102] But without God's revelation no man can make any judgement which he can justify before his conscience. Thus it will become abundantly clear to him that his cleverness will not help him to traverse heaven,[103] but that he must first become, in his inward being, a complete fool,[104] Isaiah 29, 33; Obadiah 1, 1 Cor. 1. What a strange wind that seems to the world of the flesh, of the lusts, of human wisdom! For straight away follows pain, just as for a woman in labour, Psalm 47, John 16.[105] Thus Daniel finds, like every pious man, that in such circumstances he is as little able as any one else to question God about everything.[106] That is what the wise man means in Ecclesiasticus 3, where he says: 'He who seeks to unravel the glory of God will be crushed by his magnificence.'[107] For the more our nature reaches after God the more the operation of the holy spirit recedes, as is clearly shown by Psalm 138.[108] The fact is that if man really understood the audacity of natural reason[109] he would certainly resort no more to a stolen Scripture[110] – like the scholars who brandish this fragment of it or that, Isaiah 28, Jer. 8,[111] – and would instead come to experience the operation of the divine word from the well of his heart, John 4.[112] He would no longer need to carry stagnant water into the well, Jer. 2,[113] as our scholars now do. They mingle nature and grace indiscriminately. They obstruct the passage of the word, Psalm 118,[114] which springs from the abyss of the soul, as Moses says, Deut. 30.[115] 'The word is not far from you. Look, it is in your heart etc.' You may be asking at this point how it gets into the heart. The answer is: It comes down from God on high when one is in a state of deep consternation[116] – I will leave a closer definition of this to a later opportunity. Now this state of consternation, wondering whether something is the word of God, begins when one is a child of six or

---

102. Romans 1[19ff.]; Baruch 3[14].

103. *das er mit dem kopff durch den hymmel nit lauffen kan.*

104. Isaiah 29[13f.]; 33[18]; Obadiah 1[8]; 1 Corinthians 1[18ff.]

105. Psalm 48[6]; John 16[21].

106. *das ym aldo alle ding gleych so unmůglich seindt wie andern gemeinen menschen von Gotte zurforschen.*

107. Ecclesiastes 3[11, 14]; *der wirt von seinem preiss vordruckt*; a very free quotation.

108. Psalm 139[6].

109. *den vorwitz des natůrlich liechts.*

110. One appropriated at second hand, without personal experience in the Spirit.

111. Isaiah 28[10]; Jeremiah 8[8].

112. John 4[14].

113. Jeremiah 2[13]; *Ja er dorffte der faulen wasser in brun nit tragen*; 'put up with the stagnant water in the well' (Williams); the Lutherans imagine grace can redeem nature before the Law has purged our sinful nature (Hinrichs).

114. Psalm 119[11, 139].

115. Deuteronomy 30[14].

116. *verwunderung*; cf. Goertz, p. 71.

seven, as Numbers 19 signifies.[117] Hence Paul quotes Moses and Isaiah in Romans 10,[118] speaking there of the inward word which is to be heard in the abyss of the soul through the revelation of God. Now anyone who has not become conscious and receptive to this through the living witness of God, Romans 8,[119] may have devoured a hundred thousand Bibles, but he can say nothing about God which has any validity. It should be clear enough from this to anyone, then, how far removed the world still is from faith in Christ. As yet no one wants to open their eyes or ears. But if a man is to become conscious of the word and of his receptivity to it, then God must free him from his fleshly lusts, so that when God's movement[120] invades his heart – to put to death all the pleasures of the flesh – he can make way for him there, so that God's working may be unimpeded. For a man who behaves like an animal has no ear for what God says in the soul, 1 Cor. 2.[121] The holy spirit must direct him to consider earnestly the pure and straight-forward meaning of the law, Psalm 18.[122] Otherwise his heart will be blind and he will dream up for himself a wooden Christ[123] and lead himself astray. Just look, then, at our passage! At how agonising it was for that good man Daniel to have to expound the vision to the king, and how eagerly he urges and beseeches God to help him.[124] Similarly, if a man is to receive the revelation of God he must cut himself off from all distractions and develop an earnest concern for the truth, 2 Cor. 6,[125] and learn by the practice of such truth to distinguish the authentic vision[126] from the false one. Hence Daniel says in chapter ten: 'A man should use discernment about visions, not rejecting them all etc.'[127]

Fourth, you should know that a member of the elect who wants to know which visions or dreams are of God, or of nature, or of the devil, must distance his will,[128] his heart, and his natural reason from

---

117. Numbers 19[19]; the chapter deals with the seven-fold sprinkling of the tabernacle with the blood of a red heifer; the ashes of the heifer are used to purify the unclean on the seventh day; as Hinrichs points out the verse is important for Müntzer not only here but in the Prague Manifesto, p. 358, n. 10; p. 366/29f. below.

118. Romans 10[8. 20]; Paul is referring to Deuteronomy 30[14] and Isaiah 65[1].

119. Romans 8[esp. vs. 9. 16].

120. *die bewegung von Gott*; cf. p. 97/24 above.

121. 1 Corinthians 2[14]; cf. Ecclesiastes 3[19].

122. Psalm 19[8f.].

123. Cf. p. 232/23 above.

124. Daniel 2[18].

125. 2 Corinthians 6[17]; cf. Numbers 19[20].

126. *die unbetriglichen gesicht*.

127. Daniel 10[1. 12]; more a paraphrase than a quotation.

128. *gemüth*; 'mind' (Williams).

all temporal comforts of the flesh, and must do as holy Joseph did in Egypt, Gen. 39,[129] and Daniel in this chapter. For no pleasure-loving man can accept [the guidance of God], Luke 7,[130] for the thorns and the thistles – which, as the Lord says, are the pleasures of this world, Mark 4[131] – crush any working of the word which God speaks in the soul. Hence even when God sends his holy word into the soul man cannot hear it, if he has not learnt to practise [self-discipline] for he has no insight or access[132] into his own self, into the abyss of his soul, Psalm 48.[133] As Paul, the holy apostle, teaches us, man declines to crucify his life, with its desires and vices.[134] Therefore the field of God's word is covered in thorns and thistles and thick scrub, all of which must make way for this work of God, if man is not to be found negligent or lazy, Proverbs 24.[135] Only when he sees the fertility of the field and finally the good crop will man grasp that, as long as he lives, he is the dwelling of God and the holy spirit and, what's more, that the sole reason for his creation is to seek after the signs of God's work in his life, Psalm 92, 118.[136] At times he becomes aware of this in a partial way through visual imagery, at times in a complete way in the abyss of the heart, 1 Cor. 13.[137] Secondly he must see to it that those figurative images found in dreams and visions have their parallels in every respect in the holy Bible,[138] lest the devil sneak in, and spoil the sweet ointment of the holy spirit, like the flies which die in the ointment to which the wise man refers, Ecclesiastes 10.[139] Thirdly, the elect man must pay close attention to the way in which the visions manifest themselves:[140] that they do not gush out at human prompting[141] but emerge straightforwardly according to God's unchangeable will. He must also take very good care that not one jot is missed out of what he saw, for it must all be put boldly into effect.[142] But if the devil is trying to achieve something his idle antics will

---

129. Genesis 39 (Joseph and Potiphar's wife).

130. Luke 7[25].

131. Mark 4[7. 18].

132. *er thut keinen einkehr oder einsehn in sich selber.*

133. Psalm 49[3. 16ff.]

134. Galatians 5[24].

135. Proverbs 24[30f.]

136. Psalm 93[5]; (the soul as the dwelling of God); 119[13. 46. 93. 175.]

137. 1 Corinthians 13[10ff.]

138. For example Numbers 19[20]; cf. n. 117 above.

139. Ecclesiastes 10[1].

140. *auff das werck der gesichte.*

141. *rausser quelle durch menschliche anschlege*; perhaps a reference to monastic asceticism (Hinrichs).

142. *tapffer ins werck kummen.*

betray him and his lies will eventually peep out, for he is a liar, John 8. This is indicated quite clearly in this chapter in relation to King Nebuchadnezzar and then proved by the events in chapter 3. For he lost no time in forgetting God's admonition, due without any doubt to his fleshly desire for pleasure and creaturely comforts. That is always the case when someone wants to devote himself to his pleasures continually and yet to encounter the work of God without tribulation. Such a man cannot then be over-shadowed by the power of the word of God, Luke 8.[144] It is usually when they are in the greatest tribulation that Almighty God is pleased to send genuine dreams and visions to his beloved friends, as he did for that pious man, Abraham, Gen. 15, 17.[145] For God appeared to him when he was greatly alarmed. Likewise when good Jacob was fleeing in great dismay from his brother Esau, a vision came to him of a ladder stretching up to heaven and the angels of God climbing up and down on it, Gen. 28.[146] And again when he made for home he was still immensely afraid of his brother Esau. Then the Lord appeared to him in a dream and wrestled with him, putting his hips out of joint, Gen. 32.[147] Likewise that pious man, Joseph, was hated by his brothers and had two ominous[148] visions when he was dismayed about this, Gen. 37.[149] Thereafter, too, during his heartfelt tribulation in an Egyptian prison God illumined him so fully that he was able to expound all the visions and dreams, Gen. 39, 40, 41.[150] Surpassing all this are the four dreams of the other Saint Joseph, in the first and second chapters of Matthew,[151] which challenge these pleasure-loving pigs, the smart-alecs who have never been put to the test. For the dreams reassured him when he was alarmed and dismayed; just as the wise men were instructed by the angel in their sleep not to return to Herod. Likewise the dear apostles had to pay the utmost attention to their visions, as is clearly stated in their histories. So to expect visions and to receive them while in tribulation and suffering, is in the true spirit of the apostles, the patriarchs, and the prophets. Hence it is no wonder that Brother Fatted Pig and Brother Soft Life[152] reject them, Job 28.[153] But

143. John 8[44].
144. Luke 9[34].
145. Genesis 15[1-6]; 17[1ff.]
146. Genesis 28[12].
147. Genesis 32[25f.]; *zurknyrschet*, lit. 'crushed'; the same word is used in the draft letter to Stolberg, p. 60/11f.; cf. also Letter 40, n. 44.
148. *nötliche*.
149. Genesis 37[5].
150. Genesis 39[20]; 40; 41.
151. Matthew 1[20-3]; 2[13, 19].
152. Luther.
153. Job 28[12f.]; cf. Vg., *nec invenitur in terra suaviter viventium* (Hinrichs).

when one has not yet heard the clear word of God in the soul one has to have visions. St Peter, for example, according to the histories of the apostles, did not understand the law, Lev. 11,[154] hesitating whether to eat certain foods and to have fellowship with the pagans Acts 10;[155] then he was given an ecstatic vision by God.[156] In it he saw a linen cloth with four corners let down to earth from heaven, full of four-footed animals, and he heard a voice, saying: 'Slaughter them and eat them!' Much the same happened to Cornelius, a pious man, when he did not know what he should do, Acts 10.[157] Also when Paul came to Troas a vision appeared to him in the night, and a man from Macedonia appeared before him begging: 'Come over to Macedonia and help us.' And after he had seen this vision: It was our intention, says the text in Acts 16,[158] to journey to Macedonia at once. For we were sure that the Lord had called us there. Likewise when Paul was afraid to preach in Corinth, Acts 18,[159] the Lord spoke to him in a vision during the night: 'You need not be afraid etc. No one will presume to do you harm, for I have a large following in this city etc.' What need is there to go on listing examples from Scripture? In such complex and dangerous matters, it would never be possible, for true preachers, dukes and rulers, to act in every respect blamelessly and correctly, unless they live by the revelation of God,[160] such as Aaron received from Moses, and David from Nathan and Gad. Hence to the dear apostles visions were common-place, as the text of the twelfth chapter of the histories confirms.[161] When the angel came to Peter and led him out of Herod's prison, he thought it was only a vision; he did not know that the angel was actually bringing about his release.[162] But if Peter had not been used to visions how would he have hit on the idea that it was a vision? So I conclude from this that anyone who ignorantly opposes visions, using fleshly criteria, rejecting them all (or accepting them all without discrimination), on the grounds that

154. Leviticus 11.
155. Acts 10[10ff.]
156. *im uberschwangk seins gemütes*; 'in a flush of emotion' (Williams).
157. Acts 10[3-6.]
158. Acts 16[8ff.]
159. Acts 18[9f.]
160. The German is difficult: *Es wer nimmermehr müglklich in solchen . . . sachen, als do rechte prediger hertzogen und regenten haben, das sie sich allenthalben solten bewaren sicherlich und ungetaddelt zu handeln*; 'It would never be at all possible in these far-flung dangerous matters which rightful preachers, dukes, and princes have [to deal with] that they would on all sides take heed to act securely and blamelessly, if they did not live within the revelation of God' (Williams).
161. Acts 12[7ff.]
162. *das werck seiner erlösung*: 'carrying out the work of salvation in him' (Williams).

deluded dreamers have inflicted so much harm on the world through ambitious and pleasure-loving men, will not have his way in the end,[163] but will be thwarted[164] by the holy spirit, as is recorded in Joel 2,[165] where God is clearly speaking – as in this text in Daniel – of the transformation of the world. In the last days he will bring this about so that his name is properly adored. He will release [the Christian people] from its shame, and pour out his spirit over all flesh; and our sons and daughters will prophesy and have dreams and visions etc. For if the Christian people is not to become apostolic, Acts 27,[166] where Joel is cited, what is the point of preaching at all? Of what use are the biblical references to visions? It is true – I know it for a fact – that the spirit of God is revealing to many elect and pious men at this time the great need for a full and final reformation in the near future.[167] This must be carried out. For despite all attempts to oppose it the prophecy of Daniel retains its full force – whether anyone believe it or not, as Paul says in Romans 3.[168] This text of Daniel, then, is as clear as the bright sun, and the work of ending the fifth Empire of the world is now in full swing.[169] The first Empire is explained by the golden knob[170] – that was the Babylonian – the second by the silver breastplate and arm-piece – that was the Empire of the Medes and Persians. The third was the Greek Empire, resonant with human cleverness, indicated by the bronze; the fourth the Roman Empire, an Empire won by the sword, an Empire ruled by force.[171] But the fifth is the one we see before us, which is also of iron and would like to use force, but it is patched with dung (as anyone can see if they want to) that is, with the vain schemings of hypocrisy, which swarms and slithers over the face of the whole earth. For any one who does not practise deception[172] is regarded as a real idiot. What a pretty spectacle we have before us now – all the eels and snakes coupling together immorally in one great heap![173] The priests and all the evil clerics are the snakes, as John, who baptised Jesus, called them, Matthew 3,[174]

163. *nicht wol anlauffen*; 'have a poor run of it' (Williams).

164. *wirdt sich stossen an.*

165. Joel 2[11. 28ff.]

166. Acts 2[16ff.] (false citation).

167. *eine treffliche, unuberwintliche zukünfftige reformation.*

168. Romans 3[3f.]

169. *geht itzdt im rechten schwangke*; cf. n. 22 above.

170. *knauff*; crude term for 'head', like English 'knob'.

171. *ein reich des zcwingens.*

172. *plasteucken*; *blastücken*; Williams translates: 'Whoever cannot [detect] the ruses must be an imbecile.'

173. Müntzer may have been drawing here on the *Hexaemeron* of Basil, VII, 5 (MPG 29, 1600), which deals with the strange mating habits of vipers and lampreys; (I am indebted to Dr George Dragas for this reference).

174. Matthew 3[7.]

and the secular lords and rulers are the eels, symbolised by the fishes in Leviticus 11.[175] Thus the kingdoms of the devil have smeared themselves with clay. O, my dear lords, what a fine sight it will be when the Lord whirls his rod of iron among the old pots, Psalm 2.[176] Therefore, my dearest, most revered rulers, learn true judgement from the mouth of God himself. Do not let yourself by seduced by your hypocritical priests into a restraint based on counterfeit clemency and kindness.[177] For the stone dislodged from the mountain by no human hand, is a large one now;[178] the poor laity and the peasants have a much sharper eye for it than you. Yes, God be praised, it has grown so large that if other lords or neighbours of yours thought to persecute you for the sake of the gospel, they would now be driven out by their own subjects. I know this of a certainty. Yes, the stone is now large, something which the foolish world has long dreaded. Even when it was small it rolled over it.[179] What are we to do now that it has become so large and powerful? Now that it has become so powerful, so unstoppable, striking and smashing the great statue right down to its old clay pots?[180] Hence, my revered rulers of Saxony, take up your stance resolutely on the corner stone, as St Peter did, Mt. 16[181] and let God's true, unwavering purpose be yours. He can be relied upon to keep your feet firm on the stone, Psalm 29.[182] Only seek without delay the righteousness of God and take up the cause of the gospel boldly. Then you will be on the right track. For God is at your side, closer at hand than you can credit. So why be alarmed by the phantom powers of men? Psalm 117.[183] Take a good look at the text at this point.[184] King Nebuchadnezzar wanted to kill his wise men because they were unable to expound the dream. It was no more than they deserved. For they wanted to rule the whole of his Empire with their wisdom and were not even able to carry out their

---

175. Leviticus 11[9-12]; the image of copulation evokes disgust at the collaboration of clerics and rulers.

176. Psalm 2[9]; cf. Daniel 2[44b].

177. *mit getichter gedult und gute.*

178. Daniel 2[45]; cf. n. 19 above; Hinrichs distinguishes the stone (as the Holy Spirit) from the mountain (Christ); it appears, however, to refer to the imminent kingdom of Christ.

179. *Er hat sie uberfallen;* a reference to the Reformation, now becoming radicalised?

180. *so mechtigk unvorzcöglich auff die grosse seul gestrichen;* the metaphors of Psalm 2[9], and Daniel 2[45] are now totally confused.

181. Matthew 16[18]; Christ, who as the stone in Daniel destroys the fifth Empire, is the foundation stone of the coming kingdom.

182. *Et statuit super petram pedes meos,* Psalm 39[3] (Vg.); the rock contrasts with the miry bog, the clay or dung of the previous Empire.

183. *vorm gespenst des menschen;* Psalm 118[6].

appointed duties. Our clergy today are in the same position. I know this for a fact, that if the plight of the Christian people really came home to you and you put your mind to it properly then you would develop the same zeal as King Jehu showed, 2 Kings 9, 10,[185] and as we find throughout the whole book of Revelation. And I know this for a fact that you would have the very greatest difficulty not to resort to the power of the sword. For the condition of the holy people of Christ has become so pitiable, that up to now not even the most eloquent tongue could do it justice. Therefore a new Daniel must arise and expound your dreams to you and, as Moses teaches in Deuteronomy 20,[186] he must be in the vanguard, leading the way. He must bring about a reconciliation between the wrath of the princes and the rage of the people. For once you really grasp the plight of the Christian people as a result of the treachery of the false clergy and the abandoned criminals your rage against them will be boundless, beyond all imagining. There is no doubt that you will be embittered and deeply regret all your benevolence to them in the past, since they have used most sweet-sounding words to urge calamitously wrong judgements on you, Wisdom 6,[187] quite contrary to the honest truth. For they have made such a fool of you that everyone swears by the saints that in their official capacity princes are just pagans, that all they have to do is to maintain civic order. Alas, my fine fellow, the great stone will come crashing down soon and smash such rational considerations to the ground, as Christ says in Matthew 10: 'I am not come to send peace, but the sword.'[188] But what is one to do with the sword? Exactly this: sweep aside those evil men who obstruct the gospel! Take them out of circulation! Otherwise you will be devils, not the servants of God which Paul calls you in Romans 13.[189] Have no doubts that God will smash all your adversaries into little pieces – any who dare to persecute you! For his arm is not shortened, as Isaiah 59 says.[190] Hence he is as able and willing to help you as ever; as he stood by the elect king, Josiah,[191] and the others who defended the name of God. Hence, as Peter says, you are angels when you want to do what is right, 2 Peter 1.[192] Christ has commanded us very earnestly,

184. Daniel 2[12].
185. 2 Kings 9,10.
186. Deuteronomy 20[2]; the new Daniel is also to be a chaplain to the army of Israel; clearly Müntzer sees himself taking this leadership role.
187. Wisdom 6[1ff] (a powerful passage!).
188. Matthew 10[34].
189. Romans 13[4]; this whole section reinterprets Romans 13.
190. Isaiah 59[1].
191. 2 Kings 22, 23.
192. 2 Peter 1[4] (partakers of the divine nature); 'angelic' as the apocalyptic harvesters; cf. Schwarz, p. 72; Bräuer points to Luther's use of 'angels' for the princes

saying in Luke 19: 'Take my enemies and strangle[193] them before my eyes.'[194] Why? Just listen! It is because they are ruining the kingdom of Christ[195] and, worse still, trying to use the outward form of Christian faith to defend their wickedness. This fraudulent fig-leaf[196] which they wear is an affront[197] to the whole world. Hence Christ, our Lord, says in Mt. 18:[198] 'It would be better for someone who affronts one of these little ones to have a mill-stone around his neck and be thrown into the deep sea.' Let anyone try to wriggle out of this with fancy commentaries if he likes! These are the words of Christ. Now if Christ may say this about someone affronting a single child, what is to be said when the faith of great masses of people is affronted? This is what the arch-criminals do, who affront the whole world, make it desert the true Christian faith, and who say that no one should know the mysteries of God. As Matthew 23 says, follow what they say but not what they do.[199] They deny that faith must be tested like gold in the fire, 1 Peter 1, Psalm 139.[200] This, however, makes Christian faith worse[201] than a dog's when it hopes for a piece of bread when the table is set. This is the sort of faith which the false biblical scholars display to the poor, blind world. They do not see the absurdity of this, because they preach solely to feed their stomachs, Phil. 3.[202] As Matthew 12 says, with hearts like theirs they cannot say anything else.[203] Now if you are to be true rulers, you must seize the very roots of government,[204] following the command of Christ. Drive his enemies away from the elect; you are the instruments to do this. My friend, don't let us have any of these hackneyed posturings[205] about the power of God achieving everything without any resort to your

---

in the *Magnificat* 'for Scripture calls pious, god-fearing princes angels of God', WA 7, 545, 2.

193. *würget*.

194. Luke 19[27]; a good example of Müntzer's reading of Scripture.

195. *das sie in Christo sein regiment vorterbet*.

196. *schandtdeckel*, lit. 'cover for shame'; usual meaning is 'pretext'; 'subterfuge' (Williams).

197. *ergern* can mean in Müntzer 'be a scandal to, affront', or 'make worse, ruin'; the quotation and argument which immediately follow suggests the former sense, the preceding reference to the ruining of the kingdom of Christ the latter; it seems entirely possible that both meanings are in Müntzer's mind; Hinrichs, Franz, Williams prefer the latter sense.

198. Matthew 18[6].

199. Matthew 23[3].

200. 1 Peter 1[7]; Psalm 140[10].

201. *erger*; cf. n. 197 above.

202. Philippians 3[19].

203. Matthew 12[34].

204. *so müst ihr das regiment bey der wortzeln anheben*.

205. *keyne schale fratzen*.

sword; otherwise it may rust in its scabbard. Would that this could happen! Whatever any scholar may say, Christ speaks clearly enough in Matthew 7, John 15:[206] 'Any tree which does not produce good fruit should be rooted out and thrown into the fire.' But if you discard the mask which the world wears, you will soon be able, as John 7 says, to see it[207] for what it is and to judge aright. Do judge aright, following God's command. You will have help enough for it, Wisdom 6, for Christ is your master, Matthew 23.[208] Do not, therefore, allow the evil-doers, who turn us away from God, to continue living, Deut. 13,[209] for a godless man has no right to live if he is hindering the pious. In Exodus 22[210] God says: 'You shall not let the evil-doer live.' St. Paul thinks the same, when he says of the sword that it is set in the hands of the rulers to exact vengeance on the evil and give protection to the good, Romans 13.[211] As Psalm 17 says,[212] God is your shield, and will train you for the battle against his enemies. He will make your arm quick to strike and will keep you from harm, too. But at the same time you will have to endure a heavy cross and a time of trial, so that the fear of God may be manifest to you. That cannot happen without suffering, but what will it cost you? Only the risks taken for the sake of God[213] and the vain gossip of your adversaries. For although pious David was certainly expelled from his palace by Absalom, he did in the end return to it when Absalom was swept off his feet and stabbed.[214] So, revered fathers of Saxony, you must risk this for the sake of the gospel; but God will chastise you lovingly as his most dear sons, Deut. 1,[215] while his momentary wrath is raging. For blessed are all who rely upon God at such a time. Just say stoutly, in the spirit of Christ: 'I will have no fear even if a hundred thousand enemies are encamped around me'.[216] I suspect, though, that our scholars will reprove me at this point by referring to the clemency of Christ, which they drag in to cover their hypocrisy.[217] On the other hand, however, they should consider also the zeal of Christ, John 2,

---

206. Matthew 7[19]; John 15[2.6] (pruning of branches which have no fruit).
207. the world; John 7[24].
208. Wisdom 6[1ff.]; cf. n. 187 above; Matthew 23[10].
209. Deutronomy 13[5].
210. Exodus 22[18] (Vg.): *Maleficos non patieris vivere*; (Hinrichs believes Müntzer is thinking of Luther).
211. Romans 13[4].
212. Psalm 18[35. 34].
213. *die ferligkeyt umb Gots willen gewoget*.
214. Lit., 'hanged and stabbed', 2 Samuel 15[14ff.], 18[9ff.]
215. Deuteronomy 1[31].
216. Psalm 3[6].
217. This abrupt transition begins a brief section on idolatry.

Psalm 68,[218] when he destroys the roots of idolatry; concerning which Paul says in Colossians 3[219] that the wrath of God upon the congregation cannot be averted. If he tore down what in our eyes is a minor evil,[220] he would certainly not have spared any idols and pictures that had been there. For he himself commanded through Moses: 'You are a holy people. You should show no mercy to the idolatrous. Break down their altars! Destroy and burn their images, if you want to escape my wrath!' Deut. 7.[221] These words have not been superseded by Christ, but he wants to help us to put them into effect, Matthew 5.[222] All the figurative language has been expounded by the prophets, but these are clear, unequivocal words which obtain to all eternity, Isaiah 40.[223] God cannot say, 'Yes' today and 'No' tomorrow, but remains unchangeably by his word, Malachi 3; 1 Samuel 15; Numbers 22.[224] To the objection that the apostles did not destroy the idols of the pagans I would reply thus: St Peter was a timid man. He dissembled when among the pagans, as Galatians 2 reports.[225] He is representative of all the apostles, for Christ, too, says that Peter was exceedingly afraid of death, the last chapter of John.[226] And it is easily seen that he sought to avoid giving them any pretext for his death.[227] But St Paul spoke out very severely against idolatry, Acts 17.[228] If he had been able to enforce[229] his teachings among the inhabitants of Athens there is no doubt that he would have cast down idolatry completely, as God commanded through Moses, and as reliable histories tell us took place later on through the martyrs. Hence the weakness or negligence of the saints is no reason for us allowing the godless to have their way. Since, like us, they confess the name of God they should do one of two things: either deny the Christian faith completely or do away with the idols, Mt. 18.[230] But

218. John 2[15ff.]; Psalm 69[9] (cleansing of Temple).

219. Colossians 3[5f.]

220. The tables of the money-changers (Hinrichs).

221. Deuteronomy 7[2ff.] (not an exact quotation).

222. Matthew 5[17].

223. Isaiah 40[8b]; (these words were written on the peasant flag at the battle of Frankenhausen); figurative language, whether in Scripture or dreams, is regarded by Müntzer as less authoritative, cf. p. 241/18f. above.

224. Malachi 3[6]; 1 Samuel 15[22]; Numbers 22[6].

225. Galatians 2[11ff.]

226. John 21[15-19.]

227. *Und demselbigen darumb durch solchs keyne ursach gegeben*; *demselbigen* either refers to 'death' or we should read *denselbigen*, i.e. a reference to the pagans; in the former case one would translate: 'And it is easily seen that he sought to avoid provoking his death in any way' (cf. Hinrichs).

228. Acts 17[16ff.]

229. *auffs höchst treiben.*

230. Matthew 18[8f.]

our scholars come and – in their godless, fraudulent way – understand Daniel to say that the Antichrist should be destroyed without human hands when it really means that he is intimidated already, like the inhabitants of the promised land when the chosen people entered it.[231] Yet, as Joshua tells us, he did not spare them the sharp edge of the sword. Consult Psalm 43 and 1 Chronicles 13[232] and you will find it explained thus: they did not win the land by the sword, but by the power of God, but the sword was the means used, just as eating and drinking is a means for us to stay alive. Hence the sword, too, is necessary to eliminate the godless, Rom. 13.[233] To ensure, however, that this now proceeds in a fair and orderly manner, our revered fathers, the princes, who with us confess Christ, should carry it out. But if they do not carry it out the sword will be taken from them, Daniel 7,[234] for then they would confess him in words but deny him in deeds, Titus 1.[235] The sort of peace they should offer enemies is seen in Deuteronomy 2.[236] If they want to be spiritual, and yet refuse to give an account of their knowledge of God, 1 Peter 3,[237] then they should be done away with, 1 Cor. 5.[238] But, like pious Daniel, I intercede on their behalf where they are not opposed to God's revelation. But where they do the opposite let them be strangled without mercy as Hezekiah, Josiah, Cyrus, Daniel, Elijah destroyed the priests of Baal, 1 Kings 18.[239] Otherwise the Christian church will never return to its origins.[240] The tares have to be torn out of the vineyard of God at harvest-time. Then the fine golden wheat will gain firm roots and come up well, Mt. 13.[241] But the angels who sharpen their sickles for the harvest are the earnest servants of God who execute the zealous wisdom of God. Malachi 3.[242]

Nebuchadnezzar heard the divine wisdom through Daniel. He fell down before him, after being overwhelmed by the power of the

231. The Canaanites (F.); Joshua 5[1]; cf. the parallel in Luther, WA 8, 677, 22f.; 683, 12 (Bräuer).

232. Psalm 44[4]; 1 Chronicles 14[11].

233. Romans 13[4].

234. Daniel 7[27].

235. Titus 1[16].

236. Deuteronomy 2[27ff.] (Sihon and all his people killed after refusing an offer of peace from Moses).

237. 1 Peter 3[15].

238. 1 Corinthians 5[13].

239. 1 Kings 18[40] (Elijah); 2 Kings 18[22] (Hezekiah); 2 Kings 23[5] (Josiah) 2 Chronicles 36[22f.] (Cyrus); Daniel 6[26] (Daniel).

240. *ursprung*.

241. Matthew 13[30]; note the wheat in the vineyard (!), and the 'modification' of the parable by lengthening the 'time of the harvest'.

242. Malachi 3[1-5]; cf. n. 192 above.

truth, but he was like a reed moved by the wind, as the third chapter shows. One sees much the same today: countless numbers of people embrace the gospel with great rejoicing, because everything is going smoothly for them, Luke 8.[243] But when God wants to put such people in the crucible[244] or the refining fire, 1 Peter 1[245] then, O dear! they take offence at the least little word, as Christ prophesied in Mark 4.[246] There is no doubt that many who have never been put to the test will be similarly offended by this little book, because I say with Christ, Luke 19, Mt. 18 and with Paul, 1 Cor. 5,[247] and with the guidance of the whole divine law, that one should kill the godless rulers, and especially the monks and the priests who denounce the holy gospel as heresy and yet count themselves the best Christians. Then their hypocritical, counterfeit clemency will turn to incredible fury and bitterness. It will leap to the defence of the godless and say: 'Christ never killed anyone etc.' And because the friends of God waste their breath so lamentably on the wind the prophecy of Paul is fulfilled, 2 Tim. 3.[248] In the last days the pleasure-lovers will certainly give the impression of clemency but they will deny it any power. Nothing on earth has a fairer form or appearance than counterfeit clemency. Hence every nook and cranny is full of vain hypocrites, none of whom is courageous enough to speak the real truth. In order, then, that the truth may really begin to dawn you rulers must (God willing – whether you do it gladly or not) be guided by the conclusion of this chapter, where Nebuchadnezzar installed the holy Daniel in office to judge fairly and well, as the holy spirit says, Psalm 57.[249] For the godless have no right to live, unless by the sufferance of the elect, as is written in the book of Exodus, chapter 23.[250] Rejoice, you true friends of God, that the hearts of the enemies of the cross have fallen into their boots,[251] for they have no choice but to do right, though they never dreamt of doing so. If we fear God, why should we be alarmed by rootless, feckless men, Numbers 14, Joshua 11?[252] So be bold![253] He to whom all power is given in heaven and on earth is

243. Luke 8[13].
244. *test*.
245. 1 Peter 1[7].
246. Mark 4[17].
247. Luke 19[27]; Matthew 18[6]; 1 Corinthians 5[7, 13]; cf. n. 194.
248. 2 Timothy 3[1ff.]
249. Psalm 58[10f]; Daniel 2[48].
250. *im buch des aussgangs*; Exodus 23[30].
251. *in die bruch*, lit. 'into their pants'.
252. Numbers 14[8f]; Joshua 11[6].
253. *keck*; cf. p. 70/14 above; the language and arguments used here to encourage the princes recur in almost identical form in Müntzer's letters to the peasants on the

taking the government into his own hands, Mt. 28.[254] May he preserve you, my most beloved, for ever.

Amen.

---

eve of Frankenhausen, e.g. Nr. 75.
   254. Matthew 28[18].

THE TESTIMONY OF LUKE AND THE EXPOSÉ
OF FALSE FAITH

These two writings, written at great speed, mirror the excitement and the tensions of the last few weeks of Müntzer's time in Allstedt. Since the iconoclastic attack on the Mallerbach chapel in March 1524 the pressures on the Allstedt council and people – not on Müntzer – on the part of the Saxon Elector had been growing. Property, he insisted, must be respected and the Imperial law observed. In this he was at one with the Catholic nuns of Naundorf and the Catholic prince George of Saxony.

In his *Sermon on Daniel* on 13 July Müntzer had made a last attempt to win the Saxon princes over to his understanding of the role of the godly prince. He knew he had to contend with the opposition of both Catholic and Protestant princes, and with some breaking of ranks within the Allstedt community, as the pressure became too great for men like Zeiss or Rucker. Much of this is reflected in Letters 50–67.

Behind all these political pressures, however, Müntzer sensed the hand of the Catholic and above all the Wittenberg theological opposition to him. In mid-July Luther had finally put pen to paper, stung perhaps by the *Sermon on Daniel*, and written his first polemical writing against someone within the reforming camp. There are some scattered references to this sarcastic denunciation of Müntzer in the Testimony and the *Exposé* (pp. 304/10; 306/8f. below). In essence Luther calls upon the Elector to suppress the 'Satan of Allstedt,' not as a false teacher but as a disturber of the peace, and contemptuously rejects his repeated call for an open, impartial hearing.

Müntzer had long been aware of the Wittenbergers' growing alienation from him. Bräuer[1] has traced Luther's concern right back to the beginning of the Allstedt period and documented his successive attempts, through John Lang and Justas Jonas, to bring him to heel. Thus the context of these writings is intense 'spiritual' as well as political pressure, the new 'tyranny' of the preachers.

Their aim is the now familiar one of the polemical exposé of 'counterfeit' faith, but the eschatological expectations of a new era bring it closer to the reformist mood of the Prague Manifesto. Müntzer can no longer keep silence, and although he protests his concern for dialogue he is essentially appealing over the heads of the 'authorities' to public opinion. Schwarz has shown the closeness to Taborite themes especially as regards the 'order of creation'.[2] A

1. S. Bräuer, 'Vorgeschichte', 41–70.
2. R. Schwarz, *Die apokalyptische Theologie, e.g. p. 75.*

vibrant, Savonarola-type moralism, with a yearning for purity and for justice to the poor is also evident. Again and again the apocalyptic themes of revelation, separation, imminent judgement recur.

Another aim is the exegetical one, to demonstrate – on the Wittenbergers' 'home ground' of Scripture – the harmony of Müntzer's prophetic spirit-filled understanding with that of the Gospel witness of Luke. Luke was a brilliant choice, with its interweaving of Old Testament themes, its angelic visitations, its eschatological tone in the Magnificat, its counterpointing with Genesis 1. From the very outset of this, his longest non-liturgical writing, Müntzer appears in militant guise, armed with a hammer. But it is the hammer of the word, of Jeremiah, of the true prophet against the false which he wields, not the bloody hammer of Jael, the hammer of the word which splinters rock, and scatters those who 'steal' the Lord's words. Unyielding as iron the prophet exposes the 'big-wigs', be they princes, theologians, or priests, as idolators.

We should not overlook the pastoral concern, similar to that of Letter 55, for example, to strengthen the resolution of the waverers, and no translator can fail to note the pervasiveness of the mystical terminology. If apocalyptic determines the ecclesiology, mysticism dominates his anthropology.

On the dating of the writings we know that on 1 August Müntzer submitted to Weimar for censorship a shorter form which is probably identical with the copy of the Testimony in the Electoral archives; and that the *Exposé*, the longer form, was printed prior to 29 October 1524 in Nurnberg, having been handed on by Hans Hut from Bibra. Less clear is the priority of the two writings. Hinrichs, Metzger, Franz regard the less polemical Testimony as a later form, abbreviated from the *Exposé*, for the princely censor. Elliger and Schwarz find the argument that Müntzer would be prepared, at this particular point, to tone down his writing to suit the electoral censor quite unconvincing.

Clearly caution is in place. The evidence is largely circumstantial or internal. If we assume the priority of the shorter version the addition of the polemical material against both the Wittenbergers and the princes can be seen as an index of Müntzer's mounting frustration and anger. Less easily explained, however, would be the later addition of so much superfluous and repetitive verbiage.

A careful comparison suggests that the Testimony may in fact be secondary. Frequently it reads like a clumsy abbreviation of the *Exposé*. At times the compression makes for virtual incomprehensibility (pp. 275/16ff.; 285/2f.; 287/20ff.). The beginning of the fourth section of the Testimony (p. 279/8) suggests that attention will concentrate on a 'new John the Baptist'. In fact it deals with the usurious evil-doers and the key role of the lowly. The confusion appears to arise because the careless abbreviation of the *Exposé* at this point gave undue prominence to an incidental reference to a new John the Baptist. The reference to the 'patriarch' in section 1 of B (p. 269/11) is obscure without A. Telescoping of the argument also seems evident in section 5 of the Testimony; and without the text of the *Exposé* it is hard to see to what 'experiencing the latter' refers (p. 307/8). To what does 'it' refer at the beginning of the seventh section of the Testimony? (p. 313/19). Only the *Exposé* makes it clear that 'true Christianity' is meant. Other instances, like the clipped reference to Mary at the start of section eight, point in the same direction. Moreover, is it likely that the subdivision into sections seven and eight – found only in the Testimony – would be excised in a longer version if it were secondary? The correction of the Psalm reference towards the end of the first section (p. 275/20) also suggests that the Testimony is the later writing. Many of Müntzer's writings exist in several 'drafts': the Prague Manifesto, the Stolberg Sendbrief, the letters to the Allstedters (Nos. 65–7); an analysis of them all would be valuable.

As far as structure is concerned, it is an unwieldy writing, betraying the haste with which it was written in the last weeks of July. There is little logical or historical argumentation. Continuity is poor, and the exegesis of Luke 1 is not pursued in any disciplined way. The sections are of very variable length and only of limited help in defining the train of thought.

The foreword states the objectives. Section 1 defines the gateway of faith as the fear of God, the 'overshadowing of the Spirit'; this is rarely found and unacceptable to the Biblical scholars. Section 2 argues that since faith is impossible for the fleshly-minded we have first to be freed from the 'creatures'. Section 3 insists on immediate, personal faith as the bond between the elect and God. Section 4 compares the arrogance of the tyrants and the high priests with the lowly who have the true knowledge of God. Section 5 points repeatedly to John the Baptist as the archetype of the true preacher who will point the elect to the mystical disciplines required if the Church is to be reformed. Section 6 refers to the separation of the elect from the godless. Sections 7 and 8, found only in the Testimony as separate sections, deal respectively with the eschatological gathering of the humble and with the need for total dedication to God. There follows a brief summary.

The theme of the whole book is the true exercise of authority, *christliche meisterschaft*, the Christian exercise both of spiritual and political authority. After his Allstedt experiences the power issue has become *the* issue for Müntzer, determining everything from the interior life of the individual to the gathering (or scattering) of the elect. All power is 'sacred', as the whole of creation is ordered by God. Hence power in both church and society has to be so exercised that it glorifies God alone. The prophet (with the word) and the angel (with power) are one. Whatever stands between us and the fear of God is idolatry. Conversely, wherever the true relationship of the elect with God is restored, the existing power structures are shattered.

For this is God's good world, established by him in the beginning with an innate 'order of creation'. We, who are God's 'possession' in turn have the 'creatures', all created being, for our possession (p. 316/30f.).

Yet the reality of the present world is that we have allowed our senses, our lust for the creatures, for material things, to possess us (p. 306/26f.).Our motivation is fear, not of God, but of forfeiting a 'long and lasting life' (p. 291/10f.). This drives the powerful, the 'big wigs', whether prince or priest, to tyranny – to protect their privileges – and their subjects to cowardly deference to the princely 'powder-sacks' or to the authority-figures in the church.

True Christian *meisterschaft*, exercise of authority, has to be learnt from Christ, who 'rules from the Cross'. This is most succinctly expressed in the brief *summa* at the end of the writing. Through conformity with the humiliated, suffering Jesus we will come to 'flourish and burgeon sweetly in the wisdom of the cross'. The original, paradisical order will be restored as, free from the tyranny of the creatures, we are enabled to exercise power without self-seeking.

In human terms, however, this process is an 'impossible' one, as Luke's Gospel exemplifies. It traces the beginning of the new kingdom of Christ, as Genesis does that of the original order of creation. It moves, dialectically, from 'overshadowing' to 'transfiguration', from the 'first sprinkling' of the fear of the God to our divinisation as 'this earthly life swings up into heaven' (p. 278/22).

As the veil, the 'overshadowing', of the old covenant is taken away by the birth of Christ, the light of the world, in our soul, we achieve divine wisdom, the divine image is restored within us, we become angels, fit to rule in Christ's coming kingdom. It is only the poor in spirit, like Mary, who are prepared to submit to this agonising process, in which all our hidden reservations and doubts are unmasked and Christ's spirit becomes the possessor, *besitzer*, of the soul.

Hence the *Exposé* unmasks not only the outward lies and abominations in church and society but the inward corruption of the soul where the power of evil 'is a thousand-fold more varied than outside it' (p. 304/4f.). It is when rulers reach into people's souls that they become tyrants, as he told the Sangerhausen Christians[3].

3. Cf. p. 88/28f. above.

Preachers or theologians similarly become tyrants when they make the laity dependent on them and on the bookish authority of Scripture and deflect them from engaging with their doubts and despairs. The abyss of the soul displays the depth dimension of tyranny.

Scripture itself can become an instrument of tyranny. We have to learn to use it dialectically, discovering under each text its polar opposite, allowing it to nudge us into analogous relations to God to those of the patriarchs, the prophets, the apostles. Like Mary these are not 'unique' but archetypal of the faithful in all generations, as Herod and the pharisees are of the ungodly.

Hence even if the elect have never seen Scripture the spirit of Christ can move in their hearts (p. 274/11ff.). Indeed the literalistic abuse of Scripture as a creaturely norm means that it is easier to expound 'the dominion given to us and that of God over us' to those who are ignorant of the Bible. For they seek the 'Christian Nazareth' in their souls, not in an antiquarian, Palestinian past.

Like Elijah, Jeremiah, John the Baptist, therefore, the task of the 'earnest preacher' is to lead the elect into the inner desert, to train them to discern the spirits, to separate off from the godless, to prepare for the imminent 'blow' which will reverse all previous power relationships as Christ comes to rule from the Cross.

No clear reform programme is delineated. The authority of the present secular powers is a result of the Fall. Our sin deserves such wicked rulers. As God prepares to intervene their atrocities mount, just as at the time of Christ's coming his 'godless opposite', Herod, enabled us to see his goodness more clearly. Today's princes are 'nothing but hangmen and jailors', and their arbitrary cruelty is a sign that Christ's kingdom is imminent. The lingering hope put in the godly prince in *The Sermon on Daniel* has disappeared, for even the rulers sympathetic to the Gospel are too cowardly to do anything. It is clear that, as the Magnificat says, the godless will have to be torn from their judgement seats and 'humble, coarse folk' raised up to replace them. The spiritual accomplices of the princes, like Luther, who urge the poor to submit to tyranny, manage to combine literalism with antinomianism. They are simply out to safeguard their status and privileges and will have to be replaced by the 'preacher full of grace', the 'servant of God', characterised by an undaunted sobriety from his youth which has sharpened him like a scythe; his own exemplary trials opens the eyes of others to the cross.

Thus the challenge to all conventional authority has become unbelievably radical. The undoubted personality clash between Luther and Müntzer should not blind us to this structural critique and new understanding of Christian authority. The elect are to trust neither pope nor monk nor priest, neither Catholic prince nor Protestant. Yet, apart from the 'earnest preacher' no alternative structures are outlined and too often the argument degenerates into tedious abuse, with little in the way of specific documentation.

A final word on the style. In both versions we note unevenness, repetitiveness, and a degree of obscurity. It is hardly easy reading, yet it is penned in conversational style, with frequent questions, illustrations, ejaculations, adjurations and sallies into direct speech. Some dramatic passages give us a glimpse of what Müntzer must have been like in the full flow of his pulpit rhetoric.

As a verbal cartoonist Müntzer is again quite superb: the princes as sacks of powder, the Lutherans as black crows, or copy-cats, or pussy-foots, or thieves of Scripture. We see them spreading around their poisonous additives: their glosses, their paints and their patches; or cowering behind their fig-leaves; or carrying out complicated balancing tricks.[4] Who could forget the images of the godless slithering like snakes into their lust, or clinging together like toad-spawn; or the midge with its miniscule cargo on its tail? The positive, often biblical, images are also quite striking: the sweet incense of the troubled heart, the 'Christian Nazareth' of the soul, the holy spirit as the schoolmaster of faith.

---

4 Cf. the saying 'carrying the yoke on both shoulders', i.e. being all things to all men.

A MANIFEST EXPOSÉ OF FALSE FAITH

A manifest exposé[1] of false faith, presented to the faithless[2] world from the testimony of Luke's gospel, in order to rouse our poor wretched Christian people[3] to see the error of their ways, Ezekiel 8.[4] Come on, then, lads![5] Let us, too, widen the hole in the wall, so all the world can see through and realise who the big-wigs[6] are that have so blasphemously made God into a painted puppet, Jeremiah 23,[7] Thomas Müntzer, with the hammer. Mühlhausen 1524.

Jeremiah, the first chapter:[8] 'Take heed, I have set my word in your mouth; this day I have set you above the peoples and above the kingdoms, to root out, smash, scatter, and devastate – to build up and to plant.'

Jeremiah 1:[9] 'A wall of iron has been erected against the kings, princes, priests and against the people. No matter how they struggle, a miraculous victory will be won and the might of the godless tyrants cast down.'

Foreword to the Poor, Scattered Christian People

May the spirit of the might and the fear of God be with you, most pitiable congregation![10] For to avert imminent catastrophe[11] it has

---

1. *Aussgetrückte emplössung*; the traditional rendering as *ausdrücklich* (explicit, frank) has been retained; there may well be a word-play, however, with *drucken* (to print) and *unterdrücken* (to suppress) which are closely linked and contrasted in Letter 71: Müntzer complains that he had his teachings published (*drücken*) in Nuremberg, only to have them suppressed (*unterdrücken*) p. 135/11f. above; his letters show his concern about such censorship at this time; e.g. Letters 52 and 64; cf. also the use of *aussgedrucket* for his Stolberg letter, which was printed, cf. Letter 41 B, n. 463; thus the title may reflect defiant satisfaction that his denunciation of false faith is being published; the suggestion, however, has not found favour with Germanists.

2. *ungetrewen*.

3. *der elenden erbermlichen christenheyt*; there is a parallelism in the German between the 'faithless world' and the 'poor old church', to both of which Müntzer addresses himself.

4. *zur innerung jres irsals*; Ezekiel 8[ff.] (the vision of Israel's abominations, seen through the hole in the wall).

5. *gesellen*.

6. *grosse hansen*.

7. Jeremiah 23[29].

8. Jeremiah 1[9f.]

9. Jeremiah 1[18f.]

10. *gemeyn*.

11. *das auffstehend übel zuvorkumen*; Müntzer's letters to Zeiss, the intendant of Allstedt, contain very similar language to that of the *Exposé*, e.g. No. 57: *vorkommen* (p.95/4 above); *meysterlich fetzen* (Nr. 59, n. 788).

TESTIMONY OF THE FIRST CHAPTER OF THE GOSPEL OF LUKE

Testimony of the first chapter of the gospel of Luke presented by Thomas Müntzer for the instruction of the whole people of Christ.

Widen the hole, and let everyone see who these big wigs are, Ezekiel 8.[1]

Foreword to the Gospel of Luke

May the spirit of the might and the fear of God be with you, you poor, wretched people of Christ. For to avert imminent catastrophe it

---

1. Ezekiel 8⁴; compared with A the polemical language is missing and also the identification of Müntzer with Jeremiah.

become absolutely critical that you be shown what Christian authority is,[12] following the appearance of the slanderous books[13] which intimidate you one moment and provoke you to rage the next. In our time such a disclosure is only possible by interpreting the Holy Scripture in accordance with the spirit of Christ, seeing all the mysteries and pronouncements of God as a unitary whole. For none of these pronouncements, however clear and unequivocal, can be fully comprehended in isolation since they have, hidden within them, their polar opposite.[14] To read them in isolation causes dreadful harm to the others and produces the dregs[15] from which all wicked divisions arise. This, then, is what has compelled me, wretched man though I am, to launch myself at the defences, to enlarge the breach in the fore-court,[16] although I know full well how much evil the agents of corruption are likely to inflict, in their godless way, on the servants of the Christian people. For they have flourished their literalist faith[17] and denied (as anyone can see) the gracious power of God, creating a mad, dumb and illusory God with their counterfeit preaching and faith. As a result every kind of proud abomination has become entrenched[18] in every congregation throughout the world, becoming more crazily obstinate with every passing day. That is why the radical[19] movement of the holy Christian faith must stir the wild waves to a storm of indignation, as Psalm 92 says.[20] Since no one else is

12. *mit erweysung christlicher meisterschaft; meistern* is used as a synonym for 'rule over', 'control' in p. 282/14 below, *meysterlich anrichten*, where the mighty are to be cast down for presuming to tyrannise over the Christian Faith; and in Letter 59 *meysterlich fetzen* (n. 788); the latter passage relates to Luke 5[36], the futility of putting a new patch on an old garment; this central image expresses for Müntzer the total incompatibility of the old tyrannical ways in church and state with the new coming kingdom; cf. its use in the Letter 44 to Count Ernest of Mansfeld, (p. 67/18); cf. the attacks on tyranny, especially over the soul, in Letters 55, 56; the basis of this is the tyranny over Scripture, p. 270/14; cf. Luther's trans. of 1 Timothy 17 'Wollen der Schrift Meister sein'.

13. *die schmachbücher*; not only, as Elliger p. 538 points out, those of Luther, and especially the *Letter to the Princes of Saxony* LW40, 49ff., though this is central; *allerfrechst* is understood here to mean 'enraged', 'cocky', but *frech* may be MHG, *tatkräftig*, 'ready for action', not 'cheeky', which makes no sense (Bräuer); but cf. a parallel use, clearly meaning 'insolent', in Letter 49 p. 78/22..

14. *Dann es haben alle urteyl das höchst gegenteyl bey in selber*; in German this phrase appears first.

15. *die grundtsupp.*

16. *mich fürgewendet zur wagenburg, das loch des vorhoffs weytter zu machen*; lit. 'moved forwards to the ring of waggons to enlarge the hole in the fore-court'; the *wagenburg*, the protective ring of waggons, is the fortress behind which the godless are sheltering.

17. *nachdem sie irem büchstabischen glauben also hoch auffmutzt.*

18. *also halss starrig worden ist.*

19. *gründtlich.*

20. Psalm 93[3f.]

has become critical that you should be instructed in the Christian exercise of authority, following the appearance of the slanderous books which intimidate you one moment and provoke you to action the next. In our time such instruction means interpreting the Holy Scripture in accordance with the spirit of Christ, seeing and explaining all the mysteries and pronouncements of God as a unitary whole. For none of these pronouncements can be fully comprehended in isolation since they have, hidden within them, their polar opposite, which will be harmed if omitted.[2]

So this has compelled me to launch myself at the defences, to enlarge the breach in the forecourt wall, Ezekiel 8,[3] lest people persist in a faith slyly stolen from the letter of Scripture,[4]

or even worse in one which boasts of its proud traditions and ancestry.[5]

2. As A makes clear, Müntzer means that to read one text in isolation is detrimental to the others and misleading as far as the text itself is concerned.

3. Ezekiel 8[7ff.]

4. Stolen because not authenticated by first-hand experience of the Spirit.

5. A talks more forcibly of 'proud abominations' being the tradition.

willing to grasp the rudder of the ship – because of the fierce struggle ahead[21] – I dare not stand aside; for the waters of corruption have surged into the souls of the friends of God, Psalm 68.[22] I must reveal quite frankly[23] how far the harmful poison has already penetrated. Wherever possible I will be glad to do this gently, but where it would be to the detriment of the spirit of Christ I will not allow my forbearance to be a cover-up for anyone. To set this process of explanation and demonstration in train I will have one chapter[24] published at a time, to give my opponents ample time and opportunity to reply. My only reason for refusing some hole and corner hearing[25] is that our case demands this. Christ himself shunned that breed of adders, the biblical scholars, John 7[26] and when he was heard in private[27] by Annas the only defence he would give of his teaching was to point to those who had listened to him, to the common people, John 18.[28] He said quite clearly: 'Why ask me? Ask those who heard me.' Our scholars would like to have the testimony to the spirit of Jesus brought within the walls of the university.[29] They will never succeed because their motive for pursuing learning is not to teach the common man and bring him up to their standard. What they want is to reserve to themselves the right to judge on matters of faith, using the Scripture they have stolen, though they have no credibility at all, either in the eyes of God or of man. For it is blatantly obvious to everyone that what they are after is status and material possessions. Therefore you common folk will have to be instructed, so that they can no longer lead you astray. May the same spirit of Christ come to your aid which our scholars, to their downfall, can only make the butt of their derision. Amen.

Explanation of the First Chapter of Luke

Throughout the gospel of Luke the Christian people are given clear and precious testimony that the holy Christian faith has become such

21. *von der erbsaln hertigkeit.*
22. Psalm 69[2].
23. *grēulich*; read *getreulich*, as in B.
24. This being the first chapter of Luke; the judge between Müntzer and his opponents will be the reading public throughout 'the world'; not some partial 'hole and corner' instance.
25. *Den gefehrlichen winckel*; lit. 'the dangerous corner'.
26. John 7[10ff]; cf. p. 244/29f.
27. *auffm winckel.*
28. John 18[19ff].
29. *auff die hohen schul bringen*; i.e. have Müntzer judged in Wittenberg by 'hole and corner' scholarship.

The faith I will offer the Christian people is the one by which I myself have been moved and I will, wherever possible, be gentleness itself in frankly revealing the extent of the damage already done. But where this would be to the detriment of the spirit of Christ I will resist with all the power at my command.

To begin this process of explanation I will have one chapter published at a time to give my opponents ample time and opportunity to reply. My sole reason for refusing a hole-and-corner hearing is that the cause demands this. Christ himself did the same, John 7.[6]

May he save and preserve you all, my untried brothers, from your counterfeit faith, once you have come through your time of troubles. Amen.

First.
Throughout the gospel of Luke the Christian people are given clear and precious testimony that the holy Christian faith is such a rare,

6. Both the polemic against the biblical scholars and the reference to the common man's judgement are omitted.

a rare, alien thing that it would be no wonder if a good-hearted person wept tears of blood[30] when he saw how blind the congregation of Christ really was. With his question in Luke 18[31] Christ himself said as much: 'Do you imagine that the son of man will find faith on earth when he comes?' A similar lament is raised by Isaiah, in chapter 15, and by Paul in his letter to the Romans, chapter 10.[32] So it is an unspeakable calamity,[33] as intolerable abomination, that those who themselves have no faith (as is only too obvious) set themselves up as preachers of the Christian faith to others, a faith which they have neither attained nor experienced for themselves. They have no idea what goes on in the heart of a believer.[34] They imagine, or allow themselves to believe, that faith is as easily come by as their self-opinionated blethering about it suggests.[35] Hence, my very dearest brothers, we must take this chapter to heart, from beginning to end, scrutinising it with real earnestness. Then we will find abundant evidence of how the unbelief of all the elect was disclosed.[36] Zechariah, for example, was reluctant to believe the true words of the angel Gabriel because what was promised him seemed so impossible.[37] The best example of all is Mary, who gave birth to our saviour and has been praised for this from generation to generation.[38] She wanted confirmation, and an easy access to faith.[39] They did not arrive at their faith – as the foolish world does now – in a glossy, superficial way;[40] They did not go about saying: 'Yes, all I need to do is believe, and God will bring it to pass.'[41] The drunken world dreams up for itself a poisoned faith on such a frivolous basis,[42] a faith that is much worse than that of the Turks, the pagans, and the Jews. But Mary and Zechariah were seized by the fear of God[43] until the

30. Cf. Luke 22[44].
31. Luke 18[8].
32. Probably a misprint for Isaiah 65[1ff.]; cf. 53[1](F.); Romans 10[16, 20].
33. *jamer.*
34. *wie eynem glaubigen zu mut ist.*
35. *wie sie all fast rhumretig darvon schwatzen.*
36. Müntzer uses the chapter to illustrate his dialectical understanding of faith; before reaching authentic faith the superficial character of conventional faith must be exposed and one's deep-seated unbelief allowed to surface.
37. Luke 1[18].
38. *von kinds kind.*
39. *gute ankunfft*; Luke 1[29, 34].
40. *in eyner geferbten weyss*; lit. 'in a painted way'; Müntzer frequently uses colour or paint as a symbol of a purely superficial, skin-deep faith.
41. *Gott wirts wol machen*, i.e. one can leave the rest to God.
42. *ankunfft*; cf. n. 39 above.
43. *haben sich in der forcht Gottes entsetzt.*

alien thing that it would be no wonder if a good-hearted person wept tears of blood when he saw how blind the congregation of Christ really was. With his question in Luke 18 Christ himself said as much: 'Do you imagine that the son of man will find faith on earth when he comes?' A similar lament is raised by Isaiah, in chapter 15, and by Paul in his letter to the Romans, chapter 10. So it is an unspeakable, intolerable calamity that those who themselves have no faith (as is only too obvious) set themselves up as preachers of the Christian faith to others, a faith which they have never attained or experienced for themselves. They have no idea what goes on in the heart of a believer. They think that faith is as easily come by as their self-opinionated blethering about it suggests. Hence, my very dearest brothers, we must take this chapter to heart, from the beginning, scrutinising it with real earnestness. Then we will find clear evidence that Zechariah was reluctant to believe the true words of the angel Gabriel because what was promised him seemed so impossible. The best example of all is Mary, who gave birth to our saviour and has been praised for this from generation to generation. She wanted more confirmation, and an easy access to faith. They did not arrive at their faith as the foolish world does now; they did not go about saying 'Yes, all I need to do is believe, and God will bring it to pass.' The drunken world dreams up for itself a poisoned faith on such a glib[7] basis, a faith that is much worse than that of the Turks, the pagans, and the Jews. But Mary and Zechariah were seized by the fear of God until the mustard-seed of faith overcame their unbelief, of which they became aware in great fear and trembling.

7. *leichtlicher*; cf. B *leichtfertiger*.

mustard-seed of faith overcame their unbelief, of which they became aware in great fear and trembling.[44]

Unless, we,[45] too, allow our faith to begin in this way with the greatest fear and trembling God cannot increase it or credit[46] us with it. As God himself says through the holy prophet Isaiah, chapter 66:[47] 'Whom should I look upon except the lowly person and the one who trembles at all that I say?' Hence Paul says to the Philippians in chapter 2:[48] 'You should work out your salvation with trembling and anxiety.' Oho, what an unpalatable thing this is for our nature: that faith must begin with the fear of God! Moses heard the very voice of God,[49] but he still did not want to set out in obedience to his word when he commanded him to go into Egypt, Exodus 4.[50] He had to become aware of the power of God in the abyss of the soul, as he testifies later, Deut. 30;[51] otherwise he would not have set out. God promised the patriarch Jacob many good things and gave him abundant assurances. Despite this Jacob fell out with God. He had to overcome God before he could receive the blessing which faith brings, Genesis 32.[52] Anyone who searches diligently will find testimony all through Scripture about the unheard-of conflicts which faith wages with unbelief, especially in the book of Judges, chapters 6, 7, 8.[53] Gideon had such a firm, strong faith that with three hundred men he defeated a countless host.[54] But before he was ready to embrace such a faith he spoke to the angel,[55] as if he had caught him out lying: You declare that the Lord is with you, mightiest of men. But how can that be when we are having to suffer so much misfortune? At its beginning an untried faith is fearful at every new turning and slow to respond even to the most dramatic visitation.[56] A person who comes to faith lightly is light-headed. It is the fear of God which makes way for the holy spirit, so that the elect man can be

44. Luke 1[22, 29].
45. Lit. 'anyone'.
46. *ansehen*.
47. Isaiah 66[2].
48. Philippians 2[12].
49. Lit. 'God himself speak'.
50. Exodus 4[1ff.]
51. Deuteronomy 30[11-14]: a key text for Müntzer.
52. Genesis 32[24ff.]
53. Judges 6[13]; 7[7]; 8[4ff.]
54. *ein unzelige grosse welt*; Gideon becomes an increasingly important model for Müntzer when the Peasants' War breaks out; e.g. letters Nr. 84, 88, 89 where he signs himself, 'Thomas Müntzer with the sword of Gideon'.
55. Judges 6[13].
56. *schwerlich allem singen und sagen stadt zu geben*; 'respond' in the sense of 'give way to', 'make way for'; cf. n. 77 below.

Unless we, too, allow our faith to begin in this way with the greatest fear and trembling God cannot increase it or credit us with it. As God himself has said through the holy prophet Isaiah, chapter 66: 'Whom should I look upon except the lowly person and the one who trembles at all that I say?' Hence Paul says to the Philippians in the second chapter: 'You should work out your salvation with trembling and anxiety.' Moses heard the very voice of God, but he still did not want to set out in obedience to his word when he commanded him to go into Egypt, Exodus 4. He had to become aware of the power of God in the abyss of the soul, as he testifies later, Deut. 30; otherwise he would not have set out. God promised the patriarch[8] many good things and gave him abundant assurances. Despite this he fell out with God. He had to overcome God before he could receive the blessing which faith brings, Genesis 32. Anyone who searches will find testimony all through Scripture about the unheard-of conflicts which unbelief wages with faith, especially in the book of Judges, chapters[9] 6, 7, 8. Gideon had such a firm strong faith that with three hundred men he defeated a countless host. But before he was ready to embrace such a faith he spoke to the angel, as if he had caught him out lying: You declare that the Lord is with you, mightiest of men. But how can that be when we are having to suffer so much misfortune? At its beginning an untried faith is fearful at every new turning, and slow to respond to even the most dramatic visitation. A person who comes to faith lightly is light-headed. It is the fear of God which responds to the holy spirit, so that the elect man can be overshadowed, (safe) from that which the foolish world fears, to its irreparable loss in wisdom.

8. As A shows, Jacob is meant.
9. *underschiet.*

overshadowed, safe from that which the foolish world fears, to its irreparable loss in wisdom.

Hence this overshadowing by the holy spirit should be noted both at the beginning and at the conclusion of this gospel.[57] It teaches us faith through the pure fear of God. This arouses great consternation[58] at the impossible demands on faith. For the power of the most high (described by Luke at the beginning and the end) at once drives out all counterfeit, secret unbelief,[59] the latter being unmasked by the putting on or breaking through (to the spirit) in the abyss of the soul.[60] Paul says:[61] 'You should put on Christ,' after which false faith can find no place at all. But someone who has not experienced this breakthrough has absolutely no notion of what faith is, for he continues to maintain a speculative faith which clothes his arrogant spirit like an old beggar's coat. The faithless, abandoned biblical scholars are past masters at patching this with a new patch, as our gospel says in chapter 5.[62] As a patch they use the very Scripture they have stolen. If they are asked how they have come to this lofty faith about which they blether on non-stop, or why they would not rather be heathens, Jews, or Turks, or who has instructed them, then to defend their reckless and obstinate assault on the world[63] they will resort to incredibly lame and hackneyed posturing[64] and say quite unashamedly: 'You see, I believe in Scripture!' And then they will turn to menaces and grunt away enviously, saying barefacedly[65]: 'Aha, this character is denying Scripture!' For with such calumnies they want to stop everyone's mouth much more drastically than that idiot, the pope, with all his butter-boys;[66] for they would like to still[67] the stormy movement and heart-felt anxiety of the elect, or to attribute it dogmatically to the devil. They are always going on about how Christ sent away the godless biblical scholars. The reason is that they, too, are of that ilk.[68] They poke out their thin little tongues and speak in this dainty manner:[69] 'Search Scripture, for you seem to

57. Luke 1[35], 24[49].
58. *verwunderung.*
59. counterfeit faith and secret lack of faith (!).
60. *durch das anthun oder durchgang im abgrund der seelen*; the language of German mysticism (Hinrichs).
61. Romans 13[14]; on the phrase *meysterlich fetzen* cf. n. 12 above.
62. Luke 5[36].
63. *do sie also ferlichen die welt mit stürmen und also hefftig trotzen.*
64. *fratzen.*
65. *auss dem barte.*
66. *butterbuben*; those who have a licence to eat butter during Lent.
67. *settigen*, to meet, satisfy their concerns.
68. *dess selbigen mels*, 'the same grain'.
69. John 5[39]; cf. Psalm 140[3].

Hence this overshadowing by the holy spirit should be noted both at the beginning and at the conclusion of this gospel. It teaches us faith through the pure fear of God. This arouses great consternation at the impossible demands on faith. For the power of the most high (described by Luke at the beginning and the end) excludes all counterfeit, secret unbelief, which is unmasked by the putting on or breaking through (to the spirit) in the abyss of the soul. Paul says: 'You should put on Jesus,' after which false faith can find no place at all. But someone who has not experienced this breakthrough has absolutely no notion of what faith is, for he continues to maintain a speculative faith which clothes his arrogant spirit like an old beggar's coat. The abandoned biblical scholars are past masters at patching this with a new patch, Luke 5. They use the very Scripture they have stolen. If they are asked how they have come to this faith about which they blether or why they would not rather be heathens, Jews, or Turks, or who has instructed them since they thrash around so much,[10] then they say quite unashamedly they believe in Scripture,

hoping to satisfy in this way all the elect. They talk about the way in which Christ instructed the godless biblical scholars, John 5: 'Search Scripture for you think you will gain your salvation there.' Words cannot tell how cruelly the elect are defrauded by this.

10. *auf buchen.*

think, you presume to imagine, that you will gain your salvation there.' Words cannot tell how cruelly this defrauds the poor and needy folk.[70] For all their words and deeds ensure that the poor man is too worried about getting his food to have time to learn to read; moreover they have the nerve to preach that the poor man should let himself be flayed and fleeced by the tyrants. How on earth is he to learn to read the Scripture? Yes, yes, my dear Thomas, but you are getting too fanatical! The biblical scholars should read their fine books and the peasant should listen to them, for faith comes by listening.[71] O yes, that was a fine trick[72] they discovered! It would replace the priests and monks with worse rascals than have been seen since the very beginning of the world.[73] But, God be praised, very many of the elect recognise that the roots of unbelief lie here, though they have long lain hidden. They would clearly like to continue their rank growth[74] today, and prevent the wheat coming up at all.[75] So shortly before the above mentioned words Christ speaks to these pious people, the biblical scholars:[76] 'My word will not remain with you.' And why not? Because of their unbelief, which gives no room at all[77] for the real roots of genuine faith Mt. 13, Mark 4, Luke 8, John 9, Isaiah 6.[78]

Now if these harmful roots are to be torn out precautions must be taken against the godless ways of the biblical scholars. Christ could never agree with them. For they use Scripture as a fig-leaf[79] to prevent the true nature of Christian faith from shining out before the whole world Mt. 5, 10.[80]

The son of God has said: Scripture gives testimony. The biblical scholars say: it gives faith. O, no, most beloved, you must take a much larger view of things! Otherwise you will have the most stupid form of faith on the face of the earth, just like that of the apes.[81] This is the

70. The following fiery section of about ten lines is absent in B; cf. Letters 55, p. 89/11ff.; 84, p. 151/5ff.

71. Romans 10[14ff.]

72. *griff.*

73. Cf. Letter 60, p. 103/2ff.

74. *verwildern.*

75. The German which reads 'permit the wheat', is corrected at the end of the tract. (F.)

76. John 5[38]; cf. n. 69.

77. *keyn stat geben wil*; cf. n. 56; here the mutual exclusiveness of true and false faith for Müntzer is particularly, almost spatially, graphic; cf. B; it is not just a matter of wheat and tares above the ground, as it were, but of the roots of faith or unbelief which have to be tackled; cf. Deuteronomy 29[28] and n. 36 above.

78. Matthew 13[1ff.]; Mark 4[1ff.]; Luke 8[4-15]; John 9[39-41]; Isaiah 6[9f.]

79. *schanddeckel*; pretext.

80. Matthew 5[16]; 10[26ff.]

81. 'Apes' in the sense of 'copy-cats'; cf. n. 100 below.

It is obvious that the roots of unbelief lie hidden here and entwine themselves with the pure wheat with disastrous results. Hence shortly before the above mentioned words Christ says: 'My word will not remain with you.' Why not? Because of their unbelief, which gives no room for the real roots of genuine faith (Matthew 13, Mark 4, Luke 8, John 12,[11] Isaiah 6).

Now if these roots are to be torn out precautions must be taken against the godless ways of the biblical scholars. Christ could never agree with them. For they use Scripture as a fig-leaf to prevent the nature of faith from shining out to the whole world, Matthew 5, 10, John 9.[12]

The son of God has said: Scripture gives testimony. The biblical scholars say: it gives faith. O, my dear brothers, you must take a much larger view of things! Otherwise these most unscrupulous arch-rascals will seduce you, and you will have no faith at all. Hence the truth that

11. John 12$^{39f.}$
12. John 9$^{39-41}$.

way in which all the poor folk[82] are led astray by these supercilious bacchanalians.[83] Hence the truth that has been suppressed[84] must some day emerge boldly into the open, having slept for so long. Things have come to such a pass that if a Christian told the poor folk that he had learned the Christian faith from God himself, no one (given our present lack of readiness)[85] would believe him, unless he harmonised the account he gave of how all the elect should be taught by God[86] with Scripture; John 6, Isaiah 54, Jeremiah 31, Job 35, Psalms 17, 24, 33, 70, 93;[87] many other passages of Scripture also urge everyone to be taught by God alone.

If someone had never had sight or sound of the Bible at any time in his life he could still hold the one true Christian faith because of the true teaching of the spirit, just like all those who composed the holy Scripture without any books at all. And he would have the fullest assurance that he had such faith from the one true God and not from the fraudulent god of the devil[88] or from his own natural reason. So he must always be ready to explain exactly how he came to his faith[89] to any who have a tried and genuine faith, tried like gold in the fire of the severest, heart-felt anguish.[90] Otherwise disdain and contemptuous derision would be the sole reaction of those delicate types who have never given the slightest thought to true faith at any time in their lives. For they imagine that one should just believe the fictions with which the arch-seducers sally forth.[91]

If we Christians are now to join harmoniously, Psalm 72,[92] with all the elect, of every sect[93] and tribe and of every faith, as is clearly

82. *der arm hauff.*

83. *bachanten*; perhaps *Vaganten*, wandering scholars, bletherers. (F.)

84. *verhaltene = vorenthaltene*, 'kept back'.

85. *wie wir noch geschickt sind*; Hinrichs suggests: 'although we are prepared (to concede this)'; but cf. F., p. 421/27; a misprint for *ungeschickt* (Scott)?

86. *wen er mit der schrifft durch seyn berechen nicht übereynstympte, wie alle ausserwelten sollen von Got gelert werden*; Müntzer is distinguishing in this paragraph between Scripture as corroborative testimony to a God-given faith, and Scripture as the sole norm of faith; as the next paragraph shows, for Müntzer faith is possible without Scripture; but this priority of personal faith has been denied by the scholars and lost sight of by the common man.

87. John 6[45]; Isaiah 54[13]; Jeremiah 31[33f.]; Job 35[10f.]; Psalm 18[28]; 25[5, 14]; 34[4-8, 11]; 71[17]; 94[10, 12]; the references in B to John 8 and Psalm 112 are probably a copyist's slip for John 6, Psalm 17. (F.)

88. *vom abgekunterfeyten des teufels.*

89. *berechen mit aller ankunfft.*

90. 1 Peter 1[6f.]; F. suggests Ecclesiasticus 2[5].

91. *man soll glauben, wie die ertzverfürer rausser faren mit irem gedicht.*

92. Psalm 73(?); more accurate in B: Psalm 68[33](F.); cf. Luther's quite different use of this psalm in the *Letter to the Princes*, LW 40, 57.

93. *unter allen zertrennungen*; in B *secten.*

has been suppressed must some day emerge boldly into the open, having slept for so long. Things have come to such a pass that if a Christian told ordinary Christians that he had learned the Christian faith from God himself, no one (given our present lack of readiness) would believe him, unless he could prove from Scripture how all the elect should be taught by God, John 8, Isaiah 54, Jeremiah 31, Job 35, Psalms 17[13], 24, 33, 70, 93; many other passages of Scripture also urge this.

If someone had never had sight or sound of the Bible at any time in his life he could still have a true faith because of the teaching of the spirit, just like all those who composed Scripture without any books. And he would have the assurance that he had such faith from the one true God and not from the fraudulent god of the devil or from his own natural reason. So he must always be ready to explain exactly how he came to his faith to any who have a tried and genuine faith, tried like gold in the fire. Otherwise disdain and contemptuous derision would be the sole reaction of those who have never striven for true faith at any time in their lives; just think that one should believe what the arch-seducers say.

If we Christians are now to raise our voices in harmony, Psalm 67 with all the elect, of every sect and tribe and of every faith, as is

---

13. not Ps. 112, misread by F. (Bräuer).

testified to us in the text of the historian of the apostles, chapter 10,[94] then we must know how someone who has been brought up from his youth among unbelievers feels, and who has come to experience the true work and teaching of God without the benefit of any books.

To this end one should use Scripture to form a friendly judgement about the excellent works and testimony of such people, and to instruct each one of them, whether Jew or Turk, distinguishing the spirits and seeing which are of God and which of the devil, 1 John 4.[95] Then our scholars will strut in demanding miracles, as is the wont of the godless biblical scholars, Mt. 12.[96] With a curt judgement they surrender to the devil anyone who says a single word against them; they make the spirit of Christ the butt of their derision, and, raising their voice and their pens, are audacious enough to say: 'This Spirit business is all very well,[97] but my writing is what really deserves praise; the real achievement is mine[98] etc.' They can be recognised by the fact that they plan ceaselessly, night and day, to slay those who speak a word about the spirit of God, just like the biblical scholars before they brought Christ to the cross.

They told Christ that the law of God did not predict him; today they say much the same, indeed much worse: that one should not begin with the spirit of Christ, or boast of having it, for anyone who does this shows obvious signs of being a false prophet. For (according to them) faith should come from Scripture, though these godless, delicate creatures can give no explanation or reason[99] to justify the acceptance or rejection of Holy Scripture except on the grounds that it has been handed down from of old, and so has been accepted by many. But this smarmy, copy-cat way[100] to justify their beliefs can also be used by the Jew, the Turk and all other peoples.

But what Mary and Zechariah, Abraham, Joseph, Moses and all the patriarchs tell us is the very opposite, for after the stirring[101] of the holy spirit in the abyss of the heart they paid no heed at all to the instructions of these abandoned and godless good-for-nothings, as Isaiah says in chapter 8.[102] For their decisions[103] and proposals cast disrepute on the work of the spirit of God.

94. Acts 10[1ff.] (the centurion Cornelius).

95. 1 John 4[1ff.]

96. Matthew 12[38]; 'But this spirit has still to prove that he is of God's people by a single miracle', Luther's *Letter to the Princes of Saxony*, LW 40, 59.

97. Lit. 'Spirit here, Spirit there'.

98. *ich habs gethon.*

99. *bewegung*, Beweggrund, 'motivation'.

100. *affenschmaltzische weyss*; cf. n. 81 above.

101. *anregen.*

102. Isaiah 8[12].

103. *vereynung*, perhaps 'conspiracy'.

testified to us in Acts 10, then we must know how someone who has been brought up among unbelievers feels, and who has come to experience the true work and teaching of God without the benefit of any books.

To this end one should use Scripture to form a friendly judgement about such excellent works, and to distinguish the spirits, seeing which are of God and which of the devil. Then along come our biblical scholars, without either faith or experience, and surrender such people to the devil; they make the spirit of Christ the butt of their derision, and plot and plan night and day how to slay such people, just like the biblical scholars before they brought Christ to the cross.

They told Christ that the law of God did not predict him; today they say much the same, indeed much worse: that one should not begin with the spirit of Christ, but faith should come from Scripture, although these godless men can give no reason to justify the acceptance or rejection of Scripture except on the grounds that it has been handed down from of old, and so has been accepted by many. The Turk and the Jew can do the same.

But what Mary and Zechariah, Joseph, Moses and Abraham and all the patriarchs tell us is the very opposite, for after the stirring of the holy spirit they paid no heed at all to the instructions of these abandoned and godless good-for-nothings, as Isaiah says in the eighth chapter about the decisions and proposals of their assemblies.

They declare, without becoming scarlet with shame: The holy Christian Church has agreed on this or that, this article is heresy, and so is this teaching. Yet they lack the slightest glimmering of understanding[104] and cannot bring forward the slightest argument why they have been attracted to the Christian faith rather than any other. Hence they are mercenary creatures,[105] these evil comforters of our poor, wretched, sad and grief-stricken fellow-men.

Second.

Anyone paying careful attention will be sure to find that Christian faith is quite impossible for a fleshly man, 1 Cor. 3.[106] Indeed if he goes on to look at this text he will see that this is also true of all right-believing people like Mary, Zechariah and Elizabeth; it is enough to make the hair of any sober, single-minded,[107] earnest, painstaking, well-tried man stand on end. Just see how this text treats it.

The angel declared to the mother of God:[108] 'Nothing is impossible for God.' Why, my most beloved? Why? Because of course, for our natural reason it was quite impossible, inconceivable, unheard-of, 1 Cor. 2; Isaiah 64.[109] Just as happens to all of us when we come to faith:[110] we must believe that we fleshly, earthly men are to become gods[111] through Christ's becoming man, and thus become God's pupils with him – to be taught by Christ himself, and become divine,[112] yes, and far more – to be totally transfigured into him, so that this earthly life swings up into heaven, Phil. 3.[113]

See what an impossible thing this was to all the godless and to the elect, when they hesitate![114] John 10, Psalm 81. They wanted to stone Christ to death when he spoke these words. O, my dear masters, how foolish the world becomes when the voice of God is declared to it properly, summoning it, when faith at first seems so impossible, to watch and wait to the end, Psalm 39.[115]

Now, now, why does Brother Soft Life or Father Pussyfoot[116] react

---

104. *nit das allergeringste seüfftzen.*
105. Cf. John 10[12].
106. 1 Corinthians 3[1].
107. *langweyligen*; the opposite of worldly distraction, *Kurzweil*; cf. p. 78/7ff.; p. 240/22 above.
108. Luke 1[37].
109. 1 Corinthians 2[9]; Isaiah 64[3f.]
110. *in der ankunfft des glaubens.*
111. *sollen götter werden durch die menschwerdung Christi.*
112. *vergottet seyn.*
113. Philippians 3[20f.]
114. John 10[33ff.], Psalm 82[5ff.]; important texts for Müntzer!
115. Psalm 40[1f.]
116. *leysentret.*

For they say: The Church has agreed on this or that; this is heresy, and so is that. Yet they know nothing about the true origin of faith, not a word about its true motivation.

Second.

Anyone paying careful attention will find that Christian faith is quite impossible for a fleshly man, 1 Cor. 3. Indeed if he goes on to look at this text he will see that this is also true of all experienced[14] people like Mary, Zechariah and Elizabeth; it is enough to make the hair of any sober, single-minded, earnest, painstaking,[15] well-tried man stand on end. See how this text treats it. The angel declared to the mother of God: 'Nothing is impossible for God.' Why, my most beloved? Why? Because of course, for our natural reason it was quite impossible, inconceivable,[16] unheard-of 1 Cor. 2; Isaiah 64. Just as happens to all of us when we come to faith: we must believe that we fleshly, earthly men are to become gods through Christ's becoming man, and thus become God's pupils with him – to be taught by Christ himself, and by his spirit, and become divine, to be totally transfigured into him, so that this earthly life swings up into heaven, Phil. 3.

See what an impossible thing this was to all the godless and to the elect, when they hesitate! John 10, Psalm 81. They wanted to stone Christ to death when he spoke these words. O, my dear masters, how foolish the world becomes when the voice of God is declared to it properly, summoning it, when faith at first seems so impossible, to watch and wait to the end Psalm 39.

Now, now, why does Brother Soft Life or Father Pussyfoot react

---

14. *wolgeubten*; in A *wolglaubigen*.
15. *bittern*; cf. A *biddern*.
16. *ungeachts*; cf. A *ungedachts*.

so vigorously, even agitatedly? Job 28.[117] You see, he rather fancied the idea of trying out all the pleasures he had planned, and of holding on to his status and his prosperity, and yet combining this with a well-tried faith, although the son of God had criticised the biblical scholars for precisely this, John 5,[118] when he declared: 'How can you possibly come to faith as long as it is your own reputation that you are pursuing?'

Another impossibility is outlined in Matthew 6,[119] where the pleasure-loving unbelievers are told: 'You cannot serve God and mammon.' Anyone who lets such honours and goods take possession of him[120] will in the end be left forever empty by God, as God says in Psalm 5.[121] Their heart is vain. This is why powerful, self-willed unbelievers must be torn down from their seats, because they hinder the advancement of the true, holy Christian faith in themselves and in the whole world, just when it is about to burst forth in all its pristine truth.

For example, when the grace of God was manifested by the birth of John and the conception of Christ Herod was the ruler, with his pious blood, which oozes out of the sack from this world's noblefolk.[122] This was in order that the height of goodness and nobility should be seen more clearly in the light of its godless opposite.[123] Just as in our time – when God is sending his light into the world – the godless, senseless human powers and authorities betray themselves by all manner of arbitrariness, and by openly ranting and raging with all their might against God and all his anointed ones Psalm 2, 1 John 2.[124] Some are now really beginning to fetter and shackle their people, to flay and fleece them, menacing the whole people of Christ in the process, and cruelly torturing and killing their own subjects and others with ruthless severity. As a result, God who sees the struggles[125] of his elect, will not endure their lamentations any longer and is sure to shorten the days for his elect, Mt. 24.[126] Otherwise folk would have

---

117. Job 28[15ff.]

118. John 5[44].

119. Matthew 6[24].

120. *wer dieselbigen ehr und gütter zum besitzer nimpt*; on 'possession' cf. Prague Manifesto, p. 357, n. 6 below.

121. Psalm 5[9f.]; cf. Luke 1[52].

122. Lit. 'the pious blood'; this sarcastic term seems to introduce a reference to the massacre of the innocents, Matthew 2[16]; Müntzer uses *pulversack* to indicate a man of violence; the 'sack' is a graphic image for a body, stuffed either with gunpowder, or with worms; perhaps here it characterises the bloodthirsty tyrant; cf. p. 284/23 below.

123. Cf. the interesting parallel in his understanding of Scripture, p. 262/9 above.

124. Psalm 2[1ff.]; 1 John 2[16-20].

125. *nach dem ringen*; cf. Mark 13[20].

126. Matthew 24[22].

so vigorously, even agitatedly? Job 28. You see, he rather fancied the idea of trying out all the pleasures he had planned, and of holding on to his status and his prosperity, and yet combining this with a well-tried faith, although the son of God had criticised the biblical scholars for precisely this, John 5, when he declared, 'How can you possibly come to faith as long as it is your own reputation that you are pursuing?'

Another impossibility is outlined in Matthew 6, where the self-indulgent are told, 'You cannot serve God and mammon.' Anyone who lets these honours and riches take possession of him will in the end be left forever empty by God, Psalm 5. Their heart is vain. This is why unbelievers who hold power must be torn down from their seat, because they hinder the advancement of the true, holy faith in themselves and in the whole world, just when it is about to burst forth in all its pristine truth.

For example, when grace was manifested by the birth of John and the conception of Christ Herod was the ruler, in order that the height of goodness and nobility should be seen more clearly in the light of its godless opposite. Just as in our time – when God is sending his light into the world – the godless authorities betray themselves by ranting and raging against God and his Christ, Psalm 2.

Some are now really beginning to chain and fetter their people, to flay and fleece them, threatening the whole world[17] in the process, and cruelly torturing their own subjects. As a result, God does not want to witness their lamentations any longer and is sure to shorten the days of his elect Mat. 24. Otherwise men would have accepted Christ's

17. 'The people of Christ' in A.

accepted Christ's becoming man without thinking about it properly[127] and the outcome would have been nothing but pagans and devils, and much worse sects than at the beginning. Hence Paul says, 1 Cor. 10,[128] that God is completely faithful to his loved ones, not loading more on them than they can bear, although man's nature always thinks that too much has been laden onto it. The kind and almighty father only lays aside the birch when the child has recognised his guilt, and agrees that it has merited such wicked authorities, one side being as coarse as the other.[129]

How does that help us, my dearest friends, to understand this gospel? See how this text, without beating about the bush, describes Herod, in whose time Christ and John were conceived and born:[130] He has torn down the mighty from their seat, since they presume to exercise authority over the Christian faith and to subject it to their will, although they themselves have no intention at all of learning how faith comes about. On the one hand they refuse to let anyone learn about it, on the other they set about condemning everyone. The sole reason they want to be supreme is so that everyone should hold them in awe, honour and respect. At the same time they try to anathematize[131] the gospel in the most scandalous ways they can think up. Here the true nature of Herod, that is, of secular rule, is explained, as prophesied by holy Samuel, 1 Samuel 8,[132] and by the truly visionary prophet Hosea, Hosea 13:[133] 'In his rage God has given the world lords and princes; and in his exasperation he will do away with them again.'

Since man has fallen from God to serve the creatures[134] it is only just that he has (to his cost) to fear the creature more than God. Hence Paul says to the Romans in chapter thirteen[135] that princes are not there to frighten men into good deeds but to threaten doers of evil deeds with the hangman. Hence they are nothing but hangmen and jailers; that is the whole scope of their trade. For what else are evil deeds but man's preferring the creature to God, rendering the former attention and fear and esteem? Ah! and why does that come about? Because (as is all too evident) no one has enough earnest zeal to make God his first priority in all that he does and leaves undone. Ah yes,

---

127. *durch keyn recht betrachten*; i.e. if there had been no suffering involved.
128. 1 Corinthians 10[13].
129. *mit umbstendigkeyt beyder grobheyt.*
130. Luke 1[52].
131. *verketzern.*
132. 1 Samuel 8[4ff.]
133. Hosea 13[11].
134. *von Gott zun creaturn gefallen.*
135. Romans 13[3].

becoming man without thinking about it properly and the outcome would have been nothing but pagans and devils, and much worse sects than at the beginning. Hence Paul says I Cor. 10 that God is completely faithful to his loved ones, not loading more on them than they can bear, although man's nature always thinks that too much has been laden onto it. The kind father only lays aside the birch when the child has recognised his guilt, and agrees that it has merited such wicked authorities.

How does that help us to understand this gospel? See how this text describes Herod, in whose time Christ and John were conceived: He has torn down the mighty from their seat, since they presume to exercise authority over faith and to subject it to their will, although they themselves have not learnt how faith comes about. Yet they set about condemning everyone. The sole reason they want to be supreme is so that everyone should hold them in awe, honour and respect. At the same time they try to anathematize the gospel in the most scandalous ways. Here the nature of secular rule is explained, as prophesied by holy Samuel, 1 Samuel 8, and by the visionary prophet Hosea, Hosea 13, 'In his rage God has given the world lords and princes; and in his exasperation he will do away with them again.'

Since man has fallen to serve creatures it is only just that he has to fear the creature more than God. Hence Paul says, Romans 13, that princes are not there to frighten men into good deeds but to deter them from evil deeds. For what else are evil deeds but man's preferring the creature to God? Ah! and why does that come about? Because no one sets God alone before his eyes in true, earnest and pure fear, as Christ commanded so firmly and forcefully, Luke 12, like God through Moses Deut. 6. Mary, too, has described the advent of her faith (which is a pattern for all the elect) in a similar way: 'His mercy is from generation to generation upon all who fear him.'

what prevents the fear of God from becoming pure is the hunger for human favour, Psalm 18,[136] although Christ issued a hard, really forceful prohibition of this Luke 12,[137] like the earlier one by Moses, Deut. 6.[138] Mary, too, has described the advent of her faith (which is a pattern for all the elect) in a similar way:[139] 'His mercy is from generation to generation upon all who fear him.'

When the spirit of the fear of God is given due attention[140] by the elect then the whole world, whether it wants to or not, will learn to fear an upright champion of the dignity of God, as is said of David in the first book of the history of the patriarchs 1 Chr. 14.[141] But unless someone fears God alone from the abyss of his heart God cannot be gracious to him, as anyone can see by noting the negative corollary of Mary's words.[142] We cannot be liberated from the hands of all who hate us; nor can the generous mercy of God illumine our darkness (of which we are not even aware) until we have been emptied by the fear of God to begin receiving his endless wisdom. Hence the clear words of Psalm 144:[143] The Lord does the will of those that fear him; the fear with which they are filled in the wisdom, and the understanding, and the knowledge of God, Coloss. I.[144] Thus the world will not open its eyes to the advent of faith.

For this reason it has to devote all its intelligence and all its energies to great and mighty efforts in the service of a poor, wretched, pathetic sack of powder,[145] shamelessly preferring it to God. Thus the world is too coarse to perceive God's judgement. As a result the wisdom of God, the true Christian faith, has become so alien, rare, hidden, unknown, and totally impossible that no tongue can describe it, no eye lament or bewail it enough. A man who has been caught up (in the fear of God)[146] cannot hear or read too often that the true, precious wisdom of God, the true Christian faith, has been dishonoured and scorned. For those who lack the spirit and have no fear of God have been received into the Christian fold and have to be given public respect; no one can deny this if he keeps his eyes open.

Abraham, as chapter 20 of the book of creation, describes,[147]

---

136. Psalm 19[10].
137. Luke 12[4f., 8f.]
138. Deuteronomy 6[4f.]
139. Luke 1[50]; cf. p. 266/21ff. below.
140. *recht versorget wirt.*
141. 1 Chronicles 14[17].
142. *auss dem gegenteyl der wort Marie.*
143. Psalm 145[19].
144. Colossians 1[9].
145. Cf. n. 122 above.
146. *ein entsetzter mensch.*
147. Genesis 20[11ff.] (declares Sarah his sister!).

When the spirit of the fear of God is given due attention by the elect, Psalm 18,[18] then the whole world will learn to fear a righteous man, as is told of David in the book of the history of the patriarchs, 1 Chr. 14. But unless someone fears God alone from the abyss of his heart God cannot be gracious to him, as anyone can see by noting the negative corollary of Mary's words. We cannot be liberated from the hands of all who hate us; nor can the generous mercy of God illumine our darkness (of which we are not even aware) until we have been emptied by the fear of God to begin receiving his wisdom. Hence the clear words of Psalm 144: The Lord does the will of those that fear him. Thus the world will not open its eyes to the advent of faith.

For this reason it has to devote all its intelligence and all its energies to great and mighty efforts in the service of a poor, pathetic sack of powder, shamelessly preferring it to God. Thus the world is too coarse to perceive God's judgement. As a result the wisdom of God, the Christian faith, has become so hidden, unknown, and impossible that no tongue can describe it, no eye lament or bewail it enough. A man who has been caught up (in the fear of God) cannot tire of hearing or reading how deplorably Christian faith, has been dishonoured and scorned. For those who lack the spirit[19] and have no fear of God have been received into the Christian fold and have to be given public respect; no one can deny this.

Abraham, as chapter twenty of the book of creation described,

---

18. Psalm 19[10].
19. *genadlosen*, for *geystlosen*, (A), as Hinrichs suggests?

conducted all his affairs in Gerar in the fear of God, and it was by this that the angel of God recognised him, Gen. 22.[148] He was terribly alarmed,[149] and if he had not known the fear of God working within him he would have been unable to draw the line between the impossible and the possible. The same happened to Zechariah and Elizabeth[150] although they were righteous people in the eyes of both God and the world. They feared God above all things; yet they were unable to distinguish between the possible and the impossible since the spirit of the fear of God which heralds faith had not been revealed to them. So Zechariah could not believe the angel, understandable enough in the circumstances,[151] since his wife was both old and barren. The only conclusion seemed to be that she could never become pregnant.

O, my most beloved brothers, what else is this gospel really reminding us of? That faith, when first kindled,[152] confronts us with things so impossible that our delicate friends could never dream of them coming to pass. The whole senseless, deluded world brandishes its own false gloss, saying with its sharp little tongue:[153] Now, now, there really is no problem about preaching the gospel and fearing God alone, while simultaneously revering unintelligent rulers who offend against all equity and do not accept the word of God. Indeed, for God's sake, one ought to be obedient to the good gentlemen[154] in every respect. Welcome to you, then, you defender of the godless! That must be grand, really grand, to serve in this laudable manner two masters who are opposed to one another,[155] as the counsellors of the rulers do. Aha, how inventive the clever mind becomes in such situations, preening and adorning itself most fetchingly with the pretence of love for its neighbours. Yes, it is quite impossible, today more so than at any time since the corrupt kingdom started, for the world as a whole to bear the terrible blow.[156] Indeed to countless people it all seems pure[157] fantasy. They are bound to consider that a ploy like this can never be launched and executed: to tear the godless from their judgement seats and raise up humble, coarse folk in their

148. Genesis 22[11f.] (sacrifice of Isaac).
149. *entsetzt*.
150. Luke 1[5-25].
151. *ey nach gelegner sach*.
152. *mit alle seynem ursprunge*.
153. Cf. p. 270/30 above.
154. *junckern*.
155. Luke 16[13].
156. *den puff halten*; cf. p. 245/14ff. above.
157. *mechtig gross*; Müntzer may be contrasting the size of the stone (Christ) which will destroy the old kingdom and the unbounded fantasy attributed to him by Luther.

wandered around in Gerar in the fear of God. He conducted all his affairs in the fear of God, and it was by this that the angel of God recognised him, Gen. 22. He was terribly alarmed, and if he had not know the fear of God working within him he would have been unable to draw the line between the impossible and the possible. The same happened to Zechariah and Elizabeth although they were righteous people in the eyes of both God and the world. They feared God above all things; yet they were unable to distinguish between the possible and the impossible since the spirit of the fear of God which heralds faith had not been revealed to them. So Zechariah could not believe the angel, understandable enough in the circumstances since his wife was barren. The only conclusion seemed to be that she could never become pregnant.

O, my most beloved brothers, what else is the gospel really reminding us of? That faith, when first kindled, confronts us with things so impossible that untried, fleshly people could never dream of them coming to pass. The whole senseless, deluded, world brandishes its own false gloss, saying: Now, now, there really is no problem about preaching the gospel and fearing God alone, while simultaneously revering unintelligent rulers and being obedient in every respect. That must be grand, really grand, to serve in this laudable manner two masters. Aha, how inventive the clever mind becomes in such situations, adorning itself with love for its neighbours. Yes, it is quite impossible, today or at any time since the corrupt kingdom started, for the world as a whole to bear the terrible blow. Indeed to countless people it all seems pure fantasy, that a ploy like this can be executed: to tear the godless from their judgement seats and raise up humble folk in their place.

place.[158] On this point they shut their ears to Mary, although she is their most beloved matron; they will not let her open her mouth. O Mary, how much harm will your words continue to cause because of your admirers, who want to govern other people, but could not deal with a louse down their shirt[159] if they had to?

To the world and its scum, the biblical scholars, with their untested faith, nothing seems more impossible than that the lowly should be raised up and separated off from the evil-doers. Yes, that is the whole difficulty, the real rub![160] They refuse to give any attention to the text in Matthew 13[161] about the separation of the godless from the elect. On this question they have taken up the old idea of a pair of scales, dreaming of angels armed with long spears separating the good from the bad on the Last Day.[162] It seems [163] they can turn up their nose at the holy spirit. They have the nerve to say that God never reveals his judgements. Hence they repudiate angels who are true messengers, coming (as Malachi says) to divide off the good from the evil. But you cannot really hold that against our pious people, the biblical scholars, for, as anyone can see, they are *neutrales*, that is arch-hypocrites supreme, who could surely carry the yoke on both shoulders. They declare barefacedly, these most trustworthy[164] people, that no one can know who is chosen or damned. O, yes, they have such a strong faith, one so mightily assured that its sole concern is to defend the godless. Still, though, it is a fine enough faith and will do a lot of good yet: for it will certainly produce a subtle nation; just as the philosopher Plato wove speculations in his *Republic* and Apuleius in his *Golden Ass*, and just like the dreamers Isaiah spoke of in chapter 29.[165] To legitimise their wantonness they brandish the text of St Paul in 2 Timothy 2[166] as a fig leaf, as is their custom. They say: 'The Lord knows who are his.' This is true, my dear fellow, but you must abandon this plucking of

158. Luke 1[51f.]

159. Lit. 'on their chest'.

160. *Ja, da da ist der recht schwer gantz reyf.*

161. Matthew 13[47-50].

162. *Sie haben daselbst imaginirt, auss eynem alten balcken visiert, die engel mit langen spiessen, die sollen absündern die gutten von den bösen zum jungsten tage;* Müntzer's point is that it is convenient for the separation to be put off until then; the custodian angels, and St Michael with his scales, appear frequently in contemporary art; Maron's reference to the Danzig painting by 'Hans Memling' is unconvincing: 'Thomas Müntzer als Theologe des Gerichts', ZKG 83 (1972), 201 n. 63; Dismer, p. 98, n. 5, sees it as a reference not to a set of scales (*balcken*) but to a measuring-stick (*Visierhölzchen*).

163. Lit. 'I think'.

164. *die vilglaubertgen*; possibly a play on *bart*, beard, in B, *glaubwirdigen*.

165. Isaiah 29[8]; as F. comments the whole sentence is ironic; F. refers to the *Golden Ass* III, 24 when Lucius, yearning to fly, is turned into an ass.

166. 2 Timothy 2[19].

On this point they shut their ears to Mary, although she is their most beloved matron; they will not let her open her mouth. O Mary, how much harm will your words continue to cause because of your admirers, who want to govern other people, but could not deal with a louse down their shirt?

To the world and the biblical scholars,[20] with their untested faith, nothing seems more impossible than that the lowly should be raised up and separated off from the evil-doers. Yes, that is the whole difficulty, the real[21] rub! They refuse to give any attention to the text in Matthew 13 about the separation of the godless from the elect. On this question they have taken up the old idea of a pair of scales, dreaming of angels armed with long spears separating the good from the bad on the Last Day. It seems they can turn up their nose at the holy spirit. They have the nerve to say that God never reveals his judgements. Hence they repudiate angels who are true messengers of God, coming to divide off the good from the evil. But you cannot really hold that against our pious people, the biblical scholars, for they are *neutrales*, that is, people who could carry the yoke on both shoulders. They declare bare-facedly, these most trustworthy people, that no one can know who is chosen or damned. O, yes, they have such a strong faith, one so mightily assured that it has no sense at all.

Still, though, it is a fine enough faith and will do a lot of good yet: for it will certainly produce a subtle nation; to legitimise their wantonness they brandish the text of St Paul in 2 Timothy 2, as a fig leaf, as is their custom. They say: 'The Lord knows who are his.' This is true, my dear fellow, but you must abandon this plucking of texts out of context and make way for the word which immediately

20. Their characterisation as 'scum' in A is omitted.
21. *schire*, in A *gantz*.

texts out of context and make way for the word which immediately follows in the text: 'Let him who seeks the name of God depart from evil deeds.' However great a sinner he may be, the conscience of the elect man will direct him away from his sins, as long as he senses the movement of the spirit during his time of tribulation, as Psalm 39 testifies.[167] But the conscience of the godless does not do this, as Psalm 35 points out.[168] It is always on the look-out for fornication and greed and arrogance. No foul trick is beneath him. That is how he sallies forth. Never again can he set his face against wickedness, although like Judas he may manifest a gallows-bird's repentance during Holy Week.[169] But in the ground of his heart what he is after – like the rich man in this gospel, Luke 12[170] – is a long and lusty life. He wants to be of good cheer all the day long. He honestly thinks that it was for this that he was created.[171]

Third.

Thirdly, one has to understand how the heart of the elect is always moved by the power of the Most High to return to its origin. Therefore he is continually saying, Psalm 50:[172] 'O Lord, my sin is before my eyes always. Do not take your holy spirit from me.' In this state of fear the spirit of God becomes so manifest that the heart is completely melted and ready to receive the gift of God. Now God cannot spurn the rueful and humbled heart; he really has to listen to it, since it makes truly good incense, giving out the sweetest scent,[173] though one which is altogether lost on many a God-fearing man. Because he lacks understanding, its fullness[174] is quite beyond him, Psalm 30, until it is disclosed in the great trial out of which understanding[175] finally comes,[176] Psalm 33; 1 Peter 2.

See now how Zechariah[177] went into the temple, as the Law commanded, just as in Psalm 5,[178] 'I will go into your house, I will pray before your holy temple in holy fear, that you may lead me into your righteousness on account of my enemies.' Zechariah himself explains that in this song of praise: that we may serve God in holiness

---

167. Psalm 40[1f., 12f.]
168. Psalm 36[1ff.]
169. *wiewol er auch mit Juda in der marterwochen ein galgenrew hat*; Matthew 27[5].
170. Luke 12[16-21].
171. Cf. p. 292/5f. below.
172. Psalm 51[3, 11].
173. Ephesians 5[2].
174. *mit irer menge*; Psalm 31[9-13].
175. *in die verstendige anfechtung.*
176. Psalm 34[19]; 1 Peter 2[9f., 19ff.]
177. Luke 1[8f.]
178. Psalm 5[7f.]

follows in the text: 'Let him who seeks the name of God depart from evil deeds.' However great a sinner he may be, the conscience of the elect man will direct him away from his sins, if he senses the movement of the spirit during his time of tribulation, as Psalm 39 testifies. But the conscience of the godless does not do this, Psalm 35: the godless man says.[22] It is always on the look-out for fornication and greed and arrogance. No foul trick is beneath him. Never again can he set his face against wickedness, although like Judas he may manifest a gallow's-bird's repentance during Holy Week. But in the ground of his heart what he is after – like the rich man Luke 12 – is a long and lusty life. He wants to be of good cheer all the day long. He honestly thinks that it was for this that he was created.

Third.

Thirdly, one has to understand how the heart of the elect is always moved by the power of the Most High to return to its origin. Therefore he says, Psalm 50: 'O Lord, my sin is before my eyes always. Do not take your holy spirit from me.' Then the spirit of the fear of God becomes so manifest that the heart is completely melted. Now God cannot spurn the rueful and humbled heart; he really has to listen to it, since it makes truly good incense, giving out the sweetest scent, though one which is altogether lost on many a God-fearing man. Because he lacks understanding, its fullness is beyond him, Psalm 30, until it is disclosed in the great trial out of which understanding finally comes, Psalm 33; 1 Peter 2.

See now how Zechariah went into the temple, as the Law commanded, just as in Psalm 5, 'I will go into your house, I will pray before your holy temple in holy fear, that you may lead me into your righteousness on account of my enemies.' Zechariah himself explains that in this song of praise: that we may serve God in holiness and righteousness and cast aside all fear of men. That is the one, true, tested

---

22. *dixit iniustus*, the opening words of Psalm 35 (Vg.).

and righteousness and cast aside all fear of men. That is the one, true, tested faith which is well pleasing to him. How can we put it most plainly? Every man should beat a track into his own self[179] and then, when he is moved, realise that he himself is a holy temple, 1 Cor. 3, 6[180] destined for God from all eternity, and that he has been created for this alone: to accept the holy spirit as the schoolmaster of his faith and be receptive to[181] all the workings of the holy spirit, John 14, 16; Rom. 8.[182] He should realise, too, that this same temple has been grievously devastated by the unlearned priests. O, all creatures[183] should look with compassion at this universal failure to recognise such abomination[184] in the holy place. The poor folk cannot enter into themselves because of the poison of the godless. Everyone still hangs around outside the entrance to the temple[185] and waits until things take a turn for the better.

The ordinary folk have always imagined, and to this day still do so, that the priests must know about faith since they have read many fine big books about it. And so the poor common man says: O yes, these men with their red and brown birettas are fine fellows. Surely they must know what is right and what is wrong? But in fact these people (although they claim to be Christians) are quite lacking in judgement. Despite the most urgent command of Christ to distinguish the false servants of Christ from the true ones, Mt. 7[186] they pay no attention and spend all their energies accumulating material goods.[187] Hence each of them stays outside the temple, his great unbelief preventing him from entering into his own heart. The business of getting his daily bread stops him recognising his unbelief. It is about this that the holy spirit laments in Jeremiah.[188] What's more, now that the ordinary folk have got used over a long period of time to relying implicitly on the priest and biblical scholar he has become a dumb idol. He knows much less about God than a block of oak or a pebble. The words of Psalm 30 are fulfilled:[189] 'The lips of the perfidious are stilled.'

---

179. *in sich selber schlahen.*

180. 1 Corinthians 3[16f.]; 6[19].

181. *all seiner wirckung warneme.*

182. John 14[26]; 16[13]; Romans 8[14].

183. Note the reference in the previous few lines to the whole purpose of creation which is being thwarted by the present clergy.

184. Cf. Matthew 24[15], here related to the temple of the soul.

185. Cf. Luke 1[10, 21].

186. Matthew 7[15].

187. *vil creaturen*, 'creatures' used in negative sense.

188. Cf. Lamentations 2[12]; 4[5].

189. Psalm 31[18].

faith which is well pleasing to him. How can we put it most plainly? Every man should beat a track into his own self and then, when he is moved, realise that he himself is a holy temple, 1 Cor. 3, 6 destined for God from all eternity, and that he has been created for this alone: to accept the holy spirit as the schoolmaster of this faith and be receptive to all the workings of the holy spirit, John 14, 16; Rom. 8. He should realise, too, that the same temple has been grievously devastated by the unlearned priests. O, all creatures should look with compassion at this universal failure to recognise such abomination in the holy place. The poor folk have never entered into themselves. Everyone still hangs around outside the entrance to the temple and waits until things take a turn for the better.

The ordinary folk have always imagined, and to this day still do so, that the priests must know about faith since they have read many fine books about it. And so the common man says: O yes, these men with their red and brown birettas are fine fellows. Surely they must know? But in fact these people have poor judgment. Despite the urgent command of Christ to distinguish the false servants of Christ from the true ones, Mat. 7, they pay no attention, and spend all their energies accumulating material goods. Hence each of them stays outside the temple, his great unbelief, which he refuses to recognise, preventing him from entering into his own heart. It is about this that the holy spirit laments. Now that the ordinary folk have got used over a long period of time to relying implicitly on the priest and scholar he has become a dumb idol. He knows much less about God than a block of oak. The words of the prophet are fulfilled, Psalm 30: 'The lips of the perfidious are stilled.'

Then Jeremiah runs around in every direction,[190] through all the alley-ways, trying to find one man who is exerting himself to attain divine faith and judgement. He comes to the poor peasants and asks them about faith. They direct him to the priests and the biblical scholars. Yes, the poor, wretched peasants know nothing about it, since they have put their trust in the most poisonous people. So the prophet reflects:[191] O God, the peasants are poor, care-worn folk. They have spent their life in a grim struggle for bread in order to fill the throats of the most godless tyrants. What chance have such poor, coarse folk of knowing anything? Jeremiah goes on in chapter 5:[192] I thought: Lord, Lord I will go to the big-wigs.[193] Surely they will look after the poor folk and deal with them like good shepherds. They will make due provision in word and deed for their faith and judgment. I will talk with them about this; they will certainly know. Sure, sure, in fact they knew much less than the sorriest (peasant) did.

This is what the holy spirit prophesied through Hosea, chapter 4:[194] There is no desire for the knowledge of God on the earth. Like people, like priest Isaiah 24.[195] One blind man always leads another and they fall together in a heap into the ditch of ignorance and ruin, Mt. 15.[196] In such cases each tried to pretty himself up with the other's filth. In fact all share the guilt for the whole Christian congregation worshipping a dumb God.

How has this come to pass? Simply because every peasant wanted a priest, to ensure them an easy time.[197] Now they are no longer so enthusiastic, for nowhere in the world is there much concern to encourage a true priesthood. On the contrary, the world tends to knock a true priest's head off, so that it rolls at his feet. A really good ministry tastes like bitter gall to it. One has to come out with the truth. When you consider the nobility of our souls we are much coarser than the unthinking beasts. Absolutely no one knows about anything except usury and the wiles of this world. When something is said about God, the saying of Solomon comes to mind:[198] Anyone who delivers a long sermon to a fool gets as his answer: 'Eh! What's that you said?' It is as if you were talking to someone half asleep.

---

190. *gerings rummer.*
191. Jeremiah 5⁴.
192. Jeremiah 5⁵.
193. *zun grossen hansen.*
194. Hosea 4⁶.
195. Isaiah 24².
196. Matthew 15¹⁴.
197. *darumb das sie gutte tag hetten*; they did not want a preacher who would challenge their easy-going ways; cf. p. 301/9f. below.
198. Proverbs 23⁹; a lively, if inaccurate rendering.

Then Jeremiah runs around in every direction, through all the alley-ways, trying to find one man who is exerting himself to attain divine faith and judgement. He comes to the poor peasants and asks them about faith. They direct him to the priests. O, they know nothing about it. So the prophet reflects: O God, the peasants are poor people. They have spent their life in a struggle for bread in order to fill the throats of the tyrants. What chance have such poor, coarse folk of knowing anything? Jeremiah goes on in the fifth chapter: I thought: Lord, Lord I will go to the big-wigs. Surely they will have faith and judgment. Sure, sure, in fact they knew much less than the sorriest (peasant) did.

That is what the holy spirit prophesied through Hosea, chapter 4: There is no desire for the knowledge of God on the earth. Like people, like priest, Isaiah 24. One blind man leads another and they fall together into the ditch of everlasting ruin, Matthew 15. In such cases each tries to pretty himself up with the other's filth. In fact all share the guilt for the whole Church worshipping a dumb God.

How has this come to pass? Simply because every peasant wanted a priest of his own, and because they had a good time. Now they are no longer enthusiastic, for in the world there is little concern to encourage a true priesthood, for a really true ministry tastes like bitter gall to it. One has to come out with the truth. When you consider the nobility of our souls we are much coarser than the unthinking beasts. Absolutely no one knows about anything except usury and the wiles of this world. When something is said about God, the saying of Solomon is fulfilled: Anyone who delivers a long sermon to a fool gets as his answer 'Eh! What's that you said?'

Hence we poor, wretched, pathetic Christians can only relate to God on the basis of what we have stolen from the book, and if this were to be taken from us (as is possible) there would be no way at all to help this coarse Christian people. Isn't that quite calamitous? But as yet no one takes it to heart. They think it should be hushed up. O what great, wretched blindness! If only everyone would learn to see with at least half an eye, John 9, Isaiah 6.[199]

Fourth.

If, on the other hand, the Christian people is to be set on its feet again then the usurious evil-doers must be done away with and put in charge of the dogs, for they are hardly fit to serve, and yet are supposed to be prelates of the Christian churches. The poor, common folk must exercise itself in the recollection of the spirit; it must learn to sigh, Rom. 8,[200] to pray and long for a new John,[201] for a preacher full of grace, whose faith is solidly based on the experience of his unbelief; for he has to know what it feels like to be a notorious unbeliever, and he has to know that his faith measures up to his passionate desires, Eph. 4, Psalm 67.[202] If this were not the case then this untried Christian faith would be much worse than the blasphemies of the devil against God in the abyss of hell.

Therefore someone[203] must arise who will point men to the revelation of God's little lamb, who comes from the father as the judgement[204] of the eternal word. In this passage you can see very well that the people drew its own conclusions about the length of time Zechariah spent in the temple. For the people could work it out quite well; they concluded from his long delay in the temple that he must have had a vision.[205]

Thus on that occasion people's minds were not so completely and resolutely closed as they are at the present time. Because of the scoundrelly biblical scholars the Christian people has not the least intention of believing that its God is nigh at hand, Deut. 4, Jeremiah

---

199. John 9[39ff.]; Isaiah 6[10].

200. Romans 8[22, 23].

201. The Baptist; cf. p. 280/17f. above.

202. Ephesians 4[7f.] Psalm 68[18]; *er mus der emsigen begir masse an dem masse des glaubens wissen.*

203. Cf. n. 201 above; cf. p. 262/11ff. above, p. 300/20ff. below; obviously a reference to Müntzer.

204. *urteyl;* 'the form' (Hinrichs); Maron argues that the sense of 'judgement' even 'last judgement' should not be lost, 'Thomas Müntzer als Theologe des Gerichts', 195ff.

205. Luke 1[22].

Hence we poor, wretched, calamitous Christians can only relate to God on the basis of what we have stolen from the book, and if this were to be taken from us (as is possible) there would be no way at all to help this coarse Christian people. Isn't that quite calamitous? But as yet no one takes it to heart. They think it should be hushed up John 9, Isaiah 6. O what great wretchedness! If only everyone would learn to see with at least half an eye.

Fourth.
If, then, the Christian people is to be set on its feet again[23] then the common folk must pray and long for a new John, for a preacher full of grace, whose faith is solidly based on experience; for he has to know what it feels like to be a notorious unbeliever, and he has to know that his faith measures up to his inclinations or desires, Eph. 4. Psalm 67. If this were not the case then this untried Christian faith would be much worse than the blasphemies of the devil against God in hell.

Therefore someone must arise who will point men to the revelation of God's little lamb, who comes from the father as the judgment of the eternal word. In this passage you can see very well that the people drew its own conclusions about the length of time Zechariah spent in the temple. For the people could work it out quite well; they concluded from his long delay in the temple that he must have had a vision.

Thus on that occasion people's minds were no so resolutely closed as they are at the present time. Because of the scoundrelly priests the Christian people has not the least intention of believing that its God may disclose his will to it.

23. Some fierce polemic omitted here.

23,[206] and may disclose his will to it. Just see how nervous[207] people have become about revelation these days, as Micah prophesied they would, Micah 3.[208]

Almost all of them say: Look, Scripture amply stills our needs, thank you, we don't believe in any revelation; God no longer speaks like that. Just imagine if such people had lived at the time of the prophets! Would they have been any more inclined to believe in them, or would they not rather have struck them dead? For they tap around in Holy Scripture so blindly that they refuse to open their eyes and ears to the way in which it exhorts us in the most emphatic manner possible that it is by God alone that we should, and indeed must, be taught.

If, on the other hand, anyone is to be filled with the good things of God which never pass away, then he must submit to long discipline and then be made empty by his suffering and cross so that his measure of faith may be filled up with the highest treasures of Christian wisdom, 2 Coloss., Eph. 4.[209] Everyone must receive the knowledge of God, the true Christian faith, not from the stinking breath of the devilish biblical scholars, but from the eternal, powerful word of the father in the son as explained by the holy spirit, so that in his soul he may know its length and width and breadth and depth and height Eph. 3.[210]

In short, there is no alternative: men must smash to pieces their stolen, counterfeit Christian faith by going through real agony of heart, painful tribulation, and the consternation which inevitably follows. Then a man becomes very small and contemptible in his own eyes; to give the godless the chance to puff themselves up and strut around the elect man must hit the depths. Then he can glorify and magnify God and, with his heart-felt tribulation behind him, can rejoice whole-heartedly in God, his saviour.[211] Then the great will have to give way to the lowly and be humiliated before the latter. O, if only the poor, rejected peasants knew that how useful it would be to them. God despised the big-wigs, like Herod and Caiaphas and Annas, and took into his service the lowly, such as Mary, Zechariah and Elizabeth. For that is the way God works, and to this day he has not changed 1 Cor. 1, Mt. 11, Luke 10.[212]

---

206. Deuteronomy 4[7]; Jeremiah 23[23].
207. *schewh.*
208. Micah 3[6f.]
209. Colossians 2[2f.]; Ephesians 4[9].
210. Ephesians 3[18].
211. Luke 1[47].
212. 1 Corinthians 1[26ff.]; Matthew 11[25]; Luke 10[21].

Just see how shy people have become of revelation these days, as Micah warned the world in chapter 3.

Almost all of them say: Look, Scripture amply stills our needs, thank you, we don't believe in any revelation; God no longer speaks like that. For they tap around in this Scripture so blindly that they refuse to open their eyes to the way in which it exhorts us in the most emphatic manner possible that it is by God alone that we should, and indeed must, be taught, if one is to be filled with the good things of God which never pass away, having submitted to long discipline and then been made empty by one's suffering and cross so that one's measure of faith may be filled up with the highest treasures, 2 Coloss., Eph. 4. Every member of the elect must receive the knowledge of God, the true holy Christian faith, from the mouth of God, so that he may know its length and breadth and height and depth, Eph. 3.

In short, there is no alternative: man must put away his stolen, counterfeit Christian faith by going through real tribulation and consternation, so that his soul can magnify God and, with his tribulation behind him, can rejoice wholeheartedly in God, his saviour. Then what is great will be confronted by what is lowly. God despised the great and took to himself the lowly. Luke 10, Mt. 11, 1 Cor. 1.

In men's eyes Zechariah was contemptible because his wife was barren; in accordance with the Law Mary, too, was completely despised, Mt. 13.[213] O, my dear friends, these were not great personalities[214] with pompous titles like those in the church of the godless now, Ps. 26.[215] Many poor, coarse folk imagine that the big, fat, greasy, chubby-faced types know everything about coming to the Christian faith.[216] O, my most dear friends, what sort of knowledge can they have, when they deny that we have any movement of faith, and curse and outlaw anything that goes against them, using the crudest abuse? For they have spent their life in drinking and gorging themselves like animals. From their youth on they have been brought up in the most delicate way; not one bad day have they had throughout their life; nor have they the least desire or intention to put up with one for the sake of the truth; or to exact one cent less interest for their money. And such people want to be regarded as judges and protectors of the faith. O, you poor Christian people, as a result of these clumsy dolts, you have become nothing but a chopping-block.[217] How wretchedly you are provided for because of them!

Fifth.

If the holy church is to be rejuvenated by the bitter truth a servant of God must step forward,[218] full of grace, and endowed with the spirit of Elijah, Mt. 17, 1 Kings 18, Rev. 11.[219] He must get everything into full swing.[220] Many of you really will have to be aroused to sweep the Christian people free of its godless rulers, with burning earnestness and the utmost zeal. The common folk, too, will first have to be chided very severely about its unbridled lusts, which pass the time so intemperately and divertingly that there is no resolute will[221] to take the faith earnestly. That is why so few people can say anything about the first movement of the spirit. Yes, it is all so laughable to them because they have never tasted the patient endurance[222] which is the

---

213. Matthew 13[55].
214. *grosse köpff.*
215. Psalm 26[4f.](!).
216. *gut urteyl über die ankunfft des christenglaubens beschliessen.*
217. Cf. p. 292/30 above.
218. Cf. n. 203 above.
219. Matthew 17[3ff., 11f.]; 1 Kings 18[1ff.]; Revelation 11[3] (Elijah as one of the two witnesses of the new age).
220. *in den rechten schwanck bringen.*
221. *on alle eynbleybenden muth.*
222. *langweyl*; contrasted with the previous reference to *verkurtzweylen* ('pass the time divertingly'); cf. n. 107 above.

Yes, they were people of the lowest standing. Zechariah was contemptible because of his barrenness;[24] in accordance with the Law Mary, too, was completely despised, Mt. 13. O, my dear friends, these were not great personalities with pompous titles like those in the church of the godless now Ps. 26. Everyone thinks that the big, chubby-faced types know about the Christian faith. What sort of knowledge can they have, when they curse and outlaw our coming to faith, using the crudest abuse? For they have spent their life in drinking and gorging themselves from their youth on and not a bad day have they had throughout their life; nor have they the least intention to put up with one for the sake of the truth. And such people dare all the same to claim leadership in matters of faith.

Fifth.
If the holy Church is to be rejuvenated by the truth a servant of God must step forward, full of grace, and endowed with the spirit of Elijah, Mt. 17, and must get everything into full swing, with the utmost zeal. For our Christian people will have to be chided very severely indeed about its lusts, so that they can put away all luxuriousness, intemperance and come to know the advent of faith in

24. *seiner unfruchtbarkeit.*

only way to discover the work of God Psalm 39.[223] The first step is the sprinkling, Numbers 19, by which the waters of divine wisdom are troubled, Ecclesiasticus 15.[224] Then in his sadness man[225] will become aware that God is setting quite extraordinary things in motion in him. His first step, therefore, is to tremble before the name of God, which is disclosed to him in the first movement of the work of God. For the whole of his life he will never rest from seeking this same name whole-heartedly, until God graciously gives him to understand that his own name has been inscribed in heaven from all eternity, Luke 10.[226] Otherwise he has no chance at all of having peace, joy and righteousness in his conscience, though this is his entitlement, as Romans 14, John 17 and Ephesians 1 point out.[227] He will have to go tapping around after the true God in darkness and the shadow of death. Falling time and time again, his feet will be led on the way of peace while experiencing the very opposite. All his desires will reach out towards the first sprinkling,[228] the gentle sighing breath of the holy spirit.[229] But it demands the continued application of all his diligence, for the holy spirit never allows him to be complacent, but drives him on restlessly, pointing him to the eternal good. A coarse person can only be brought to understand that after he has fallen into the most coarse and doltish sins. The unpolished man has to be continually gnawed and bitten and pricked, as Psalm 31 says,[230] so that he turns to God from his sins and learns to hate them. After all the creaturely lusts man must turn to God, for his natural self would collapse otherwise.[231] Not till then does he confess his unbelief and cry out for the doctor, whose boundless mercy is so great that he can never leave anyone in the lurch if he is poor in spirit like this.[232] Here is the origin of all goodness, the true kingdom of heaven. Now man becomes hostile to his sins and embraces righteousness with all sincerity; only now is he assured of his salvation and comprehends properly that God has driven him from the evil to the good by his unchangeable love, and from the sins through which his unbelief was

223. Psalm 40[2].
224. Numbers 19[19]; Ecclesiasticus 15[17, 3] (Vg.); cf.p. 239/27ff. above.
225. Lit. 'Then the sad man'.
226. Luke 10[20].
227. Romans 14[17]; John 17[13]; Ephesians 1[4].
228. Cf. the Prague Manifesto, p. 366/29f. below.
229. John 20[22].
230. Psalm 31[4] (Vg.) *conversus sum in aerumna mea, dum configitur spina*.
231. *es künd anderst seyn natürlichs wesen nicht bestehen*; B is simpler; sin is both hateful and pleasurable; until one turns to God, one cannot escape it.
232. Cf. Luke 5[31]; the emphasis on lack of true faith, so characteristic of Müntzer, may come from Jesus' healing miracles; righteousness as healing rather than justification?

the heart. The first happens with the sprinkling, Numbers 19, with the water of wisdom, Ecclesiasticus 15. Then the elect man will become aware that God is setting quite extraordinary things in motion in him. Therefore he trembles before the holy name of God and for the whole of his life he will never rest from seeking this same name wholeheartedly, until God graciously gives him to understand that his own name has been inscribed in heaven from all eternity, Luke 10. Otherwise he has no chance at all of having that peace, joy and righteousness which is his entitlement in the kingdom of God, Rom. 14, John 17, Eph. 1. He will come to know the true God in darkness and the shadow of death so that his feet will be led on the way of peace. All his desires will reach out towards the first sprinkling, Rom. 8.[25] This sprinkling and first breathing of the holy spirit would never cease, if man could keep his conscience pure by battling away chivalrously.[26]

Hence he sighs whenever he defiles himself and notices more and more clearly the pricks of a heavy conscience,[27] Ps. 31, so in the end he has to turn away from the creaturely lusts to God; not till then does he confess his unbelief and cry out for the doctor, who can never leave anyone in the lurch if he is poor in spirit like this. Here is the true kingdom of heaven. Now man becomes really hostile to his sins and is assured of his salvation and sees clearly that God has driven him from his sins and unbelief by his unchangeable love Jer. 31.

25. Romans 8[22f., 26].
26. *durch ritterlichen streit.*
27. Lit. 'the burden and pricks of the conscience'.

detected;[233] now he becomes altogether free, as described in Jeremiah 31.[234]

This, then, is how true faith must gain the victory, 1 John 5,[235] after it has overcome the world, whose existence within the heart is a thousand-fold more varied than outside it. After coming to this earnest recognition faith overflows; nothing can stop it from growing in the believer, from increasing its capital.[236] It is then, my literalistic fellow, that you learn how heavy your pound is. But you cannot weigh it until you have the scales of divine judgment to measure your heart, Psalm 118.[237] If, however, you choose to deride this increase of holy faith your own cheeks will flame in humiliation when it comes to your downfall, Proverbs 1.[238] But how can it be found?[239] According to the thieves of Scripture one is supposed just to believe in Scripture, without any recourse to the most secure testimony of all – that of the spirit – and then to creep away and get involved in all manner of usurious dealings,[240] in which the godless cling together like toad-spawn,[241] as Psalm 54 instructs us.[242] Usury and interest and dues prevent anyone coming to faith. The longer it goes on the more the damage being done to the world spreads and deepens so that even the way to any sort of human faith[243] becomes barred.

Intelligent judgements cannot be arrived at under such circumstances, and if we do not better ourselves very soon we will have lost our natural reason as well – because of the selfish way in which we all pursue our fleshly pleasures, Psalm 31, Isaiah 1.[244] Hence John the baptiser called the people, with their biblical scholars, a brood of vipers, Mat. 3, Luke 3,[245] since nothing but poison is produced when one preaches to pleasure-loving men. They garner

---

233. *gespôret = gespürt.*

234. Jeremiah 31 esp.vs. 3, 31ff.

235. 1 John 5[4].

236. *bleybt des glaubens überschwanck unvorhindert zu wuchern, zuzunemen in im*; cf. Luke 19[11-27].

237. Psalm 119[75]; *in erfoderung deynes hertzens*, to call your heart to judgement (Hinrichs).

238. Proverbs 1[26].

239. *Wie wolt sichs finden?*; cf. Luke 19[20f.]

240. An abrupt shift from a positive to a negative assessment of *wuchern*, increasing capital.

241. *wie krôtenreych*; 'kingdom of toads', perhaps in contrast to 'kingdom of heaven', p. 302/28 above; in B the normal term for toad-spawn is used on p. 305/7, and the reference to the snake, line 26, is reminiscent of the passage in the *Sermon to the Princes*, p. 244/29 above.

242. Psalm 55[10f.]

243. *dem menschlichen glauben*; explained by the following sentence.

244. Psalm 32[9]; Isaiah 1[3].

245. Matthew 3[7]; Luke 3[7].

True faith now appears, grows and increases all its spiritual capital.[28] It is then, my dear fellow, that you learn how heavy your pound is. Yes, it is so heavy that the mad, senseless world can never put it in the scales of judgement; it is always wanting to believe but slithers into its lusts like a snake. Hence John called pleasure-loving men a brood of vipers, Mat. 3, Luke 3. The godless cling together like toad-spawn in their counterfeit faith, since many share their views and despise true, genuine faith for being so rarely found and so impossible in its demands.

28. B is very substantially shorter at this point, omitting the pointed references, for example, to taxation; the compression makes the sense of the passage hard to follow.

the very worst from the very best, as today's Christians do with our precious faith. It would have been better for them if they had remained heathen like their fathers. Preaching to them is like talking to pigs in their filth, Mat. 7, Peter 2.[246] They rush off into the sea and suffocate, Mat. 8.[247] Anything one says to them about the manner or gravity of coming to faith, is a complete waste of time. They excuse themselves with lame, hackneyed posturings: Yes, we are poor sinners; but Christ did not despise sinners, so what right has this pharisaical type[248] to despise us? If I speak to them of the faith they have stolen they retort by excusing their sins, and justify themselves by referring to their pretended faith and love. They deny the visitation of God, for they have no desire to put on the blessed salvation proclaimed by the mouth of all the prophets from the very beginning. As a result they are left empty and without faith and love, although they most sturdily boast of having both. In reality they have not a scrap [249] of either, since they are such obvious hypocrites, swearing by the saints that they are pious Christians, although in fact they use every possible device to cast down faith everywhere. How can anyone who is stuffed with every kind of lie and goes on, like these thieves of Scripture, stuffing the world with them, Jeremiah 8[250] be a man of divine faith?

Christ was conceived by a pure virgin of the holy spirit, so that we should realise the harm caused by sin from the very beginning, for it came through our first parents, by the lust for the fruit of the forbidden tree, Gen. 3.[251] This threw the human body into disorder,[252] so that all the lusts of the body became obstacles to the working of the holy spirit, Wisdom 9.[253] All the days of a man's life are not sufficient to realise the harm that has been done and to combat it by determined self-renunciation, Ecclesiastes 2.[254] Now if someone who is negligent in such matters pretends a tearful penitence,[255] despite his intemperate life, while in fact looking like someone who has vomited, and keeps

---

246. Matthew 7[6]; 2 Peter 2[22].

247. Matthew 8[32].

248. Lit. 'spirit'; cf. Luther's *Letter to the Princes of Saxony*, LW 40, 57; the next four sentences are omitted from B.

249. *trümleyn* ('fragment').

250. Jeremiah 8[8f.]

251. Genesis 3[1ff.]

252. *verrücket*; as Dismer points out, p. 12 n. 3, Mary's body remains for Müntzer *unvorruckt*, like her chastity, F. p. 169/9f.; p. 175/2.

253. Wisdom 9[13ff.]

254. Ecclesiastes 2[11].

255. *ein saltzricht angesicht* (B *saltzig*); lit. 'a salty face'.

That is why they are not sober or free from lust though they even try to excuse their wicked life with lame, empty posturings: Yes, we are poor sinners; but Christ did not despise sinners, so what right has this pharisaical type to despise us?

Christ was conceived by a virgin of the holy spirit, so that we should realise the harm caused by sin from the very beginning, Rom. 5, and all the lusts became obstacles to the holy spirit. All the days of a man's life are not sufficient to experience the latter, Eccles. 2. Now if someone pretends a tearful penitence about such a weighty and serious matter, while in fact looking like someone who has vomited, and keeps on saying: Believe, believe! till the mucus bubbles out of your nose; his conduct is befitting to pigs rather than men.

on saying: Believe, believe! till the mucus bubbles[256] out of your nose; his conduct is befitting to pigs rather than men.

Anyone can blether on about faith as much as he wants. But these pleasure-loving, ambitious types have no credibility at all, for they have not practised what they preach. Hence Christ says in John 10:[257] The sheep should not listen to the voice of the strangers. Faith is alien to them, and they to it, for salvation is far from them, Ps. 118.[258] That is why they are beasts of the belly as well, Phil. 3.[259] They preach what suits them, but what they really pursue is the belly. Yes, yes, to keep it in good trim they gladly, reverently accept shining pieces of gold. They need hardly a hundredth of it, and yet they set themselves up as our evangelists. Therefore their teaching is without power, as it says at the end of the same seventh chapter of Matthew.[260] The sole and only outcome of their teaching is the freedom of the flesh. Hence they poison the Bible for the holy spirit. Sometimes one hears of them striking out on the right track for a while but it does not last long. No one can be reformed by them, for their teaching is a stolen one, Jeremiah 23.[261] So it leads no one to search his heart.

John,[262] however, is a very different preacher, an angel testifying to Christ, one mirrored[263] in all true preachers. They must be praised, like him, not for their meritorious deeds, but for their earnestness, a fruit of the undaunted[264] sobriety by which they aim to set all lusts aside, allowing the powers of the soul to be disclosed, so that the abyss of the spirit may emerge through all the powers and the holy spirit can then have his say, Psalm 84.[265] A preacher has to be wondrously driven to such disclosure from his very youth in a life of self-denial. Hence John was sanctified in the womb of his mother as an archetype of all preachers. Paul says that he was ordained from his mother's womb to proclaim the priceless riches of Christ.[266] This is why the preachers must know who it is that sends them out to the harvest, Mat. 9, John 4,[267] for which, like a strong scythe or sickle, they have been sharpened by God from the beginning of their lives. Not

---

256. *pflastere* (B *plostert*); lit. 'blooms'.
257. John 10[5].
258. Psalm 19[155].
259. Philippians 3[19].
260. Matthew 7[29].
261. Jeremiah 23[30].
262. John the Baptist again; Luke 1[15-17].
263. *angezeygt*.
264. *tapffer*.
265. Psalm 85[9-13].
266. Galatians 1[15f].
267. Matthew 9[38]; John 4[35-38]; cf. Joel 3[13]; Revelation 14[14ff].

Anyone can blether on about faith as much as he wants. But these pleasure-loving, ambitious types have no credibility, for they have not practised what they preach. The sheep should not listen to the voice of the strangers, John 10, for they are beasts of the belly Phil. 3. They preach what suits them, but what they really pursue is the belly. Yes, yes, they gladly, reverently accept shining pieces of gold. They need hardly a hundredth of it, therefore their teaching is without power, Matthew 7, at the end of the chapter. The sole and only outcome of their teaching is the freedom of the flesh. Their teaching is certainly heard, but no one is reformed, for their teaching is a stolen one, Jeremiah 23. So it leads no one to search his heart.

John, the angel who testifies truly to Christ, and is mirrored in all true preachers, was praised for his sobriety, not because of his works but because of his earnestness which aims to set all lusts aside, allowing the powers of the soul to be disclosed, so that the abyss of the spirit may emerge and the holy spirit can then have his say. A preacher has to be wondrously driven in this way from his very youth beyond his will[29]. Hence John was sanctified in the womb of his mother as an archetype of all preachers and Paul says that he was ordained from his mother's womb to proclaim the priceless riches of Christ. For we preachers must know who it is that sends us out to the harvest, for which, like a fine strong scythe or sickle, we have been sharpened by God from the beginning of our lives.

29. *uber seinen willen*; Scott notes the difference from A.

everyone can execute this office, even if he has read every book that has been written! For he must first have the assurance[268] of faith possessed by those who wrote the Scriptures, if it is not to be a mere war of words, a thievish blethering.

Sixth.

So it[269] can never condone the shameless pleading of those scoundrelly arch-hypocrites who want to be kinder than God himself, and defend the godless and accursed false preachers. They say: Whether a priest is good or bad, he can still administer the mysteries of God and preach the true word. These depraved defenders of their fellows, the godless, (one crow doesn't scratch out the eye of another) are clearly quite blind to the clear and unequivocal text in Exodus 23,[270] where God says – admittedly in relation to a lesser matter – 'I show no favour to the godless; you should not make his case look any better[271] than it is'. Moreover they offend much more against Psalm 49,[272] where the ordinances for the servant of God and the word he preaches are set out, and God says to the godless preacher: 'Who authorised you to preach about my righteousness? You take the testimony about my covenant into your mouth, and yet loath all correction.' As if he were saying: Do you really mean to preach to the world about my dear crucified son in order to fill your belly, not knowing that one's life has to be conformed to his? Rom. 8.[273] Do you really mean to be a schoolmaster to others, when you have not learned the knowledge yourself?

Hence the man who has put all worldly things behind him,[274] and has been roused by God from the desolation of his heart must take himself off and work zealously among the delicate, pleasure-loving types, who become as hard as adamant when it comes to accepting the truth. By his exemplary trials he must open others' eyes to the cross which he has come to know from his youth and must cry out into the wretched, desolate, erring hearts of the God-fearing, who are now beginning to watch out for the truth Luke 12.[275] O, how gladly they would come to true faith, if only they could come across it! The yearning of people like this is described in Psalm 62:[276] 'O God, my God, I have been waiting on you, in order to get light. My soul thirsts

---

268. *sicherheyt.*
269. The office of preaching; cf. Luther's *Letter to the Princes of Saxony*, LW 40, 57.
270. Exodus 23[1].
271. *schmücken* (not quite the Biblical text!).
272. Psalm 50[16f.]
273. Romans 8[29].
274. *der allergelassenste mensch.*
275. Luke 12[35ff.]
276. Psalm 63[1ff.]

Not everyone can execute this office, even if he has read every book that has been written! For he must first have the assurance of faith possessed by those who wrote the Scriptures.

Sixth.

So it can never condone the shameless pleading of those arch-hypocrites who want to be kinder than God himself and defend the godless and accursed preachers. They say: Whether a priest is good or bad, he can still administer the mysteries of God and preach his word. These depraved defenders of the godless act contrary to the clear text, Exod. 23, where God says: 'I am the enemy of the godless.' Then they err even more, this time against Psalm 49, where God says to the godless: 'Who authorised you to talk about my righteousness? You take my testament into your mouth, and yet loath all correction.' As if he were saying: Do you really mean to preach to the world about my dear crucified son in order to fill your belly, not knowing that one's life has to be the same as his? Rom. 8. Do you really mean to be a schoolmaster to others, when you have not learned the knowledge yourself?

Hence, dear brothers, a preacher who is full of grace must preach from the desert, that is from exemplary trials in which he has borne the cross, and must cry out into the desolate, wretched, erring hearts of the God-fearing, who are now beginning to watch out for the truth. O, how gladly they would come to true faith, if only they could come across it! The yearning of people like this is described in Psalm 62: 'O God, my God, I have been waiting on you, in order to get light. My soul thirsts for you. O, the countless troubles my flesh

---

30 *vorstehen ader vornemen.*

for you. O, the countless troubles my flesh has known in a desert land, trackless and waterless! There I learned that this is the way to experience your strength and glory.'[277] It is by his overshadowing[278] that the power of God is transmitted. How right it is to rejoice about the true preachers whom God is sending to earth in our time so that the true testimony of faith may come to light. Hence this text says:[279] 'Many will rejoice in him' etc. Hearts will be awakened from their negligence, which leads them to tarry in unbelief, prompting them to depart from it and to engage themselves in true faith through their common rediscovery of the testimony of Christ. You must keep the whole context in mind here, relating all the words to one another, if you are to understand what I am saying both about faith and about its impossibility.

The chosen friend of God experiences an overflowing, gladsome joy when his fellow and brother comes to faith in the same way as himself.[280] For example the mother of God gives her testimony to Elizabeth and vice-versa. We must do the same, too. Paul and Peter went into conference, and thought about the gospel given to Peter by the revelation of the father, Matthew 16, and to Paul by a heavenly revelation Gal. 2,[281] (although the poisonous black crow casts scorn on the latter, as is to be seen from his abusive book).[282] The time is fast approaching when everyone will have to give an account of[283] how he came to faith. Surely it is this which constitutes a true Christian church, that the godless are separated off from the chosen; for the former have never been saddened by their unbelief or even recognised its existence. How, then, should they know anything about true faith?

The present church is a real old whore by comparison, which can still be put right, though, by burning zeal. The tares will first have to suffer the attentions of the winnowing-shovel. But the time of harvest is certainly with us, Matthew 9.[284] Dear brothers, from all sides we hear the tares crying out that the time of harvest has not yet come. O, the traitor betrays himself: A true Christianity for our days will soon be in full swing despite all the previous corruption, Matthew 18,[285] for

277. The free rendering is best understood by consulting the Vg.
278. Cf. p. 270/3ff. above; n. 318 below.
279. Luke 1[14].
280. durch solche gleychformige ankunfft; probably conformity with Christ's sufferings is also hinted at, cf. p. 310/21 above.
281. Matthew 16[17]; Galatians 2[2].
282. Letter to the Princes of Saxony, LW 40, p. 50.
283. brechen, in B berechnen.
284. Matthew 9[37].
285. Matthew 18[7ff.]

has known in a desert land, trackless and waterless! There I learned that this is the way to experience your strength and glory.' How right it is to rejoice about the true preachers whom God is sending to earth in our time so that such testimony may come to light. Hence this text says: 'Many will rejoice in him' etc. Hearts will be awakened from unbelief to faith by the unanimous testimony to Christ. (You must keep the whole context in mind here, if you are to understand[30] me.)

The chosen friend of God experiences an overflowing, gladsome joy when his fellow-citizen[31] comes to faith in the same way as himself. For example the mother of God gives her testimony to Elizabeth and vice-versa. We must do the same, too. Paul and Peter went into conference, and thought about the gospel given to Paul by a heavenly revelation and to Peter by the revelation of the father, Mt. 16, Gal. 2. All the elect will have to give an account of how they came to faith. It is this which constitutes a true Christian church, that the godless are distinguished from the chosen.

Seventh.
The present church is a real old whore by comparison, which can and must still be put right, though, by burning zeal. The tares will first have to suffer the attentions of the winnowing-shovel. Then it will be in full swing.

31. *mitburger*; cf. *mitbruder* in A.

after the damage has been remedied and unbelief punished corruption will be followed by reform.

The gospel will spread even more fully than in the time of the apostles, Matthew 8.[286] From many lands and strange nations great numbers of the elect will appear who will be far superior to us lazy, negligent Christians. O, my dear masters, do not be so confident about this mad faith of yours, surrendering everyone (yourselves excepted) to the devil, as you have been in the habit of doing. For these usurious evangelists with their high opinion of themselves are taking this anathematising to new heights. They imagine that no one is a Christian unless he accepts their literalist faith.

Look at the way in which, long ago, people were plucked from the multitudes of the heathen and brought into fellowship with the Jews: Raab from Jericho, a wife of Salmon who begat Boaz of her Mat. 1; Naaman of Syria who was brought to faith by Elijah;[287] Job, the Edomite, was chosen by God;[288] Jethro was chosen by Moses,[289] Cornelius by Peter,[290] the officer whose faith the Lord Jesus regarded as far surpassing that of Israel, Luke 7; in Jerusalem the heathen woman was ranked far ahead of the Jews, Matthew 15.[291]

Hence many will be gathered in from the wild and alien heathen, to the discomfiture of the false thieves of Scripture; for – as I have heard – at present the heathen are quite taken aback by our faith and are repelled by our licentious behaviour. They are often overcome by grief in a way which transcends all natural reason and so are assured that they are inclined and destined for eternal life, Acts 13.[292] Like all of us the heathen and the Turks lack the true testimony to faith; otherwise countless numbers of them would become Christians. To appreciate this you only need to realise that if a Jew or a Turk were to live among us – and was supposed to be bettered by the sort of faith we have at present – he would gain about as much as a midge could carry on its tail – or rather much less. For no people under the sun condemns, curses and calumniates its own law so deplorably as today's Christians do, especially these scoundrelly literalists who provoke the worst trouble and yet presume nonetheless to judge the whole world. They cannot believe that God has no wish to bestow on them a single cent's worth of goods. Hence every nook and cranny is

286. Matthew 8[11f.]
287. Matthew 1[5]; 2 Kings 5[9ff.]
288. Job 1[ff.]
289. Exodus 18[1ff.]
290. Acts 10[1ff.]
291. Luke 7[1ff.]; Matthew 15[22-8].
292. Acts 13[48].

The gospel will spread even more fully than in the time of the apostles Mat. 8. From many strange lands and nations great numbers of the elect will be far superior to us lazy, negligent Christians. O, my dear masters, do not be so confident about this mad faith of yours, surrendering everyone (yourselves excepted) to the devil.

Look at the way in which, long ago, people were plucked from the multitudes of the heathen and brought into fellowship with the Jews: Raab from[32] Jericho, a wife of Salmon who begat Boaz of her, Mat. 1; Naaman of Syria who was brought to faith by Elijah; Job, the Edomite, was chosen by God; Jethro was chosen by Moses, Cornelius by Peter, the officer whose faith the Lord Jesus regarded as surpassing that of Israel, Luke 7, in Jerusalem the heathen woman was praised far above the Jews, Mt. 15.

Hence many will be gathered in from the wild and alien heathen, for they are quite taken aback by our faith; they are assured by this experience of desolation that they are destined for eternal life Acts 13.[33] The heathens and Turks lack only the true testimony to faith; otherwise countless numbers of them would become Christians. To appreciate this you only need to realise that if a Jew or a Turk were to live among us – and was supposed to be bettered by the sort of faith we have at present – he would gain about as much as a midge could carry on its tail.

For no people under the sun condemns, curses and calumniates its own law so deplorably as today's Christians do. They cannot believe that God will not bestow on them a single cent. Hence every nook and cranny is full of usurers and traitors, Ps. 54.

---

32. 'and', cf. 'from' in A.
33. Very compressed and virtually incomprehensible; cf. A.

full of usurers and traitors, Ps. 54.[293] And those that should stand in the vanguard of the Christian people – and are called princes for that reason – prove conclusively, every time an issue or plan crops up, their lack of faith by fearing, because of their fellow princes, to do right, Isaiah 1.[294] They imagine they would be driven out if they were to stand by the truth, which they only pretend to accept because it has not brought any persecution upon them. They like being called the best Christians of all, but they juggle around[295] to find a way to excuse their godless fellow-princes, and declare barefacedly that if their subjects were persecuted by their neighbours for the sake of the gospel they would not spring to their defence. They want to be good, sturdy jailers and executioners of common thieves, that is all. Those pious people, their priests, who preach the gospel to them, pay court to old women with great wealth.[296] They are worried that they might end up begging for their bread. Yes, indeed, what fine, evangelical people they are! What a firm, strong faith they have! What good fortune for anyone who puts his trust in their plausible posturing and blethering! With their monkish idol in the van their bragging and boasting about their literalistic faith beggars description.

To be honest, my most beloved brothers, I cannot hide my preference for giving the most elementary instruction to heathens, Turks and Jews about God and his ordering of things:[297] to give an account of the dominion given to us and that of God over us. For these very clever thieves of Scripture totally deny the existence of this, fulfilling what Jude and Peter say in their epistles:[298] like irrational animals their knowledge[299] brings them to grief; they completely reject it.[300] Their mad faith robs them of all rhyme and reason; they rail against anything which they do not choose to accept, just shutting their eyes and ears to it. When I refer them courteously to what the Bible teaches in its first chapters about the creatures being our possession and we God's, they reject it all as wild fantasy. Hence I say that if you are not prepared to learn the proper interpretation of the beginning of the Bible, then you will understand neither God nor the

293. Psalm 55[11].
294. Isaiah 1[23]; lit. 'fellows'; cf. B 'tyrants'; note the play on words: *vorstehen* (lead) and *fürsten* (princes).
295. *gauckeln hin und her*.
296. Cf. Letter 51.
297. *von Gott und seyner ordnung zu reden*; on Müntzer's concept of God's order cf. p. 357, n. 6 below; Müntzer expresses a similar preference to teaching the ignorant folk at Mühlhausen to the more sophisticated ones in Allstedt, cf. Letter 68, p. 120f.
298. Jude[10]; 2 Peter 2[12].
299. Their instinctive, natural knowledge.
300. God's order.

And those that should stand in the vanguard of the Christian people prove conclusively, every time an issue or plan crops up, their lack of faith by fearing to do right because of the tyrants. They imagine they would be driven out if they were to stand by the truth. The priests pay court to rich old women for their money. They are worried that they might end up begging for their bread. Yes, what a fine faith they have! What good fortune for anyone who puts his trust in their blethering! Their bragging and boasting about their literalistic faith beggars description.

To be honest, dear brothers, I cannot hide my preference for instructing rather heathens, Turks and Jews rather than us Christians about God's dominion over us and about ours over the creatures. When I say anything about this, they say I am fantasising. Hence I say that if you are not[34] prepared to learn the proper interpretation of the beginning of the Bible, then you will understand neither God nor the creatures and God will humble you by making the heathen flourish.[35]

34. 'Not' (*nit*) omitted by mistake.
35. *grosse jungen*; cf. *grassingen* in A (Hinrichs).

creatures nor the relationship between them, (to the glory of his true name) and God will bring you to complete discomfiture by making the heathen flourish,[301] so that your descendants will spit at the memory of you.

However much our biblical scholars may grunt away and grind their teeth[302] this gospel, as interpreted in the light of the whole of holy scripture, reveals to them, and their all too mortal idols, the error of their ways.

Jesus was conceived in Galilee, at Nazareth, and there too he was brought up, Matthew 3.[303] The evangelists described exactly how it was. If anyone harmonises the gospels[304] he will find it set out quite clearly. There is an excellent reason for this, as anyone can see by reading John, chapter 7.[305] The mad, raging, irrational thieves of Scripture thought in their fleshly minds that it was quite out of the question for Jesus of Nazareth to be Christ, because he was brought up in Galilee! They kept to the Scripture, but abandoned its spirit, as the godless do to this day. They rebuked poor Nicodemus for the simplicity of his faith.[306] They pointed him to Scripture and imagined they had hit the mark. But God led them around by the nose. Their great blindness prevented them from seeing the whole of Scripture as a unity, and they paid no attention to the wondrous working of God, just as today our envious fantasts seduce the common folk to every sort of intemperance, as anyone can see. Although it is just to prevent this sort of thing that holy Scripture has been left to us negligent creatures as our sole comfort here on earth.

If these thieves of Scripture had not loved it for the sake of their belly they would have known the time of the birth of Christ from Daniel[307] and the town where the birth took place from Micah,[308] and from Isaiah[309] and others they could have learned how our saviour would be brought up.

The whole trouble was, then, (as it still is for the world) that Christ was a contemptible person, one of humble parentage. And yet he had the effrontery to instruct and chastise too pointedly the chubby-cheeked people of substance, those who were out for their own

---

301. *grassingen*; growth of young grass (Hinrichs); possibly a reference to the coming of the Prince of Peace in Psalm 72 esp. v. 16; cf. p. 320/10f. below.

302. Lit. 'rage intensely'.

303. Matthew 3[13].

304. *ein gut monotesteron drauss macht.*

305. John 7[41, 52].

306. John 7[50ff.]

307. Daniel 2[44]; 12[1ff.]

308. Micah 5[2].

309. Isaiah 7[14]; 9[6f.]; 11[1f.]

However much our biblical scholars may rage, this gospel, as interpreted in the light of the whole of holy scripture, reveals to them the error of their ways.

Jesus was conceived in Galilee, at Nazareth, and there too he was brought up. The evangelist described exactly how it was. There is an excellent reason for this, as anyone can see by reading John, chapter 7. The mad, raging, irrational thieves of Scripture thought in their fleshly minds that it was quite out of the question for Jesus of Nazareth to be Christ, because he was brought up in Galilee! They kept to the Scriptures, but abandoned its spirit, as the godless do to this day. They rebuked poor Nicodemus for the simplicity of his faith. They pointed him to Scripture and imagined they had really hit the mark. But God led them around by the nose because their great blindness prevented them from seeing the whole of Scripture as a unity, and they paid no attention to the work of God, just as today our smart alecs[36] seduce the common folk to every sort of intemperance. Although it is just to draw our attention to this sort of thing that holy Scripture has been left as our sole comfort.

If these thieves of Scripture had not loved it for the sake of their belly they would have known the time of the birth of Christ from Daniel and the town from Micah, and from Isaiah, how our saviour would be brought up.

The whole trouble was, then, (as it still is for the world) that Christ was a contemptible person, one of humble parentage. And yet he had the effrontery to instruct and chastise too pointedly the chubby-cheeked people of substance, those who were out for their own

36. *jecken.*

pleasures. For he preached the wisdom of his heavenly father so clearly that they were unable to refute him, and he performed such miracles that they could not reject them, John 9.[310] So one of them says to the other: 'Where does all his wisdom and strength come from? He is a joiner's son. Isn't his mother's name Mary? Etc., What is he up to then? And they were all angry with him.' Matthew 13, Luke 4.[311] The godless do the same nowadays, when someone rebukes their pretences, their pomp, their false, slick wisdom. O, how often the eternal word has concealed itself[312] in chosen men, in our Christian Nazareth, that is to say among the burgeoning elect, who flourish and burgeon sweetly in the wisdom of the cross,[313] though every pussy-footing pleasure-lover has regarded them as mad and idiotic. That is the wicked way of the world: that which should really better it brings out the worst in it. Ah, my most beloved, that is the wisdom of the cross, with which God greets his elect. For although there is nothing good to be seen in the world, wherever one peers, one is not supposed to take offence at anything, while all the world takes offence at what the very best have done, saying it is all a devilish illusion.

How the elect would abound with the grace of God if they abandoned their own will there, too, and left everything for the sake of God! On this Christ is quite explicit: 'Whoever does the will of my father, is a mother to me,' Matthew 12, Mark 3, Luke 8.[314] For our sake he handed over his mother at the cross and described her as our companion. Like her we are terrified by God's greeting when God wants us to become gods through his son becoming man, that is, when he tests our faith like gold in the fire. We think: Oh, what will come of all this? Just as Mary's natural reason led her to be sceptical of the angel,[315] so we distrust the upright preachers who explain and expound the cross and the impossibility of faith so that we can understand it; although the true kingdom of David is where Christ rules from the cross and we are crucified with him.[316] And what is the house of Jacob but your soul that has been emptied by the crushing of your loins, by the doing away of your lusts.[317] There the power of the almighty brings to birth in our suffering the impossible work of God,

---

310. John 9[32f.]
311. Matthew 13[55ff.]; Luke 4[22].
312. *geschwunden.*
313. Cf. n. 301 above.
314. Matthew 12[50]; Mark 3[35]; Luke 8[21]; cf. the prayer about Mary as our companion, cf. p. 402 below and the accompanying note.
315. Luke 1[34]; cf. pp. 266/27–277/1 above.
316. Romans 6[6]; Galatians 2[19].
317. Genesis 32[32].

pleasures. For he preached the wisdom of his heavenly father so clearly that they were unable to refute him, and he performed such miracles that they could not reject them. So one of them says to the other: 'Where does all his wisdom and strength come from? He is a joiner's son. Isn't his mother's name Mary? Etc., What is he up to then?' And they were all angry with him, Mt. 13, Luke 4. The godless do the same nowadays when someone rebukes their pretences. O, how often the eternal word has concealed itself in chosen men, in our Christian Nazareth, that is to say among the burgeoning elect, who flourish in the wisdom of the cross, though every pussy-footing pleasure-lover has regarded them as mad and idiotic. Ah, my most beloved, that is the wisdom of the cross, with which God greets his faithful.

Eighth.

Oh, how full of grace men would become if they sought to do the will of God there, too, for Christ is quite explicit: 'Whoever does my will etc., Mt. 12, Mark 3. The mother of God is our companion. Like her we are alarmed by God's greeting when God wants us to become gods through his son becoming man, that is, when he tests our faith. We think: Oh, what will come of all this? Just as Mary's natural reason led her to be sceptical of the angel, so we distrust the upright preachers who expound the cross and the impossibility of faith; although the true kingdom of David is where Christ rules from the cross and we are crucified with him. And what is the house of Jacob but the soul that has been emptied by the crushing of our loins, by the doing away of our lusts. There the power of the almighty brings to birth his work in our suffering, the overshadowing of the attested[37]

---

37. *bezeugten*, lit. 'witnessed'.

by the overshadowing of the sacred old covenant, which is completely transfigured[318] by the light of the world, the true genuine son of God, Jesus Christ.

To sum up. This first chapter is about the strengthening of the spirit in faith. Its message is simply that almighty God, our dear Lord, wishes to give us the most glorious Christian faith through Christ's becoming man. All we need to do is to be conformed to his life and passion through the overshadowing of the holy spirit, so bitterly resisted[319] and so coarsely mocked by this fleshly world. Hence the spirit is given only to the poor in spirit (who recognise their unbelief).

These concluding words are confirmed by everything that is said throughout the chapter and especially by the most gladsome hymns of Mary and Zechariah[320] in which the warm mercy which flows from the spirit of the fear of God is so clearly described. This is the holy covenant which God swore to keep with Abraham and all of us, Rom. 4,[321] who serve him in holiness and in righteousness; it[322] will truly be valid in his eyes. He who does not truly fear God cannot be renewed daily in the knowledge of God, which he needs if he is to understand faith and the work of God in him. Cannot learn either how to give an account of his faith. Since it meets with contempt, such faith is a rare thing, given and nurtured by God in great tribulation. May the spirit of Christ, a butt of derision to the godless, be with you. Amen.

---

318. *durchglastet*; on overshadowing cf. p. 270/2ff. above; cf. 2 Corinthians 3[14-18]: the transfiguration in the Spirit.

319. *fleyschentz*; in contrast to living by the Holy Spirit to live in a fleshly way (Hinrichs).

320. Luke 1[46ff., 67ff.]

321. Romans 4[13].

322. i.e. our righteousness, cf. Romans 14[23].

covenant, being completely transfigured by the light of the true, genuine son of God, Jesus Christ.

To sum up. This first chapter is about the strengthening of the spirit in faith. Its message is that almighty God, our dear Lord, wishes to give us the most glorious Christian faith through Christ's becoming man. All we need to do is to be conformed to his life and passion through the overshadowing of the holy spirit, so mocked by this world. Hence the spirit is given only to the poor in spirit (who recognise their unbelief).

These concluding words are confirmed by everything that is said throughout the chapter and especially by the most gladsome hymns of Mary and Zechariah in which the warm mercy which flows from the spirit of the fear of God is so clearly described. This is the holy covenant which God swore to Abraham that he would keep, that if he served him in holiness and in righteousness it would truly be valid in his eyes. He who does not truly fear God cannot be renewed daily in the knowledge of God. Cannot progress, in giving an account of his faith to the Christian people. That is why faith is a rare thing, given and nurtured by God in great tribulation. May Jesus Christ help you. Amen.

VINDICATION AND REFUTATION

The primary purpose of this writing is, as the title suggests, a refutation of Luther's *Letter to the Princes of Saxony* (LW 40, 49–50) of July 1524 and a vindication of his own position. It is undoubtedly the most personalised and polemical of all his writings, reflecting the bitter harvest-tide of 1524, as Allstedt slipped from his grasp and he shouldered yet again the burdens of exile. Especially towards the end of the writing argument collapses into a cascade of (remarkably imaginative) abuse. Throughout the treatise his rage keeps breaking through. Theological or spiritual themes are certainly not absent, but are only attacked as it were, in the by-going. The focus is personal.

Much interest centres, however, on Müntzer's analysis of the reformation movement, his reflections on the divergent careers of Luther and himself, of the contrast between the 'soft life' of Wittenberg and the life of the wilderness, the cave of Elijah, which is to be Müntzer's lot. The radical themes of the *Exposé* are developed further; the integration of faith and politics, the divine and the creaturely. Every line pulsates with the controversy of the time – 'situation theology' indeed.

The eschatological perspective is provided by John 8, on which the *Vindication* is an extended meditation. Thus exegesis, political radicalism, theological reflection and personal polemic swirl together in a thick soup which can be supped only with circumspection.

We have only indirect evidence for the dating. Franz suggests it could have been begun in Allstedt, prior to his departure on 7 August, but finished in Mühlhausen between 15 August and 19 September. Elliger doubts whether the turbulent last days in Allstedt would have allowed him leisure to write, and the hectic activities in Mühlhausen suggest to him that he may not have written it until he arrived in Nuremberg at the beginning of October. It is clear that it was printed by Hieronymus Hölzel in Nuremberg some time before 17 December (when it was discovered and confiscated by the Council).

The reference to Luther's quarrel with the authorities in Orlamünde on 24 August (p. 342/10) suggests that the earliest date possible for its completion would be around mid-September.

At all events, it emerged at a time of acute crisis in Müntzer's life, the abrupt termination of his ministry in Allstedt after the summons to Weimar on 1 August led to a disintegration of his support in the Allstedt Council. Müntzer, of course, realised that it was the alliance of Luther and his Elector which had stymied his plans.

The *Vindication* is poorly structured, comparing unfavourably with Luther's *Letter to the Princes of Saxony*. It is neither a systematic exegesis of John 8 nor a point by point rebuttal of Luther's letter. Like the *Exposé* it begins with an electrifying image – Elijah in his cave, ruthlessly determined to resist the godless. There follows immediately Müntzer's prayer that he will be equally resolute, and a dedication of the treatise to Christ, king of kings, the sole prince recognised by the godly.

Müntzer's persecution at the hands of Luther is seen as predictable, given the age-old conflict between the spirit of Christ and those lions of literalism, the biblical scholars, who, as in John 8, dub it devilish. He rejoices that he may share in the suffering of his master. As for Luther and the Pharisees before him, he repeats the now familiar arguments that they lack both the motivation and the personal experience of the spirit to penetrate to the truth of Scripture.

As a result they fail to see that the Gospel and the Law are complementary. The Law is understood here, in a double sense, individually and politically, as the hard, but royal road of suffering, the chastisement of the holy spirit, but also as divine righteousness in political affairs. Accustomed to the 'soft life' and in the pocket of princes who refuse to exercise justice, Luther has a dual motive for declaring the Law superseded.

His indictment of Müntzer for stirring up insurrection misses the point. The power of the sword, like that of the keys, rests with the whole community. The princes have usurped this right by claiming lordship over all creation. Their hypocrisy is a natural ally of Luther's deviousness. In fact, only the godly can be trusted to exercise justice. To achieve this an insurrection may be justified.

Müntzer stresses the simplicity, straightforwardness of his own approach, preaching the gospel which is good news to the sad at heart. It is this which accounts for the popularity of his message of which Luther is so jealous.

From this point he begins to deal with the particular criticisms of Luther: that he has no real claim to be a martyr, that he enjoyed Luther's protection, and that he makes arrogant claims to special inspiration; he also takes issue with Luther's portrayal of his own, non-violent progress from Augsburg to Worms. The violence of the language shows that many of Luther's shafts have hit home. He ends by repeating that he is weary of polemic and by explaining the circumstances of his flight from Allstedt.

The debt of the *Vindication* to John 8 is very considerable. The Johannine polarities of light and darkness, truth and lies, of the children of God and of the devil, provide an attractive dualistic framework for Müntzer to interpret his own situation. The virtual identification of himself with Christ and of Luther with the blind, worldly Pharisees is basic. In the trickery of the latter (the woman in adultery!) their persecution of true teaching, their attribution of an evil spirit to Jesus, their own self-glorification, he sees a dazzlingly clear mirror of the way in which the Wittenbergers are treating him. Luther, too, judges according to the flesh, fails to understand the origin of faith, and – by substituting himself for Christ as pope, saviour, son of God – proves that the devil is his father. His lust for honours and titles shows that he knows neither Christ nor his Father. All in all, therefore, Müntzer sees Jesus' vindication of himself against the Pharisees in John 8 as the model for his own *Vindication*.

Apart from Luther's *Letter* and John 8 Müntzer draws on many other sources, indeed there are reminiscences of almost all his previous writings. The theme, for example, of the true exercise of power, so central to the *Exposé*, is presented again, in more personalised and politicised form, and once again it is closely related to the order of creation.

It is the perversion of this order by the princes which is the root cause of all 'usury, theft and robbery'. Likewise, in the religious sphere, the new biblical scholars distort Scripture because they are 'distracted by the creaturely lusts', and their interpretations of Scripture become devious and complex. Elijah and Müntzer, on the other hand, are straightforward and simple, because their hearts are pure. 'But I say with Christ; whoever is of God, hears his words.' They recall the rational, clear explanations of Jesus which captivated even the human reason of the godless.

Reflecting on the course of the Reformation Müntzer believes that although, like Saul, Luther began by doing some good he must now step aside for the new David, i.e. Müntzer. For he has embarked on an unholy alliance with the princes, making himself another pope, which detracts from the honour due to God alone and tyrannises over the people. To restore the order of creation, when 'the people will go free and God alone will be their Lord', an insurrection may well be justified. His logic leads him relentlessly to such astonishing radicalism. The Reformation must go on to embrace the princes as well as the priests. Ahab will be humbled by Elijah!

The flaws of the *Vindication* are manifest: the moralising, *ad personam* polemic, the wild accusations, the simplistic, dualistic categories. One wonders who would have read it, if it had not been suppressed!

Yet it certainly is colourful! It abounds in vivid imagery – the monkeys trying to cobble shoes, the sustained metaphor of the Lutheran carrion-crow, the scholars blotting their great tomes, the variations on the theme of roasting. A whole menagerie of animal images is offered. Müntzer's language, one senses, is straining at the limits of expression. From now on he will be committing himself, as the shadows of war gather, to action.

VINDICATION AND REFUTATION

A highly provoked Vindication[1] and a Refutation of the unspiritual soft-living Flesh in Wittenberg, whose robbery and distortion of Scripture[2] has so grievously polluted our wretched Christian Church.[3]

Thomas Müntzer of Allstedt.

From the cave of Elijah, whose zeal spares no one. 3 Kings 18; Matthew 17; Luke 1; Revelation 11;[4] Anno MDXXIIII.[5] O Lord, deliver me from the calumnies of men that I may keep your commandments,[6] and I will proclaim the truth hidden in your son, lest the wiles of the evil-doers continue to flourish.[7]

To his Eminence, the first-born prince and almighty lord, Jesus Christ, the kindly king of kings, the valiant leader[8] of all believers, to my most gracious lord and true protector, and to his grieving and only bride, the poor Christian Church.

All glory, fame and honour, all dignity and splendour and acclamation[9] be given to you alone, eternal son of God. Philippians 2.[10] Your holy spirit has always suffered the fate[11] of being treated by these merciless lions,[12] the biblical scholars, as the worst of devils, John

---

1. *Schutzrede*, i.e. statement in one's own defence; *apologia*.

2. Cf. p. 180/28 above; to the now familiar theme of robbery, Müntzer adds that of perversion of Scripture, *mit verkerter weysse*; cf. Letter 66A, n. 903; the topos of *die Verkehrten die Gelehrten* (scholars) was common in later Anabaptism (Bräuer).

3. *Christenheit*.

4. 1 Kings 19[9ff.] or perhaps a reference to 1 Kings 18[40], the merciless slaughter of the priests of Baal, as Schwarz suggests, p. 63 n. 4; Hans Hut uses the same image of Elijah in his cave on the title page of his Augsburg *Sendbrief* (Bräuer); Matthew 17[10ff.]; Luke 1[17]; Revelation 11[3-6].

5. Printed in Nuremberg prior to 17 December 1524 (when it was confiscated by the magistrates) by Hieronymus Hölzel. (F.)

6. Cf. Proverbs 7[1f.] (Vg.).

7. This whole sentence is in Latin; the source of the second half of the sentence cannot be traced; there may be an echo of 1 Corinthians 2[7f.], (Vg.) or of Jude v. 14f. (Vg.).

8. *hertzogen*, lit. 'Duke'; the whole dedication is closely modelled on Luther's *Letter to the Princes of Saxony* (LW 40, p. 49); everything Luther attributes to the Elector Frederick and Duke John of Saxony Müntzer attributes to Christ.

9. *titel*, lit. 'title'; cf. p. 342/17 below.

10. vs. 9ff.; cf. n. 8 above.

11. *sölich glück gehabt*.

12. *gnadlossen lewen*; possibly a play of words here; the biblical scholars are not only '*geistlos*', as the title of the work suggests, (bereft of the Spirit) but lack grace, mercy (*Gnade*) as well.

8;[13] although the holy spirit was yours in inexhaustible measure from the very beginning, John 3,[14] and all the elect have received it from your fullness, John 1,[15] and it has dwelt in them. 1 Cor. 3, 6; 2 Cor. 1; Eph. 1, Psalm 5.[16] You give it to all who hasten towards you, according to the measure of their faith, Eph. 4; Psalm 67.[17] Anyone, on the other hand, who does not have it to give infallible testimony to his own spirit[18] has nothing to do with you, O Christ;[19] Romans 8 [20] gives you the irrefutable testimony to that, Psalm 92.[21]

Hence there is nothing so very surprising about Doctor Liar,[22] that most ambitious of all the biblical scholars, becoming a more arrogant fool every day, covering himself up with your Holy Scripture and most deceitfully arming himself with it, but in no way renouncing fame and easy living. For the last thing he intends is to make you his first concern, Isaiah 58.[23] As if he had access (through you, the very portal of truth) to your judgements,[24] he is insolent to your very face, utterly despising your true spirit for, driven by his raging envy and his most bitter hate, he has betrayed his true colours[25] by denouncing me. Without true or just cause he has made me a laughing-stock among his scornful, jeering, ruthless companions and has jeeringly traduced my name in the eyes of the simple, making me out to be a satan or a devil, although I am a ransomed member of your body.[26] Such scandalous conduct can never be made good.[27]

In you, however, my joy is full, and your gentle consolation satisfies me completely, for as you have proclaimed so graciously to

---

13. John 8[48ff.]; John 8 is seen by Müntzer as the basis for this whole writing cf. p. 347/9f. below; this is almost a word for word rejection of Luther's lament in the *Letter to the Princes of Saxony* that it has always been the fate of the Word to be attacked by the devil (Hinrichs, p. 166).

14. John 3[34]; *one masse von anbegin*.

15. John 1[16].

16. 1 Corinthians 3[16], 6[19]; 2 Corinthians 1[21f.]; Ephesians 1[13]; Psalm 5[8, 12f.]

17. Ephesians 4[7f.]; Psalm 68[18]; the Temple, referred to throughout this psalm, generally means for Müntzer the heart of the believer, the temple of the Spirit, cf. p. 292/3f. above.

18. Romans 8[9, 16].   19. *ist dir Christo nit zustendig.*

20. v. 9.   21. Psalm 93[5].

22. *doctor lügner* = Luther; the pun is closer in German; more than a mere term of abuse, it has eschatological overtones (John 8[44]); cf. Hinrichs, p. 171.

23. *und nichts weniger will mit dir auffs forderste zu schaffen haben*; an alternative translation, if we read *nichtsdestoweniger*, would be: 'nevertheless he claims that you are his first concern'; Isaiah 58[6ff.] (the contrast between true and false piety).

24. *urteyl*; Müntzer's usual term for the living word of Scripture.

25. *meldet sich deutlich unwidderuflich*; note Müntzer's identification of the cause of the Spirit with his own.

26. *dein erworben glied in dir.*

27. *zur unerstatlichen ergernuss.*

your real friends[28] in Matthew 10: 'The pupil will not have it any better than the master.'[29] Now if they were blasphemous enough to call you Beelzebub, my innocent leader[30] and comforting saviour, how much more will they do this to me, your tireless warrior,[31] once I have shaken off that flattering rascal at Wittenberg and followed your voice, John 10.[32] Yes, this is how things are bound to be, if one is not prepared to let soft-living and self-willed men[33] get away with their counterfeit faith and their pharisaical dodges, but sees to it that their fame and pomp declines.[34] Even you[35] were not able to get them to recognise your superiority.[36] They preferred to think that they were more learned than you and your disciples. Indeed they probably were more learned, with their stubborn literalism, than our Doctor Lampooner[37] can ever be. Even though their fame and reputation were so widespread throughout the world they had no right to devise clever plans against you, trying to refute you from the clear word of Scripture, as in their reproof of Nicodemus, John 7 and in their arguments about the Sabbath, John 5, and in chapter 9.[38] They mobilised the whole of Scripture against you with all the energy at their command, saying that you would and should die for daring to confess boldly that you were a son of God,[39] born of the eternal father, as we confess of your spirit. Hence they said: We have a law, and according to it he must die. For they twisted the text of Deuteronomy 13 and 18[40] to refer to you, and refused to look at it in a broader context. I am now being treated in exactly the same way by that sly robber of Scripture,[41] who pours out his scorn at just those points where Scripture is clearest, in his fiery jealousy calling the spirit of God a devil.

The whole of Holy Scripture is about the crucified son of God and nothing else (as is evidenced, too, by all the creatures[42]) which is why he himself explained his ministry by beginning with Moses and going

---

28. *deinen hertzlichen frewnden*, i.e. the 'friends of God'.

29. Matthew 10[24].

30. Lit. 'Duke', cf. n. 8 above.   31. *landtßknecht*.   32. John 10[4f.]

33. *gutdunckler*; those guided by what seems right to them, not by the Spirit.

34. *iren namen und pracht zu nidergen*.

35. Christ.

36. *Du vermöchtest dasselbig auch nit vor in uberhaben sein*; Hillerbrand: 'Thou wert not immune from this experience.'

37. *der doctor Ludibrii*; another pun; *ludibrium* = mockery, idle play.

38. John 7[50ff.]; 5[9f.]; 9[14ff.]

39. *einen son Gottes*.

40. Deuteronomy 13[1-5]; 18[10f., 20].

41. *schrifftsteler*; yet another pun, on *Schriftsteller/stehler* = author/robber; Luther is again meant.

42. A reference to Revelation 5[8f.?] For a general comment on Müntzer's 'theology

on to all the prophets, showing how he had to suffer and enter into the glory of his father. The last chapter of Luke sets this out clearly.[43] Paul, too, having searched the law of God more penetratingly than all his companions, Gal. 1, says that he can only preach Christ, the crucified, 1 Cor. 1.[44] For he was unable to find in it anything else than the suffering son of God, of whom Matthew 5 says that he did not come to rob the law of its force or to tear up the covenant of God, but on the contrary to complete, explain and fulfil it.[45]

The hate-filled biblical scholars were unable to recognise any of this, for they did not search Scripture with their whole heart and spirit as they ought to have, Psalm 118, and as Christ commanded them, John 5.[46] They were like the monkeys who tried to emulate the cobbler and succeeded only in ruining the leather. And why was this? Because they wanted the comfort of the holy spirit but never once reached the ground [of their soul] through sadness of heart,[47] as one must if the true light is to shine out in the darkness and empower us to be children of God[48] – as is clearly explained in Psalm 54 and Psalm 62 and John 1.[49]

So if Christ is merely accepted on the testimony of the old and new covenants of God but preached without any manifestation[50] of the spirit the result may be much more confusion and monkeying around than the Jews and the pagans caused. Anyone can see with his own eyes that today's biblical scholars do exactly the same as the Pharisees did of old. They boast of their competence in holy scripture, cover every book with their writing and their blots and blether on more and more every day, saying: Have faith, have faith! Yet all the time they deny the source[51] of faith, deride the spirit of God and really believe in nothing at all, as you see. None of them will preach unless they get a stipend of forty or fifty florins. Indeed, the best actually want more

---

of the creatures' cf. p. 357 n. 6 below; here a parallel is drawn between the consistent biblical testimony to the suffering of Christ and what appears to be the universal human experience; the previous paragraph has already underlined the way of the Cross as common to Master and disciple and the impossibility of those with material concerns understanding Scripture; suffering is the royal path for the friends of God.

43. Luke 24[27, 44].
44. Galatians 1[11-16]; 1 Corinthians 1[23].
45. Matthew 5[17].
46. Psalm 119[2]; John 5[39].
47. *und sein ir leben langk durch traurigkeyt des hertzens auff iren grund nye kommen.*
48. This biblical term was used in German mysticism to indicate true discipleship; cf. n. 28 above.
49. Psalm 55[2-9]; Psalm 63, (David in the wilderness); John 1[4f.]
50. *eröffnung*; 'enlightenment' (Hillerbrand).
51. *ankunfft.*

than a hundred or two hundred florins, bringing to pass the prophecy of Micah 3: 'The priests preach for the money they get out of it.'[52] They want their peace and their easy life[53] and their lofty status, and yet they boast that they understand the source of faith. In fact, however, they do the absolute opposite, for they scold the true spirit for being an erring spirit and a satan, using Holy Scripture to cover themselves.[54] The very same happened to Christ when he proclaimed by his innocence the will of his father. This was quite abhorrent to the biblical scholars, and quite beyond them, John 5, 6.[55]

You find exactly the same thing continues to our day. When the godless are caught out[56] by the law they declare airily: Oh, it is no longer in force. But when it is explained to them quite correctly that it is written in the heart, 2 Cor. 3[57] and that one must follow its instructions to discover the right ways to the source of faith, Psalm 36 [58] then the godless man assaults the just man, brandishing Paul in his face, but a Paul so clumsily understood that even children would dismiss it all as a Punch and Judy show, Psalm 63.[59] He still wants to be the wisest man on earth, and boasts that there is none to equal him. What's more he describes all humble folk[60] as deranged spirits[61] and closes his ears as soon as the word 'spirit' is spoken or written. He has to shake his clever head, for, as Proverbs 18 says,[62] the devil cannot abide it when one starts talking to him about the origin[63] of faith, since he has been cast out. So he resorts to deception, 2 Cor. 11.[64] Using the highest register[65] of the musician, the double octave,[66] he sings the following melody from Paul's letter to the Romans, chapter 12: 'One should not bother oneself with such high matters, but adapt them for the humble folk.'[67] He fancies this gruel, but only because he is afraid

---

52. Micah 3[11].

53. *gute gemach*.

54. *mit dem deckel der heyligen schrifft*.

55. John 5[16ff., 30]; 6[38–40]; note Müntzer's virtual identification of himself with Christ; cf. n. 25 above.

56. *beschlossen*.

57. 2 Corinthians 3[3].

58. Psalm 37[23, 31].

59. *dass es den kindern auch zum poppenspill wirdt*; Psalm 64[4].

60. *armselige menschen*; poverty of spirit is meant.

61. *schwimmelgeyster*.

62. Proverbs 18[2].

63. *anfang*.

64. 2 Corinthians 11[13ff.]; there may be a reference to the scoffer being cast out in Proverbs 22[10].

65. Lit. 'alphabet'.

66. *disdyapason*: 'an interval of two octaves or a fifteenth' (Webster); Müntzer is drawing attention to the dissonant character of Luther's faith. (Hinrichs).

67. Romans 12[16].

to breakfast on soup.[68] He commends simple faith, but fails to see what is necessary to have this. That is why Solomon describes a man like this as a numskull, as the 24th chapter of Proverbs puts it: 'The wisdom of God is quite beyond the fool.'[69]

Like Moses, Christ began with the origins[70] and explained the law from beginning to end. Hence he says: 'I am a light to the world.'[71] His preaching was so truthful and so well thought-out[72] that he even captivated the human reason of the godless, as the evangelist Matthew describes in chapter 13 and as Luke, too, indicates in his second chapter.[73] But as Christ's teaching was beyond them and his person and life beneath them they took offence at him and his teaching and had the effrontery to say[74] that he was a Samaritan and possessed by the devil.[75] For their judgement was based on fleshly considerations, which greatly pleased the devil, and they were bound to blurt it out, being in good odour with the world which enjoys being Brother Soft Life, Job 28.[76] They undertook everything with an eye to the world's approval, Matthew 6, 23.[77]

The godless flesh in Wittenberg treats me in exactly the same way when I strive for the purity of the divine law, Psalm 18[78] by pointing to the beginning of the Bible, to what its first chapter says about the ordering of creation,[79] and explain how all the sayings of the Bible point to the fulfilment of the spirit of the fear of God, Isaiah 11.[80] Also I refuse to tolerate his perverse way of treating the new covenant[81] of God without first dealing with the divine commandments and the

---

68. *es grauset im vor der suppen zum frweessen.*

69. Proverbs 24[7].

70. *ursprung*; after *ankunfft* and *anfang* the third word used for 'origin', here the origin of the created world and of the law; cf. n. 42 above.

71. John 8[12].

72. *verfasset.*

73. Matthew 13[54]; Luke 2[47]; cf. n. 42 above.

74. *aus dem barte*; lit. 'out of their beards'; the opposite to mumbling into one's beard. (Hinrichs).

75. John 8[48].

76. *bruder sanfftleben*; Job 28[13]; cf. Vg.: '*nec invenitur (sapientia) in terra suaviter viventium*'.

77. Matthew 6[1-5. 16ff.]; 23[5ff.]

78. Psalm 19[8f.]

79. *durch den anfangk der biblien und ordenung des ersten undterschaydts derselben*; Hinrichs derives *anfangk* from *anfangen* in the sense of 'tackle', 'approach'; however the context suggests a relationship in Müntzer's mind between (1) the *origin* of the world and its order, Genesis 1. (2) the *beginning* of the Bible and its unity, and probably also (3) the origin or *source* of faith; cf. n. 70 above; cf. also Dismer, p. 7 n. 5.

80. Isaiah 11[1ff.]

81. The New Testament.

source of faith, which one can only reach[82] after chastisement by the holy spirit, John 16.[83] For it is only after the law is understood that the spirit punishes unbelief, which no one can understand until he has first embraced it himself, and as fiercely as the most unbelieving pagan. From the beginning, this is the way in which, testing themselves by the law, all the elect have come to understand their unbelief, Romans 2, 7.[84] I confess[85] Christ with all his members as the fulfiller of the law, Psalm 18,[86] for God's will and work must be completely carried out by observance of the law, Psalm 1, Romans 12.[87] Otherwise no one could distinguish belief from unbelief,[88] except in a counterfeit way, like the Jews, with their Sabbath and Scripture, who never came to understand the true ground of their faith.[89]

All I have done to that wily black crow[90] released by Noah from the Ark as a sign is this: like an innocent dove I have flapped my wings, covered them with silver, which has been purified seven times[91] and gilded my back, Psalm 67,[92] and flown over the carrion on which he likes to perch. How I loathed it! I will let the whole world know his hypocrisy towards these godless rascals, as seen in his book against me.[93] He is, in brief, their advocate. It is quite clear then, that Doctor Liar does not dwell in the house of God, Psalm 15[94] since he does not despise the godless, but denounces many God-fearing men as devils or rebellious spirits in order to serve the interests of the godless. The black crow knows this very well. He pecks out the eyes of the pigs to turn them into carrion, he blinds these pleasure-loving people. For he is indulgent about their faults in order to eat his fill of their wealth and honours and especially of the fine-sounding titles at their disposal.[95]

The Jews wanted to see Christ insulted and humiliated on every occasion, just as Luther now tries to treat me. He denounces me

---

82. *erkundiget = erkundet*, experienced. (F.)

83. John 16[8].

84. Romans 2[12]; 7[6f.]; the law, for Müntzer, reveals not sin, but unbelief; this unbelief, now recognised as such, and latent in nominal Christians as much as pagans, can be chastised by the holy spirit, and the way is open for faith to emerge.

85. *setze*.

86. Psalm 19.

87. Psalm 1[1f.]; Romans 12[2].

88. Not to be misunderstood in a formalist sense; Müntzer's concern is for the existential dimension of faith.

89. Lit. 'their ground'.

90. Luther, the carrion crow, is compared with Müntzer, the dove; cf. Genesis 8[7f.]

91. Cf. the Prague Manifesto, p. 363/6 below.

92. Psalm 68[13].

93. Cf. n. 8 above.

94. Psalm 15[4].

95. A splendidly mixed metaphor!

fiercely and reproaches me with the mercifulness[96] of the son of God and of his dear friends.[97] This is his retort to my preaching about the earnestness of the law, and the punishment of unspiritual sinners. For (even if they happen to be rulers) this is not abolished but is to be executed with the very greatest severity. Paul instructed Timothy (and through him all pastors) to preach this to the people, 1 Tim. 1.[98] He says clearly that (punishment) will visit all who combat and try to subvert sound teaching. No one can deny this. It is stated clearly and unambiguously in Deuteronomy, chapter 13, and Paul pronounces the same judgement against the unchaste sinner. 1 Cor. 5.[99] Although I have had my sermon[100] printed in which, arguing from Scripture, I told the princes of Saxony quite frankly that if they were to avert an uprising[101] they must use the sword: that, in short, disobedience must be punished, and neither great or small would be exempt, Numbers 25.[102]

Despite[103] all this that indulgent fellow, Father Pussyfoot,[104] comes along and says I want to stir up an insurrection. This is how he understands my letter to the mine-workers.[105] He says one thing, but suppresses the most vital point[106] for, as I expounded quite clearly to the princes, the power of the sword as well as the key to release sins is in the hands of the whole community. From the passages in Daniel 7, Revelation 6, Romans 13, and 1 Kings 8 I pointed out that the princes are not lords over the sword but servants of it.[107] They should not act as they please, but execute justice, Deut. 17.[108] Hence it is a good old custom that the people must be present if someone is to be judged properly by the law of God, Num. 15.[109] Why? So that if the

96. *güttigkeit*.

97. Cf. Luther's denunciation of Müntzer's 'Pharisaical spirit'. LW 40, 57; cf. also *Exposé*, n. 248.

98. 1 Timothy 1[9ff.]

99. Deuteronomy 13[6ff.]; 1 Corinthians 5[1-5]; key texts for Müntzer.

100. *Sermon to the Princes*, cf. pp. 230ff. above.

101. *empörung*.

102. Numbers 25[4].

103. *gleichwol*; follows on from the *Wiewoll* (although) at the beginning of the previous sentence.

104. *vatter leisendritt*, lit. soft-step.

105. John Zeiss wrote to Duke John of Saxony on 25 August 1524 that Müntzer had written a ferocious letter to the Mansfield miners, encouraging them to wash their hands in the blood of the tyrants; Förstemann, *Neue Mitteilungen aus dem Gebiet historisch-antiquarischer Forschungen* 12 (1868), p. 203, quoted by Franz, p. 571, n. 1.

106. *das allerbeschaydenste*; cf. n. 125 below.

107. Daniel 7[27]; Revelation 6[15ff.]; Romans 13[1]; 1 Samuel 8[7]; again, key texts for Müntzer.

108. Deuteronomy 17[18ff.]

109. Numbers 15[35]; examples of how Müntzer put this into practice are found in his later letters, esp. Nrs. 82–86.

authorities try to give a corrupt judgement, Isaiah 10[110] the Christians present can object and prevent this happening, since anyone spilling innocent blood will be accountable to God, Psalm 78.[111] There is no greater abomination on earth than the fact that no one is prepared to take up the cause of the needy. The great do whatever they please, as Job describes in chapter 41.[112]

The poor flatterer tries to use Christ to cover himself, adducing a counterfeit type of clemency which is contrary to Paul's text in I Timothy 1.[113] In his book about trade, however, he says that the princes should not hesitate to join the thieves and robbers in their raids.[114] He suppresses here, however, the basic reason[115] for all theft. He is a herald,[116] who hopes to earn gratitude by approving the spilling of people's blood for the sake of their earthly goods; something which God has never commanded or approved. Open your eyes! What is the evil brew[117] from which all usury, theft and robbery springs but the assumption of our lords and princes that all creatures are their property?[118] The fish in the water, the birds in the air, the plants on the face of the earth – it all has to belong to them! Isaiah 5.[119] To add insult to injury, they have God's commandment proclaimed to the poor: God has commanded that you should not steal. But it avails them nothing.[120] For while they do violence to everyone, flay and fleece the poor farm worker, tradesman and everything that breathes, Micah 3,[121] yet should any of the latter commit the pettiest crime,[122] he must hang. And Doctor Liar responds, Amen. It is the lords themselves who make the poor man their enemy. If they refuse to do away with the causes of insurrection how can trouble be avoided in the long run? If saying that makes me an inciter to insurrection, so be it!

He[123] has absolutely no sense of shame. It reminds one of the Jews in

---

110. Isaiah 10[1]; i.e. one oppressive to the poor.

111. Psalm 79[10].

112. Job 41 (Leviathan as a symbol of the powerful).

113. I Timothy 1[7-11].

114. *Trade and Usury*, LW 45, 269f.; in fact, Luther is critical of the princes' failure to see that the peace is kept.

115. *ursprung*.

116. *heerholt*; Hinrichs suggests a play of words: Luther is favourable (*hold*) to bloodshed (*heer* = army).

117. *grundtsuppe*; lit. 'dregs'.

118. Cf. Letter 91, p. 159/1ff.

119. Isaiah 5[8].

120. *es dienet aber in nit*.

121. Micah 3[2ff.]

122. *am allergeringesten*.

123. Luther.

John 8 who brought to Christ a woman who had been caught committing adultery.[124] They were putting him to the test. They would have cheerfully denounced him as an evil-doer if he had sought to disobey the stern command of the father. On the other hand if he had dismissed the woman without giving any judgement[125] he would have been considered an advocate of law-breaking. In the gospel Christ clarified his father's sternness by his own clemency. The clemency of God extends to all the works of his hand, Psalm 144.[126] This is not annulled[127] by the penalty of the law, which the elect man does not desire to evade, for – as Jeremiah and Psalm 6 say – he wants to be chastised justly but not in wrath.[128] For wrath was not with God in eternity, but springs from the perverse fear men have of God. They shrink from the pain and do not see how, through all this pain, God is leading them out of their delusions[129] and into his eternity.

All evildoers who, although members of the Christian community, perpetuate the original transgression of Adam[130] must, as Paul says, be justified by the law,[131] so that the godless Christians who resist the wholesome teaching of Christ can be swept out of the way by the sternness of the father, and so that the just can have time and space to learn the will of God. For not a single Christian would be able to devote himself to such meditation in the tyranny which would ensue if anyone could punish evil by the law.[132] For then the innocent person would have to let himself be afflicted, since the godless tyrant would use the following words as a pretext for this attack on the pious: I have to make a martyr of you, for Christ too suffered and you should not resist me, Matt. 5.[133] That would be a great calamity. Very precise distinctions have to be drawn, now that the persecutors claim to be the best Christians.

The devil uses many clever wiles in his campaign against Christ and

---

124. John 8[3ff.]
125. *one beschaydt.*
126. Psalm 145[9].
127. *verruckt.*
128. Jeremiah 10[24]; Psalm 6[1ff.]
129. *durch drügnuss*; *Trügbilder* (phantoms arousing fear). (F.)
130. *Alle ubelthäter der ursprünglichen misshandlung der gemaynen christenheyt.*
131. Romans 2[2].
132. *so das ubel durch gesetz zu strafen sölte frey seyn*; if even the godless had the right to punish sin by the law the elect would never survive, jurisdiction must be in the hands of the elect, not the present authorities (Hinrichs); Hillerbrand translates: 'Not a single Christian could ever follow his contemplation under such tyranny, if evil were far from being punished by the Law ...' This makes good sense, but is not an obvious reading of the German.
133. Matthew 5[39].

his followers, 2 Cor. 6:11.[134] On one occasion he may use indulgent flattery, as when that fellow Luther defends the godless with the words of Christ; on another occasion he shows ruthless severity applying, for the sake of worldly possessions, a corrupt system of justice.[135] But the holy spirit, the finger of Christ, 2 Cor. 3,[136] has not imbued [this ruthlessness] with any of the friendly severity of the law or with the crucified son of God. For the holy spirit leads those who seek the divine will to understand its most severe mercy in the light of both of these, 1 Cor. 2.[137] But he despises the law of the father and uses that most precious treasure, Christ's mercy, for his own hypocritical ends, using the patience of the son to negate the zealous concern of the father for the law, John 15, 16.[138] In the process he despises the power of the holy spirit to distinguish between the two, so that in the end one is vitiated by the other and judgement vanishes from the face of the earth, Jer. 5.[139] The impression is spread abroad that the sole reason for Christ's patience is to allow the godless Christians to afflict their brethren.

Christ was denounced as a devil when he pointed out to the Jews what Abraham had done[140] and when he provided them with the best possible guidance[141] about punishing and forgiving. Punishment is to be carried out with due severity. That is why he did not abolish the law, for as he said in the seventh chapter of John and just before the eighth: Your judgement should be just and not guided by appearances.[142] The only judgement demanded of them was that laid down in the law: that they should judge according to the spirit of the law. Likewise they should forgive according to the spirit of Christ, in the light of the gospel, so that the cause of the gospel would be furthered and not hindered, 2 Cor. 3, 13.[143] It is because of this distinction I make that Doctor Liar makes me out to be a devil, saying

---

134. 2 Corinthians 6[14]; 11[14f.]

135. *furzuwenden von der zeitlichen gûter wegen sein verderbliche gerechtigkayt.*

136. 2 Corinthians 3[3].

137. *durch dye aller ernste gûttigkeyt zu eröffnung gôtliches willens entgegen helt mit vergleichung bayder*; the collocation of severity and mercy is important for Müntzer; *gûttigkeyt*, clemency or mercy, becomes mere indulgence at the expense of others unless yoked to the law; conversely, a positivistic understanding of the law, unrelated to the old and new covenant, simply undergirds tyranny; 1 Corinthians 2[2]; cf. Romans 11[22].

138. John 15[10]; 16[15].

139. Jeremiah 5[31].

140. John 8[39-52].

141. *undterschayd*; elsewhere translated 'distinction'.

142. John 7[24]; i.e. there is no contradiction between this and Jesus' merciful treatment of the woman in John 8 (Hinrichs).

143. 2 Corinthians 3[6], 13[10].

like his biblical scholars: What is wrong, then, with my teaching and writing? The sole fruit of your work is insurrection. You are a satan, nothing but a satan etc., Look, you are a Samaritan, one possessed by the devil.[144]

O Christ, I consider myself unworthy to bear such costly suffering for the same cause as you. Of course, the view of my adversary finds many complaisant and corrupt judges. Like you I say to the proud, puffed-up, wily dragon: Are you listening to me? I am not possessed by the devil; what I am trying to do through my ministry is to proclaim the name of God, which is comfort to the sad but to the healthy illness and ruin, Isaiah 6, Matthew 9, 13, Luke 8 and 4.[145] And if I were to say that I would give it up because of the bad name it gives me, and because of the lies with which I am smeared, then I would be on the same level as you, Doctor Liar, with all your perverse polemics and abuse. You could not help quarrelling with the godless. But after that had happened you installed yourself in the place of the evil-doers whom you had just been belabouring[146] so ferociously. Now you realise that things might go too far you are trying to off-load your name on to another man, to whom the world is completely opposed anyway, and to affect purity,[147] as the devil is wont to do, so that no one may spot your wickedness. Hence the prophet calls you, Psalm 90[148] a basilisk, a dragon, a viper and a lion, since in your inimitable way you either flatter people with your poison or rage and rant against them.

The blameless son of God compared the ambitious biblical scholars most convincingly with the devil and left us to form our judgements on the basis of the gospel and in harmony with [God's] immaculate law, Psalm 18.[149] They thirsted for his blood, and would be satisfied with nothing less, for they said, John 11:[150] 'If we let him go[151] then all the people will believe in him; the common man will attach himself to him; look, already they are beginning to swarm around him. If we allow him to carry out his mission then we are done for, we will be nothing but poor wretches.' In just the same way along came that Caiaphas, Doctor Liar, and gave his princes sound advice. He managed it splendidly, saying that he was worried about his fellow

144. LW 40, 54.
145. *verstockung und kranckheyt*; Isaiah 6[8ff.]; Matthew 9[12]; 13[14f.]; Luke 8[36f.]; 4[18f.]
146. *aussgewessert*; like beating flax (Hinrichs).
147. *dich schône brennen*; cf. n. 174 below; lit. 'burn yourself beautiful'; a false refinement or purification by fire; cf. Satan in 2 Corinthians 11[14].
148. Psalm 91[13].
149. Psalm 19[7f.]
150. John 11[48].
151. *so wir in lassen bezemen.*

countrymen near Allstedt. As the whole land will testify on my account, the honest truth of the matter is this, that among the poor people there was such a thirst for truth that every road was crammed with people from far and near, who had come to hear how worship was conducted in Allstedt, with its biblical praise and preaching.[152] Although he nearly burst himself with his exertions he was unable to achieve anything of the sort in Wittenberg. One can see very well from his German Mass his holy rage about it.[153] Indeed Luther was so vexed that he succeeded first of all in getting his prince to prohibit the printing of my liturgy. But since the command of the Wittenberg pope was not heeded, he thought to himself: Wait! I will work out a fine plan to smash this little pilgrimage to smithereens. The godless man has a sharp, inventive mind for thinking out this sort of thing, Psalm 35.[154] For, as is obvious, his tactics were to establish his teaching by fomenting the hatred of the laity against the priests. If he had possessed a true love which was prepared to chastise, he would never have set himself up in place of the pope, as he has now, and he would not have played the hypocrite with the princes. You find all this clearly described in Psalm 9. He has translated this psalm and applied it to the Pope but it has been rather nicely realised in his own person too.[155] For he wants to make Saint Peter and Saint Paul into jailers, lending their support to his common hangmen.[156]

But our Doctor Liar is a simple man when he writes that I should not be stopped from preaching; just see to it, he declares, that the spirit in Allstedt keeps his fists to himself. Look, dear brothers of Christ! Isn't he learned? Yes, indeed, he is learned. Even after another two or three years the world will fail to realise how much fraudulent, murderous damage he has done. But by writing in this way[157] he hopes to wash his hands of any guilt in the matter so that no one notices that he is a persecutor of the truth. For he declares brazenly that the great persecution his teaching has to bear proves that it is the true word of God. It also surprises me very much that the shameless monk can bear to be so atrociously persecuted, used as he is to good malmsey and whorish fare.[158] That is what one expects of the biblical

---

152. Müntzer's *German Service Book* and *German Mass*.

153. Either *Concerning The Order of Public Worship*, (1523) by Luther (LW 53, 11ff.) or Paul Speratus' German translation of Luther's *Formula Missae* (1523) (Hinrichs).

154. Psalm 36[4f.]

155. Luther's translation of Psalm 10 appeared in 1524; traditionally taken to refer to Antichrist, Luther interpreted it as referring to the Papacy.

156. The Princes.

157. *Letter to the Princes of Saxony*, LW 40, esp. p. 57.

158. *bey dem guten malmasier und bey den hurnköstlein.*

scholar, and he has no alternative but to take this course, John 10:[159] 'It is not because of your good deeds that we are taking action against you, but because of your blaspheming that we will stone you.' They spoke to Christ in the same way as this fellow speaks against me: You should be expelled not because of your preaching but because of the threat to public order.

My very dearest brothers, in all honesty it is no simple matter which is before us at the moment. You have not the slightest idea of what is involved, for you imagine that everything will be all right, if you give nothing more to the priests. What you do not know is that you are now a hundred times, a thousand times worse off then before. From now on they will shit on you with a new logic,[160] twisting the word of God. Against this, however, stands the command of Christ, Matthew 7.[161] If you really take it to heart no one will be able to deceive you, whatever he says or writes. But what you must do is be watchful, just as Paul warned his Corinthians, saying, 2 Cor. 11:[162] 'See that your mind is not distracted from the simplicity of Christ.' By this simplicity the biblical scholars understand the full treasure of divine wisdom, Col. 2,[163] contrary to the text in Genesis 3[164] where a single command from God was enough to warn Adam against the harm that might befall him, if he allowed himself to be distracted[165] by the creaturely lusts, instead of finding his sole delight in God, as it is written: You will find your delight in God.[166]

One great objection advanced by Doctor Liar against me is that his teaching is straightforward[167] and, will, he thinks, burrow its way through all obstacles.[168] Preaching then, does not really worry him, for sects there must be; and he requests the prince not to prevent me preaching.[169] This had been my hope: that he would allow the matter to be dealt with by discussion, giving me a hearing before the world and making himself available and dealing with the matter by discussion alone. But he turns everything upside down and sets about getting the support of the princes. Everything was cut and dried from

159. John 10[33.]
160. *mit einer newen logiken.*
161. Matthew 7[15f.]; (beware of false prophets).
162. 2 Corinthians 11[3].
163. Colossians 2[3]; simple discipleship is replaced by theological doctrine (Hinrichs).
164. Genesis 3[3].
165. *vermanchfeltigt*; simplicity, oneness (*Einfältigkeit*) is eroded by the multiplicity (*Vielfältigkeit*) of the world; cf. p. 346/1ff. below.
166. Psalm 37[4].
167. *ainfeltig*, cf. n. 165 above.
168. *wils alls durchgrübeln.*
169. LW 40, 57.

the start[170] to prevent anyone saying: Well, well, now they themselves want to persecute the gospel; they should let me preach and not hinder it. But I am supposed to keep my hands idle and refrain from writing anything for the printers. What a fine business that is, exactly like the Jews saying: 'It is not because of your good deeds that we are taking action against you, but because of your blaspheming.'[171] Those truly pious people said that even if someone took an oath, it was only valid if he swore by the gift on the altar. They were always using tricks like that, Matthew 23, Luke 11.[172] It did not prevent them being pious people. No, no, they do no harm! Providing you believe that one should show consideration for the weak!

The blasphemy could never have worried the Jews, as you can see from the gospel. Nor like Luther were they really concerned about good deeds. Hence God reproved them with the deeds of Abraham, John 8.[173] But fierce hatred was stoked up in the Jews, who affected purity before the people, just as our virgin Martin does now.[174] O, the chaste woman of Babylon, Revelations 18![175] He claims that he will deal with everything by discussion, but refuses to start discussing my case, so it can be justified or condemned. All he does is urge the mighty that no one should follow my teaching since it leads to insurrection. Anyone who wants to judge this matter fairly should neither love insurrection nor, on the other hand, should he be averse to a justified uprising.[176] His outlook must be a balanced one;[177] otherwise he will either hate my teaching too much or have ulterior reasons for loving it too much. This is the last thing I want.

It would certainly be more profitable for me to spend my time instructing the poor people with good teaching rather than getting myself entangled with this blasphemous monk, who now makes himself out to be a new Christ, one who has purchased so many good things for the Christian people by his blood and striven as well for this noble cause: that priests may take wives. What should I answer to that? Perhaps I will find nothing to say, for (or so you think) you have an answer to everything. Look how nobly you sacrificed the poor priests to the chopping block, saying in your comment on the Emperor's first edict:[178] It had to be endured, in order to safeguard the

170. *wie es dann eyn angelegter karrn war*; lit. a hitched-up waggon, i.e. a conspiracy.
171. Cf. n. 159 above.
172. Matthew 23[18]; Luke 11[39].
173. John 8[39f.]
174. Cf. n. 147 above.
175. Revelation 18[3ff.]
176. *füglicher empörung*; 'righteous retaliation' (Scott).
177. *ein gantz vernünfftiges mittel halten*; 'steer a sensible middle course' (Scott).
178. The fourth article stipulated that the secular authorities should not hinder the punishment of married clergy, as laid down by Canon Law; Luther while deploring

teaching you had initiated. For in your hypocritical way you would be happy enough to have them taken away. In this way you would steadily accumulate new martyrs and could have sung a song or two about them,[179] and would then have been confirmed as a genuine saviour. Then indeed you would sing – as only you can – Nunc dimittis etc.,[180] for all to sing after you. All you need to do, monk, is dance and the whole world falls at your feet.

But if you are a saviour, then a mighty strange one! Christ renders all glory to his father, John 8[181] and says: 'If I pursue my own honour then it is nothing.' But what you want from the people in Orlamünde is a great title.[182] You go and steal (like the black crow you are) the name 'son of God' and expect the gratitude of your prince. Have you not read, you most learned wretch, what God says through Isaiah in chapter 42: 'I will give my glory to no one?'[183] Why not call the good people what Festus is called by Paul in the histories of the apostles, chapter 25?[184] Why do you call the princes 'Your Eminences'? For the title does not belong to them but to Christ, Hebrews 1, John 1, 8.[185] Why do you call them 'High-born'? I thought you were a Christian, but in fact you are an arch-heathen, making them your Joves, your Muses; perhaps not born from the shame of women, as the Wisdom of Solomon puts it, chapter 7,[186] but out of the forehead. It is all too much, too much!

You should be ashamed of yourself, you arch-wretch! Are you trying to patch up a hypocritical accommodation[187] with this erring world? Luke 9.[188] You who wanted to judge all men! You choose well, though, the objects of your insults. The poor monks and priests and merchants cannot defend themselves. So it is easy for you to insult them! But the godless rulers are to be immune from criticism, even if

---

its harshness, advised against resistance; it was 'a precious thing' to suffer injustice for the sake of the Gospel. WA XII, 65f.; Brussels was described as *der Christen fleisch bank* in Eberlin v. Günzburg's Life of Jakob Probst, *Ausgew. Schriften* II (Halle, 1900), p. 110 (Bräuer).

179. Refers to Luther's hymn to the Brussels martyrs of 1523: 'A new song here shall be begun', LW 53, 214ff.

180. Luke 2².

181. John 8⁵⁴.

182. Refers to Luther's controversy with the followers of Karlstadt in Orlamünde in 1524, who declined to address Luther with his customary titles; WA XV, 345.

183. Isaiah 42⁸; the reference is to the titles given by Luther to the princes; cf. Hebrews 1⁵⁻⁹.

184. Acts 25¹ff; Paul gives Festus no title at all.

185. Hebrews 1³f; John 1; 8¹².

186. Wisdom 7².

187. *heüchlen zuflicken*.

188. Luke 9²⁵.

they tread Christ underfoot. But to satisfy the peasants you write that the princes will meet their end through the word of God,[189] and in your gloss on the latest Imperial edict you say: The princes will be cast down from their seats.[190] You prefer them, though, to the merchants. You should give your princes a tug at the nose too! Is it not conceivable that they have merited it more than the others? What concessions do they make? On the interest they charge, on their extortions? But though you have scolded the princes you can give them fresh courage again, you new pope, by presenting them with monasteries and churches. Then they will be happy with you. That's what I would advise you, lest the peasants take matters into their own hands.[191] You are always talking about faith and alleging that I want to do battle with you while shielded and sheltered by you, but that just illustrates my uprightness and your folly.[192] I have been as much shielded and sheltered by you as a sheep by a wolf, Matthew 10.[193] Is it not a fact that you had more power over me there than anywhere else? Couldn't you take that into consideration? What other consequences could that have had? The reason I was in your princedom was to give you no excuse.[194] Under your shield and shelter you say. Oho! how you give yourself away! I take it you're a prince too? What right have you to puff yourself up about your shield and shelter? In all my letters I dispensed with his shield and shelter.[195] I requested him not to alarm his own people just because of the goat shed and the statue of Mary at Mallerbach.[196] Because of this he was all for attacking their hamlet or township, regardless of the fact that the poor folk there sit in anxiety day and night for the sake of the gospel.[197] Do you imagine that the whole province doesn't know how you shield and shelter them? God have mercy on the Christian people. Is not he who has created it its protector? Psalm 110.[198]

You say that I complain about my great sufferings although they amount to no more than three years of exile and chasing around from

---

189. *Letter to the Princes of Saxony*, LW 40, p. 49f.

190. *Zway keyserliche uneynige und wydderwertige gepott den Luther betreffend*, 1524, WA XV, 255.

191. *der pawer möcht sonst zufallen*; F. suggests *dazwischentreten* – (intervene); this whole section is, of course, heavily sarcastic.

192. LW 40, 50.

193. Matthew 10[16].

194. The excuse, presumably, for ignoring Müntzer.

195. Cf. the letter to Duke John of Saxony of 7 June 1524, p. 80/35ff. above.

196. Near Allstedt; the chapel was burnt down in Easter 1524 by a group from Allstedt; the verger's hut is described as a goat-shed (F.); cf. Letters 48, n. 575, and 50 above.

197. Cf. Letter 50, p. 81/1ff.

198. Psalm 111[9]; note the reference to the eternal covenant.

one place to another.[199] Let us see what the truth of this is. You have libelled and abused me by your pen[200] to many honest fellows, as I can prove. You have opened your great coarse mouth and denounced me as a devil. Naturally, that is how you treat all your opponents. Like a black crow all you can do is cry out your own name. You and your unroasted[201] Laurence of Nordhausen know very well the reward already bestowed on evil-doers – to kill me etc. You are no murderous or rebellious spirit, Oh, no! But you incite Duke George like a hound of hell, urging him to fall upon the land of the Elector Frederick and break the common peace.[202] But, of course, that is not to stir up an insurrection, for you are the cunning serpent, which slithers over the rock, Proverbs 30.[203] Christ says in Matthew 10 and 23:[204] 'If they pursue you in one place, flee into the next.' But this messenger, the very arch-chancellor of the devil, says that if I am pursued it shows that I am a devil. He tries to prove this from Matthew 12,[205] producing an interpretation contrary to the holy spirit whom he derides, so shooting himself in the foot, Psalm 26.[206]

He goes to great lengths to make the divine word ridiculous and an object of scorn. He says I call it a heavenly voice and claim that the angels speak with me and so on.[207] My answer: I have no cause to boast of almighty God's dealing with me or words to me; whatever I declare to the people comes through the testimony of God from the Holy Scripture.[208] I try, God willing, not to preach my own fancies. Should I do so, however, I will gladly suffer correction by God and his dear friends and be subject[209] to them. To the scoffer, however, I am under no obligation at all, Proverbs 9,[210] for it is forbidden to eat

---

199. LW 40, 50.

200. Lit. 'with your feather', your quill pen; possibly a play on the 'crow' theme.

201. *ungepraten*; the third century martyr, Laurence of Rome, was said to have been roasted to death on a grid-iron; the first evangelical preacher in Nordhausen, Laurence Süsse, whose life was undignified by such heroism, is 'unroasted;' cf. p. 119/1 above.

202. The basis for this claim, as Hinrichs gently puts it, is not evident; it is probably a misunderstanding of Luther's ironic reference to Duke George's 'clemency', LW 40, 50.

203. Proverbs 30[19]; the arbitrariness of the quotation reflects the deterioration of the argument; the snake (or dragon, or Leviathan (n. 112 and p. 338/8 above)) like the lion – n. 12 above – and the false prophet herald Armageddon; cf. Revelation 16[13].

204. Matthew 10[23]; 23[34].

205. Matthew 12[43]; cf. LW 40, 50.

206. *Hawet darüber sich in die packen*; tr. by Scott; Psalm 27[12].

207. LW 40, 51.

208. *dann allayn was ich durchs gezeügnuss Gottes dem volck auss der heyligen schrifft vorsage.*

209. *urpüttig.*

210. Proverbs 9[7].

the jay, Leviticus 11,[211] i.e. to imbibe the filth of the godless scorner. I am at a loss to know where you get your idea from, since – coming from the Harz as you do – surely you would like the mystery of the divine word to be called a set of heavenly bagpipes?[212] Then the devil, your angel, could have piped your little tune. Monk, whenever you are to dance, all the godless play court to you.

I speak of the divine word with its manifold treasures, Colossians 2[213] which Moses offers for our instruction in Deuteronomy, chapter 30, as does Paul in Romans, chapter 10.[214] Psalm 84[215] says that it will be heard by those who turn whole-heartedly from their old ways and are taught by the spirit to give equal weight to the mercy and to the righteousness of God in all their decisions.[216] You, however, deny the true word and present a mere pretence to the world. This is what makes you into an arch-devil: lacking all understanding you distort the text of Isaiah[217] and make God the cause of evil. Surely that is God's most terrible punishment upon you? You remain blinded, and yet set yourself up as a guide for the world's blind and try to blame God[218] for your being a poor sinner, you poisonous little worm with your stinking humility. You have conjured up such fantasies from your Augustine; truly a blasphemous thing: to pour contempt on man's free will!

You say that I resort at once to forcing faith on people, not giving anyone time to consider. But I say with Christ; Whoever is of God, hears his words.[219] Are you of God? Then why do you not hear it? Why do you deride it, and stand in judgement over things you yourself have never plumbed?[220] Are you only now giving some thought to what you should be teaching other men? You should be called a crook, not a judge.[221] The poor Christian people will eventually realise how right your fleshly understanding was to oppose the unerring spirit of God. Let Paul pronounce his judgement

---

211. Leviticus 11[15]; an unclean bird; member of crow family.
212. Müntzer regards Luther's home county of Mansfeld as part of the Harz territories, where folk music made much use of the bagpipes; to counter Luther's ridiculing of his 'heavenly voice' he pictures Luther dancing to 'heavenly' bagpipes (Hinrichs).
213. Colossians 2[3]; cf. n. 163 above.
214. Deuteronomy 30[11]; Romans 10[8]; (God is near at hand).
215. Psalm 85[8f.]
216. Cf. n. 137 above.
217. Isaiah 40[2, 6ff.]; cf. WA VII, 144.
218. *Got in pussem stossen.*
219. John 8[47].
220. *befunden.*
221. *ein krummer denn ein richter*; a word play on 'crooked' and 'upright'.

on you, 2 Corinthians 11.[222] You have always acted straightforwardly, your symbol should be an onion, with its nine skins, as straightforwardly as a fox. See, you have become a real black fox,[223] howling loudest before day-break. And now that the real truth is dawning it is the lowly and not the mighty whom you want to blame. What you do, as we Germans say,[224] is to climb into the well, like the fox who stepped into the bucket and ate the fish. Then he enticed the silly wolf into the well by the other bucket and so he sailed up and the wolf stayed down. The same fate will befall the princes who follow you, and these noble roosters whom you whip up against the merchants. In chapters 13 and 34 Ezekiel gives his judgement on the fox when referring to the beasts, the wild animals whom Christ calls the wolves, John 10.[225] They will all suffer the same fate as the foxes that have been trapped, Psalm 72.[226] When the people begin to pay attention to the light, the little dogs, Matthew 15,[227] will pursue the foxes right into their dens, and all they will be able to do at first is snap at their mouths. But the bold dog[228] will so shake the fox by its fur that it will have to leave the den. Its days of gobbling hens will be over. See here, Martin, has your nose not told you that it is a fox that is being roasted, like the ones given to the greenhorns at a hunting lodge instead of a hare? It serves you right, you Esau,[229] that Jacob has pushed you aside. Why have you sold your inheritance for the sake of a meal?

Ezechiel 13 and Micah 3 will tell you.[230] You have confused the Christian people with false beliefs and now that troubles have come[231] you cannot put them right. So you play the hypocrite with the princes and imagine that as long as you acquire a great reputation all has gone well. You never tire of prattling about how you stood up before a very threatening assembly at Leipzig. Do you think you can deceive everyone? You had such a good time at Leipzig that you drove out of the city gate with a wreath of carnations on your head

222. 2 Corinthians 11[13ff]; cf. n. 162, n. 163, n. 165 above.

223. *prandtfuchs*; really means a fox with black ears, feet and brush; here a burning, raging fox (Hinrichs); cf. the 'burning' theme in n. 147, n. 174 above.

224. The story of Reynard The Fox.

225. Ezekiel 13[4]; 34[25]; John 10[12].

226. Psalm 73[18ff].

227. Matthew 15[27]!

228. *fryschhundt*.

229. The sequence of thought is hard to follow; perhaps the fox's fur points to Esau, the 'hairy man'; or is it simply that Luther, the 'first-born' of the Reformation, is being replaced by Müntzer and his ilk?; cf. Genesis 25[24ff], 27.

230. Ezekiel 13[3-9] (false prophets like foxes); Micah 3[5-8] (false and true prophets).

231. *nun die noet heergeet*.

and drank good wine at Melchior Lotter's.[232] And when you were at Augsburg you were immune from danger there too, for you could lean on Staupitz as an oracle to help you, though he has now deserted you and has become an abbot.[233] I would not be at all surprised if you were to follow him, for truly the devil cannot abide the truth, he cannot cease from his wiles. Yet, as the writing about insurrection shows, the prophecies against his abominations unnerve him.[234] This is why his language about the new prophets is like that of the biblical scholars about Christ, John 8.[235] That is why I have used almost the whole of that chapter for this judgement of mine.[236] In 1 Corinthians 14,[237] Paul says this about the prophets: A true preacher has to be a prophet and indeed – though the world may laugh this to scorn – the whole world must become prophetic if it is to judge who the false prophets are. Who are you to judge others when you abdicate from your own ministry in the Monk-Calf book?[238] You claim to have punched me in the mouth, but that is not the truth at all.[239] The lie is buried a pike-staff deep in your throat,[240] for I have not been near you for six or seven years.[241] But if you have made a fool of the good brothers[242] who did call on you this will surely be revealed one day.

232. Luther sported some carnations at the famous debate in Leipzig with John Eck 1519, and stayed at Lotter's home, which had a wine-shop; (Hinrichs); cf. LW 40, 53.

233. *dann Stupicianum oraculum stundt hart bey dir*; learning of a papal plan to arrest Luther Staupitz tried to gather money to enable Luther to flee Augsburg. (Hinrichs)

234. Cf. Luther's *Sincere Admonition . . . against Insurrection and Rebellion*, LW 45, 51ff.

235. John 8[52].

236. *urteyl*; in fact a careful examination of John 8 throws much light on this whole writing.

237. 1 Corinthians 14[1-5].

238. In a tract on the interpretation of two 'abominable figures', the Papal ass at Rome and the 'Monk Calf' at Freiberg in Meissen, (in 1522 a deformed calf had been born near Freiberg) Luther had declined to interpret the significance of the 'Monk Calf' 'because I am not a prophet'. *Deutung der zwo grewlichen figuren, Bapstesels zu Rom und Mönchkalbs zu Freiberg in Meißen funden*, (1523) WA XI, 380.

239. Luther claimed that 'the spirit of Allstedt . . . has been once or twice in my cloister in Wittenberg and had his nose punched.' LW 40, 52.

240. *du leugst in deinen halss spiesstief*.

241. Hinrichs claims that Luther may not have meant Müntzer himself when he spoke of the 'spirit of Allstedt', but have been referring to the meeting with Stübner and Storch in 1522; Müntzer denies having been in Wittenberg since his early stay there; Dismer, p. 260ff., argues that this is correct, dating his stay 1517/18; a lecture copied by Müntzer in Wittenberg in 1517/18 is shortly to be published by Ulrich Bubenheimer, 'Thomas Müntzers Nachschrift einer Wittenberger Hieronymus-vorlesung', ZKG 99 (1988).

242. Stübner and Storch, the 'Zwickau prophets'.

For that is what is meant by the saying[243] that you should not despise the humble, Matthew 18.[244]

The insane folly of your boasting simply sends one to sleep. That you stood up at Worms before the Empire[245] is to the credit of the German nobility, whose great mouths you smeared with honey, for they were quite sure that your preaching would present them with monasteries and foundations on the Bohemian pattern.[246] These you now promise to the princes. If you had vacillated at Worms, the nobility would have stabbed you, not released you, as everyone knows. You have absolutely no right to book this to your account, to boast, as you do, that you were once again prepared to risk your noble blood. You and your followers resorted to crazy tricks and deceptions. You let yourself be captured at your own suggestion and then pretended it was against your will.[247] Anyone who had not seen through your rascally behaviour would swear by the saints that you were a pious Martin indeed. Sleep softly, dear flesh! I would prefer to smell you roasting in your arrogance in a pot[248] or in a cauldron by the fire, Jeremiah 1,[249] smitten by God's wrath, and then stewing in your own juice. May the devil devour you! Ezekiel 23.[250] Your flesh is like that of an ass; it would be a long time cooking and would turn out to be a tough dish indeed for your mealy-mouthed friends.[251]

My most beloved brothers in Christ, at first I was weary of this quarrel because of the offence it was bound to give to the common man, and if Doctor Liar had allowed me to preach or had confuted me in public or allowed his princes to judge the matter when I was before them in Weimar,[252] when they questioned me at the instance of this very monk, then I would have been much happier to leave this matter alone.

In the end it was decided that the prince should leave the matter in the hands of the awful Judge on the Last Day. He declined to take measures against the tyrants who use the pretext of the gospel to

243. *Es wirt sich anderst nit reymen*; Hinrichs takes this to be a reference to Luther's statement that he punched 'the spirit' on the nose.

244. Matthew 18[10].

245. Cf. LW 40, 53; the Diet of Worms in 1521.

246. Secularisation of church property on the Hussite model.

247. *und stelltest dich gar unleydlich.*

248. *im hafen*; Luther had talked of Müntzer smelling 'the roast', LW 40, p. 52, and the theme of roasting recurs throughout this writing.

249. Jeremiah 1[13].

250. Ezekiel 24[1-13]; 23[46f.]

251. *deinen milchmeulern*; lit. 'milk-mouths', cf. 1 Corinthians 3[2].

252. On 1 August 1524 Duke John summoned him to Weimar; cf. his letters, Nrs. 64–68, pp. 110–121 above.

violate his sphere of influence.[253] It would be good if the courts[254] were instructed in the same way too; the peasants would approve of that. It would be good to leave everything to the Last Judgement; this would give the peasants a great case.[255] When they[256] should be doing what is right, they say: I leave it to the Judge; in the meantime, however, the rod of the godless is to be used.

When I returned from the hearing at Weimar I intended to preach the earnest[257] word of God. Then along came the magistrates and sought to hand me over to the worst enemies of the gospel. When I got wind of this there was no more tarrying for me. I swept their dust from my shoes,[258] for it was crystal clear to me that they had more respect for their oaths and duties than for God's word.[259] They proposed to serve two masters who opposed one another,[260] although God would quite clearly have stood by them; he who had delivered them from the power of the bear and the lion would also have delivered them from the hands of Goliath, 1 Kings 17.[261] Although Goliath put his trust in his armour and his shield, David would teach him a lesson.[262] Saul, too, began by doing some good, but it was David who, after lengthy wanderings, had to bring it to fruition, which is a symbol of you, O Christ, in your dear friends.[263] You will zealously care for them to all eternity. Amen.

ANNO MDXXIIII

Vulpis, fecisti merere mendaciter cor iusti, quem dominus non contristavit. Confortastique manus impiorum tuorum, ne

---

253. *in sein pfleg fallen*; Duke George of Saxony and Count Frederick von Witzleben (cf. Letter 57, n.734) will be the tyrants referred to; Müntzer is complaining that their actions are endangering subjects of the Elector, but that the latter refused to take action to support the League of the Elect.

254. *dem gericht*; lit. 'court'; the thought is telescoped and the meaning not quite clear; Müntzer seems to be arguing for consistency; if questions of justice were universally left to God's Last Judgement that would suit the peasants; in fact, however, this is only done selectively, where the peasants' interests are at stake; verbal protestation and the realities of power remain poles apart; cf. the *Exposé*, p. 288/6ff. above.

255. *gute sach*; I follow here the punctuation of Elliger, p. 622.

256. The princes.

257. *ernste*, 'earnest', 'severe'; rather like the Puritan 'painful'.

258. Luke 10[11]; Müntzer left Allstedt on 8 August.

259. Cf. Letters 66, p. 114/16ff., 67, p. 117/15ff.

260. Cf. Matthew 6[24].

261. 1 Samuel 17[36f.]

262. *lernen*; 'larn him'!

263. Not least Müntzer himself.

revertantur a via sua mala, ob id peribis et populus dei liberabitur a tyrannide tua. Tu videbis deum esse dominum. Ezechielis 13. capitulo.[264]

Translated this reads: O Doctor Liar, you wily fox.[265] With your lies you have saddened the heart of the just man, whom God did not cause to grieve. For you have strengthened the power of the godless evil-doers, so that they could continue on in their old way. Therefore your fate will be that of the fox that has been hunted down;[266] the people will go free and God alone will be their Lord.

264. Ezekiel 13 refers to the false prophets; Müntzer's quotation for the Vulgate appears to be from memory; it is loosely based on v. 22, and 20; in v. 4 the false prophets are described as 'foxes'.

265. Not, of course, in the Latin.

266. Again Müntzer cannot resist the temptation to elaborate; cf. Song of Songs 2[15].

INCIDENTAL WRITINGS AND NOTES

This section gathers together most of the literary remains of Müntzer which were not dealt with in his correspondence. However the liturgical material: the Officium St. Cyriaci, from his time in Frose 1515–16, and the translation of Psalm 119$^{161-176}$ has been omitted, as have the extracts from Pliny and Diogenes Laertes in Müntzer's hand. Some pieces in the 'letter-sack' have not been included; two style letters by Ambrosius (Emmen), the Czech version of the Prague Manifesto, Latin notes by Duke George of Saxony, a list of Plato's writings, the Historie Thomas Müntzer, and some other fragments.

This is the most neglected section of Müntzer's work. The material varies greatly in importance, from quite central writings such as the Prague Manifesto to slight jottings on the back or the margins of letters. Its fragmentary character reminds us how much of Müntzer has been lost.

These sermons, prayers, hymns, shopping-lists, book-lists, odd scraps of notes do, however, throw considerable light on Müntzer's everyday concerns, and on the largely pastoral, devotional, non-polemical character of his concerns. A high proportion is in Latin. They not only supplement what we know elsewhere, but focus our attention on Müntzer's views on some subjects in a quite fresh way: on discipleship, the nature of Christ, the role of women, on the 'order of things'.

The Prague Manifesto rightly takes pride of place. For all the solid scholarly attention it has received in recent years, there is still little consensus on its interpretation, and a critical edition of its various versions remains a desiderandum. The 'Propositions' of Egranus have been helpfully analysed by Elliger, although many problems still remain. With the notable exception of Dismer the sermons and expositions of Scripture have been unfairly neglected in the past, while the notes and jottings are still more virgin territory. It is, above all, puzzling that Müntzer's marginal notes on Tertullian have not been transcribed previously. Without them our knowledge of Müntzer is unbalanced. It is to be hoped that, with this edition, at least a beginning has been made.

The final documents on Müntzer's interrogation and 'recantation' and on the background to his life again show a heavy debt to Franz's work. There have been, however, some revisions and additions, not least the mysterious Rumherius letter, and the Mühlhausen articles. It seemed appropriate that the moving letter by his wife, Ottilie von Gersen, should have the last word.

1. Prague Manifesto

The Prague Manifesto, as the first major statement of Müntzer's views, is of primary importance. The existence of no less than four manuscript versions of it, a shorter and longer German one, a Latin one, and an incomplete Czech one, indicates the weight attached to it by Müntzer himself. Yet both the circumstances of his visit to Prague, the relationship of the various versions to one another, and the actual content or message of the Manifesto still remain to some extent obscure.

Prague, it appears, was to be Müntzer's Jerusalem. His last days in Zwickau had been filled with foreboding. He therefore set out for Prague as much with martyrdom in mind as with any anticipation that the true reformation was about to begin there (Letter 24).

He appears to have made a brief exploratory visit first to Žatec (Saaz), just inside Bohemia, between the end of April and the beginning of June.[1] It is not clear why he rushed back to Germany – to settle his affairs, perhaps, or to secure the impatiently awaited companionship of Stübner, one of the 'Zwickau prophets' (Letter 22) and, he hoped, others (Letter 23). His sense of insecurity seems to be reflected in the letter to Nicholas Hausmann of 15 June (Letter 25) which makes no mention at all of his imminent departure.

Hence his initial welcome in Prague around 21 June must have surpassed all his expectations. For the first time in his life he was honoured and feted. Accommodation was provided for him in the Collegium Carolinum, by 23 June he was preaching in Latin and German in the University chapels and welcomed as an *emulus Martini*,[2] a disciple of Luther. The contrast to his recent treatment in

---

1. On the visit to Prague cf. Gritsch, pp. 45ff.; Elliger, pp. 181ff.; Elliger's conclusions rest largely on the study by Vaclav Husa, 'Tomas Müntzer a Čechy', *Rozpracy Českolovenské Akademie Vêd. Ročník* 67 (1957), 1–102.

2. On the outer side of a copy of Melanchthon's disputation thesis which he had copied and taken with him to Prague, Müntzer has written the words '*Emulus Martini apud Dominum distat duo semimiliaria a Praga*'; as Elliger, p. 184, n. 19, comments, the meaning of the last 5 words has yet to be clarified; but cf. the odd verbal similarity to the Latin version of the Prague Manifesto where the hearts of the preachers are said to be a thousand miles away from the word of God *plusquam mille miliaria distant ab ipsis*, F. p. 508/30; Rupp, *Patterns of Reformation* (London, 1969), p. 172f., prints the Latin text, which is available in facsimile form in Husa, op. cit., and makes the point that '*aemulus Martini*' could refer to Melanchthon:

'Question to be debated by M[aster] Thomas Müntzer:

Human nature loves itself for its own sake more than anything else; it cannot love
    God for his own sake
Divine as well as natural law commands that God should be loved for his own sake
Since we cannot do this, the law brings about a servile fear of God
What is feared must be hated. The Law, then, leads us to regard God with hate

Zwickau must have been quite extraordinary. Yet by the end of his five-month stay, when he seems to have penned the Manifesto, the wheel of fortune had turned once more. He had been constrained to leave his comfortable quarters, to content himself with small groups of listeners; by the end of November he had to suffer the indignity of something like house-arrest and probably his expulsion from the city.[3]

It seems probable, therefore, that the Manifesto reflects not only the bitter experiences of his Zwickau days – the scorn of his humanist opponent, Egranus, and his dismissal by the city authorities – but the further humiliations he had suffered in Prague.

If we accept the shorter German version (A) as the first draft the more intemperate tone of the Latin (C) and larger German (B) versions may reflect his mounting frustration and anger as the warm welcome was replaced by suspicion and repression. There are close correspondences between the Latin version and B; contrary to the traditional view, Elliger has argued for the priority of the former.[4] It is worth noting that the Czech version, based on B, was never completed, no doubt indicating the waning enthusiasm for Müntzer's mission.

As hate cannot be the starting-point for love, so servile fear cannot be the starting-point for filial fear

It follows that servile fear cannot be the starting-point for penitence

Therefore righteousness is Christ's gift

All our righteousness is attributed to us gratuitously by God

Therefore to say good deeds, too, are sins is not dissimilar to the truth

The mind cannot assent to any proposition that is beyond reason or experience

Nor can the will of itself constrain the mind to agree by images (eiconibus)

This agreement is faith or wisdom

As to the Catholic faith, it is not necessary to believe any points which go beyond those to which Scripture testifies

The authority of councils is subject to the authority of Scripture

Therefore to doubt the [indelible priestly] character, transubstantiation etc. does not incriminate one of heresy

Acquired faith is a delusion

To offend in one instance, is to be guilty of all

The commandments are to love your enemy, not to seek vengeance, not to swear, to have all things in common

The laws of nature are habits coeval with the soul's creation

Nature yearns more for the good life than merely for life itself

God is one, the sum of all things is in the divine attributes (*categoriis*)'.

3. Stübner reported on his return to Wittenberg that stones had been thrown at him, but – miraculously – they had all missed their mark; cf. Elliger, p. 213.

4. Elliger, pp. 202ff.; Wolgast, *Thomas Müntzer: Ein Verstörer der Ungläubigen* (Gottingen/Zürich, 1981), p. 26, even speculates that the sole purpose of B was as a basis for the Czech version; de Boor argues that the (undated) Latin edition may have been the first, its arguments being condensed in the shorter German version, and

The shorter German version is dated 1 November. It is in Müntzer's own hand. The large placard-like format in which it was written and the date chosen certainly appear to suggest a parallel to Luther's 95 Theses four years previously. If so a new, more far-reaching Reformation was being proclaimed. B, three times larger, is dated 29 November; it is a contemporary copy, with a generous harvest of errors. The Latin version is simply dated 1521, and is in Müntzer's own hand.

The ostensible aim of all the versions is to summon the Czech people to reassert their historic role as the pioneers of a genuine, apostolic renovation of the Church, rejecting both the Roman obedience and practice and a mere wordy Biblicism, and embracing an authentic, personal, Spirit-filled faith. The reference to John Hus is natural in this context; on 7 July there had been a militant demonstration in his memory.

Müntzer begins by presenting his credentials. His previous preaching career at Zwickau is not mentioned; indeed apart from his birthplace no evidence at all is presented for his outrageous claim to have surpassed all others in his zealous pursuit of the truth. Given his denial that he had learnt anything from intermediaries – clergy, monks, or scholars – and his emphasis on immediate revelation from God, such evidence would in any case have been redundant. His zeal and his readiness to suffer bear sufficient witness to the truth of his claims – as do Christ and all the elect.

In sharp contrast to this stands the hypocrisy and unprofessional conduct of the old clergy, the so-called leading Christians, who have failed to instruct him, and others like him, about the nature of salvation, about the waters or abyss of the Spirit, the time of trial and self-emptying, the order of creation and the relation of the parts to the whole.

Müntzer does not reprove the clergy in Lutheran manner for concealing or repressing Scripture, but for presenting it in undigested, disparate pieces, thus manifesting lack of pastoral concern and their own spiritual deadness; for such texts are cold, 'stolen' testimonies to their own 'dumb' God. Lacking revelation themselves they cannot, like Ezekiel, digest truth but can only, like storks ingest and disgorge it. The references to the scorn with which they treat

---

then, presumably after the break with the Prague authorities, extended and sharpened in the larger German version, which was complemented by the Czech version; each version has its own readership and orientation in mind and care should be taken to distinguish them; 'Zur Textgeschichte des Prager Manifestes', in M. Steinmetz and W. Trillitzsch (edd.), *Thomas Müntzer: Prager Manifest* (Leipzig, 1975), pp. 7–15.

those who claim such revelation will reflect Müntzer's own treatment at the hands of Egranus and Agricola.

For Müntzer this denial of personal revelation, by refusing entrance to one's soul of its true 'possessor', the Spirit, makes nonsense of faith. It also prevents the restoration of the order of creation. Hence, such clergy are possessed by the Devil. Their reluctance to be conformed to Christ in his suffering, removes the key of true knowledge from the elect and hardens the wicked in their ways.

The result is the ruin of the church, its submergence in worldly concerns and standards. Unlike the primitive church, it lacks both the certainty of election[5] and the missionary authority of those with immediate experience of faith. Its censorious dogmatism cloaks licentiousness and inner fraudulence, which may well attract cataclysmic judgement.

The time of harvest, then, is at hand. Already Müntzer is sharpening his sickle for this. The separation of the godly from the ungodly which should have taken place long before will now be enforced. Only B contains explicit chiliastic prophecy[6] but all the versions warn of an impending attack, by the Turks, within a year, according to A,[7] if his warnings are not heeded. If, however, they do respond, the new church will arrive in their midst, to the joy of the elect everywhere.

The Latin version is generally less taut than A, adding many Biblical references and much pointless invective, as well as some expansion, though hardly clarification, of Müntzer's understanding of the process of salvation. Like B, which is still more self-indulgently moralistic and polemical, it is a less successful piece of writing than A and its appeal to the 'cultural élite'[8] must have been minimal.

The weaknesses of the Manifesto are obvious. Even in A the logic is at best opaque, the language frequently obscure or 'coded'; rational, historical or theological analysis is only sporadically present. It begins disastrously with the insistence on Müntzer's personal authority, and generally it is a reflection on Müntzer's own immediate past experience, rather than an engagement with the fluid, but highly complex religious situation in Bohemia; no positive or coherent programme for reform is offered. As a clarion-call to action it was, in fact, an unmitigated failure, a bizarre misreading of the situation in and around Prague. Despite the desire to reach 'the whole world' the Manifesto never saw publication. Müntzer's exaggerated

---

5. Cf. Müntzer's letter to Luther in July 1520, p. 20/32f. above.
6. Cf. p. 371/19ff. below.
7. Cf. p. 360/25 below.
8. Cf. Elliger, p. 192.

expectations of Bohemia were replaced thereafter by an ominous silence. Perhaps they foreshadow the hopes he would later pin on the peasants in 1524–5.

Yet the fascination of the Manifesto remains. It adumbrates, not least in its appeal to Eastern Europe, countless themes of the later, so-called Radical Reformation: the 'separation' of the godly, faith in 'the people' as opposed to the authorities, distrust of scholarship, the need for immediate revelation; a primitivist ecclesiology, some sensitivity to other faiths. Its Biblical basis may be relatively tenuous, unlike Müntzer's later writings, but its intricate counter-pointing of apocalyptic and mystical language and themes will often be repeated in the future.

It does, then afford us a glimpse into the emergence of Müntzer's own independent thinking. The *Sermon to the Princes*, for example, will take up the themes of the seven-fold holy spirit and the third day of sprinkling; the centrality of the order of creation recurs throughout his later writing as does his understanding of Scripture as testimony to the living word in the soul. The programmatic call for the true preacher, with its perhaps unexpected succession of gentle, maternal images, and its concern for the 'poor, poor, poor people' will be taken up by Müntzer himself in his Allstedt ministry.

Shorter German Version (A)

I, Thomas Müntzer of Stolberg, do declare before the whole church and the whole world – wherever this letter[1] may be shown – that I can testify with Christ and all the elect who have known me from my youth up, to having shown all possible diligence, more than any other man known to me, in pursuing[2] better instruction about the holy and invincible Christian faith. For at no time in my life (God knows I am not lying) did I learn anything about the true exercise of the faith from any monk or priest, or about the edifying time of trial which clarifies[3] faith in the spirit of the fear of God, showing the need[4] for an elect man to have the seven-fold gift of the holy spirit.[5] I have not heard from a single scholar about the order of God implanted in all creatures, not the tiniest word about it;[6] while as to understanding the whole as a unity of all the parts[7] those who claim to be Christians have not caught the least whiff of it – least of all the accursed priests. I have heard from them about mere Scripture, which they have stolen from the Bible like murderers and thieves; in chapter 23 Jeremiah

1. *dysse bryff* (plural on analogy of Latin *litterae*).
2. lit. 'to have or gain'.
3. *vorclereth*.   4. *inhaldungk*.
5. In the margin *frucht* (fruit), and above this Isaiah 11a; cf. C, n. 4.
6. There are few more controversial areas in Müntzer's thought than his 'theology of the creatures' or teaching on the order of God; Rupp sees some closeness to a natural theology; H.-J. Goertz, (*Innere und Äussere Ordnung in der Theologie Thomas Müntzers*. Leiden, 1967) regards it as the link between his mystical theology and his revolutionary political programme, a fusion of 'inner' and 'outer' order; R. Schwarz, p. 125, sees Müntzer's concept of order as the 'quintessence' of his chiliastic world view; W. Ullmann sees it as a radical new understanding of salvation history, cf. p. 000; it is certainly of central importance to Müntzer and recurs again and again in his later writings; it signifies the restitution of right relationships between God and man, on the one hand, and between man and the creatures, on the other, as envisaged in Genesis I, p. 387/16; cf. Jeremiah 31;[36] but forfeited by Adam, p. 388/3ff.; God alone, as uncreated, being, is to be feared, p. 87/17f., p. 235/15f., and trusted, p. 215/19; for this to happen we have to be conformed to Christ, p. 396/21f., and freed from our lusts, p. 199/12ff., and our love of wealth and honour, p. 292/23f., indeed of all creaturely supports, including the words of Scripture themselves, p. 359/26ff. Then instead of being 'possessed' by pleasures, p. 280/10f., God himself will 'possess' our soul cf. Letter 31 n. 293, and p. 389/5ff.; being 'in order' ourselves, we will then exercise our rightful authority over the creatures, which belong to all the elect and not to the tyrannous princes, pp. 255f.; the Biblical basis for this is set out in an appendix to 'On Following Christ', p. 398; cf. Dismer, pp. 7ff.; cf. also the last three of Melanchthon's theses, p. 353, n. 2 above.
7. *das gantze eyn eynygher weck alle teyle*; cf. 1 Corinthians 13[9]; the Platonic contrast between oneness or simplicity and multiplicity, or distraction (cf. the *Vindication*, p. 340/17ff.) is wedded with that of the sole lordship of God over his creation and that of Christ, saviour and head, over his members, p. 70/26f.; it is in the abyss of the soul that all partial vision becomes whole, p. 241/18f.; cf. B. p. 363/12f.

describes this theft as stealing the word of God from the mouth of your neighbour;[8] for they themselves have never heard it from God, from his very mouth. In my opinion these really are fine preachers, consecrated for just this purpose by the devil. But St Paul writes to the Corinthians, in the third chapter of the second epistle,[9] that the hearts of men are the paper or parchment on which God's finger inscribes his unchangeable will and his eternal wisdom, but not with ink; a writing which any man can read, providing his mind has been opened to it; as Jeremiah and Ezekiel[10] say, this is where God writes his laws, on the third day, that of the sprinkling: when man's mind is opened up. God has done this for his elect from the very beginning, so that the testimony they are given is not uncertain, but an invincible one from the holy spirit, which then gives our spirit ample testimony that we are the children of God.[11] For anyone who does not feel the spirit of Christ within him, or is not quite sure of having it, is not a member of Christ, but of the devil, Romans 8.[12] Now the world (led astray by many sects) has for a long time been yearning desperately for the truth; thus the saying of Jeremiah,[13] has been fulfilled: the children have clamoured for bread but no one was there to break it to them.[14] For there were many, and there still are [many] today, who have flung bread to them like dogs,[15] that is, the letter of the word of God; but[16] they have not broken it to them. Oh! note this, note this! They have not broken it to the children. They have not explained the true spirit of the fear of God which would have informed them truthfully that their status as children of God could never be forfeit. That is the reason why Christians are such effeminate creatures about (defending the truth);[17] so they can chatter away about God not speaking to people any more, as if he had suddenly become dumb;[18] they think it enough to have it written in books, so they can vomit it out undigested[19] like a stork [disgorging] frogs to her young ones in the

---

8. Jeremiah 23[30].

9. 2 Corinthians 3[3].

10. Jeremiah 31[33]; Ezekiel 36[25f.]; Numbers 19[12]; cf. *Sermon to the Princes*, n. 117; this reference to the opening-up of the mind or reason (*vornunft*) occurs only in A; cf. Letter 31, p. 46/16f.

11. Romans 8[16].

12. Romans 8[9].

13. Lamentations 4[4].

14. Cf. Matthew 7[9].

15. Cf. Matthew 15[27].

16. *adder*.

17. *memmen*; 'knaves' (Rupp); the linguistic evidence, unfortunately, makes a trans, such as 'womanish men' inescapable; cf. Grimm VI, 2005.

18. Cf. *Exposé*, p. 298/5f. above.

19. *rôch*; i.e. undigested.

nest. They are not like the hen which goes around with her children and keeps them warm;[20] nor do they spread abroad in people's hearts the goodness of God's word (which lives there in all the elect) like a mother giving milk to a child, but they treat the people like Balaam;[21] they mouth the empty words, but their heart is a good hundred thousand miles removed from them. It would be no wonder if this stupidity had provoked God to smash us to smithereens along with our clownish faith. Not is it any surprise to me that all the nations of men deride us Christians, and spew us out, if no one can do better than [to assert]: It is written here, it is written there.[22] Yes, my dear sirs, this wonderful proof has been dreamt up in the hen-house. If a simple man or an unbeliever were to come into one of our gatherings, and we tried to bowl him over with our chatter he would say: 'Are you mad or stupid? What is your scripture to me?' But if we learn the real living word of God we will win over the unbeliever and speak with obvious authority[23] when the secret places of his heart are revealed so that he has to confess humbly that God is in us. Look, Paul testifies to all this in the first epistle to the Corinthians, chapter 14,[24] saying there that a preacher needs revelation; without it he should not preach the word. The devil believes in the truth of the Christian faith.[25] If the servants of Antichrist deny all this, then God must be mad and stupid, since he has said that his word will never pass away.[26] Would that not be the case if God had ceased to speak?

Take note of this text, if you happen to have any brains in your head: Heaven and earth will pass away, my word will never pass away.[27] If it is only written in books, nowhere else, and God spoke only once and then vanished into thin air, then it surely cannot be the word of the eternal God. Then it is just a creaturely thing, entering the memory in an external way,[28] all of which is contrary to the true order and contrary to the rule of the holy faith, as Jeremiah says.[29] That is why all the prophets speak in this way: 'Thus says the Lord';

20. Cf. Matthew 23[37].

21. *machen in den leuten, Balams weyse*; *aus* is crossed out before *in*; cf. Numbers 22–24; (Balaam speaks God's word, but is slower to recognise the angel of the Lord than his ass).

22. A theme which Müntzer continues to develop, e.g. in the *Exposé*, p. 270ff. above.

23. *richten sichtlych*.

24. *andern*, i.e. 'second', crossed out and replaced by 14; 1 Corinthians 2 does seem at first sight more relevant, e.g. vs. 4, 10; chapter 14 deals with speaking in tongues; cf. esp. vs. 23, 24, which refer to outsiders.

25. James 2[19].

26. Isaiah 40[8]; a favourite text of Müntzer.

27. Matthew 24[35].

28. *in dye gdechnusz von auszwennig eyngeczoghen*; cf. p. 404/4 below.

29. Jeremiah 31,[33] another favourite text.

they do not say: 'Thus said the Lord', as if it were past history; they speak in the present tense.

This intolerable and noxious canker from which the Christian people suffers has moved me in pity to read the history of the early fathers with all diligence. Find that after the death of the apostles' pupils the immaculate virginal church became a whore by the adultery of the clergy; it was the fault of the scholars, who always want to sit up top, as Hegesippus writes and then, after him, Eusebius in Book 4, chapter xxii.[30] Nor do I find any council giving a convincing account of its faith in the infallible word of God in terms of the entire living order;[31] there was nothing but child's play. All this has been possible because of the loose rein[32] God has given men, so that all their works might be manifest. But, God be praised, it can never be the case that the Christian church is made up of monkeys and monks,[33] for the elect friends of God's word must also learn to prophesy, as Paul teaches,[34] so that they can really experience the friendly and oh! so generous-hearted way in which God speaks with all his elect. In order to bring such teaching to the light I am willing to sacrifice my life for God's sake. God will do wonderful things with his elect, especially in this land.[35] For the new church will begin here, this people will be a mirror for the whole world. Therefore I summon every single person to help in the defence of God's word. And let me also point out to you[36] openly, in the spirit of Elijah, those who have taught you to sacrifice to the idol, Baal.[37] If you refuse God will let you be struck down by the Turks in the coming year.[38] I know for sure that what I say is in fact the case. I am ready to suffer for it what

30. Eusebius, *Ecclesiastical History* IV, 22, 4–6; cf. Letters 7–9; Hegesippus, a second-century writer, is quoted by Eusebius as an authority on the early church; a theme later taken up in the *Sermon to the Princes*, p. 232/2ff. above; note the intense manner in which he reads history; cf. C. p. 377/12.

31. *nach gestrackter lebendyger ordenungk*; cf. C, p. 377/19f.; *gestrackt*: fully stretched out, like a weaving (?)

32. *den vorhencklichen willen Gots.*

33. *pfaffen und affen*, lit. 'priests and monkeys'; the polemic of A against the clergy and scholars is more succinct than B and C but pulls no punches; only C explicitly calls for a choice to be made between Müntzer and the Czech priests (p. 378/21) but the reference in both A (l. 23 below) and B (p. 371/12) to Müntzer's acting in the 'spirit of Elijah' implies this; the differences between the versions should not be exaggerated.

34. 1 Corinthians 14[1ff.]

35. Bohemia.

36. *dyr* (singular); there is little social reference, and only one mention of 'the people'.

37. 2 Kings 2[15]; 1 Kings 18[18–40]; Elijah is of course a Messianic figure; cf. Mark 9[12].

38. One of the very few instances of which we know where Müntzer makes a specific prediction.

Jeremiah had to bear.[39] Take it to heart, dear Bohemians. It is not just I, but God himself, as the saying of Peter[40] teaches me, who commands you to give an account of your faith. I will give you an account of my faith, too; if I do not master the knowledge of which I make such boast then may I be subject to temporal and eternal death.[41] I can offer no higher pledge. With that, I commend you to Christ.

Prague in 1521 on the day of All Saints.[42]

39. i.e. imprisonment and contempt.
40. 1 Peter 4[5].
41. *so will ich seyn eyn kint des czeytlichen unde ewygen todts*; cf. Matthew 23[15].
42. 1 November 1521.

Larger German Version (B)

A PROTESTATION CONCERNING THE SITUATION IN BOHEMIA[1]

I, Thomas Müntzer, born in Stolberg and living in Prague, the city of the dear and saintly warrior[2] John Hus, intend to fill the sonorous marching trumpets[3] with the new song of praise of the holy spirit. With my whole heart I make my testimony and raise a bitter complaint to all the churches of the elect, to the whole world, too, wherever this letter may reach. Christ and all the elect, who have known me from my youth, stand by this undertaking[4] of mine. I declare, pledging all that is most precious to me as warranty,[5] that I have applied myself with special diligence and the utmost industry to reach a better understanding of how the holy, invincible Christian faith was founded[6] than that of other men. I make bold to affirm the truth that no tar-salved priest, no spirit-dissimulating monk[7] was able to tell [me] anything about the ground of faith, not the tiniest point. Like me many other men have complained that, although labouring under genuinely intolerable burdens,[8] they have never once been comforted, or enabled to be confident that in all their desires and deeds they have been led by faith, but had to work their own way through them.[9] They had not been able, either, to discover the

1. *Der Bemen sache betreffende protestation.*

2. *kempers*; Latin version: *athleta*.

3. *dye lautbaren unde bewegliche trummeten*; cf. Letter 45, p. 67/32f.; note the allusion to the militant Hussite tradition, and to the coming judgement declared in Psalm 98[1, 6, 9].

4. *antragen.*

5. Cf. A, p. 361/6 above.

6. *gegrundet*; it is the ground of ongoing faith, not primarily its historical basis, in which Müntzer is interested.

7. *kein pechgesalbeter pfaffe, keyn gar geystscheynender münnich.*

8. *untrechtliche unde warhafftige drucknusse*; the Czech version, as translated by Wolfgramm, speaks of the deceptions of the monks; following this, F. takes *drucknüsse* to mean *Betrüge* (deceptions); cf. the reference to this later in the *Sermon to the Princes*, p. 237/30ff. above; in the Latin version, however, the term *angustia*, p. 372/12 below, would suggest *Bedrücknis* (oppression) as the meaning; it appears that both meanings were in Müntzer's mind; the Czech version, in Wolfgramm's words, was 'verily no good translation' and its value for explicating B must be limited; cf. Eberhard Wolfgramm, 'Der Prager Anschlag des Thomas Müntzer in der Handschrift der Leipziger Universitätsbibliothek', *Wissenschaftliche Zeitschrift der Karl-Marx-Universität Leipzig*, 6 Gesell-und Sprachwissenschaftliche Reihe, Part 3, (1956/7), 295–308, esp. p. 298f.

9. *das sie vorsichtlich muchten alle yre begyre unde werck in glauben haben gefuret und sich do selbest dorcherbytet hetten*; from the Czech version Wolfgramm translates the last phrase, 'and raised themselves therein'; but this makes no sense here; cf. Philippians 2[12f.]

wholesome trials and the edifying abyss[10] by which the mind of the predestined man is emptied, nor would they ever be able to. For they had not been seized by the spirit of the fear of God which is the sole aim and solid ground of the elect, who are overwhelmed and drenched by such a flood of it (as the world cannot abide).[11] In short each man must have the spirit seven-fold,[12] otherwise he cannot hear or understand the living God. I declare freely and frankly that I have never heard any donkey-farting doctor whisper the tiniest fraction or slightest point about the order (established in God and all creatures),[13] far less speak openly about it. Not even the most distinguished Christians (I mean the hell-grounded[14] priests) have ever caught a whiff of what the whole is, and what is incomplete,[15] how a measure distributed in equal parts is superior to all its parts.[16] 1 Cor. XIII, Luke VI, Ephesians IV, Acts II, XV, XVII.[17] Time and again I have heard mere Scripture from them, which they have stolen[18] in rascally fashion from the Bible like confidence tricksters and cruel murderers. They are accursed by God himself for such theft, for he declares in Jeremiah XXIII:[19] Know this, I have said to the prophets: They steal my words, each from his neighbour, for they betray my people; I have not spoken to them at all but they dare to use[20] my words, making them taste rotten[21] with their stinking lips and whore-sick[22] throats. For they deny that my spirit speaks to them. Then with scornful, keen words of derision they jab at one,[23] at those who say that the holy spirit gives them an invincible testimony that they are the children of God, Romans VIII, Psalm CLXXXXII.[24] It is not

10. *nutzbarlichen abegrundt.*

11. A remarkably mixed metaphor; the solid ground becomes a flood!

12. Cf. C, n. 4.

13. *von der ordennünge (in Got unnd alle creaturn gesatzth)*; cf. A, n. 6.

14. *hellegruntfesten.*

15. Wolfgramm, on the basis of the Czech text, suspects an omission and suggests: 'what the whole is, or the completely perfect'; the Latin version supports this view (F.); cf. p. 372/22 below.

16. *welches ist ein gleichteilende mass alle teyle uberlegen.*

17. 1 Corinthians 14 (speaking in tongues); Luke 6[1-10] (the literalism of the Pharisees); Acts 2 (Pentecost); Acts 15[esp v. 28] (council of Jerusalem led by Holy Spirit); Acts 17[27f.] (God not far off); the reference is to the following sentence; Dismer, p. 14 n. 1, relates it back to the wholeness, unity in the Spirit.

18. *gestalten.*   19. Jeremiah 23[30ff.]   20. *ermessen.*

21. *faulfressigk*; colourful abuse of the clergy is a feature of B.

22. *hurnsuchtigen.*

23. *stechen eynen monnich*; 'monk' (missing in C) makes little sense; 'flourishing their monasticism' (Wolfgramm) does not convince; a copyist's error for *mensch* (person) or *monig* (madly)?

24. Romans 8[16]; perhaps Psalm 89[7] (Vg. 'in the sons of God') (F.) or Psalm 93[5] (the soul is the house of God for Müntzer).

surprising that those abandoned[25] men have the audacity to oppose the latter for in the above mentioned chapter[26] Jeremiah expressed their views: 'Who has been in the council of the Lord? Who has seen or heard God speak? Who paid heed, or who can say that he has heard God speak?' On these highly-honoured, oak-blocks[27] of men, hardened against all that is good, Titus, chapter one,[28] God is going to pour out in our days his invincible anger, for they deny the saving basis[29] of faith, though they are the ones who ought to fling themselves forward like an iron wall[30] to defend the elect from the blasphemers who oppose them, as Ezechiel says in chapter III etc.[31] But that is the sort of person they are, for all that emerges from their hearts, brains and jaws is ridicule for such matters. What man would want to say that these were fitting servants of God to testify to the divine word? Or that they are the undaunted preachers of the divine graces,[32] when they are besmeared with the oil of the sinner by the Papal Nimrod,[33] Psalm CXL,[34] which flows down from the head to the feet, polluting and poisoning all the Christian churches? In other words, they originate from the devil who has utterly corrupted their hearts, as it is written in the fifth psalm,[35] for the latter are vain, lacking their owner,[36] the holy spirit. That is why the consecrator who consecrated them is the devil, their real father, who, like them, declines to hear the real, living word of God, John, Isaiah XXIV, and Hosea IV.[37] Zechariah XI,[38] too, says that they are like scarecrows among the rows of peas. So to sum up a great deal: they are abandoned, John chapter 3,[39] condemned long ago. Indeed, they are no insignificant criminals, but abandoned reprobates, found throughout the whole world from the very beginning, and ordained

---

25. *verdampten.*

26. Jeremiah 23[18].

27. *voreychenblochysse*; cf. Letter 59, p. 101/15 (F.); Müntzer frequently uses 'wooden' as a metaphor e.g. *Exposé*, p. 300/18 above; cf. n. 98 below and C, p. 376/22 below; probably the most vivid example is in the *Sermon to the Princes*, p. 234/5 above.

28. Titus 1[16] (Vg. – *ad omne opus bonum reprobi*).

29. *das gruntlich heyl des glaubens.*

30. Jeremiah 1[18]; cf. *Exposé*, p. 260/12 above.

31. Ezekiel 3[8ff.]; the Czech version: 'against the opponents and blasphemers'.

32. Cf. p. 373/11 below.

33. *vom hunrotussen babst*; the Czech version followed here; Dismer reads *hunnenrottischen*, p. 68, n. 3; on Nimrod cf. Letter 31, n. 2.

34. Psalm 141[5].

35. Psalm 5[9].

36. *besitzer*; cf. A, n. 6.

37. John 8[38, 41, 44]; Isaiah 24[5f.]; Hosea 4[6].

38. Zechariah 11[17]; Jeremiah 10[5] (scarecrows in a melon patch).

39. John 3[18].

to plague the poor people which is so very coarse[40] as a result. They have no claim on God or men, as Paul expresses clearly enough in Galatians[41] where he describes the two types of men. So as long as heaven and earth stand[42] these criminal, turn-coat priests will not be of the slightest use to the churches, for they deny the voice of the bridegroom,[43] which is the real and certain sign that they are devils pure and simple. For how can they be the servants of God, bearers of his word, which, with their whore's countenance, they deny? For all true priests need revelation, if they are to speak with conviction, Corinthians XIV.[44] But they say, with their hardened hearts, that this is impossible; so it is only right – since they imagine they have gobbled up the whole of Scripture – that they should be struck down by Paul's words in the second epistle to the Corinthians, chapter three,[45] as if by thunder and lightning, for there he distinguishes between the elect and the damned. For some the gospel and the whole of Scripture is a closed book,[46] Isaiah XXIX and XXII on the key of David and on the closed book, Revelation V.[47] Ezekiel ate the rolled-up scroll.[48] Christ says in Luke XI[49] that the priests steal the key of this closed book; they lock Scripture up and say God cannot speak to man in his own person. But where the seed falls on the good field, that is, in hearts full of the fear of God, then they become the paper or parchment on which God writes the real holy scripture with his living finger, not with ink.[50] It is to this that the outward books of the Bible bear true testimony.[51] And there is no surer testimony to authenticate the Bible than the living speech of God when the Father addresses the Son in the heart of man. This Scripture can be read by all elect men, who seek interest for their talents.[52] But the damned will surely fail to do that; their heart is harder than a pebble, from which the master's chisel always slides off. That is why they are called stony by our dear Lord;[53] the seed that falls there bears no fruit, although they welcome

---

40. *grob.*
41. Galatians 4[22ff.]
42. Matthew 24[35].
43. Cf. Song of Songs 5[2].
44. 1 Corinthians 14[1ff.]; cf. Jeremiah 3[3].
45. 2 Corinthians 3[14-18]; de Boor suggests 4[3].
46. *zcugelassen*, for *zugeslossen* ('open' for 'closed') as in the Czech version. (F.)
47. Isaiah 29[11]; 22[22]; Revelation 5[3]; cf. 3[7].
48. *hat vorflossen auffgegessen*; F. suggests *vorflossen aufgeslossen*, but the text can stand; cf. Ezekiel 2[9ff.] (*involutus liber* (Vg.)); the contrast is with the priests who thought they could gobble up Scripture; cf. l. 12 above.
49. Luke 11[52].
50. 2 Corinthians 3[2f.]; Exodus 31[18].
51. Cf. *Exposé of False Faith*, p. 272/26 above.
52. Matthew 25[16f.]
53. Matthew 13[5].

the dead word[54] with joy, with great joy and praise. There are, by my soul, others, apart from students and priests and monks, who welcome bookish truth with warm flattery[55] and pomp. But when God wants to write something in their hearts there is no people under the sun which is more opposed to the living word of God than they are. Nor do they suffer any trials of faith in the spirit of the fear of God; for they are despatched into the lake where the false prophets will be tormented with Antichrist from generation to generation, amen.[56] Nor do they want the spirit of the fear of God to alarm them. That is why they never stop deriding the trials of faith,[57] for they are the people of whom Jeremiah speaks in chapter VIII;[58] for they have no experience of their own which they could employ in the explanation of the holy Scripture. Their only way to write is a hypocritical one which throws away the authentic words, and even though they use them they will never pay heed to them from eternity to eternity. For God only speaks through the readiness of the creatures to suffer,[59] which is what the hearts of unbelievers lack. For they become more and more hardened. For they cannot and will not empty themselves,[60] for their foundation is a slippery one, and they screw up their face in disgust at their owner.[61] That is why they fall away at the time of trial, they shrink away from the word that has become flesh.[62] The unbeliever absolutely refuses to become conformed with Christ by his suffering;[63] he wants to achieve it all by honey-sweet thoughts.[64] That is why these abandoned priests take away the real key[65] and say this sort of approach is fantasy and clownery and declare that nothing is more impossible. These very men are now condemned to eternal damnation from top to toe, so why should I not damn them too, John 3?[66] They were not sprinkled with the spirit of the fear of God on the third day; how, then, are they to be purged on the seventh day, Numbers XIX?[67] For they have been despatched into the abyss of the pit.[68] But I do not despair of the

54. *tode wort*; expanded in accordance with the Czech. (F.)
55. *kutcelen*.
56. Revelation 19[20]; 20[10].
57. Czech version continues: 'and treat it as a game'. (F.)
58. Jeremiah 8[8].
59. *leidligkeyt*.
60. Czech version adds: 'of their fleshly desires'. (F.)
61. God owns, possesses the soul; cf. A, n. 6; cf. Jeremiah 23[12].
62. John 1[14].
63. Romans 8[29].
64. Cf. *Sermon to the Princes*, p. 246/18 above.
65. Cf. p. 374/28 below.
66. John 3[18f.]
67. Cf. *Sermon to the Princes*, n. 117.
68. Cf. n. 56 above.

people. Oh, you really poor and pitiable little group, how thirsty you are for the word of God! For it is abundantly clear that no one, or hardly anyone, knows where they stand or what group[69] they should join. They would gladly do what is best, but have no way of knowing what this is. For they do not know how to react or comply with the testimony which the holy spirit utters in their hearts. Therefore they were much too alarmed at the spirit of the fear of God, and the prophecy of Jeremiah[70] was fulfilled in them: 'The children have asked for bread, but no one was there to break it to them.' Oh, oh, no one broke it to them. There were plenty of money-grubbing scoundrels[71] who flung down before the poor, poor, poor little people the dry as dust, popish[72] texts of the Bible just as one flings bread to the dogs.[73] But they did not break it to them through the knowledge of the holy spirit, that is, they did not open their mind to recognise the holy spirit within themselves. For all the priests[74] gathered together in one group would not be able to instruct one single man that he was prepared for eternal life. What need is there to say any more? These are the gentlemen who just eat, drink and are merry;[75] they plot day and night, search for ways to nourish themselves and get good livings, Ezechiel XXXIV.[76] They are not like Christ, our dear Lord, who compares himself to a hen which keeps her children warm.[77] Nor do they give milk to the disconsolate and deserted ones from the inexhaustible well of God's counsels. For they have not made trial of faith. They are like the stork which gathers up frogs from the fields and the swamps and then disgorges them undigested to its young ones in the nest. That is what the usurious, interest-exacting priests are like, who gulp down the dead words of Scripture and then pour out[78] the mere letter and the untried faith (which is not worth a louse) upon the poor, really poor people. The end-result is that no one is sure of his soul's salvation. For these same Beelzebub-like fellows bring a single piece of holy Scripture to market.[79] Hey, a man doesn't know if he deserves God's hate or love![80] The abyss from which this poison rises is

69. *houffen*; Latin: *sectae*.

70. Lamentations 4[4].

71. Czech: 'priests'. (F.)

72. *dam patischen* (Czech: popish) *unerfarnen*; mistake of copyist.

73. Matthew 15[27].

74. Czech: 'bald pates'.

75. *pastalen* (?); mistake of copyist? Following the Czech Wolfgramm suggests a connection with *Pastete*, a good dish.

76. Ezekiel 34[2, 8, 10].

77. Matthew 23[37].

78. *schuten*; a close parallel on p. 455/1 below; Czech version ended with the previous sentence; note the concern of B for the 'people'.

79. *zcu margke*.

80. Ecclesiastes 9[1].

that each whore-riding[81] priest acknowledges the most treacherous and wicked princes of the devil, as the Revelation of John declares.[82] Thus they have scattered the sheep of God[83] so badly that none can be seen any more among the churches. For no one is there to separate the good from the reckless mob[84] which is unknown (to God). Nor is there any recognition of the infirm[85] and the healthy, that is, no one heeds the utter corruption of the church by those abandoned men. For the sheep do not know that they should hear the living voice of God. That is, that they all should receive revelations, Joel 2, and David in Psalm LXXXVIII.[86] For the task of the real pastors[87] is simply to bring all the sheep to this point, to be refreshed by the living voice, for the knowledge of God is what only one master teachers, Matthew XXIII.[88] Because this has not happened for a long time, in many respects the elect are all too similar to the damned or have been completely swallowed up.[89] So that virtually the whole world came to think that it was not necessary for Christ himself to preach his own gospel to the elect. I affirm and swear this by the living God: anyone who does not hear from the mouth of God the real living word of God, and the distinction between Bible and Babel,[90] is a dead thing and nothing else. But God's word, which courses through heart, brain, skin, hair, bone, marrow, sap, might, and strength surely has the right to canter along in a quite different way from the fairy-tales told by our clownish, testicled doctors. Otherwise no one cannot be saved; otherwise no one can be found. The elect man must clash with the damned and his forces must collapse before the latter. Otherwise you will not be able to hear what God is. Anyone who has once received the holy spirit as he should can never again be damned, Isaiah chapter LV and LX, John VI.[92] Oh, oh! Woe, woe to those preachers who teach in the manner of Balaam,[93] for the words are directed to their jaws, but their hearts are more than a thousand times a thousand miles away. That is why the people live without real pastors,[94] for the

---

81. *hurnhengestiger.*
82. Revelation 16[13ff.?]
83. Ezekiel 34[5].
84. *frischen haufen.*
85. *pittalischen*; F. suggests *pestalischen* since the Latin version speaks of leprosy.
86. Joel 2[28]; Psalm 89[7] (cf. n. 24 above).
87. *herten*, shepherds.
88. Matthew 23[10].
89. *voschlunden.*
90. Cf. Luther's *Letter to the Princes of Saxony* (1524), LW 40, p. 50.
91. *dan unser nerrisschen, hodenseckysschen doctores tallen.*
92. Isaiah 55[11. 13]; 60[15f., 21]; John 6[39f.]
93. Cf. A, n. 21.
94. Matthew 9[36].

experience of faith is never preached to it. The Jewish and heretical priests may well say such sharp measures are not necessary. They say that one can surely flee the anger of God with good works and with costly virtues. From none of these, however, do they learn what it is to experience God, what real faith is, what robust virtue is, what good works are after the reconciliation[95] with God. So it would be no surprise[96] if God had reduced us all, body and soul, the elect with the damned, to dust and ruins in a much worse flood than the one long ago and it would be no wonder if he had damned all the people who had succumbed to the seductions of the accursed ones. For our faith bears more resemblance to that of Lucifer and Satan; and it is coarser than wood and stone. It does not seem unreasonable that all other peoples describe our faith as monkey-play, for it is obvious – one cannot deny it – that the unbelievers have asked us for a full account[97] of our faith. The answer we proudly produced for them came out of the hen-house, great big books full of blots, saying: In our law we have this or that written, for Christ has said this, Paul has written that, the prophets have predicted this and that, the holy church, our mother (in the whore house) promulgated this and that; yes, great things – this thing, that thing – were presented by that Nero, the holy, most wooden pope and chamber-pot[98] in Rome in his coal-shed, and especially in his excommunications which, so the strawbrained little doctors tell us, should not be treated with contempt either, for the sake of the conscience. Let my good reader substitute other words or formulations if he will, but they cannot prove the Christian faith with a dry-as-dust[99] Bible, however much they may chatter away. Oh, beware, beware! Oh, woe, woe, woe to these hell-fire, Asmodaean[100] priests, who are openly seducing the people. Even now, no one will open their eyes and ears, when arguments of this or similar nature are produced for unbelievers. Do you imagine that they do not have a brain in their heads, as well? They probably think to themselves: what sort of proof is one from books? Those who wrote them may well have lied. How can one know if it is true? There is no doubt that the Turks and the Jews would like very much to hear our invincible ground, as would many of the elect. But the devil's priests screw up

95. *eintragen.*

96. *Drumb wir es nicht wunder.*

97. *dicke rechenschafft;* Wolfgramm suspects an echo here of the report that the Sultan Suleiman II demanded tribute from the Hungarian king in May 1521.

98. *allerhultzeister bapst und pruntztopf* (*hultz = holz;* wood).

99. *unerfaren* (not experienced).

100. Asmodeus was, according to Tobit, the worst of demons, jealously killing off seven successive bridegrooms of Sarah until Tobias came to the rescue; Tobit 3, 6, 7, 8.

their noses and prepare to condemn them, although they have no right to judge since they deny that any man has this.[101] They speak with mere words: 'He who believes and is baptised will be saved.'[102] This is the well-grounded account they give of the faith to its opponents – this and nothing else! The only possible explanation – it is certainly my understanding of the situation – is that they are so mad, foolish and senseless that they try to present the faith to its enemies in this simplistic, barren way. One should discard this sort of apologia for the faith like old rags, and it should be cast into the abyss of hell with its proponents. It is really much madder than stupidity itself. Who can deplore or lament it as it deserves? But is there no blood in our body and being either, if things have become so mad and foolish as this? Doesn't one feel a little spark that will soon awaken to kindle a fire? Yes, one feels it and I feel it too. It has moved me to great and bitter pity that the Christian church has been so badly crushed that God could not afflict it worse if he wanted to wipe it out altogether, which he will not do except for the thin-shitters,[103] who taught them to worship Baal; they richly deserve to be sawn apart, as Daniel says:[104] For they have not executed the judgements of God. I have read here and there in the history of the early fathers, and find that the immaculate, virginal church, after the death of the pupils of the apostles, soon became a whore because of the seductive priests. For the priests have always wanted to sit up at the top, as Hegesippus and Eusebius plainly testify, and others too.[105] Because the people allowed its right to choose the priests to fall into disuse, from that time on the convening of a proper council proved impossible. If anyone did want one, it was the devil's doing, for what was dealt with in the councils or consultations was mere child's play: bell-ringing, chalices and cowls, lamps and locums, the adoration of masses; as to the real living word of God not once, not once did they jerk open their jaws, nor did they as much as mention the order (of creation).[106] Such errors had to take place[107] so that all men's deeds, those of the elect and those of the damned, could flourish freely until our time when God will separate out the tares from the wheat,[108] since one can now see by the clear light of noon who has been seducing the church for so long. All the extremes of scoundrelly behaviour had to come to the light. O ho,

101. *unde haben doch nicht das gerichte, das sie leukens, das es ein mensche haben kann.*
102. Mark 16[16].
103. *lapscheyssern.*
104. Daniel 3[29].
105. Cf. A, n. 30.
106. Cf. A, p. 360/11.
107. Cf. 1 Corinthians 11[19].
108. Matthew 13[30].

how ripe the rotten apples are! O ho, how rotten the elect have become! The time of the harvest has come! That is why he himself has hired me for his harvest. I have sharpened my sickle,[109] for my thoughts yearn for the truth and with my lips, skin, hands, hair, soul, body and life I call down curses on the unbelievers.

In order to achieve this best, I have come into your land, my most beloved Bohemians. All I ask of you is to be diligent in studying the living word of God from the mouth of God himself, for through this you yourselves will see, hear and grasp how the whole world has been seduced by the deaf priests. Help me for the sake of the blood of Christ to fight against these high enemies of the faith. I will confound them before your very eyes in the spirit of Elijah.[110] For the new apostolic church will start in your land and then spread everywhere. I will be prepared so that when the people in the churches address a question to me in the pulpit I will satisfy every single person. If I cannot demonstrate such mastery and knowledge then let me be liable to temporal and eternal death. There is no greater pledge that I can offer. Anyone who scorns this warning is already doomed to fall into the hands of the Turk. After the wild rage of the latter the real Antichrist will reign in person, the real opponent of Christ, who will soon afterwards give the kingdom of this world to his elect for all time.[111]

Prague on Catherine's day in the year of the Lord 1521.

Thomas Müntzer wants no dumb God to worship but one who speaks.[112]

109. Joel 3[13]; in Revelation 14[14-20] the sickles are wielded by 'one like the son of man' and by the angels of judgement.

110. Cf. A, n. 37.

111. Explicit apocalyptic language, a feature of B; cf. also pp. 366/7ff., 31; 368/1f.

112. Cf. Isaiah 41[23] (if gods, should tell the future), Jeremiah 10[5].

Latin Version (C)

I, Thomas Müntzer of Stolberg, will sound a new song in Prague on the sonorous marching trumpets,[1] with that beloved athlete of Christ, John Hus; I make my testimony with a deep sigh[2] to the whole church of the elect and the whole world, wherever this letter may be shown; and I believe that I have laboured more intensively than any of my contemporaries to be, in the end, found worthy of that richer, sound knowledge of the invincible and holy Christian faith which I have now secured. I affirm boldly that no sacrificing priest,[3] no monastic hypocrite was able to do this for me; Christ and his elect, who have known me from my youth, add their testimony to mine; nor could they bring to a single living person, when he was assailed by grievous and real oppression of spirit, the infallible disciplines of the orthodox faith; nor could they explain in the spirit of divine fear how the mind of the elect must profit from being emptied, and then must plumb the most profound abysses of temptation; for all the elect cling to this anchor and long for the seven-fold spirit,[4] and unless someone has been infused by it that number of times he has no possibility of hearing or understanding God. Nor did I hear one of the play-acting[5] scholars open his mouth to expound even the slightest point about the order which is innate[6] to God and the creatures. Nor, finally, did those who were prominent among the nominal Christians (I mean the pestiferous priestlings) ever sense what is whole or perfect, the whole criterion for understanding the nature of the parts.[7]

All too often, however, I heard from them icy words of Scripture, which like sly thieves and notorious bandits they most scandalously stole from the biblical books. Indeed God himself execrates this theft, saying:[8] 'Behold I [warn] the seers, who have filched my oracles, each one from his neighbour,' for they deceive my people and usurp my words,[9] which I have never spoken to them, and which in their stinking lips are depraved, losing their true nature; for they deny that my spirit speaks to men down the centuries.[10]

---

1. Cf. B, n. 3.

2. *ingemiscens*; cf. Romans 8[22ff.]

3. *sacrificulum*; cf. Psalm 119[99].

4. Isaiah 11[2]; Revelation 1[4]; 3[1]; 4[5]; 5[6]; Lohmann, p. 25, sees the influence of Tauler here, with his stress on the spirit of fear.

5. larvatis (masked) – Müntzer's usual use of this word; cf. p. 377/2 below; or 'bewitched'; Trillitzsch: *besessen* (obsessed).

6. *congenitum*.

7. Cf. A, n. 7.

8. Jeremiah 23[30].

9. Ibid. vs. 13, 21, 31.

10. Cf. Theses 21, 22 attributed to Egranus, p. 382 below.

With the fiercest scorn they deride those who affirm that the holy spirit speaks, and testifies to us;[11] they set their face against this, piling up their blasphemy: 'Who was present at the council of the Lord, to hear and witness his speeches? Who has heard and considered his word?[12] Upon these men the Lord is about to send down his most dire displeasure in our time, because those who ought to set themselves up as an iron wall[13] to defend the people of God against its calumniators are denying the real goal of faith.'[14]

But it is these very men who live this abomination, breathe it forth, and vomit it out.[15] What mortal man would call them chaste dispensers of the manifold grace of God[16] and undaunted preachers of the live, not the dead word? For they have been ordained at the hands of the papist corrupter and anointed with the oil of sinners that flows down from the head to the heels.[17] This is to say: it is from the apostasy of the devil that their madness originates, and then proceeds into their inmost hearts, which (as Psalm Five attests[18]) are vain and bereft of the spirit, their owner;[19] as a result they are consecrated by their father, the devil, who, like them, does not hear the living word of God, to be a plague upon the people, John 8, Isaiah 24, Hosea 4.[20] For they are idols, very similar to daemons, Zechariah eleven,[21] that is, if I may sum up, they are men who are damned, John, the third chapter,[22] nay, most damned, having no hereditary claim on God or men, as the apostle to the Galatians declares,[23] expounding Genesis.

Hence as long as heaven and earth endure,[24] they will be of no benefit to the church which hears the voice of the bridegroom,[25] they themselves viciously rejecting it from the start.[26] How, then, can they be ministers of God, bearers of the word which, with their whore's countenance,[27] they deny? For certainly revelation is necessary for all priests, but they say this is quite impossible, contrary to the apostle,

11. Romans 8[16].
12. Jeremiah 23[18].
13. Cf. B, n. 30.
14. *scopum fidei.*
15. Cf. p. 378/2f. below.
16. 1 Peter 4[10].
17. Cf. B, n. 34.
18. Psalm 5[9].
19. B, n. 36; cf. n. 40 below.
20. B, n. 37.
21. ibid., n. 38.
22. John 3[18].
23. Galatians 4[22ff.]
24. Matthew 24[35].
25. Song of Songs 5[2].
26. 1 Peter 5[8].
27. Jeremiah 3[3].

1 Corinthians 14.[28] It is because of this that the latter elsewhere shakes with his thunder-claps those obstinate men to whom the gospel of God has been closed.[29] He says exultantly that the hearts of the elect are tablets;[30] into which, by the finger of God which furrows them, the mysteries of the living word are ploughed;[31] all who seek interest for their talents, can read these with the greatest of ease.[32] The wicked, like the Marpesian rock,[33] will repel the mason's chisel for all time; in fact the Lord calls these very wicked men stony ground, on which the corn fell in joy and sweetness.[34] Indeed, as Ezechiel points out,[35] the hearts of the damned are stony, especially of priests and men of a similar grain[36] who are quick to be complacent and content with their edicts, saying:[37] 'We are wise, and the law of the lord is with us.' But when their faith comes under scrutiny there is no people on earth which opposes the holy spirit and the living word more strenuously than these useless Christian priests. In his eighth chapter, Jeremiah certainly turns these points most cogently against those who cannot understand that all Scripture must be complemented by the experience of faith and that this is altogether infallible.

In short, these men have a lying pen,[38] for they reject the living word (which no created being can understand unless it is ready to suffer), and they usurp words which they will never ever hear themselves. Moreover the hearts of the wicked will be hardened for the worse. When they should empty themselves,[39] these slippery creatures draw back, abhorring him who from the heavens possesses[40] all things including themselves; this is, at the time of most edifying temptation they withdraw from the incarnate word. On no account is the wicked man willing to be conformed to Christ[41] by his own suffering, which is why he takes away the key of knowledge[42] from those who seek it.

This entrance to life he calls perverse and impossible. This is why he

---

28. 1 Corinthians 14[1ff.]
29. 2 Corinthians 4[2]; cf. B, p. 365/15f.
30. 2 Corinthians 3[3].
31. Exodus 31[18]; cf. p. 44/16f. above.
32. Matthew 25[16f.]
33. *Aeneid* VI, 471; WA 18, 675.
34. Matthew 13[5].
35. Ezekiel 11[19].
36. *farinae*.
37. Jeremiah 8[8f.]
38. ibid.
39. Cf. p. 372/14 above.
40. *possessorem*; cf. A, n. 6; F. suggests: 'abhorring in their arrogance the owner ...'
41. Romans 8[29].
42. Luke 11[52].

already stands under judgement[43] while still in the flesh and with death still ahead of him. But the people of God which is sprinkled on the third day desires intensely to be washed on the seventh,[44] as long as it feels the most constant testimony in the heart. From here comes its burden of anxiety, its wretched uncertainty as to which sect it should join.[45] Yet for a long time all men have hungered and thirsted after the righteousness of faith. And we see the prophecy of Jeremiah vindicated:[46] 'The little ones sought bread and there was no one to break it to them.' There were many who flung down to them whole texts of the books of the Bible as if they were dogs.[47] But they could not be instructed in the knowledge of the fear of God. Ah, ah, they were not able to break it to them, they did not nourish the sons of God with the infallible certainty of predestination, so that they might proceed in the seven-fold divine power[48] to see the most direct way to the living God. Pastors who have begun like this, and do not feed themselves,[49] are made mothers to the sheep, supplying milk from the breasts of that inexhaustible[50] consolation by which they themselves are comforted by God.[51] While wicked men are like storks, avidly gathering frogs from the fields and swamps. Then they vomit out this undigested food to the chicks in the nest. Similarly all the wicked, after hunting down the divine words in books, gulp down these dead things, and as a result the poor ordinary people are rendered uncertain about their salvation. They dare, then, to claim in their preaching that they and all men are uncertain whether they deserve hate or love.[52] What are they achieving, may I ask, but the scattering of the divine sheep? They do nothing to cure the sores of the latter for they cannot distinguish between leprosy and health. They do not separate the wicked from the elect, because they do not feed the sheep on the living voice; thus they give ear to the voice of strangers[53] and great contagion results; that is, they do not teach the path by which they may become empty[54] and so hear and grasp the most sure preacher of the real gospel, Jesus Christ, with their whole soul, flesh, skin, marrow and bones.

43. John 3[18f.]
44. B, n. 67.
45. *Hinc illa eadem pressura.*
46. Lamentations 4[4].
47. Cf. B, p. 367/12.
48. *numine.*
49. Ezekiel 34[2, 8, 10]; i.e. pastors with a certainty of predestination.
50. *inhaustae*; for *inexhaustae* (F.); (B: *unausscheplichen*).
51. Isaiah 28[9].
52. Ecclesiastes 9[1].
53. John 10[5].
54. *vacent* for *vagentur* (F.); (B: *das dye schaffe dohin alle gefurt werden*); Trillitzsch: 'in which way they can become empty'; cf. n. 39 above.

Anyone who has once received him as he should, can never be damned. Isaiah 55 and 59, John 6.[55] Oh, woe, woe and eternally woe to those preachers in the very likeness of Balaam.[56] For the word of God may be found in their mouths but their hearts lie more than a thousand miles away.[57] Which is why they have reduced virtually all the people to sheep skulking around[58] without shepherds. No experience of faith is required of men;[59] and they prattle on coldly about fleeing the wrath of God. Ah ha, with good works and some wondrous virtues, too, the rage of God can be evaded – or so they say. They fail to understand God, faith, Christian virtues, good works. In their dizziness of spirit[60] they are stunned into insensibility. With this in mind it would be no wonder if the Lord were to embroil the elect with the reprobate in a general cataclysm once again because of faith like this, more stupid than things of wood and stone. Nor am I in any doubt why the different peoples throughout the whole world have pronounced the Christian faith one of presumptuous stupidity. Frequently the unbelievers have demanded that Christians justify their faith only to meet with various supercilious replies: 'We've got it all in our law; this is written, that is written; Christ calls, Paul re-echoes, the prophets make their predictions.' This edict of holy mother church strengthens the prostitute[61] of souls, the papist, wooden high-priest of Rome, decreeing it in his Babylonian brothel. This sort of reasoning only hardens our adversaries still more, for they think to themselves: 'What? If their prophets, Christ and Paul lied, how would we know if they are telling the truth?' Without doubt many Jews and Turks make a considerable effort to listen to, and try to understand, the arguments for our faith;[62] with a snore[63] we pronounce them impious without the authority of the holy spirit, and it is the carelessness of the priestlings which brought about this disaster. They tend to say:[64] 'Anyone who believed and was baptised cannot be harmed.' This is the sort of apologia that is given for the faith and nothing else.[65] Ah, it deserves to be cast out of their pathetic

---

55. B, n. 92.

56. A, n. 21.

57. Isaiah 29[13].

58. *delitescentem*; Matthew 9[36]

59. Cf. Müntzer's letter to Melanchthon; p. 44/5 above.

60. *In vertigine spiritus inconcussi obtunduntur*: Trillitzsch: 'and are blinded by dizziness of spirit without being struck low'; Isaiah 19[24]; cf. pp. 18/16, 29/19 above.

61. *prostibulum*; the devil (?); cf. Proverbs 7; Hosea 2[5].

62. *firmamentum fidei nostrae*.

63. *roncho nostro*; B: *runtzeln yre nasen*.

64. Mark 16[16].

65. A similar argument is developed in the *Exposé*, p. 314/28ff. above.

lungs, it really deserves to be expelled into the dust with these men.[66] For it is madder than all their pompous antics. Who can lament this as it deserves? Who has dared to cure such mad frenzy? For it has burst out and been carried up to the very clouds of the heavens. So I am moved to weep in pity, and from the depths of my being I lament and deplore the ruin of the true church of God, which so afflicts it that it does not feel the Egyptian darkness.[67] The Lord could not grind it down any more without destroying it altogether, which he will only do to the impious imposters who have taught it to worship Baal. They deserve, they richly deserve to be cut apart by men and angels.[68] For they do not call to mind the just judgements of God.

I have read and reread the histories of the Early Fathers. I find that after the deaths of the pupils of the apostles the immaculate and virginal church of Christ was contaminated, prostituted and exposed to hag-like[69] adultery by the activities of the perfidious priestlings. Hegesippus, Eusebius and several others testify to this.[70] And because the people neglected the elections of the priests none of the councils provided a genuine apologia for the faith after their imposture had begun; for at them the order of creation[71] and the authority of the voice of God[72] did not speak in harmony; as a consequence God's wondrous dispensation handed them over to boys' vanities, as they themselves say, to fantastic ceremonies,[73] so that they should act like baby boys until the essence[74] of both the wheat and the tares is winnowed out and all those works which prevail in the blind world can be plucked out at the imminent harvest.[75]

Rejoice, then, most dear friends, for your slopes are whitening [with the harvest].[76] For I am sharpening my sickle to put it into the harvest, having been hired by heaven for a penny a day.[77] 'For my mouth will meditate on the supreme truth and my lips will hold the impious in contempt;'[78] it is in order to detect and to destroy these

---

66. *Ach digna, quae pelleretur minutiis pulmonum* ...; cf. Psalm 18[41f.]; F. rejects Clemen's view that the coughing-up of blood is meant.

67. *qua ipsa percussa non palpat Egyptiacas tenebras*; cf. Exodus 10[21].

68. Daniel 3[29].

69. *rugoso*, lit. 'wrinkled'.

70. Cf. A, n. 30.

71. *ordo rerum*.

72. The living word of God (B).

73. Cf. B, p. 370/28f.

74. *natura*.

75. Trillitzsch transcribes *instantissima; intanstissima*, however, appears the correct reading.

76. John 4[35].

77. Matthew 20[2].

78. Proverbs 8[7].

latter, most beloved Bohemian brothers, that I have entered your renowned region, desiring only that you should receive the living word by which I live and take breath, lest it should return empty.[79] Embrace it, and help to ensure that your mass priests are put to the test. You will realise that you have been seduced in the clear light of noon.[80] I assure you that your coming glory will equal the ignominy and hate you met at the hands of the Romans.[81] I know for sure that the northern regions will hasten towards the flow of ripening grace.[82] Here the renewed apostolic church will take its beginning and spread out into the whole world. Hurry, therefore, not to me but to his word (I have sought no emolument from you) which is about to run forth speedily.[83] Just grant a place to the preacher who is coming. I will be prepared to meet every questioner's point. But if you should pay no attention to my admonition, the Lord will deliver you into the hands of those who have their eye on your frontiers and will make you a by-word to every tribe among the nations.[84] If I have lied about the living word of God, which issues from his mouth[85] this very day, may I suffer the lot of Jeremiah;[86] I offer myself submissively to the torments of present and future death; a more weighty pledge I do not possess. I urge and adjure you in the name of the crimson blood of Christ to judge between me and your priests and the Roman ones; the judgement is for you to make, 1 Corinthians 14.[87] I know for sure that none of them believes with assurance, for in their fantasies and incurable avarice and inexplicable perversity they have reduced the holy church of God to chaos and confusion; but the Lord will build up, console and reunite this fragmented, derelict and scattered [church] until it sees the God of gods dwell in Zion from eternity to eternity, amen. In the year of Christ 1521.

I, Thomas Müntzer, beseech the church not to worship a mute God,[88] but a living and speaking one; none of the gods is more

79. Isaiah 55[11].
80. Deuteronomy 28[29].
81. The Papal Church.
82. *in profluvium germinatis gratiae ruitura*; cf. Psalm 48[2].
83. Psalm 147[15].
84. Jeremiah 18[16] (Vg.).
85. Deuteronomy 8[3].
86. F. cites Jeremiah 23[34ff.], where the 'burden of the Lord' is mentioned, surely the opposite of what Müntzer means here; cf. A, where the burden is the suffering, *leyden*, of Jeremiah, p. 360/26f.
87. 1 Corinthians 14[24]; an important text for Müntzer; the writing degenerates in these last few lines into a hasty sprawl, indicating perhaps the strong emotions felt by Müntzer.
88. Cf. Müntzer's letter to Melanchthon, p. 43/18 above.

contemptible to the nations than this living one to Christians who have no part in him.[89]

89. *quam vivus Christianis expertibus.*

2. Egranus

Propositions Attributed to Egranus (Zwickau? prior to 16 April 1521?)

Propositions of that upright[1] man, Dr Egranus. (*in Latin*).

1. Christ[2] is not the saviour of all the elect, or of those who were under the Law, of those who lived prior to the Law or outside its jurisdiction.
In the margin: Under the Law only the prophets knew the Christ who was to come.

2. Christ did not come into the world to teach us to bear our sufferings patiently and so follow in his footsteps, but he suffered so that we might have complete security,[3] free of affliction[4] of any kind.
In the margin: The saying of St Peter about the suffering of Christ.

3. The Fathers of the old Law did not have the grace of Christ,[5] since this was in the nature of things impossible, but all who followed possessed it because, as upright men, their powers never deserted them.

4. Circumcision could not convey or signify grace, just as the Eucharist does not confer the remission of sins or impart the holy Spirit, for it is simply a sign, instituted to commemorate the Passion.[6]

5. The Passion was not so agonising[7] as the loose talk of many folk suggests, and the sole benefit it confers is a disposition to good works. Human death cannot be agonising, either, but is a gentle dissolution[8] of soul and body.

6. The remission of sins occurs without any punishment being exacted; it is enough if heart–felt contrition is present as happens in the case of thieves; for the contrition comes from man's own resources.

The use of Scripture by the doctors (of the Church) against heretics was an illegitimate one.[9]

---

1. *probi*; of course sarcastic; on Egranus cf. Letters 15, 20, 40.

2. χριστος; presumably an echo of Erasmian universalism: Socrates, and others who lived a rational and ethical life, will be saved; cf. Elliger, p. 134f.

3. *securissimi*; cf. Thesis 95 of Luther's *Ninety Five Theses*. *Ac sic magis per multas tribulationes intrare celum, quam per securitatem pacis confidant.*

4. *amaritudine*, 'bitterness'; underlined; it is linked by a line to the marginal note, i.e. 1 Peter 3[18, 14].

5. χριστι; Egranus did deny that ancient Israel had true faith in Christ and therefore access to forgiveness in him; cf. Elliger, p. 135.

6. Egranus argues that the Eucharist is only a memorial token left us by Christ, not a vehicle of forgiveness, but affirms the Real Presence; cf. Elliger, p. 139.

7. *amara*; not an accurate rendition of Egranus' views; cf. Elliger, p. 141f.

8. *resolutio*.

9. At the bottom of the page, in small writing – in effect a marginal note.

6. [sic!] Punishment is not to be sought after;[10] for man knows himself well enough from his own resources.[11] It is right, therefore, to reject temptations to one's faith which are not of this world, the temptation of hell[12] etc. These are nothing but fantasies produced by human inclinations.

7. The only experience of faith we can have in this world is derived from books. This is why neither the layman nor the unlearned – however much they have been put to the test – can make any judgements on matters of faith, but judgement on all such matters pertains to those with mitres but no experience at all.[13]

8. The Old Testament is not binding on Christians, for it was only given to the Jews.[14]

9. The New Testament should be understood in its literal sense and none other. Hence the gospel accounts require no interpretation but suffice for salvation as they are, even though they were written not about us but about the blind and the dumb.[15]

10. In the Lord's Prayer it is not Christ,[16] the living bread, which should be sought, but that bread which we share with the Turks and all unbelievers. The Lord's Prayer should not be interpreted either.

11. It is wrong to interpret each text of Scripture by reference to another one, because things which are scriptural cannot be compared with one another. But we should treat each with respect,[17] allowing all the authorities to stand on their own, and not intruding others, so that each can be given its due weight.

12. The apostle Paul is not so difficult as many imagine. He is quite straightforward; what he says at times about the Jews and the Gentiles has nothing to do with us.

13. Romans, chapter seven, is not dealing with a dual nature in man, as the Martinians imagine, but with that of the Jews, which has nothing to do with us.

14. Romans, chapter eight, says we are completely free from the Law. So we are quite right to reject the Ten Commandments. We can

---

10. *pene non optande.*

11. *ex propriis viribus*; cf. the marginal notes on Tertullian, p. 422/1f. below.

12. *temptatio inferorum*; cf. Thesis 94 of Luther's *Ninety-Five Theses!*

13. *infulatos inexpertissimos.*

14. Again, a distortion of Egranus, as is the following thesis; a marginal note by Müntzer on Tertullian's *Against Marcion* reads: 'against Egranus', i.e. his destruction of the law, p. 411/25 below.

15. A reference to the miracle stories, or to spiritual blindness?

16. χριστος.

17. *observari sinceritas*; Elliger, p. 153, regards this as a fair reflection of Egranus' views.

recognise sin through the Gospel without their help; moreover, unlike the Jews, we do not need to sanctify the Sabbath.[18]

15. The fear of God should not be instilled in men's breasts; after all, the New Testament is silent about it, and perfect love casts out fear.[19]

16. The last chapter of Mark's Gospel is apocryphal and an evangelical Coronis.[20] Therefore Mark is not a witness to the resurrection of the Lord.

17. No one has to believe what his intellect cannot grasp. For man's rational faculties are most ample, and are not surrendered to the obedience of faith; this is completely unnecessary, anyway; indeed, it is the height of folly for something free to be made captive.

18. God is omnipotent, but not over our free will; this is obvious in the case of a sailor whose efforts snatched his ship from disaster, and the only way God could save him was by giving him assistance.[21]

19. Prior to the dispensation of grace it was by his uprightness[22] that Abraham earned the name of father of the nations, just as Zechariah and Elizabeth were just in the eyes of the Lord before the angel spoke to them.

20. The Pelagians, whom the unlearned call heretics, are better Christians than that most unlearned man, Augustine, than that most awkward fellow, Bernard,[23] than all these wandering Martinian men. For they preach that man is saved or damned by his own volition. They did not comfort themselves in this world like Manichaeans.[24]

21. Only the apostles had the holy Spirit. It was not necessary for other men, because the Church had been put on a firm enough footing by the labours of the apostles. For four hundred years no one has been more learned than Egranus. He is the first apostle to the people of Zwickau.[25]

22. For a thousand years no man has had the holy Spirit; the Church is not ruled by it either.[26]

18. Elliger, p. 156, points out that Egranus' intention is to free the confessional from a legalist approach.

19. 1 John 4[18]; there is no clear evidence that this represents Egranus' view.

20. In Greek mythology Coronis was the mother of Aesculapius, whose cult is associated with healing and the symbolic serpent. Egranus rejected the Marcan authorship of chapter 16; cf. Elliger, p. 157.

21. No doubt an exaggerated form of something Egranus actually said, Elliger, p. 162.

22. *probitate.*

23. *Bernhardo inconvenientissimo etc.*

24. *Nec Manichei fuerunt in mundo*; one cannot imagine Egranus speaking in this way.

25. The preceding two sentences, written at the bottom of the page, are headed 2a and placed after proposition 17 by Franz, but the correct reading is 21; they are clearly an addition to this clause.

26. Again probably a distortion of Egranus' views; we have, in fact, little from

23. There are four spirits, as is obvious from Pomerius and 'Sleep Safely' and Paratus.[27]

24. When I was bound in chains in Chemnitz,[28] the only spirit I entertained with any seriousness was tossed about by the fury of the waves and, in the end, by the lust for money.

I will defend these axioms against the whole world and especially against that ass, Thomas Müntzer. In the valley of St Joachim.

Egranus about the Spirit.

27. *ut patet ex pomerio et dormi secure et parato*; these collections of sermons are meant to illustrate the four-fold interpretation of Scripture.

28. Egranus, who was in Chemnitz prior to coming to Zwickau is described as motivated only by greed and opportunism; possibly a reference to Ephesians 4[14]; certainly to Acts 20,[22] (Vg.) *alligatus ego spiritu*, of Paul about to leave for Jerusalem.

3. Sermons and Expositions of Scripture

(a)   *1520.   Two Sermons from Zwickau. (in Latin)*

Thomas[1]

I.   On the birthday of the Virgin Mary (8 September 1520). He read out from the beginning of the Gospel of Matthew:[1] who Uriah's [wife] was,[2] who had been Uriah's wife.

Mattheus cur Christi carnalem nativitatem descripserit.[3]

Messae opus

In the Gospel before us we must see why Matthew describes the earthly birth of Christ and why it is being dealt with[4] today. For when Matthew was preaching that Christ had been the Messiah, it must have been objected that his works had not preceded him. For it had been predicted by David and Isaiah[5] that the work of the Messiah would be to bring the whole world under his power. Likewise that he would gather together all the Jews who had been scattered, Isaiah 2.[6] Likewise that there would have to be peace throughout the earth, so that weapons would be turned into plough-shares and bill-hooks, Isaiah 2.[7] Likewise that he would take away death, Isaiah 25,[8] casting down death for all eternity and that God would wipe away the tears from every face and the disgrace of his people from the whole earth etc. Likewise that Christ, who was supposed to be the Messiah, should not be born in Galilee, but of the root of David in Bethlehem in

Christi nativitas

Judah, John 7.[9] For all these reasons, therefore, Matthew was constrained to describe the birth of Christ. Now in the lineage of Christ 14 patriarchs, 14 kings and 14 priests are to be found.[10] This accounts for the wondrous joy of the Blessed Virgin and the praise and adultation accorded her, for the Virgin Mary is also titled a patriarch as the daughter of Abraham; a queen, as one of the lineage of David; and a priest.[11] Matthew could not have shown that Christ was descended from David unless he had added Mary's name in the Gospel.[12] For by Jewish law Gentiles were incorporated by

---

1. Matthew 1[6]; the account of the sermon by 'Thomas' is by the town clerk, Stephan Roth; cf. Franz, p. 517.

2. *quae fuit Urie* (Vg.); then repeated in German.

3. Matthew; why he described the earthly birth of Christ.

4. *assumatur.*

5. Isaiah 45[1] (Vg.: *ut subjiciam ante faciem ejus gentes*); cf. Psalm 46[4] (Vg.).

6. Isaiah 11[12].

7. Isaiah 2[4].

8. Isaiah 25[8].

9. John 7[41f.]

10. Matthew divides the descendants of Abraham into three groups; the first beginning with Abraham, the second with David, the third with Shealtiel.

11. Mary's name makes up the third group of 14.

12. Joseph's 'legal' fatherhood of Jesus was apparently not enough to prove his descent from David.

marriage.¹³ That is how it is shown that both Christ and Mary have descended from David. But the birth of the Virgin Mary is described in the Song of Songs 6.¹⁴ It is she who advances like the surge of the dawn, as beautiful as the moon, as outstanding as the sun, as terrible as the serried ranks of an army on parade. The comparison of the Blessed Virgin with the dawn is legitimate and to the point. For just as the dawn comes between¹⁵ night and day, so the Virgin Mary is the mediator¹⁶ between God and man. And as the dawn precedes the sun, so Mary preceded Christ, the sun of righteousness. And as the dawn brings sweetest sleep to sick people who have been restless and getting weaker¹⁷ throughout the night so Mary brought us, who are sick and burdened by most grievous sins, the most pleasing sleep,¹⁸ that is, Christ, who carried away our sins and our sick, bad conscience, Isaiah 53.¹⁹ And just as dawn drives away the birds of the darkness so Mary drove away the devil, it being said of her in Genesis 3: She has bruised your head etc.²⁰ For by her humility and chastity which were hers not of nature but by a superfluity of grace, the Virgin Mary ground to nothing all the power of the devil. And just as the dawn arouses all the birds of the light to sing and the other animals to toil and work, so by her birth Mary aroused both men and angels since she had to complete the number of the former and the former completed the number of the angels.²¹ That is why the Church sings: Your birth, virgin mother of God, has proclaimed joy to the entire world etc.²²

See one of Bernard's sermons on the birth of the Blessed Virgin.²³

Praise of the Virgin Mary
Jerome says in his letter²⁴ on the Assumption of the Blessed Virgin:

13. All the four women mentioned in the genealogy, seen as precursors of Mary, were aliens: Tamar, Rahab, Ruth, and Bathsheba (Uriah's wife).

14. v. 7f.; in the margin: 'the birth of the Virgin Mary'.

15. *media est.*

16. *mediatrix*; in the margin: 'the Virgin Mary is compared with the dawn'.

17. *laborantibus et deficientibus*, lit. 'struggling and losing strength'.

18. *somnum*; in view of the following demonstrative pronoun 'hoc', which is in the neuter gender, F. suggests that *somnium* (dream) is meant; this, however, makes little sense, and loses the parallel with the sleep brought by the dawn; a grammatical slip seems more likely.

19. Isaiah 53⁴ᶠ·

20. Genesis 3¹⁵; this verse is usually applied to Christ, as a Messianic prophecy; cf. Müntzer's prayer, p. 402/11f. below.

21. Müntzer frequently compares the elect to angels; cf. Luke 20³⁶.

22. Cf. Roman Antiphonal.

23. MPL 183⁴³⁷⁻⁴⁴⁸; cf. also the preceding sermon on the Assumption of the Blessed Virgin, which makes frequent comparisons of the moon and the sun and sees Mary as *mediatricem ... apud solem justitiae*, ibid., p. 438.

24. MPL 30,ᵉˢᵖ· ᵖ· ¹²⁶; the letter is in fact written not by Jerome, but by Paschasius Rodbertus, addressed to Paula and Eustochium. (F.)

Although I want to meet your requests,[25] I really do fear that I will be shown up as an inadequate and unworthy extoller [of Mary], especially since I lack both the sanctity of life and the eloquence which are needed to extol the blessed and glorious Virgin Mary in a worthy manner; for – to tell the truth – anything which human words can say falls far short of heavenly praise; because she has been proclaimed and extolled by divine and angelical praises, foretold by the prophets, adumbrated[26] by the patriarchs in sign and allegory,[27] displayed and made manifest[28] by the evangelists, greeted with all reverence and honour by the angel. Moreover the latter defines her nature and status[29] with divine authority when he says: Hail, Mary, full of grace, the Lord be with you, blessed are you among women. For it is only right that such honours be attributed[30] to the Virgin Mary, that she should be full of grace; who gave glory to the heavens and to the earth peace; who bestowed faith on the nations, [setting] an end to vice, a pattern for life, and a rule for morals etc.

II.   Chastity.

Thomas

There is no more eminent virtue in heaven and on earth than chastity: it is what Christ counsels in Matthew 11.[31] To keep one's chastity deserves lasting[32] praise, but victory in chastity is seldom attained! People should not be coerced into chastity. You cannot force boys into monasteries etc. without committing mortal sin.

25. *dum vestris cupio parere profectibus*, lit. 'advances'; Paula and Eustochium had requested a sermon on the subject.
26. *praesignata*.
27. *figuris et aenigmatibus*.
28. *exhibita et monstrata*.
29. *qualis et quanta esset*.
30. *Talibus namque decebat virginem Mariam oppignerari muneribus*, lit. 'pledged'.
31. Matthew 19[12].
32. lit. 'perpetual.'

(b)   *Copies of Notes for Sermons*

Romans 4, Luke 8, Exodus 4,[1] preached after St. Vitus' day[2] (15)23.
  1.   Doing many works, doing none at all; both are wrong. The Jews did many, the heathen none.

1. Romans 4 (Abraham's faith and righteousness); Luke 8[4ff.] (the parable of the sower; for Müntzer the 'thorns' represent our worldly lusts); Exodus 4 (Moses' slowness to respond to God's call); cf. esp. v. 24, where God is about to kill Moses.
2. 15 June.

2. Faith comes before works, as in the case of Abraham;[3] the Law brings knowledge.
3. While we think soberly we can give the work of God due respect.
4. Anyone who wants faith must endure the work of God and not be entangled in creaturely things; like Abraham, who was not entangled in this way.
5. The work of God is as bitter as the abyss of hell.
6. First unbelief has to get the better of counterfeit faith, and one has to stand before God quite helplessly.
7. It is God's doing[4] that he deprives man of all comfort.
8. To start with, the best thing is to pass one's whole life under review and suffer enough to balance the damage done by the lusts of the flesh.[5]
9. First one should pray for the work of God.[6]
10. This is what is meant by contemplating and sorting out the order of things:[7] first the four elements and the heavens, then the plants, then the animals, then man, then Christ, then God the Father Almighty, who is uncreated; then one understands everything in them.

On Romans 5, Mark 9, Exodus 7.[8] Preached on the sixth feast day after St. Vitus' day.[9]

11. All man's thoughts are false; for there is no good in him;[10] this is inborn in him from Adam, because his reason does not adhere to the supreme order of things.
12. But man's reason is good, if it endures the work of God.
13. No one can know if he is pious unless he has endured the work of God.
14. The soul has to be emptied of all delight in creaturely things.[11]
15. God awakens within us the desire for faith when he plants it in us.

3. *Der glaube ist vor dem gesetze wie in Abraham*; cf. Romans 4[10]; but for Müntzer this is as yet an untested faith, as in Genesis 17[17].
4. *Werckunge*; cf. *werck Gottes* in clause 3 above.
5. *so vil leiden, wie die lusth vorhindert hat.*
6. i.e. in one's soul.
7. *Dye ordenunge zu betrachten und zcu machen*; on the 'order' of creation cf. the Prague Manifesto, A, n. 6, p. 357 above.
8. Romans 5 (Adam and Christ in the context of justification by faith); Mark 9[2ff.] (Transfiguration); Exodus 7 (the plagues in Egypt and the hardness of Pharoah's heart).
9. 20 June.
10. Cf. Romans 3[11f.]
11. *von aller ersettunge der creaturn.*

16. The works of God ensure that one has no wish to deny the testimony of God and cannot do so.

17. The opposite to Adam[12] is Christ, for just as [Ad]am[13] distorts the order of things and entangles himself with creaturely things, so Christ held fast to the highest[14] and despised creaturely things.

On Romans 6, Mark 10, Exodus 8.[15]

18. If we are to do penance for sin, then our life must be a sad one, and God must give us as many pains as the pleasures we enjoyed from our sins. The guilt of sin is the doing of creaturely things.[16] Sin is misuse of creaturely things.

May praise be to God in all eternity.[17]

Christ is risen[18] [from] torment and misery an[d defeat]. Adam's all – we should be ... glad of this. Christ will be our comfort.

12. Cf. Letter 46, p. 70/24ff. above.
13. Abraham (F.)
14. *zum obersten gehalten.*
15. Romans 6 (freedom from law is not licence to sin); Mark 10[23ff.] (Jesus predicts suffering and death for himself and his followers); Exodus 8 (Pharoah's hardness of heart continues, as do the plagues).
16. *vorwirckunge der creaturen.*
17. In Latin.
18. A corner has been torn from the back of the paper, hence much of the text is lost: *Christus ist erstanden [...] marter und jummers un[d ...] Adams alle das sollen wir [...] fro sein. Christ wyll unser trost sein*; it is part of a well-known medieval song, sometimes sung in the Mass; Bräuer has pointed this out and suggests the reconstruction: *Christus ist erstanden [von] marter und jummers un[d schaden]. Adams alle das sollen wir [alle] fro sein ...*

(c) On the Incarnation of Christ (1524)[1]

The whole of Christ's incarnation must be fully understood if one is to partake of it fruitfully; otherwise the precious mysteries of God will become mere monkey-play;[2] for Christ, the authentic son of God, became human for this reason alone: that the holy Spirit should become manifest[3] in the hearts of the elect, John 7,[4] that [Spirit]

1. Böhmer, *Studien zu Müntzer*, p. 30, suggests that it was written towards the end of 1524 but it may well be earlier; there are many similarities in its language and thought about the Eucharist, with Müntzer's Eucharistic hymn, cf. p. 399f. below; the title was added later, and not by Müntzer; cf. Dismer, p. 40 n. 5; a lucid, attractive, largely unpolemical treatment of the Eucharist, it emphasises the importance of the sacraments for Müntzer.
2. Pure external rites, lacking the spirit of Christ; cf. *Vindication*, p. 330/19ff. above; the reference is to the Eucharist.
3. *erclert.*
4. John 7[39].

which, as St Luke shows in chapter 2,[5] grew in the sight of God and man; so before anything else we too must become fully aware of this primary reason. Christ took upon himself flesh and blood to release us by his heavenly understanding from our rationalistic, sensual, bovine understanding[6] John 10.[7] The word of God must make us divine[8] by taking captive our understanding for the service of faith, 2 Cor. 10.[9] It must also eradicate the fleshly, bovine lusts so that we begin to hunger for the best food of all, which is to do God's will, John 4.[10] God's wisdom and understanding and knowledge pour into us, Col. 1,[11] after all our understanding and reasoning has been laid low by heart-felt grief. It was in this way that Christ grieved his beloved disciples, as Matthew depicts for us in chapter 26;[12] when Jesus was about to give them his body he so saddened them by the [mention of] betrayal that each of them said to him: 'O, Lord, is it me?' Then he gave them to eat, and said: 'Take and eat. This is my body.' The same with the cup. An awesome, bitter food was being set before them. That was the manifestation of God's eternal will; for Christ did not come to do his own will but the will of his father, John 5.[13] The will of Christ was manifested most clearly when Christ's human will had the struggle in the garden, when he said: 'Not my will but yours be done,' and when he said 'My God, my God, why have you forsaken me?'[14] There it is expressed most clearly. Hence Christ compared himself with a seed of corn, John 12,[15] which is thrown into the earth; this gives us an image of how we should grow in his spirit; that is why the things of God can only be handled in a seemly way if the true and fruitful preaching of the death of his dear son has explained them.[16] Anyone who has not become, like the Easter lamb, a sheep destined for death,[17] Rom. 8, Ps. 43, will be unable to grasp the mystery of his death in the sacrament. An untried person, without experience of faith, can be likened to a dog to which a piece of bread is thrown; those who are bovine grasp

5. Luke 2[52].

6. *vornunfftigen sinlichen vichischen vorstande*, a very odd collocation!

7. In John 10 'the Jews' do not understand or believe in Jesus, cf. vs. 6, 20f., 26, 38.

8. *vorgoten*.

9. 2 Corinthians 10[5].

10. John 4[34]; cf. p. 400/11 below.

11. Colossians 1[9]; *kunst*, 'knowledge', is of God's will.

12. Matthew 26[21ff.]

13. John 5[30].

14. Luke 22[42]; Matthew 27[46].

15. John 12[24]; cf. the Eucharistic hymn, p. 399/8 below.

16. Luther's influence is evident here; I follow Dismer's corrections (p. 43) of Franz: *gehandelt*, not *behandelt*, *fruchtbaren*, not *furchtberen*.

17. *eyn schaff des todes*; Romans 8[36]; Psalm 43[22] (Vg.) *oves occisionis*.

merely the bare flesh, nothing more, 1 Cor. 3.[18] Since the flesh of Christ is a hindrance to the disciples, Christ has to remove it from their eyes, John 16,[19] and make them exceedingly sorrowful; otherwise he could not have bestowed the holy Spirit on them. Thus Paul says in 2 Cor. 5,[20] where he is clearly preaching about the death of Christ: 'Though we once knew Christ according to the flesh, now we no longer know him according to the flesh.' Christ brought about a renewal of his flesh,[21] which those without experience of faith exclude[22] from the sacrament, saying that he has the same height, weight, breadth and length as when he hung on the cross etc. If this were the case what use would Christ be to us, in a form like that? In holy Scripture, after all, he has left us no special testimony to [support] this sort of empty talk, but Christ says: 'This is my body, which is given for you.' That must be understood to mean this: the body of Christ is offered, is sacrificed on the cross, just as we should be sacrificed to God, Rom. 6.[23] Thus the body of Christ was set before the disciples in this way[24] so that the spirit of Christ, by which he was really zealous to face suffering, Luke 12[25] might remind timid hearts of him. Christ pointed to himself, as if to say: Ah, my most beloved, see how completely willing I am to give my body over to this gallows, to the cross; that is how you, too, should react when you have to die for my sake, as I did for the sake of the father, John 20.[26] Only after Christ's body had been offered was the sacrament effective, for in it the strength of the blood and flesh of Christ is passed on to us in a genuine disclosure of the divine testimony;[27] that is why it is called a sacrament, a holy sign; it is not just that the bread and wine point to the being[28] of Christ, but his flesh and blood are present in their very being, in a way which enables the spirit of Christ to be

18. 1 Corinthians 3[1ff.]; Müntzer's metaphors become very mixed, but the meaning is clear enough: without the spirit one cannot see beyond the outward realities.

19. John 16[6f.]

20. 2 Corinthians 5[16].

21. *hat eyne vornewrung gethan an seynem fleysch.*

22. *abwerffen.*

23. Romans 6[5ff.]

24. *dargestallet* = 'dergestalt' (F.); the reference seems to be to the appearance to Thomas with the signs of the nails in his side, John 20[27]; Dismer, p. 44, understands *dargestellt* (presented), and cites John 20[21].

25. Luke 12[4f., 50].

26. John 20[21].

27. *das sacrament, welchs ist dye abgehende crafft vom bluthe und fleysche Christi in wahrhafftiger erfindung gotlicher gezeugnuss*; the image in Müntzer's mind appears to come from John 7[38], the 'rivers of flowing water' pouring from the wounds of Christ, which is combined with the Thomas story, cf. *Protestation,* p. 192/14f. above.

28. *wesen.*

passed on from them into the hearts of the elect.[29] If one does not treat the sacrament like this, one cannot be saved, or to put it positively with John 6:[30] 'He who eats my flesh and drinks my blood remains in me and I in him.' But if Christ had simply spoken about his flesh in the foolish manner mentioned above[31] without any thought of us remembering it later[32] and said nothing about the power of the spirit being passed on from the flesh and the blood then he would not have said shortly afterwards in the same chapter:[33] 'The words which I have spoken are spirit and life.' Judas, together with the godless, was as upset[34] by Christ as the priests are at me, because I remove the sacrament with its little box[35] from those with no understanding, and say in plain language[36] that it is the devil they are handling, for they do not want to come to terms with the power of Christ. May God preserve you from that, Amen.[37]

29. *ist nach solcher weyse do, wye der geyst Christi darvon abgeht in dye hertzen der ausserwelten*; a mystical rather than a symbolic understanding of the sacrament.

30. John 6[54].

31. Cf. the 'empty talk', i.e. the purely fleshly understanding of Christ in p. 390/13 above.

32. *ane alle betrachtung weyter erinnerung*; cf. the reference to *erinnern* 'remind' in p. 390/18 above.

33. John 6[63].

34. *gar schelligk*.

35. *mit der buchse*, i.e. the pyx containing the consecrated host.

36. *auss dem barte*, lit. 'out of the beard', quite openly; cf. *Exposé*, p. 316/9 above, *Vindication*, p. 332, n. 74 above.

37. This ending suggests that our text is incomplete; as Dismer, p. 39, points out, there appears to be a reference back to an initial statement at the beginning of the text; that the text begins with *dye*, without a capital letter, supports this view; Dismer argues convincingly that it is a copy of authentic Müntzer material.

(d) *Sermon on the Parable of the Unmerciful Servant.*[1]

The kingdom of heaven is like a king who wanted to settle his accounts with his servants.[2] The sum of this whole gospel is to be found in the Lord's prayer: Release us from our debts.[3] The judgement of God is perfect, too terrible even for the deeds of the saints to come under his scrutiny: All flesh shall perish.[4] For men must render account for every idle word.[5] Now if this is true of the word what does he do about our deeds, what about our hidden deeds and

1. May only be a copy, though in Müntzer's hand, of a text unknown to us (F.); the frequent MS abbreviations may suggest this.

2. *R(egi), q(ui) v(oluit) rationem p(onere) cum servis suis*, Matthew 18[23] (Vg.).

3. Matthew 6[12] (Vg.).

4. Job 34[12, 15]; cf. Psalm 130[3] and Job 15[15].

5. Matthew 12[36].

the inexpressible wickedness of our heart, as Job says?[6] When he cleanses[7] he will not declare or find any man innocent, not even a child who has lived on earth but one day. Thus all the saints cry out, saying with the prophet: Do not enter into judgement with your servant, because no man alive will be justified.[8] Because the Lord wants the law he has given to be observed throughout one's life; not a single jot or tittle is to be lacking;[9] the whole is to be kept. It is because of this that all the saints are so terribly agitated, saying with the virgin apostle:[10] 'If we say we have no sin, we lead ourselves astray, and truth is not in us.' With the apostle let them cry out, groaning most vehemently: Who will free me from the body of this death?[11] Who will provide my head with water enough to lament day and night[12] my tribulations, my sins, my depravity etc? By this cry the unrighteous person is justified. He groans like this, and his sins are no longer taken into consideration by God. For to God alone have they attributed this honour, because he alone is holy. Apart from him 'there is not one, who does good, not even one'.[13] And they are sanctified by this confession of faith, believing in their heart in his righteousness, and, with the apostles deserve to sit in judgement, as the text clearly says: 'You who have followed me, will sit on the seats of judgement over the 12 tribes of Israel.'[14] Likewise the apostle Paul: 'How will God judge this world etc.?'[15] The Lord will judge the entire world together with those who confess their sins and forgive others theirs; he will only damn those who have not released their neighbour from his sins. The king will settle accounts with his servants when he examines those sins which are beyond faith.[16] Man is a servant, who has been created to sanctify the name of the Lord in all his deeds and be disciplined by them to know God with unfeigned faith and strengthen his weakness by crying out and saying: Lord, in all my deeds I am a useless servant,[17] help my unbelief,[18] without you I cannot please you.[19]

6. Job 22^5? (F.); cf. Psalm 19^{12}.

7. *Mundans hominem non faciet, non reperiet innocentem*; Psalm 18^3 (Vg.) *ab occultis meis munda me*; cf. Psalm 50^2.

8. Psalm 143^2.

9. Matthew 5^{18}.

10. *cum virgineo apostolo*; 1 John 1^8.

11. Romans 7^{24}.

12. Jeremiah 9^1.

13. Psalm 14^3; 53^3; Romans 3^{12}.

14. Matthew 19^{28}.

15. Romans 3^6.

16. *extra fidem*; cf. Hebrews 11^6.

17. Luke 17^{10}.

18. Mark 9^{24}.

19. Hebrew 11^6.

The account is settled when our conscience has disturbed us; as it is written of the steward:[20] 'What shall I do? The Lord will take my stewardship away. I lack the strength to dig, and to beg would shame me.' Throughout Scripture, then, we are disturbed by such stern judgement, because even a just man is scarcely able to face it with equanimity.[21] For he failed to do everything in a praiseworthy way, he did not fulfil a single precept, he owes ten thousand talents. Even if he has obeyed every law, he cannot trust in his own deeds because he only has the righteousness which pertains to the law and he will die an eternal death if he perseveres in this.[22] That is why one of the servants is sacrificed, all the servants in this one Christ, who assumed the form of a servant and who did not consider it robbery to be equal with God.[23] One stands for all, he who alone is righteous, who alone has been pleasing in the eyes of the eternal father; all the others are auctioned off. What does auctioned off mean? That they should renounce themselves, and so come to terms with their wretchedness, not trusting in their own deeds etc., in wife and in sons. Though he gives all that he has in exchange for his soul he will not be able to pay what he owes. Everything he can give is tawdry. What, then, is to be done? Surely he must despair? Far from it! But he must fall on his face with an unfeigned will to serve. Be patient, behold, I am all yours.[24] That is why you have made me, who was your adversary, your debtor. Grant what you exact, and it will be done as you will.[25]

20. Luke 16³.
21. *qui(a) iustus vix stabiliter computare non potest*; cf. 1 Peter 4¹⁹; the text is clearly corrupt, though the meaning is clear enough.
22. Circled in the margin are the words *usura in peccatis*. 'usury in sins'.
23. Philippians 2⁶ᶠ· (Vg.).
24. Cf. Matthew 18²⁹.
25. Augustine, *Soliloquia* I, 1, 5; *Confessions* 10, 37 (*da quod jubes, et jube quod vis*).

(e) Interpretation of 1 Corinthians 7

Response concerning the saying 'each one according to his calling'[1] etc. 1 Cor. 7.

The calling of each man is to keep the commands of God, as it is written: Fear God and keep his commandments.[2] This refers to every man.[3] That is why St Paul says:[4] Any of you that has been baptised has put on Christ; and is not a Jew, or a Greek, or a freeman, is not masculine or feminine. For you are all one in Christ. Just as little as

1. In Latin; 1 Corinthians 7²⁰; not in Müntzer's hand.
2. In Latin; Ecclesiastes 12¹³.
3. *Hoc est omnis homo.*
4. Galatians 3²⁷ᶠ·, in Latin, based on the Vulgate.

one's trade or business makes one a Christian, that is, furthers one's faith or piety or righteousness – for no one does joinery or works as a blacksmith in order to become pious; he does it to earn his bread and help his neighbour – similarly cowls, shaven heads, singing, bell-ringing, special foods, times, or places[5] contribute as little to making monks and nuns pious as eating, drinking, sleeping and other natural activities further piety, or as outward activities like these make one spiritual – not to mention bringing one to perfection. But if it is faith which makes us pious by making Christ our righteousness, with all his works and sufferings, then we should exercise and activate Christ within us all the more by love, which would then be Christ's work, too, and very good. For good works are fruits of love,[6] Galatians 5. And whatever is not of faith is sin,[7] Rom. 14. Our fathers instituted some ceremonies, as Christ did the sacraments, to exercise faith, to crucify the old man and to form Christ within us. But we have now turned these exercises into good works and enforced them with strict commands, excommunications and threats,[8] and as time went on this sort of superstition increased; we believed that we became pious, righteous and blessed through illusions[9] like this, that we atoned for our own sin and that of others; although they are nothing but works which we ourselves have chosen to do,[10] and about which Christ says:[11] They worship me in vain, teaching as dogmas the commands of men. In this manner they deny Christ, who alone justifies us without any works of our own and reject his commands for the sake of our tradition. W:D:[12] this we are as little instructed to do as wicked men are to steal, practise usury, rob, commit unchastity. Why don't you remain in the world if you want to remain in your calling? Why don't you let any of these stay in their vocation?[13] Paul says:[14] Circumcision is nothing and the foreskin is nothing; what matters is keeping the commandments of God. Let each one stay in the calling

5. *steten.*
6. Galatians 5[22].
7. Romans 14[23].
8. *und swer gebot, ban und furcht darauff gelegt.*
9. *gespenst.*
10. *eytel selbst erwelte werck.*
11. In Latin; Matthew 15[9], based on Vulgate; in margin Mat. 15.

12. The initials of the inquirer about the meaning of vocation? It appears that the question is whether the inquirer(s) should enter the monastic life; this, and the Lutheran flavour, suggest an early date for this writing; Bubenheimer wonders if it is a genuine writing by Müntzer.

13. *Wurumb list ir disser ke(i)n nicht in sua vocatione.*

14. 1 Corinthians 7[19ff.]; closely based on Latin of Vulgate; in margin 1 Cor. 7; in the margin there is a pointing hand; a piece of paper glued onto the corner obscures two or three letters of two lines of the page.

to which he was called. If you were called to be a slave, do not worry about it, but if you have the chance to be free make use of it. I will employ Paul's advice here, will take the sword from you and thereby ...[15] If you have the chance to be free, then make use of this; you have been bought with a price, do not become slaves of men.[16]

Amen.

15. *Will euch das swert nemen und do mit tzu* ...; Dismer, p. 239, suggests the addition of *slan* (*schlagen*): 'I will take the sword from you and hit out with it', Paul's 'advice' being Romans 13[4] or 1 Corinthians 5[13b] (Root out the evil-doer); this seems speculative; there is a close parallel in the *Sermon to the Princes*, p. 250/13 above; cf. p. 248/23ff. above; cf. Acts 16[27], where Paul prevents the jailor using his sword on himself by not fleeing precipitately.

16. 1 Corinthians 7[21, 23], based on Vulgate.

(f) On Baptism (1524, after 15 August)[1]

If baptism is to be properly administered in the house of God, Psalm 68,[2] with due attention to godly zeal, then all the clearest places in holy Scripture dealing with the baptism of Christians must be dealt with in the presence of all the people.[3] In olden times one spent the whole day and night of Easter in this way. Therefore, my dearest [friends], let us in peace and unity abandon our wrong ways so that all the peoples will say, as in Deut. 4:[4] 'O what a wise and understanding people that is.' O, what excellent people! With what dignity they administer initiation into their faith! Many unbelievers would then fall down and confess Jesus Christ with us, 1 Cor. 14[5], just as I want you, my dearest [friends], to come to know him again by the right understanding of Christian baptism through the grace of Christ. Amen.

See now, my dearest [friends], would it not be better for baptism to be held twice a year with the people in this reverent frame of mind, and dispensed to the children in a way that gave them, throughout

1. The dating is uncertain, but the reference to the loss of his property suggests some time after the flight from Allstedt on 7 August; Dismer, p. 191 n. 4, noting linguistic similarities to the *Protestation or Proposition*, prefers a date early in 1524; there are, however, as Scott notes, similarities to Letter 70, of September 1524; cf. p. 133/20ff. above; the original is lost; the copy in Müntzer's possession of his capture is on the back of Letter 72, of March 1525, and by the same hand.

2. Psalm 69[9], 'For zeal for thy house has consumed me'; this and the 1 Corinthians citation below are also found in Müntzer's treatment of baptism in the *Order and Explanation of the German Church Service*; the attitude to godparents, however, is quite different; cf. p. 178/8f. above.

3. *yn gegenwertigen alles volks*.

4. Deuteronomy 4[6f.].

5. 1 Corinthians 14[25]; baptism is not induction into a 'Christian' society, it is a missionary event.

their life, a vivid memory of how they had received it?[6] That would deter them from sins. To tell the real truth it would then be dealt with in a much more respectful way and be taken far more to heart than by giving the godparents the responsibility.[7] I know for a fact, and there is no doubting this, that at no time in his life has any godparent or sponsor dreamt of worrying whether his godchildren would adhere to what he had pledged. And the fruit of the institution of godparents was what one might expect from a basis like that. I defy you scholars – the whole host of you – to produce just one little straw[8] about this institution of godparents or this strange fantastic faith. I fully expect that you will confront me with the master from the briar bush,[9] Book 4 of the Sentences, on circumcision being transformed and baptism instituted in its place. Prove this from clear Scripture and from the fruits of faith and I will cede the point to you. Otherwise you must hold the cats aloft,[10] so know what you have to expect. With that, God be with you; do not take offence, my most beloved. We are disputing about a good and blessed matter. As far as our temporal goods are concerned we have had our fill of contention, but a dispute is worth it when truth gains the victory, through Jesus Christ and by his grace. Amen.

End of this little book.[11]

6. The meaning seems to be that baptism is to be administered to children of an age to understand it; cf. *Protestation or Proposition*, p. 191/3ff. above.

7. Cf. *Protestation or Proposition*, p. 193/17 above.

8. *eyn stiplein*; i.e. not a scrap of evidence from Scripture or the fruits of faith.

9. Peter Lombard, *Sententiarum libri* IV; the first two distinctions of Book IV refer to the transition from circumcision to baptism. (F.); cf. the explanation of the briar bush as 'heathen ways' in the *Protestation or Proposition*, p. 203/9f. above.

10. *die kaczen halten*; take the abuse showered on the loser, possibly referring to a traditional punishment (F.); or is there a reference to the popular tug-of-war game, the *Strebkatz*? A pamphlet, *Die Lutherisch Strebkatz*, was published in 1524 in Worms by P. Schöffer; cf. Scribner, *For the Sake of Simple Folk*, p. 60.

11. This suggests that it was drawn up for publication.

(g) On Following Christ[1]

No teaching about conformity with God[2] should be permitted which has not been produced by people in conformity with Christ,[3] because the blue-bottle flies have polluted the anointment of the holy Spirit.[4]

1. The similarities of the thought and language of this piece of writing with *On Counterfeit Faith*, esp. sections 9, 10, 12 are legion, beginning with the emphasis on conformity with Christ, cf. p. 220/6ff. above; cf. *Protestation*, p. 207/2 above; it is a somewhat untidy scrawl, written at speed, perhaps, but without a single correction; in Müntzer's hand.

2. *keyne gotformige lere.*

3. *christformige menschen.*   4. Ecclesiastes 10[1]; cf. pp. 57/7f., 86/17 above.

For through the negligence of such men unspeakable harm and shame[5] has been visited upon the poor, wretched and miserable Christian people, which nowadays cannot be lamented enough and should be before our sorrowful eyes the whole time. Ah, alas, al(as),[6] the godless have run off with the key to holy Scripture in their arrogant, headstrong way.[7] At no time in their life have they contemplated, or been inclined to follow the Son of God through the door by which he entered,[8] rather – lamentable though this is – they say that one can indeed be saved by just having a simple faith.[9] Ah, dear God,[10] doesn't that mean stealing the key of David[11] and closing off the way by which people could follow together a life in conformity with Christ.[12] Although in fact the disciple cannot be better than the master.[13] The master has come and given his example and his pupils must do the same as he did, must set out on the way.[14] In short, through the trial of their faith they are to take the path of their master; one has to be pointed towards the lamb by the whole of Scripture, not only how it has borne the sin of the world, but also how the lamb has been choked to death, and can only open (the door) to those who follow it wherever it goes. Though it does not recognise the others at all, this lamb[15] makes all the elect into sheep who hear the voice of those servants of God[16] who are in conformity with Christ, but who pay absolutely no attention at all to the voice of the murderous, luxury-loving men whose only contribution to the Christian people is that of Judas, who muttered about the expensive ointment being poured onto the head of Christ.[17] What else can that mean except that these delicate biblical scholars with their pointing fingers[18] do not want man to have to learn from the anointing of the spirit but to believe them, who have stolen a piece out of holy

---

5. *smacheit* = Schmach, contempt; cf. *Protestation*, p. 207/8f. above.

6. Some loss of the text at the margin here and elsewhere.

7. Cf. *Counterfeit Faith*, p. 224/5 above.

8. Cf. John 10[1ff.]

9. *wan man slecht auffs eynfeltgs gleube*; cf. *Counterfeit Faith*, p. 220/13f. above.

10. *trauter Got*.

11. Isaiah 22[22]; Revelation 3[7].

12. *unde czuslyssen, das dye menschen nicht eyngen ym fusspfad christformiges lebens*; cf Psalm 139[24], Proverbs 4[14f.]

13. Matthew 10[24]; cf. *Vindication*, p. 329/1f. above.

14. *mussen dye bane ennausen*.

15. The metaphor is again very mixed; the Lamb becomes the shepherd who knows his own sheep, and the door of the sheepfold; cf. John 10[1ff.]

16. A characteristic modification; in John 10[3] it is Jesus' voice that the sheep hear, not that of the *christformige gotsknechte*.

17. John 12[5]; note the references to 'ointment' in the writing.

18. *dye czarten spytzfingeryssen scrifftgelerthen*; cf. *Counterfeit Faith*, p. 216/5f. above.

Scripture;[19] like the murderous, confidence tricksters they are[20] they do not know what they are saying or thinking; they do not even understand themselves.

Written below in a different pen (in Latin)

Possessor; Genesis 14d, Exodus 15;[21] until the people whom you possessed passed through, 34 Exodus 6, and that you may possess us.[22] Psalm 73a. Why, O God, have you rejected?[23] Psalm 138[24] O Lord you have tested, you have possessed my inmost being 4 Proverbs a[25] 8 Prover... 11 Prover.[26] 16.8.[27]

---

19. Cf. Prague Manifesto p. 357/15f. above; cf. *Counterfeit Faith*, p. 218/9ff. above.

20. lit. 'the deceptive, murderous thieves'; *Counterfeit Faith*, p. 221/7 above.

21. Genesis 14[22f.] (Vg.); Exodus 15[16]; Abraham recognises only God, the creator, 'possessor', of heaven and earth as his benefactor, not the king of Sodom; Israel 'belongs' to God; on the concept of discipleship as 'possession' in Müntzer cf. n. 22, n. 26 below, *Exposé* n. 120, and pp. 45/2f., 46/3 above; cf. also Dismer, p. 9f.

22. Exodus 34[9b]; 62[ff.] refers to God's covenant with Abraham, Isaac and Jacob to 'possess' Israel as his people, and to invest them with 'possession' of the Promised Land.

23. *ut quid deus repulisti*; Psalm 74[1] refers to God's anger with the sheep of his flock.

24. Psalm 138[1, 13] (Vg.).

25. Proverbs 4[7], in *omni possessione tua acquire prudentiam*.

26. In Proverbs 8 Wisdom, God's first creation or possession, (v. 22 *Dominus possedit me*) stands at the door and appeals to men to follow her, not evil and folly; Proverbs 11 compares the righteous with the godless; cf. v. 29.

27. Proverbs 16[16]; 18[15?] (Vg.).

4. Eucharistic Hymn, attributed to Müntzer[1]

1.

All thanks and praise; Lord God of hosts,
For giving us what we need most.
Heavenly food to us you bring,
Praise eternal, Lord we sing.
   In Christ's dying
   Wholeness lying
From corruption's grip us prying.

2.

Here was ground the grain of wheat,
Which the cost of sin did meet.
Here was broken life's true bread,
As the prophets had foresaid.
   Bread for living
   Christ's the giving
Here, upon this sore Cross stretching.

3.

They haste, such blessings to partake,
Beneath the Cross their place to take,
Who seek on earth to do his will,
Conformed to him upon the hill.
   By our suffering
   Christ's completing,
And the Father's kingdom gaining.

---

1. This hymn first appeared in the 1529 Augsburg collection, *Form und ordnung geystlicher gesang*; it was attributed to T.M., i.e. to Müntzer, by Sigmund Salminger; the 1533 edition adds that it is to be sung to the melody of *Pange lingua*; Salminger belonged for a while to the group of Augsburg Anabaptists around Hans Hut, and it is the latter who was regarded as the author by Anabaptist circles, who continued to use it till the mid-seventeenth century; some Mennonite scholars today still maintain this attribution to Hut; however, as Bräuer points out, its emphasis on the role of the Spirit accords well with Müntzer's understanding of the sacraments, and – while absolute certainty about Müntzer's authorship may not be possible – this hymn does constitute a unity with the other twelve hymns in Müntzer's Liturgy and Mass; there are, of course, also apologetic motives for minimising any influence by Müntzer on Anabaptist hymnody; cf. S. Bräuer, 'Thomas Müntzers Liedschaffen', LJ 41 (1974), 45–102, esp. 53f, 56, 99f; a variant version of 5 verses, sung in Anabaptist circles near Erlangen in 1527 is reproduced in Gess II, (Berlin, 1917) p. 248, together with various testimonies to the continuing influence of Müntzer's teachings, prayers and hymns in Anabaptist circles, e.g. the woman from the Neunheiligen group who in 1534 admitted she had heard Müntzer preaching in Mühlhausen ten years before 'and from him she had learnt the Lord's Prayer ... and several hymns'; ibid., p. 360.

(The translation by Müntzer of Psalm 119, which follows this hymn in Franz's edition, p. 531, is not reproduced here.)

4.   Now as the food you are receiving,
See Christ's spirit all pervading.
His life on earth must take its ending,
Wholeness from the Father sending.
    The proof is clear
    The bread is near
    Thus his praise eternal hear.

5.   This bread a higher truth describes,
For we in nature live our lives.
From day to day require instruction,
True food is the spirit's unction.
    The Lord's cruel pain
    We must explain
    Unique his body and its fame.

6.   Thus by him the bread was broken,
While the words were clearly spoken:
As often as you this do eat,
In memory my death repeat.
    Good heed paying
    That my sharing
    Men repaid with crucifying.

7.   Take, then, the body of the Lord,
And as the spirit strikes a chord;
Within our hearts true God we know,
And godly love begins to glow.
    On his vine
    His spirit mine
    His body given as the sign.

5. Jottings and Notes

(a) *Notes in his own hand*[1]

This is the day which the Lord has made,[2] truly the most glorious of days, for it alone can comfort those who are languishing after every manner of sadness; it is the day longed for after darkness, or the light I hope for after darkness, where he dwells who holds hell in sway. After his passion Christ rested for three days and nights in the grave, thus signifying that rest in which we shall contemplate God. These three days, then, are mentioned in synecdoche,[3] as when we name the whole of something after a part. For just as someone is described as being white if his face is that colour, so Christ, who is part of the human race, is the only one to be described as just, and yet, through him, all are said to be just, as it says in Romans 3.[4] God confirms this figure miraculously on the human level, as is obvious in the case of the children of Israel. When some of them had sinned, while others remained[5] innocent, sometimes both groups were punished because of the wicked, and sometimes both were rewarded because of the good. In the same way God miraculously governs all things in our own day, until his own have been tested and the reprobate cast out from the sight of God. For these latter are wandering around in circles.

The devil[6] did not plant his feet in the truth. Scripture in the hands of the reprobate is to be regarded in the same way as Christ treated it when the devil sought to exercise his tyranny over him;[7] and became utterly confused as a result, citing it as perfidiously[8] as our own contemporaries[9] do – to their own perdition. Christ cites Scriptures to the impious in order to reduce them, being impious, to confusion at every point.[10] He learnt nothing from them for, as Matthew 22 says:

1. In Latin; it is not certain if Müntzer composed the first paragraph.

2. Psalm 118[24]; the day of victory, of the Resurrection; in margin, written in different ink: *abduc, apage sic cruentos impios*, 'lead off, take away the wicked, so stained with blood'; possibly a reference to 2 Kings 24[3f.]

3. *per* συνο(κ)δοχεν.

4. Romans 3[23f.]; cf. p. 70/26ff. above.

5. *extiterunt*, written above the line. (F.)

6. This paragraph is separated by a line from the previous one, and appears to be in different ink. (F.)

7. Matthew 4[1ff.]

8. *infideliter*.

9. *sicut nostri*.

10. For Müntzer confusion is the mark of ungodliness, order of true piety; this comment is important for his use of Biblical quotations in his writings.

'Do this and you will live.'[11] He who has never died to self [only] seems to live.[12]

11. It appears that Matthew 23[3] is meant.

12. *Videbatur vivere, qui nunquam fuit sibi mortuus*; cf. Ezekiel 13[19], quoted in Letter 13, p. 18, n. 85.

(b)   *Prayer*

O eternal kindly God, who sets before us today[1] the death of the precious Virgin Mary, who brought your son into the world, vouchsafe to us that we may contemplate the quite wondrous testimony of your holy word; for it is written in the most worthy gospel, that we are to confess her as a companion[2] in life eternal through Jesus Christ, our Lord, your son and hers, he who with you, lives...

Below, in another ink, and in Latin

I will put enmity between you and the woman, between your seed and her seed. He will bruise your head and you will strike at his heel[3], Isaiah 7,[4] Matthew 12,[5] Luke 2,[6] John 2,[7] Mark 3. The mother and brothers of Jesus come, and when Jesus had seen his mother and the disciple whom he loved standing there, he says (to his mother)[8]; Ezekiel 44,[9] the seventh chapter of Acts about Mary the mother of Jesus.[10]

1. 15 August (?); in his own hand.

2. Probably a reference to Matthew 12[46ff.] (cf. n. 5, n. 8 below); *eyne genossen*; after *eyne* follows *im* or *un* and perhaps two letters are missing; cf. *Exposé*, p. 320/23f. above.

3. Genesis 3[15]; cf. p. 385/15f. above; Eve as the antitype to Mary.

4. Isaiah 7[14] (the birth of Immanuel).

5. Matthew 12[46ff.]; Mark 3[31ff.] (Jesus declares that everyone who does God's will is his mother etc.).

6. Luke 2 (Jesus' birth and childhood).

7. John 2[1ff.] (the wedding at Cana).

8. *dicit ma(tri suae)*; John 19[26f.]

9. Ezekiel 44[25(?)]   10. Acts 1[14].

(c)   *Note in his own hand*[1]

A lascivious faction – that is what the present reprobate church is. Amos 6, Psalm 25.[2]

1. Notes in Latin for what appears to be a meditation from Amos on the corruption of church and society; Dismer, pp. 23ff., remarks on the surprisingly infrequent use by Müntzer of Amos (only 10 citations), and suggests that this collection of quotations may be preparatory work for the *Protestation or Proposition*.

2. Amos 6[1, 4ff.]; Psalm 26[4ff.]

Keep silent; make no mention of the name of the Lord. Amos 6.[3]

God does no great deed without first revealing it to his prophets. Amos 3.[4]

They do not know how to do good;[5] and then again, in the palaces of the wicked princes [lies] plunder;[6] the wicked hate him who speaks honestly.[7] Amos 5.

In that time the prudent man will keep silence;[8] the earth cannot sustain all the words of God. Amos 7.[9]

3. Amos 6[10].
4. Amos 3[7].
5. Amos 3[10].
6. *repine in edibus principum impiorum*; cf. Amos 3[10] (Vg.) *thesaurizantes . . . rapinas* .
7. Amos 5[10].
8. Amos 5[13].
9. Amos 7[10].

(d)   *Notes on the back of letters*

It[1] is in its entirety that all knowledge of created things must be approached;[2] it is excellent, for it treats of the work of his hands and so, when it is grasped in its entirety, it is as praiseworthy as the knowledge of God. For when it is referred to God, the knowledge of things is excellent.

Iron, which had been cold, becomes watery[3] when placed in steamy heat due to the contrasting nature of the elements.

If the world were to last for ever the land would fill the whole framework of the world, as we see most clearly in condensation.[4]

Virtue went out from him, it is a sacrament;[5] it heals all. A grain of mustard seed does not have taste added to it but simply has the substance; yet in this nucleus too, the husk is bitter. This is why the Lord did not adduce the grain of wheat to indicate the bitterness of the soul, for the tastes would be added later.[6] For it is in bitterness that the soul has to be filled by God because in this way it is emptied.

1. This note is written in his own writing on the back of a draft of the letter to Michael Gans on 15 June 1521; cf. p. 33 above; Elliger, p. 198 n. 71, slightly amends the text of Franz.

2. *In toto exordienda est omnis scientia creaturarum*; cf. Letter 57 to Zeiss: *Der wylle Gottis ist das ganze uber alle seyne teyle*, cf. p. 97/19 above.

3. *aquosum*; cf. his marginal comments on Tertullian, p. 421/3 below!

4. *totam machinam mundi, ut videmus clarissime in resolutione.*

5. Cf. p. 390/24ff. above.

6. *propter adiectitios sapores*; cf. Matthew 13[31]; for Müntzer the mustard-seed is a good figure for the Kingdom of God not only because it begins small but begins with bitterness.

For if God were nothing, the order of things would demand this lest the order of things in these matters should perish.[7]

7. *ne hiis periret tali(s ord)o rerum*; the words, in tiny writing, are written around the mark left by a seal; there is a loss of text at the margin; fragments of letters are as yet undeciphered; it would be unwise to assume that the text is intact.

Memory in its two forms:[1]
In my memory I will be mindful and my soul will wane within me.[2]

1. Written on the back of the letter of the Erfurt monks to Müntzer who mention their prayers for him, cf. p. 41 above.
2. The whole text reads:
Memoria de utraque specie:
Memoria memor ero et tabescet in me anima mea; there may be a reference to 2 Timothy 1³ᶠ; the two forms of the *vis memorativa*, retention and recall, may be meant here; or the outward sensory material and its inward appropriation (I am indebted to my colleague, Dr Guy Hartcher, for these suggestions).

(e) *Note in his own hand*

Peace and joy be with you[1] in the overshadowing of the holy Spirit. You judge me to have rushed in with misplaced zeal,[2] and conclude that the habitation of my brain must have been consumed by hot fever for a while.[3] Now I have always deferred to your ability, though not to that of the others;[4] I hope you will now see to whose malicious trick you have deferred. From the beginning I have not believed the Christians,[5] since I saw more clearly with every passing day that none of them trusted God to provide them with temporal things.[6] As to my judgement on these matters, I would have preferred to have been led to higher things by an appeal to my good will, not arrogantly constrained by human authority.[7]

1. In Latin; it appears to be preparatory material for the first part of Müntzer's letter to Luther of 9 July 1523 (Nr. 40).
2. κακοξηλίαν; cf. Nr. 21, pp. 29ff. above, and Nr. 40, p. 56/18ff.; *nec tam arrogans sum*; p. 58/24.
3. *parumper caumate adustam.*
4. Cf. Nr. 40 *sincerissime inter ceteros pater*, p. 55/29.
5. *ego a principio christianis non credidi*; this strange phrase is explained by Nr. 40: *Nec credendum est illis gloriantibus de Christo*, p. 57/22f.; *a principio* is also there, p. 56/2.
6. *In dies experiebar nullum confidere deo de recipiendis temporalibus*; cf. the reference to Nr. 40 to *animal ventris*, p. 56/11; *in dies expertus* also recurs, p. 56/5.
7. *superbissime*; cf. *superbo oculo*; ibid., p. 56/17.

On the reverse side of the piece of paper, Extracts from Basil.[8]

Basil, ch. 6. Religious authority denies that judgement can be found among the judges of this world;[9] he cites Paul, Corinthians 6.[10]

Basil c. XXIV. On the condemnation of knowledge directed against God; on unjustifiable obedience.

Ch. 3. A monk does not partake of milk, but of solid food. c. 16.

A prelate teaching contrary to the Gospel is sacrilegious. A brother should be warned. c. 17.

8. Müntzer appears to have used the Paris edition by J. Bade, 1520, 1523, of the works of Basil; cf. the Rule of St Basil in MPL 103: Interr. 5, 397; 13, 506; 2, 492; 15, 506f. (F.)

9. There may be some echoes of the Basil notes in the letter to Luther; to the *iuditium* (p. 57/5f. above) (judgement) of the divine will; the true *scientia Dei*, p. 56/26ff.; the need to reprove an erring brother, p. 56/17f.

10. 1 Corinthians 6[1].

(f) Notes in his Hand[1]

About the Knights of St. John. About the prelates.[2] About the sermon criticising the prelates. About the monastery, the three girls.[3] (About) the abbot . . .[4] About Mark on the tenants.[5] About the three vessels of holy water.[6] About the famulus[7] being safe. About the mother's death; she died destitute, he received the garment.[8] About the restitution of the missal. About singing the Mass about the hanging of the thieves[9] in the hangman's church.[10] About Illmenau, the valley of tears in the Sequence,[11] and the Gospel about the hanging of the

1. In Latin; these notes, according to Franz, refer to Stadtilm, being on the reverse side of a letter from Theodericus Greif, identified by Bräuer as a public notary in Erfurt, (not *Puff* (F.)) which apparently urges Müntzer to warn eleven inhabitants of Stadtilm to pay their taxes, on pain of excommunication, to the provost in Illmenau. Many of the notes seem to refer to legal cases, and there are similarities with the language of the *Vindication*.

2. There follows an illegible word.

3. *De monasterio tribus puellis.*

4. *(De) abbate*; edge of paper cut, and loss of text.

5. *De Marco hospitum*; perhaps a reference to Mark 12[2ff.]? Cf. the reference to the parable of the vineyard on p. 393/10f. above.

6. *De tribus cantaris; or* 'about the three tankards'.

7. Perhaps this and the next note refer to the Ambrosius Emmen. (Müntzer's famulus) and his mother.

8. *tacuit nuda, recepit vestem.*

9. *de furibus suspendendis*; the following note suggests a reference to Matthew 27[38ff.]

10. *in des henckers kirchen*; this phrase in German; Müntzer regularly refers to the princes as executioners, because they 'bear the sword', cf. *Vindication*, p. 339/22 above; the reference to this 'hangman's church' is unclear.

11. Cf. the Sequence, *Veni sancte spiritus*, 'Help us in our weary pilgrimage through this valley of tears'; Illmenau is mentioned in Greif's letter.

thieves.[12] About the monastery of the Friars Minor in Magdeburg. About the school and the boy being sold.[13] About the sausages [being eaten] in the inn on Friday.[14] About the executioner's church. About the Carthusians. About the death of Thomas.[15] About the priests.[16]

You[17] are not a friend of Caesar, O life of the damned,[18] because you love yourself intensely. Anyone who makes himself king contradicts Caesar.[19]

12. Cf. Matthew 27[38ff.]

13. *De scola et puero vendendo.*

14. Breaking the fast.

15. *De Toma mortuo*; reference unclear; the Latin would seem to exclude any prophetic reference to his own death.

16. There follows a list, in Latin, of Plato's writings, which has been omitted.

17. Luther, described by Müntzer in the *Vindication*, p. 343/20f. above, as a self-appointed prince; cf. John 19[12].

18. *o vita reproborum*; cf. *Vindication*, p. 337/2f. above.

19. Three other brief notes, which follow in F. p. 536f., which contain forms of address, and two quotations have been omitted.

(g)   *Fragment of a Letter(?)*[1]

In Christ Jesus, whose light and truth have dawned on us, my dearest brothers, Thomas Müntzer of Stolberg, master of arts and bachelor of holy scripture,[2] preacher in the town of Zwickau. To the most pious and outstanding men, lords, magistrates, the most constant adversaries of the awful Roman tyrant. To be delivered to the most upright magistrates.... Who[3] yearned for the pure teaching of Christ, so that they might become more effective in smashing down all the defences of the perverse tyrant who resists the divine spirit.

1. Franz, p. 537, describes the above as *Grussformeln*, forms of greeting; Boehmer suggested they were designed for submission to the Prague magistrates; Bräuer/Kobuch see it as a fragment of a letter, perhaps to the provincial Diet (*Landtag*); the names of the addressees have been heavily blotted out.

2. Of interest for its documentation of Müntzer's claim to hold these degrees; there is no need to doubt this claim; cf. G. Vogler, 'Thomas Müntzer als Student der Viadrina', in G. Haase, J. Winckler (edd.), *Die Oder-Universität Frankfurt* (Weimar, 1983) p. 249f.

3. *Que.*

(h) Entry by Müntzer in a Book[1]

1.   Agabus, the prophet. 4 prophetesses foretold the future, Act. 21.[2] The Spirit of JESUS appeared in a vision to Paul who then leaves for Macedonia, Act. 16. The vision of Cornelius, Act. 10.[3] On five occasions a dream is mentioned: in the first two chapters of Math. 1 and 2, when an angel appeared to Joseph and the wise men were warned in dreams not to return to Herod;[4] Ananias had a vision about St Paul, Act. 9,[5] and Peter the vision about the sheet with the four-legged creatures[6] and in [chapter] eleven he tells of his vision.[7] Agabus in the same [chapter] foretells a famine by the prophetic spirit which can be in visions.[8] Peter, being accustomed to visions, thought he had seen a vision, Act. 12 and 13;[9] about the true and false prophets,[10] about the saying of God:[11] 'Set apart Paul and Barnabas to the work for which I chose them.' Likewise, Act. 18,[12] the Lord spoke by night to Paul in a vision. Likewise to the Corinthians 12.[13]

1. In the library of the church of Gera there was in the eighteenth century the following book, since disappeared: *Liber trium virorum et trium spiritualium virginum, in quo visiones Hermae, Uquetini, F. Roberti, Hildegardis, Elisabethea eht Mechthildis etc.* Paris 1513. With it was bound John Tauler, *Sermones die da weissend auf den nechsten waren weg.* Augsburg (Otmar), 1508; both in folio; the one-time Superintendent of Mühlhausen, Jerome Tilesius, had noted in the book (in Latin): 'This book belonged to Thomas Müntzer, who began the peasant rising in Thuringia and spread many errors in the church, especially that of Mühlhausen ... What is written on the margin of the facing page and in the other pages is in Müntzer's own hand; they show what manner of things that "enthusiast" (in Greek) dreamed of'; Franz claims to find his text in B. G. Struve, *Acta Litteraria ex manuscriptis eruta*, Bd. I, (Jena, 1703) 196f., but there are considerable minor variations from the latter.
2. Acts 11[28]; 21[9f.]
3. Acts 16[9]; 10[3-8].
4. Matthew 1[20]; 2[12].
5. Acts 9[10].
6. Acts 10[11f.]
7. Acts 11[5ff.]
8. Acts 11[28].
9. Acts 12[9].
10. Acts 13[6] (the false prophet Bar-Jesus).
11. Acts 13[2].
12. Acts 18[9].
13. 2 Corinthians 12[1ff.] (*not* 1 Corinthians 12[14](F.)); as Tilesius notes at the end, these scattered notes do not make complete sense 'since they are mainly composed of exclamations.'

(i) Marginal Notes on Cyprian and Tertullian[1]

The Works of Cyprian

Sermon Three: On the value of Patience:

Christ who is innocent, or rather innocence and justice itself, is reckoned among the evil-doers.

1. The volume in which Müntzer's marginal comments are found is in the Sächsische Landesbibliothek in Dresden; cf. W. Ullmann, 'Ordo Rerum', *Theologische Versuche* 7 (1976), 125–40; with the year 1521 on the cover, it contains the *Opera Cypriani*, in Erasmus' 1520 Basel edition and the *Opera Tertulliani*, in Beatus Rhenanus' 1521 Basel edition; the inside cover of the Cyprian book informs us that it belonged to Müntzer; both books have extensive underlining and even in the Cyprian volume some of the marginal comments may be Müntzer's; as to the Tertullian volume, 'The title-page itself is full of underlinings and marginal comments which certainly are by Müntzer, of a historical and doctrinal nature. The same is true of the margins, and of the text of the Life of Tertullian, as well as of the sketch of his Theology by Beatus Rhenanus.' Ibid., p. 127; there are further underlinings and marginal comments in the prefaces of Beatus Rhenanus to Against the Valentinians and On Penitence, in the preface of Konrad Pelikan to the Index to Tertullian, and in the latter itself; most of the important comments are added to On Patience; On the Flesh of Christ, On the Resurrection; Against Marcion, Book 4, also has a few very significant theological comments; without reproducing the whole book there are, of course, difficulties in evaluating the comments as Franz, p. 539, remarks; the fifteen notes reproduced by the latter are however inadequate and are supplemented here by others; *all* the marginal notes on The Flesh of Christ, and on The Resurrection of the Flesh have been reproduced; Ullmann is cautious about dating the comments, which are in three different types of writing, according to the pen and ink used; the Tertullian volume did not appear until 1521, and at least one of the comments presupposes the break with Luther and so must be after Letter 40, i.e. 9 July 1523; the comments do, however, reflect Müntzer's early interest in Augustine, Jerome and Eusebius (pp. 15/13; 360, n. 30 above), and the references to Origen may suggest that Müntzer's reading of the latter and of Eusebius alerted him to the earlier pre-Nicene Fathers; Ullmann, p. 128.

Müntzer's marginal comments are often little more than working notes, sub-headings, exclamations, which were never designed for any other eyes. As such, the temptation to 'over-interpret' them should be resisted, especially as we lack his comments, say, on Augustine and Eusebius. Tertullian's influence should not be over-estimated.

His notes on *The Flesh of Christ* (de carne Christi) and on *The Resurrection of the Flesh* (de resurrectione mortuorum) have been transcribed from a film of the book mentioned above, in the possession of Dr. Siegfried Bräuer and by kind permission of the Sächsische Landesbibliothek, Dresden; the Tertullian texts are taken from *Tertulliana Opera* Pars II (Corpus Christianorum S.L. II, Turnhout, 1954) 871–917; 919–1012; no attempt to indicate Müntzer's underlining has been made, nor to date the comments.

They do show Müntzer 'at work', and the precision and care, but also the independence with which he reads Tertullian is not unimpressive. The comments above or below the text tend to be of a more evaluative nature and are marked with an asterisk.

Index to the Works of Cyprian:
Nothing without the consent of the people[2]

Title page of Tertullian's Works:
Cyprian a reader of Tertullian[3]
Almost all the Councils were anti-Christian
★ Tertullian lived at a time when priests were still elected – to meet the danger from Antichrist should those who are themselves damned hold sway over Christians

Preface by Beatus Rhenanus:
Satanic Councils, nearly all of them
The Councils are always thinking of establishing a faith other than the ancient one
The Roman pontiff cannot determine anything
Tertullian, Chrysostom, Gregory said that the Last Day of Judgement was at hand
None of them had revelations
The authority of the proceedings of the Councils is nil

Müntzer wrestles with the text more as a theologian than a humanist. Contemporary or polemical references are very limited. Some of the themes, such as the nature of the Resurrection, do not recur in any obvious way in his later writings.

On occasions he adds a reference to the Spirit when Tertullian only mentions the Scriptures, to the elect where only Christ is spoken of, to the Church being able to survive without the Bible, where the text only speaks of the complementarity of Scriptural and 'natural' revelation. His special vocabulary of the 'creatures' or 'returning to the origin' crops up. He differs sharply from Tertullian on the simultaneity of the Last Judgement and the Coming of Antichrist. Above all, and most interestingly, he is sharply critical of Tertullian on several occasions for failing to refute the heretics from 'the order of things'.

At other points he appears to attribute to Tertullian an interest in 'the order of things' which is not an obvious reading of the latter. No doubt Tertullian's emphasis on the drama or history of salvation, and on the 'work of the hands of God' encouraged him. Ullmann's warnings against a glib reading of a natural theology into Müntzer's comments deserve attention. The incarnational theology of Tertullian may well be a factor in Müntzer's attempts to understand God's sovereignty over the world and the individual soul in a holistic fashion.

The ambivalant attitude to the flesh, the mention of dreams, the emphasis on Mary as an antitype to Eve, the critique of allegorical exegesis and speculative theology, even the belligerent, confident manner in which Tertullian mounts his offensive are all of interest for the later Müntzer, and even the most superficial glance shows parallels or similarities to the Prague Manifesto, the Propositions of Egranus, the *Exposé*. Until careful analysis has taken place, however, caution is indicated in assessing their importance.

2. In the text of the index: he wanted nothing done without the consent of the presbyters and people.

3. Ullmann, p. 128, suggests that Müntzer came to Tertullian by way of an

As long as living theology prevails, the true church grows[4]
Today's heretics are worse than the ancient ones
Insane Marcion
All the Scriptures have to be harmonised
* The Scriptures differ from one another most directly and diametrically unless they are all harmonised against the most insane men
He fears the petty councils of the fathers of the demoniacs
Four councils of the apostles were sound
Marcion, the archetype of the Erasmians and the Picards, distinguishes between the Old and the New Testament
How wretched the ancient fathers were!

On the Life of Tertullian by Beatus Rhenanus:
The Roman Church made everything good schismatic.
You see beyond all doubt that the Roman Pontiff was the cause of all error, heresy, superstition, perversion and hatred and was a hellish morass[7]
He mocks the Romans with [their] anathema
[Tertullian] was contemptuous of the anathemas of the Romans

On the admonition to the reader about certain teachings of Tertullian:
They ought to be searched out and known by every man in the world[5]
We should be versed more in the meaning of the matter than the sound of the word
God is body, that is essence[6]
The soul in dreams
The soul is made from the material of the body
On the substance of the bread
These masked theologians are the worst, the worst
I am astonished Christians engage in such puerile ceremonies
The cleric wants to eat his bread in luxury, not by the sweat [of his brow]
Just look at the stupidity of the Councils
About the living word they said nothing

---

interest in Cyprian, and notes that the underlining in the Preface to Tertullian shows a particular interest in the relation of Origen, Augustine and Chrysostom to the North African Fathers; the world of North African Christianity, with its primitivism, enthusiasm, legalism certainly seems to offer instructive parallels to Müntzer.

4. *dum viva theologia in usu evenerit crescit vera ecclesia.*

5. Beatus Rhenanus argues that the highest mysteries of faith should be adored, not investigated.

6. *Deus est corpus, id est essentia*; essence in the sense of a real existent.

They prohibited visions at the Council of Worms[7]

True visions were denounced by those Jews (large, sprawling writing)

They wanted charity to be shown alike to the damned and to one's neighbour

O ho ho![8]

Everything about confession is wrong

Outside the true church of the elect no sin is forgiven

The sin of the priestlings was always obnoxious to the laity

He defends the worst of the priests

It is a very great sin to know one's wife even for procreation

The soul is born by the transmission of the seed

On Patience:

He vehemently commends patience

The evil of impatience is a good[9]

It is untrue[10]

His treatment of 'Do not judge' is primitive

O feeble patience!

It is said of the patience of the saints who do not know the destiny of their adversaries that to God they are vessels of wrath; why is the same not said concerning men given sure knowledge by revelation?

Against Hermogenes:

On the margin of the Preface by Beatus Rhenasus:

The philosophers are the patriarchs of the heretics

The pride of the priests

Against philosophy

Against Marcion:

All heretics deceived the church of God by the pretext of clemency

Against Egranus

On the Flesh of Christ

Marginal Notes by Müntzer	*Preface by Beatus Rhenanus*
Christ was born of an inviolate body	Text: modern theologians say Mary's womb was closed

---

7. Not clear to which of the many synods held at Worms this refers.

8. Text: Do whatever the priest commands, as if from God.

9. Inverts text: 'Evil is impatience for the good.'

Marginal Notes by Müntzer		*On the Flesh of Christ*
The argument	II, 2	i.e. against Marcion
He is refuted by his own words		i.e. Marcion
He proves nothing from the order	III, 1	Marcion argues that it is impossible or unseemly for God to be born; in Tertullian's view this is to judge God by human categories.
The nativity of Christ is to be proved from the innocence of Christ and the sin of Adam[10]		
Being infinite he is unchangeable	III, 4	Marcion's argument against the Incarnation
Here he is a sharp controversialist	5	i.e. Tertullian
Jacob	6	The struggle with the angel (Gen. 32^{24-6})
On the substance of the angels who appear[11]	7	i.e. in human likeness
The heretics' branded conscience[12] is replete with nausea	IV, 1	i.e. with disgust at the sensual
He is amazed the heretics manage to love themselves	IV, 5	In view of Marcion's disgust at the processes of birth etc.
★God chooses the foolish things to confound the wise		Quote by Tertullian, 1 Corinthians 1^{27}
★Marcion is the foundation of the Turks[13]		

10. Text: One must not repay evil with evil.
11. The epiphanies in the Old Testament.
12. *cauteriata conscientia*; cf. 1 Timothy 4^2.
13. Cf. the *Protestation*, sections 11, 13; Ullmann, p. 13, sees this as an indication that salvation is for all peoples; this seems unlikely.

Why do you not argue from the order of things?	V, 3	Tertullian quotes Mark 8³⁸: 'Whoever is ashamed of me ...'[14]
On the contrary, denying the Scriptures[15]	4	The famous Tertullian passage: it is certain because it is impossible etc.
How can he be true if his [Christ's] words are not true?	5	Tertullian is actually arguing that if Christ is not a genuine man, his words cannot be true
The God of Marcion	6	In text: without the spirit of God
★All very elegantly proven from nature	7	The two natures of Christ from spirit and flesh in man
Christ said the Spirit had neither flesh nor bones	9	Quote from Luke 24³⁹
He [Christ] has borrowed his flesh from the stars	VI, 3	The argument of Apelles, Philumena
★None of the doctors wrote about the order; as a result they could not vanquish a single heretic, except by the Scriptures, which can be compared and wrapped up in some obscure explanation[17]	VI, 5	Tertullian refers to the abuse of Scripture by the heretics[16]
He provides his reason with an explanation		Christ came with a human body because he came to die
They do not prove that the angels took their flesh from the stars; all bodies are made according to their constellations	VI 9	

14. Vg.: *Qui enim me confusus fuerit* ...; the 'order of things' as the opposition to such 'confusion'.

15. *contra negantem Scripturis*; this relates to the previous comment.

16. Cf. the 'Propositions' of Egranus, p. 380/25f. above.

17. Cf. the *Exposé*, p. 314/26ff. above.

Marginal Notes by Müntzer		*On the Flesh of Christ*
O ho! Everything has its cause.	10	
Contrary to the order		
★The sophistry of the heretics	12	When they argue against the full humanity of Jesus because he said: 'Who is my mother etc.?'
Many things were done for the sake of temptation	VII, 3	i.e. to tempt Jesus – Luke 10²⁵ Matthew 19³
He then silences¹⁸ these heretics with the letter	4	Marcionites take the question to Jesus about his mother and brothers too literally
It was in the letter that all the doctors err, fondling the darkness everywhere¹⁹	10	
The understanding of this matter	13	Jesus gave priority to the word of God
They are cut down by Marcion, the first of that sect	VIII, 1	
It is to the Spirit that this authority refers	6	1 Corinthians 15⁴⁷ refers not to heavenly flesh but to the Spirit
All things are to be taken back to their origin	IX, 1	
He compares flesh with the earth	2	What is the flesh but the earth converted into its forms?
The flesh of CHRIST is like our flesh	4	
★The amazement of people at Christ and his elect when they taught	5	It was Christ's words, deeds, virtue which caused astonishment (no mention of elect); cf. Matthew 13⁵⁴

18. *quiescit.*

19. A reference to Exodus 10²¹; cf. also the Latin version of the Prague Manifesto, p. 377/7 above; this again appears to be a criticism of Tertullian.

The prophets being silent		The Marcionites ignore the prophetic predictions of Christ's unbecoming appearance
It proves that the flesh of Christ is not heavenly	7	Matthew 27[30], Mark 15[19], Luke 22[64] cited
He ridicules the heretic	8	i.e. Marcion's view that a suffering Christ cannot be from the heavens
The carnal soul is never without desires	X, 3	The soul is never without the body
All the heretics were ignorant of the order	XI, 1	Probably a reference to XI, 4, 'Everything that is, is a body of its own kind'
The soul is not body	5	
Everything we are is soul	XII, 1	A direct quote from Tertullian
What the soul is ignorant of		
The soul developed from the vine[20]	2–3	
*The soul is ignorant about itself and can understand neither God nor the creature unless it dissolves [this ignorance][21]	5	Tertullian: Soul has self-knowledge, but none of God
Beyond all doubt you know how this denies the order of things[22]	6	The son of God descended, not so that the soul should understand itself in Christ, but Christ in itself
He bases salvation on gross ignorance	7	Marcion denied the true humanity of Christ

20. *ex traduce*; appears to mean propagation.
21. Misreads, or differs from, Tertullian.
22. Ullmann, p. 129, argues that what interests Müntzer here is that salvation is not a process in the human consciousness but a transformation of the whole cosmic order of things, of the physical, the 'natural' world but he bases this on the reading: *quomodo hic nectat ordinem rerum*; it must read: *negat*.

Marginal Notes by Müntzer		*On the Flesh of Christ*
How easily danger arises in matters which are not understood	XIII, 2	The danger of confusing one thing, or none, with another
The example of the pot and the clay		
He shows the difference between soul and body	5	
Against the error attributed to Origen	XIV, 2	The salvation of the devil
He could not save man by an angel	3	
You made him a little lower than the angels[23]	4–5	Christ in function, not by nature, an angel
The EBIONITES with the TURK	4–5	Ebionites saw Christ as merely a man
The authority of Christ	6	'But I say to you', Matthew 5[34, 39]
VALENTINIANUS (sic) says the flesh of Christ is spiritual	XV, 1	
*He proves from the Scriptures that Christ is a man		Six Scriptural texts adduced by Tertullian
MAN		
The TRICK of controversy creates heresies	2	Tertullian mentions this love of disputation
They did very well to resist; because they wanted the order of which the THEOLOGIANS were ignorant from the beginning[24]	4	Heretics do not believe in him whom they ought to believe, pagans believed in what ought not to be believed

23. Psalm 8[5.]

24. *optime contrariati sunt quia voluerunt ordinem quem THEOLOGI ignoraverunt in principio*; meaning unclear, but seems to relate to the *Merito* in Tertullian, and to suggest that the motives (of the pagans?) were good; Ullmann, p. 132, points out that Tertullian's critique of the heretics, too, is differentiated.

A HERETIC, in the
proper sense of the word, is
an unbelieving believer

They fantasised about the emptying of the flesh of Christ	XVI, 1	The Gnostic, Alexander, said his opponents needed a fleshly Christ so that he could empty, in himself, the flesh of sin
sinful flesh		Christ took it upon himself
*Just as Adam was born from the virgin earth, so it was fitting that the Second Adam should be		Against those who argue Christ not of seed of man so could not bear our flesh
Alexander syllogises	4	Criticises Gnostic syllogising of Alexander
The order of things is dealt with in a unique way here; Adam was not made of the seed of man; the same is true of Christ	5	
The authority	XVII, 3	The Word became flesh, John 1^{14}
On Eve and MARY	5	One believed the serpent, the other Gabriel
*Here again he touches on the order of things as it relates to the conception of diverse [beings]	6	Conception by Eve of Cain, by Mary of Christ, the good brother to eradicate memory of the bad
CAIN a devil from the beginning		
All to Christ and those believing in him	XVIII, 5	All is subject to Christ
Against Valentinus	XIX, 2	
*He declaims the verse, declaims (sic): who is neither of blood or the will of the flesh		i.e. against the Gnostics, who claim they are meant by 1 John 1^{13}

417

Marginal Notes by Müntzer		*On the Flesh of Christ*
Participation in the womb	3	Tertullian stresses this
FROM THE WOMB	5	
In dreams	XX, 1	Angel speaks to Joseph
He seeks to refute the heretics from the holy Scriptures	2	
Valentinus was a Platonist[24]		
Torn from the womb, who adheres to it[25] *He argues about the tearing away of the flesh of Christ	5	If (Christ) not incorporated with the womb, how could he be torn from it?
On the milk of the breasts	6	Whether a virgin could produce milk
Why she remained a virgin	7	
No Scripture is void; it is fulfilled	XXI, 3	
*He adduces the testimony of the Scriptures, passing over the testimony of the Spirit	5	The testimony of the apostles cannot be destroyed
*The womb of Mary was opened at the nativity of CHRIST	XXIII, 4	
nuptial passion		
All the heretics make a multiple Christ	XXIV, 3	Distinguish between Jesus and Christ etc.

The Resurrection of the Flesh

Marginal Notes by Müntzer	*Preface by Beatus Rhenanus*
He proves the Resurrection from the order of things	

25. Not strictly a marginal comment – the whole phrase is circled.
26. *Avellitus ex utere qui adhaeret illi.*

Some wanted to interpret
the Resurrection spiritually

The soul is propagated by
heredity

On the new prophecy
according to Montanus

The contradictions of the wicked are found on all sides	I, 2	The pagans believe death is the end; yet continue to sacrifice on behalf of the dead i.e. the eternal soul
Plato posits the eternal	4	
The world knows of the Resurrection	II, i	Although mixed with erroneous concepts the world not ignorant of The Resurrection
The Sadducees	2	We now have to deal with new Saducees
P[re]ceding		Text refers back to *De Carne Christi*
★The works of the hands of God testify many things about God		We believe in no God but the Creator
THE ORDER OF THINGS[27]	7	Tertullian refers to order of argument he will follow
The works	8	The testimony of the works of God naturally known
The resurrection of the flesh is hard to believe in		Text: easier to believe in one God
A diversity of promises suggests diverse gods	10	If one's hope changes one's God changes
Aristotle says the soul has to be dissolved	11	

27. Tertullian is making a formal point, that in a debate with heretics, the order (*ordo*) should deduced from the principles at issue; it has nothing to do with Müntzer's interest in 'the order of things'.

Marginal Notes by Müntzer		*The Resurrection of the Flesh*
The heretics invent their god in [the shape of] Christ	III, 3	Heretics derive their views from pagan standards of reason, common sense etc.
The works of the hands of God[28]		
Against all scholastics who [confuse] the natural with the divine		
Nothing but controversies among the doctors	4	Questions, debates taken over from the secular world
The letter does not overcome	IV, 1	'but divine reason is in the heart'
The disgust at natural things [mentioned] in Tertullian	2	Heretics constantly abuse and abhor the flesh
The heretics' argument about the inappropriateness of the flesh	6	Weaknesses of flesh itemised
Menander and Marcus. The body originated by the angels	V, 2	They claim the body is the work of angels
Clay to a living soul	8	Genesis 2[7, 8] cited
*The image of CHRIST before the foundation of the world		Man made in the image of God, i.e. of Christ
In the image of God, of CHRIST	VI, 3	
The heretics are contemptuous of the rude creatures; because they know nothing about the order of things	5	Man, made of clay, is work of God's hands; heretics blacken the name of the earth

28. The work of the hands of God is, as Ullmann, p. 130, points out, the 'entire living order' of the Prague Manifesto (p. 360/11 above), of which the Resurrection is the supreme example; he sees it as the very reverse of a natural theology.

Gold from the earth, flesh from the earth	6	Thus Tertullian
A VAPOROUS WIND[29]	VII, 3	By God's breath man becomes a living soul, as by fire clay is baked into a pot
Glorious clay[30]	7	By the hand of God the clay is glorious
All works in the flesh	12	The arts, scholarship, business, the whole of life is done in the flesh
The body being one with[31] the soul will rise at the judgement	13	Since body and soul are inseparable in temporal life, why not in eternal?
★Being drawn to every creature man lives in the flesh[32]		
Tertullian is talking about his ceremonies	VIII, 2	References to Christian worship and role of bodily in baptism, anointing etc.
★Ah![33] the enlightened soul!	3	As the flesh is hinted at in the imposition of hands, so the soul is illumined by the spirit
The soul is enriched in the elect[34]		The soul is enriched by God
modesty is necessary in marriage	4	Praised like virginity etc.
The flesh is pierced		By martyrdom

29. Cf. p. 423/14ff. above!

30. *gloriosus limus*! Müntzer picks up Tertullian's paradox; the following three comments are closely related.

31. *simul cum*.

32. Müntzer introduces his own vocabulary and thoughts here; Tertullian actually sees the flesh as the key to salvation at this point.

33. *Ach*! in German!

34. No mention of the elect in Tertullian.

Marginal Notes by Müntzer		*The Resurrection of the Flesh*
To offer Christ one's powers[35] is to die for him	5	Reference to martyrdom
God's care for us is no trifling one	IX, 1	
God loves our flesh	3	God's power to restore disintegrated bodies
Giving more honour to the more reputable	4	
The glory and ignominy of our flesh	X, 1	Contrasting Biblical passages about the flesh
The act of the flesh is repudiated	3	Paul rejects not substance of flesh but its acts
The flesh is the temple of God	4	As God's temple must not be violated
The greatest friends of the flesh are the heretics	XI, 1	Heretics both enemies and devotees of flesh
He argues in a pious and Christian way from created things to the Resurrection[36]	9	God, able to create *ex nihilo*, can also raise from the dead
The restoration of the flesh is easier than the creation of the world		
★The nature of things is reviewed here	XII, 2	The rhythms of day and night, of the seasons etc.
The DAWN of the day after the night a likeness of the rising again of the flesh		
Everything returns	4	The revolutions of the seasons
A very fine conclusion about the resurrection of the dead	7	'Therefore this whole revolving order of things is a witness to the resurrection of the dead'

35. *vires*; relates to the previous comment; of the draft letter to Stolberg, p. 60/9ff. above, and esp. p. 59, n. 434 above.

36. There appears to be some closeness to a natural theology here; cf. the following comments.

Nature assists prophecies	8	Nature was there as an instructress before the prophets
All for the sake of man	9	Designed for man
To hold the creature in contempt is the height of ignorance Nature teaches		
The Phoenix	XIII, 2	No clearer documentation of Resurrection
All plagues are divine parables	XIV, 1	No reference to plagues, but to works of God in nature as parables
The reason why the flesh rises again	XIV, 3	Begins to explain the reason
The perfect judgement of God	10	The necessity of the resurrection is the necessity for judgement
The perverse inclination to the creatures is condemned	XV, 3	
All works are in the flesh		Whatever soul does is in, with, and through the flesh
The face mirrors all intentions	XV, 5	(Thus Tertullian)
The comparison of our flesh with instruments	XVI, 3	Heretics unwilling to allot any instrumental role to the flesh
The comparison too inexact	10	A vessel or instrument can be laid aside, the flesh is a body's present to the soul
In its own way the soul is bodily	XVII, 2	The soul has its own kind of solidity, by which it can feel and suffer
He buttressed the meanings of Scripture from nature	XVIII, 1	i.e. Tertullian

Marginal Notes by Müntzer		*The Resurrection of the Flesh*
For even without Scripture the Christian truth endures[37]	XVIII, 3	Persuaded even without the divine voice
The soul does not fall into the sleep of the body; the sp[irit] is awake	9	Agitated in dreams
★The soul is at its most powerful in dreams		
They pronounce certainties about uncertain matters	XIX, 1	The heretics prescribe certainties about uncertain matters, i.e. declaring. Resurrection should be understood spiritually,
The excessive love of allegories	2	allegorically
The custom of the heretics	6	Do not deny Resurrection, but say it is not in *our* flesh
Not all things are simply images	XX, 2	Some things are images, some truths; some shadows, but some bodies
ISAIAH	8	Prophets described the historical realities of exile etc.
He routed allegories It is dangerous not to believe in the Resurrection	XXI, 4	Our 'reward' and our 'peril' are dependent on the Resurrection
Inconstancy cannot be ascribed to our God	5	If God's judgements clear about individual cases, how much more so his universal judgement; no inconstancy can be attributed to Him
It is one thing for salvation to be at hand, another for it to be present	XXII, 7	Jesus' predictions that salvation at hand

---

37. Goes well beyond Tertullian here.

*Elijah about to come, Antichrist in his own person	11	Salvation, the day of judgement is still to come, the coming of Elijah and the Antichrist
On the spiritual Resurrection	XXIII, 3	Paul sees us as spiritually dead, but about to rise physically
PAUL WANTS TO KNOW HIS SALVATION in his understanding	8	Philippians 3$^{12-14}$ cited
The trumpet of God is the word of the Gospel	XIV, 7	The trumpet has not yet sounded for the Last Judgement; but it can be called the word of the Gospel
He cites Revelation	XXV, 1	Revelation 6$^{9-11}$
The whole	3	i.e. of salvation, is yet to come
He expounds (how) the Lord reigns	XXVI, 4	Exultation of saints at fruits of the divine kingdom terror of profane
Garments	XXVII, 2	White garments refer to purity of the flesh
Fasting	3	Isaiah 58$^{6ff.}$ cited
Closed cellars where the flesh is salted	4	Tertullian suggests Isaiah 58^8 is a symbol of Resurrection
The leprous hand	XXVIII, 1	Exodus 4^6
He proves the Resurrection most firmly from the clear [words of] Scripture and from allegories	XXIX, 1	
EZECHIEL		Ezekiel 37$^{1-14}$ cited as prophecy of Resurrection
Heretics fashion allegories out of Ezechiel	XXX, 1	They make it an allegory of Israel

Marginal Notes by Müntzer		*The Resurrection of the Flesh*
The vision of the bones		
The intention of the revelation is to be maintained	XXXI, 7	We should retain the meaning of the 'divine proposition', i.e. as a prophecy
The beasts will not be raised	XXXII, 3	Reference is to Enoch 61⁵: 'And I will command the fish of the sea to vomit up the bones they have eaten ...,' but Tertullian denies this means all animals will be raised at the Last Judgement
To the Jews in parables	XXXIII, 3	Jesus may have spoken to the Jews in parables, but not to all
a parable expounded by CHRIST	5	Reference to Jesus' explanation of the parable of the sower
Each participates in the other	XXXIII, 9	Soul and body are one
He does not allow the flesh to perish eternally	XXXIV, 4	Would be unjust of God to allow part of man to perish when he saved him
The body and soul of the wicked will be sent to Hell	XXXV, 1	An eternal killing of both body and soul in hell
human power is not to be feared	XXXV, 1	It cannot harm the soul
The ASTUTENESS OF THE HERETICS	5	They dispute about what is meant by a body; and whether it is punished eternally in hell
The flesh rises again by the will of God	9	For all the hairs on our head are numbered ...
To eat of the tree of life, of the bodily disposition	13	i.e. it is an indication of bodily nature; cf. Revelation 2⁷

With a clear voice the Lord affirms the Resurrection, Luke	XXXVI, 2	Against the Sadducees, Luke 20$^{27-34}$
The Sadducees of the Jews, of the Christians	7	The heretics of the Jews paralleled by the Christian Saducees, who deny the bodily Resurrection
He shows the flesh profits nothing	XXXVII, 1	This to be understood in context of John 6$^{51ff.}$
To the mortified flesh the spirit is profitable	5	The Spirit gives life to the mortified flesh
The resurrection of judgement	8	Reference to John 5^{29}
*He refutes the Heretics with a broken battering-ram^{38}		
*He frequently cites the Apocalypse	XXXVIII, 4	Revelation 6^{9}
O lame pretence!		
Paul on the Resurrection	XXXIX, 3	Acts 23^{16}
Moses professes the Resurrection	5	Cf. Acts 26^{22}
The Athenians derided the Resurrection	7	Not immortality of soul, but Resurrection
Heresies are inevitable because of the false understanding of the Spirit and of the Scriptures	XL, 1	Tertullian mentions only the false reading of the Scriptures
The outward man is in decay	2	Paul does not distinguish between two different types of men; all combine inner and outer, soul and flesh
A glory which exceeds	8	2 Corinthians 4^{18}

38. *quassante ariete*; presumably Tertullian's use of Scriptural proofs is being criticised, rather than arguing from 'the order of things'.

Marginal Notes by Müntzer		*The Resurrection of the Flesh*
The body will be crowned with the soul	14	Both suffer at present, both will be glorified
A[men]		
He lets the coming of Antichrist coincide with the day of judgement like the monk Martin Luther; but I dissent.		Tertullian is expounding Thessalonians 4[15-17]
★The judgement of Christ will be long in coming[39] Many of the elect condemned the wicked man		
He believes in Purgatory	XLII, 3	Tertullian talks of change even after the Resurrection
On the corpses once whole		How is the mortal element of those alive at time of the Coming of Christ to give way to inmortality?
On an eternal devotion in the fatherland[40]	XLIII 1	Probably refers to longing for our heavenly home, cf. 2 Corinthians 5[6]
★He does not abide in the Lord at once	4	Only the martyrs move straight from the life of the body to being with God
Transposition of words[41]	7	Refers to interpretation of 2 Corinthians 5[10]
The body should be mortified on account of the Resurrection	XLIV, 7	Bearing the mortification of the Lord in our bodies, 2 Corinthians 4[10], i.e. the life that broke the gates of death
All heretics claim to be spiritual	8	While we live we cannot exhibit true, perfect oneness with Christ

39. The words after '... Martin Luther' have been added in a different ink.
40. *de eterno studio in patria.*
41. *Hyperbaton.*

He wrote a commentary on the soul[42]	XLV	Tertullian, referring to the simultaneous conception of the soul and the body refers to his commentary on the soul
Every word should build up faith		Ephesians 4^{29} quoted
He gives precepts, obviously (?) healthy[43]		Presumably refers to the quotations from Ephesians 4^{25-32}
He derides these people	14	Who identify the 'old man' with the flesh; why don't they just rush to die?
The difference is a moral one	15	The new thing is the moral, not the 'substantial' difference
★The Holy Spirit is not to be grieved in the hearts of the elect		Cf. Ephesians 4^{30}
It is not the flesh the apostle condemns but its works	XLVI, 1	i.e. The works of the flesh
Many live in the body according to the Spirit and not according to the flesh	3	Thus Tertullian
The Holy Spirit who dwells in us will raise up our mortal bodies. Here Paul is crystal clear	6	Romans 8^{11} cited
The sense of the flesh is death	12	The 'operation', the sense of the flesh, not its nature is the cause of death
The life of the world he calls the 'old man' Romans 6	XLVII, 1	Thus Tertullian, quoting Romans 6^6

42. *de Anima.*
43. *dat precepta ap[er]t[issime] salubria.*

Marginal Notes by Müntzer		*The Resurrection of the Flesh*
He gives the firmest proof	13	Romans 5²¹; if sin reigns in death, and grace is even reigning in a parallel way in eternal life, then the dissolution of the body in death must be paralleled by its integration
Those who flee the light of the Scriptures⁴³	17	1 Thessalonians 5³ 'May God make you holy in every part', i.e. the body too is to be sanctified
He argues convincingly and clearly about the Resurrection	XLVIII, 7	1 Corinthians 15 cited, the parallel between Christ's Resurrection and ours; his was in the flesh, therefore ours also
To fight against beasts	12	Cf. 1 Corinthians 15³²; i.e. dangers to the flesh
What manner of bodies are restored to those who die?	XLIX, 4	1 Corinthians 15³⁵, ⁴⁸ᶠ·
*The first man of DUST, of clay, the second heavenly man the word of God		1 Corinthians 15⁴⁷

44. *Lucifuge Scriptarum.*

(j) Hebrew Proper Names[1]

Naas	snake[2]
Amon	son of sorrow[3]
Jabes	dry grief[4]
Gilead	heap of witnesses[5]
Gibea	valley of sin[6]
Saul	an abuse sought out[7]
Basek	vain splendour and destitution[8]
Gilgal	mud-hole for pigs[9]
Sissera	knocking out of the rejoicing tooth[10]
Hazor	a creature of wrath
Balim	gape[11]
Astaroth	bed-mate, stark naked[12]
Gerubaal	to be avenged by Baal
Bedan	pre-eminent in judgement
Japhthah	opening
Samuel	claimed by God
Rachel	egg, seeing God

1. This list, thought by Wilhelm Eilers to be evidence of original Hebrew scholarship on Müntzer's part, (F.p. 540) has been shown by Hans Peter Rüger to be largely dependent on Jerome: on the latter's Liber de interpretatione hebraicorum nominum, on the text of the Vulgate, and on another writing in the Jerome tradition, a forerunner of the anonymous Libellus de interpretatione nominum proprium, 'Thomas Müntzers Erklärung hebraischer Eigennamen und der Liber de interpretatione hebraicorum nominum des Hieronymus,' ZKG 94, 1/2, 83–7; Müntzer's sole originality lay in amending the form of some words in the Vulgate to make them closer to the Hebrew; frequently he conflates or abbreviates Jerome's rendering; as Rüger points out, he did contemplate buying all Jerome's works in 1520 (cf. Letter 8), which would have included Jerome's book on the interpretation of Hebrew names, and Hebrew grammar figures in his Book-list of 1520 (cf. p. 444/4 below); the notes below are taken from some of the comparative data provided by Rüger.

2. Identical with Jerome.

3. A conflation of Jerome's *filius populi mei vel populus moeroris*.

4. A conflation of 1 Chronicles 4⁹ (Vg.) *quia peperi eum in dolore* with Jerome's *exsiccata vel siccitas*; cf. the Libellus: *Siccitas vel confusio; Tristitia, sive dolor.*

5. *Galaad, id est, tumulus testis* Genesis 31⁴⁸ (Vg.).

6. Note here (and in n. 5 above), the correction of the Vg. (*Gabaath*).

7. Jerome: *expetitus vel abutens.*

8. Jerome: *Bezec fulgur vel contemptus vanus sive micans; egestas.*

9. Jerome: *Galgala volutatio* (wallowing) *sive revelatio.*

10. Müntzer has confused 'Sissera'; (according to Jerome: *gaudii exclusio*) with 'Sennaar'; (according to Jerome: *excussio dentium*); with spectacular results.

11. *maulaff.*

12. *cubile futter, totus nudus*: the German *Bett* (cubile) *futter* literally means 'bed pasture' or 'bed fodder', i.e. what the woman 'receives' from the male in intercourse. Grimm I, 1735; IV, 1071f.

Aseka	strong trap[13]
Damin	blood
Goliath	crossing over strong revealing them
Geth	press
Michal	water from all
Ramath	vision of death
Naroth	conspicuous
Ephrata	fruitfulness, fruit-bearing[14]
Jeremias	sublimity[15]
Helchias	part of the Lord
Sellum	peaceable
Hanameel	gift of God
Benyamin	son of God
Saruia	bond in narrowness
Anathot	obedience
Baruch	blessed
Neri	my light
Masias	creation, work of the Lord
Michmas	touched, humility
Jonathas	donation of God
Beth auen	home of idolatry
Ephrata	dusty, fertile
Bethoron	house of wrath
Socho	bower[16]
Secu	fountain hidden by branches
Achila	my acceptance
Abisai	my father, incense to me
Joab	hostile paternity[17]
Ahimilech	my brother the king, kingdom of my brother

13. Jerome: *fortitudo sive decipula.*
14. *ubertas* καρποφορία.
15. Libellus: *Celsitudo Domini vel sublimitas Domini.*
16. *eyn laubrothe.*
17. Jerome: *inimicus vel est pater.*

INTERROGATION AND 'RECANTION' OF MÜNTZER

(a) *Standard Form of Interrogation*[1]

You should ask the prisoner:
   Where he comes from?
   How he earns his living?[2]
   Why he took part in this rebellion against L(andgrave)
   Ph(ilip), our gracious Lord etc?
   Who their leader was?
   Who started the rebellion and organised its spread among the
      people?[3]
Then to state what their intentions and plans[4] had been, and what they
   would have done if things had gone as they had hoped?

(b) *Confession of Master Thomas Müntzer, previously pastor in
Allstedt, now discovered among the rebel horde at Frankenhausen: made
voluntarily*[5] *on the Tuesday after Cantate, 1525:*
1.   He does not want anyone to adore the holy and most revered
sacrament in an external way, but only in the spirit; but each
individual should be allowed to decide for himself.
2.   Says that he has distributed the sacrament to the sick and has
himself partaken of it in the afternoon, after he has eaten, or, if it
proved more suitable for people, in the evening;[6] has taken wine and
bread and consecrated them.
3.   In Klettgau and Hegau, in the neighbourhood of Basel,[7] he issued
some articles, drawn from the Gospel, on how one should govern,

---

1. The interrogation of the ordinary captives after the failure of the Peasants' War
seems to have followed a fairly standard pattern. The following form of questions
was found among the statements made by the Hersfeld and Fulda captives. A leader
like Müntzer would, of course, have to submit to much more extensive questioning.
(F.)
   2. *was sein handel und gewerb sei.*
   3. *ins volk gepildet hab.*
   4. *was ir furne(me)n und anschlag seien gewesen.*
   5. *in der gute,* i.e. without torture being used; the interrogation took place in the
castle of his arch-enemy, Ernest von Mansfeld at Heldrungen; it began on 16 May,
the day after the defeat of Frankenhausen; its revised text was already published by
the beginning of June, and in view of this propaganda use caution is in place about its
complete accuracy as a record of Müntzer's replies.
   6. *in der nacht.*
   7. Müntzer appears to have arrived here at the beginning of December 1524; cf.
Elliger, pp. 634ff.

from which, later on, other articles were devised;[8] they would have liked him to join them, but he declined with thanks. It was not he who started the rising in that region; they had already risen in rebellion. Oecolampadius and Hugwald[9] instructed him to preach to the people in that region. So he had then preached that the rulers there were unbelievers, that the people, too, were unbelievers, and that a day of reckoning was sure to befall them. The letters which they had written to him were in a sack in the keeping of his wife at Mühlhausen.

4.[10]　Says that the castles are grievously oppressive and bristling with compulsory dues and other forms of exploitation of their subjects.

5.　Says he declared that when they ride out [in public] the princes should be accompanied by eight horses, a count with four, a gentleman by two, but no more than that.

6.　The original members of his alliance had been Balthasar Krump, a tanner, and Baltzer Stübner, a glazier, both of Allstedt; they had started the rebellion with him. The castellan[11] was involved too, although he had begun by denouncing it. The alliance was directed against those who persecute the Gospel; the register in which the names of those who had covenanted themselves together were inscribed had been in the possession of the two men mentioned above.

7.　Master Tilmann Banz, the preacher at Sangerhausen, had urged him to write a letter to the congregation there, encouraging them to stand by the Gospel and take measures against those who obstructed it; and this he had done.

8.　Says that he had words with Dr Strauss[12] in Weimar, when Duke John of Saxony etc. summoned him there.[13] At the time[14] when Strauss was debating with the Franciscans he had told the brothers that, in his view: If all the Lutherans intended to do was to harass these people – the monks and the priests – then they were leaving as much undone.[15] Since then [Strauss] had written him in a letter to Johann

8. *daraus furder andere artigkel gemacht*; Elliger is probably correct in suggesting that Müntzer is disclaiming responsibility for the later articles; his own original articles have not been found; Elliger, p. 651.

9. Müntzer was invited to a meal by the Basel reformer, at which the humanist Hugwald was present; it appears to have been a quite friendly affair; cf. Elliger, pp. 630ff.

10. This paragraph is only found in the Leipzig edition, not in the MSS.

11. Cf. the letters to Zeiss, Nrs. 46, 57, 58 above.

12. Jacob Strauss, pastor in Eisenach; cf. p. 126/11 above.13. On 1 August 1524.

14. This disputation was at the beginning of December 1522; it is not absolutely clear whether Müntzer was personally present, but in view of his colloquy with the Weimar court preacher, Wolfgang Stein, at the same time, it seems more than likely; cf. p. 455, n. 1 below; cf. Elliger, p. 238.

15. *hetten sye es gleych so mer underlassen*; cf. p. 18/24f. above; *or*: they had 'all the more [reason] to desist.' (Scott).

Koler[16] in Mühlhausen: If the journey did not deter him, he would gladly come to Mühlhausen and drive him out; perhaps it was because he would have liked to be there himself.

9. The reason he had dishonoured and upbraided[17] my gracious lord, Count Ernest von Mansfeld, prince of this territory, was the complaint of his subjects that the word of God was not being preached to them; it was actually proscribed, and he would not let them go to hear it. He had ordered them to report this state of affairs, each to his own lord. If it still was not preached, then they should come to him. He would preach to them himself, and no one should let themselves be hindered from coming.

10. The people of Mühlhausen admitted him and Hans Rotte,[18] a furrier, and the distiller near St Blasius welcomed him.

11. Was at Mallerbach[19] and saw the people from Allstedt carrying some images out of the church and then going on to burn the church; preached a sermon that it was licentiousness[20] and superstition to bring figures made of wax into [the church];[21] it was not commanded by God. The verger was urged to leave the place; this had happened. After that the church, as mentioned above, was burnt down.

12. The house of Apel von Ebeleben[22] was plundered and demolished by the Mühlhausen brothers; the brothers' grievances against the house were set out in various articles, not known to him. They were partly the Twelve Articles of the Black Forest peasants and partly others.

13. The Mühlhausen Council did not agree to join the alliance itself, but allowed the common man to covenant himself.

14. Klaus Storch and Marx Stübner had been with Luther in the same little room in Wittenberg in which he had been.[23] That man Luther had denounced them, saying that he had given the Allstedt spirit one on the chopper;[24] he himself had not been there on that occasion.

---

16. An ex-member of the Franciscans in Mühlhausen; probably the 'preacher sent by Martin from Wittenberg' mentioned in a letter of 9 January 1525 from Sittich von Berlepsch to Duke George of Saxony. (F.)

17. *beschediget und geschulden.*

18. Hans Rotte the Younger became secretary of the Mühlhausen 'Eight' and of the Committee, as well as to Müntzer himself. (F.)

19. Cf. Letter 50 above.

20. *eyn spelunkge*; a cellar, usually a beer-cellar, drinking-den; hence wider meaning of house of depravity, ill-fame.

21. Votive offerings brought to this pilgrimage church.

22. He was present during part of the proceedings and obviously had a personal interest in them, cf. p. 439/6 below; the reference is to the 12 Articles of Upper Swabia.

23. The 'Zwickau prophets'; cf. p. 58/27 above; Luther had spoken with them in 1522.   24. *uber dye schnausse gehauen.*

435

15. Master Gangolf,[25] the chaplain to the hospital, took responsibility for one detachment, in which the men of Heringen and Greussen had served.

Confessed under Torture:[26]

1. Heinrich and Hans Gebhart, of the Hundegasse in Zwickau, were weavers and with their followers[27] had thrown in their lot with the alliance.

2. Master Heinrich Pfeiffer[28] had contended that one castle in each district[29] was enough; one should destroy the others.

3. Had pronounced judgement on Matern von Gehofen and the other servants of C(ount) Ernest on behalf of the congregation, and had agreed to it, and had done so because he was afraid.[30]

4. Had sought refuge and assistance in Mühlhausen because he had liked it there and because it was a fortified city. His chief supporters[31] there had been Hans Kule near All Saints and the two mentioned above,[32] the furrier and the distiller near St Blasius.

5. Admits that if he had taken the castle at Heldrungen he and all his followers had intended to cut off the head of Count Ernest, and that he had often talked of doing this.

6. He had launched the rising with the aim of making all Christians equal[33] and of expelling and doing to death the princes and gentry who refused to support the Gospel.

25. He had recently arrived in Heldrungen as a captive.

26. At least initially there seems no great difference in the type of questions posed; the fact that they were posed and answered under torture obviously was not felt to diminish the propagandistic value of his confessions.

27. *sambt irem anhange.*

28. The ex-monk Pfeiffer had been both the real reformer of Mühlhausen since 1523 and the leader with Müntzer of the social unrest which led to their joint expulsion on 27 September 1524; after his triumphal return on 13 December he was joined by Müntzer in February and both worked closely together in the ecclesiastical and social transformation of the city which led to its pivotal role in the Peasants' War; he was executed with Müntzer on 27 May 1525; on Pfeiffer cf. Letter 70 n. 1.

29. *pflege.*

30. Together with the priest, Stephen Hartenstein and George Buchner, Matern von Gehofen had been captured by the rebels and executed on 13 May as an emissary of Count Ernest; this incident, a revenge killing for the death of one of the 'brothers', had particularly provoked the wrath of Count Ernest; cf. Elliger, p. 744f.; the form of the confession, here as elsewhere, suggests the repeated application of the thumbscrew; in the printed edition of the *Confession* the reference to 'fear' reads, 'was afraid of Count Ernest and of the commune'; neither version makes much sense, unless it is a clumsy attempt at self-exculpation; possibly Müntzer meant a reference to the 'fear of God'.

31. *Seyne principal.*

32. p. 435/12f. above.

33. *das dye christenheyt solt alle gleych werden.*

7. The chief supporters of the covenant in Allstedt had been:
Balthasar Krump
Bartel Zimmermann
Peter Warmuth
Nickel Ruckert   of Allstedt
Andreas Krump
Bischoff of Wolferode

8. The articles which they held and sought to put into practice were:
All things are to be held in common[34] and distribution should be to each according to his need, as occasion arises. Any prince, count, or gentleman who refused to do this should first be given a warning,[35] but then one should cut off his head or hang him.

9. Others who had been in the covenant were:
Hans Rodeman
Peter Schutze   of Thalmansfeld
Peter Beher
Tile Fischer of Wimmelburg
Tilmann Banz of Sangerhausen
Peter Rodeman likewise

The register in which the members of the alliance[36] are listed, is in the hands of Balthasar Krump in Allstedt.

10. He had also formed an alliance in his youth[37] in Aschersleben and Halle when he had been a vicar[38] there. In it had been Peter Blinde of Aschersleben, Peter Engel, a verger at Halle, Hans Buttener and Kunz Sander at the Stone Gate of the same city. It was directed against Bishop Ernest of blessed memory.

11. If things had turned out as he had hoped and planned he had meant – and that had been common knowledge among all the members of his covenant – to appropriate all the land within a forty-six mile radius of Mühlhausen and the land in Hesse, and to deal with the princes and gentry as described above.[39] About this all of them were pretty well informed.

12. The people of Mühlhausen had lent him eight waggon-loads of

---

34. In Latin, *omnia sunt communia*.

35. *des erstlich erinnert*.

36. *verbundtnus*, used here as a synonym for *bund*, covenant.

37. *in der jugent*; *or*: 'among the youth'.

38. *collaborator*; he probably left the university in Leipzig in 1508/9, or 1512/13, for Aschersleben and then Halle; we have no real information about what was probably a youthful ploy in Halle rather than a genuine conspiracy against Ernest of Saxony, archbishop of Magdeburg; cf. Elliger, p. 30f.

39. Elliger, p. 796 suggests that Duke George may have wished to incriminate Mühlhausen with this particular confession; 1 Prussian mile = 4.6 miles (Scott).

fire-arms.[40] A small cannon had been lent to the Frankenhausen contingent by von Stolberg.[41]

Fragment with further statements of Müntzer.

1. In Zwickau the two parishes of St Katherine and of Our Lady had chosen him as their preacher. I was there for a year, too, and my testimony was very well received.

2. Master Heinrich Pfeiffer first took the field on behalf of the people of Salza.

3. Master Heinrich Pfeiffer started the first rebellion in Mühlhausen; has preached there for a year and a half.

4. Had discussed with the peasants of Klettgau and Hegau near Basel whether they wanted to join forces with him at Mühlhausen and this area. To which they said that if they were paid for it they would come.

40. *acht karn buchsen.*

41. Count Bodo von Stolberg, acting to save his son, Wolf, a captive in the rebel hands (F.); the so-called *halbe schlange* weighed about 13 cwt., firing 7 pound shots.

The 'Recantation' of Thomas Müntzer[1]
17 May 1525

The following points were made by Thomas Müntzer voluntarily, after due consideration, and based on his own knowledge of the facts, in the presence of our noble and well-born lord Philip, count of Solms, of Master Gebhard, count and lord of Mansfeld etc., of Master Ernst of Schönburg, lord of Glauchau and Waldenburg, of our gracious, steadfast and prudent lord, Apel von Ebeleben, knight, of Simon von Greussen, Hans von Berlepsch and Christopher Laue.[2] He requested them to remind him of them, in case they slipped from his own memory, so that he could recite them to every one before his end and affirm them with his own lips.

First, as far as one's obedience and obligations to the authorities were concerned, he had preached the very opposite and with such lack of restraint[3] that those subjects who heard him had listened to him with an equal lack of restraint. He had then embarked with them on this outrageous, wanton insurrection, rebellion, and revolt; he begged them for the sake of God not to be led astray by what he had done,[4] but to live in obedience, especially to the above authorities – being ordained and established by God – and to forgive him.

Secondly, in reference to his preaching of all manner of fanciful and erroneous ideas about the most venerable sacrament of the holy and divine Body of Christ[5] contrary to the universal order of the Christian church,[6] and in a manner calculated to create unrest and lead folk astray, he intends to submit peaceably and in all respects to what the same holy Christian church has always accepted and still accepts, and to die in every respect as one who is truly incorporated in it and is once again a reconciled member of it, begging them to testify to this

---

1. Apart from its last request there is nothing in the language or thought of this alleged recantation to support its authenticity, and much to the contrary. As Elliger, pp. 806ff., points out:
(1) Philip of Solms and Gebhard of Mansfeld, as sympathisers with the reforming cause, could not have endorsed its sentiments about the Eucharist and the unity of the Church.
(2) Its unconditional obeisance to the secular authorities cannot be reconciled with the tone or language of his letter of the same day to the people of Mühlhausen, cf. p. 000.
It is best understood therefore as a clumsy piece of propaganda by the winning side.
2. It is interesting that only persons of secondary rank and importance are mentioned as being present.
3. *gar zu mylde.*
4. *doran nit zu ergern.*
5. *fronleychnams Christi.*
6. *auch widder ordnunge gemeyner christlichen kirchen.*

before God and the world, to pray to God on his behalf, and to forgive him in a brotherly way.

Finally, he requests that his recent letter[7] should be sent to the people of Mühlhausen and that all his goods should be left to his wife and child.

Took place in Heldrungen, on the Wednesday after Cantate 1525.

7. Cf. Letter 94, esp. p. 160/26ff. above.

INFORMATION ABOUT MÜNTZER'S LIFE

(a) Old City of Brunswick

1. The Council of the Old City of Brunswick presents Thomas Müntzer to an altar benefice in St Michael's Church in Brunswick.[1] Brunswick, 6 May 1514.

To his honour, Master Henning Breyer, priest of the parish church of St Michael of the town of Brunswick in the diocese of Hildesheim, our most gracious master and friend, the patricians and magistrates of the same ancient city and town are desirous in all things to be devoted to your service.[2]

To the altar of the holy and glorious virgin Mary situated in your church, now vacant because of the death of Master Johann Opperman its latest holder, the right of patronage or presentation being known to pertain to us, we duly present to you by these documents his reverence Master Thomas Müntzer, priest[3] of the diocese of

---

1. When and why Müntzer first came to Brunswick is unknown; Elliger, p. 50, argues that he was first active in Brunswick in 1518; this document, the evidence of Müntzer's close relationship with Claus Winkeler, Hans Pelt's agent, of his tutoring of the sons of Brunswick citizens in Frose from 1515, and his relationship to Hans Pelt and the Rector of St. Martin's school in Brunswick present, however, overwhelming evidence of a much earlier stay; cf. Letters 1–4, above; this document was probably found in his 'Briefsack' or collection of papers, on his capture; this led to the conclusion that it had not been presented to Henning Breyer, the parish priest of St Michael's, and that the benefice had never been taken up (F., p. 553); Bubenheimer points out that while the document certainly had to be presented by its bearer (*exhibitorem*) to the parish priest, the role of the latter was largely formal; there would be no legal necessity for him to retain it after Müntzer's installation on 6 May 1514; Müntzer might well require it to secure the payment of his stipend from the City Council; hence the burden of proof lies with those who argue that he did *not* take up the benefice; in fact it seems likely that he held it for more than seven years, until his reforming concern about pluralities led him to dispense with it (cf. Letters 26, 28 above); nor does the evidence of Müntzer's residence in Frose (cf. Letters 1–3) conflict with this; the liturgical duties at St. Michael's were light and the stipend correspondingly small; in 1514 he will have begun by residing in Brunswick; there is confirmation of this by John Agricola; and may have shared a house with Ludolf Wittehovet (cf. Letter 2); but some time before July 1515 he left for Frose, either delegating his duties to a vicar or commuting between Brunswick and Frose; he then returned to Brunswick in 1517/18, and stayed with Hans Pelt (cf. Letter 4 and the remark by the Franciscan Bernard Dappen in 1519 about his recent expulsion from Brunswick); (cf. p. 447/16f. below); cf. Bubenheimer I, 41–4, 48–54; ibid., 'Thomas Müntzer ... in Braunschweig' NAK 65, 1–30; and S. Bräuer, 'T. Müntzers Beziehungen zur Braunschweiger Reformation', Th.Lit.Z. 109, 636–8.
2. Text as amended by Bubenheimer, in Latin.
3. By this time, then, he was ordained as priest.

Halberstadt, the bearer of these present letters, so that you may vouchsafe to instal and invest the same Master Thomas at the said altar, endowing him with its real and corporeal possession, and seeing to it yourselves, as far as is within your power, that in respect to all its dues, fruits and rights full satisfaction is given him in accordance with the praiseworthy custom of your above-mentioned church.

As witness thereof the privy seal of the town of Brunswick, as currently used, is appended to these letters patent of ours. In the year of our Lord fifteen hundred and fourteen on the sixth day of the month of May.

(b) *Shopping-list.*[1] *(Orlamünde, End of June 1519)*

The vineyard of Dr Carlstadt is being cultivated[2] and the rent has been paid. If the doctor wants to sell his vineyard for twelve old schock[3] I can arrange for a buyer; as the pastor in Uhlstadt writes, it can be paid off in three years. Has also had to pay a levy on the vineyard for the military campaign.[4] Also some money for the barrel in which the wine is kept.

Pigs:[5] 2 sows, 1 castrated pig,[6] 1 boar at [the house of] Augustine Smith by the water-wheel in the Judenstrasse[7] near Pisch.

The accounts to be paid by Peter and Paul's day or at the Easter fair at Leipzig.

Order me bright brazil-wood for dyeing. The Chapter. The Schoolmaster.[8] 1 measure of saffron for $2\frac{1}{2}$ gr(oschen.) For all this I have given you $12\frac{1}{2}$ (gr(oschen). 2 strong screws, with wide holes, to go through the large lock, at 10d. each.

Three lock screws at 8d. each.

Lettuce seed in Leipzig – basilisk seed, beetroot seed, marjoram seed, lavender seed, hyssop seed at 1d. – you will find all that in front of Peter's Gate.

Peter de Crescensiis in German.[9]

1. Given to Müntzer as he left for the Leipzig Disputation by Karlstadt's vicar in Orlamunde, Conrad Glitsch (F.); Dismer, p. 262f., argues that there is no evidence for Müntzer's presence in Leipzig during the Disputation.
2. *ist bestalt.*
3. A measure of sixty; equivalent to 20 groschen.
4. *herfart geld.*
5. Presumably for sale. (F.)
6. *1 hackisch.*
7. Jews' Street, in Naundörfchen; though since 1442 no Jews lived there. (F.)
8. *Capitulam* (not clearly legible); *Schulmeister.*
9. The leading authority on agriculture in the Middle Ages (d. 1370); in 1493 first translation into German. (F.)

Martin Luther's sermon. *On the Three Kinds of Righteousness.* And then his *Appeal*.[10]

Similarly the first Leipzig edition.[11]

The *Resolutions*[12] from his recent disputation. Eck's *Resolutions*[13] against Karlstadt. The tract of Karlstadt on true penitence.[14] He should send me the latter's 'Chariot'[15] and everything which is being published by these men at this time.

He should write and tell me what lectures Martin, Karlstadt, Melanchthon are giving.

He should greet Doctor Karlstadt, Martin, Otto,[16] Master Eisleben,[17] my lord Hermann,[18] and all my benefactors.

10. 1518 Kawerau Nr. 51, 53.

11. 1518 Kawerau Nr. 49, cf. WA 2, 3.

12. 1518 Kawerau Nr. 45; LW 31, pp. 79–252.

13. Ingolstadt, 14 March 1519.

14. Karlstadt had declared his intention of writing on this subject, but apparently failed to do so. (F.)

15. The 'chariot' refers to a lost wood-cut by Cranach, to which Karlstadt had added appropriate comments; a chariot carrying the true doctrine ascends to heaven, while another goes down to hell with the false scholastic doctrines. (F.)

16. Otto Beckmann (1476–1556), Professor in Wittenberg, a friend of Luther and Karlstadt but remained in the Old Church; from 1523 pastor in Warburg. (F.)

17. Agricola.

18. Tuleken or Tulichius; cf. Letter Nr. 8, n. 15.

(c) *List of Books (End of 1520)*[1]

(Lor)enzo Valla ... *On the Freedom of the Will*[2] 8 shillings.

(D)iogenes Laertius, *On the Mores and Lives of the Philoso(phers)*[3] 24.

Eras(mus) of Rotte(rdam), *Against the Barbarians*[4] 19.

1. This list was written on the inside of Müntzer's draft letter to his father (Nr. 14); it is not clear if it is a bookseller's list, though this is suggested by the fact that almost all the books date from 1519 and 1520; Müntzer may have secured a list of new publications from a bookseller known to him – at the Leipzig Fair – for example – or been given favourable terms as a bulk purchaser (F.); (we should not assume that he bought all the books mentioned here); I follow Bräuer's suggestion that later folding has obscured the fact that there are two separate lists, each in different hands, one listing humanist writings almost exclusively (51ᵛ, 54ʳ), and concluding with four books, listed in Müntzer's own hand, the other theological writings of Karlstadt, Alveld, and Luther (52ʳ⁻ᵛ); the latter are, in turn, subdivided into three 'books'; if this refers to the common practice of binding smaller books together (F.) Book III would have been very large indeed; more work needs to be done on many aspects of this list.

2. *do lit ar*; 1516, Vienna; 1518, Basel.

3. This is the only known reference to a Latin edition before 1524.

4. Strasbourg, Cologne, 1520; two editions in Basel, 1520.

Conrad Celtis, *Two Elegies*[5] 3.
Philip Melanchthon, *Address to Youth*[6] 3.
Erasmus of Rotterdam, *Certain Letters*[7] 6.
Phillipus Novenianus of Erfurt, *Elements of Hebrew*[8].
Lucian, *Fugitives from Bilibilis*[9] 3.
John Gertophius, *Retort to Edward Lee*[10] 3.
Erasmus of Rotterdam, *The Precepts of Cato*[11] 10.
Rudolph Agricola, *Works*[12] 16.
Erasmus of Rotterdam, *Two Apologies*[13] 7.
von Hutten, *About Medicine, On the French Sickness*[14] 11.
Aesop's Fables[15] 7.
Martin Dorp, *Discourse on the Letters of Paul*[16] 7.
Peter Mosellanus *Discourse on the knowledge of different languages*[17] 8.
Ulrich von Hutten, *Letter to Martin Luther*[18] ½ sheet.
D. M. L., *On the Power of Indulgences against Franciscus Seylerus*[19] 2.
Martin, *Appeal*[20] 1.
Oecolampadius, *Paraphrase of Solomon's Ecclesiastes*[21] ½.
Diodorus (S)iculus,[22] 22.
Lorenzo Valla, *On Pleasure etc.*[23] 28.
Erasmus of Rotterdam, *On the Instruction of Princes*[24] 50.
Johannes Reuchlin, *Letters of Celebrated Men*[25] 27.

5. Leipzig, 1520.
6. Wittenberg, 1518; Basel, Haguenau, 1519.
7. Most recent edition, Strassburg, 1519.
8. Leipzig, 1520.
9. Pirckheimer's translation appeared in Haguenau in 1520.
10. Retort to ... E.L. ... who was the first to dare to bespatter the most pure Erasmus with dirt. Basel, 1520.
11. Frequently printed, 1517, 1518, 1520, in Leipzig.
12. Basel, 1518.
13. Against Latomus, Paris, 1518; Cologne, 1520.
14. Mainz, Basel, 1519.
15. Very often printed, 1515, 1517, Leipzig.
16. Basel, 1520.
17. 1513, 1518, Leipzig; 1519, Basel.
18. 1520, Wittenberg; WA Br 2, Nr. 295.
19. Not by Luther, as the initials suggest, but by Karlstadt; Wittenberg, 1520.
20. 1519; cf. LW 31, 297ff.
21. Augsburg, 1520.
22. 1516, 1517, Vienna.
23. 1483, Louvain; 1519, Basel.
24. Very frequently printed, including 1518, 1520, Basel.
25. Haguenau, 1519; the famous satire on Reuchlin's Dominican opponents in Cologne.

Erasmus, *Paraclesis* or exhortation to the wholesome study of Christian philosophy etc.[26] 2.

In all, 538(?) sheets @ 2 sestertii, which makes 2 f(lorins) 3 g(roschen) 3 pence.[27]

Bishop Claudianus, *On the soul*,[28] costs 25 shillings.

Gregory Nazianzus.[29]

Florinus.[30]

Cassianus.[31]

Book I

In Defence of Divine Grace[32] 14.

An(dreas) Karlstadt, *Epitome*[33] 4.

Andreas Karlstadt, *On the Canonical Scriptures*[34] 13.

Andreas Karlstadt, *Apologetic Conclusions*[35] 5.

John Eck, *Defence against the polemics of Karlstadt*[36] 4.

Karlstadt, *Defence against Eck*[37] etc. 7.

Karlstadt, *Against Eck, who manifestly said*[38] 7.

Bodenstein, *Appeal*[39] 1.

On the power of Indulgences against Francis(cus) Syler[40] 2.

Confutation of Andreas Karlstadt against his defensive letter etc.[41] 7.

On the Papal Holiness[42] 7.

Bodenstein, *Appeal to the Council*[43] 1.

26. 1519, Leipzig; Eng. tr. by John Olin (ed.), *Christian Humanism and the Reformation*, pp. 92ff.

27. The figure 538 (F.) must be very dubious; it is very hard to decipher; it is not clear whether these calculations – working out the price by the number of sheets of paper – relate to the list of humanist books only; cf. n. 1 above.

28. Basel, 1520, edited by Mosellanus; Claudianus was a 5th-century presbyter and philosopher.

29. Perhaps one of Oecolampadius' Latin translations of the great fourth-century Church Father.

30. Not traced; could it refer to Irenaeus' letter to Florinus (end 2nd century)?

31. Perhaps John Cassian's *Institutes*, Lyons 1516; Cassian (c. 360–435) was one of the great interpreters to the Wester Church of Eastern monasticism.

32. By Carlstadt; Wittenberg, 1519.

33. Freys and Barge, Nr. 13.

34. Wittenberg, 1520.

35. Wittenberg, 1518.

36. Augsburg, 1518.

37. Wittenberg, 1518.

38. Wittenberg, 1520.

39. Wittenberg, 1520.

40. Identical with n. 19.

41. Wittenberg, 1520.

42. Wittenberg, 1520.

43. Identical with n. 39.

The Chariot in the heavens[44].

Book II
Alfeld, *On the Apostolic See.*[45] 10.
Jo. Lonicerus, *Against the Romanist*[46] 5.
Confutation of the inept and impious pamphlet supporting Martin Luther[47]
   3.
A most fruitful and edifying little book on the Roman See[48] 3.
M.L. *On the Roman Papacy*[49] 8.
Augus(tine) von Alfeld, *A pious collection*[50] 2.
The New Alfeld Bible[51] 2.
Alfeld, *Sermon on the sacrament of confession*[52] 3.
Alfeld, *Tractate on the communion in both kinds*[53] 7.
Alfeld, *Malagma*[54] 6.
Alfeld, *A Sermon against Martin*[55] 2.
Alfeld, *On the married estate*[56] 5.
The Louvain Condemnation of the books of Martin etc.[57] 4.
Against the doctrinal statement of certain Louvain masters[58] 6.
Martin Luther, *To the nobility*[59] 12.
Thomas Radinus[60] 8.

Book III
A German Theology[61] 9.
Sermon on the power of excommunication[62] 1.

44. Cf. p. 443, n. 15 above.
45. Alfeld was one of the early Catholic controversialists who took up the battle against Luther, who dubbed him the 'Leipzig ass'; Lemmers, Nr. 1.
46. 1520; Lonicerus (Lonitzer) was Luther's famulus.
47. Lemmens, Nr. 3.
48. Lemmens, App. I, Nr. 2.
49. Kawerau Nr. 104; Luther's response to Nr. 32; Wittenberg, 1520; LW 39, 51ff.
50. Lemmens, App. I, Nr. 4.
51. Lemmens, App. III, Nr. 2.
52. Lemmens, App. I Nr. 8.
53. Lemmens, App. I, Nr. 6.
54. Ibid., Nr. 3.
55. Ibid., Nr. 5.
56. Ibid., Nr. 7.
57. This condemnation of Luther by the Louvain and Cologne theologians was frequently printed in 1520 together with Nr. 45.
58. Cf. WA 6, 181–95.
59. Luther's famous *Appeal to the Nobility of the German Nation*, LW 44, 115–217.
60. His *Discourse* on Luther; Rome, August 1520, and reprinted by Melchior Lotter in October, Wittenberg.
61. Luther's edition of the full text appeared no less than nine times between 1518 and 1520; cf. LW 31, 75ff.
62. August 1518; Kawerau Nr. 56.

Sermon on three-fold righteousness[63] 1.

M.L. Amended sermon on two-fold righteousness[64].

Doctor Martin, *Appeal*[65] 1.

Ulrich von Hutten, *Letter*[66] 1.

Insane Bull of the Pious Pontiff[67] 1.

Martin Luther, *Against the Bulls of Antichrist*[68] 2.

A revelation and vision of Sigismund,[69] 1.

M.L. Sermon on the preparation for death[70] 2.

M.L. Fourteen Words of Consolation[71] 4.

On the Babylonian Captivity[72] 11.

M. On Freedom[73] 3.

Mar. On Good Works[74] 14.

M.L. On Good Works[75] 14.

An Open Letter[76] 2.

63. 1518.

64. 1519; cf. LW 31, 297ff.

65. 1518 or 1520; Kawerau Nr. 51 or 121.

66. Cf. n. 18.

67. Hutten's edition of the Bull threatening Luther with excommunication; Wittenberg, 1520.

68. Kawerau Nr. 117.

69. Basel, 1520.

70. 1519; LW 42, p. 97ff.

71. 1520 Kawerau Nr. 98.

72. 1520; LW 36, p. 3ff.

73. *The Freedom of a Christian,* 1520; LW 31, p. 327ff.

74. The Latin translation did not appear until 1521.

75. 1520.

76. 1520.

(d) Sermons of Müntzer in Jüterbog 1519

... But at that time[1] another master of that same sect arrived called Thomas, at whose instigation I do not know. He had been expelled from the town of Brunswick not long before.[2] (Günther) had him

1. After Lent 1519 the preacher at St Nicholas, Franz Günther (cf. Letter 7 n. 1), was summoned by the Guardian, or superior, of the Franciscans to explain his conduct in criticising Catholic practices such as fasting. The Franciscan Bernard Dappen, the reporter on these sermons of Müntzer, had been instrumental in raising the issue; more complaints soon followed however and Günther judged it best to beat a tactical retreat, no doubt arranging with the Council for his substitute, at least temporarily, to be Thomas Müntzer, fresh from his stay in Wittenberg; cf. Elliger, p. 49ff; Manfred Bensing, Winfried Trillitzsch, 'Bernhard Dappens "Articuli contra Lutheranos"', *Jahrbuch für Regionalgeschichte,* 2 (1967), 113–47; cf. S. Bräuer, 'Müntzerforschung von 1965–1975,' LJ 45 (1978), 107ff.

2. Elliger, p. 51, suggests early October 1518.

preach in his stead, by what authority I do not know, but perhaps he anticipated that this other man, being unrestrained by reason, would undertake what he himself did not dare to do, because he feared our gracious lord, the bishop of Brandenburg.[3]

Therefore, on the holy day of Easter,[4] preaching in the church of our glorious Lady against the Father Superior who had preached the Passion there, he launched a fierce polemic in the following words:

The Passion of Christ has been preached here by someone who said that the Bible was neither in Greek nor in Hebrew. Pray to God, then, for a man who can err so wretchedly, that in his extreme mercy God may deign to illumine him, lest he perish in his error. When this was reported to the Father Superior, he said that he had never said that the Bible was not in Greek or in Hebrew but that the inscription on the holy cross had been written in the Hebrew, Greek and Latin languages, (as) the simple Gospel text teaches, and that he then went on to mention the division of the vestments of Christ – that the soldiers divided the vestments of Christ into four parts, one part to each soldier, and that lots were being taken for the seamless tunic. He interpreted this in the way of St. Augustine, namely that by the four parts of the vestments is signified the Christian faith spread into the four parts of the world and that the seamless tunic represented the unity of this Christian faith and after that he mentioned that this unity now appears to be broken in many respects, for I scarcely know whether we are Christians or Bohemians or Greeks or pagans, since some say the Bohemians are better Christians than we are and others say one should not fast, others that one should not confess, etc.[5]

So when I[6] preached to the people on the second day of Easter I repeated this statement of Master Thomas from the pulpit, for my astonishment at the presumptuous way in which he had spoken against the Father Superior knew no bounds. I said to all those who were listening: I do not know, dearly beloved, what I should say, for in these modern times of ours one preaches this, another that, Master Prattle[7] this, and I am quite sure that, if a Runkarius[8] or some master of the Bohemians' heresy were to come to this place preaching his errors and saying that his preaching was the Gospel of Christ,

---

3. A second complaint against Günther had been sent to the bishop of Brandenburg, claiming that he had spoken libellously against the Abbess of St. Mary's nunnery; Elliger, p. 56.

4. 24 April.

5. Clearly refers to Günther, but the testimony to the influence of Bohemia is also interesting; cf. Hans Pelt's comments in Letter 28, p. 40/28f.

6. Dappen.

7. *Quatles*; presumably a nonsense name, used in derision.

8. Heretic, Waldensian. (F.)

certainly some would be very happy to listen to it with open ears, like the Athenians bending their ears to novelties.[9] But while I was proclaiming this to the people, Master Thomas together with Master Franz,[10] stood outside the wall of the cemetery listening to what I was saying. For his part, Master Thomas used those words as a pretext to inveigh against me fiercely and libellously in the sermon which he gave on the evening of the same day after the second Vespers,[11] and when this was reported to me I steeled myself to attend his preaching, so that I might observe for myself if this were the case. When I did this on the third day of Easter[12] after Vespers when he was preaching and neglecting the Gospel – although at the sermon which the Father Superior held after lunch in obedience to the holy Roman church and on the writings of the approved doctors, namely St Bonaventura and St Thomas, he said he was going to expound it[13] – Master Thomas rushed eventually into this pronouncement: First, that the Pope ought to celebrate a Council every five years but four hundred years had elapsed with only three Councils having been celebrated.[14] Likewise he asserted secondly that a Council should be held even against the will of the Pope and that the Pope was the head of the Church as long as the other bishops tolerated him, and he said many things contrary to the reverence due to the Pope. Likewise he said that the canonisation of the saints was once a matter for the General Councils, but St Bonaventura and St Thomas had been canonised by one man, namely the Pope, thus insinuating that their canonisation had not been a legitimate one. Likewise he said that no one can prove that either of the aforesaid doctors had converted a single heretic,[15] and that if anyone could prove this he would gladly forfeit his neck.[16] Likewise that the doctrine of the aforesaid doctors and of other scholastics is declared acceptable by the Church; and prostitutes and pimps[17] are sanctioned in the towns.[18] Likewise that the aforesaid doctors rely on natural reason in their arguments and that all such

9. Acts 17[20f.]

10. Franz Günther.

11. Major feasts of the Church were celebrated by two vespers, on successive days.

12. 26 April.

13. Presumably either interrupting the sermon, or adding an unsolicited advertisement about his own forthcoming sermon!

14. With Luther's appeal to a Council on 29 November, 1518, the Conciliar issue was, of course, livelier than ever; it is linked here with an attack on scholasticism.

15. An early testimony to Müntzer's missionary concerns.

16. *vellet privari capite suo.*

17. *lenonosque*, for *lenonesque*.

18. The scholastic doctrine is as ineffective for moral regeneration as for missionary expansion; licensed brothels were common in German cities, as elsewhere in Europe, by the late Middle Ages.

arguments are of the devil. Likewise that all bishops are required to visit those in their charge each year and to examine their faith as a rector examines his young pupils in the schools, and that if this were done there would not be the (black) bats[19] of citations, admonitions and excommuniations which he called diabolical letters. Likewise that at one time holy fathers were installed as bishops but in modern times tyrants are installed, who feed themselves and do nothing of any value.[20] Likewise that priests once brought allegations against their bishops in the councils and those found guilty were deposed and removed to the monasteries of the holy father Benedict and other priests were installed in their stead, and that they did not act the tyrant by imprisoning priests[21] as some other tyrants are wont to do. Likewise he said that they are flatterers and seducers of an erring people, calling good evil and evil good;[22] they know neither Greek nor Hebrew unless it be scrounging and malingering.[23] Likewise he said, not once but repeatedly, that for more than four hundred years the holy Gospel had lain under a bed,[24] and that already very many had been forced to risk their necks[25] for demanding its recall. As to the insults publicly directed in this sermon at me in this gathering of the whole populace I will say nothing, because I am a brother of the Order of Minors, whose calling it is to love their enemies, according to the Gospel and their Rule.

19. Isaiah 2[20].

20. The historical and humanist thrust of the argument is unmistakable; the Church's teaching and pastoral care should return to the standards of the Early Church; cf. Müntzer's purchases of historical and patristic material around this time (Letter 8).

21. *sacerdotes incarcerandum*.

22. Isaiah 5[20].

23. *questen und stincken*; an interesting parallel is the denunciation of John Eck as *mit dem questen wydel verwandelt* in *Eyn kortze anred zu allen missgunstigen Dr. Luthers und der Christlichen Freyheit*, J. A. 1522/Matthis Maler, Erfurt; there could be a reference here to sprinkling holy water with the *quest*, or bunch of leaves.

24. *sub scamno*, lit. 'bench'; cf. Mark 4[21].

25. *colla extendere*, i.e. be martyred; cf. n. 16 above.

(e)   Rumherius

Langius Rumherius to N. Gord ... mo[1] (Elsterberg, 31 October 1520.
To the excellent, most excellent Master N[icholas] Gord ... mo,

1. In Müntzer's 'letter-sack'; Nr. 55 of the Lichtdrucke; it is apparently in the hand of Moritz Reynhart (cf. Letters 17, 22) and may come from Elsterberg (Bräuer/Kobuch); it is a riddle from beginning to end; Franz, p. 16 n. 4, suggests that it is from a brother Langius Rumthirius, i.e. a monk from Romschütz, living in Altenburg, to his superior; Bubenheimer has hinted that it may be a pasquill, along

my greatly loved friend in Christ, a devoted and vigilant[2] man, in these favourable[3] times much exercised in preaching.[4]

Many greetings! Reverend Father, many devoted greetings and my sincere love in the Lord, with my humble subjection and service under the yoke[5] of my prayers. I know, most reverend Father, that your devoted paternity has spent no little time on good letters.[6] Nor has it escaped me that he expended no little time on sacrosanct theosophy,[7] (which teaches a Christ without a Cross). Nor your continuous toil, your vigils, burning the midnight oil.[8] They have consumed your energy;[9] for your sagacity and your industry has attained the point where there is nothing at all in theology which is hidden from you; for you have examined the most obscure and indeed intimate things[10] with extraordinary industry (not hiding your light under a bushel). So it is only right that I should flee to your amplitude in the matter before me, in a strange quest,[11] driven rather by my urgent need; I flee as to an asylum. If you leave me without your protection I really am done for,[12] as is the whole family of our monastery.[13] So do not withhold your hand, but rather take up the

---

the lines of the Dunkelmännerbriefe, *Amtsblatt d. Ev.-Luth. Kirche in Thüringen* 40 (1987), viii, 66.

2. *speculative.*

3. *secundis.*

4. *multum trito contionatissimo*; an odd phrase.

5. *iugi servitute.*

6. The fullsome language suggests a humanist context.

7. *sacrosancta theosophia*; the natural meaning seems to be that the addressee was himself attracted to 'theosophy'; the bracketed phrase which follows is the strongest evidence for the letter being a persiflage; Egranus, of course, would be an ideal candidate! cf. his 'Propositions', esp. 2, 5, 21, pp. 380ff. above.

8. An almost Faustian picture!

9. *Vestram operam luserunt*; meaning unclear.

10. *penetralia et quidem intima*; together within the reference to nothing being hidden (*reconditum*) to Müntzer, there are quite close verbal similarities to Engelhard Mohr's letter to Müntzer of 1523, which speaks of the latter revealing *varia humanumque penetralium abscondita* (Letter 39 p. 55/1 above); cf. also Müntzer's claims for his unique industry and insights at the beginning of the Prague Manifesto, where he does not 'hide his light under a bushel' either, p. 357 above; could the letter he addressed to Müntzer? cf. Matthew 5[15] (Vg.).

11. *explorat[i]o[n]e*, or *expolat[i]o[n]e* (?); the latter, which could perhaps = *spolium*, robbery, seems improbable.

12. Again these are close verbal similarities to Johann Caphan's letter to Müntzer (Nr. 16, p. 24 above) where he also talks of *Ream meam* (here: *in re mea*) of *actum est mecum* (here: *de me actum est*); Caphan also uses the phrase *te latere nolo* (here: *Nec latet me*); but all these, of course, are common enough phrases.

13. *nostra conventus familia.*

sword of the word of God,[14] so that we will be safe under the shadow of your wings.[15] For in it[16] we are perishing, expecting shipwreck;[17] among us, in Altenburg[18] the preaching continues in its accustomed way: 'Let us work while we have time; light came into the world; I am a flower of the field',[19] and it is taught that we should be bound by this to do good works so that we may taste the joys of eternity; but unfortunately the preacher(?) heard these things[20]; it was barked out[21] against us that this kind [of person] understands these words of Paul not to be about good works such as fasts, alms, prayers and so on,[22] and that these words 'I am the light of the world, the flower of the field' cannot refer at all to good works; to put it briefly,[23] we are regarded as heretics. We are represented as ignorant of the Scriptures, as hypocrites, possessing nothing but having everything.[24] So I pour out my complaint about these matters to your paternity, longing for a remedy and for your protection, lest we be sent into exile.[25] Farewell in (our) most gentle Christ;[26] do write to us. For we are at the canonisation of Wolfgang, 1520.[27]

> Brother Langius Rumherius
> Your beloved in Christ.

14. Ephesians 6[17] (Vg.);the request seems to be for preaching to support his case; note the emphasis on preaching in the opening greeting, and *passim*.

15. Psalm 16[8] (Vg.).

16. *in quo*, referring back to the 'sword of the word of God'.

17. Moritz Reynhart uses the same term *naufragium*, (shipwreck) in Letter 17, p. 25/9 above; the greeting is in the same high-flown style, and quite similar language.

18. *Aldeburgia*; for evidence of criticism of the Franciscans in Altenburg at an early date cf. *Duae Epistole*: Henricii Stromeri Auerbachii ... Leipzig, 1520 (Bubenheimer).

19. Galatians 6[10] (Vg.) John 1[9] (Vg.) Isaiah 40[6] (Vg.).

20. *sed infeliciter audivit hec concio*; translation uncertain; lit. 'the sermon heard these things'.

21. *latratum est*.

22. *hec Pauli verba non de bonis operibus que ieiunia ... et cetera idem genus intelligit*; translation uncertain.

23. *ut paucis multa obsolavari(?)*.

24. Who is criticising him? It sounds like the criticism of monasticism by reforming groups.

25. What is meant by exile? How, if this is a genuine letter, is the addressee to exert his influence?

26. *dulcissimo*; a 'sweet' as opposed to a 'bitter' Christ?

27. i.e. 31 October.

(f) Zwickau Receipts

(a) 9 October 1520

I, Thomas Müntzer, received from the honourable[1] council of the town of Zwickau as a stipend for the preaching of the word of God fourteen and a half florins, in the year of our Lord, 1520, on the day of St Denys.

(b) 16 April 1521

I received from the Zwickau Council twenty-five florins (on the Tuesday)[2] after the Lord's day called *Misericordia domini*, which I witness with my own hand.

Thomas Müntzer, who uses truth for his battle in this world.[3]

1. *magnifico*; the second receipt is significantly less deferential!
2. Franz suggests the insertion of these words; Müntzer left Zwickau on a Tuesday.
3. *qui veritate militat in mundo.*

(g) His Mother to Ambrosius Emmen.[1] Late autumn 1520?

This letter is for Ambrosius Emmen.

My dear son!

I am still well. You should know that. I have a daughter now; you should know that too. But it was not kind to me or your father to stay away, when I asked you to come home.

But if you are pursuing some studies I am not going to regret giving you what I did, and I am quite content for you to stay where you are. Your father, though, is very angry that you have gone to the Greek(?) school.[2] He has forbidden me to send you as much as a cent.

However, I have managed to get together twelve groschen and nine pence behind your father's back; that was all I could get together in secret.[3] But if you don't come home over the winter, then go to the Leipzig Fair, to Thomas Emmen, who will tell you what is happening and give you whatever I send you. For if it is the case,[4] that a student

1. Found in Müntzer's papers; Lichtdruck 56; the warm relation of Müntzer and his famulus is confirmed by Letter 68 above; there may be a reference to Emmen on p. 54/21f. above; if the reference is to the 'Greek' school, presumable the Council school in Zwickau is meant (F.); Emmen will have met Müntzer in Zwickau.
2. *in di grege schoel.*
3. *dan ych en nyt me tzo wegebrengen heymlych.*
4. *dan weritz sch.*

can't come home, then I won't complain too much; for you, too, know what your father is like, and how he treats me. For I have to steal it secretly behind his back.

F[riendly] g[reetings].[5]

Ambrosius Emmen

5. F.g.; probably *f*[*runtliken*] *g*[*escreven*] (Bubenheimer); unclear what is meant; on the back, in Ambrosius Emmen's hand; (in Latin) 'Wherefore thunder and lightening on 6 February?' with a hand pointing to the right.

(h) *1522 Colloquy of Master Wolfgang Stein, of Zwickau and of Thomas*[1]

The knowledge[2] of God is what is required.
What might this knowledge of God be?
It can only be gained through faith and experience of faith.
What is faith?
It can only be taught by someone who has experience of faith.
What is experience of faith or how can it be acquired?
From the knowledge of God.[3]
It can only be taught by someone who has the spirit and the knowledge of God.
How can the knowledge and the spirit of God be gained?
It can only be taught by hazards and toil.[4]
You[5] have to let things become really bitter for you, for things really became bitter for me.
There is no faith unless Christ and the experience of faith are there, the true works of faith.[6]
And I believe it is to be gained from Scripture and the Gospel and Christ.[7]

1. The date of the colloquy between the Court Preacher, Stein, a predecessor of Müntzer in Zwickau, and Müntzer is probably December, 1522, following the colloquy of Stein, Jacob Strauss and the Franciscans in Weimar (F.); cf. Elliger p. 237f. and Müntzer's *Confession*, p. 434/26ff. and n. 14; Spalatin recorded the discussion, mainly in Latin.
2. *scientia*.
3. The argument, such as it is, is relentlessly circular.
4. *periculis et laboribus*.
5. This sentence in German; is Müntzer addressing Stein or is it, more generally, the call of Christ to all his disciples? Cf. Letter 18, p. 26, n. 147 above.
6. *Fidem non esse nisi Christum et experientiam fidei vera opera fidei*.
7. *ex scriptura et Evangelio et Christo*; perhaps a retort by Stein?

454

Ha,[8] my dear fellow, I would shit a mighty work[9] into your Scripture, Gospel and Christ, if you lacked the knowledge and the spirit of God.

He[10] thinks and speaks ill of the Wittenbergers, describing Doctor Luther Doctor Karlstadt, Phil. Mel(anchthon) and even Doctor Lang as fatuous.

8. This sentence reverts to German.

9. *ich schiss dir eyn werk*; cf. p. 367/27 above; faith without the 'works' of 'experience', of 'Christ' (i.e. suffering) is empty; presumably a retort by Müntzer to an accusation that he was confounding faith with works.

10. Müntzer.

(i)   The Mühlhausen Articles[1] (mid-September 1524)

[In the name of] Jesus. Set of conditions.[2] To the praise and glory of God[3] the Mühlhausen communities of St Nicholas, St George, St Margaret, with the linen-workers of St Jacob,[4] joined by many from other trades as well, have discussed how the city should be governed. Their judgement has been determined from the word of God. However, if in any way their decisions should be contrary to the word of God, let them be amended and altered.[5]

(1)   That a completely new Council be appointed. Why? To ensure that actions are taken in the fear of God;[6] that old hatreds do not linger on; that arbitrariness ceases; since the evildoer and the dispenser of justice deserve equal punishment;

1. These articles, which constitute a revolutionary programme, have to be read in conjunction with Letter 70, pp. 132ff. above; they were despatched to the villages around Mühlhausen in an abortive attempt to win them for the cause; Elliger, p. 581f. argues that 'For reasons of style and content, it is likely that Pfeiffer had the primary role in producing this document'; Duke George's official in Salza, Sittich von Berlepsch, made a copy of it 'from Heinrich Pfeiffer's own manuscript', ibid., p. 581, n. 58; yet Müntzer's language and ideas also surface unmistakably; a degree of participation by him, both in the preparation of the articles and even the choice of Bible passages seems certain; on the other hand, there are terms which are not found in Müntzer's writings elsewhere, and the final draft may come from Pfeiffer; translated from A. Laube, H. W. Seiffert, *et al.* (edd.), *Flugschriften der Bauernkriegszeit* (2nd ed., Cologne/Vienna, 1978), pp. 80–82; there are frequent minor variations in the Weimar MS, SA Weimar Reg. N. 837, B1.8ʳ–10ᵛ (W).

2. *Das bedingen.* Not found in Müntzer's writings elsewhere.

3. lit. 'to the praise of God'.

4. The first three are suburbs of Mühlhausen; St Jacob is in the inner city; W. omits Mühlhausen.

5. Cf. the last words of Müntzer's *Order and Explanation*, p. 179 above; and Letter 13, p. 20/4f. above.

6. Not the fear of man, cf. Letter 70, p. 133/26 above.

Romans 1, Luke 19 on the self-willed servant;[7] lest there be a half-baked mixture[8] of those outside and those inside; from which the community is bound to suffer; for it is a hard thing to have judges who are themselves guilty.[9]

(2) That righteousness and judgement be exercised in accordance with the Bible or command of the holy word of God.[10] Why? To ensure that the poor are treated in the same way as the rich, as in Zechariah 17, Leviticus 19 and 26, John 7, Matthew 5, Luke 18.[11]

(3) That no fixed term of office be given for the Council, neither one year nor two. Why not? To prevent them doing whatever they fancy; not puffing themselves up and lording it over others, but exercising true judgement. Judas in his canonical writing, and 2 Peter 2 on the seed of godless people; Deuteronomy 16 on godless rulers.[12]

(4) That the Council be instructed, on pain of death, namely by execution, to do justice and forsake injustice. Why? So that justice may be upheld and injustice be duly punished. Isaiah 5, Luke 19, on those who resist the rule of God; Numbers 14, Deuteronomy 4, 20 on unjust judges; and in Numbers 25[16] God commanded the unjust rulers to be executed when they refused to obey God's commandment to punish evildoers.[13]

(5) No one should be compelled to govern, and if someone is unwilling another should be appointed. Why? Lest any one have any excuse. Luke 19 on the lazy servants and 1 Peter 5, Exodus 23[14] on not joining the godless hordes[15] in their injustice; Matthew 7 on the good building; Deuteronomy 13, not even father and mother should be obeyed contrary to God's will, as in Luke 14.[16]

(6) That they be provided with sufficient for their sustenance.

---

7. Romans 1[32]; Luke 19[22, 27].

8. *ein kuche*, a hopeless confusion of the elect and the godless, all 'baked together'.

9. A frequent theme of Müntzer.

10. Cf. the text of the linen-workers' submission: *aus enphel gottes und noch der heilgen biblien der heilgen geschrift*, AGBM II, 49, quoted in Elliger, p. 582.

11. A frequent theme of Müntzer, e.g. in Letter 25, p. 34/16f.; Zechariah 7[9f.] (W. = ch. 7); Leviticus 19[15] and 26[2f.]; John 7[24]; Matthew 5[3-6(?)], 19(?) (W. = ch. 7, cf. vs. 1ff.); Luke 18[22ff.]

12. Judas[4, 8, 15] (W. – 'Judas in his letter'); 2 Peter 2[1f., 18]; Deuteronomy 16[19].

13. Isaiah 5[1-7 et passim]; Luke 19[27]; Numbers 14[3, 9, 26ff., 37]; Deuteronomy 4[24-6], 20[16-18]; Numbers 25[4f.(?)]; cf. also Romans 2[1-3]; cf. Müntzer's *Sermon to the Princes* p. 250/13ff.

14. Luke 19[20-27]; 1 Peter 5[2]; Exodus 23[2].

15. Letter 70, p. 133/29 above, speaks of the 'turncoat rabble of the godless'.

16. Matthew 7[24-7]; Deuteronomy 13[6-10] (father and mother not actually mentioned!); Luke 14[26].

Why? To remove any occasion for greed, and to prevent the flaying and fleecing[17] [of the poor]; as Exodus says, the greedy, arrogant and foolish liars, filled with hate, are unfit to govern[18] as Acts 20 says about government, and Matthew 10 about the worker being worthy of his hire, and 1 Corinthians 9 on due provision; and Luke 3, Be content with your pay.[19]

(7) To seal [their decisions] with the new seal or the privy seal and to use it for the honour of God and the welfare of the city. Why? So that all deceit and falsehood can be prevented and averted, as Luke 16 says: The children of this world are wiser than the children of light in their generations.[20] Jeremiah 2; the people is shrewd in the pursuit of wickedness;[21] while the doing of good is beyond it. Genesis 6, the flesh[22] is always inclined to evil. Romans 6.[23]

(8) If they refuse to look to the common good and to be instructed,[24] we will put together [a record of] all their wrongdoing on paper, how they acted contrary to the common good some 20 years ago, and have it published,[25] so that it can be seen what sort of people they are. Why? So that every one can see and hear how they treated us. Then everyone will say that they have been given far too much indulgence, and that people have put up with them far too long,[26] as Psalm 82 says: You should cover their face with shame; then, O God, they will seek your name.[27] Deuteronomy 6, Ruth 7 and Matthew 21,[28] on the servants who were reluctant to give their master his fruit; the master had the servants die a miserable death and entrusted his vineyard to other workers.

(9) Unless all this is settled according to the word of God we, the above-mentioned, are not prepared to come to any agreement with them. Why not? In order that God's righteousness and equity should come first, and all fraudulent power and self-

17. Another phrase much used by Müntzer.
18. Exodus 18²¹.
19. Matthew 10¹⁰; 1 Corinthians 9⁴⁻⁷; Luke 3¹⁴.
20. Luke 16⁸.
21. Jeremiah 2⁸, ¹³, ²²⁻⁵.
22. Genesis 6⁵; lit. the flesh of people.
23. Romans 6¹⁶.
24. *sich weissen lassen*; cf. *weysslich, eyn weisse volk, der weyssheit gotlichen wortes* in Letter 70, F. pp. 447/23, 448/16, 26, all emphasising the need for instruction, wisdom.
25. Much of Müntzer's Letter 70 is devoted to the use of printing as a weapon against the Council, p. 133.
26. Cf. Letter 70 '... have shown far too much patience', p. 133/21 above.
27. Psalm 83¹⁶ᶠ.
28. Deuteronomy 6²⁽⁷⁾; Ruth 4¹⁴; Matthew 21⁴¹.

seeking be relegated. We are not prepared to come to terms with the councillors or with the Eight[29] or with the guilds or with the community unless they propose something which is more in the common interest and more in accordance with God's truth and righteousness than we have. 1 Thessalonians 5:[30] Test everything and hold to what is best.

(10)   If our opponents hinder the new council being confirmed in office by their procrastination we will see that they pay dearly for it.[31] Why? Because they have refused to obey our Council, which we have given them in accordance with the word of God, so it is only fair that they should pay the piper, Exodus 21, 22, 23, Proverbs 1.[32]

(11)   In this whole matter we want action taken without vacillation, without any delay, and in accordance with the word of God. Why? If the execution of God's commands is to be thwarted, then we want you[33] to tell us what our dear Lord and his only son Jesus Christ, together with the Holy Spirit, has done to you, to make you unwilling to have him overrule your wretched sack of worms? In what way has he lied to you, or betrayed you? For he is righteous?[34] Psalm 10 and 14, Deuteronomy 10.[35]

Decision. It is our considered and unanimous decision that all our actions and dealings should be measured against the commandment and righteousness of God, to see if they are contrary to [the will of] the people or of God. Should they be agreeable to the people but contrary to [the will of] God, or agreeable to God, but contrary to [the will of] the people then we intend to choose one of the two;[36] we would much prefer to have God as our friend and the people our enemy than to have God as our enemy and the people as our friends; for it is a grievous thing to fall into the hands of God. Genesis 7, Exodus 15, Romans 3 and 9, Matthew 14 on the Last Judgement and

29. *mit achtmann*; the representatives of the Mühlhausen city districts, leaders of the artisan opposition to the patrician Council.

30. 1 Thessalonians 5[21].

31. *unsern schaden … erholen*, i.e. recover our losses, exact retribution.

32. *den schaden abtetten*, i.e. do away with the loss, settle their account; Exodus 21–3, especially 23[20, 27]; Proverbs 1[24–32].

33. *Euch*; the peasants, in this case the inhabitants of Horsmar, near Mühlhausen, are being addressed and criticised for their passivity and deference to the authorities ('sack of worms'); they were not responsive to this adjuration.

34. Cf. Jeremiah 2[5].

35. Psalm 11[5–7]; 15[1–5]; Deuteronomy 10[12, 17].

36. *under zweien eines erkiessen*; another recurrent theme in Müntzer's writings; cf. Letter 54, p. 86/14 above.

Luke, chapter 21, Matthew 10: You should fear him who has the power to cast body and soul into the fires of hell etc.[37]

[In the name of] Jesus. We write this to you, Christian brothers, so that you know the course you have to follow.[38]

37. Genesis 7[1-24] (Noah's ark); Exodus 15[11]; Romans 3[5f., 19]; Matthew 14 = 16[27] (W. – Mt. 24 – cf. vs. 37ff., 45ff.); Luke 21[22ff., 34f.]; Matthew 10[28].

38. W. adds: the advice of Müntzer, alias the Allstedter, to the village of Horsmar.

(j) Müntzer's wife Ottilie von Gersen to Duke George of Saxony[1]
19 August 1525

Eminent, high-born prince, gracious Lord, I am at all times Your Princely Grace's most willing servant. Poor, wretched and deserted as I am, I humbly ask Your Princely Grace to hear my complaint. When I was before Your Princely Grace last – at the Swan Inn in Mühlhausen, and begged in my misery for my belongings[2] through the mediation of the noble Ernest von Schönburg, the comforting assurance of Your Princely Grace that they would be returned was reported to me by the noble Ernest von Schönburg.

But this did not in fact happen. So in my misery I left for Nordhausen and spent some four weeks there. And then in my extremity of need I came again to Mühlhausen and petitioned the honourable Council for [the return of] my belongings through the honourable Erasmus von Warn, then a captain of the troops sent

1. The letter is in the hand of the clerk of Dr. Johann von Otthera, Johannes Helmolt (Bräuer/Kobuch); cf. Letter 68 n. 7; transcribed by Bräuer/Kobuch from the State Archives, Dresden, Geh. Rat Loc. 9135, Aufruhr zu Mühlhausen, Bd. 1, Bl.103[r-v]; on Ottilie von Gersen or Görschen cf. Elliger, pp. 374–6; it is possible that she was one of the 16 nuns from the Widerstedt convent of whom 11 found refuge in the castle of Allstedt; according to John Agricola she bore Müntzer a son on Easter Day 1524, the father demonstrating his spirituality by showing no pleasure at the news! As a nun married to a cleric, in defiance of the Imperial Edict of 1523, she was – quite apart from Müntzer's role in the Peasants' War – bound to be particularly obnoxious to the strongly Catholic Duke George; he will have heard of her own active disruption of the Vespers at Mülverstedt in January 1525, with a group of other women, distracting the prior and monks by their 'unlustige handlunge', unseemly conduct; cf. Gess II, 8.

2. gerette; in his very last letter Müntzer had begged the Mühlhausen Council not to make his wife destitute, p. 160/27 above; cf. also the same request in his 'Recantation', p. 440 above; however, on his death his widow was left to the mercy of the victors; it appears there was little; her household goods were taken; we read nothing in the letter about her infant son, who may perhaps have died in the chaos after Frankenhausen; she was pregnant, bereaved, impoverished; at the beginning of September 1525 Duke George instructed the Mühlhausen Council, presumably as his response to her letter, to '. . . see to it that she doesn't leave, and to inform us if she gives birth'; we hear no more of her after that.

against Mühlhausen by Your Princely Grace, and a relative of mine. The Council responded positively. I should come to them and my belongings would be returned. So under great hardships I again came to Mühlhausen. But, whatever the reason may have been, nothing came of it; so I left to stay for a while with good friends in Erfurt, but then came again to Mühlhausen again because of the widespread distress so that I could secure the belongings promised me by the honourable Council. But it bore no fruit. And through all this I have devoured all my substance. Hence it is my humble request that Your Princely Grace will have regard to my terrible misery and poverty and for the mercy of God graciously write to the Mühlhausen people, so that I might secure my belongings again – so that I can move to my friends[3] from whom I expect comfort and help in my distress. I will be for all time in Your Princely Grace's debt for this and Your obedient servant. I have heard, too, that it is Your Princely Grace's good opinion that I should return to the convent, as I myself have requested,[4] but according to Your Princely Grace's favour and wishes; for Your Princely Grace can adjudge the matter more graciously than my feeble capacity is able to express. I will always be indebted to Your Princely Grace and be Your Princely Grace's obedient servant etc. Saturday after the Assumption of Mary, 1525.

Ottilie von Gersen

3. *fruntschafft.*
4. *do ich dan vor gebetten wyl habe.*

SELECT BIBLIOGRAPHY

The aim of this bibliography is to itemise books and articles which were of immediate value in preparing this edition; for a comprehensive Müntzer bibliography reference should be made to Hans J. Hillerbrand, *Thomas Müntzer: a bibliography*. (*Sixteenth Century Bibliography*, IV), St. Louis, 1975 (defective); Max Steinmetz, 'Thomas Müntzer in der Forschung der Gegenwart', *Zeitschrift für Geschichtswissenschaft* 23 (1975), 666–85; Siegfried Bräuer, 'Müntzerforschung von 1965 bis 1975', *Luther-Jahrbuch* 44 (1977), 127–141; 45 (1978), 102–39; also invaluable are the annual Literature Reviews of the *Archive for Reformation History*; cf. also the forthcoming review article by Tom Scott in the *Journal of Ecclesiastical History* 39(1988); (for English translations cf. Introduction, n. 1); a general overview in *Reformation Europe: A Guide to Research*, edited by Steven Ozment. Centre for Reformation Research, St Louis, 1982.

Sources

'Bernhard Dappen, "Articuli ... contra Lutheranos". Zur Auseinandersetzung der Jüterboger Franziskaner mit Thomas Müntzer und Franz Günther', intro. by Manfred Bensing, text by Winfried Trillitzsch, *Jahrbuch für Regionalgeschichte* 2 (1967), 113–47.

Carl E. Förstemann, *Neues Urkundenbuch zur Geschichte der evangelischen Kirchenreformation*, Vol. I. Hamburg, 1842.

Flugschriften der Bauernkriegszeit, edited by Adolf Laube, Hans Seiffert etc. 2nd ed. Cologne/Böhlau, 1978.

Conrad Grebel's Programmatic Letters of 1524: with facsimiles of the original German script of Grebel's letters, edited by John C. Wenger. Scottdale Pa. Herald, 1970.

Dr Martin Luthers Werke. Kritische Gesamtausgabe. Weimar: Hermann Böhlaus Nachfolger, 1883ff.

Luther's Works (the 'American Luther'), general editors: Jaroslav Pelikan and Helmut Lehman. Philadelphia and St Louis: Concordia, 1955ff.

Thomas Müntzers Briefwechsel, edited by Heinrich Böhmer and Paul Kirn. Leipzig and Berlin: Teubner, 1931.

Thomas Müntzers Briefwechsel. Lichtdrucke Nr. 1–73 nach Originalen aus dem Sächsischen Landesarchiv Dresden, edited by H. Müller. Leipzig, 1953.

Thomas Müntzer. Politische Schriften, edited by Carl Hinrichs (Hallische Monographien, 17). Halle: Niemeyer, 1950.

Thomas Müntzer: Schriften und Briefe, Kritische Gesamtausgabe. In collaboration with Paul Kirn edited by Günther Franz (Quellen und Forschungen zur Reformationsgeschichte, 33). Gütersloh: Gerd Mohn, 1968.

Thomas Müntzer: Politische Schriften, Manifeste, Briefe 1524/25, edited by Manfred Bensing and Bernd Rüdiger, 2nd ed. Leipzig, 1973.

Thomas Müntzer: Ausslegung des andern unterschyds Danielis des propheten. Aussgetrückte emplössung des falschen Glaubens. Hochverursachte Schutzrede. Facsimile edition edited by Max Steinmetz, together with modernised text by Otto H. Brandt. Berlin, 1975.

Thomas Müntzer: Prager Manifest. Intro. by Max Steinmetz, with a contribution on the history of the text by Friedrich de Boor; new version of text and translation by Winfried Trillitzsch; facsimile of Latin MS by Hans-Joachim Rockar. Leipzig: Zentral-antiquariat der DDR, 1975.

Thomas Müntzer: Theologische Schriften aus dem Jahre 1523, edited by Siegfried Bräuer and Wolfgang Ullmann. 2nd ed., Berlin: Evangelische Verlagsanstalt, 1982.

'Der Prager Anschlag des Thomas Müntzers in der Handschrift der Leipziger Universitätsbibliothek', edited by E. Wolfgramm, *Wissenschaftliche Zeitschrift der Karl-Marx-Universität Leipzig* 6 (1957). Gesellschafts- und sprachwissenschaftliche Reihe, pp. 295–308.

The so-called 'Lichtdrucke' of Müntzer's 'Letter-sack', compiled by H. Müller (Leipzig: C. G. Röder, 1949), a facsimile copy of outstanding quality of the contents of 'Alte Briefe und Zettel, welche zum Theil Thomas Müntzer, zum Theil andere on ihn als D. Andr, Carlstadius, Joh. Agricola Islebensis pp. geschrieben', originally Loc. 10327 in the Dresden Landeshauptarchiv, and now in the Moscow Lenin Library, was made available to me by courtesy of Dr. Siegfried Bräuer; as was the microfilm of Müntzer's marginal notes on Cyprian and Tertullian, by kind permission of the Sächsische Landesbibliothek, Dresden.

Books and Articles

The Anabaptists and Thomas Müntzer, edited and translated by James M. Stayer and Werner O. Packull. Dubuque and Toronto: Kendall-Hunt, 1980.

Richard Bailey, 'The Sixteenth Century's Apocalyptic Heritage and

Thomas Müntzer', *Mennonite Quarterly Review* 57 (1983), 27–44.

Georg Baring, 'Hans Denck und Thomas Müntzer in Nürnberg 1524', *Archiv für Reformationsgeschichte* 50 (1959), 145–80; also in A. Friesen and H.-J. Goertz (edd.), *Thomas Müntzer*, pp. 132–77.

Harold S. Bender, 'Die Zwickauer Propheten, Thomas Müntzer und die Täufer', *Theologische Zeitschrift* 8 (1952), 262–78; also in A. Friesen and H.-J. Goertz (edd.) *Thomas Müntzer*, pp. 115–31; Engl. trans. in *Mennonite Quarterly Review* 27 (1953), 187–203; and in abbreviated, unannotated form in J. M. Stayer and W. O. Packull, *The Anabaptists and Thomas Müntzer*, pp. 145–51.

Manfred Bensing, 'Thomas Müntzer und Nordhausen 1522. Eine Studie über Müntzers Leben und Wirken zwischen Prag und Allstedt', *Zeitschrift für Geschichtswissenschaft* 10 (1962), 1095–1123.

—— 'Idee und Praxis des "Christlichen Verbündnisses" bei Thomas Müntzer', *Wissenschaftliche Zeitschrift der Karl-Marx-Universität Leipzig. Gesellschafts- und Sprachwissenschaftliche Reihe* 14 (1965), 459–71; also in A. Friesen and H.-J. Goertz (edd.), *Thomas Müntzer*, pp. 299–338.

—— *Thomas Müntzer und der Thüringer Aufstand 1525* (Leipziger Übersetzungen und Abhandlungen zum Mittelalter, Reihe B, 3) Berlin: VEB Deutscher Verlag der Wissenschaften, 1966.

—— *Thomas Müntzer*, Mit 74 Abbildungen. 3rd ed. Leipzig: VEB Bibliographisches Institut, 1983.

Peter Blickle, *Die Revolution von 1525*, Munich: Oldenbourg, 1975; Eng. trans. by T. A. Brady and H. C. E. Midelfort, *The Revolution of 1525. The German Peasants' War from a New Perspective.* Baltimore, London: Johns Hopkins University Press, 1981.

Heinrich Böhmer, *Studien zu Thomas Müntzer.* Leipzig, 1922.

Siegfried Bräuer, 'Zu Müntzers Geburtsjahr', *Luther-Jahrbuch* 36 (1969), 80–3.

—— 'Die erste Gesamtausgabe von Thomas Müntzers Schriften und Briefen', *Luther-Jahrbuch* 38 (1971), 120–31.

—— 'Thomas Müntzers Liedschaffen. Die theologischen Intentionen der Hymnenübertragungen im Allstedter Gottesdienst von 1523/4 und im Abendmahlslied Müntzers', *Lutherjahrbuch* 41 (1974), 45–102.

—— 'Hans Reichart, der angebliche Allstedter Drucker Müntzers', *Zeitschrift für Kirchengeschichte* 85 (1974), 389–98.

'Die Vorgeschichte von Luthers "Ein Brief an die Fürsten zu Sachsen von dem aufrührerischen Geist"', *Luther-Jahrbuch* 47 (1980), 40–70.

—— 'Thomas Müntzers Selbstverständnis als Schriftsteller', in Siegfried Hoyer (ed.), *Reform-Reformation-Revolution.* Leipzig, 1980, pp. 224–32.

—— 'Thomas Müntzers Beziehungen zur Braunschweiger Frühreformation', *Theologische Literaturzeitung* 109 (August 1984), 636–8.

—— 'Thomas Müntzer und der Allstedter Bund,' in *Täufertum und radikale Reformation im 16. Jahrhundert*: Akten des internationalen Kolloquiums für Täufergeschichte des 16. Jhs. gehalten in Verbindung mit der XI. Mennonit. Weltkonferenz in Strassburg, Juli 1984. Edited by Jean-Georges Rott and Simon Verheus. Baden-Baden, Bouxwiller, 1987.

—— 'Thomas Müntzers "Fürstenpredigt" als Buchbinder-material: Zum Fragment eines bisher unbekannten Exemplars des Allstedter Druckes der "Ausslegung des andern vnterschyds Danielis"' Th Lit.Z 112 (1987) Nr. 6, 415–24.

Ulrich Bubenheimer, 'Thomas Müntzer in Braunschweig', *Braunschweigisches Jahrbuch* 65 (1984), 37–78; 66 (1985), 79–113.

—— 'Thomas Müntzer und der Anfang der Reformation in Braunschweig, *Nederlands Archief voor Kerkgeschiedenis* 65 (1985), 1–30.

Ulrich Bubenheimer, 'Luther-Karlstadt-Müntzer: soziale Herkunft und humanistische Bildung...' *Amtsblatt der Ev.-Luth. Kirche in Thüringen*, 40, no. 8 (April, 1987), 60–8.

Claus-Peter Clasen, *Anabaptism. A Social History, 1525–1618*. Switzerland, Austria, Moravia and South and Central Germany. Ithaca, London: Cornell University Press, 1972.

Helmut Claus, 'Zur Druckgeschichte der in Sachsen veröffentlichten Schriften Thomas Müntzers', in *Der deutsche Bauernkrieg und Thomas Müntzer*, edited by Max Steinmetz etc., pp. 122–7.

Otto Clemen, 'Das Prager Manifest Thomas Müntzers', *Archiv für Reformationsgeschichte* 30 (1933), 73–81.

Rolf Dismer, Geschichte Glaube Revolution. Zur Schriftauslegung Thomas Müntzers. Theological Dissertation: Hamburg, 1974.

Andrew Drummond, 'Thomas Müntzer and the Fear of Man', *Sixteenth Century Journal* 10 no. 2 (1979), 63–71.

—— 'The Divine and Mortal Worlds of Thomas Müntzer', *Archiv für Reformationsgeschichte* 71 (1980), 99–112.

Mark U. Edwards, *Luther and the False Brethren*. Stanford, Cal. Stanford University Press, 1975.

Walter Elliger, *Thomas Müntzer: Leben und Werk*. 2nd ed. Göttingen: Vandenhoeck und Ruprecht, 1975.

Günther Franz, *Der deutsche Bauernkrieg*. Aktenband. Darmstadt: Wissenschaftliche Buchgesellschaft; 5th ed., 1980.

—— *Der deutsche Bauernkrieg*. Darmstadt; 6th ed., 1962.

Robert Friedmann, 'Thomas Muentzer's Relation to Anabaptism', *Mennonite Quarterly Review* 31 (1957), 75–87.

Abraham Friesen, 'Thomas Müntzer in Marxist Thought', *Church History* 34 (1965), 306–27.

—— 'Thomas Müntzer and the Old Testament', *Mennonite Quarterly Review* 47 (1973), 5–19; also in A. Friesen and H.-J. Goertz (edd.), *Thomas Müntzer*, pp. 383–402.

—— *Reformation and Utopia*: The Marxist Interpretation of the Reformation and its Antecedents. Wiesbaden: F. Steiner, 1974.

—— 'Die ältere und die marxistische Müntzerdeutung', in A. Friesen and H.-J. Goertz (edd.), *Thomas Müntzer*, pp. 447–80.

—— 'The Radical Reformation Revisited', *Journal of Mennonite Studies* 2 (1984), 124–76.

Hermann Goebke, 'Neue Forschungen über Thomas Müntzer bis zum Jahre 1520. Seine Abstammung und die Wurzeln seiner religiösen, politischen und sozialen Ziele', *Harz-Zeitschrift*, 1957/1959.

Hans-Jürgen Goertz, *Innere und äussere Ordnung in der Theologie Thomas Müntzers* (Studies in the History of Christian Thought, 3) Leiden, 1967.

—— 'Der Mystiker mit dem Hammer. Die theologische Begründung der Revolution bei Thomas Müntzer', *Kerygma und Dogma* 20 (1974) 25–53; also in A. Friesen and H.J. Goertz (edd.), *Thomas Müntzer*, pp. 383–444; also in Eng. trans. by Elizabeth Bender, *Mennonite Quarterly Review* 50 (1976), 83–113, and in unannotated, abbreviated form in J. M. Stayer and W. O. Packull (edd.), *The Anabaptists and Thomas Müntzer*, pp. 118–32.

—— 'Schwerpunkte der neueren Müntzerforschung', in A. Friesen and H.-J. Goertz (edd.), *Thomas Müntzer*, pp. 481–536.

—— ' "Lebendiges Wort" und "Totes Ding". Zum Schriftverständnis Thomas Müntzers im Prager Manifest', *Archiv für Reformationsgeschichte* 67 (1976), 153–78.

Leif Grane, 'Thomas Müntzer und Martin Luther', in *Bauernkriegs-Studien*, ed. Bernd Moeller (Schriften des Vereins für Reformationsgeschichte, 189) Gütersloh, 1975; and in A. Friesen and H.-J. Goertz (edd.), *Thomas Müntzer*, pp. 74–111.

Eric W. Gritsch, *Reformer Without a Church*: The Life and Thought of Thomas Müntzer 1488(?)–1525. Philadelphia: Fortress, 1967.

Carl Hinrichs, *Luther und Müntzer; ihre Auseinandersetzung über Obrigkeit und Widerstandrecht* (Arbeiten zur Kirchengeschichte, 29) Berlin: de Gruyter, 1952.

Karl Holl, 'Luther und die Schwärmer', in idem, *Gesammelte Aufsätze* I. Tübingen, 1923, pp. 420–67.

Karl Honemeyer, 'Thomas Müntzers Allstedter Gottesdienst als Symbol und Bestandteil der Volksreformation', *Wissenschaftliche Zeitschrift der Karl-Marx-Universität, Leipzig*. Gesellschafts- und

Sprachwissenschaftliche Reihe 14 (1965), 473–7; also in A. Friesen and H.-J. Goertz, *Thomas Müntzer*, pp. 213–26.

—— *Thomas Müntzer und Martin Luther, Ihr Ringen um die Musik des Gottesdienstes.* Untersuchungen zum 'Deutzsch Kirchenampt' 1523. Berlin: Merseburger, 1974.

Joyce L. Irwin, 'Müntzer's Translation and Liturgical Use of Scripture', *Concordia Theological Monthly* 43 (1972) 21–8.

Illustrierte Geschichte der deutschen frühbürgerlichen Revolution, ed. Adolf Laube, Max Steinmetz, Günter Vogler. Berlin: Dietz, 1974.

Günther List, *Chiliastische Utopie und radikale Reformation.* Die Erneuerung der Idee vom tausendjährigen Reich im 16. Jahrhundert (Humanistische Bibliothek R.1., Bd 14), Munich, 1973.

Annemarie Lohmann, *Zur geistigen Entwicklung Thomas Müntzers* (Beiträge zur Kulturgeschichte das Mittelalters und der Renaissance, 47). Leipzig, Berlin, 1931.

Johannes Luther, *Die Titeleinfassungen der Reformationszeit.* Leipzig, 1909–13.

Josef Macek, 'Die böhmische und die deutsche radikale Reformation bis zum Jahre 1525', *Zeitschrift für Kirchengeschichte* 85 (1974), Heft 2, 5–29.

Gottfried Maron, 'Thomas Müntzer als Theologe des Gerichts. Das "Urteil" – ein Schlüsselbegriff seines Denkens', *Zeitschrift für Kirchengeschichte* 83 (1972), 195–225; also in A. Friesen and H.-J. Goertz (edd.), *Thomas Müntzer*, pp. 339–82.

Erwin Mühlhaupt, 'Welche Schriften Luthers hat Müntzer gekannt?', *Luther-Jahrbuch* 46 (1975), 125–37.

Michael Müller, 'Die Gottlosen bei Thomas Müntzer – mit einem Vergleich zu Martin Luther', *Luther-Jahrbuch* 46 (1979), 97–120.

Thomas Müntzer, Anfragen an Theologie und Kirche, ed. Christoph Demke. Berlin: Evangelische Verlagsanstalt, 1977.

Thomas Müntzer, edited by Abraham Friesen and Hans-Jürgen Goertz (Wege der Forschung, 491) Darmstadt: Wissenschaftliche Buchgesellschaft, 1978.

Thomas Nipperdey, 'Theologie und Revolution bei Thomas Müntzer', *Archiv für Reformationsgeschichte* 54 (1963), 145–79.

—— *Reformation, Revolution, Utopie.* Studien zum 16. Jahrhundert. Göttingen: Vandenhoeck und Ruprecht, 1975.

Heiko A. Oberman, 'Thomas Müntzer: van verontrusting tot verzet', *Kerk en theologie* 24 (1973), 205–14.

John S. Oyer, *Luther Reformers Against Anabaptists.* The Hague: Martinus Nijhoff, 1964.

Steven E. Ozment, *Mysticism and Dissent.* Religious Ideology and Social Protest in the Sixteenth Century. New Haven, London:

Yale University Press, 1973.

Werner O. Packull, *Mysticism and the Early South German-Austrian Anabaptist Movement, 1525–31*. Scottdale, Pa.: Herald, 1977.

Wolfgang Rochler, 'Ordnungsbegriff und Gottesgedanke bei Thomas Müntzer. Ein Beitrag zur Frage "Müntzer und die Mystik"', *Zeitschrift für Kirchengeschichte* 85 (1974), 369–82.

Hans Peter Rüger, 'Thomas Müntzers Erklärung hebräischer Eigennamen und der Liber de interpretatione hebraicorum nominum des Hieronymus', *Zeitschrift für Kirchengeschichte* 94 (1983), 83–7.

Gordon Rupp, *Patterns of Reformation*. London: Epworth, 1969.

—— '"True History": Martin Luther and Thomas Müntzer', in *History, Society and the Churches*: Essays in honour of Owen Chadwick, edited by Derek Beales and Geoffrey Best. Cambridge University Press, 1985, pp. 77–88.

Martin Schmidt, 'Das Selbstbewusstsein Thomas Müntzers und sein Verhältnis zu Luther. Ein Beitrag zu der Frage: War Thomas Müntzer Mystiker?', *Theologia Viatorum* 6 (1959), 25–41; and in A. Friesen and H.-J. Goertz (edd.), *Thomas Müntzer*, pp. 31–53.

Reinhard Schwarz, *Die apokalyptische Theologie Thomas Müntzers und der Taboriten* (Beiträge zur historischen Theologie, 55) Tübingen: Mohr, 1977.

Tom Scott, 'The "Volksreformation" of Thomas Müntzer in Allstedt and Mühlhausen', *Journal of Ecclesiastical History* 34, Nr. 2 (1983), 194–213.

—— *Thomas Müntzer. Theology and Revolution in the German Reformation*. London: Macmillan, 1989.

Robert Scribner, *For the sake of simple folk: popular propaganda for the German Reformation*. (Cambridge Studies in oral and literate culture; 2) Cambridge University Press, 1981.

Gottfried Seebass, 'Das Zeichen der Erwählten', in *Umstrittenes Täufertum 1525–1975*, edited by Hans-Jürgen Goertz. Göttingen: Vandenhoeck und Ruprecht, 2nd ed., 1977, pp. 138–64.

Johann K. Seidemann, *Thomas Müntzer*. Dresden, Leipzig, 1842.

Hans Otto Spillmann, *Untersuchungen zum Wortschatz in Thomas Müntzers deutschen Schriften* (Quellen und Forschungen zur Sprach- und Kulturgeschichte der germanischen Völker, N.F., 41). Berlin, New York: de Gruyter, 1971.

James M. Stayer, 'Thomas Müntzer's Theology and Revolution in Recent Non-Marxist Interpretation', *Mennonite Quarterly Review* 43 (1969), 142–52.

—— *Anabaptists and The Sword*. Lawrence, Kansas: Coronado, 1972.

David C. Steinmetz, *Reformers in the Wings*. Philadelphia: Fortress, 1971.

Max Steinmetz, *Das Müntzerbild von Martin Luther bis Friedrich Engels* (Leipziger Übersetzungen und Abhandlungen zum Mittelalter, Reihe B, 4) Berlin, 1971.

—— 'Thomas Müntzer in der Forschung der Gegenwart', *Zeitschrift für Geschichtswissenschaft* 33 (1975), 666–85, and in Eng. trans. by J. M. Stayer (abbreviated and unannotated), in J. M. Stayer and W. O. Packull (edd.), *The Anabaptists and Thomas Müntzer*, pp. 133–43.

Georg Strobel, *Leben, Schriften und Lehren Thomas Müntzers ...* Nüremberg, Altdorf, 1795.

Wolfgang Ullmann, 'Ordo rerum: Müntzers Randbemerkungen zu Tertullian als Quelle für das Verständnis seiner Theologie', *Theologische Versuche* 7 (1976), 125–40.

Günter Vogler, 'Thomas Müntzer als Student der Viadrina', in *Die Oder-Universität Frankfurt. Beiträge zu ihrer Geschichte*. Weimar: Hermann Bohlaus Nachfolger, 1983, pp. 243–51.

Paul Wappler, 'Thomas Müntzer in Zwickau und die "Zwickauer Propheten"', *Schriften des Vereins für Reformationsgeschichte*, 182. Gütersloh, 1966; (orig. 1908).

Johannes Werner, 'Thomas Müntzers Regenbogenfahne', *Theologische Zeitschrift* 31 (1975), 32–7.

George H. Williams, *The Radical Reformation*. Philadelphia: Westminster, 1962.

Eike Wolgast, *Thomas Müntzer*: Ein Verstörer der Ungläubigen (Persönlichkeit und Geschichte, 111/112). Göttingen, Zürich: Muster-Schmidt, 1981.

Gerhard Zschäbitz, *Zur mitteldeutschen Wiedertäuferbewegung nach dem grossen Bauernkrieg*. Berlin: Rütten und Loening, 1958.

—— 'Die Stellung der Täuferbewegung im Spannungsbogen der deutschen frühbürgerlichen Revolution', in G. Brendler (ed.), *Die frühbürgerliche Revolution in Deutschland*. Berlin: Akademie Verlag, 1961, pp. 152–62; and in Eng. trans. by W. O. Packull (abbreviated and unannotated) in J. M. Stayer and W. O. Packull, *The Anabaptists and Thomas Müntzer*, pp. 28–32.

INDEX OF PEOPLE AND PLACES

INDEX OF BIBLICAL REFERENCES